THE MAKING OF MIDDLEBROW CULTURE

THE MAKING OF MIDDLE/BROW CULTURE

JOAN SHELLEY RUBIN

THE UNIVERSITY OF NORTH CAROLINA PRESS

CHAPEL HILL & LONDON

The paper in this book meets the
guidelines for permanence and durability
of the Committee on Production
Guidelines for Book Longevity of the
Council on Library Resources.

Manufactured in the
United States of America

96 95 94 93 92
5 4 3 2 1

Permission to reproduce quoted matter
can be found on pages 415–16 of this
book.

Library of Congress Cataloging-in-
Publication Data
Rubin, Joan Shelley, 1947–
    The making of middlebrow culture / by
Joan Shelley Rubin.
        p.   cm.
    Includes bibliographical references and
index.
    ISBN 0-8078-2010-5 (alk. paper). —
ISBN 0-8078-4354-7 (pbk. : alk. paper)
    1. Books and reading—United
States—History—20th century.
2. Literature—Appreciation—United
States—History—20th century.   3. Art
appreciation—United States—History—
20th century.   4. United States—
Popular culture—History—20th century.
5. Middle classes—United States—
History—20th century.   6. Self-
culture—History—20th century.
I. Title.
Z1003.2.R83   1991   91-22241
028'.9'0973—dc20   CIP

An earlier version of part of chapter 3
appeared in the *Journal of American
History* 71 (March 1985): 782–806. Essays
based on some of the material in chapter 6
were published in *American Quarterly* 35
(Winter 1983): 499–517, and in *Mass Media
between the Wars*, edited by Catherine L.
Covert and John D. Stevens, pp. 3–19. ©
1984 by Syracuse University Press.

For Tai, with love

CONTENTS

Acknowledgments, ix

Introduction, xi

Chapter 1. Self, Culture, and Self-Culture in America, 1

Chapter 2. The "Higher Journalism" Realigned:
Stuart Pratt Sherman, Irita Van Doren, and *Books*, 34

Chapter 3. Why Do You Disappoint Yourself?: The Early History of
the Book-of-the-Month Club, 93

Chapter 4. Classics and Commercials:
John Erskine and "Great Books," 148

Chapter 5. Merchant of Light:
Will Durant and the Vogue of the "Outline," 209

Chapter 6. Information, Please!:
Book Programs on Commercial Radio, 266

Notes, 331

Bibliography, 373

Index, 405

Permissions, 415

A section of illustrations can be found following page 198.

ACKNOWLEDGMENTS

The making of this book has its own history, stretching over more than a decade. Three people deserve special mention because they believed in the project from the beginning. Like the "steady sellers" he has described as fixtures of the Puritans' world of print, David D. Hall's advice and encouragement have been important to me year in and year out. Early in my work, several conversations with the late Warren Susman convinced me to continue exploring what then felt like an unmanageable subject. Finally, as always, David Brion Davis's generosity and interest have been invaluable and sustaining.

Many others gave me the benefit of their learning and counsel. Stanley Engerman, Richard Wightman Fox, David Hollinger, Christopher Lasch, and Robert Westbrook read the entire manuscript with care, insight, and sensitivity. Several additional scholars aided my investigation by commenting on earlier drafts, sharing ideas, or furnishing various kinds of assistance: James Baughman, Casey Blake, George Cotkin, the late Catherine Covert, Lynn Gordon, Robert A. Gross, James Hoopes, Michael Kammen, Bruce Kuklick, Fred Matthews, Jean Matthews, Doris Meadows, Richard Pells, Elisabeth Perry, Lewis Perry, Janice Radway, Raymond A. Schroth, S.J., Holly Cowan Shulman, Janet Tighe, Christopher P. Wilson, Daniel Wilson, and Mary Young. I am especially indebted to Roland Marchand and Susan Smulyan for helping me to gather materials on the history of radio.

For support and understanding, I am grateful to my colleagues Owen S. Ireland, Kathleen Kutolowski, Bruce Leslie, Kenneth P. O'Brien, Lynn Parsons, and Robert Strayer, and to Marcia Boyd, Elsa Dixler, Stanley Engerman, Kate Fisher, Ruth Freeman, Gail Gilberg, Trish Harren, Joanna Heal, Patricia Hogenmiller, Barbara Orenstein, and Leonard F. Salzman. My sisters, Cynthia and Linda Rubin, and my parents, Pearl and Sydney Rubin, made countless contributions ranging from archival errands to patient listening.

Clifton Fadiman kindly granted me an interview. Linda Cranmer allowed me to examine the unpublished John Erskine papers then in the possession of her family. Of the numerous librarians who facilitated my research, I owe special thanks to Bernard Crystal of the Rare Book and Manuscript Library, Columbia University; the refreshingly unbureaucratic interlibrary loan staff of the University of Rochester Library; and the reference department at the University of Rochester.

It is a pleasure to acknowledge the deft guidance of Kate Douglas Torrey and her associates at the University of North Carolina Press. Closer to home, Brenda Peake assembled the bibliography and performed other secretarial tasks with unusual efficiency and good cheer. Barbara Thompson conscientiously retrieved bibliographical information and helped check quotations.

The following gave me not only funds for research but also the gift of time: a National Endowment for the Humanities Fellowship for College Teachers (1983–84); a State University of New York College at Brockport sabbatical leave (1985–86); an American Council of Learned Societies Research Fellowship and a Spencer Foundation Small Grant (1988–89). An additional stipend from SUNY Brockport in 1988–89 was only one expression of my college's unwavering commitment to this project.

My greatest debt is to my husband, Tai C. Kwong, and to my two growing sons, David Rubin Kwong and Michael Rubin Kwong. I thank them for baseball, Ninja turtles, music, Chinese food, perspective, joy, and their inestimable contribution to my own sense of self.

INTRODUCTION

On rainy summer afternoons, the inhabitants of the cottages for rent along the New England coast or the lakes of the Midwest sometimes grow restless. Tired of Monopoly and finished with the stack of current fiction imported from home, they fasten their attention on the well-worn books that, like the mismatched china and frayed rag rugs, furnish the house. Among the faded volumes on the shelves, certain titles turn up with the faithfulness of an old friend: John Erskine's *The Private Life of Helen of Troy*, Will Durant's *The Story of Philosophy*, Stuart Pratt Sherman's *My Dear Cornelia*, William Lyon Phelps's *Autobiography with Letters*, the collected essays of Alexander Woollcott, a novel or two by Dorothy Canfield Fisher. Published in the 1920s, 1930s, and 1940s, such works are all but unknown today. Yet, amid the mystery stories and ancient magazines abandoned by departing vacationers, they testify to an unjustly neglected phenomenon of that era: the emergence of American middlebrow culture.

In the three decades following the First World War, Americans created an unprecedented range of activities aimed at making literature and other forms of "high" culture available to a wide reading public. Beginning with the Book-of-the-Month Club, founded in 1926, book clubs provided subscribers with recently published works chosen by expert judges (Fisher among them). "Great books" discussion groups, which Erskine pioneered, and, eventually, a set of classic texts themselves furnished comparable access to older volumes. Colleges and universities, accommodating an expanding student body, augmented their curricula with extension programs in the humanities and other disciplines, some offered on the new medium of radio. By the 1930s broadcasting also routinely enabled literary critics such as Woollcott and Phelps to bring their commentary directly into American living rooms. Innovations in print journalism—the establishment, for example, of the *New York Herald Tribune*'s *Books* under Sherman's editorship and the *Saturday Review of Literature* under Henry Seidel Canby—similarly enlarged the critic's opportunity to guide readers through the increasingly bewildering task of book selection. In addition, publishers, responding to the demand for culture in organized, manageable parcels, nurtured authors like Durant who could "outline" and simplify specialized learning.

At the same time, older institutions such as correspondence courses, night schools, and women's study clubs flourished; it was a "golden age" for the speaker on the lecture circuit. Public libraries facilitated the dissemination of knowledge with revamped cataloguing, open stacks, and information services. As early as 1927, when Fisher compiled a survey of such ventures for the Carnegie Corporation, so many versions of what she called "voluntary education" were engaging American readers that her systematic inventory disintegrated into a chapter she helplessly titled "everything else." Had she taken stock again in 1950, she would have had even greater difficulty achieving comprehensive coverage of the field.[1]

By that date, however, a single phrase frequently replaced precise characterizations of the popularization of literature in the preceding decades: instead of Fisher's careful treatment, the phenomenon was routinely subsumed—and abandoned—under the rubric "middlebrow culture." The reference to the height of the brow originally derived from phrenology and carried overtones of racial differentiation. Transformed into a description of intellectual caliber, "highbrow" was, in the 1880s, already synonymous with "refined"; twenty years later, "lowbrow" came to denote a lack of cultivation. Shortly thereafter, as is well known, Van Wyck Brooks commandeered both "highbrow" and "lowbrow" in the service of social criticism. Condemning the division in American life between effete guardians of art and practical, vulgar materialists, Brooks looked in vain for a "genial middle ground" on which cultural life could thrive.

In 1933 Margaret Widdemer, ignoring Brooks's wider political concerns, mapped that terrain in an innocuous essay for the *Saturday Review* called "Message and Middlebrow." Paring the label down to a description of the reading public, Widdemer identified as middlebrow the "men and women, fairly civilized, fairly literate, who support the critics and lecturers and publishers by purchasing their wares." Located between the "tabloid addict class" and the "tiny group of intellectuals," middlebrows represented, in Widdemer's view, simply "the majority reader."[2]

In other hands, though, the word acquired more potency. Virginia Woolf, in an essay published in *The Death of the Moth* (1942), derided the middlebrow as a person "betwixt and between," devoted to "no single object, neither art itself nor life itself, but both mixed indistinguishably, and rather nastily, with money, fame, power, or prestige." Observing that the middlebrow outlook consisted of "a mixture of geniality and sentiment stuck together with a sticky slime of calf's-foot jelly," she warned lowbrows to resist efforts to "teach them culture." Her assumption that highbrows and lowbrows were naturally allied against the "pernicious pest who comes between" them and her association of "middlebrow" with the corruption of taste by commercial interests reverberated through every subsequent discussion of the term. In 1948, for example, the art critic Clement Greenberg, bitterly seconding Woolf's view, emphasized the "insidiousness" of middlebrow culture—its capacity for "devaluating the precious, infecting the healthy, corrupting the honest, and stultifying the wise." The task of the avant-garde, Greenberg warned, was to fortify itself against a middlebrow "penetration" that had become "infinitely more difficult to detect and block."[3]

Shortly thereafter, the *Harper's* editor Russell Lynes, writing in a decidedly different vein, partially rehabilitated the middlebrow sensibility by poking fun at the siege mentality of the avant-garde. Lynes developed the fullest analysis up to that date of the relationships among the "brows." The highbrow, Lynes contended, linked culture with "every aspect of daily life, from the design of his razor to the shape of the bottle that holds his sleeping pills." Self-appointed guardians of aesthetic standards, highbrows stood as a "bulwark against the enticements of Hollywood and the advertising agencies." They were, in a word, "serious" about books and the arts. The lowbrow, Lynes explained, wanted "to be comfortable and to enjoy himself without having to worry about whether he has good taste or not." As devotees of jazz and comic books, lowbrows adopted an attitude toward the arts of "live and let live." Lynes reserved his most finely drawn definition for the term "middlebrow," which he subdivided into "upper" and "lower." In the first group fell the highbrows' chief patrons: publishers, museum directors, and other "cultural do-gooders." *Their* audience, the lower middlebrows, was consonant with Fisher's subject: they were the book-club members, the "course takers who swell the enrollments of adult education classes," the lecture-goers "hell-bent on improving their minds as well as their fortunes."[4]

Incorporating quotations from Greenberg's and Woolf's diatribes, Lynes dished out a good deal of anti-intellectual satire: his highbrows wished that "all middlebrows, presumably, would have their televisions taken away, be suspended from society until they had agreed to give up their subscriptions to the Book-of-the-Month." But none of his stereotypes entirely escaped his gently contemptuous tone. The playfulness of Lynes's interpretation made it a prime candidate for appropriation by the mass media. In its issue for April 11, 1949, *Life* featured not only a paraphrase of Lynes's "three basic categories of a new U.S. social structure" but also an accompanying visualization: drawings of Lynes's four brow sizes juxtaposed to sketches of each group's preferences in such areas as clothes, furniture, salads, and drinks as well as reading and sculpture. Even *Life* writer Winthrop Sargeant's "defense" of the highbrow sustained Lynes's note of flippant parody.[5]

Lynes's essay thus had the effect of firmly fixing the language of the "brows" in the popular lexicon while softening its critical edge. In 1960, however, Dwight Macdonald, whose *Partisan Review* article "Masscult and Midcult" remains the most famous critique of American middlebrow culture, irreversibly heightened that term's pejorative connotations. Writing in the same spirit of dead seriousness that motivated Woolf and Greenberg, Macdonald revived their view that "midcult" was more harmful than mass culture because it was the enemy within the walls: "It pretends to respect the standards of High Culture while in fact it waters them down and vulgarizes them." Singling out, once again, the Book-of-the-Month Club, along with the *Saturday Review*, the figures associated with the *Great Books of the Western World* publishing project, and such authors as Archibald MacLeish, Stephen Vincent Benét, and Thornton Wilder, Macdonald deplored the tendency of proponents of "midcult" to debase the "discoveries of the avant-garde" by reducing them to banality and commercialism. "It is one thing," he explained in a footnote, "to bring High Culture to a wider audience without change; and another to 'popularize' it by sales talk in the manner of Clifton Fadiman or Mortimer J. Adler." Unlike his adversary Gilbert Seldes, who believed in the viability of raising "the level of our culture in general," Macdonald rejected the idea that democracy permitted—and required—a broadly diffused commitment to art. Placing his hopes instead in the creation of "smaller, more specialized audiences," he concluded: "So let the masses have their Masscult, let the few who care about good writing, painting, music, architecture, philosophy, etc., have their High Culture, and don't fuzz up the distinction with Midcult."[6]

Macdonald's dismissive argument not only gave up on middlebrow culture as a means for improving the quality of American life in the future, it also licensed the scholarly neglect of middlebrow efforts in the past. In the years since "Masscult and Midcult" appeared, students of American literature—loyal, like Macdonald, to the avant-garde—have ordinarily focused on figures who have viewed themselves as alienated: expatriates, writers for "little magazines," modernists. Chronicling twentieth-century critical movements, they have usually moved from the Seven Arts group through New Humanists, Menckenites, Marxists, and New Critics, with nary a Book-of-the-Month Club judge in sight. The recent interest in literary institutions of Janice Radway, Gerald Graff, and others has restored some middlebrow representatives—notably Erskine and Canby—to partial view, but the factors animating their careers largely remain obscure.[7]

Similarly, historians, compensating for years of inattention to the working class, have emphasized the nature of popular taste. When not engaged in studies of intellectuals such as the coterie clustered around the *Partisan Review*, they have concentrated on the development of amusement parks, the movies, the sporting scene, and other varieties of mass entertainment. Like their colleagues in literature, they have thus reified and perpetuated the conventional dichotomy between "high" and "popular" culture, overlooking the interaction that went on between the two. Those few historical accounts that have mentioned the diffusion of the humanities in the post–World War I period, moreover, have typically followed Macdonald's and Greenberg's lead in treating the phenomenon solely as an extension of consumerism. In a monograph on the 1920s, for example, Ellis Hawley, noting the "successful launching of the Book-of-the-Month Club" and the spread of other "packaged cultural experiences," nonetheless viewed such "products" merely as "symbols of social refinement" that could be purchased in the same way as toasters and Model T's.[8]

The primary task of this book is to redress both the disregard and the oversimplification of middlebrow culture in the 1920s, 1930s, and 1940s by illuminating the values and attitudes that shaped some of its major expressions. In picking examples for close examination, however, I faced Fisher's problem: how to select from among the plethora of possible case studies? Because I am interested in unconscious conflict as well as explicit motivation, in individual lives as they intersect with wider social movements, and in the evolution of the literary critic as cultural mediator, I chose to limit my purview to efforts which encompassed, in addition to entrepreneurs, an identifiable critical presence. Hence my decision to explore the following five subjects: the *New York Herald Tribune*'s *Books* section; the early Book-of-the-Month Club; the initial ideology behind the "great books" movement; the vogue of the "outline" volume; and the spectrum of literary programming on the radio. Those topics, each of which occupies a chapter herein, enabled me to consider, among others, Sherman, Irita Van Doren, Fisher, Canby, Erskine, Mortimer Adler, Durant, Phelps, Woollcott, Mark Van Doren, and Clifton Fadiman. Hence my omission, as well, of a strictly business undertaking like the *Reader's Digest*. For some of the same reasons, but, in addition, because the data on audience response were largely unavailable or problematic, I have emphasized the artifacts middlebrow ventures created rather than their impact on readers. Recognizing the desirability of incorporating the latter dimension, however, I have used whatever documents about audience I could find and, where fruitful, speculated about a text's possible appeals.

Within each chapter, I investigate the definition of the cultured person and, more broadly, the vision of the self implicit in the reviews or commentaries my protagonists created; the sense of role, purpose, and authority middlebrow writers evinced; the meaning of the form, as well as the content, of the projects to which they attached themselves; the responses of academic critics and the avant-garde to the challenge of middlebrow initiatives; and, where appropriate, the nature of the advertising accompanying new literary commodities. By thus charting what I like to call the "middleness" of middlebrow culture, I hope to contribute to the redrawing of the boundary between "high" art and popular sensibility that historians such as Lawrence W. Levine and David D. Hall have recently undertaken for different times and places.[9]

In addition, my exploration of the middlebrow perspective serves a second aim: to reassess the fate of the so-called genteel tradition in modern America. When George Santayana introduced that label in 1911 to describe an attenuated Calvinist strain in nineteenth-century American literature and philosophy, he provided a convenient epithet for the perpetrators of the dichotomy between "highbrow" and "lowbrow." Highlighting its repressive aspects and condemning its tendency to render American artists "starved and abstract," both Santayana and Brooks depicted gentility as a yoke to be shaken off. Throughout the twenties the Younger Generation, self-consciously announcing that it had enacted that escape, reiterated Santayana's and Brooks's message—and proclaimed the death of its captors. The title of Malcolm Cowley's collection of essays about American literature between 1910 and 1930—*After the Genteel Tradition*—summarized the younger writers' sense of a complete break with the past. Subsequently, adopting Cowley's perspective, literary historians have assumed that the triumph of modernism rested on the demise of nineteenth-century critical strictures.[10]

The idea that, by the First World War, the genteel tradition had vanished as a force in American life has enjoyed equally wide currency among cultural and social historians. In *The End of American Innocence* (1959), for example, Henry F. May depicted the period 1912–17 as a time when insurgent intellectuals struck fatal blows against the Victorian faith in optimism, morality, and progress. The United States after those years, May concluded, was a fundamentally different civilization from the one that had preceded it. More recently, the same scholars who have analyzed the rise of popular amusements have predicated their interpretations on the destruction of "the genteel middle-class cultural order." Even a monograph which views the public library system as the last bastion of gentility nevertheless declares that the "genteel tradition tottered and collapsed in the second decade of the new century." Concomitantly, historians concerned with the organization of knowledge in America have predominantly assumed that the genteel critic's stance as generalist gave way to a relentless, all-pervasive process of specialization.[11]

My endeavor, by contrast, has been to demonstrate that genteel values survived and prospered, albeit in chastened and redirected form, throughout the 1920s, 1930s, and 1940s. Although it is indisputable that the avant-garde flourished after World War I, and equally true that mass entertainment overrode Victorian proscriptions, I contend that the terrain of middlebrow culture proved solid ground on which the genteel outlook could be reconstituted. By delineating the presence of mingled, competing ideals—for example, of both "character" and "personality"—that argument assists the ongoing effort among historians to understand with more depth and precision the consequences of the United States's shift from a producer to a consumer society.

Although not my principal focus, I have, along the way, also pursued a third objective. Especially in my discussions of Sherman, Canby, and Erskine, where the topic is most germane, I have tried to connect the making of middlebrow culture to the current interest in the phenomenon literary scholars call canon formation. The phrase denotes the designation of some writers as "major" and, in Sharon O'Brien's phrase, "the exclusion or marginalization of others" on the basis of "social, political, and ideological assumptions." Given their tenuous position in the historical record, middlebrow figures appear, from one angle, victims of that process. Yet, because of their efforts as book reviewers and list makers, many of them can also be seen as canonizers themselves. Erskine's construction of the "great books" syllabus is the most obvious example of middlebrow canon making, but the designation of the "book-of-the-month" or the announcement on the air of the season's "best books" represent other instances of the same activity. Recognizing that fact, I have conceived of my project as, in part, a reinforcement of the premise that Graff, Radway, Jane Tompkins, Richard Brodhead, Annette Kolodny, and other scholars have so convincingly established: that the shape of the canon has always derived from the experiences and presuppositions of the literary establishment.[12] But I also wanted to counteract the tendency to depict canonizers monolithically: that is, merely as dictatorial members "of a privileged class and of the male sex." Almost conspiratorial in some formulations, that view presumes that the figures who devised exclusive book lists did so arrogantly and unhesitatingly; that they harbored no reservations, conscious or otherwise, about their warrant to act as literary experts; that (except for a desire to subordinate those threatening them) their own variable psychological requirements had no effect on their choices.[13] By shedding light on the particular needs and beliefs middlebrow critics brought to their literary judgments, I mean to suggest otherwise.

While the intent governing those three aims has been to replace categorical accounts of the subject with a more intricate, historically based exploration of the making of middlebrow culture, I have nonetheless not discarded the term "middlebrow" because, despite its pejorative connotations, it remains serviceable as descriptive shorthand. If my goal has been to move beyond some of those connotations, however, I do not pretend to have used the word more neutrally than did Lynes or Macdonald. On the contrary, throughout my research, I have been keenly aware of my attitudes—both positive and negative—toward my material. On the one hand, I recognize, and deplore, the extent to which Macdonald's position slighted the legitimate needs and aspirations of millions of "average intelligent readers" (as the Book-of-the-Month Club termed them). To anyone dedicated, as I am, to democratic values, the promise that middlebrow ventures would put more books in the hands of more people is a highly attractive one. Along the same lines, I have been impressed by the allegiance of many of the figures I have investigated to their own version of democratic ideology and have accordingly argued against the temptation merely to berate them as self-protective "custodians of culture."

On the other hand, while I reject Greenberg's and Macdonald's automatic equation of mediation with mediocrity, I share their dismay at the middlebrow critic's failure consistently to maintain aesthetic standards. Acknowledging that measures of literary quality are not self-evident truths but, rather, social constructs, I nonetheless adhere to the now unfashionable view that learning to apprehend the workings of form and language in the books that critics have, over time, judged "best" affords readers a richer life—a deeper humanity—than they might otherwise experience. Like the more truculent castigators of "midcult," I see the rise of American consumer society not simply as a spur to the commendable democratization of "high" culture: to my mind, as middlebrow popularizers accommodated consumer priorities, worthwhile aesthetic commitments were also lost in the bargain. ⌐

In arriving at that position, I have been influenced by a writer—similarly out of favor today in some circles—who yoked together both democratic values and a rigorous concern for literary quality: F. O. Matthiessen. Matthiessen saw criticism as "both an aesthetic and a social act." He assigned the critic a "central responsibility to the text before him," insisting that "he must judge the work of art as a work of art." In that connection, he argued in 1949 that "wise standards are the greatest need in American life and literature today." At the same time, he held that, for critics to stimulate "the works of art that we need most," they must be attuned to the literature and politics of their age, fashioning criteria from "the demands of our own environment" as well as from the legacy of the past. Matthiessen's egalitarian assumption that readers deserved the insights of uncompromising but engaged authorities in order to share in literature's "chief gift"—the "extension of our sense of living by compelling us to contemplate a broader world"—has been my own starting point. Despite its susceptibility to elitist applications, I believe his perspective still offers more prospects for human fulfillment than a situation in which market considerations rush in to fill the vacuum created by an unchecked relativism.[14]

A similar ambivalence marks my approach to the genteel tradition. At their best, genteel critics wanted people to be engaged with society and yet to possess a sense of competence and wholeness that was not contingent on the judgments of others. Although perhaps unattainable, that ideal strikes me as a more salutary vision of the self than the fragmented "personality" American consumer culture encouraged. Genteel intellectuals also dedicated themselves to fostering a widely shared aesthetic sensitivity. I have tried to recover those attitudes and thus to expand the meaning of "genteel tradition" beyond the associations Brooks and Santayana imposed upon the words. Aware of its dangers and limitations, I have rather reluctantly retained the phrase (and employed it interchangeably with "Arnoldian") because, like "middlebrow," it is language in common usage among historians. While, as Edwin Harrison Cady noted in 1949, it is probably impossible to strip "genteel tradition" of its negative references, my goal is at least to restore some shadings to it.[15]

Yet those shadings include darker as well as lighter hues. Along with my admiration for the genteel tradition's finest hopes, I understand what Brooks and Santayana meant by their attacks. Like them, I reject the lifelessness gentility at its worst engendered and sympathize with the individuals I discuss who sought "experience" outside its confines. If the text which follows is thus laced with my own "middleness" about my subject, perhaps that is only appropriate in a work where the emphasis is on unresolved tensions and contradictions—on the complexities that made American middlebrow culture in the years between 1917 and 1950 the reflection of a society in transition.

THE MAKING OF MIDDLEBROW CULTURE

SELF, CULTURE, AND SELF-CULTURE IN AMERICA

"I venture to ask," a reader of the *Ladies' Home Journal* wrote the critic Hamilton Wright Mabie in 1906, "if you would be so kind as to give some idea how to start right to obtain culture. I have plenty of time and a good library at my disposal, but no money to employ teachers." Mabie's advice was straightforward—to "read only the best books." Yet the exchange depended on a number of unspoken assumptions: that culture could be dissociated from wealth; that it could be acquired; that the process of doing so entailed reading certain books and avoiding others; that becoming cultured required time; that cultured individuals (in this case, Mabie) commanded deference from those who timidly "ventured" to join their company.[1]

Those understandings were part of a definition of culture that had evolved in America since the colonial period. Even restricted to its association with "high" art (as opposed to its broader, anthropological denotation of a "way of life"), the term reflected the interplay of several distinct ideological traditions. At its base was a model of cultivation forged by the gentry who, in the eighteenth century, populated the "great houses" of the Eastern seaboard. The ideal combined the British legacy of insistence on fine manners, proper speech, and elegance with the demand, in the American setting, for moral substance. Mere drawing-room performance—the display of wit, beauty, and similar attributes of refinement—was counterposed to "true gentility," in which those exterior signs corresponded to inner virtues such as tolerance and dedication to reason.[2]

Diffused throughout the colonies, culture in these early years nonetheless remained largely an accompaniment of political and economic power. The elite who set the standard of "high style" were the same people who provided leadership for colonial governments. Similarly, not only was genteel culture compatible with wealth, it depended on it—because the pursuit of refinement was expensive. Aspirants to gentility were avid consumers of parlor furnishings, rare wines, fine china—and books—that bespoke their sense of propriety and grace. Moreover, practical businessmen were also considered "men of letters" whose involvement in commerce did nothing to disqualify them as cultured individuals.[3]

Even so, by the 1790s figures like Elihu Hubbard Smith and Charles Brockden Brown had begun concluding that commercial success might impede, rather than nourish, literary and artistic achievements. Their discouragement about the love of gain they observed in the postrevolutionary era coincided with a larger development: the emergence, in both Europe and America, of the romantic artist as critic of industrialism. Reacting against an increase in imitative, mechanical production, romantics fostered an idea of "Art" as the domain of a "superior reality." Culture became linked with "imaginative truth"; it was, as Raymond Williams has put it, the "court of appeal in which real values were determined, usually in opposition to the 'factitious' values thrown up by the market and similar operations of society."[4]

Nineteenth-Century Definitions of Culture

After 1800 those two tendencies—to associate genuine cultivation with inward virtue and to counterpose it to materialism—deepened and spread. The democratization of property ownership and the rise of republicanism enhanced the prospect that Americans of more modest means could attain the respectability formerly limited to the aristocracy. Although the relationship between money and "the best people" remained ambiguous, many writers of popular advice manuals stressed that genteel conduct did not depend on financial resources. By the same token, when George Ticknor, a founder of the Boston Atheneum, met the British entrepreneur William Roscoe in 1815, he saw as unusual and impressive Roscoe's capacity to combine literary and business acumen. By 1851 the term "gentility" described "all who were well brought up and well educated." Moreover, the same democratic doctrines which generated widespread aspirations to refinement disjoined gentility and political leadership. Winning votes became less a matter of possessing culture than of being able to juggle the needs of various interest groups, of which the gentry itself was one.[5]

As economic and social barriers to refinement fell, however, they also eliminated the reliability of privilege as a predictor of cultured behavior. Moreover, despite the growing element of antipathy to the marketplace within the official definition of culture, the greater availability of consumer goods meant that it was increasingly possible to contravene that part of the ideology in practice. That is, officially, gentility denoted moral and intellectual qualities that could never be bought. Yet middle-class Americans in the mid-nineteenth century scrambled to purchase replicas of luxury items (carpets, upholstery, watches) in order to mimic the upper echelons of society. Such goods made it both easier to acquire an aura of refinement—to regard gentility itself as a commodity—and more difficult to sift imposters from the authentically respectable. The problem was compounded by the faceless, confusing, potentially anarchic crowd populating the expanding urban environment.[6] In response, Americans intensified their attachment to the idea that a person's actions certified the presence or absence of the inner qualities comprising "true gentility." Essayists, novelists, journalists, ministers, and educators developed a language that honed the observer's sense of those qualities so that they would be readily recognizable.

The most important entry in this lexicon was "character." In broad outline, the word denoted integrity, balance, and restraint, traits which well served the needs of an economy dependent on diligent producers. Animated by a firmly grounded sense of the self as interior, persons of character were also, paradoxically, selfless. Public-spirited and cognizant of moral obligation, they were committed more to the fulfillment of duty than to uninhibited self-expression. Possessors of character won prestige and "reputation" by exhibiting it to others. Yet the ideal approximated the set of attributes David Riesman labeled "inner direction" in the sense that its exemplars determined their behavior according to what Riesman called an internalized "psychological gyroscope." The conformist aspects of "inner direction"—the tendency to follow the gyroscope unthinkingly—were often implicit in expectations of character as well. But in some formulations, notably those of Emerson and Charles Eliot Norton discussed below, the ideal left room for the trait from which Riesman tried so hard to distinguish "inner direction": the exercise of independent, reflective choice he denominated "autonomy."[7]

In addition, the effort to identify genuine culture drew on the contrasting terms "fine" and "fashionable." Such figures as Catharine M. Sedgwick, Caroline Kirkland, and N. P. Willis celebrated ordinary Americans of "fine" bearing and simple circumstances whose actions, Sedgwick remarked, "expressed conscious dignity, independence, and painstaking benevolence." At the same time, those writers deplored the adherence to "mere convention" rampant among the "fashionable" but indolent rich. (Confusingly, some authors conflated "fine" and "fashionable," relying on "true" and "Christian" as antonyms for both, but the underlying dichotomy the two sets of adjectives established was identical.) This antithesis not only reinforced the view that the opportunity for culture was available to anyone, it further disentangled refinement and wealth. The divisions observers like Sedgwick postulated had special implications for women. Although they were largely excluded from authority outside the home, women's putative superior sensitivity to "fineness" empowered them to exert leadership and realize prestige within the limited sphere of "polite culture."[8]

A related pair of words—"taste" versus "fashion"—accomplished the same thing. Despite the determination of moralists to separate them, the terms often overlapped. By the 1840s, however, "tasteful" had become roughly synonymous with "fine" or "true" in the sense that the exhibition of all three qualities supposedly derived from internalized moral standards. By contrast, the fashionable man, as Horace Bushnell stated, wore his soul "on the outside of him." Assuredly, the idea that culture entailed the observance of "taste" did not obliterate the tie of either of those qualities to income. "Taste" presumed participation in the marketplace and guided buyers in making appropriate selections. Yet, although inextricably bound to the spread of consumer goods, the exercise of "taste" was supposed to harmonize one's possessions with one's nature—to assist in expressing self-control and building character. It was not (at least in theory) a process of amassing those goods solely to impress others.[9]

By the mid-nineteenth century, Americans were deeply involved in invoking "character," "fineness," "taste," and "culture" in order to resist "vulgarity" and fend off the specter of the "confidence man." The popularity of grammars and dictionaries designed to defend refined speech from the incursions of informality and slang reflected that preoccupation. So did the high demand for etiquette manuals. Anchored in the premise that " 'manners are the outward expression of the internal character,' " etiquette writers taught how to discern and display inward civility in the form, for example, of discipline at the dinner table. Although the system of rules actually tended to weaken the very concept it was supposed to strengthen—by providing more opportunity for gesture without substance—overtly, it shored up the reassuring assumption that appearance mirrored reality.[10]

At roughly the same time the speech and etiquette authorities were dispensing their formulas for sorting genteel individuals from vulgar ones, other writers were enunciating ideas of culture and character in a less worldly context. The Harvard moral philosophers who shaped Unitarian theology—figures such as Joseph Stevens Buckminster, Andrews Norton, and William Ellery Channing—articulated a complex moral and aesthetic vision of gentility. To them, the attainment of a cultured sensibility was part of a larger task: the achievement of salvation. Specifically, in place of the belief in innate depravity, Unitarians substituted the view that sin lay in the failure to sustain inward harmony. Virtue consisted in the practice of "self-mastery" and moderation. "Character," the hallmark of the ethical individual, was central to the Unitarians' vocabulary: one's obligation, they preached, was to engage in character development—which they also called " 'a progressive purification of the personality' "—in order to do honor to divine creation.[11]

Culture, or, as Channing emphasized, "self-culture," was integral to that process. Obtained through the reading of literature and other forms of study, it consisted "not chiefly, as many are apt to think, in accumulating information" but instead in nurturing a mind and spirit consistent with "Christian character." Channing conceived of self-culture in organic imagery. "To cultivate any thing, be it a plant, an animal, a mind," he explained in 1838, "is to make it grow." That development, Channing believed, was intrinsically worthwhile. "The ground of a man's culture," he explained, "lies in his nature, not in his calling. . . . His powers are to be unfolded on account of their inherent dignity, not their outward direction." But the end of growth was also a means to further goals that stood in contradistinction to personal aggrandizement. Channing briefly acknowledged that self-education was "practical" and could improve the worldly lot of those who pursued it. Nevertheless, real self-culture, he insisted, acted to "depress" those "desires, appetites, passions which terminate" in the individual, while exalting human responsibilities to ameliorate society and to serve God.[12]

In the Unitarian scheme, the possessor of self-culture exhibited two forms of taste: moral and aesthetic. Moral taste was the quality of taking delight in the perception of virtue. Aesthetic taste described a similar response to beauty. It is true that, for Norton and his colleagues, literature which was not morally sound could not be aesthetically pleasing either. Yet, in light of the changes the meaning of culture would subsequently undergo, what is striking about the Unitarian framework is the degree to which the Harvard philosophers at least attempted to sustain allegiance to art and goodness alike.[13]

As the Unitarians delineated their version of gentility, they also formulated a role for the "man of letters" charged with defining and exemplifying culture. Such figures were expected to comprise, in Daniel Walker Howe's phrase, a "literary moral elite." Although functioning as writers and critics rather than ministers, they were to provide the same intellectual leadership the clergy had traditionally supplied. This stance equipped critics to make literary judgments with untrammeled authority. Broadly speaking, the Unitarians' sense of purpose was often coupled to antidemocratic rhetoric. Buckminster, for example, decried the "pernicious notion of equality" that undermined reverence for classical education, while Norton blamed democracy for "a poisonous atmosphere, which blasts everything beautiful in nature and corrodes everything elegant in art."[14]

Those views, however, did not license retreat to smug disengagement. Rather, "men of letters" were duty bound to remain immersed in democratic society—guiding, criticizing, and elevating it. Relying on their counsel, the "average man" would not so much surrender to their dicta as engage in "obeying his own instructed mind." In sum, the Unitarians' aristocratic prejudices coexisted with a drive to help all Americans, regardless of class, become, in Howe's words, "not only more religious, but also more cosmopolitan, more sensitive, and more compassionate—in short, more fully human." That commitment propelled the Harvard moral philosophers to seek audiences for their message outside their immediate circles: Channing's "Self-Culture," for example, was a lecture before an association of workingmen, while Buckminster helped found a periodical to promulgate the Unitarian outlook.[15]

A short distance from the Unitarian stronghold of Boston, the so-called New Haven scholars, clustering around Yale College, provided, from the 1840s through the 1880s, a complementary interpretation of the requirements of culture. There Presidents Theodore Dwight Woolsey and Noah Porter attempted to foster in their students "inner growth" through "full and harmonious training." Drawing on the German ideal of *Bildung*, they sought to instill "not erudition, so much as culture; not facts, not reflection, not feats of memory . . . but the power of subtle and ready thought, and of apt and finished expression." Distinguished from mere information, culture was, in the New Haven view, also a corrective to materialism. Woolsey and Porter assumed—indeed, hoped—that college graduates would exhibit the results of their "liberal" education in the public realm; the acquisition of prestige through the display of refinement remained a part of the New Haven ideal. One of the graduates' functions, Porter explained in his 1871 inaugural address, was to "soften" the "vulgarities" endemic to American society and introduce "amenities into our social life." But Porter was quick to differentiate that form of social performance from the flaunting of "cheap glitter" and "showy accomplishments" in the service of economic self-interest.[16]

Attached to an exclusive educational institution, the New Haven scholars imbued their own roles as facilitators of culture with the same tensions about democracy the Unitarians manifested. They, too, relied on the concept of an elite that would, by instruction and example, assist the masses in attaining salvation; to that end, they adopted a tone that was unequivocal and definitive. Yet their presumption of authority was largely bounded by their locale. Connected to the New York publishing world through the firm of Charles Scribner, they nonetheless remained aloof from the metropolitan scene and the influence it afforded.[17] Thus, the New Haven group represented a tributary, rather than the main stream, that carried the ideology of genteel culture forward to the twentieth century. The broader currents emanated from Unitarianism, not only by extension of the Harvard moralists' outlook but also by way of reaction against it. They swirled with particular force through transcendentalism, cresting in the thought of the figure who, perhaps more than any other individual, both typified and defined the cultured person for mid-nineteenth-century Americans: Ralph Waldo Emerson.

"Culture," Emerson declared in 1867, "implies all which gives the mind possession of its own powers." That formulation both perpetuated Emerson's Unitarian heritage and allied culture (or, again, "self-culture") with his own concept of "self-reliance." To cultivate the self, in Emerson's view, was to achieve a sense of proportion, a state of spiritual harmony, and the intellectual independence that Riesman would later call autonomy. It was, in addition, to acquire the aesthetic sensitivity that Emerson, like his contemporaries, designated "taste." Such qualities were "interior," not "easily disturbed by outward events and opinion." Moreover, in Emerson's scheme, as in Channing's, culture was intimately linked with character: the latter term retained its meaning as the expression, in demeanor and action, of integrity and balance within.[18]

Thus, Emerson added his voice to those who cast the true gentleman or lady as a foil for the pretender who exhibited merely a veneer of refinement. Self-reliance, attained through self-culture, shone in "a beauty which reaches through and through, from the manners to the soul." (Reversing the figure, Emerson also found the Quaker symbol of the "inner light" a congenial representation of the way culture radiated outward.) Finally, both culture and character rested on the human ability to exercise "moral sense." As Emerson made the connection, "The foundation of culture, as of character, is at last the moral sentiment." That is, Emerson joined the Unitarians in coupling self-development with self-denial in order to improve the common welfare. "Taste," too, was embedded in morality: "Beauty," Emerson wrote, "is with Truth and Goodness the triple face of God."[19]

As the last phrase reminds us, however, Emerson went further than the Unitarians in insisting that human beings embodied not only ethical potential but also godliness. This premise, the radical core of transcendentalism, introduced alongside Emerson's depiction of the autonomous individual a competing vision of self-abnegation that went far beyond the altruism implicit in the moral obligation to advance the human race. As Emerson veered away from Unitarian rationalism, self-culture became a process designed to approximate God within the individual. Its ultimate goal was to tear down the boundaries perceived to separate humanity, nature, and divinity. That objective might seem to sanction the pursuit of pure experience as a means of entering the realm of the universal and infinite. Emerson's most famous passage linking culture with a romantic, unfettered, expressive self appeared in the "introductory" to his 1837–38 lecture series "Human Culture." "Culture in the high sense," Emerson declared, "does not consist in polishing and varnishing, but in so presenting the attractions of nature that the slumbering attributes of man may burst their sleep and rush into day. The effect of Culture on the man will not be like the trimming and turfing of gardens, but the educating the eye to the true harmony of the unshorn landscape, with horrid thickets, wide morasses, bald mountains, and the balance of the land and sea."[20]

Yet even such metaphors of fervid awakening and unrepressed wildness did not, in fact, signify the abandonment of control, proportion, and self-sacrifice. As David Robinson has argued, Emerson in the late 1830s prescribed a more active form of discipline than the Unitarians did—he insisted that individuals fully exercise, rather than stifle, the "latent power" within them—but self-denial remained for him an essential attribute of the cultured person. So encumbered, one could never quite enact a complete surrender to self-annihilating experience. At the same time, the organic image of culture as the "unfolding" of one's divine "nature," while encouraging the release of inner feelings, also implicitly checked the tendency to sanction self-expression for the sake of a given person's "growth" alone. Emerson's sights were always on revealing the divinity in humankind as a whole. To pursue and exemplify the "ideal" was a "duty" that precluded hedonistic self-absorption.[21]

Emerson's understanding of the role of the critic was similarly complicated by a tension between his democratic individualism and his concern to spur cultural change. That is, his announcement, in "Self-Reliance," that "nothing is at last sacred but the integrity of your own mind" summarized his rejection of the idea that readers owed allegiance to the judgments of a "literary moral elite." The distinguishing feature of the "American Scholar," as depicted by Emerson in 1837, was self-trust, not reverence for "accepted dogmas." At the conclusion of an essay entitled "Books," Emerson made that principle the basis for a thoroughly egalitarian model of book reviewing: in place of deference to critical expertise, he imagined a "literary club" in which members would "report" on a book, after which each listener would "decide whether this is a book indispensable to him also."[22]

Still, Emerson differentiated the "scholars" who comprised his "club" from the "farmer," the "tradesman," the "attorney," and others. Even in his early writings, he attributed to the former the function—and the special prerogatives—of "delegated intellect." Moreover, by the time Emerson wrote "The Progress of Culture" in 1867, he had begun endorsing a "knighthood of virtue" comprised of the "few superior and attractive men" equipped to "calm and guide" the people. Emerson himself enlisted in that cadre in both the substance and style of his prose. With specific reference to book selection, he offered "practical rules" for reading, mingling homage to personal taste ("Never read any but what you like") with two other principles that exalted the classics: "Never read any book that is not a year old" and "Never read any but famed books." The heart of "Books" was an annotated list of the authors Emerson found "vital and spermatic"—a roster of "best books" (e.g., the works of the Greeks, Shakespeare, the "Bibles of the world") presented without apology or reticence. More generally, Emerson's interest in convincing his audience to pursue self-culture shaped his use of a literary strategy David Robinson has called "the Orphic voice": a predilection for the aphoristic sentence, delivered in the form of an "authoritative pronouncement" and "tinged with an aura of mysticism." This sermonlike quality in Emerson's prose reinforced, in language and tone, his assumption that his unregenerate readers required the benefits of his tutelage and counsel in order to guarantee "the gradual domestication of the idea of Culture."[23]

Thus, the Emersonian contribution to definitions of the cultured person sustained earlier conceptions of refinement even as it strove to overturn the rationalistic theology which buttressed them. It looked forward as well to the stance of a slightly younger generation of critics and reformers—to those writers who, between the Civil War and the turn of the twentieth century, so assiduously applied genteel strictures to literature and society that they have come to be known, collectively, as the major codifiers of the "genteel tradition" in American letters. The New York representatives of that tradition included a number of didactic poets and editors—Richard Watson Gilder, E. C. Stedman, Richard Stoddard—who exuded prudishness and superficiality. But the Boston wing of the group, and the New York component which identified with it, were more intellectually rigorous and substantial. The "Brahmin" version of gentility, expressed in such institutions as the *North American Review*, the *Atlantic Monthly*, and the Saturday Club, bridged both the Unitarian and transcendentalist viewpoints. Among its chief representatives, Charles Eliot Norton, the son of Andrews Norton, best symbolized the tie to Unitarianism, yet Norton managed to couple his disdain for the blandness of late transcendental thought with an affectionate respect for Emerson and a sense of their mutual connection to the Boston milieu.[24]

Together with such colleagues as George William Curtis, James Russell Lowell, Frederick Law Olmsted, and E. L. Godkin, Norton perpetuated the association of culture and character while strengthening the vocation of the writer as educator of public taste. As the central link in the Anglo-American chain of intellectuals David D. Hall has labeled the "Victorian connection," Norton provides the clearest reminder that the genteel vision of culture was not just a domestic development. Emerson's travels in England during the 1830s and 1840s, when he visited Thomas Carlyle and Arthur Hugh Clough, helped pave the way for Norton's transatlantic relationships with both of those writers. Norton also befriended, among others, John Morley, Leslie Stephen, and Goldwin Smith. Those figures shared with Norton and his circle a commitment to John Stuart Mill's liberalism; they assigned to the "best men" (like themselves) the task of freeing society at large from superstition, conformity, mediocrity, and debilitating economic competition.[25]

Culture, from their perspective, was thoroughly severed from any automatic association with wealth; rather, its diffusion held the greatest promise of counteracting materialism. Thus equipped, individuals could resist the temptations thrown up by the pace and pressures of a rapidly changing world. "To restore the balance of our lives, in these days of haste, novelty, and restlessness," Norton wrote in 1860, "there is need of a larger infusion into them of pursuits which have no end of immediate publicity or instant return of tangible profit—of pursuits which . . . should introduce us into the freer, tranquiller, and more spacious world of noble and everlasting thought." While Norton himself was no stranger to showmanship in the classroom, he still presumed a correlation between inward culture and outward manner. There is a "great need of men who may keep up the standard of cultivation," he declared in 1874, "without aiming at the cheap personal distinction for which most men strive."[26]

Character remained a synonym for culture in the vocabulary of this international community. Norton advised C. C. Stillman in 1899 to render "service" to others in the form of "influence" by "force of character." Elsewhere, he used the term to summarize the end of education as "the development of the breadth, serenity, and solidity of mind . . . the attainment of that complete self-possession which finds expression in character." That language—especially the phrase "complete self-possession"—inflected Norton's formulation, like Emerson's, with the capacity for independent choice associated with autonomy. But Norton's reference to "breadth" also deserves special mention as an allusion to a relatively new and increasingly troubling phenomenon: the rise of specialization. Norton, who lived long enough into the early twentieth century to see professionalization in full swing, wrote James Loeb in 1907: "It is a great pity that so many of our American scholars, old and young, have preferred the methods which lead only to the acquisition of facts often of no importance, to those which lead to the nobler cultivation of the intelligence and of the taste, and to the appreciation of the true ends of the study of language and of literature." James Russell Lowell summarized the issue metaphorically: "Special culture is the gymnastic of the mind, but liberal culture is healthy exercise in the open air." Thus, members of the genteel tradition took a stand as unreconstructed generalists, appropriating culture and character as weapons in their cause.[27]

Perhaps even more important in the lexicon of the "Victorian connection" was "discipline," which was closely allied with the notion of "training." Both words figured in Norton's 1867 definition of culture as "whatever discipline or training fits a man to make the best use of all his faculties"; the latter appeared as well in Thomas Wentworth Higginson's pronouncement that "culture is the training and finishing of the whole man." Similarly, E. L. Godkin described culture as "the breaking-in of the powers to the service of the will." In particular, "discipline" and "training" described the means by which the literary critic gained both ethical and aesthetic discrimination. Those qualities were as inter-twined for mid-Victorian genteel intellectuals as for their Unitarian predecessors. Norton's chief concern was that critics take responsibility for the "condemnation of pretension and inaccuracy, of false reasoning, of corrupting thought." This capacity to join "uprightness of character and justness of mind," Norton made clear, demanded "long and careful preparation": the "ideal critic's" powers had to be "trained" by "faithful study" of "the best products of literature in ancient and modern times." But while Norton believed that beauty was "the ultimate expression and warrant of goodness," he demanded that criticism make not only "thought accurate" but also "perception fine." That is, as they defined "the best," he and his colleagues, for all their moralism, insisted, in Daniel Aaron's phrase, "on the centrality of style, structure, form, clarity—on the craft of writing."[28]

Hence, Norton valued Dante's use of language as much as his didactic message. Similarly, Higginson, in an 1867 essay entitled "Literature as an Art," identified stylistic attributes—"simplicity," "freshness," and "choice of words"—as the qualities that lifted books to the "domain of pure literature." Critical "training" encompassed acquiring the ability to read a variety of works with "delicacy of feeling" and "insight of imagination." As Lowell explained, a "true scholar" learned to appre-ciate Wordsworth "for his depth of sympathy with nature," Herbert "for the naked picturesqueness of his style," and Herrick for his "sen-suous paganism." In short, in addition to ethical awareness, culture meant, in Higginson's words, educating "one's aesthetic perceptions to the very highest point."[29]

These imperatives, moreover, did not simply govern the genteel critics' private sensibilities. The emphasis on moral and aesthetic "training" shaped their understanding of their public roles as well. Their purpose, as they saw it, was not just to exemplify culture but to replicate it in others—to help readers replace what Olmsted called the "lack of *habits* of discipline" with a grasp of the "standards" that would enable them to discern the "best." Thus, for example, Norton in the 1890s created a series of anthologies—the Heart of Oak Books—to help instill "a taste for good reading," an objective he connected with mastering "control of the will" and "the quickening and growth of the moral sympathies." Conveying his sense of mission, Norton described the office of critic as one of "public instructor"; Lowell called it "a kind of priesthood."[30]

Both of those images rested on a paradox at the heart of the learning experience: that people in search of self-reliance could attain it only by becoming dependent on a superior authority outside themselves. The politics of Norton's circle expressed that paradox. Genteel liberalism, grounded as it was in a belief in individual freedom, entailed a commitment to the preservation of democracy; yet, increasingly, the "Victorian connection" concluded that, without the guidance of an educated minority, the majority would all too readily find itself entrapped in what Norton labeled a "paradise of mediocrities." To insure, in Norton's words, "the success of democratic institutions" required "the intellectual and moral training of the people" by an elite imbued with a sense of "patriotic duty." In that spirit, genteel critics made rigorous judgment the heart of their enterprise. To shrink from asserting their expertise—to exude " 'good nature' " instead—was to abet "the great enemy to excellence in literature and reform in politics."[31]

One member of that self-appointed elite—Matthew Arnold—so fully epitomized the transatlantic genteel tradition that the term "Arnoldian" can stand as a summary of its attitudes toward culture, character, discipline, training, democracy, and critical authority. Arnold's thought was not initially as important to Norton and his colleagues as Mill's; nor, when he launched his attacks on American society in the 1880s, did it always find favor among those who applauded his literary criticism. Yet eventually Arnold became the most influential disseminator of the genteel aesthetic. As Henry James declared, "I shall not go so far as to say of Mr. Arnold that he invented [culture], but he made it more definite than it had been before—he vivified and lighted it up." Arnold's famous definition of culture as "the best that has been thought and said in the world" became a slogan for allegiance to "standards," reverence toward the classics, and deference to critics skilled at sorting edifying books from the useless or harmful. Arnold's other well-known injunction, to pursue "sweetness and light," conveyed his double concern with beauty and truth. Like his American counterparts, he set those qualities over against materialism, or what he called the "faith in machinery" accompanying industrialization. An alternative as well to the mere display of "outward gifts and graces," culture was, finally, a barrier against the ultimate lack of discipline—the "anarchy" that ensued from "doing what one's ordinary self likes" rather than pursuing the "best."[32]

Arnold's plan for resisting that threat captured the essence of the genteel tradition's politics: he proposed to "do away with classes" by designating "the great men of culture" as "the true apostles of equality." Such individuals, Arnold claimed in a key passage, "are those who have had a passion for diffusing, for making prevail, for carrying from one end of society to the other, the best knowledge, the best ideas of their time; who have laboured . . . to humanise [knowledge], to make it efficient outside the clique of the cultivated and learned, yet still remaining the best knowledge and thought of the time." The last phrase was crucial; while Arnold's brigade of critics was always to remain engaged with the public, it was not to let its mediative function interfere with its concerted exercise of judgment. What is more, though he eschewed pedantry, Arnold made it clear that the process of pursuing perfection would not admit shortcuts; culture was "an object not to be gained without books and reading," which demanded "disinterested and active" attention.[33]

Armed with those convictions, Arnoldian intellectuals established museums, parks, symphony orchestras, and libraries. As Hall reminds us, Olmsted's career was a prime example of the "passion for diffusing": he not only designed Central Park but also served as a trustee of the Metropolitan Museum of Art. Along with Norton and Godkin, he was especially committed, as chapter 2 will relate, to inculcating genteel values through the mechanism of the "higher," or noncommercial journalism. In that way, Arnoldian critics transmitted and solidified all of the premises that came to animate Hamilton Wright Mabie's *Ladies' Home Journal* correspondent. Her anxiety was a measure of their success.[34]

Instruments of Diffusion—and Subversion

As genteel critics and reformers joined novelists, theologians, and philosophers in shaping a nineteenth-century ideology of culture, the institutions they founded took their place alongside other agencies which served as sources for refinement or sites at which it could be calibrated. One such testing ground was the theater or the concert hall. Lawrence W. Levine has forcefully insisted that, in the antebellum period, popular audiences routinely embraced performances that later came to be associated exclusively with "high" culture. Shakespeare, for example, was as much a part of the working-class world as folktales about Davy Crockett. Shakespearean language and style accorded with the spirit of the camp meeting, the melodrama, and the political debate. Burlesqued and revised to fit the needs of the times, Shakespeare was integrated into the cultural life of the nation as a whole. Levine has related a similar story about opera, which at first absorbed such eclectic materials as popular tunes, sword fights, and band renditions. Only later, in his view, after Arnoldian elitists engaged in the "sacralization of culture," did the stage and the opera hall come to exhibit the divisions between "high" and popular art twentieth-century Americans customarily draw.[35]

This argument contains a valuable warning against imputing to the past the analytical categories of the present. Yet, for all its merits, Levine's interpretation is still a picture of a one-way street. If, as is now clear, Shakespeare was not the exclusive property of an educated minority, the fact remains that, even in the years before the 1850s, when matters were most fluid, the exuberant spectacles of the popular stage were never permissible entertainments for aspirants to respectability. Those Americans sought from the early 1800s a theater of "refined sentiment" that blended decorum, obedience to authority, and reverence for European forms. As Levine himself has related, a figure like Washington Irving, for example, felt at odds with the frequenters of the gallery, who annoyed him by making animal noises and other disruptive sounds. To respond instead with polite applause was to differentiate oneself from the uncultivated. Richard Bushman's appraisal of the relationship between the vernacular and the genteel in the eighteenth century applies to the later period as well: "Exchange and assimilation went on constantly, but the porousness of the boundaries does not mean that no boundaries existed." It is true that, gradually, entr'acte juggling routines were excluded from evenings of Shakespeare, the opera became isolated from other musical events, and symphony orchestra conductors made a virtue of remoteness from the untrained listener. These developments, however, reflected not so much a new religion of culture as the elaboration of a doctrine that had long had faithful adherents.[36]

A second source of refinement—although it also had other consequences—was the burgeoning American publishing business. In the first decades of the nineteenth century, changes in technology and distribution methods made possible a revolution in the manufacture and sale of books and periodicals. The introduction of such innovations as the power-driven cylinder press and new paper-making machinery dramatically lowered the cost of book production. Improvements in transportation and communication, together with the consolidation and reorganization of the industry, made publishing after 1840 more and more a national, rather than a local, activity. Those developments eradicated what remained of the authority of "steady sellers"—the devotional texts that had formed the core of traditional literacy in seventeenth- and eighteenth-century New England; they engendered in its place an abundant print culture characterized by the casual, widespread reading of fiction, journalism, and instructional volumes on myriad subjects. Publishers marketed books by subscription through traveling agents or mail order advertising to help satisfy the demand for such works.[37]

Undergirding the efforts of etiquette writers, Unitarians, and Arnoldians alike, the transformation of publishing assisted the democratization of gentility by exposing more people to its moral and aesthetic ideals. That is, the market permitted what might be called a process of "desacralization," facilitating Arnold's directive to spread the "best" throughout society. From the beginning, the spread of print also carried an attendant risk: that audiences, misappropriating or even ignoring their genteel instructors' meaning and intentions, would seize on cheap novels rather than serious literature. Until the 1850s, however, proponents of culture tended to emphasize only the positive side of the publishing revolution. For example, Channing hailed "the multiplication of books, and their distribution through all conditions of society" as a force for "an unspeakable good to the individual" and the "stability of nations" alike.[38]

During the second half of the nineteenth century, the "desacralization" fostered by an expanding American book trade gained even more momentum. In the absence of an international copyright law, reprint "libraries" offering inexpensive editions of fiction mushroomed in the 1870s and 1880s. The distribution of such works through newsdealers as well as booksellers added to their accessibility. Similarly, between 1885 and 1905 almost eleven thousand different periodicals were published in the United States. In roughly the same period—1880 to 1900—American book publishers produced a threefold increase in titles and adopted new, aggressive marketing techniques to peddle them to the public. Sales of books by subscription agents also continued to multiply. The growth of lending libraries made this surfeit readily available to book borrowers as well as purchasers.[39]

Even when those trends tended to present refinement in unabashedly commodified form, they still had the potential to bolster Arnoldian values by dispersing them. The editors of popular periodicals, John Kasson has written, "participated in the commercialization of American culture; but in their public postures they resolutely directed their gazes above the coarse and vulgar realities of everyday life to the lofty realm of the ideal." Varieties of mass image reproduction—lithographs, photographs, engravings—could likewise serve to familiarize audiences with the genteel aesthetic.[40]

At the same time, the expansion of publishing, by making it more difficult to discern "the best" amidst the mountains of volumes published, partially enhanced the stature of genteel critics. As expertise came to be viewed as the antidote to bewilderment, Americans cast public officials and educators as advisers about book selection. Noah Porter's popular *Books and Reading: Or What Books Shall I Read and How Shall I Read Them* (1871) was a response to that mandate. Porter's volume was characteristically reassuring: he issued his edicts about appropriate books in the unequivocal, definitive tone that Godkin and Arnold prescribed for disseminating literary judgments. The promise of guidance inhered as well in later anthologies and collections of essays like Norton's Heart of Oak series and Charles Dudley Warner's thirty-volume *Library of the World's Best Literature* (1897), to which Norton contributed an article.[41]

Yet Arnoldian critics were increasingly aware after 1850 that the spread of print could subvert as well as consolidate their authority. As recalcitrant audiences evaded genteel control by grabbing up "trash," Lowell observed: "It may well be questioned whether the invention of printing, while it democratized information, has not also leveled the ancient aristocracy of thought. . . . [I]t has supplanted a strenuous habit of thinking with a loose indolence of reading which relaxes the muscular fiber of the mind. . . . The costliness of books was a great refiner of literature. . . . The problem for the scholar was formerly how to acquire books; for us it is how to get rid of them." Similarly, Godkin's famous indictment of "Chromo-Civilization" (1874) tied "mental and moral chaos" to the ease with which Americans could "see and own pictures" and acquire a "smattering" of knowledge from periodicals.[42]

From this perspective, efforts such as Porter's volume of advice on book selection appear as attempts to intervene in the marketplace. Porter's text, for example, explicitly treated the growth of the publishing industry as a threat to morality. In contrast to Channing, who was content merely to allude to the importance of choosing the "best" books, Porter felt compelled to supply general principles of book choice and lists of acceptable volumes. Offering predictable warnings against sensational novels, he also fended off attacks on the primacy of discipline, insisting that the entertaining "quick read" had no place in Christian nurture. Even so, the salient feature of such interventions was the genteel critics' optimism that they could counteract the tendency of the publishing explosion to foster vulgarity rather than refinement.[43]

Higher education was a third arena in which some Americans could discover and display the attributes of culture. In the mid-nineteenth century, its structure was in flux: the old-time college, largely devoted to training young men for the ministry, was receding before the rise of the research university. In this process, the idea that higher learning existed to inculcate "mental discipline" lost ground to a number of rival philosophies of education. The New Haven scholars, with their emphasis on self-cultivation, represented one departure from earlier pietistic priorities; so did Emerson, in his capacity as lecturer on the importance of student-centered instruction. The widely held position—enunciated by Charles W. Eliot of Harvard, Andrew Dickson White of Cornell, and Charles R. Van Hise of Wisconsin, among others—that universities should serve utilitarian purposes subordinated the shaping of taste and character to the goal of preparation for "real life." Eliot, moreover, was working toward his "new definition of the cultivated man," which made scientific knowledge an integral part of culture. Still other educational theorists envisioned universities as centers of pure research—Johns Hopkins University being the chief example.

Yet, although its appeal would soon prove almost irresistible, in principle the advocates of practicality and research rejected a curriculum devoted entirely to specialized learning. "We must beware," Hopkins's president Daniel Coit Gilman warned, "lest we make our schools technical instead of liberal, and impart a knowledge of methods rather than principles." Many university presidents not only continued to champion the character ideal but also embodied it. Both Eliot (who was Norton's cousin) and Gilman radiated independence, moral virtue, and reason. Similarly, Robert LaFollette pronounced University of Wisconsin president John Bascom "a man much of [Emerson's] type, both in appearance and in character." While the presidents' symbolism of professional accomplishment aided the proponents of utilitarianism by contributing to modern conceptions of "career," their model equally served to reinforce the idea that the purpose of college education was the shaping of the "inner man."[44]

In addition, there remained a group of educators who more actively opposed specialization: the partisans of "liberal culture." Giving "mental discipline" a cosmopolitan, secular turn, this faction essentially represented the academic wing of the genteel tradition. As a member of the Harvard faculty, Norton was, of course, in this category; so, too, was his colleague Barrett Wendell. But numerous other instructors, at places like Williams and Amherst, Yale and Princeton, also resisted the attractions of scientism and the pressure for expediency. Instead, they offered students the opportunity to become exemplars of broad knowledge, humanistic feeling, and proper conduct. The introduction of the elective system in the 1870s—which Eliot spearheaded—entrenched the advocates of specialization and research as the dominant influence on the nation's campuses, fortifying the university's capacity to undermine genteel values. Nevertheless, American higher education still offered to the proponents of "liberal culture" an opportunity for diffusing their generalist creed. Beleaguered but steadfast, those professors continued to defend their belief that the classroom was to be a refuge from narrow vocational concerns and a "retreat" from mediocrity and materialism.[45]

A fourth institution—the public lecture system in which Channing and Emerson participated—complemented the university by serving as a source of culture for a broader audience than the privileged population of matriculated undergraduates. Locally sponsored between 1826 and 1845, and part of a growing national network thereafter, public lecturers appeared at such forums as lyceums, mechanics' institutes, and, later, Young Men's Mercantile Libraries and Chautauquas. Although literature occupied a significant proportion of the lecturers' subject matter, the system as a whole tended to facilitate less the acquisition of refinement than the accumulation of eclectic information. Because all knowledge might someday be useful, mid-nineteenth-century lecture-goers voraciously amassed disparate collections of facts—some about topics as remote from "the best that has been thought and said in the world" as "The Honey Bee" or "Chemistry Applied to the Mechanic Arts."[46]

Moreover, like the dissemination of advice about speech and conduct, and the spread of print generally, public lecturing allowed people to adopt refined behavior without undergoing the process of moral development the lecturers themselves had in mind. Emerson's addresses are a case in point. For one thing, because he was often judged difficult to understand, his audiences were smaller for topics like "Books" than for apparently practical subjects like "Wealth." But, in addition, by the 1850s some of Emerson's listeners at his more popular performances were transforming his critique of American materialism into maxims for commercial success. The more he gained in celebrity, the more it became possible to regard mere attendance at his lectures as proof of cultivation.[47]

Despite those features, however, the lecture system also expressed and shored up genteel premises in several ways. First, lecture audiences typically demanded that facts be interpreted—that speakers present them in a manner capable of inspiring as well as educating and diverting. Thus, listeners evinced some desire for a refined sensibility as well as a command of data. Second, in terms of personnel, many of the best-known figures on the lecture circuit were also eminent in genteel literary circles: not only Emerson but Lowell, George William Curtis, Oliver Wendell Holmes, and, representing the New York contingent of the same tradition, the popular poet and travel lecturer Bayard Taylor. Their roles as acclaimed speakers enlarged their cultural authority. Most important, the lyceum movement, at least in the antebellum period, shared with the genteel ideology of culture a common assumption about the self. That is, the popular lecture served the process of "individual self-creation": it promised not to equip listeners with job skills but, rather, to endow them with the resourcefulness and inner strength the boundless conditions of American life seemed to require. Although lecturers' messages could be applied in ways at odds with genteel expectations, the mid-nineteenth-century view of "useful knowledge" rested on and reinforced the conviction that self-reliance was possible.[48]

Further Challenges to Self-Reliance and Liberal Learning

By the late 1800s, however, even as the theater, the publishing industry, the university, and the lecture system were continuing to strengthen genteel definitions of character and culture, accelerating forces in American society were challenging that faith in self-reliance and intensifying the problem of recalcitrant audiences. On the broadest level, massive immigration, urbanization, and industrialization severely limited the extent of compliance with genteel strictures. New immigrants, holding fast to their heritages, often remained impervious to the efforts of genteel critics to impose "discipline" and "standards." Along with other urban workers, they flocked instead to amusement parks, dance halls, vaudeville shows, and similar forms of uninhibited popular entertainment. Likewise, as immigrants and workers gained political power, they threatened traditional patterns of deference to white Anglo-Saxon Protestants. Beginning in the 1880s, ethnic groups demanded representatives sensitive to their quest for the American dream—a quest carried out on their own terms. In response, both upper- and middle-class Americans, Levine has written, felt lost in a "new universe of strangers," beset by "a sense of anarchic change, of looming chaos, of fragmentation."[49]

More specifically, the inhabitants of that universe experienced growing difficulty sustaining a belief in the autonomous self. Technological advance created a diffuse malaise about "overcivilization"; the intrusion of doubt into Protestantism weakened its call to duty as well as its theological framework; and the rise of an interdependent national market made it more difficult to believe that anyone could be "self-made." In this context, even Norton lamented that "the man of to-day . . . cannot get along alone" and was more "helpless" than his predecessors. Yet, to the end of his life, Norton was guided by a conviction that "self-possession" was desirable and attainable. By contrast, many finde-siècle observers concluded, in Jackson Lears's words, that "modern man seemed to lack any irreducible core of individuality; selfhood consisted only in a series of manipulatable social masks." William Dean Howells summarized that view in a memorable analogy: human beings were like onions—"nothing but hulls, that you keep peeling off, one after another, till you think you have got down to the heart at last, and then you have got down to nothing."[50]

To reintroduce Riesman's terminology, by the turn of the century "other direction" tended to supplant "inner direction"; concomitantly, the character ideal gave some ground to a vision of the self predicated on "personality." Although they shared with representatives of character an interest in self-development, exemplary personalities (as the word was most widely used after the early 1900s) sought "growth" for its own sake. Instead of achieving "self-control," they attained "self-realization" and "self-expression" by the therapeutic release of emotion. "Letting go" and the pursuit of intense experience through immersion in "real life" superseded boundedness and restraint. In that sense, the emphasis on personality lodged a protest against the potential for the culture of character to discourage spontaneity and sensuousness. At the same time, successful personalities continually sought confirmation that they were on the road to "well-being" by gauging the responses of others. The man or woman with "magnetism" and attractiveness knew how both to please and to stand out from the crowd. Thus, while it contained laudable elements of liberation, the advice-manual authors' declaration that "Personality is the quality of being Somebody" entailed its own form of repression: enslavement to the judgment of other people—with Nobody inside.[51]

Two caveats are in order here: one about context, the other about chronology. To begin with, the concept of personality as what F. Scott Fitzgerald described as "an endless series of successful gestures" did not always or exclusively capture the meaning writers who employed the word had in mind. As already noted, the Unitarians invoked the term in their call for service to divinity. Similarly, the Protestant theologian Walter Rauschenbush upheld the commitment to character development but labeled it "personality," or "the fullness of humanity that permits breadth of sympathy and maturity of judgment." Moreover, Randolph Bourne, Van Wyck Brooks, and others in the so-called Seven Arts group of intellectuals appropriated the same word to advance the cause of radical politics, using it to signify their opposition to the stultifying effects of capitalism on creativity. Within that framework, "experience" likewise served spiritual and political purposes larger than individual gratification. John Dewey talked of "self-realization" but saw that process within the framework of character; he advocated not a conscious quest for personal growth but a sense of selfhood arising out of moral action undertaken to benefit society as a whole. Walt Whitman's declaration, in "Democratic Vistas" (1871), that culture "must have for its spinal meaning the formation of a typical personality of character" provides a striking reminder of the difficulty of sorting out the associations with the two terms and of taking account of the particular setting in which they appear.[52]

In addition, as the example of Emerson's lecture audiences shows, even the most common twentieth-century understanding of the imperative to build personality had its nineteenth-century antecedents. Likewise, Emerson's romantic leanings foreshadowed later quests for "real life." Nor, it must be reiterated, did the notion of character preclude garnering social approval. Still, while its elements were incipient earlier, what Warren Susman called the full-fledged "culture of personality" differed from the official norms of the mid-1800s in two key respects: First, the type of social performance that increasingly preoccupied Americans after the First World War bore no necessary connection to inward traits. Second, the modern seeker of personality typically shed the larger moral justification for self-culture that figures like Channing and Emerson always maintained.

Furthermore, although the precise periodization involved remains a matter of controversy, the rise of personality as a standard of self-definition was inextricably linked to the expansion of mass consumer culture.[53] Beginning in the late nineteenth century, such developments as corporate organization, efficient, large-scale distribution networks, and specialized advertising made an unprecedented variety of goods available to working-class as well as middle-class Americans. That climate of abundance overtook the producers' ethic of scarcity, encouraging instead the search for infinite "growth." That is, the emphasis on control and self-sacrifice attending the concept of character ill served an economy that required continual spending on proliferating goods. Additionally, Lears has noted, "the therapeutic injunction to 'let go' eased adjustment to the rhythms of life under corporate capitalism"—to a cycle of "degrading" work and "revitalizing" leisure. Perhaps more fundamentally, in the widening consumer culture "the fragmented self became a commodity like any other, to be assembled and manipulated for private gain." In a faceless, corporate milieu, the ability to attract attention and seduce others by concocting "winning images"—to be, in other words, a "confidence man"—acquired greater value than discipline or industry. As part of that process, the fabrication of a performing self equipped to create favorable impressions in variable circumstances came to depend on the acquisition of products and services. By the 1920s and 1930s these included elocution lessons, charm courses, and beauty aids. Advertisers made the prospect of self-realization through pleasing others the heart of campaigns for items ranging from home furnishings to toilet paper.[54]

Again, it would be a mistake to overstate the discontinuity this transformation entailed with respect to ideas of culture, because the exercise of "taste" always implicated exemplars of character in consumption. But one feature of the pervasive consumer ethos was that the distinction between "taste" and "fashion" tended to collapse. The sense that the self was a series of purchases now sanctioned the inclination to regard culture as one more commodity; the emphasis on projecting images challenged the idea that one's possessions were to reflect an inward *self*-possession; and the stipulations that buyers should observe restraint, exercise discipline, and foster the moral order were subordinated to an endless search for items that would, above all, supply personal gratification and influence over others.[55]

A further threat to genteel ideology in the late 1800s arose as the trend toward specialization gathered momentum outside of, as well as within, the university. The rapid expansion of information and the splintering of occupations into discrete pursuits requiring particular skills cast serious doubt on the value of liberal culture altogether and narrowed the definition of "useful knowledge." In a society in which opportunities were increasingly circumscribed by a person's ability to display the learning and credentials that would impress other people, the best course might be not to build the capacity to meet any eventuality but to concentrate one's energies on acquiring immediately practical "know-how." To the extent that Emerson's listeners turned his "Orphic voice" into slogans applicable to business, they revealed this tendency in its nascent stage. By the turn of the century, numerous other commentators had joined Godkin in bemoaning the "fad of imitation culture" and assailing the clamor for facts that competed with the demand for aesthetic and moral training. James L. Ford's satire on the pursuit of "culturine" appropriately depicted the situation in metaphors of commodification and consumption: Americans, he complained, wanted "information . . . put up in small capsules, and sold in boxes containing one dozen each." These they could swallow in order to project a more attractive self at the dinner table. That frame of mind weakened the authority of generalist critics, whose stance as "experts" broadly versed in liberal learning now verged on a contradiction in terms.[56]

Arnoldian Criticism as Humanistic Reform

Given the strength of the various challenges to their outlook throughout the nineteenth century, it is easy to see, especially in the American context, a current of fear underneath the Arnoldian critics' principled position. Their insistence on "standards," on the importance of training, and on distinguishing true from false culture appears designed to stave off threats to their own power. Figures like Olmsted and Norton, Levine has explained, seized upon culture as "a life raft in an unpredictable and turbulent sea." Once aboard, they tried to navigate as much as possible according to rules of public decorum—rules which they alone determined. These they attempted to impose on a heterogeneous society at the expense of spontaneity and pluralism. Employed as a bulwark against change, genteel moralism might eventuate in the overweening attention to propriety of which Santayana and Brooks complained; at its worst, it could be used to support racism or claims of Anglo-Saxon superiority.[57]

Yet, as Levine acknowledges, to construe the genteel tradition entirely in terms of social control is to oversimplify the matter. Arnoldian critics deserve credit for their democratic convictions and their sense of civic responsibility. More than that, a thorough account of their viewpoint demands recognition of the degree to which genteel ideology was itself an attempt to wrest power from an entrenched establishment. Whether they saw themselves as educators or priests, genteel intellectuals were fundamentally reformers. The museums and journals they founded were efforts to assert authority apart from existing religious, educational, and literary institutions. Their estrangement from what they saw as the cruder aspects of popular culture militated against their impulse to plunge into the task of reform. But their antiestablishment origins make one thing abundantly clear: in Hall's words, the "Victorian connection" did not "begin with cultural hegemony and live in quiet desperation watching it decline."[58]

This is not to dismiss the repressive potential the genteel understanding of culture always entailed. Nor is it to ignore another of its perils: that an exaggeration of the emphasis on "beauty" or form would lead to self-involved decadence.[59] Yet, if they veered toward aestheticism, critics such as Norton at least made qualities of mind, rather than dollars in the bank, marks of the successful individual. More broadly, the genteel belief in aesthetic training was essentially humanistic. Grounded as it was in a vision of self-reliance, it presumed the capacity of all readers, once "trained," to grasp the elements of literary style and accorded them a basic right to have their lives enriched in so doing. Lastly, one must recognize that many Americans, themselves adrift in uncharted waters, turned to Arnoldian critics for comfort and guidance not only because they wanted thereby to gratify their desire for prestige or to differentiate themselves from the working class, but also because they sought stability, insight, and pleasure in the books to which they were directed. Although many social historians have often overlooked them, those hopes were as legitimate, as poignant, and as human as any of the fantasies played out at Coney Island or the movies.

Dr. Eliot's Five-Foot Shelf

In any case, the historical processes that undermined nineteenth-century suppositions about self and culture did not so much result in the "decline" or disappearance of the genteel tradition as endow its Arnoldian program with a set of characteristic tensions. While the book clubs, "great books" groups, radio programs, and similar efforts generated in the three decades following World War I afford the fullest view of those conflicts, it is worth a brief look at the most famous predecessor of such middlebrow forms to see the direction in which things were headed by 1909. This was Charles W. Eliot's "Five-Foot Shelf of Books," also known as the Harvard Classics. During his Harvard presidency, Eliot had from time to time hypothesized in speeches about a five-foot shelf of books that would furnish a liberal education to anyone willing to devote fifteen minutes per day to reading them. When the publisher Robert Collier proposed that P. F. Collier and Son create such a collection, Eliot agreed to lend his—and Harvard's—name to the venture, as well as to choose the books for inclusion and prepare an editor's introduction.

The completed project captured Eliot's intermediate position as a proponent of the elective system who nonetheless championed education "which broadened the sympathies and opened the mind." It also marked him as a figure who combined respect for experts with the moralistic insistence that such authorities be "cultured men of old families" committed to "community, duty, and self-sacrifice." The texts he selected revealed his persistent allegiance to the ancients and to venerable English writers. In his introduction, Eliot reiterated the connection between culture and the mid-nineteenth-century understanding of self-creation, identifying the goal of his reading program as the development of the "liberal frame of mind" that great books "enriched, refined, and fertilized." The attainment of that goal, he contended, demanded self-sacrifice and "a resolute spirit." Yet he also identified a liberal education with a list of great books, a move which, to some observers, smacked of the substitution of specific knowledge for a refined sensibility. Additionally, his willingness to quantify the time required for reading suggested cramming rather than training, undermining the idea that culture required sustained effort.[60]

Hence, the early rhetoric surrounding the Harvard Classics satisfied the need for access to "the best" while simultaneously addressing the desire for information and making it consumable. Eliot's continuing depiction of culture as interior, together with his refusal explicitly to associate learning with ease, signified that the "Five-Foot Shelf of Books" was, as initially conceived, predominantly an index of the tenacity of genteel strictures, but the apparatus for loosening those strictures was present nonetheless. The same themes surfaced in the early advertising for the volumes. One of the first advertisements featured a portrait of "Dr. Eliot" beneath the banner "The Harvard Classics," language that both traded on and perpetuated the prestige of the university and the importance of the "best." Flanking the portrait were two quotations from Eliot, their symmetrical position mirroring the duality underlying the enterprise as a whole: on the right, Eliot's comment that the "studious and reflective recipient" of a liberal education would attain a "liberal frame of mind"; on the left, although joined to a qualifying phrase about "rereadings and memorizings," the reference to "fifteen minutes a day." A more famous early advertisement pictured Eliot reading to his grandson—an allusion, in a different way, to traditional values. The combination was a winning one, the sale of the volumes surpassing Collier's expectations.[61]

The Post–World War I Situation

By the time Eliot died in 1926, the United States was even more thoroughly and visibly an interdependent, bureaucratic, urban, secular, and mass society than it had been in the late nineteenth century. As numerous writers of the 1920s attested, the word "standardization," formerly denoting uniformity in the manufacturing process, acquired fearful associations: the demise of the country storekeeper, the sameness of towns flashing by in train windows, the "lock-step" nation simultaneously eating "tabloid" dinners. The ability to muster a successful impression correspondingly seemed more urgent.[62] In consequence, the pressure to acquire information in order to mold personality could easily overwhelm the impetus to build character through reading the classics. Culture, explained Albert Edward Wiggam in *The Marks of an Educated Man* (1925), involved "getting along with other people," or "get along-ableness." Reflecting that premise, the advertisements for Eliot's volumes in the 1920s and 1930s shed most of their genteel overtones. Some attached purchase of the set to business rewards. But an even more frequent appeal linked an aura of cultivation to the achievement of social success. One advertisement intimated that acquiring the volumes would result in admission to a country club. Another substituted a picture of dinner guests seated around a table for the portrait of Eliot. As Everett Dean Martin described it, "There are two men and a beautiful woman. She is talking to the man on her right, and is evidently fascinated with his brilliant conversation. The man on the left sits dumb and miserable and unnoticed; he cannot join in such sophisticated and scintillating discussion. We are informed that the poor man has neglected to read his fifteen minutes a day." The ultimate in such pitches appeared in 1932, when an advertisement revealed "How to Get Rid of an Inferiority Complex" by purchasing the set. (Around the same time, a blurb for a two-volume collection of Emerson's writings urged, "To fully realize what magnetism there is in your own personality, read CULTURE, WEALTH, BEHAVIOR, POWER.") Yet, however skewed toward "impression management," those appeals were still predicated on the assumption that readers would benefit—psychically as well as socially—from familiarity with the literary canon genteel critics had constructed.[63]

Whatever the underlying strains the decade encompassed, the booming economy of the 1920s tended, in some quarters, to weaken even that barely Arnoldian stance. "Not long ago," James Truslow Adams noted in 1929, "a despatch from Washington announced that 'the highest standard of living ever attained in the history of the world was reached last year [1926] by the American people.'" That triumph, related not to the disciplined study of the classics but to technological innovation, practicality, and occupational specialization, made it tempting to dismiss culture altogether as irrelevant to success—now defined as the ability to buy consumer goods. This was the "flip side" of the dissociation of culture and wealth: status, one might conclude, belonged not to those refined, dutiful individuals detached from commercial pursuits but to those in business, literate or not, whose "know-how" showed them to be the masters of modern conditions. The expansion of business education at the nation's universities reflected the new mood. As Adams complained, Arnold's definition of culture was "far removed from giving the degree of Bachelor of Arts to a student who has learned how to truss and dress poultry or has compassed the mysteries of how to sell real estate and run an apartment house."[64]

Alternatively, if they "bought" it at all, newly rich entrepreneurs, staking their claim to prestige on the basis of wealth alone, might see culture as merely good for the pocketbook. Intent on convincing the Boosters Club to support a symphony orchestra, Chum Frink explained in Sinclair Lewis's *Babbitt*: "I don't care a rap for all this long-haired music. . . . But that isn't the point. Culture has become as necessary an adornment and advertisement for a city today as pavements. . . . The thing to do then, as a live bunch of go-getters, is to *capitalize Culture*; to go right out and grab it."[65]

But other characteristics of the post–World War I era tended to buttress, rather than to erode, the ideology of culture as it had evolved throughout the nineteenth century. At many universities the ideal of liberal education still held its own, striking an uneasy truce with specialization; it even made something of a comeback at institutions like Harvard and Amherst. Thus, the dramatic rise in the number of college graduates between 1920 and 1930 from a half-million to more than one million meant, if not necessarily an increase in the study of classic texts, at least more exposure to the idea that broad reading was intrinsically worthwhile as well as socially rewarding. Similarly, the doubling of high school enrollment in the same period increased the number of people who wanted "to continue some contact with the better printed word." The continued growth of the book market, which the prosperity of the decade fostered, also made the materials of culture more accessible than ever: American publishers issued over ten thousand new titles a year in 1929, as opposed to just over six thousand in 1920. The shortening of the work week and the spread of the eight-hour day gave at least some parts of the population more opportunity to encounter those titles. To be sure, the book industry worried about competing with automobiles, movies, and radio for Americans' extra leisure hours. Yet radio itself, in the form of literary and other educational programs, also provided "the opportunity to guide reading without the painfulness of the review."[66]

The contested worth of culture by the interwar period magnified the ambiguities surrounding the role of the literary expert. More than America's well-known anti-intellectualism was involved. The widespread experience of success in the marketplace tended to overturn the presumption that their superior knowledge entitled critics to special treatment from unschooled readers. At the same time, the anonymity of modern life and the anxiety that "standardization" would lead to the "chain-store mind" made it more difficult for experts to insist that the route to autonomy lay in the self-abnegation the genteel tradition had demanded. Instead, they increasingly leaned toward perpetuating the fiction, if not the reality, of their audiences' ready-made capacity for independent judgment. Moreover, the political developments of the early twentieth century had rendered the elitist aspect of the genteel outlook less tenable: as Progressives came to terms with pluralism, they heightened both the rhetoric and the practice of democracy; as the nation justified its participation in World War I, it repeatedly invoked the vocabulary of egalitarianism. In this context, critics who asserted "the best" without allowing for a reader's own preferences risked the charge that they were out of step with American values.[67]

But the conditions for enhancing critical authority were also present. The prestige of experts in the social sciences, at a high-water mark by 1917, continued to spill over into the humanities. Even more than in the nineteenth century, readers overwhelmed by spiraling numbers of book titles required guidance in selecting the "best"—if only to draw the attention of others. The rise of literary modernism, by challenging conventional uses of form and language, presented another source of confusion.

In addition, America's preoccupation with consumption triggered a debate about the nature of "civilization" within its borders. Was it possible, more thoughtful observers wondered, to be simultaneously a consumer society and a repository of artistic achievement? Would such a society offer future artists adequate traditions on which to draw? As Adams queried, "Can a great civilization be built up or maintained upon the philosophy of the counting-house and the sole basic idea of a profit?" Harold Stearns's collection of essays *Civilization in the United States* (1922) was the most famous—and most negative—commentary on those questions. But the issue informed other documents of the period. Alarmed librarians studied American reading habits and urged their colleagues to make serious books more attractive to a straying public. Ironically, because it rested on the desire for increased revenue itself, O. H. Cheney's *Economic Survey of the Book Industry, 1930–31* condemned such entrepreneurial techniques as price-cutting, best-seller "ballyhoo," and the production of "excessive numbers of titles." To the segment of the population which shared those fears of rampant materialism, the critic who offered a way to maintain both affluence and standards commanded respect and gratitude.[68]

Given that matrix of rival impulses and understandings about culture and criticism, one can thus detect two styles of expertise among the middlebrow authorities of the early twentieth century: one diffident and subjective, the other pontifical and prescriptive. These styles sometimes coexisted in the same individual—just as the institutions to which middlebrow critics attached themselves mingled character and personality, autonomy and the "social mask," aesthetic training and information, repression and experience, democracy and elitism. In general, the history of middlebrow culture provides a powerful illustration of the shift from producer to consumer values in America. At the same time, such an account furnishes an equally powerful reminder that that transformation, if far-reaching, was also partial and uneven. The "middleness" evident in the examples which follow supports both conclusions.

THE "HIGHER JOURNALISM" REALIGNED

STUART PRATT SHERMAN, IRITA VAN DOREN, AND BOOKS

The American affinity for diagnoses of declension—for seeing in the present a waning of earlier glories—has informed artifacts ranging from the Puritan sermon to Jay Gatsby's romantic remembrances. To those familiar expressions of the lament for the past, one might add an example drawn from the history of middlebrow culture: the jeremiad concerning American book reviewing. Writing in *Harper's* for October 1959, for instance, the novelist Elizabeth Hardwick castigated the book-review sections of the *New York Times* and *New York Herald Tribune* as blander and less rigorous than they used to be. "The flat praise and the faint dissension," Hardwick complained, "the minimal style and the light little article, the absence of involvement, passion, character, eccentricity—the lack, at last, of the literary tone itself" had turned such publications into mediocre repositories of "slumberous acceptance." The source of the malady, she argued, was a slavishness to "simple 'coverage'" of new books, regardless of their quality and significance. Commercial pressures were less responsible for that approach, Hardwick thought, than an editorial failure to encourage "seriousness" and "independence of mind and temperament." Looking to British alternatives like the *Times Literary Supplement*, she concluded her remonstrance with the hope that, "for the great metropolitan publications, the unusual, the difficult, the lengthy, the intransigent, and above all, the *interesting*, should expect to find their audience."[1]

Hardwick's essay prompted a heated rejoinder from the book publisher Cass Canfield. Chiding Hardwick for a "basic lack of understanding" of the medium, he insisted that one function of the newspaper book supplement was to emphasize the "news value" of books. Because, unlike Hardwick's British models, they served a large audience, such periodicals, according to Canfield, could not survive if they failed to provide "coverage." Unconvinced, Hardwick replied that Canfield seemed to regard the book sections of the *Times* and the *Tribune* as "trade journals giving out news and information about the publishing business and offering reviews as a bonus."[2]

Nineteenth- and Early-Twentieth-Century American Book Reviewing: An Overview

Hardwick's and Canfield's exchange—part of the discourse that led to the founding of the *New York Review of Books* in 1963—had a longer history than Hardwick's perception of a fall from grace implied.[3] The question of whether attention to new books should take the form of "news" or "criticism" had shaped American book reviewing since the nineteenth century. The distinction between the two conceptions was more a matter of emphasis than a hard and fast line. "News" subsumed both blurbs and reviews that mainly described a book in factual terms. By contrast, Stanley Edgar Hyman noted, "critical" reviewers, primarily treating "books as literature," judged a work's relationship to aesthetic or moral principles and strove to inculcate those principles in their audience.[4]

The "news" approach, always predominant, was virtually the only mode of presentation in the daily press during the antebellum period. Newspapers typically carried book notices—unsigned, brief announcements of new works—rather than full-fledged reviews. Such notices reflected the pressures of the marketplace: publishers frequently prefabricated favorable ones and assured their use by purchasing advertising—or made the same bargain in return for words of editorial praise. A lack of critical rigor characterized even the *New York Evening Post*, where William Cullen Bryant, as a poet turned editor, might have been expected to provide more literary direction. In the New York press in the 1840s, the only notable exception to the general absence of genuine critics was Margaret Fuller, who contributed essays on books and other subjects to Horace Greeley's *Tribune* two or three times a week between 1844 and 1846. Although the practice remained controversial, the appearance of some signed book-review columns in the 1850s added accountability to the system. Room still remained, however, for a publisher like James T. Fields actively to influence favorable publicity by cultivating personal relationships with writers. Fuller's colleague on the *Tribune*, George Ripley, who began a thirty-one-year tenure as literary editor in 1847, supplied serious reviews attentive to "the dignity of the language"; nonetheless, the former Brook Farm founder was characteristically undemanding in his own assessments and lax about the credentials of his contributors. Even though better than the offerings of its competitors, the *Tribune*'s book columns usually consisted of "a few drops of comment" which were "swamped by oceans of scissored quotation."[5]

The approach of the Civil War further diminished the prospects for literary criticism in American newspapers, which were filled instead with political and, eventually, military bulletins. When William Dean Howells, armed with a letter from Fields, approached the *Evening Post* in 1860 about serving as its literary editor, he was rejected. The postwar climate was similar. As Allan Nevins wrote in 1922 about John R. Thompson, the literary editor Bryant finally hired in 1867, he "could not have made the *Post* a good literary organ in the present-day sense. It did not want critical or analytic reviews. An entertaining summary or paraphrase would appeal far more to the general reader." Thus, Thompson "confined himself largely to what was explanatory or descriptive." In part, Nevins observed, that posture resulted from an anxiety that American literature was too frail to be subjected to exacting scrutiny; its delicate condition required that critics avoid severe judgments in order to insure its survival.[6]

Yet Thompson's successor, George Cary Eggleston, also argued that newspaper reviewing positively required an emphasis on paraphrase.

Responding to an 1877 article in the *Atlantic Monthly* by E. S. Nadal that accused book reviewers of collusion with advertisers and deference to their friendships with authors, Eggleston defined the reviewer's role: "To tell newspaper readers what books are published, and what sort of book each of them is, so that the reader may decide for himself what books to buy. His work is not so much criticism as description. It is in the nature of news and comment upon news, and the newspaper reviewer rightly omits much in the way of adverse criticism." Fields's affiliation with the *Atlantic Monthly* lent irony to Nadal's holier-than-thou critique. Yet Eggleston preserved his attacker's stature by sending readers who wanted what Nevins called more "elevated, analytic, and rigid" reviewing to another form of journalism: the magazine.[7]

The emergence of several new periodicals in the 1850s and 1860s, and the revitalization of older ones, had made Eggleston's directive viable. The founding of *Putnam's Monthly* (1853), the *Round Table* (1863), the *Galaxy* (1865), and the *Atlantic Monthly* (1857) itself reflected American efforts to imitate the British quarterly or monthly review. In embarking on such ventures, the exemplars of the genteel tradition willingly became journalists—but they regarded their calling as "higher" than that of the ordinary newspaper reporter. Imbuing their editorial stance with their belief in discipline, autonomy, and morality as components of culture, they conceived of themselves as carrying out their mandate to educate public taste. The characteristic form such periodicals adopted—what Walter Bagehot called the "review-like essay and the essay-like review"—was, in a sense, a compromise between the genteel commitment to training and the demands of a middle-class readership eager for education without excessive effort. If it was a step in the direction of the twentieth-century penchant for "outlines" because it made "laborious analysis conveniently impossible," it nonetheless enabled the writer to instruct a wide audience with reasonable thoroughness and authority. Thus, when the *North American Review*, since 1815 the subdued voice of the New England Unitarian establishment, passed into the hands of James Russell Lowell and Charles Eliot Norton in 1864, they made publishing trenchant essays about books for the purpose of elevating standards one of their prime objectives. The same agenda governed the appearance, a year later, of the *Nation*, which became the most important American organ of both liberal social policy (that is, government by the "best men") and the genteel aesthetic. Its founders—Norton, E. L. Godkin, Frederick Law Olmsted, and George William Curtis among them—declared in its first issue that one "principal object" of the weekly was "to promote and develop a higher standard of criticism." In its self-conscious practice of the "higher journalism," the *Nation* explicitly underscored the difference between its purpose and Eggleston's, setting itself against the prevailing tolerance of newspaper reviewers for sentimentality, sensationalism, and mediocrity.[8]

In the second half of the nineteenth century, the book pages of other genteel magazines—the *Century*, *Harper's*, *Scribner's*, as well as the *Atlantic* and the *North American Review*—reinforced the polarity between newspaper and magazine reviewing. (Somewhere in the middle were new literary journals like the *Bookman* and the *Critic*, entirely devoted to material about books and authors, that contained a sizable amount of gossip and trade news.) Beginning in the 1880s, however, there developed a significant innovation in newspaper reviewing—in which both the *Nation* and Eggleston's own sheet played a part. In 1881, three years after Bryant's death, the *Evening Post* and the *Nation* merged under the ownership of Henry Villard. By this arrangement, Godkin took over as editor-in-chief of the *Post*. The *Nation*, edited by Wendell Phillips Garrison, Villard's brother-in-law, became a weekly version of the paper, its contents largely reprints of articles that had previously appeared in the *Post*.

The merger produced no radical transformations in the tone and spirit of either publication. Despite its dismal record in literary criticism, the *Evening Post* and the agenda of the "higher journalism" had overlapped for some time. In the face of James Gordon Bennett's sensational *Herald*, the *Post* had remained staunchly serious and reserved; concomitantly, its circulation—almost twenty thousand in 1860—was less than a quarter of the *Herald*'s. Bryant's son-in-law, Parke Godwin, a contributor to the newspaper since the 1830s and its editor between 1878 and 1881, was sympathetic to the aims of men like Norton and Lowell; he had moved from the *Post* to an associate editorship at *Putnam's* and then back again. A critic and scholar himself, Godwin had approximated some of the impulses behind the creation of literary magazines by instituting at the *Post* a two-page Saturday supplement containing "book notices, essays, fictional sketches, and other miscellaneous matter." In addition, the paper had early advocated the civil-service reform measures that were at the heart of the *Nation* editors' politics.

The takeover nonetheless did clear the way for genteel commitments to the elevation of taste to displace the treatment of books as news. Garrison, who had been part of the original *Nation* staff and who now added literary editorship of the *Evening Post* to his responsibilities, adhered to the premise that contributors ought to be "specialists" in the subject matter of the books they were evaluating. That term denoted not so much the triumph of scientific expertise as the survival of the *Nation*'s founders' emphasis on training and discipline within the framework of broad liberal culture. Thus, Garrison marshaled as newspaper reviewers distinguished literary figures both within and outside the academy, many of whom were already familiar to readers of the magazine: Norton, Henry Adams, Goldwin Smith, Thomas Wentworth Higginson, Francis Parkman, John Fiske. Younger writers for the paper in the 1880s included George Woodberry, W. C. Brownell, and Brander Matthews. In consequence, as Nevins phrased it, the "dominant tone" of the *Post*'s literary section was "authoritativeness—it was not clever, it was not newsy, but it was definitive." By contrast, "people who wanted bright belletristic literary pages were disappointed. . . . There was a decided deficiency in news of literary personalities." Garrison's retention of the practice of publishing most articles anonymously, moreover, minimized the opportunity for reviewers to enhance their own celebrity.[9]

If the caliber of its literary columns revealed the critical potentialities of the daily press, however, the *Evening Post* remained an anomaly in American journalism. Although it perpetuated the *Nation*'s sense of mission, it inherited as well the magazine's animus against vulgarity, a quality which, in the era of the tabloid, meant that it exercised authority without power. When Paul Elmer More served as the *Post*'s literary editor between 1903 and 1909, he sustained the principle that "the goal of the honest reviewer is to *form* the reader and the future writer, not merely to guide them in one instance." He also pursued that goal as literary editor (1906–9) and editor (1909–14) of the *Nation*—still influencing the *Post*'s book department in the latter position. Yet More's transformation of both journals into outlets for his particular critical program, the New Humanism, further distanced the *Post* from the mainstream.[10]

Instead of following the *Post*'s example, most book sections in newspapers throughout the country during the late nineteenth and early twentieth centuries continued to emphasize reporting about, rather than evaluating, literature. Obviously, among reviewers there was a tremendous range in talent and in the willingness to go beyond factual description: literary editors at the *Chicago Evening Post*, for example, included Francis Hackett and Floyd Dell, both accomplished writers, while at the *Chicago Tribune* the conservative reviewer Elia W. Peattie never hesitated to voice her moralistic opinions. Still, when Adolph Ochs of the *New York Times* created the *Saturday Review of Books and Art* in 1896 (it came out on Sunday beginning in 1911), he did so in the belief that "books could be treated as news." Although its tabloid format and allusive title gave it the look of a magazine, this premise undercut the supplement's resemblance to the critical weekly. Unlike the *Nation*, the *Times* hired a series of book-review editors, starting with Francis Whiting Halsey, who were largely undistinguished in, and unconnected to, the circles of New York's literati. After some initial resistance from publishers who feared that readers would overlook advertisements segregated from the rest of the paper, the *Times* supplement eventually became preeminent in terms of advertising dollars and circulation.[11]

Similarly, at the *New York Tribune*, Ellen Mackay Hutchinson, who started covering books in 1882, was more noteworthy as a pioneering woman journalist than as a critic. Her husband, Royal Cortissoz, who in 1897 took over from her as book-review editor and held the post until 1913, earned his primary reputation as the *Tribune*'s art critic from 1891 to the early 1940s. In general, Bliss Perry complained in 1914, "there were never so many Saturday and Sunday literary supplements and other guides to the book buyer; but there was never, even in the Eighteen-Thirties, any less actual criticism in proportion to the number of books published." Perry specifically condemned the tendency of those media to overpraise shoddy works—an indictment Henry James had issued earlier, More reiterated in 1911, and subsequent critics perennially reinvoked down to Hardwick's time.[12]

By the same token, while the *Century*, the *Bookman*, and the *North American Review* sometimes came under attacks similar to Perry's, and in any case were on the wane, new journals of opinion like the *New Republic* emerged alongside survivors such as the *Atlantic* and the

Nation. (The latter separated from the *Post* in 1917 and moved left politically.) Although there was some crossover in personnel (Hackett, for example, becoming the *New Republic*'s literary editor), this development tended to deepen the disparity between magazine and newspaper reviewing. Moreover, newspapers, in the view of observers like More and Perry, were especially subject to the commercial pressures the growth of publishing generated. Resurrecting the charges Eggleston had earlier dismissed, Perry excoriated the "system of control which the advertiser of books tends to exercise over the literary columns of the periodicals which print his advertising matter and review his books." This "system," Perry said, was a "Silent Bargain" between the young reviewer, desirous of job security, and the paper's managers, bent on maintaining advertising revenue. As Perry explained, if unfavorable notices threatened relations with publishers, the "counting-room" often succeeded in getting the reviewer to "take a more 'reasonable' attitude of mind. That is all." More blamed "two rough forces—journalism and advertising"—for the "shallow" quality characterizing "all but a small circle of reviewing periodicals." Prophesying no immediate change in that situation, he shortly retreated to a professorship at Princeton.[13]

Such tirades did nothing to offset either the consolidation of the "news" approach or the power of advertising. On the contrary, during the 1920s the increase in educated readers, the continuing boom in book production, and the postwar intellectual ferment made newspaper publishers increasingly regard new titles as both journalistic and commercial opportunities. As Harry Hansen, book reviewer first for the *Chicago Daily News* and later for the *New York World-Telegram*, explained, they saw "that there was a larger audience for books and reviews; they discovered that the [book] publishers had larger revenues to spend for book advertising; and they found that the book section could be used as a quality argument with other advertisers." One outcome of those perceptions was the proliferation of daily book-review columns, including Hansen's own, in which timeliness was everything. In the mid-1930s, when Florin L. McDonald sampled the aims of thirty-five newspaper book-review editors, almost 80 percent defined their goal as "to serve as a guide to selection," while only 13 percent saw their objective as "to shape the readers' tastes."[14]

The set of assumptions comprising the "higher journalism," however, did not simply vanish from American newspapers under the weight of that trend. The same factors that enhanced the "news" treatment of books renewed some individuals' faith in the "higher" possibility of fostering critical acumen in a wide public as well. New York City, the nation's largest book market, seemed especially fertile ground for the hybrid configuration of the newspaper book supplement. Gradually (but not sufficiently to overturn its "news" approach), "more opinion crept into reviews" in the *Times*.[15] In 1920 the *Evening Post* decided to establish its own weekly supplement, the *Literary Review*. After a change in ownership four years later, the section's editors, headed by Henry Seidel Canby, broke away to found the *Saturday Review of Literature*. That same year, the *New York Herald Tribune* created its Sunday supplement, *Books*, which remained attached to the newspaper.[16] Both the *Saturday Review*, which the following chapter will address at greater length, and *Books* combined aspirations to "criticism" with an awareness of "news value." As such, they represented the adaptation of the *Nation*'s founders' legacy to the exigencies of American society after the First World War. That realignment is particularly striking in the case of *Books*, for it was lived out in the career of the supplement's first editor, Stuart Pratt Sherman.[17]

"Two Stuart Shermans": New Humanism and Its Discontents

To students of American literature, it may seem a commonplace to say that Stuart Sherman mediated between the genteel tradition and a sensibility hospitable to modernism. His migration from disciple of Paul Elmer More and Irving Babbitt to champion of Sinclair Lewis and Theodore Dreiser has permanently earned him such designations as "radical conservative."[18] The varied landmarks on that journey—a self-portrait embedded in a book on Matthew Arnold, a period as *Nation* contributor, a spirited exchange about naturalism with H. L. Mencken, his departure from academia to edit *Books*—have led some writers to describe Sherman's career as inconsistent and muddled. Others, notably Richard Ruland, have argued for the essential unity of Sherman's position by emphasizing the democratic premises of both his early pleas for standards and his later sympathy with contemporary

American writers. In either case, however, Sherman ordinarily stands as a figure located between two sets of aesthetic principles.[19]

This focus on Sherman as New Humanist knight-errant has nonetheless obscured the broader shift in values his life and work reflected and, in particular, the commentary it provided on genteel visions of character and culture. Moreover, the connections between Sherman's career and the parallel activities of figures such as Canby have been left out of account. Yet Sherman's transition from university professor to book-review editor and popular essayist, always portrayed as idiosyncratic, embodied precisely those tensions that animated middlebrow culture generally. As Canby himself remarked, Sherman was "a representative man . . . responsible for the early nineteen hundreds in America as truly as Roosevelt and Wilson, Mencken and Dreiser, the movies and the automobile."[20]

Born in 1881, Sherman had a pioneer's childhood, living first on an Iowa farm and later in the rough-and-tumble atmosphere of Los Angeles and Arizona. His mother's New England origins, however, determined his education: two years after his father's death from tuberculosis in 1892, he moved to Vermont and Massachusetts to complete his schooling. As an undergraduate at Williams College between 1900 and 1903, he studied Latin and comparative literature. His affinity for faculty members such as John Bascom (on his way to the University of Wisconsin presidency) reflected his developing outlook. Like Robert LaFollette, Sherman described Bascom as "one of the last of the transcendentalists." The "gift" of this "white-haired, unbent, stately old professor of moral philosophy" to his students, Sherman recalled in 1908, was his personification of integrity, self-sacrifice, and liberal culture. "He told us," Sherman wrote, "that, if we would live true to our own clearest vision, we must not hope for the world's success; that . . . in every moment of deepest trial, whether triumphant or tragic in issue, we must stand utterly alone; yet not alone, because upheld by the hands of men before us who had embraced disaster like a bride. . . . He conducted no doctor's dissertations that we remember, but he showed us the face of truth and the austerest beauty of character." Outside the classroom, Sherman pursued his own vision by writing poetry. Some lines from his Williams days—"The cake and wine you too may share / I keep the black bread for myself"—suggest that he mingled his emulation of Bascom's steadfast idealism with a more melancholy sense of life's limitations.[21]

This mood and set of loyalties, perhaps deriving in some measure from the early loss of his father, well befitted Sherman for his next undertaking: graduate study in English at Harvard. There he found the faculty divided over the merits of philology. As Thomas R. Nevin has noted, "Philology was the application of German positivism to letters, a laboratorial reduction of literature to its historical and mechanical parts." It was, in other words, the literary version of specialization and scientific method. Among the proponents of that approach at Harvard, George Lyman Kittredge was particularly powerful, as Sherman himself later caustically reported, in steering graduate students toward narrow analyses of textual "facts." For his part, although he took Kittredge's courses, Sherman resisted Kittredge's "overlordship." Never interested in minute linguistic and bibliographical research, he found an alternative in the teaching of one of Harvard's surviving generalists: Irving Babbitt.[22]

A classical scholar by training, Babbitt had acted on his own antipathy to specialization by deciding not to obtain a Ph.D. Barred from Harvard's classics department, he taught courses on French literature and criticism instead. When Sherman encountered him, Babbitt was in the midst of formulating the position he would first widely publicize in *Literature and the American College* (1908) and eventually elaborate in works like *Democracy and Leadership* (1924). With fervor and relentless conviction, he articulated in his lectures a philosophy so compelling, Sherman recalled, that he drove his listeners "into a reconstruction of [their] entire intellectual system."[23] Deepened and extended by Babbitt's ally Paul Elmer More, whom Sherman met at Babbitt's home, that philosophy—denominated the New Humanism—addressed most of the issues with which middlebrow critics were also concerned: it encompassed, among other things, a vision of selfhood, a definition of culture, a conception of literary criticism, a model of education, and an attitude toward democracy.

Babbitt and More's principal assumption was that human nature entailed two selves: a "lower self," ridden by impulse, instinct, and passion, and a "higher self," the locus of restraint and the source of art and spirituality. From this dualism, Babbitt derived the conclusion that human progress depended on the capacity to exercise what he called the "inner check": the balance and control necessary to tame those baser qualities. Explicitly counterposed to the romantic celebration of natural, untutored genius, Babbitt and More's view equally condemned a mechanized, materialistic society that indulged the wish for physical comfort while leaving spiritual needs unsatisfied. Empowering the "higher self" meant substituting for the lures of boundless individualism and transient desire an attachment to the permanent, universal features of existence.[24]

In the effort to fortify those absolutes, the New Humanists relied on each person's ability, lodged in the faculty of imagination, to grasp what they called "standards": measures of the degree to which both art and moral conduct expressed the timeless achievements of humanity. This position brought their understanding of culture so close to Matthew Arnold's invocation of the "best" that Arnold became the New Humanists' patron saint. In particular, Arnold's approbation of classical writers corroborated the regard Babbitt and his followers accorded the ancients as models of devotion to the "higher" life. More broadly, Arnold's dictum about culture became, in J. David Hoeveler's words, "the general prescription for the entire Humanist program."[25]

It followed that the function of the literary critic was rigorously to champion restraint and antinaturalism, assessing works in both aesthetic and ethical terms. After 1910, when Joel Spingarn first formulated his countervailing definition of criticism as "impressionism," that stance came into sharp contrast with the idea that the critic's obligation was to gauge how successfully a book permitted its audience to reexperience the artist's feelings. To put the matter in a wider context, "impressionism" was another version of a commitment to self-realization; the function of criticism, some of its followers went so far as to declare, was not "pedagogical" but "to provide a means of self-expression for the critic." Against the impressionistic neglect of everything but the portrayal of emotion, Babbitt defined criticism's aim as "judgment and selection and only secondarily comprehension and sympathy." In addition to monitoring contemporary literature, New Humanists were to apply "standards" retroactively, for only in that way could the critic foster the consciousness of tradition that (as Arnold had also maintained) would weaken the temptation of settling for immediate gratification. It was their determination to reassess the past in light of New Humanist doctrine that, as Ruland has explained, led Babbitt and More to rediscover and reshape the canon of American literature.[26]

The New Humanist formulation of the critic's role was a statement as much about politics as art: it presumed that most people required the guidance of a select group of leaders in order to learn the meaning of "standards." Although Babbitt and More viewed the possibilities of democracy more negatively than Sherman eventually did, New Humanism in its original version reiterated Edmund Burke's and Arnold's prescription for government by a "natural aristocracy" or "saving remnant." By positioning right-thinking critics as members of such an elite, Babbitt and More thus made them responsible for insuring both order and enlightenment. Criticism, in other words, became not simply a vehicle for appraising style and content but also an instrument in the arduous struggle to preserve and advance society as a whole.[27]

One way in which critics might wage that struggle was through the academic lecture or scholarly article. Charged with educating public taste, arbiters of literature's aesthetic and moral properties might appropriately convey their insights within the university, where they could raise the next generation's awareness of standards. In that setting, however, success was constrained by the democratic and scientific influences Babbitt opposed.[28] Another alternative lay outside the academic battleground, in the field of journalism. The essay and the book review, as the *Nation*'s founders had earlier concluded, could serve as devices for enlightening the public, but only if they bore no resemblance to the tolerant bulletins reflecting the "news" approach. Reviews were to shun emotion, pull no punches, and avoid dwelling on personal idiosyncrasies. Thus conceived, they became, in structure and style, verbal correlates of the New Humanist struggle to subdue the "lower self": restrictions on digression (the structural equivalent of indulging impulses) and effusion (the language of passion) served the cause of "higher" truth. More's editorship of the *Nation* was predicated on that translation of ideology into literary form.

George Santayana's famous conflation of New Humanism with the genteel tradition—he called the former "the genteel tradition at bay"—has made it seem obligatory to disentangle the two outlooks. Scholars have rightly pointed out that New Humanism rested on a much more cogent, specific analysis than genteel writers ever constructed; that the complacency characterizing the less intellectually penetrating exponents of gentility like Richard Stoddard and E. C. Stedman had no counterpart in the reactionary manifestos of Babbitt and More; and that the genteel tradition actually celebrated the romanticism the New Humanists decried. Babbitt and More's insistence on the dualism of human nature does, on the face of it, contradict the Emersonian faith in an integrated self. As Babbitt noted with respect to Emerson, whom he partly admired, the trouble with the idea of "self-reliance" is that not every self is reliable.[29]

Yet it is also worth reiterating the similarities Santayana's labels imply. Unity was not absent from the New Humanist lexicon; if not a goal of self-development, it remained an aim of social evolution, whereby individuals rose above the demands of the ego to join in the universal life of the soul. More generally, the emphasis the New Humanists placed on self-discipline, intelligent control, moderation, and duty furnishes a striking example of the perpetuation of the character ideal by twentieth-century intellectuals. Finally, both groups identified the same agency—the practice of the "higher journalism"—as a weapon by which the crusade for civilization could be waged. Even without the obvious mutual dependence on Arnold, Babbitt and More unmistakably echoed, if in a different key, many of the values Norton, Godkin, and their colleagues had intoned.

Sherman responded to Babbitt's precepts with missionary zeal. While still at Harvard, he proselytized among his friends and family, writing his sister, for example, that her readiness to "assimilate the point of view of these wretched modern writers in whom is no sweetness, nor strength, nor peace" had "very considerably disturbed" him. He accepted an instructorship in English literature at Northwestern University in 1906, where he presented the New Humanist point of view in his mentor's own style: his technique, he told a friend, was to "use Babbitt's method—pound and pound on central ideas till their ears ache." The next year he took up an appointment at the University of Illinois in Urbana; the position shaped a commitment to state universities that would color Sherman's later definition of his role. There he was able to ignore the claims of philologists and to assume, like Babbitt, the mantle of resident generalist. Among his early students was Carl

Van Doren, who worked with Sherman before leaving for graduate school at Columbia; when Van Doren's brother Mark became an undergraduate in 1910, he, too, became Sherman's protégé.[30]

Thus established, in the spring of 1908 Sherman sent the *Nation* a lengthy letter to the editor excoriating American graduate training in literature along the lines Babbitt was then sketching. The essay made a companion piece to John Erskine's plea, published in the same pages a few months later, to approach "great books" as recent works. Ironically, given the New Humanists' antipathy to pragmatism, Sherman's depiction of "pseudo-scientific specialists" linked the essay as well to William James's condemnation of "The Ph.D. Octopus" five years earlier. Yet Sherman augmented the familiar attack with an original argument about the relationship between academia and journalism. The technical scholarship of the graduate schools, Sherman noted, drove students of "real literary taste and power" out of the university before they had the opportunity to acquire "the culture that Arnold meant." So exiled, they turned, uneducated, to "hackwork," while the academy suffered for want of talent. Instead of this bifurcation, Sherman called for an educational program that would supply teachers and writers capable of guiding readers in their search for lasting values. "The scrupulous Darwinian," Sherman wrote, "will at once retort that the guides I am asking for are mere popular lecturers, flimsy generalizers, belle-lettristic triflers. I admit that I think we need more generalizers, though it is not essential that they be flimsy generalizers. If talking in a comprehensive way about the great men and great ideas of the world is to be popular, then we do direfully need more popular men—more men like Lowell, Arnold, Leslie Stephen, John Morley."[31] That sense of purpose, explicitly linked to the practitioners of the "higher journalism," made Sherman's eventual editorship of *Books* not the surprising rupture in his career it has sometimes been made to appear but, rather, the logical outcome of his early vocational commitments.

Sherman's piece on graduate training permitted him, moreover, to bridge the worlds of scholarship and journalism himself even while retaining his university appointment. It so impressed the editor of the *Nation*, Hammond Lamont, that he invited Sherman to spend the summer of 1908 filling in for an editorial writer on leave from the magazine and the *Evening Post*. Relocated in New York, Sherman composed a series of essays assailing "decadence" in literature and departures from the traditional curriculum in education. He also did unsigned book reviews. The following spring he was offered a permanent position on the *Nation* staff. Although he decided to remain at Illinois, he became, for the next ten years, "virtually a staff contributor." His early appraisals enforced with biting irony New Humanist injunctions against sentimentality and "the new-fangled 'reality,' " although his biographers Jacob Zeitlin and Homer Woodbridge pointed out that his flexibility was also evident in his regard for O. Henry's stories and the "platitudinous" writings of a popular philosopher. Later, after More had assumed the *Nation* editorship, Sherman grew still more vigilant against aestheticism and literary naturalism.[32]

Yet, even in this period, Sherman exhibited tendencies which made Babbitt and More distinctly uncomfortable. One was his optimism about democracy, particularly as represented by the state university. In May 1913 Sherman published in the *Nation* an article entitled "Education by the People," in which he defended institutions like his own as centers of culture in no way inferior to private Eastern colleges. The next year he told More that "if you happen to be living in a 'democratic' government and wish to have your way in it, you must use upon the people either Gatling-guns or infinite patience and flattery"—the latter method promising to have "a more refining and uplifting influence upon the people." In another essay, he evinced more sympathy to Rousseau than More could tolerate.

At this time, Sherman also brought his politics to a project that enabled him to engage in his own reformulation of the American literary canon: *The Cambridge History of American Literature.* As an editor of the volume (along with Erskine, Carl Van Doren, and Erskine's former teacher William Peterfield Trent), Sherman furthered Babbitt and More's aim of fashioning a viable tradition. Yet, as Ruland has shown, Sherman read the past more democratically than they did. His article on Benjamin Franklin for the *History* portrayed him as a kind of premature Arnoldian who accepted the rule of the people because it was inevitable; his essay on Henry James (begun for the volume but published later) condemned James's "aesthetic aristocracy." Such writings established the arc of the intellectual trajectory that would ultimately lead Sherman out of the New Humanist movement altogether.[33]

There was, however, another largely overlooked source of Sherman's growing heterodoxy—one that had less to do with purely intellectual matters than with temperament and emotional need. When Sherman left Harvard for Northwestern, he had carried with him his intention to be a poet. A colleague recalled that in 1906 there were "two Stuart Shermans." One was the "scholar" and "ambitious young teacher"; the other, "one of the most romantically minded persons I have ever known," was the Sherman who composed sonnets inspired by Lake Michigan. This poetic cast of mind, dissociated from his sober professorial demeanor, manifested itself as well in the overwritten but fundamentally earnest letters he sent his friends. To Homer Woodbridge's invitation to Christmas dinner, for example, he replied characteristically: "This bridge between the dark infinities is stormfully crowded with many forms and voices, and shadows from either abyss.— Yet the mere human at the viscera of me yearns, yearns, Sir, at the thought of that young Pig." In remarks like those, Sherman's reliance on theatrical, allusive diction seems part playful posturing, part a way of harnessing literary convention to express feelings that threatened otherwise to escape his control. Still the keeper of the "black bread," he remained vulnerable to "melancholy"—"tormented" by an awareness of the distance between a "Dream" of "Harmony" and a disappointing "Reality."[34]

Sherman's poetic aspirations and mannerisms gradually gave way, over the next several years, to teaching and criticism. What did not disappear, one senses, was the inner life that had engendered them. Extraordinarily shy, he was also capable of sudden bursts of anger and sarcasm. Those qualities made him seem, to some observers, distant and baffling.[35] More directly, in a highly revealing letter to Woodbridge shortly after he arrived at Illinois, Sherman described the costs of his decision to forgo creating "Art." Man, he reported, was "a hungry living case enclosing the cadaver of a soul." His own spirit was "nearly dead," stifled by his academic responsibilities. Sometimes he attained "a certain well-being" by "the polishing and staining of wood"—but "carpentering" brought only temporary peace. "It can't be sustained," he told Woodbridge. "It's drugging, no more. One wakes again with the intensest psychic belly-ache." Two years later, after watching some builders mixing mortar outside his window, he recorded in his journal, "Brain sensation as of nausea at 'intellectual life.' "[36] That portrait of a divided self beset by unfulfilled longings argues that when Sherman assented to Babbitt and More's view of human existence as a struggle between higher obligations and the wish to gratify untamed impulses, he knew in a deep-rooted way what they were talking about. But Sherman's self-diagnosis also makes it possible to see him in a setting other than the familiar New Humanist one. As the chapters which follow will show, it immediately links him to Erskine, another failed poet who transferred a search for experience to criticism, and to Will Durant, who quested after "the healing unity of the soul." It also invites comparison to the "anti-modernists" Jackson Lears has delineated, some of whom made woodworking and other crafts anodynes for fragmented selfhood.

Notwithstanding the latter connection, Sherman's own use of medical imagery should not obscure the fact that his initial response to disunity was not the therapeutic pursuit of growth but the further renunciation of uncontrolled self-expression. Yet, to introduce a different metaphor, Sherman's surging feelings kept threatening to break through the seawall of the character ideal and of New Humanist doctrine. The most significant aspect of this tension was that it led Sherman to protest the form as well as the substance of his mentors' position. In a letter to More of December 1912, Sherman both substantiated the fact that New Humanist interdictions had ordained a particular form of criticism—the stock "*Nation*-essay"—and rebelled against it: "I have meditated very frequently upon the '*Nation*-essay'—from the point of view of an outsider," he wrote. "In the space at our disposal it is necessary to be very curt. And I think we contributors—and you as well—are paying a penalty for this curtness. We get the credit for having *no aesthetic appreciation*. . . . We break their [writers'] necks in a *Nation*-essay and wash our hands of them. We ought to have space to show that we, too, understand all the seductions of their hyacinthine locks *before* we break their necks. . . . [W]e should oppose enthusiasm to enthusiasm." His desire for more freedom to give himself over to an artist's "seduction," Sherman reported, had lain "smouldering for years." More's reply only threw the nature of the prescribed form into sharper relief. The "hard fact remains," he insisted, "that the *Nation* is not a general magazine and only by some sacrifice can give a meager nine columns to an essay. The side lights, the romantic appreciation, suffer no doubt; but most of the people who complain of the resulting 'harshness' would be satisfied with nothing less than an overflowing measure of gush. . . . [A]n excess of judgment over 'appreciation' is no bad thing these days, and 'enthusiasm' makes me afraid."[37]

Sherman and More's exchange is a reminder that the editorship of a literary periodical outside the university did not necessarily involve a more democratic orientation than the practice of academic criticism. While Sherman continued to regard the *Nation* as the most appropriate outlet for his essays and reviews—and was even given the chance to succeed More as editor—his unhappiness about the limitations the magazine's tone and style imposed would resurface later on.[38]

Both the intellectual and emotional countercurrents in Sherman's outlook during the 1910s coalesced in his most important work of the period, *Matthew Arnold: How to Know Him* (1917). By the time he wrote it, the professor had thoroughly won out over the poet in terms of Sherman's day-to-day activities. He had become chair of the Urbana department and was busy trying to build a top-flight faculty; among his recruiting efforts was an unsuccessful attempt to woo Erskine from Columbia. Although he occasionally still wrote poems, his teaching and scholarship consumed most of the time not devoted to administration. Yet the Arnold book, which Sherman's biographers characterized as a chronicle of "the same conflicts of temperament and reason" plaguing Sherman, acknowledged that poetic impulses could be buried only by an act of will. The first chapter seems especially autobiographical: it depicts the young Arnold giving an "outlet" through poetry "to the stream of his instinctive and spontaneous feelings, which was frequently of a poignant melancholy"; it notes Arnold's "duplex" nature—the "poet and the critic in him . . . contending for supremacy"; and it records the outcome of the contest as a triumph for "character" (his biographers' term).

Arnold thus emerges from Sherman's account as an embodiment of the New Humanist ideal. (Sherman, in fact, identified More as his "living model" for the study.) Sherman venerated his subject as a figure who "had made a clear, still, cool place at the center of his consciousness in which he saw the 'realities of life' in their eternal aspects and with their permanent values. . . . [H]e had acquired a wholesome tranquillity about the universe . . . which enables a man of his rigorous social sense and fundamental seriousness to do his duty lightly and even gaily." That description apparently negated Sherman's earlier conclusion that at the human core lay only a shriveled soul. The same passage celebrating Arnold's self-mastery, however, suggests why Sherman's own victory in the struggle against "lyric impulse" ultimately proved precarious and incomplete: it regretfully calls "the purely individual passion for self-expression" the "birthright of every poet" and registers a continuing dichotomy between "the serene melancholy of Arnold's inner life and the blitheness of his outward demeanor."[39]

Similarly, Arnold's critical stance, as Sherman presented it, affirmed the judicial, as opposed to the impressionistic, approach, while leaving space for voicing the enthusiasm and feeling Sherman found lacking in the *Nation*-essay. Arnold, Sherman primarily argued, equated morality and artistic merit, insisting that the critic evaluate works in terms of the degree to which they illuminated the question of "how to live." Impatient with those of his contemporaries who appealed "to no authority outside themselves," he took instead as his mission "the discrimination of values" in the light of classical examples and what he saw as timeless principles. In a key formulation of the link between culture and discipline at the core of the genteel outlook, Sherman declared: "If you compare all these passages as you are directed to compare them, if you make an earnest effort to perceive the stylistic distinctions which Arnold tells you are there, you will find the process highly exciting to your esthetic sensibility; you will undergo an esthetic discipline which you will never forget, and which will leave you with a sense of augmented power in these matters." By focusing on the cultivation of aesthetic sensitivity, and by describing the outcome of Arnold's lessons as the interior benefit of "augmented power," Sherman furnished a benchmark with which to measure the space between the original Arnoldian program and its middlebrow descendants.[40]

At the same time, Sherman rescued Arnold from the charge that he was insensitive to beauty for its own sake. In most of his *Essays in Criticism*, Sherman wrote, "the really decisive part is played by personal taste, functioning, to be sure, under classical discipline." The task of criticism, in Sherman's paraphrase, was to "reckon" the "stimulus to the heart and conscience" with "the stimulus to esthetic sensibility," so that readers would not only "know the best" but "love" it as well. Preserving, in that way, a place for emotion, Sherman also indicated that discipline exacted a price: no doubt mindful of his own experience, he wistfully remarked that as the "discipline of [Arnold's] feelings approached completion there was relatively little feeling left to discipline." This subsidiary theme of homage to "emotional impulse" once more distinguished Sherman from Babbitt, who, reviewing *Matthew Arnold* in the *Nation*, accused Arnold (and implicitly Sherman) of succumbing to "the romantic fear of precise analysis" and of harboring a Bergsonian inclination to view life as a "'perpetual gushing forth of novelties.'"[41]

In addition, Sherman's book on Arnold implemented the democratic values he had begun espousing in his reviews and communications with More. These were clear in a number of ways. Most obvious was the portrait of Arnold as radical conservative—as a man who wanted the "'something better' in the future to be much more widely distributed than 'what was good' in the past," a figure "so passionately aristocratic that he wanted to make all men aristocratic." Less patent but equally revealing of Sherman's position was the nature and tone of the book as a whole. *Matthew Arnold: How to Know Him* was part of a series of works (including one by William Lyon Phelps on Browning and another by George Edward Woodberry on Hawthorne) edited by Will D. Howe for a general audience. In undertaking a volume for what was somewhat sneeringly called "Howe's How in Literature," Sherman himself endorsed the Arnoldian program of diffusing "sweetness and light." In so doing, he assented not only to the idea that ordinary people required exposure to what critics judged "the best" but also to the premise that they were entitled to culture in undiluted form. Thus, although Howe's venture to a degree anticipated the vogue of the "outline" and even the "how-to" book, the difference between the "knowing" of the title and the "appreciating" that Phelps, for one, purveyed remained salient in Sherman's case. As his directive urging the reader to practice discipline reveals, he made the cornerstone of the Arnold study his faith that anyone might, through effort, grasp both Arnold's aesthetic principles and his wider message. The result was a volume that surpassed others in the series by presenting more than excerpts sprinkled with a few biographical and critical remarks. Sherman's contribution minimized biography in favor of textual analysis, combined clarity with complexity of interpretation, and served scholars and lay readers alike.[42]

If *Matthew Arnold* announced Sherman's credo as critic, *On Contemporary Literature*, published the same year, represented the application of theory to practice. It was this collection of revised *Nation* articles that hurled him into the controversy for which he is best remembered. Hewing more closely (and with less ambivalence) to the New Humanist line than did the Arnold book, the essays rejected relativism in criticism and naturalism in philosophy, affirming instead Sherman's allegiance to the "instructed and disciplined heart." The most provocative section, "The Barbaric Naturalism of Theodore Dreiser," amalgamated Sherman's antipathy toward Dreiser's failure to display the "higher self" with his admiration for the American Puritan, a figure More had already endowed with Arnoldian virtues. Dreiser's depiction of humans as animals, Sherman insisted, under-mined the Puritan legacy of exercising "the inner check upon the expan-sion of impulse." To that thesis, Sherman also added an element of ethnic prejudice fueled by Germany's territorial aggression in World War I, a bias that would become more blatant in *American and Allied Ideals* (1918).[43]

This inflammatory combination sparked Sherman's well-publicized debate with Mencken, who, entirely missing Sherman's feel for aes-thetics, attacked his adversary as a repressed and repressive enemy of art. *On Contemporary Literature* also provoked rancorous assess-ments from reviewers like Francis Hackett and Burton Rascoe. Sher-man's approbation of the Puritans particularly earned him the con-tempt of figures such as Randolph Bourne and Van Wyck Brooks, just then leading the assault on Puritanism as a prime source of the bank-ruptcy of American aesthetic traditions. When Sherman subsequently contrasted his preference for the "once dominant Puritan stock" to the spectacle of immigrants resisting assimilation, the *Nation* itself de-nounced him as a practitioner of "Ku Klux Kriticism." Even Carl Van Doren began openly retreating from his mentor's corner.[44]

Sherman's response, extending into the early twenties, was to depict Mencken as pandering to a vulgar "new public now swarming up the avenues of democratic opportunity." By encouraging "learning without study" and by subjecting literature to a spurious "democratization," his adversaries, Sherman contended, cut themselves off from the best hope for a genuinely democratic diffusion of standards. He especially faulted young "Bohemians" for their insistence on a liberation that precluded contact with the practical "builders of American civiliza-tion." Increasingly drawn to native subjects himself ("How interesting American literature is after all," he had written Carl Van Doren in preparing the *Cambridge History*, "when you really get down to it!"),

Sherman instead continued basing his American canon on a national heritage of moral idealism that combined respect for popular democracy with aspirations to an "aristocracy of talent." In this effort, Emerson and Thoreau joined the Puritans as examples of Humanist concern with the "higher self"; likewise, Whitman became an impassioned advocate of "distinction" for the "average man." Eventually, Sherman even added Sinclair Lewis to his pantheon because Lewis attempted to foster (by constructing counterexamples) "'the highest standard of manners and morals in America.'"[45]

Sherman's reading of American literary history thus contained an answer to the question of whether "business civilization" was an adequate resource for the art of the future. His discovery of a "great tradition" in American letters was a ready-made "usable past" that anticipated Brooks's similar investigation in the 1930s. To the critic W. C. Brownell, he summarized his evolving position:

> The line I have taken and intend to follow is the encouragement of the native tradition, with all its imperfections on its head, the Puritan, the pioneer, the Jacksonian strain, the adventurous, daring, exploring, spirit, democracy. . . . I got a couple of volumes of [Santayana's] *The Life of Reason* and *The Sense of Beauty*, and *Poetry and Religion*, and these with the works of Arnold and your books and whatever appeared in the older *Nation* style—the Charles Eliot Norton tradition, and Babbitt's and More's books— whatever, in short, was most hostile, on the surface, to the earthy, rough Jacksonian element in our life and literature seemed the things to cultivate. They seem so still. . . . [But] I want to get the Emersons and the Jacksons together, and their offspring to intermarry. I believe the American breed will profit by the misalliance.[46]

As everyone noticed at the time, the controversy between Sherman and his opponents (who entirely missed the complexities of his political position) was a generational as well as a literary dispute. Sherman ruefully imagined the youthful "radicals" dancing and howling "in happy derision, 'Go up, bald head!'" Yet the two factions had more in common than they knew. Not only did both sides espouse a program of cultural renewal in order to offset the damaging effects of materialism, but Sherman in fact was also far less contented with the hermetic atmosphere of the library and the parlor than Bourne and his colleagues thought. Echoing his earlier misgivings about an academic vocation, and revealing the same restlessness that impelled many younger figures' quests for "real life," Sherman wrote Carl Van Doren in 1918 that he "waver[ed] between the delight of losing touch with the world in the pages of Giraldus Cambrensis and the Grettir Saga, and on the other hand wishing I were a muddy journalist cuffing and taking cuffs in the thick of the struggle." (A few years later he openly condemned Babbitt and More for keeping "too far from the scene of action.") The clash with the "shivering young Davids"—as Ludwig Lewisohn called Mencken, Hackett, Brooks, Bourne, and Sherman's other opponents—was, even for Sherman as defeated Goliath, a kind of moral equivalent of war, with the same regenerative possibilities Bourne himself ascribed to the front in World War I.[47]

Thus, although he resented his critics' failure to understand that his Americanism was not a statement of racial superiority but a desire to preserve certain shared values (arguably a hairsplitting distinction), he paradoxically found in the initial period of conflict about *On Contemporary Literature* greater peace than at perhaps any other time in his life. Within the classroom, he attained some satisfaction in his effort to "mould character through teaching English." His goals became expressly Arnoldian ones: "not to divulge information but to . . . sensitize the mind" and strengthen "the bonds of a common culture." Allan Nevins, one of his early students, remarked on the "sprightliness" and engagement that differentiated his teaching in this period from the reserved, constricted style he had exhibited upon his arrival at Illinois.[48]

Yet, despite the augmented sense of self the limelight seems to have generated, Sherman's journals and correspondence suggest that the Arnoldian serenity for which he strove still eluded him. A journal entry recording his determination to "say each day" that "to-day I am to acquit myself like a man, a believer in ideas, a gentleman, a person with standards" bespeaks the need to impose that ideal on other impulses. More specifically, his bout of "cuffing" did not sufficiently fulfill his desire to transcend the confines of academia. Once again, Sherman voiced his objections to the "academic point of view": "I am not quite reconciled to that. I shall never be. It lacks two virtues one cannot do without and touch at greatness: courage and love." If "courage," in that statement, referred to the importance of action, "love" was freighted with the wish for emotional expressiveness that remained a plaintive melody in Sherman's repertoire.[49]

The Limits of Character

Around 1921, when Sherman turned forty, that longing culminated in what his biographers, writing well before the idea of such a mid-life passage became fashionable, identified as a "definite crisis" that "press[ed] itself insistently upon him." His malaise reflected deeper cultural tensions than historians of merely literary matters have recognized. In Zeitlin and Woodbridge's words, Sherman began to reexamine "the point of view of those who claimed that fulness and richness of living rather than restraint were the true satisfactions of men." By 1924 he was recording in his journal a paean to "richness of personality" that sympathetically noted the antagonism of youth to "Arnold, More, et al." He planned a novel in which a successful but joyless Puritan fell in love with a gay, carefree French woman. He resolved to "gather up and concentrate and intensify" so as to "live in personal relations with my world." Sherman's most sustained, public communication of his changed outlook appeared in an essay entitled "Forty and Upwards," which proclaimed his intention to leave off "hammering out his 'solid character.'" Wrapping his yearnings for renewal in metaphors similar to Emerson's, he announced a new creed that made dedication to growth, rather than to moral principle, its chief article: "Unfold leaf by leaf. . . . Push on into untrodden forests, up unexplored valleys, seeking new springs of refreshment, crying at the foot of every mountain ridge, 'Let us see what is on the other side.'" With that proclamation, Sherman (distancing himself from the genteel tradition more fully than many of his middlebrow colleagues ever did) became a certifiable apostle of the culture of personality.[50]

While, to some of his adversaries, Sherman's reorientation appeared unprecedented and capricious, it was, however, only the breaking of the dam that had tenuously contained his desire for self-expression since his days as an aspiring poet. Moreover, in no sense did Sherman entirely abjure the character ideal; in fact, his simultaneous loyalty to elements of both personality and character might be read as another version of the contest between the Emersonian and Jacksonian factions informing his politics. In most (though not all) of his writing, he continued to reveal a belief that he possessed an interior source of power and emotion—an "inner ecstasy and mysticity and rapture" that made his conception of personality more than a "set of social masks." In an essay entitled "The Shifting Centre of Morality" that beautifully documents the modern American's changing view of selfhood, Sherman even explicitly deplored the tendency to turn away from one's Emersonian "inner monitor" toward an "external" and "socially-centered" ethic. "Intelligently or otherwise," he complained, "our young people seize upon current philosophy to help them construct an entire universe for themselves which shall have no 'insides.' In the violence of their reaction against the idealism and inwardness of their fathers, they rejoice in their intention of living on the surface of things." Yet Sherman never saw that his own decision to become an explorer whose only compass directed him to become "more and more intimate with life" might lead to precisely the aimless self-absorption he here condemned.[51]

Sherman's restlessness in the early 1920s was exacerbated by the structural obstacles facing anyone who wanted, as he now did, to embrace the profession of critic in the same way "Browning and Tennyson gave themselves to poetry"—obstacles arising from the prior inability of the "higher journalists" to institutionalize their role. To Ellery Sedgwick, the editor of the *Atlantic Monthly*, Sherman posed the issue as a question: "How to develop and reward a professional literary class, distinct, on the one hand, from the journalist and popular novelist, and, on the other, from the damned professor. Do you see how this can be done?"[52]

Unable to solve that institutional dilemma, Sherman also continued to search for an appropriate mode of expression. What had earlier been merely a frustration had become by this time a major discontent—in part because, after More's departure in 1914, the *Nation* no longer seemed the logical outlet for Sherman's ideas. Although he still sent it pieces occasionally because Carl Van Doren was literary editor, the journal seemed "to have drifted from its moorings" in both politics and literature. "Dreiser, Symons, Lewisohn—what next?" he wrote Van Doren in 1920. "Is Lewisohn going to take control? . . . Some of the stuff Lewisohn gets off would make fifty years of *Nation* editors squirm in their graves." The changed tenor of the *Nation* reflected the growing influence of the "radicals" generally. "Where can one get a hearing, except in an occasional old-fashioned monthly," Sherman complained to More, "for anything but the radical point of view?"[53]

To external issues of power, however, was added the impact of Sherman's internal rebellion. In a letter to Canby, who had approached him about writing for the *Evening Post*, Sherman again revealingly translated his revaluation of character, discipline, and self-control into a matter of form. Invoking an image of release, he told Canby: "For some time, I have 'sort-of' hankered to pull out an essay-stop which is somewhere in my melodeon. But nearly everything I have done for years has set out under the flag and pretext of a review. I hanker for the freedom of the 'informal essay' and particularly for the 'personality' of it, as allowing an expression of 'suppressed desires'; and flatter myself that once the outlet is found, I might produce like a flowing well." Similarly, he wrote Sedgwick at around the same time, "I have long felt a desire to develop a somewhat different style than these [weekly "organs of opinion"] foster—something less journalistic; more, in a certain sense, personal; with more undertones and overtones; utilizing more of one's experience, feeling, etc."[54]

Both the philosophical and structural tensions prompting Sherman's reassessment of the character ideal, and its equivalent in literary form, eventuated by 1924 in two new projects. The first, at Sedgwick's suggestion, was a series of articles for the *Atlantic Monthly* that became *My Dear Cornelia* (1924). This work, usually dismissed by chroniclers of Sherman's career, reveals as much, if not more, about his mentality in the early 1920s as his critical efforts. The book was a fictional exploration of the fate of genteel morality in the freer climate of the postwar years. Three main characters appeared. One, Cornelia, a wealthy, well-bred, middle-aged woman alarmed by the younger generation's drift away from chastity, temperance, and religion, explicitly symbolized beleaguered gentility. (She was, Sherman told Sedgwick, intended to represent the *Atlantic*'s typical reader.) Another, Cornelia's husband Oliver, defended "modern" practices, flouting Prohibition and condoning his daughter's smoking. To the role of mediator between the genteel and the "modern," Sherman assigned an old flame of Cornelia's, now a professor of literature—a figure transparently a spokesperson for Sherman himself.

Much of *My Dear Cornelia* consisted of Sherman's argument that, because Victorian writers had anticipated the naturalists in valuing passion over chastity, the "decline" of virtue was illusory. Responding to Cornelia's revulsion at contemporary novels, the "professor" also contended that sexually explicit literature actually fostered traditional morality by demonstrating that a focus on sex alone dead-ended in disgust and the "irreducible hell" of a "disintegrated personality." By that logic, Sherman effected the rapprochement with literary naturalism that colored his criticism from the early 1920s on. Within the same framework, he also offered his starkest endorsement of an exterior view of selfhood. In place of his earlier lament that his soul was only a "cadaver," he now celebrated the absence, "beneath the skin," of anything more than "viscera and vacancy." As the professor told Cornelia, "The interesting and precious and desirable self isn't 'inside.' . . . It doesn't exist till it gets outside. . . . In so far as people . . . really give themselves adequately to each other in love or in friendship, and impart happiness with the gift, they give a self that is externalized, objectified, and tangible." Yet, again, one must remember that Sherman recorded in a letter the experimental nature of his attempt to "see how much of a case can be made out for the 'externalized life.'" To the same correspondent, he remarked, "I confide that Cornelia is in reality a picture of a 'lobe' of my brain, dressed up something like a lady and held off at arm's length so that I can look at her from another critical lobe." No image conveys more succinctly the "middleness" of the middlebrow critic than that ambivalent self-portrait.[55]

The Founding of Books

The "Cornelia" essays were, of all of Sherman's writings, the most popular with the general public. They also earned him the acclaim of reviewers who (like Irwin Edman in the *Nation*) admired his pose between two generations.[56] In the wake of this success, Sherman embarked on a second, more momentous venture reflective of his reorientation: his editorship of *Books*. Although the circumstances in which he resigned from Illinois are still a bit cloudy, this much is clear. Beginning in 1913, the *New York Tribune* had run a weekly two-page book section containing reviews by members of the newspaper's staff. Heywood Broun, one such rotating reviewer, broke away from the pack and in

1919 inaugurated a book column that gave the *Tribune* a certain sparkle, but he moved it to the *World* two years later. Sherman's nemesis
Burton Rascoe took over as literary editor in 1922, presiding over a
tabloid section called "Book News and Reviews" and infusing it with
his enthusiasm for writers in rebellion against gentility. When, two
years later, the *Tribune*'s owners, Ogden and Helen Rogers Reid,
purchased the *New York Herald*, however, they decided to go forward
with a plan for an even more ambitious literary supplement.[57]

The specific impetus to establish *Books*, a project Helen Rogers Reid
especially championed, derived from an awareness that, in Royal Cortissoz's words, "the psychological moment is here." Cortissoz, still the
Tribune's art critic and a member of the Reids' inner circle, observed a
year before the merger: "The Greenwich Village dodge [presumably,
the literate public's gravitation toward avant-garde periodicals] is tot-
tering. The Times, with its huge circulation, goes in for seriousness in
its literary department. So does the Herald. So does the Evening
Post." By comparison, Helen Reid admitted to John Macrae, president
of E. P. Dutton and Company, the *Tribune*'s book department had
lacked influence. Taking advantage of the widening audience for mainstream review media, *Books* would, Reid hoped, outstrip its competition and achieve the "same dominating position in the book world which
the *Tribune* has maintained so long in the fields of drama, art, and
music." As director of the *Herald Tribune*'s advertising department,
Reid also wanted to increase the amount of book-ad copy the paper
carried.[58]

Cortissoz's analysis of the way to put the *Tribune*'s book section
"back on the map" had included a suggestion for a new literary editor.
(Rascoe, given to what Cortissoz obscurely called the "I-Me-I business" and to what Alfred Kazin labeled "indignations" and "hot ideal-
isms," had proved a liability.) To Geoffrey Parsons, the editorial-page
writer who had the Reids' ear about the paper's cultural departments,
Cortissoz commended "one man" who would "bring us renewed prestige and prosperity." "His name," he announced, "is Stuart P. Sherman. . . . He is the sanest, soundest critic we have. He is as light in
touch, as entertaining, as he is scholarly. He is a progressive if ever
there was one but he has standards and balance." Accurately capturing
Sherman's mediative position, Cortissoz continued, "Now I can't stress
too much that Sherman is both competent and READABLE. He never

writes the stodge that you meet in The Times so often. He is not superficial as The Herald is. He is nearer The Evening Post's mode, only he is better, more amusing." In conclusion, he urged Parsons to handle the paper's literary editor as he would popular columnists like Mark Sullivan, Don Marquis, or the authors of sports and radio features—that is, to invest money in his salary, shower him with publicity, and "make him comfortable."[59]

Nothing came of Cortissoz's idea until after the *Herald* and *Tribune* merger. In April of 1924, though, the Reids dispatched their managing editor to visit Sherman in Urbana and offer him the editorship of *Books*. Sherman's eventual acceptance of the position had something to do with his continuing desire to implement more fully his democratic commitments. But the key factor in his decision to resign from Illinois seems less a matter of principle than of emotions. By this time, his psychological crisis had not only heightened his long-standing reservations about academia but also colored his relationships on campus. An exchange of Christmas greetings a few months earlier with university president David Kinley, for example, had turned into a telling confrontation. Kinley's poem to Sherman read in part:

> . . . .
> O'er a mass of filthy writing
> Praised as showing good technique,
> You pour a flood of thought delighting,
> Form and phrase alike unique.
>
> . . . .
> Houses are of marble builded,
> E'en if some prefer them mud!
>
> . . . .
> Be marble yours this Christmastide!
> Be marble yours this glad New Year!

Sherman's response, a numbered series of "meditations of a piece of marble," was aggressively hostile: "We talk of 'character': immediately the chisel and mallet are in our hands, and we are sculptors," he wrote, "and our material is marble. Chips fly. Chips of what? . . . Is the imposition of marble qualities on flesh and blood and brain the task of educators, or embalmers?" In closing, he repeated the directives he had postulated in "Forty and Upwards" to "unfold, leaf by leaf" and explore new "forests" and "valleys"—opportunities he clearly felt the president obstructed. That alienation, now laced with personal antagonism, made the Reids' offer more attractive. In addition, Sherman had soured on teaching and felt unbearably burdened by chores that took time away from writing.[60]

Nonetheless, Sherman demurred until the *Herald Tribune* could promise him an assistant. His choice for the job was Carl Van Doren's wife, Irita Bradford Van Doren, then serving (as her husband and brother-in-law Mark had done earlier) as literary editor of the *Nation*. Born in 1891, Irita Van Doren grew up in Alabama and Florida as the eldest of four children. When she was nine years old, her father was murdered; thereafter, her mother supported the family by giving music lessons and selling preserves. With that model of resourcefulness and independence before her, Van Doren graduated (at age seventeen) from the Florida State College for Women at Tallahassee and in 1909 moved to New York to study for a Ph.D. in literature at Columbia. There she met her future husband—they were married in 1912—and began work on a dissertation she titled "How Shakespeare Got the Dead Bodies Off the Stage." Like Fisher, Durant, and, ultimately, Sherman, Canby, Erskine, and Carl Van Doren, however, she left academia to follow other interests. At first, these amounted to activities traditionally attached to the role of academic wife: she helped Carl conduct research for his books and bore three daughters. (In addition, she compiled the index for the *Cambridge History of American Literature*, a fact predictably omitted, as efforts of faculty wives so often are, from a recent account of that enterprise.) Living in Greenwich Village when the avant-garde's rebellion against Victorianism was in full swing, she also made friends in literary and artistic circles, in part through her sister Margaret's marriage to the publisher Charles Boni.[61]

Van Doren joined the editorial staff of the *Nation* in 1919—a move that, given Carl's position on the magazine, was arguably merely an extension of her domestic status. Even so, Sherman, in a tone that seems only half joking, asked: "But, really, Irita, haven't you anything to do at home? . . . Let us have one good old fashioned family left in the City." Heedless of that advice, she became, three years later, the *Nation*'s advertising manager. Comfortable with the idea of promoting consumption, Van Doren expanded both the types of advertisements the magazine solicited and her own responsibilities. When she took over the literary editorship the next year, she was similarly assiduous in pursuing potential reviewers—Sherman among them. Although she failed to wrest a contribution from him, Sherman was thus well aware (despite his antifeminist remarks) of her competence and editorial skill when the *Herald Tribune* came forward with its proposition. Despite his growing differences with Carl, his well-established friendship with the Van Doren family also made Irita the logical person to assist Sherman on what Van Doren herself regarded as "the great adventure."[62]

By the terms of their arrangement with the Reids, Sherman's editorship of *Books* was to entail a weekly essay; in line with Cortissoz's initial recommendation, he was not obliged to involve himself in the day-to-day coordination of the supplement. The tasks of assigning reviews, reading proof, overseeing personnel, and so on were exclusively Van Doren's, whose title was associate editor. This division of labor left Sherman free to continue thinking of himself as "a man of letters (and nothing else)."[63] Although little survives to indicate what directives, if any, the *Herald Tribune* management provided the staff of its new book section, throughout the summer of 1924 Sherman himself considered at length how to combine that role with the demands of serving a newspaper audience. His journal entries of the period form an unusually rich statement of the fate of the "higher journalism" by the mid-1920s.

On the one hand, Sherman cast the critic as an "explorer" whose "principal function" was to discover "the secret of felicity" which eluded most Americans. That assignment, which perhaps echoed Tocqueville's famous description of the American's "bootless chase" of happiness, conformed to Sherman's program in "Forty and Upwards." Adopting a position close to the "impressionist" emphasis on feelings he had earlier renounced, Sherman contemplated the future of his career in phrases that suggest Whitman: "I am going to write, so far as possible, . . . about happiness, and where it is, and how it got there; and every paragraph that I write shall have the word, or the record of happiness in it." Hence, a list of great critics Sherman developed while vacationing in Europe featured Swinburne and others capable of "communicating literary joy," while faulting Babbitt's "worship of will" and "air of universal condemnation."[64]

On the other hand, Sherman qualified his conviction that the "maximum of happiness" equaled the "maximum of expression" by reiterating the New Humanist theory of inner control. "The power which drives the engine," he noted, "also applies the brake." More important, he continued, at least initially, to conceive of literature as a "partner" of "morals"—even if he now wanted to "widen the meaning of moralist" to mean "student and master of *mores*." Nor was he content to detach from the critic's charge the Arnoldian mission of diffusing civilization. Still an educator at heart, he described his new responsibilities as substituting "one classroom for another." Adopting a different metaphor, he wrote, "I should like to be an architect, [in order to be] of use to the republic, to many people; to be of use in ways that they understand . . . [creating] a new beauty; rooted in the ground, reaching towards the skies . . . Till the whole nation becomes a city-state, like the old Greek states, *civitas*—civilized." Using language strikingly similar to that of Canby, whom Sherman at this juncture identified as feeling "so much alike" him "about critical and literary matters," he saw the newspaper review as a force for positive standardization—that is, for replacing a destructive sameness with a uniformly higher level of taste. In his view of himself as "public instructor," Sherman thus brought to *Books* a variant of the moral framework governing the founding of the *Nation*.[65]

Sherman, however, was more willing than his predecessors to resolve the problem of combining democracy and standards by modifying the form and style of his writing. Such concessions might have been predictable, given his own recoil from the *Nation*-essay, yet the particular lines along which Sherman proposed to recast his prose are immensely suggestive: "As you widen your audience," he proposed in his journal, "you omit your parentheses; you eliminate dependent clauses; you reduce subordination . . . ; you reduce allusion; you erase shades; you don't soften lines; you remember you are advertising—a 'Poster' not an etching." Elsewhere, he made the same point: "We don't want soliloquy. Personality. Megaphone at Stamford Bridge— jollying the American crowds—Mark Twain did it. A. France does it. Johnson did it. Now comes my chance to try it."[66] Those statements reveal the extent to which the language of consumer culture had, by the mid-1920s, infiltrated not only Sherman's sense of self but also his definition of role.

If Sherman accepted his audience as one of his "masters," moreover, he also recognized that Arnoldian "disinterestedness" could not withstand the commercial pressures his editorial position involved. The literary supplement was, he acknowledged, in part a "publisher's organ" designed to "help them move the season's crop of new books." Acceding to that expectation, Sherman arrived at the conclusion that current books ought not to be evaluated on the same scale as older works. He thus here discarded the Arnoldian critical practice of evaluating contemporary literature in light of the classics. Instead, he vowed to consider himself a "cheer leader" whose obligation was to promote "fair play" and "enthusiasm" even if the competitors in the literary game did not "break a world record."[67]

Hence, when Sherman wrote Irita Van Doren that he hoped *Books* could have more "sweetness and light" than "any other Review in the City," his language signified a reapportionment of Arnold's objectives: although he still strove for both qualities, his conception of his purpose was heavier on "sweetness"—the critic's discernment of "joy" and "beauty"—than on "light" or elucidation of the "best." At the end of his introspective summer, Sherman moved to New York to implement that idea and to seek amid the city's pinnacles of steel and concrete the restorative "forests" and "valleys" he craved.[68]

The Ambivalent Arnoldian as Editor

The first number of *Books* appeared on September 21, 1924. Sherman's opening column was prominently located, as in subsequent issues, on the left-hand side of the front page. That placement, like Sherman's billing in large print just beneath the journal's title, assisted the *Herald Tribune*'s effort to feature its literary editor as "the most authoritative interpreter of American letters in this country and abroad." As one might expect from his anticipatory reflections, however, the content of Sherman's first essay was somewhat less firmly positioned. Predominantly, he vowed to stand for "the old moralistic criticism," as opposed to the indifferent aestheticism of Spingarn. Yet he also distanced himself from genteel values by rejecting Arnold's idea that criticism be "disinterested"—here broadening the term to mean freedom from "preconceptions" as well as from the "political, practical considerations" Arnold had in mind. Promising his readers the benefit of judgments rooted in his "knowledge" and "beliefs," he simultaneously licensed the expression of his impressionistic tendencies by giving equal standing to his "unanalyzed prejudices, intuitions, and emotional capacity." He thus left open the possibility that an emphasis on individual "happiness" might overtake his moral agenda.[69]

Over the next two years, that is essentially what happened. The process, though, was less linear—and less thorough—than Ruland has implied in concluding that, as soon as Sherman went to *Books*, "posterity lost a critic of insight and power who never returned to significant work in the world of letters." Especially during the first few months, Sherman's lingering New Humanist sympathies were still often in evidence. In a discussion of William Crary Brownell, for example, he affirmed the virtue of "self-denial" as a means to the "ideal sphere." In fact, his laudatory summary of Brownell's viewpoint—in language diametrically opposed to the metaphors of "Forty and Upwards"—is an index of the persistent ambivalence surrounding Sherman's quest for self-expression: he commended the "aspiration to achieve rather than to experience, to reach a goal rather than to explore the unknown" in an effort to attain "perfection." On the matter of standards, Sherman even more blatantly attacked a position he himself had at least privately articulated. Assessing one of Canby's collections of *Saturday Review* pieces, he chided his fellow editor as if fending off a menacing doppelgänger: Calling Canby a "sportsman" and a "good scout," Sherman depicted him as turning "from the academic cloister to current literature with a determination to encourage the game—to encourage, in fact, all kinds of games. He enjoys them all so much that he rather hates to commit himself to any."[70]

Despite his own assent to the "cheerleader" conceit, Sherman, for his part, did not hesitate to announce that Dreiser had "the imagination of a chemist"; that Twain's *Autobiography* was "pretty bad"; that a novel by May Sinclair was facile and sentimental. Toward his predecessor and enemy Rascoe, he directed intellectual rigor combined with unambiguous contempt. At times, he continued to reject literary modernism on the grounds that it glorified amoral behavior. Thus, he applauded Robert Louis Stevenson's decision to "shun the treatment of 'modern love,'" faulted the poetry anthologist Louis Untermeyer for "his gross confusion of 'modern' with 'good,'" and warned his audience away from Ford Madox Ford's "devastating cynicism." In service to the project of inculcating aesthetic awareness he had pursued in *Matthew Arnold*, he sensitized readers to "psychological veracity," economical delineation of character, "luminous" language, and fidelity to truth.[71] His own level of diction strikes one today as uncompromisingly high, as if to use words like "lambency" was to set an example of the linguistic precision he valued in other writers.[72]

Yet these instances of adherence to aesthetic stringency and "the old moralistic criticism" grew less frequent as Sherman acceded to his desire to celebrate personal freedom. By the end of 1925 he had acknowledged the seductive nature of Anatole France's hedonism, derided the stifling atmosphere of Barrett Wendell's New England, and reiterated the potentially liberating notion that "the surface is everything."[73] While such perceptions remained consistent with Sherman's emotional history as frustrated poet, they made his overall outlook just as noncommittal as the attitude of which he accused Canby. In his preface to *Critical Woodcuts*, his first collection of *Books* articles, Sherman defended the evolution of his position in terms that announced his resignation from the post of moral arbiter: "No man," he declared, "should state very emphatically what 'the good life' is until he has found it." Retracting the premises of his initial essay for the supplement, he remarked: "The first duty of a commentator on current literature . . . is to present a fairly full and veracious report of what is going on. He will have his own convictions regarding the permanent value of various parts of the contemporary spectacle. . . . But his first duty is not to exploit his own predilections; it is rather to understand the entire 'conspiracy' of forces involved in the taste of his day." Similarly, in an October 1925 review, he declared his intention to supply "understanding" rather than explicit "adverse criticism," language which harkened back to his exchange with More about the drawbacks of the *Nation*-essay's rigorous form.[74]

Sherman's reconception of his responsibilities drew him closer to the idea that book reviews should be primarily a type of news. Although that outlook rested on a long tradition, it had particular meaning in the context of the 1920s, when the acquisition of specialized knowledge seemed increasingly essential for personal advancement. Sherman's promise of thorough, reliable reporting could ease readers' anxieties about sorting through the number of volumes piling up on bookstore counters. As one advertisement for the supplement proclaimed, *Books* presented "the complete picture of current literature" so that readers would not "miss" the works they "want to read." Moreover, in much

the way Frederick Winslow Taylor's ideology of "scientific management" used the rhetoric of self-fulfillment to organize the individual for
industrial productivity, this information served the priorities of a consumer society, in which "using books efficiently" (as copywriters for the
"Five-Foot Shelf" put it in 1924) came before the slow accretion of
liberal culture. "The less time you have for reading," the same ad
phrased it, "the more important it is for you to consult 'BOOKS' in order
that none of your reading time may be wasted." As Hardwick later
recorded about comparable reviews in *Time*, some publishers even
concluded that the magazine's audience, "having learned *Time*'s opinion of a book, feel that they have somehow already read the book, or . . .
at least taken it in, *experienced* it as a 'fact of our time.' They feel no
more need to buy the thing itself than to go to Washington for a
firsthand look at the latest works of the Republican Administration."[75]

Those assurances enhanced Sherman's stature as an expert, cloaking
him with the same "authoritativeness" Nevins ascribed to the *Evening
Post*'s reviewers. Yet the matter was complicated. Sherman's reportorial stance simultaneously implied a reallocation of authority from
critic to reader. His decision "on all possible occasions to keep his
theoretical and didactic mouth shut"—to reduce, in other words, his
function as transmitter of standards—left his audience free to weigh his
remarks in terms of their own criteria. As the New Humanist critic
Norman Foerster put it, his aim was "to subdue rather than to cultivate
the personal equation, to understand and explain rather than judge."
This diffident style of expertise accommodated a democratic resistance
to the power of elites and preserved the ideal of the autonomous self.
Sherman's own democratic leanings, once channeled into a vision of his
membership in the "saving remnant," now occasionally surfaced in
expressions of sympathy with the "sheep" and descriptions of himself
as "an inveterate and incorrigible average man."[76]

Average readers, however, did not always perceive this shift as in
their best interest. Sherman's 1925 exchange with a reader named John
A. Slade, whom *Books* dubbed "The Man in the Street," nicely captures
the tensions his contraction of his role entailed. As Slade noticed,
Sherman's pledge to keep "his own predilections" at bay competed with
his increasing reliance on autobiographical impressions. In other words,
the exploration of personality expanded to fill the void left by abandoning adjudication of "the best." Thus, Slade complained that Sherman

had reduced criticism to "personal likes and dislikes" which were not meeting his need to know what he ought to read. Although he characterized himself as a seeker of "information," Slade's definition of the term required the reviewer to adhere to "critical standards" and to tell him whether or not a book was "good." Sherman's reviews, he complained, have "just that subjective flavor which makes the reader say: 'Oh, well, that's the way it affects him.'" In reply, Sherman argued for the reader's autonomy and against his own expertise, insisting that "you have in your own mind some of the material needful for a judgment, *with standards*."[77]

At the same time, Sherman told Slade not to "sit around and kick against your own salvation"—thus retaining for himself the power to dispense grace. Similarly, Sherman's actual practice of continuing to write reviews based on aesthetic and even moral premises moderated his reinterpretation of his role. His evaluations remained erudite and subtle, with minimal plot summary and few lapses into the quotable epigrams on which many of his middlebrow contemporaries relied. For the most part, Sherman stayed focused, if not always on the texts at hand, at least on the historical contexts in which they appeared. Nor, as the next chapter will demonstrate, did Sherman go as far in deprecating his special qualifications as did his counterparts on the Book-of-the-Month Club board. To the extent that he disavowed authority while asserting it, however, he was as much a mirror as a recorder of the "'conspiracy' of forces"—here tugging at ideals of democracy—that shaped "the taste of his own day."

Sherman's gradual embrace of journalism without its "higher" aims had other implications for his relationship to both literary movements and consumer culture. From one standpoint, Sherman's ambivalent posture was a victory for modernism. Out of "chivalry," "curiosity," and "the need for restoring the balance," he began turning his broadened perspective toward works he called "new, difficult, questionable and forever caviare to the general." Thus, the forays he had made in that direction before assuming the *Books* editorship now gave way to regular excursions into the modernist camp. If he disparaged Ford, he commended D. H. Lawrence for his "incomparably vital interpretations of nature"; if he resisted modern poetry, he acclaimed Virginia Woolf for a sensibility that was basically "classical." In an essay lauding Sherwood Anderson and even favorably alluding to Dreiser, Sherman declared himself "heart and soul in sympathy" with their ambition to "express the color and passion of contemporary life." For these reasons, Van Wyck Brooks (himself in a different sort of retreat from his earlier cultural criticism) extolled Sherman for extricating himself from the "morass" of his previous moralism and landing in a "stronger position than ever."[78]

Arguably, Sherman's "middleness" on the merits of modern literature was just what was required to ease a conservative reading public toward unfamiliar genres. To an audience he himself identified as still suspicious of mysticism, symbolism, and psychology, the example of a figure with unimpeachable credentials and strong links to the past welcoming those approaches might well serve the avant-garde cause. Yet there was, of course, the catch that Sherman's newfound tolerance also extended to books that were far from "caviare." Whatever the stultifying aspects of the New Humanist conception of standards, that credo at least prevented the excessive praise that Sherman sometimes bestowed on works conventional at best. In these instances, Ruland is right that Sherman's "power" utterly failed him. The most flagrant example of his runaway enthusiasm was his statement, in a review of Don Marquis's dramatization of the New Testament, that it "should affect us as the tragedies of Aeschylus and Sophocles affected the Greeks"—a judgment so overblown that he himself qualified it by adding "—religiously" when the essay was reprinted in *Critical Woodcuts*. With evident relief, he hailed Louis Bromfield as "a novelist who will please you" and accorded "a large place in American fiction" to the admittedly "second-line" writer Charles G. Norris.[79]

It was this streak of indiscriminateness that Edmund Wilson attacked in his *New Republic* essay "The All-Star Literary Vaudeville" (1926), perhaps the most famous critique of overpraise in American book reviewing. "Even Stuart P. Sherman," Wilson wrote, "once so savage in the opposite camp, has become as benevolent as Carl Van Doren and now occupies what has perhaps become, from the popular point of view, the central desk of authority, to which each of the performers in the all-star circus, from Ben Hecht to Ring Lardner, steps up to receive his endorsement." Sherman and his fellow reviewers, according to Wilson, were inclined to "forget critical standards"; as a result, he observed, "it is scarcely possible nowadays to tell the reviews from the advertising." Functioning as "salesmen" for "contemporary literary goods," they tended to "convey the impression that master-pieces are being manufactured as regularly as new models of motor-cars."[80]

Wilson's metaphor aptly connected Sherman's approach to the priority Americans in the 1920s placed on both display and expertise. What is more, his appraisal of that stance in terms of the marketplace points the way to the deeper ramifications of Sherman's ambition to "remember you are advertising" as it played itself out in print. In the service of his wish to explore personality, Sherman constructed his *Books* essays less as assessments of particular works than as occasions to expatiate on an author's entire corpus—and on his own experience. As such, they typically began by offering readers the same sort of memorable visual images for which advertising copywriters strove—for example, a glimpse of Lawrence with "a shag of hair across the forehead, eyes alert, defiant, glinting like a squirrel's, snubby nose sniffing the air, and a big bush of a beard." Along with the simplified syntax he had prescribed for himself, Sherman also created sentences strikingly similar in impact to the "windswept" technique the publisher Max Lincoln Schuster developed at the same time to sell his firm's books. The following excerpt from Sherman's description of Carlyle, which, as published, went on for fifteen lines, was typical. Employing the second person to intensify the sense of Carlyle's reality (as if he were still alive), it immersed readers in a rhythmic series of evocative phrases: "They have made of your peasant childhood, of your struggling, passionate early manhood, of your thwarted loves and bitter rages, of your religious ecstasies and despairs, . . . of your wild humors, of your small personal habits, of your physical infirmities, even of your most intimate bursts of spleen and affection—they have made of these things a rich legend, like the stories of Alexander and Arthur, which passes from babbling mouth to greedy ear, and grows in passing." Thus, Sherman enabled readers to feel (without too strenuous an effort) the immediacy of his subject matter.[81]

Those effects were the result of Sherman's considered decision to laden his prose with emotional appeal. In a letter to his son, written after he had worked on *Books* for a few months, he explained: "Your vulgar reader can dispense almost with thinking if you prod his senses sharply. This is an aspect of the literary art which since I have been writing for the large audience of a newspaper I think about more frequently than when I wrote for a more academic audience." Although Sherman did not give up "nuance" without some regret, that assessment of the stylistic needs of his readers was worthy of Bruce Barton or John B. Watson.[82]

In addition to matters of structure and style, moreover, there was a more directly political link between Sherman's shift away from his moral agenda and the ethos of American consumer culture. Whereas Babbitt and More had indicted the mechanical comforts and paltry satisfactions American materialism engendered, the matrix for Sherman's *Books* essays was a rejection of any need for social change. In part, Sherman's complacency proceeded from the democratic orientation he thought of himself as acting upon. In a rave review of Will Durant's *The Story of Philosophy*, for example, he emphasized the "average man's" hunger for knowledge and read the book's popularity as a sign of a thriving American civilization. Yet Sherman approved equally of what he saw as the source of such intellectual vitality: the belief in progress accompanying the rise of a consumer economy. In an address to the publishing industry entitled "Finding the Intelligent Public and Enlarging It," he gave Henry Ford credit (along with writers and inventors) for enabling Americans to envision a future even "more rational, more scientific, more beautiful," with "more of health, comfort, [and] refreshment" than they currently enjoyed. His role at *Books*, he declared, was "to interpret this new world to our public."[83]

Thus, within the pages of the supplement itself, he worshipfully reported, "I never step into the all-day thunder of a subway or watch an eighteen-story apartment house rushing toward heaven, or the big driving rods of our political and religious and educational machinery in action, without an almost overwhelming sense that colossal creative minds are at work, imitating God and rivaling many of the productions which were pronounced good in the first chapter of Genesis." In another essay, he underscored his admiration for the same qualities Lewis satirized in *Babbitt*. "I am a strong believer in the American bourgeoisie," he wrote, "and feel great pride in its virtues and its achievements"—among them "energy, organization, 'pep,' system, efficiency and a cheerful sentimentalism." To be fair, this acquiescent mentality competed with Sherman's sense that Americans were unduly afraid of nonconformists and with his conciliatory attitude toward political radicals. Yet, arguing the case against censorship before the prime advocates of those "virtues"—the Rotarians of New York City—he was capable, by the mid-1920s, of advising "successful executives" to regard literature as an "information department" that would help them expand their markets.[84]

Any chronicle of Sherman's accommodations to consumer values— manifest in his quest for self-expression, his role as newsgiver, his absorption of advertising techniques, and his occasional boosterism— must, however, record two countervailing points. First, no one who reads Sherman's *Books* essays can fail to be struck by the effectiveness of his style, even when the content it conveyed was off the mark. His poetic leanings, his struggle for a freer self, his painful awareness of life's limitations on "happiness"—these facets of his sensibility shaped passages like the following description of Carlyle, which resonates to Sherman himself: "Perhaps more and more we shall learn to smile indulgently and dismissively at his politics and to look with increasing respect and curiosity into his revolutionary and epoch-making art— into that style which grows constantly more supple, voice-like and expressive . . . and into that fashion of painting man which results from seeing with perfect distinctness his waistcoat and his shoe buckles, and also the stars behind him and the deep, dark space behind the stars." For that lucidity and pathos, as much as anything, Carl Van Doren was right when he placed Sherman's *Herald Tribune* writing "not in the history of news, but in the history of literature itself," and eulogized him as "the least merely journalistic" of reviewers.[85] —

Second, his career encompassed the irony that his effort to flee the confines of gentility and academia did not, in the end, procure him the "happiness" he sought. Although he worked mainly at home, he did like his colleagues on the *Herald Tribune* staff and especially enjoyed nosing about the office on the day the paper went to press. With Irita Van Doren, his biographers noted, "there was something more than cordial harmony." This was true, but not quite in the way they meant. Sherman admired Van Doren's competence, spirit, and judgment. In July of 1925 he sent her a letter full of compliments about her work: she was "so wise, so generous, so sympathetic . . . so unerringly right . . . so resourceful, prescient, original, clear-sighted, swift, tenacious," and so on. Yet a few weeks after writing that adoring tribute, he chided Van Doren for not replying to his letters unless they were "part of the routine of the office." Sherman coolly added: "As one of thirty applicants for attention, I got 1-30 of the time at the disposal of the Editor for applicants. Never at any time have I raised a shadow of doubt regarding your Efficiency." Thus, the *Books* environment, if more congenial than Urbana, had its own conflicts.[86]

Moreover, Sherman found the schedule press deadlines enforced at least as onerous as his academic obligations had been. Much of the time he relished his work load, "slogging away" but having "quite a bit of fun out of it." His biographers saw the pressure only as a stimulus, without which he grew depressed. The work itself, however, was also a source of dismay. To Ellery Sedgwick, Sherman declared that he was "attached to a wheel"; to Oswald Garrison Villard, that he had "a really heartfilling sense of life as one damned thing after another." By the spring of 1926 he was expressing his dissatisfaction in terms that suggest alienation from the marketplace: he told Sedgwick that he was ultimately "hoping to live through this business that I am in, and retire to a life of perfectly free writing activity." Sherman's real interest in, and pleasure from, his job offset those sentiments, yet they mark his persistent frustration at failing to become "a man of letters and nothing else."[87]

Beyond the day-to-day stresses that burdened him, one also senses that, however much Sherman encountered the richer fare New York offered—the literary gatherings, the excursions to galleries and plays, the urban ambience—he continued to take "black bread" as his portion. Unable to replicate the austere tranquillity of a figure like John Bascom, he could not give himself over, either, to the lure of living "on the surface of things." To his colleague Isabel Paterson, he spoke of his determination to spend more time on "the avowed pleasures of life" and then perceptively added, "I would, you know, approach amusement in that way, as a duty." Torn between self-control and self-expression, he also continued to evince the same dichotomy between "inner melancholy" and outward demeanor he had attributed to Arnold years before. Who, he asked in one telling *Books* essay, "is really contented with the present quality of our personal lives?" For all his paeans to New Era prosperity, he regretted, inside, the waste of "passionate power" on "the shuttle trains of a business which hurries us from places where we feel no joy in staying to places where we find no joy in going."[88]

Perhaps, if Sherman had lived longer, he would have achieved some greater measure of serenity. As it was, he died of a heart attack while swimming in Lake Michigan on August 21, 1926. He was forty-four years old. By an odd coincidence, one aspect of his death perpetuated the tensions of his life. The newspaper stories lamenting his loss competed for space with obituaries for two other figures, one representing the genteel tradition, the other the culture of personality: Charles W. Eliot and Rudolph Valentino.

Other Features of Books

Sherman's *Herald Tribune* reviews did not, of course, appear in a vacuum but existed within the context of *Books* as a whole. Each issue carried, along with Sherman's lead essay, a number of other features. These eventually included a children's books page, a column for book collectors, correspondence from readers, news of "Books Abroad," a column about reissues of older works, and, together with publishers' advertisements, a full page of classified ads. Four regular departments stand out as departures from the spirit of the "higher journalism." One, a listing of the week's best-selling books, was hardly a *Books* invention, yet it strengthened the identification of culture with news and fed the desire for successful social performance. So did a compilation of the week's new titles, which differed from similar lists in the old *Nation* by providing brief summaries of each book's contents.

The other two noteworthy items—the anonymous "Letters to a Lady in the Country" and Isabel M. Paterson's "Turns with a Bookworm"— deserve fuller comment. The former, largely written by Sherman himself, is just as neglected as his "Cornelia" essays—and just as revealing. The origin of the "Letters" lay partly in an aim that governed *Books* into the 1930s: the plan of making it a truly national periodical. Both editor and publisher shared that goal, Sherman because of his commitment to widening his audience, the Reids because they wanted to increase circulation. "The trouble with every paper that is published here," Sherman explained in the words of a fictitious alter ego, "is that it is edited for Manhattan Island, which is as detached from the rest of America as the Basques are detached from Europe. . . . What you need is a link between the city and the provinces, which will show people out there that you are thinking about them, are conscious, you know, that they exist."[89]

Because of his years in the Midwest, Sherman himself was well suited to supply that link. Aware of his own provinciality, in 1923 he had confided to Irita Van Doren his plans for a sketch of "our new metropolitan type"; a few months later, congratulating her on her *Nation* editorship, he had identified Van Doren herself as a fascinating representative of the type and urged her to write an autobiographical article. "Letters to a Lady in the Country," the ostensible correspondence between a transplanted Kentuckian and a woman back home, served the same function. Further manifesting his accommodation of consumer culture, Sherman made Paul, the New Yorker, an ex-poet who worked as an advertising man but retained his literary bent; for romantic interest, he married Caroline, the "country" resident, to Paul's best friend. Beginning with the first issue, the "Letters" ran in *Books* almost weekly until the spring of 1926.[90]

Through that medium, readers across the country glimpsed Sherman (as Paul) lunching with authors and attending publishers' parties. Caroline's part of the exchange, eventually written by Sherman's assistant Garreta Busey, helped win the loyalty of non–New York readers by giving equal time to rural pleasures. The most significant aspect of the feature, however, was the contrast it provided to Sherman's sober front-page reviews. While those remained grounded in the genteel aesthetic, here was personality in its shallowest form—morsels of literary gossip or one-line book recommendations. About the dinner celebrating Robert Frost's fiftieth birthday, for example, Sherman wrote, "I managed to get one of the waiters to let me peep through the door while the speaking was going on; and I saw him and Carl Van Doren and Wilbur L. Cross and Dorothy Canfield and Louis Untermeyer and Walter Prichard Eaton all making speeches." His June 6, 1926, "letter" described the wedding of publisher John Farrar to Simon and Schuster's crossword-puzzle whiz Margaret Petherbridge. "And so, as you have such a sharp little tooth for 'inside information,'" Sherman had Paul tell Caroline, "I'm sending you [this] book . . . without waiting to read it myself."[91]

Thus, the combination of his two *Books* contributions (his reviews and the "Letters") allowed Sherman to express simultaneously his ambivalent vision of the self. The "Letters" alone also permitted Sherman another forum for pitting self-expression against restraint: Paul competed with Caroline's husband, Jim, by sympathizing with Caroline's desire for the intense experience of "apple-green sunsets," while Jim remained the prisoner of disciplined emotion. In light of that symmetry, Sherman's comment to Busey about concealing his authorship of the "Letters"—"I want as long as possible to remain two persons: it is truer to life!"—takes on broader meaning.[92]

For all the breezy charm of the "Letters," however, the supplement's center of wit and personal revelation was Paterson's "Turns with a Bookworm," a part of the *Herald Tribune* since 1922.[93] A novelist with no special qualifications for criticism other than a love of literature and a lively mind, Paterson was a frequent reviewer for *Books*; in that capacity, she once declared Elinor Wylie's sonnets "the most beautiful in the English language" and pronounced *The Great Gatsby* "a book of the season only." The column, however, was her major claim to fame. Describing her role as the "pleasant office of gossip to the literary fraternity," she signed the feature "I. M. P." and lived up to the image of the acronym. In a typical example from 1924, she began by mentioning that Sinclair Lewis had passed through New York on the way to Europe and concluded with these social notes: "Matrimony is coming in again among the literary younger set. Gilbert Seldes has been honeymooning abroad; nearly got killed in a motor smash in Italy. . . . Alyse Gregory and Llewellyn Powys were married recently. She is managing editor of the *Dial*." Additional references to comings and goings, glimpses of works in progress, and literary opinions filled the remaining space.[94]

In one of his "letters" to "Caroline," Sherman summarized Paterson's appeal in language that provides a decisive commentary on his own outlook: "What I like is personality," he has "Paul" announce. "It seems to me the very marrow of literature, and I am ready to quarrel with all the highbrows and high hats who try to banish it. For example, in 'Books' I always read first Isabel Paterson's sharp 'Turns with a Bookworm.' I enjoy her page more than going to a party. I encounter personality in it at more frequent intervals. . . . It's all bosh to say I don't care for personality. I care for nothing else."[95]

Beyond that allure, Paterson's column encompassed strategies that some of her contemporaries would exploit more fully. Predominantly, she set herself up as an "insider" who offered access to an exclusive realm of culture and sophistication. Yet she also implied that culture was not dependent on the actual reading of books. "With mingled pain and horror," Paterson declared, "we discover that of 'A List of Forty Important American Books of 1924' we have read only three! . . . Well we didn't exactly read all of all three, either. . . . [We] got tied up in one sentence that we couldn't make out what it meant, and, escaping with our life, didn't venture again." That tone of scatterbrained anti-intellectualism reinforced Paterson's message of access by flaunting her lack of critical expertise. Although her frank, glib judgments sometimes alienated members of her audience, Paterson's promise of "inside dope" was popular: as *Publishers' Weekly* commented in 1939, "Paterson readers seem to be divided into two camps—those who love her and those who take her as their Sunday morning hair shirt—but everybody reads her!"[96]

Alongside *Books*'s departments were the reviews—a front-page critique juxtaposed to Sherman's, eight or so other major ones highlighted in the table of contents, ten or fifteen more signed contributions, and, mostly near the back of the journal, several unsigned brief notices. Many of the figures who regularly wrote for the supplement in the 1920s lived in the New York area and clustered around Irita Van Doren: Carl Van Doren covered history, biography, and fiction, often in the front-page space; Mark Van Doren did poetry; Mark's good friend Joseph Wood Krutch reviewed both fiction and literary criticism; the Van Dorens' Columbia colleague Irwin Edman handled philosophy and social science. Lewis Gannett, whom Irita helped recruit in 1928 to write the *Herald Tribune*'s weekday book column, also sometimes appeared on Sunday. Other reviewers, outside the Van Doren network, were just as identified with New York: Erskine, Hendrik Van Loon, the novelists Alice Beal Parsons and Lorine Pruette, Malcolm Cowley, the poet Babette Deutsch. A notable addition in the 1930s was the writer and editor Constance Lindsay Skinner.

In addition, however, a number of far-flung contributors, many located at universities, helped *Books* acquire the national flavor it sought: novelists Zona Gale and Ellen Glasgow, from Wisconsin and Virginia, respectively; the Arkansas journalist Charles J. Finger; academics Jacob Zeitlin (Illinois), Frederic J. Paxson (Wisconsin), Louise Pound (Nebraska), Walter Prichard Eaton (Massachusetts), and Albert Guerard (Texas and California). (After Sherman's death, they were joined by Constance Rourke, Gerald W. Johnson, and Stewart Holbrook, from Michigan, Baltimore, and Oregon.) A 1934 letter to Irita Van Doren from the theater critic Sheldon Cheney indicates the extent to which the policy of counterbalancing a New York perspective had become, by that time, one of *Books*'s hallmarks: "I particularly like your way of going out for reviews to authorities in other parts of the country," Cheney wrote, "thus escaping what is sometimes a narrowness of the metropolitan viewpoint."[97]

At the same time, occasional reviews by British writers such as Lawrence and John Galsworthy, as well as (until 1932) a weekly department entitled "Books Abroad," enhanced the journal's cosmopolitan quality. Moreover, leaving aside Sherman's hospitable viewpoint, the goal of broad appeal did not, in the mid-1920s, result in as much adverse response to modernism and experimentation as one might expect. In general, *Books* reviewed (rather than ignored) major works by avant-garde writers, but not on page one.[98] Some, like the assessment of Hemingway's *In Our Time* as revealing "promise of genius," were highly enthusiastic. More often, such reviews tended to take an arms-length position, bringing departures from conventions of form or content to the attention of readers who liked that sort of thing. This assessment of Fitzgerald's stories was typical: "They show why Mr. Fitzgerald is admired by just the reviewers who admire him." The only genre to take a real beating was modernist poetry. Assenting to one reviewer's statement, in a condemnation of Marianne Moore, that critics had "nourished the work of Pound, Stevens, Cummings, and Eliot beyond its true worth," *Books* tended to bury reviews of works by major experimental poets. For example, the week a notice of William Carlos Williams's *In the American Grain* appeared on an inside page, T. S. Stribling's novel *Teeftallow* was featured opposite Sherman's column. In that respect, *Books* failed even as a record of "what is going on."[99]

Personality, "Fairness," and News: Books *after Sherman*

In the years following Sherman's death, the legend grew up that he would not have perished in the waters of Lake Michigan if he had not been ravaged already by the soul-destroying effort to write honest criticism in a society that did not value it.[100] That melodrama, if it contained some truth, omitted Sherman's complicity in his own demise.

It drew its force, however, from the fact that, once deprived of Sherman's critical authority (however inconsistently exercised), *Books*'s aspirations to instruct as well as report withered away.

The key figure in this phase of the "higher journalism"'s realignment was Irita Van Doren, who succeeded Sherman as editor and remained in that role for almost forty years. Because she was already handling every aspect of the supplement's production, her appointment to the editorship was virtually automatic. Less clear was the question of what to substitute for Sherman's lead essays. Van Doren filled the gap by inventing the job of "visiting critic." Over the next five years, such figures as Virginia Woolf, Rebecca West, André Maurois, Ford Madox Ford, E. M. Forster, and Ellen Glasgow made month-long appearances on *Books*'s front page. The device continued to enhance *Books*'s cosmopolitan aura and introduced readers to a remarkably distinguished group of authors, yet Sherman's coherent sense of purpose dropped out of sight. As Van Doren remarked to Jacob Zeitlin when she initiated the "visiting" arrangement, "I must now make a virtue of variety, whereas our chief strength before was in the unity of those first page impressions."[101]

Of interest here is Van Doren's assumption that she herself could not supply that unity by making explicit an editorial outlook of her own. Her promotion, she informed one well-wisher after Sherman's death, was "largely a matter of change in title," but that was true only because Van Doren subtracted criticism from the editor's responsibilities. Even though she was, if not as erudite as Sherman, perceptive, knowledgeable, and articulate, she insisted, throughout her career, that she was not a writer, and she proved it: she did no reviews, never penned more than a sentence or two to *Books*'s readers, and refused the opportunity to publish the insightful commentaries she prepared for the *Herald Tribune*'s "Books and Authors" luncheons.[102]

It may be that Van Doren's failure to find her own voice stemmed entirely from what she called an "instinct" for editing rather than writing. Still, she had tried her hand at reviewing while on the *Nation* staff and, as Mark Van Doren noted, "told stories and described things in a way that could make us wonder why she had never admitted the possibility of herself being a writer." A reply to Harry Scherman's suggestion in 1963 that she undertake a memoir points to a possible explanation. "There should be at least one Van Doren," she joked, "who doesn't write." Did she, consciously or unconsciously, curtail her writing out of deference to, or fear of competition with, her husband and brother-in-law? To put the matter in a wider context, was her decision to continue assigning reviews, reading proof, running the office—to be, in other words, a superb administrator behind the scenes but not to step out in front with an educational or critical mission—as much the outgrowth of gender expectations as of her actual skills? Assuredly, thanks to Helen Rogers Reid's efforts, there were "more women in positions of responsibility on the *Tribune*" than on any other major American newspaper—Dorothy Thompson and Marie Meloney as well as Van Doren among them. Yet Van Doren's decision to restrict the extent of that responsibility out of the conviction that she had nothing to say seems all too characteristic a response of women, while the men who preceded and surrounded her had no such modest self-perception.[103]

In addition, Van Doren undoubtedly faced a pressure to maintain the first page of the book review as an arena for the "literary vaudeville." Her own critiques would not immediately have satisfied the demand for stars; the "visiting critic" strategy did so. Thus out of the limelight, however, Van Doren exercised another sort of influence (arguably also typical of women): the force of her personality. Soft-spoken yet vivacious, she was, in her brother-in-law Mark's words, "utterly affectionate and charming." Her polite southern manners, radiant warmth, and "wonderful gift for enjoyment" endeared her to almost everyone she met. Her friends—Erskine, Edman, Woolf, West, Vincent Sheehan, Edna Ferber, John Gunther (to name a few)—were legion and devoted. Divorced from Carl Van Doren in 1937, she had a special, touchingly intense relationship with Wendell Willkie. (In contrast to the expectations of candidates in the 1980s, Willkie, though married, barely concealed their affair when he ran for president in 1940, and no one raised a fuss.) To Helen Rogers Reid, she was confidante and adviser. Her colleagues on the *Tribune* staff, such as her assistant, Belle Rosenbaum, were unfailingly loyal; the contributors she mustered returned her extraordinary kindness by developing "a deep desire to please her." Her charm, Mark Van Doren noted, concealed a "will of iron" that revealed itself in her demand for "good writing and good thinking"; she was a "superb copyreader" as well as a delightful companion. "I don't know whether it's your natural Southern sweetness, or my professional respect for your skill as an editor," wrote Lewis Mumford, capturing both those qualities, "but I find you very hard to resist, and have almost given up trying to." Yet her dominant trait was, in Mark Van Doren's words, that "she was personal . . . as few persons have ever been."[104]

One is tempted, given such glowing tributes, to see Van Doren as a representative of the culture of personality at its best. Her capacity for intimacy and openness had its positive effects on *Books*: it won her reviewers despite inadequate pay for contributions and resulted in the discovery of new talents like Alfred Kazin and Henry Steele Commager. Her style also apparently filtered through to *Books*'s readers: when the supplement conducted a direct-mail advertising campaign in the mid-1930s, many people responded to Van Doren's form letter by replying not to the business office but to her personally, as if she cared about each subscriber.[105]

Yet, as Van Doren's successor Richard Kluger has pointed out, there was a way in which her congeniality eventuated in an unwillingness to publish assessments that might be rigorous but uncivil. Her humane approach, Malcolm Cowley recalled, also meant that she sometimes kept reviewers on her staff too long. More than that, Van Doren's definition of "good thinking and good writing" did not encompass the Arnoldian commitments that had shaped at least part of Sherman's approach. A 1939 interview with *Publishers' Weekly* furnished a rare exposition of her editorial policy: "Since *Books* is published as part of a large newspaper," she observed, "it must count among its potential readers people of every variety of taste and opinion, . . . and since books are published which represent all these tastes and opinions, it seems only fair to review them from the point of view from which they were written, so that they will ultimately find the audience for whom they are intended." In an undated radio address, probably from the late 1930s, Van Doren elaborated on this principle as it applied to the assessment of fiction. Acknowledging that "the majority of the novels published are second or third grade" but assuming that *Books* had an obligation to review them, she explained that "we can only try to prejudge these novels sufficiently to get them into the right hands—not to send a tough, hardboiled story to some one who likes graceful, poetic writing; nor a charmingly written book to some one primarily interested in action and adventure stories." The same was true of poetry:

"We would not ask Carl Sandburg," she declared, "to review T. S. Eliot."[106]

The language of "fairness" similarly characterized Van Doren's description of a good review. The "fair" appraisal, Van Doren noted in her radio broadcast, was not so balanced as to say nothing; like Sherman, she acknowledged and welcomed contributors' expressions of their opinions. Yet, "if a review seems unfair, biased or uninformed, as sometimes happens," she admitted, "we get in touch with the reviewer, talk it over, and, if he is willing, get him to rewrite it. If not, we send the book to another reviewer."

This rhetoric, another manifestation of Van Doren's humane temperament, drew on the ideal of "objectivity" that governed modern journalism as a whole. By awarding equal standing to readers of varying tastes, it also seemed to serve democratic values. Yet, although Sherman would hardly have described himself as "unfair," it contrasts with his view—potentially equally democratic—that readers deserved exposure only to the "best." Absent from Van Doren's formulation is the belief that the "second or third grade" should not find an audience at all and that the differences between Sandburg and Eliot, for example, were a matter of literary quality. Missing also is the critic's charge to adhere to aesthetic and moral principles in the conviction that they would engender a more adequate culture. Van Doren's remark that "we see no point in taking some slight or unimportant book and breaking it like a butterfly on a wheel" represents the antithesis of More's comment that "an excess of judgment over 'appreciation' is no bad thing."[107]

Van Doren's premium on unbiased reporting had particular repercussions in the 1930s. Although the outpouring of nonfiction that characterized American publishing during the Depression dominated *Books*'s front page, experimental fiction like John Dos Passos's *1919* continued to fare reasonably well. Political radicalism as a basis for criticism, however, was another matter. During the decade's debates over "proletarian literature," when critics on the left urged that literary judgments serve revolutionary ends, individual volumes advocating that view (for example, Granville Hicks's *Proletarian Literature in the United States*) were sometimes favorably reviewed. Yet *Books*'s unwillingness to endorse any doctrine aside from "fairness" meant that the supplement typically balanced praise for left-wing perspectives with equally strong counterarguments. Hence, Ben Ray Redman, writing about the reissue of Hicks's *The Great Tradition*, cautioned that "economics is not the whole answer to the life, or art, of man." Similarly, Mary Colum dismissed as a demand for "propaganda" Edmund Wilson's celebration of Marx's place in "the intellectual kingdom of magnificence, nobility and justice." This approach, which treated political convictions like any other piece of information, appeared to situate *Books* "above the battle." Yet, as Joseph Freeman noted at the time, such neutrality was itself a "political weapon"—one, in the case of the *Herald Tribune*, thoroughly consistent with the Reids' Republican loyalties.[108]

In terms of the issue of critical authority, the doctrine of "fairness" returned even more power to readers than Sherman had. As Foerster noticed, a literary journal like *Books*, especially without Sherman's editorial presence, gave equal weight to every reviewer's claims. "Instead of requiring conformity to a standard of its own," Foerster argued, "it voices the opinion of many minds, each able in its own way but often fundamentally in conflict with other minds." The result of this version of democratization, Foerster concluded, was that "the review that criticizes a given book must itself be criticized by the reader," who was not always equipped to identify the victor in such a "battle of the wits." For his part, Foerster (from the vantage point of the political right) doubted whether "a review which is virtually an open forum, making the inexpert reader the judge of the conflicting expert writers," could "shape opinion" in a way that would adequately resist the "disintegrating forces everywhere at work." Yet Foerster's contemporary Maxwell Bodenheim made a similar argument from the left, prefacing a denunciation of Sherman, among others, with the comment that the effort to "escape from dogma" was "making every reader his own critic and reducing printed criticism to an undistinguished, indecisive, and unnecessary melée."[109]

Although the feature originated elsewhere and never purported to supply reviews, in a sense the fullest expression of Van Doren's commitment to neutrality for its own sake was May Lamberton Becker's "Reader's Guide" column. Becker had started a literary question-and-answer department in the *New York Evening Post* in 1915. The column carried over into the *Saturday Review of Literature*, where it ran until Becker moved it to *Books* in 1933.[110] The "Reader's Guide" printed inquiries from readers in search of particular types of books—novels about doctors, for instance, or (for a women's club) biographies of queens. Becker also tracked down answers to puzzlers like "What three heroines of literature were hanged?" She replied by personal letter to readers whose inquiries she did not publish; she also prepared 750 different book lists for her correspondents. The content of Becker's "guidance" consisted mainly of supplying the authors and titles of the volumes she recommended, together with brief annotative remarks and enough homey philosophizing to glue together the various queries. In that way, the "Reader's Guide" was frankly a vehicle for information, which Becker transmitted by "conducting" an acritical exchange. In marked contradistinction to the tenor of Hamilton Wright Mabie's advice column, Becker told her audience that, from her point of view, "there are no best books, only books best for certain people for certain circumstances, sometimes even under certain conditions."[111]

Of course, critical principles necessarily shaped Becker's choices, infiltrating phrases such as "peculiarly satisfying" and "most successful." Such language was minimal, however, and the rationale behind it never apparent. One might thus claim that, by issuing absolute pronouncements, she arrogated *more* power to herself than Sherman did. Yet, functioning as an expert, Becker nonetheless made lack of judgment and subservience to her clientele the essence of her sense of purpose. The measure of the column's success, she reported in a 1949 reminiscence, was when readers "began to tell me about books as well as ask me about them." The description of Becker in *Publishers' Weekly* and elsewhere as "reference librarian to the country at large" further illuminates the point. The image conjures up the library patron, request already in mind, who solicits professional service and then walks away from the reference desk with taste and autonomy uncompromised. What is more, the role Becker adopted, which Amy Loveman played as well when she took over Becker's post at the *Saturday Review*, had affinities to Van Doren's style as editor: it involved carrying out discrete tasks, dealing personally with readers, more or less silencing one's own voice. Again, it does not seem coincidental that the figures who thus carried to the extreme the self-effacement potentially inherent in the position of newsgiver were women. In any case, Becker's undertaking accorded perfectly with the pluralism and relativism that Van Doren's belief in "fairness" subsumed.[112]

Van Doren's quest for an illusive objectivity was not the only way in which her editorial approach allied *Books* with the newspaper to which it belonged. While Sherman had only gradually and defensively considered himself a reporter, Van Doren actively and unambivalently embraced the "news" tradition in book reviewing. For example, she took pride in the fact that in 1933 *Books* became the "first weekly book review to departmentalize the reviewing of popular fiction." That is, in addition to the humorist Will Cuppy's older feature "Mystery and Adventure," it began consigning "New Popular Novels" to a section edited by Lisle Bell. (Sometimes the department was called "This Week with the Novelists.") As *Publishers' Weekly* explained, this practice "grew from the editor's conviction that popular novels have a large and legitimate audience who are interested not so much in critical reviewing, but in news of the latest publications." That outlook, moreover, had an impact even on the style of reviews not "departmentalized." While *Herald Tribune* reporter Ishbel Ross noted that Van Doren tried "to strike the medium between the reportorial type of review and pure criticism," Ross also remarked: "The current trends are played hard and [Van Doren] believes in a tie-up between book reviewing and the news whenever possible. She has a theory that the first paragraph of a review should be informative, much like the news lead of a story for the front page, and wherever possible should provoke the reader's interest at once."[113]

Similarly, after 1931, when reviews of the "outstanding book of the week" superseded the "visiting critic" on the front page, they acquired banner headlines with timely messages: "First Six Books on Technocracy Out This Week," for example. Even modernism could thereby lose its oppositional edge and become just another news item, as when the review of Gertrude Stein's latest book appeared under the subhead "Louis Bromfield Hails Her 'Autobiography' as a Literary Event." The same technique recurred on the inside pages. One reader reflected the success of such strategies (as well as the ambiguities involved in the concept of the nonjudgmental expert) by complimenting Van Doren in 1934: "May I say that your downright straight-news treatment of books is a joy? . . . The whole section always reads as if it were founded on the conviction that books *are* news to a great many people—people, like me, who live far away from the center of things, and who depend upon book reviews to tell them what's worth reading."[114]

By accelerating the movement away from discipline and training,

Books during Van Doren's tenure as editor thus exhibited even greater congruence with consumer values than it had in Sherman's day. This was true, moreover, in ways that were more directly commercial. Under the terms of the "Bookstore Plan" instituted in 1933, the *Herald Tribune* contracted with certain booksellers to mail *Books* to selected customers. Originally the bookstores paid the newspaper for the "service" and, because the mailing wrapper carried the store's name, received advertising in return; soon, the customer bore the charge. As part of the bargain, the stores were responsible for sending to the *Herald Tribune* their weekly tally of leading sellers. The results appeared in a chart (eventually occupying a full page) entitled "What America Is Reading," which replaced the small best-seller list formerly published. The compilation had a number of effects: it enhanced *Books*'s status as a national medium, gave bookstores additional advertising, contributed to the health of the publishing industry, got more books into the hands of readers, and provided the data necessary for them to keep up with the crowd. Specifically, thanks to this device, by 1939 *Books* acquired approximately sixty thousand additional paying subscribers reached through 142 bookstores nationwide.[115]

A related development was the increase in the supplement's advertising linage in the same period. Almost tripling between 1924 and 1927, declining somewhat during the early years of the Depression, and then rising steadily thereafter, book-ad space in the *Herald Tribune* reflected more than the publishing industry's adoption of aggressive promotional strategies. It also resulted from Helen Rogers Reid's concerted efforts to increase her newspaper's advertising revenues. By 1939 she had succeeded in garnering almost 40 percent of the total volume of book advertising in the New York area. As Royal Cortissoz remarked to Reid when her ambitions began paying off: "What you have done to the darling old paper! . . . I chuckle and chuckle. Queen Mary said that when they examined her heart they would find 'Calais' engraved upon it. When they look into mine they'll find 'The full page ads!' "[116]

Books's greater implication in the marketplace during Van Doren's editorship did not mean that it became the passive victim of insidious commercial forces or even that it enforced Perry's "Silent Bargain." Although the supplement's relations with advertisers are almost impossible to document, what evidence there is indicates that, on more than one occasion, Reid resisted publishers who made positive reviews a condition of advertising in *Books*. In 1924, for example, Dutton's John Macrae refused to take out extensive ads unless the newspaper, by its "method of reviews," led "the public to buy the books they want"; in 1935 the head of Bobbs-Merrill, declaring that an unfavorable assessment of a book would waste his firm's advertising budget, similarly announced that his house would do business where it got the best reviews. Unmoved, Reid insisted that her paper's policy was "to have critics state their honest convictions with complete independence." Nor was it *Books*'s practice, as was the case on the *Chicago Tribune* during World War I, to handle space limitations by giving preference to works from those publishers who advertised in its pages.[117]

Yet observers subsequent to Perry suspected that the market exerted more subtle influences on the shape of periodicals like *Books*. For one thing, the "practically universal respect for advertising," complained James Orrick, reversed the relationship between critic and book promoter: advertising managers wooed publishers by calling attention to the number of reviews a journal carried; when publishers responded by placing ads in advance of a book's appearance, editors were more likely to award the book a prominent review. That is, they judged "the importance of a book by the news value of the advance literary notes and the amount of advertising space the publisher has taken." In this way, "instead of leading, the critic follows those he exists to lead." For another thing, business considerations appeared to require a "dumbing down" of reviews. As James Truslow Adams declared in 1931, the literary editors of "one of the best book review sections in the country" (his reference is unclear) were "bluntly told to 'cut out the high-brow' to meet the increased moronism of an increased circulation." Finally, throughout the Depression, economic collapse seemed to place special pressures on editors and critics. The difficulty of selling any books in hard times, Henry Seidel Canby noted, increased the temptation to engage in "blurbing," pushing "kind-hearted, standardless reviewers to the first page."[118]

During the 1930s such perceived subservience to commercialism alienated from *Books* writers as different as Ezra Pound and Ludwig Lewisohn. Pound, who had served as "visiting critic" in 1929, ranted to Van Doren shortly thereafter: "You know perfectly well that I consider BOOKS like every other god damn American advertising medium, IS engaged in retarding the entrance into America of any and every live thought. . . . You are NOT as stupid as the groveling bugs on some of the other papers, and for that reason you are all the more RESPONSIBLE for the impossibility (wherein most americans live) of keeping in touch with what is BEING thought." More coherently but with equal vehemence, Lewisohn announced his "long suspicion" of the "chains worn by our editors": "Any intellectual rectitude is taboo. Any publisher's favorite speculation is protected."[119] Although disaffection arising from *Books*'s relationship with advertisers was only part of the story (the attractiveness of journals with more congenial politics, like the *New Republic* and *Partisan Review*, was certainly another), by 1940 *Books* had lost, among its distinguished contributors, not only Pound and Lewisohn but Cowley, Wilson, Mumford, and Brooks.

Those defections further shifted the balance of *Books*'s content from criticism to news. On the supplement's twenty-fifth anniversary in 1949, Lewis Gannett put the matter positively: "As the years passed, *Books* more and more confined itself to its essential function, of reviewing with the maximum of authority and the greatest liveliness and readability attainable as many as possible of the best books published each year." At the time of Gannett's appraisal, Becker, Cuppy, and Bell remained fixtures on the staff. Paterson's "Turns with a Bookworm" had just ended, but John K. Hutchens continued to supply literary gossip in "On the Books." Earlier in the decade, Rosemary and Stephen Vincent Benét's biographical sketches of contemporary authors were prominently featured; later, before wartime paper shortages imposed space limitations, *Books* offered photographic visits to writers' homes. Those items perpetuated Sherman's interest in personality and continued the drift away from what had remained of his Arnoldian premises at the supplement's inception.[120]

Thus, when Van Doren, in need of a statement of *Books*'s purposes for the twenty-fifth anniversary issue, reprinted Sherman's initial promise of criticism committed to moral and aesthetic judgments, she unwittingly highlighted the section's disparity between theory and practice. Geoffrey Parsons, still the dominant influence over arts coverage at the *Herald Tribune*, was more cognizant of the departures that had occurred since Sherman's time. In a 1952 memorandum calling for a reorganized book section, he declared that "the magazine was stronger and possessed more unity of design and purpose when Stuart Sherman was its top critic." As a remedy, Parsons proposed that a critic of comparable stature "play an active and constant part in picking reviewers and deciding how the books should be reviewed." In that way, he essentially registered his dissatisfaction with Van Doren's policies even while praising her "handling of copy."[121]

Yet Parsons's belief that "the section was at its best when Stuart Sherman was alive" coexisted with his view that the book supplement ought to provide "more news of books and personalities and reduction of reviews," with most assessments relegated to short notices. That tension about the book review's tone and purpose was, of course, as much Sherman's legacy as his example of erudition. (Parsons apparently forgot that he once told Sherman he had liked better the work he had done when he was still at Urbana.) Thus encumbered, the supplement remained basically unchanged until Van Doren's retirement in 1963. By then it had been thoroughly eclipsed by the *New York Times Book Review*, which had never deviated from its goal of supplying, in Kluger's phrase, "a collection of book reports to consumers on the readability of new titles." For a brief period thereafter, the *Tribune*'s revamped *Book Week*, under Kluger's editorship, recaptured some of *Books*'s early intentions and tone: aimed at "serious readers," it strove for stimulating essays by leading critics and scholars rather than coverage and "fairness" for their own sake. Soon, however, the *Tribune*, struggling under new ownership and battered by the New York newspaper strike of 1962–63, ceased publication entirely—succumbing to economic and technological realignments which no brand of journalism, "higher" or otherwise, could forestall.[122]

3

WHY DO YOU DISAPPOINT YOURSELF?

THE EARLY HISTORY OF THE BOOK-OF-THE-MONTH CLUB

Defenders of the emphasis on books as news in settings such as the *Herald Tribune* had a certain logic on their side when they argued that, given the function of the daily press, that treatment was both appropriate and necessary. As the climate of the 1920s intensified the demand for knowledge, however, the same approach came at least partially to characterize other, less inherently journalistic forms. One of these was the book club. As Norman Foerster observed, the creation of book clubs in the middle of the decade was a "natural extension" of the newspaper and the literary review, which had paved the way for the phenomenon by stressing "the book news of the day, expert opinions of authors and their writings, and advice, direct or indirect, as to the Book-of-the-Week."[1] The oldest and, in this period, largest such venture, the Book-of-the-Month Club, not only replicated the newspaper's typical mode of reviewing, it also made the news value of recent publications the core of a marketing strategy that fostered the equation of culture with information. In ways that Foerster did not see, however, the Book-of-the-Month Club simultaneously sustained a vision of the cultured self that more resembled Stuart Sherman's portrait of Arnold than it did the beneficiaries of Eliot's fifteen-minutes-a-day.

The Creation of the Book-of-the-Month Club

When Harry Scherman, a New York advertising man, started the Book-of-the-Month Club in 1926, he did so on the assumption that the nation's bookstores were not meeting the American reader's desire for new books. Scherman's savvy appraisal of the market reflected his long experience with both literature and commerce. Born in Montreal in 1887, he grew up in Philadelphia, briefly attended business and law school after college, and settled in 1907 on a career as a writer. For five years he covered cultural and political affairs for the weekly *American Hebrew*, while trying his hand at fiction and dabbling in advertising copywriting. Scherman shelved his literary ambitions in 1913 and began working full-time for the Ruthrauff and Ryan advertising firm, where he concentrated on direct-mail circulars. The following year he joined the mail-order department of the J. Walter Thompson agency. Even so, he remained connected to a group of artists and intellectuals, counting among his friends Walter Lippmann, Irita Van Doren's brother-in-law Charles Boni, and Charles's brother Albert.

In 1916 Charles Boni happened to show him a publishing gimmick—a miniature leather-bound edition of Shakespeare. Scherman decided a set of such classics had merchandising potential and convinced the manufacturers of Whitman's chocolates to include a volume in each candy box. To oversee production, he resigned his job and, with the Boni brothers, established the Little Leather Library Corporation. Joining them as partner was Maxwell Sackheim, another Thompson copywriter whose highly effective campaign on behalf of a correspondence school ("Do You Make These Mistakes in English?") became a model of selling technique.

The enterprise prospered. To augment the Whitman's order, Scherman and his associates printed additional titles, which Woolworth's sold at ten cents apiece. The Little Leather Library later issued a set of "Thirty World's Greatest Masterpieces," capitalizing on the same clamor for access to liberal culture that the "Five-Foot Shelf" exploited.

It even offered the shelf itself. That is—anticipating a theme of Book-of-the-Month Club promotion—it enabled purchasers to display their refinement by giving away "a handsome quartered-oak bookrack which will ornament any library table." Scherman did have to deal with one disaster, now a comical part of Book-of-the-Month Club lore: as leather prices rose, the publishers switched to synthetic bindings which, it turned out, smelled bad in hot weather. Despite that setback, however, by 1920 the Little Leather Library had marketed over twenty-five million volumes, many of them by mail.[2]

Thereafter, the Bonis sold their interest in the concern and went on to other undertakings, including the founding of the Modern Library, initially a reprint series intended to bring avant-garde fiction to American readers. Scherman and Sackheim sold out as well a few years later. In the meantime, though, they formed their own advertising agency and tried to apply the lessons they had learned about book distribution to further projects. Although Scherman recognized that he had tapped a profitable wellspring of customers by operating outside retail outlets, he also realized that he could not make money unless, following their first purchase, buyers were hooked into returning for additional ones. After some false starts, he devised a plan that combined the use of the mails with a subscription feature that insured the necessary "repeat business." This time, instead of the classics, Scherman tendered newly published works. The Book-of-the-Month Club, a child of advertising, was born.[3]

Aside from Scherman's own prior activities, the club was not entirely unprecedented: German book societies, which printed cheap editions for sale directly to the public, had entailed a similar arrangement since 1919, and Samuel Craig had conceived of what eventually became the Literary Guild as early as 1921. Scherman's inventiveness, however, lay in the fact that he, Sackheim, and the venture's first president, Robert K. Haas, were the first club organizers to act as distributors rather than publishers, to rely heavily on mail-order techniques, and to employ a board of expert judges to win the confidence of consumers.

Under the terms of the club's initial contract, subscribers agreed to buy one new book per month for a year, at full retail price plus postage, with no book costing more than three dollars. For their money, they also received the guidance of the Selecting Committee, or Board of Judges, comprised of five of America's most famous writers and critics:

Henry Seidel Canby, Dorothy Canfield Fisher, Christopher Morley, Heywood Broun, and William Allen White. The committee identified the "book of the month," furnished comments about it for a monthly newsletter called the *Book-of-the-Month Club News*, and generated a list of alternate selections from which subscribers could order if, after examining the judges' choice, they wished to exchange it for another volume.

Within a year, that formula had earned the club over sixty thousand members. Subsequently, Scherman and his partners modified the contract to require the purchase of only four books per year and replaced the exchange policy with the "privilege" of substituting an alternate selection in advance of the shipping date. The result was a rise in membership to 110,588 in 1929 and steadily increasing returns for the club's investors. Those trends, except during the worst years of the Depression, continued through 1946. Three innovations in the early 1930s gave the club essentially the structure it has today: the manufacture of special Book-of-the-Month Club editions, the occasional (and now routine) cutting of prices, and the implementation of the "book dividend" plan, which provided free books to members on the principle of stock dividends. All contributed to making the Book-of-the-Month Club an enduring feature of the cultural landscape and the progenitor of dozens more book clubs and other "of-the-month" marketing devices.[4]

If the public's response to the enterprise was enthusiastic, however, the attitude of the literary community was far more ambivalent. Part of the animus toward the club derived simply from the fact that it competed with publishers and booksellers. The publishing industry and Scherman initially enjoyed a brief honeymoon, allied against the Literary Guild, which began underselling both retailers and the Book-of-the-Month Club early in 1927.[5] In the spring of 1929, however, the Book-of-the-Month Club and the Literary Guild together incurred a vehement denunciation from the American Booksellers Association—and particularly from Dutton's John Macrae. The provocation for the attack was the club's designation as the March book of the month Joan Lowell's *Cradle of the Deep*, a sensational "autobiography" later revealed as a hoax. Macrae and the booksellers seized the occasion not only to ridicule the selection but to argue that the idea of a "best book of the month" was an "intellectual sham." Deploring the unwarranted advertising club selections received as "detrimental to the sale of scores of other books in the same field," the booksellers and publishers barely concealed beneath a plea for noncommercialism their desire to protect their own pocketbooks.

Yet Macrae's contention that the book clubs foreshadowed the "mechanization of the American mind" echoed the concerns of more disinterested observers. The "cultural effect," the *Commonweal* argued, "is to standardize American reading, precisely because the selection is buttressed by authority. . . . Moreover, a similarity of tone pervades almost all the selections made, so that eventually a certain kind of literature becomes the vogue." An anonymous writer in the *Bookman* for April 1927 likewise asked, "Has America a Literary Dictatorship?" Answering in the affirmative, he condemned associates of book clubs as "clever publicists and literary boosters, advocates of standardization and self advocated boards of authoritative criticism" who had promoted passivity and a decline in taste among the reading public.[6]

The booksellers eventually backed down when it became apparent that the selection of a book by a club increased its bookstore revenues as well.[7] Some publishers even began reducing the price of titles slated for club distribution, since they could count on making up the difference by a greater sales volume. Nonetheless, the depiction of the Book-of-the-Month Club as an agency for the destruction of independent judgment and literary quality continued to resurface periodically. On the club's twentieth anniversary, the *New Republic* pronounced the reading diet of its members "neither rich nor nourishing." Twelve years later, when Charles Lee surveyed a group of critics for his *The Hidden Public*, the only full-length account of Scherman's brainchild, he turned up a decidedly mixed response. Malcolm Cowley, for example, noted that, while many of the club's selections were admirable, others were "merchandise" and "pure junk." The culmination of this tradition of disaffection, Macdonald's "Masscult and Midcult," remains its most forceful expression. In turn, the club's defenders have insisted, over the years, that the venture has actually elevated American taste by making books more available. As Delmore Schwartz wrote Lee, "The BOMC . . . has been invaluable in widening the audience for serious literature." The club itself put the matter more modestly, arguing that its success proved "the intelligence of the American people" (echoing Stuart Sherman's appraisal of the popular demand for books like *The Story of Philosophy*). As for the charge of standardization, Lee and other proponents stressed the variety of titles the club had offered to members.[8]

Instead of perpetuating that debate, it seems more productive to conclude that the Book-of-the-Month Club both expanded the market for serious reading and had a standardizing effect. In an effort to convey a fresh perspective, the discussion which follows will not explore in detail the club's monthly selections. Rather, it focuses on the competing impulses and understandings implicit in the club's structure and advertising as well as in the premises of its judges. In contrast to Sherman, whose search for self-expression overtook much of his genteel outlook, the Book-of-the-Month Club held both those propensities in equilibrium—a balance that its list of titles does not, by itself, reveal.

Symptoms and Cure

When Scherman and Sackheim turned their copywriting talents toward promoting their new project, they targeted what they called the "average intelligent reader." As Canby explained, the phrase denoted someone "who has passed through the usual formal education in literature, who reads books as well as newspapers and magazines, who, without calling himself a litterateur, would be willing to assert that he was fairly well read and reasonably fond of good reading. Your doctor, your lawyer, the president of your bank, and any educated business man who has not turned his brain into a machine, will fit my case."[9] Hence, in contrast to Eliot, who envisioned the "Five-Foot Shelf of Books" as a liberal education for the workingman, the Book-of-the-Month Club aimed from the start at well-heeled college graduates. The first "test" list was the New York Social Register, with profitable results, and university alumni lists were fruitful later on.[10]

If potential subscribers had money and academic degrees, however, the club's advertising strategy implied that they had other difficulties. In accordance with Sackheim's first principle of mail-order copywriting, the advertisements identified "symptoms" and provided a "cure."[11] That technique, beautifully epitomizing the link between the therapeutic outlook and consumption, was a common one by the early twentieth century. What is striking, however, is that the particular ailment club membership promised to heal was the same one Lears and Susman detected at the center of campaigns for home furnishings and soap: the modern anxiety about the self.[12] The use of that approach in conjunction with the marketing of books thus illustrates both the versatility of the technique—its disconnection from the nature of the product advertised—and the extent to which such anxiety permeated American culture by the mid-1920s.

The early Book-of-the-Month Club advertisements, the model for the club's circulars into the 1950s,[13] created a persona who sets out to choose books but instead commits a series of self-betrayals. The shortcoming to which the copy referred most explicitly was the failure to carry out one's intentions. "Think over the last few years," the first advertisement for the enterprise began. "How often have outstanding books appeared, widely discussed and widely recommended, books you were really anxious to read and fully intended to read when you 'got around to it,' but which nevertheless you *missed*! Why is it you disappoint yourself so frequently in this way?" That pitch, which Scherman summarized as an appeal to the fear of "backsliding," was especially successful at arousing guilt among (and producing subscriptions from) male college graduates who, convinced of the value of culture, had nevertheless subordinated reading to business.[14] But the question "Why is it you disappoint yourself?"—which might have served as the modern American's motto—had greater resonances: it suggested the powerlessness of a self in conflict, one half vainly trying to prevent the other from spinning off in its own direction.

The answer the advertisements provided to that unsettling question only made matters worse, since it pinned the blame on the individual incapable of ordering his or her experience. The first advertisements typically alluded to the expansion of the book market and the resulting confusion about the "best." As an advertisement in the *New York Times Book Review* in January 1927 observed, "You know that, out of the thousands of books published, there are only a few you are interested in. You want the outstanding ones. But what are they?"[15] Yet Scherman and Sackheim did more than capitalize on a general perception of intellectual chaos; they enhanced the discomfort by implying that consumers were responsible for their own sense of disarray. "Occasionally, at haphazard and almost altogether by chance," the club's 1927 direct-mail brochure explained, the booklover "reads an advertisement or review of a book that engages his interest. . . . He says to himself, 'I must read that.' . . . Unfortunately, his memory is not always good. He stops and thinks: 'What *was* that book I wanted to read?' He cannot remember; he hasn't the time to search among the hundreds of books on the counters. . . . Perhaps afterward, in a group of bookish people, again he hears the book recommended. He confesses sadly that he had 'never got around to reading it.'"[16] In that scenario, the reader's "confession" amounts to much more than a statement about the vicissitudes of book selection; as the phrases "at haphazard" and "by chance" underscore, it is an admission that he has, through his own negligence, lost control of his will, his memory, and a good part of his world. In particular, he is victimized by time, his shortage of which is both a source and a reflection of his disorganization.

That hapless condition could in turn lead to one more self-betrayal: the inability to project to others the image of being au courant. Copy for the Literary Guild, the *Elbert Hubbard Scrapbook*, or, as noted, the "Five-Foot Shelf" was much more blatant in this regard than that for the club. Yet the presumption of a disappointed audience—the accusatory "You didn't say a single word all evening" (as one Hubbard advertisement put it)—infiltrated Book-of-the-Month Club appeals as well. "What a deprivation it is to miss reading an important new book at a time everyone else is reading and discussing it," the club's 1927 brochure announced, reminding potential subscribers that neglect of the latest books meant loss of "fine camaraderie." Other blurbs wailed, "He is Always Saying Apologetically: 'I Just Can't Find Any Time to Read Books!'" or "I'm Sorry I Haven't Read the Book Yet!"[17]

The cure for that array of symptoms, all of which might be subsumed under the heading "loss of mastery," was an "ingenious, but quite simple, system" with two major components: the imposition of time management and the use of experts. Both of those innovations made dependence on others the remedy for the ailing self. Yet, given American culture in the 1920s, Scherman's solution was just what the doctor ordered: that is, it accepted and reinforced the values of a mass consumer society while alleviating some of the distress the expansion of that society had engendered. This capaciousness functioned in several ways.

First, after 1927 members surrendered to the club's "automatic"—that is, externally controlled—schedule of distribution: one book parceled out each month, arriving unless the subscriber took the initiative of canceling it. This arrangement, perhaps Sackheim and Scherman's greatest brainstorm, was the key to the business's profits, yet it was presented to consumers as an altruistically administered prescription for the distracted reader. As Charles Lee observed, the frequently used slogan "Handed to You by the Postman—the New Books You Intend to Read" was "shrewdly directed, not only to the customer's sense of comfort, but also to his sense of intellectual fulfillment."[18] The club's newsletter, enclosed with the book, likewise furnished a victory over the inexorable flow of print, the knowledge of the next month's choice literally placing subscribers ahead of time.

Similarly, the use of expert judges appended book promotion to the areas in which the Progressive faith in bureaucracy as an antidote to disorder asserted itself. The club's 1927 brochure included full-page photographs of each member of the Selecting Committee, with captions listing their credentials, a format that made the judges into larger-than-life exemplars of mastery. Pictures of the judges routinely appeared in magazine advertisements from 1926 to 1933 and occasionally thereafter. The club's advertising assured prospective subscribers that the experts assigned to the task of "culling out of the best books from the hundreds that are published" had no financial connection (other than a salary) with the business end of the club; thus, they were free to perform in an entirely "disinterested" manner the intellectual triage the bewildered bookbuyer required. The vehicle for communicating their decision, the *News*, was depicted in the same terms. Drawing on well-worn Progressive language (one is reminded of Jane Addams's pronouncements about "carefully collected" facts), the promotional brochure specified the contents of that "simple and sensible" newsletter: "a very careful description of the next chosen 'book-of-the-month,' *explaining exactly the type of book it is*, why the judges selected it, and something about the author." Protected by such "clear and unbiased reports," readers need not fear that they would unwittingly succumb to an alluring—but bad—book.[19]

By the 1920s Scherman was hardly alone in basing a marketing campaign on what Roland Marchand has called "a public demand for broad guidance" in the face of "proliferating choices."[20] (As noted previously, *Books* capitalized on something of the same appeal.) To some observers, however, Scherman's invention of the Selecting Committee went too far in applying to book promotion strategies apparently acceptable for selling pharmaceuticals and hosiery. In a sense, the expert board was merely extending the genteel critic's insistence on diffusing awareness of the "best." Yet, as the anonymous *Bookman* writer cited earlier implied, the manner in which they did so forced the issue of passivity out into the open. The result was that, of all its features, the committee loomed largest in the attacks the club incurred during its first few years. By agreeing to identify the book of the month, the club's assailants charged, not only had the experts sold their souls to commercial interests, they had also conspired to prevent readers from actively assaying the competing judgments of reviewers. Said the *Bookman*: "The reason by which the judges arrived at their decision are [*sic*] not discussed in open court; only the result and not the process by which the conclusion is arrived at is known to those who accept the decision; the matter must in the final analysis rest on the authority of the judges alone." As Janice Radway has concluded in a rich essay informed by literary and social theory, the "transgression" of the club was to unmask this exercise of power, instead of perpetuating the fiction of what the *Bookman* author called "free critical inquiry."[21]

Nevertheless, the actual form in which the committee or board rendered its verdicts—the *News*—argues that the club's "transgressions" in the service of supplying order also included the opposite sin: the withholding, or underexercise, of critical authority. Edited by Scherman himself, the monthly mailing featured a lead article about the main selection which integrated background about the book with excerpts from the judges' comments. (Beginning in the early 1930s, Scherman merely introduced a "review" signed by a member of the board.) Briefer notices of alternate choices followed for around ten pages. While those reports made culture accessible, they also tended to substitute narrative for evaluation, information for aesthetics. The title *Book-of-the-Month Club News* makes the point most economically. The reportorial emphasis was underscored, however, by several additions to the publication (some longer-lived than others) in the 1930s and 1940s: a section of frankly "informational, not critical" summaries for books of "sectional or special" appeal; the segregation of works "For the More Serious-Minded"; a "Panorama of New Books" consisting of single-paragraph plot descriptions interspersed with illustrations; and, accompanying the glossier look the brochure acquired in the early 1940s, a collection of anecdotes about authors compiled by Scherman's wife, Bernadine Kielty.[22]

Furthermore, all news was good news, since the judges included only the books they recommended, a feature of the club's operation that Scherman defended as necessary to business. "After all," he mused, "the publishers send in books to us, go to considerable trouble, and to damn their books. . . ." Clifton Fadiman, appointed to the board in 1944, was even more candid on this score. The articles in the *News*, he observed, "are pretty largely sales talks. We're trying to be fair, but at the same time we are trying to put the book in the best possible light so that people will like it as well as we did. In that sense, the reviews are not truly judgmatical." As was true for Stuart Sherman's *Books* audience, some club patrons reacted to that practice by demanding more, not less, mediation by the Selecting Committee. In Scherman's words, "In the beginning we were pretty severely criticized by subscribers themselves for what they called favorable reviews—'All the reviews are favorable reviews.' Well, obviously they were favorable; they were recommended." That discontent might be construed simply as a sign that confident readers wished more opportunity to weigh good books against bad on their own. Yet it also suggests a desire for even greater relief from the anxiety about the ineffectual self—about making wrong decisions in a chaotic world—that reliance on experts could palliate.[23]

As it assisted the search for order, Scherman's "system" served the requirements of early-twentieth-century Americans in a second way: by helping to supply one more item for the market. Reflecting that fact, the advertising journal *Printers' Ink* referred in 1943 to the Board of Judges as a "consumer jury that passes on the quality of every bit of" the club's "merchandise."[24] In this respect, those who have described the manifestations of "midcult" as products have been partly correct. The originality of Scherman's contribution was, of course, not the transformation of books or even culture into objects for purchase. Rather, by selling an opportunity to acquire books not yet published (instead of the books themselves), Scherman created a new *kind* of cultural commodity. Experts facilitated that diversification by certifying the quality of the package as a whole. As Scherman put it, "You had to set up some kind of authority so that the subscriber would feel that there was some reason for buying a group of books, so that he'd know he wasn't buying a pig in a poke, and also that he wasn't buying books which were suspect."[25]

This facet of the club's operations likewise tended to minimize the importance of aesthetic distinctions, as the advertising man Earnest Elmo Calkins well knew. In a 1922 article for *Printers' Ink*, Calkins had urged publishers to adopt a strategy that would generate goodwill toward future purchases rather than promote specific books. He counseled "a form of advertising that will make book enthusiasts, that will sell the reading idea." Calkins likened his proposal to the campaign to sell "the motoring habit" and envisioned generic advertisements for books on billboards, in streetcars, in the movies. "You will notice," he admitted, "that I am not bothering about literary values. For the purpose of this plan a book is a book." When Calkins reprinted his essay in *Business the Civilizer* in 1928, he noted with satisfaction the extent to which the Book-of-the-Month Club had implemented his suggestions.[26]

Third, both the time management and expertise Scherman offered promised to cure the floundering self's social distress by enabling subscribers to convey the instant and favorable impression required for success in a bureaucratic, anonymous society. As the 1927 brochure explained, through the *Book-of-the-Month Club News* the reader stays "completely informed *about all the important new books*. He knows about them and can talk about them." Here the club's automatic distribution system, with its assurance that members would remain au courant, came into play, since the key to impressing others depended, in the first place, on the ability to keep up with the conversation. Moreover, by conveying knowledge of the book of the month in advance of the publication date, the *News* (like Paterson's column) served as a source of "inside dope." As R. L. Duffus remarked, it thus permitted subscribers "to become 'cultured' before anyone else could." Finally, by the 1930s subscribers who decided to select an alternate from the club's back list could consult a section in the *News* headed "Recent Books Which Have Been Most Popular With Members." Those enticements allied book-club membership with the other products for the enhancement of personality popular in the 1920s; not surprisingly, students in "charm and glamour courses" were among the groups most receptive to the club's initial mail-order campaign.[27] The club's potential for conferring distinctiveness also fed longings for upward mobility, as the early advertisement imploring would-be subscribers to join "the intellectual élite of the country" revealed.[28]

The genteel emphasis on character, and on culture as an interior process with only incidental social benefits, was correspondingly diminished. So was the earlier stress on discipline and effort, since knowing and talking about books bore no relationship to reading them carefully—or at all. (The more brazen Literary Guild, likening their selections to home furnishings, announced, "The Hall-Mark of Literary Distinction: The Guild Book on Your Table"—with no suggestion that the book would also be "in Your Mind.") Furthermore, prior knowledge of works sure to be widely read but as yet unknown gave the reader a competitive edge in a way that the classics (by definition already famous) could not. The total failure of the club's 1928 attempt to sell as alternate choices "older" books "which a newer public may not know" suggests the strength of that appeal.[29] The Book-of-the-Month Club was not the first institution to capitalize on the social advantages of familiarity with new, popular books; one can regard Dodd, Mead's creation of the best-seller list in 1895 in the same way. Sackheim and Scherman's marketing strategies, however, raised to a new level of sophistication the message that the acquisition of information was tantamount to possessing culture. As Everett Dean Martin put it (albeit with some hyperbole), the idea of selling a book "with the promise that a casual reading of it would enable [one] to appear more cultivated than [one] really was" represented "a distinctly modern contribution to educational theory."[30]

Finally, club advertising shared with promotions for the "Five-Foot Shelf" and *Books* a stress on organizing haphazard readers' time in order to maximize their opportunity for commercial pursuits. One blurb from 1927 explicitly subordinated reading to business, echoing Eliot in the process: "Yet . . . if he spent (on an average) only 30 minutes a day before bedtime, or while traveling to or from work, or in other leisure moments—he could easily read every best-seller during the year, and a great deal more!"[31] The unique structure of Scherman's venture, however, enabled Book-of-the-Month Club advertisements to emphasize not only efficiency but "convenience." The use of that word in club copy, while grounded in an appeal to rural or small-town subscribers, was only partly related to the urban locations of most bookstores. Cigarettes, the sociologist Michael Schudson has noticed, were advertised in identical language, and for identical reasons. In the affluent conditions of the 1920s, when compensation for work was increasing, time spent not working represented an expensive loss. The ability to buy cigarettes—or books—"conveniently" through the mail meant the conservation of one's resources for accumulating additional products.[32] The same meaning inhered in the depiction of the club's system as "automatic"; like the effect of the word "reliable" in cigarette advertising, the message was that buyers need not be diverted from more important activities by planning for or even thinking about their purchases. Dependence on experts could have similar consequences. The contrast between culture and work in turn further eroded the understanding that cultivation resulted from disciplined study. "You can now subscribe to the best new books—just as you do to a magazine," one advertisement announced; an "Outstanding Book Each Month," declared another, would be "Sent to You Like a Magazine"—and presumably required about as much effort to read.[33]

Countervailing Appeals in Club Advertising

If those features of its advertising and structure allied it with the values of a widening mass consumer society, however, in other ways the Book-of-the-Month Club countermanded the premise that character and self-reliance were things of the past. For one thing, while club advertisements defined the importance of reading contemporary literature in terms of social utility, they made references as well to the intrinsic satisfactions such books could supply. "There is an overpowering fascination," the 1927 brochure explained, "about good new books. . . . [I]n reading them, in enjoying them, in talking with others about them, we feel the new thought of our day actually taking shape, and we participate in its formation." Similarly, the concluding portion of the brochure recommended reading as a way of encountering the "absorbing and continuing show of life" which characterized the "age of flux we live in." Those statements, while they contained elements that suggest the preoccupation with personality (the phrase "in talking with others," the connotation of "participate"), were more concerned with the development of the mind than with a social skill. The same document also invoked genteel commitments to good citizenship by announcing that, although club members subscribed "out of pure self-interest," they indirectly played a role "in stimulating our literature and deepening our culture."[34]

More significantly, several themes of Book-of-the-Month Club advertising paid homage to the individual's prerogatives in the matter of book selection, implicitly reducing the stature of the Selecting Committee. In the wake of the *Cradle of the Deep* debacle, Scherman announced that the committee would henceforth designate an "outstanding" book each month rather than presume to determine the single "best" one. Moreover, club publicity insisted that the books members received were the ones they had "decided" they wanted to read; the experts simply facilitated acquisition of the volumes subscribers would "choose to purchase anyway." Billing the exchange privilege as a "guarantee against dissatisfaction," a phrase which made the subscriber's judgment paramount, Scherman also took precautions to declare that the method of selection "is not set up as being either final or infallible." The *News* routinely reiterated the point, reminding readers that their own tastes "should be sacred" to them. Only rarely did it advise members not to substitute an alternate for the book of the month—and then not on literary grounds but because, atypically, the club had arranged an especially good bargain.[35] The club's disclaimers about its judges' power paralleled advertisements for other products which, Marchand has pointed out, aimed to leave the purchaser " 'with the feeling that he has done his own thinking, made up his own mind.' "[36] In context, however, their function was more specific. They answered the charge that the board was a "literary dictatorship"; they placated publishers of works passed over for the main selection; they met the challenge of rising demands for democracy by permitting the conclusion that choosing books required no special understanding. Yet the "guarantee against dissatisfaction" was no less grounded in a perception of anxiety about reconstructing the self than the emphasis on the benefits of expertise. It merely assuaged that anxiety differently: by creating the illusion that the capacity for autonomy was as alive and well as ever.

The same message inhered in the repeated characterization of the Book-of-the-Month Club as a "service." As the 1927 brochure exclaimed, "All this service costs subscribers nothing." An emphasis on "service" was a mainstay of 1920s business rhetoric and shaped what might be called a genre of the period's advertising. As used by such industrialists as Gerard Swope, E. A. Filene, and Henry Ford, the term signaled an effort to define the social responsibilities of the businessman in an era when large profits were undercutting pre–World War I ideals of business leadership. Particularly, according to Morrell Heald, "the service motif helped justify and reconcile the peacetime pursuit of profit with the war-awakened sense of community." In practice, "service" became a staple of advertising copy aimed at presenting all sorts of products in a favorable light: the January 28, 1926, issue of *Printers' Ink*, for example, observed "anniversaries of service" for both AT&T and the N. W. Ayer & Son advertising agency itself.[37]

If both idealism and salesmanship shaped the "service" campaign, however, its appeal derived at least in part from the relationship the term implied between the seller and the consumer. An emphasis on "service" preserved the autonomous self; it presumed a self that antedated and controlled the marketplace, rather than one created by it. What was "served" was an individual commanding the fulfillment of some conscious desire, not a passive object of the producers' and the advertisers' manipulations. With respect to book clubs, "service" conjured up an image much like the one May Lamberton Becker projected in the "Reader's Guide." The club became a friendly local bookseller, eager to advise and assist but not to overpower the customer who entered a shop with a title or a subject already in mind. Thus, the rhetoric of "service" betokened prewar attitudes with respect to more than the concept of business leadership: it rejected the realities of the mass consumer culture America had become.

The designation of Scherman's distribution scheme as a "club" worked in similar fashion. As early as the 1880s, mail-order advertisers had organized "clubs" comprising housewives who agreed to pool their orders for goods like pots and pans (the famous Club Aluminum cookware). In part, therefore, Scherman was trading on a well-established sales technique. But in the context of book marketing, more was involved. The label allied the Book-of-the-Month Club with the tradition of women's study clubs, those locally based groups dedicated to perpetuating genteel formulations of culture by learning about the classics. It alluded as well to organizations for both men and women that promised sociability and social status. More specifically, "club" harkened back to societies for the publication of rare manuscripts which had existed in America since the colonial period. By the turn of the twentieth century, however, the "club idea" had an overarching meaning: in John S. Gilkeson's words, it gratified "the desire of Americans to set themselves apart from others" by banding together in a world grown uncomfortably anonymous and diverse. Even groups predicated on the acquisition of specialized skills, such as the collectors' clubs that flourished in the interwar period, held out that prospect of achieving a feeling of community based on shared interests and, in the event of club meetings, face-to-face contact.[38] Hence, the Book-of-the-Month Club's appropriation of "club" amounted to a re-creation, in language, of a relationship that the magnitude and impersonal nature of the enterprise, as well as of American society, precluded. Like advertisements that featured the "confidential advisor" who purportedly cared about each consumer, items inserted into the *News* sometimes capitalized on that appeal. In April 1949, for example, Scherman's letter headed "Inside the Club" told readers, "[Y]ou play a central role in this dissemination of the best thought of our time." The following December Henry Seidel Canby coupled "personal and sincere" New Year's greetings to the statement that "every member of the Club is present, in spirit if not in the flesh, at our meetings." The myth was compelling enough that one deluded subscriber, when membership was about seventy-five thousand, offered his backyard and outdoor grill for a club picnic.[39]

The backward glances involved in the "guarantee of satisfaction," the rhetoric of service, and the construct of a "club" suggest that Scherman sensed within his audience longings for a world inhabited by models of character, even as it strove to cultivate personality for the sake of impressing others. Additionally, the "service" and "club" themes indicate some resistance to the transformation of culture into a commodity, since the primary effect of such language was to obscure the fact that anyone was making money. One must be careful not to overestimate such resistance: the success of the Literary Guild, which printed its own editions and discounted them, signifies that many customers saw no conflict between getting a bargain and upholding standards. In 1930, in a climate of price-cutting in the book industry, the Book-of-the-Month Club itself began discounting—and might have earlier if Scherman had thought publishers would have complied. By 1935, when saving money was on everyone's mind because of the Depression, the club was as capable as any other advertiser of subordinating its other appeals to the promise of free samples. Yet in the late 1930s the advertising retreated to a less bold typeface for the word "free"; in general, the club, in Lee's phrase, "eschew[ed] the violent bargain look of its more raucous competitors," as if retaining its preeminence in the market demanded dissociation of culture and business. As Scherman put it, "Good taste does pay off, without any question."[40]

The Selecting Committee: Henry Seidel Canby

Such vestiges of older values tempered the degree to which Book-of-the-Month Club advertising rescinded the genteel tradition, although the balance remained heavily weighted toward the side of consumer priorities. The reverse, however, was true with respect to the outlook of the club's Selecting Committee. The judges seem, at first glance, so diverse that, but for the inescapable fact of their collaboration, discussing them together might seem artificial. Yet that is precisely the point: it is this dimension of the Book-of-the-Month Club that most strikingly suggests the persistence of Arnoldian assumptions alongside the emphasis on information, social performance, and consumption.

The chair of the original board, Henry Seidel Canby, deserves particular attention because, as the most accomplished critic in the group, he brought to his work for the club a cogent set of literary standards and an explicit sense of mission. Dorothy Canfield Fisher, the judge second to Canby in influence, also held a clearly articulated set of convictions about the functions of reading and reviewing that is worth close inspection. Their colleagues Christopher Morley, Heywood Broun, and William Allen White had less effect on selections but were still important for the image they projected to the public.

The son of a founder and president of the Delaware Trust Company, Canby was born in Wilmington in 1878. Although his family's fortunes declined somewhat in the 1890s, he spent a comfortable childhood, pursuing a love of nature and books. Formally an Episcopalian and married in the Presbyterian church, he came from Quaker ancestry, attended the Friends School, and eventually came to see himself as having an essentially Quaker turn of mind. In particular, he credited his Quaker background with shaping his predilection for "quality in everything" and for endowing him with emotional reticence and tolerance for others. The Quaker doctrine of an "inner light," which Emerson had invoked, gave Canby as well a model of the self—quiet, serene, radiant with spiritual integrity—that he retained throughout his career. About hard-boiled writers like Hemingway and Robinson Jeffers, he once wrote, "I had rather believe with the Quakers that all humanity is potentially good than run with these fellows who are obsessed with its imperfections."[41]

Looking back in his memoir *The Age of Confidence* (1934) on the period in which he grew up, Canby described it as the "last epoch of American stability." Although the industrial growth and consolidation of the era were altering traditional relationships and channeling more and more of the nation's energies into frenzied practical pursuits, Canby remembered the age as one characterized by qualities regrettably absent from the modern scene. While he deplored the drabness of the businessmen who peopled his childhood and faulted both school and church for perpetuating empty conventions, he relished the rhythm of domestic routine and ritual in Wilmington's middle-class homes. Families there understood the boundaries between parents and children— the children deferential, the parents self-denying in their acceptance of their responsibilities to guide the younger generation. "The homes I knew in the nineties," Canby lamented, "are too many of them disrupted by death and moving, yet where the members remain the spirit remains. There was a bond more indissoluble than the search for self-expression." Guests at his mother's famous terrapin suppers, surrounded by symbols of decorum, left the world of business behind: "In a community growing year by year more commercialized, more cut-throat in competition . . . , such evenings as this were (and perhaps they knew it) the last stand of the old order where a man was a gentleman first and a lawyer or banker afterward. . . . The realism of money-making was as firmly shut out as the night behind the curtains."

Even Canby's youthful butterfly chases stopped short of taxonomy, as if "spiritual self-preservation" depended on differentiating that activity from the ardent purposefulness of business. An atmosphere of stability and a distance from "greedy commercialism" also marked Canby's early schooling. If much of the curriculum was devoted to meaningless memorization, it was nevertheless unified by a code of beliefs and behavior that upheld ancient notions of right and wrong and of human perfectibility, ignoring what Canby termed the more sordid aspects of industrialism. There was, in addition, a friendliness, a tone of genial respectability, that shone in the demeanor of the men and women Canby encountered, giving his experience a quality he himself labeled essentially "genteel."[42]

When Canby enrolled as a freshman in the Sheffield Scientific School at Yale University in 1896, he found the campus a center of gentility as well, even while it was expanding to serve growing numbers of students from recently prosperous families. Canby's classmates, unquestioningly planning to become businessmen like their fathers, concentrated on using the football team or the college magazine to cement the social connections that would enhance their prospects after graduation, but they made no comparable demand on the curriculum. The result was a moment, Canby explained, when a number of the faculty felt both the freedom and the obligation to emphasize the intrinsic virtues of the liberal arts. If many of their colleagues were either indifferent, or bogged down in trivia, or (like William Lyon Phelps) indiscriminate enthusiasts, there was still a core who believed that they represented the last chance to expose the bankers and executives of the future to "any values not purely utilitarian." Touched by their message, and dreading the alternative of becoming just another member of the Wilmington business community, Canby stayed on at Yale following completion of a bachelor of philosophy degree in 1899 to pursue graduate study in English. As he worked his way up the academic ladder—he was a teaching assistant from 1900 to 1903, received a Ph.D. in 1905, and was an instructor from 1903 to 1908—he himself became an idealist with "an intensity that was almost lyrical." The struggle he engaged in, Canby noted, was "between two views of civilization, between two ideas of living. . . . Plato versus John Rockefeller, Shakespeare versus Benjamin Franklin, Milton against the stock exchange and the YMCA."[43] Promoted to assistant professor in 1908, Canby waged the conflict until 1916.

It was, however, a battle that increasingly seemed replete with hollow victories, if not out-and-out losses. For Canby found the tendency toward specialization within the university just as threatening to humane values as the rampant materialism outside it. In his own field, philology seemed as menacing as it did to Babbitt and Sherman. The premium on the obscure fact, the contempt for the professor who could address a general audience, and the insistence that the humanist amass data in the same fashion as the biologist made the university, in Canby's eyes, not so much a refuge from the outside world as a mirror of it: both entailed "a senseless race for self-defeating power" and "riches badly used." But developments on campus only paralleled, rather than inter-sected, wider trends. Yale remained an ivory tower, the emphasis on research drawing its specialists on the faculty even further away from the realities of business competition than was the case for the outnum-bered and displaced generalists. Thus, if a professor succeeded in win-ning a convert from materialism, he could offer only "skillful antiquari-anism," the "aridity of a high sweeping plateau." Instead of teaching "the transferrable values inherent in any good literature"—transfer-rable, that is, to the needs of "an American community boiling with efficient energy and hot for material achievement"—many of Canby's colleagues clung to their "cross-word-puzzle" scholarship and to the hope that their students would turn out like Victorian gentlemen.[44]

By 1911 Canby had grown restive in that insular environment. Tem-peramentally Victorian himself and intellectually committed to coun-teracting utilitarianism, he nevertheless chafed at the remoteness of the university from the forces shaping modern America. "We were puzzled idealists," he later said of himself and the other young teachers who shared his predicament, "trying to keep our footing in two worlds at once."[45] When Wilbur Cross that year revamped the *Yale Review* and invited Canby to become assistant editor, Canby found an arena for his balancing act—the first of several in which he would play out his public career. Cross, on his way to becoming governor of Connecticut, had wanted to create a journal that availed itself of the prestige of the university while shedding the dry irrelevancies of the specialist. Open-ing its pages to any serious writer or poet, the *Review* met Canby's desire for contact with living authors and for a more vibrant exchange of ideas than teaching alone was providing him. In particular, his posi-tion on the *Review* put him in touch with British writers such as John Galsworthy and H. G. Wells who in 1914 sought a forum to explain what was at stake in World War I. Those associations resulted in Canby's appointment to a liaison position with the British Ministry of Informa-tion—a greater dose of reality than he had bargained for.

When Canby returned to Yale following his wartime service, the campus seemed even less engaged in meaningful activity than when he had left. In addition, he found himself embroiled in what looked like a hopeless quest for promotion to associate professor. At this point, Canby exemplified what Gerald Graff has called "the failure of the generalists" to sustain more than a "marginal relation" to English departments that had institutionalized the research model of professionalism. (Sherman had escaped this fate only by attaching himself to a new, relatively weak department where he could set his own priorities.) Yet, if that model largely characterized the academy, it is important not to overstate the degree to which the specialist victory permeated American society as a whole. As Laurence Veysey has noted, the generalist position lived on not only in enclaves at some universities (like Sherman's) but also "to a lesser extent in the museums and the various learned societies." More than that, it was carried, like the tenants of a burning building, to havens outside ivy-covered walls: that is, to forums situated between academic and popular culture.[46]

In Canby's case, the rescue effort took the shape of a turn to journalism. In 1920, when Thomas W. Lamont bought the *New York Evening Post*, he received the offer to edit the paper's weekly *Literary Review*. In addition to extricating him from his Yale difficulties, the invitation promised to immerse Canby in the surging literary energies of the era. He liked the idea of reaching the large, earnest audiences who were devouring reviews and flocking to lectures on books. He also welcomed encounters with vigorous young writers, even though he always remained an observer of, rather than a participant in, their rebellions. Those prospects made it easier for him to bid Yale good-bye. Assembling a staff that included Amy Loveman, William Rose Benét, and Christopher Morley, Canby accepted the job and moved to New York. Within a short time, the *Literary Review* had built a nationwide subscription list (outside of the newspaper's) of eight to ten thousand readers. Four years later, after the sale of the *Post* to the Curtis family, the same group started the *Saturday Review of Literature*, backed by Lamont and the founders of *Time* magazine.[47]

In contrast to his counterpart at *Books*, Canby imposed no urgent psychic quest on his role as literary editor. Yet he brought with him, and continued to develop, a number of assumptions forged in his earlier experience and strengthened by the circumstances of the postwar period. Later he applied the same convictions to his role as Book-of-the-Month Club judge. Instructive for their additional commentary on the "higher" journalism in its twentieth-century phase, those premises also display the mix of self-interest and principle with which Canby approached the process of canon formation.

Canby as Critic

Like Sherman (and Norton before him), Canby continued to envision himself, in his editorial office, as a professor who had only shifted the location of his classroom. His governing purpose, he announced, was to "make criticism first of all a teaching job." Similarly, in an allusion to his wartime function, he identified the reviewer as a "liaison officer" between readers and their books: a go-between motivated by an "instinct to teach" who "grasps" and "estimates" a work and then "explains," "interprets," and "in so doing necessarily criticizes, abstracts, appreciates." Although that formulation might seem almost tautological, it precluded certain other possibilities: on the one hand, that critics be scholars, dedicated to transmitting the results of their original research; on the other hand, that they be what Canby called prophets, willing to conduct "reconnaissance" about the likelihood that a given work or literary trend would prove enduring. The title of his two-volume series of essays and editorials, *Definitions*, summarized his view of his task: not "fundamental, creative criticism" or "taking sides" but the preparatory work of relying on established tenets to set new books upon their appropriate "planes" and sort them "into their categories." In that way, Canby thought, he would provide "what Arnold meant by seeing steadily and seeing whole."[48]

The need for this broad educational campaign, Canby believed, stemmed from several factors. One, a consequence of specialization, was a gap in the hierarchy of American book-review media. The family magazine and the newspaper column reached general readers but typically limited literary pronouncements to benign approval. The rise of "intellectual weeklies" such as the *New Republic* raised the standard of reviewing, but mainly for titles related to the "social philosophies" they sought to impart. At the same time, scholars assessed new work in their disciplines only for the benefit of their colleagues. The *Nation* had grown stodgy; the *Times* and the *Tribune* (before Sherman came on the scene) combined the worst elements of scholarly pretentiousness and overpraise. This situation, as Canby regarded it, required more than mediation between reader and text; it demanded a "liberal journal of catholic criticism," like the *Saturday Review*, that would "bring to the interpretation of new books for the intelligent reader the trained thinking and real erudition of the universities."[49]

But the problem went deeper than the structure of the nation's periodicals. Although Canby never described himself as middlebrow, he appropriated the terms "highbrow" and "lowbrow" to analyze a dangerous condition in American society as a whole: the threat of vulgarization. "Lowbrows," as Canby defined the word, were those who "guess and have no taste," as opposed to "highbrows" who "know and have taste." If academics, critics, journalists, and other intellectuals did not make common cause with each other and with the educated public, they would find themselves overrun by the vulgar masses. The "lowbrows," Canby warned, "are breeding by millions and already they control nine-tenths of the published word."[50]

Behind this alarming picture lay Canby's understanding of the forces assaulting "the mind that reaches for the best." One was the increasing dominance of the trends he had resisted at Yale—rampant materialism and its accompanying evil, standardization. By the 1920s, in Canby's view, technological innovation, mass production, and advertising had combined to produce a society riddled with "the vulgarities of signboards, cries of cheap newspapers, noisy hustle of trivial commercialism, and the flatness of standardized living." That development had "shut out the view of fields, sky, God, the value and purpose of life itself." In particular, like Thoreau (whom he counterposed to the standardized citizen), Canby lamented that Americans had "sold our individualism" to the inventions of the "machine age." In an essay entitled "Easy Come, Easy Go," he also charged advertising, the raison d'être for the boom in throwaway magazines, with fostering "the glib practice of seeing the world by paragraphs." Likening the United States to the declining Roman Empire, he deplored the "spread of general information" if it meant that "most reading is to be by excerpt, and most education to consist of knowing the easy parts of many kinds of learning."[51]

Another source of vulgarization, though Canby might not have put it quite this way, was the spread of democracy. Specifically, he was troubled by the growing presence of the immigrant in American life, fearing that "alien swarms" would annihilate the "older," "everyday" Americans such as himself. Like the Progressive proponents of the "Americanization" movement, Canby believed immigrant Jews (potentially part of "our best reading population") and other minorities could only make themselves "at home" in their adopted country if they were reeducated in the values of the "Anglo-American tradition." By the same token, he urged magazine editors (and presumably strove himself) to "recapture . . . especially the 'old American'" facet of their audiences in order to stave off the decay of culture. More generally, Canby voiced dismay that the "slow uplifting of the masses" had "scattered" the "important parts of real aristocracy": "fineness of spirit, the willingness to do without rather than do badly, the preference for quality over quantity, pride in achievement rather than pride in recognition, hate for the cheap, the easy, the vulgar." It was time, he declared, for the aristocratic impulse to reassert itself.[52]

That analysis—born, in part, of Canby's class prejudice and racism—undeniably entailed a move to preserve his own power. Yet, as in the case of Sherman, Canby's endorsement of aristocracy coexisted with a type of democratic politics. His prewar volume of essays on education, *College Sons and College Fathers* (1915), argued that a sharp dichotomy between vocational and "cultural" training jeopardized democracy by driving a wedge between leaders and workers. Both the schools and the universities, he stressed, were obligated instead to provide an "irreducible minimum of cultural training" to all citizens, creating a bond of "intellectual sympathy" between the masses and the "cultured classes." Such a common core of learning would insure the full participation of every American in the government of the nation. Thus, he concluded, the liberal arts were as practical and efficient as anything the vocationalists proposed.[53]

Canby incorporated a similar perspective into his activities on behalf of "adult education in the value of books." Rejecting what he labeled "the barbarism of the dead hand," he cautioned against literary judgments rooted in dogmatism, pedantry, and contempt for the public. "We have not made a perfect democracy," he acknowledged, "but perhaps more men, women, and children have been happy in America than elsewhere in world history." His efforts, as educator turned critic, to foster the "progressive refinement" of that population rested on his sense that therein lay the "only chance for democracy" to survive. If he regretted "debasement" and the "withering" of "fine traditions," and if he disapproved of Marxism and the movement for proletarian literature, he sanctioned "a society whose standards are broader than they are high" and welcomed the vital, new energies the decline of deference had unleashed. Poised in still another mediative position—between the mummified conservatism of the academic neo-Egyptians on the right and the recklessness of the neo-Gauls on the left—he was, in his words, a neo-Greek who exemplified the "liberal mind."[54]

Finally, as it addressed the consequences of specialization and the peril of vulgarization, Canby's educational project also attempted to arrest the erosion of conventional morality. "I am not an uncritical admirer of the Puritan," Canby wrote. "But I object still more strongly to the anti-Puritans." Here the enemy was not so much the masses or the "alien swarms" as the avant-garde. Condemning those "rebels" whose sole "philosophy" consisted of "their own desires," he urged the resuscitation of duty as a primary motivation in American life. In a similar vein, he observed that "a slow swinging away from discipline and self-restraint," under way throughout the nineteenth century, had deplorably culminated in devotion to excess and purposeless experiment in modern America. The casualty of this development was Emersonian self-reliance, the effort "to discipline and refine the emotions to deeper harmonies and finer perceptions" in order to "make life coherent."[55]

As he was well aware, Canby's generalist posture, antipathy to commercialism, complex politics, and emphasis on self-control could be "translated into terms of criticism," thus furnishing "better grounds than mere timorous necessity for resisting the chaotic, the incoherent, and the unrestrained in literature and all art." To move from Canby's premises to his critical practice, the *Saturday Review* became, in his hands, a manual for rendering that translation.[56] Faced with the "cascading torrent" of fiction marked by "commercialized sentimentalism" and written like "bad advertisements," Canby and his like-minded colleagues resolved to consider only "serious" works. Without buying into the narrow New Humanist conception of the endeavor, they pledged themselves to uphold standards. That effort would also combat standardization, since contact with good writing gave the individual "an intenser sense of his own reality in a society which is always trying to make him a number and a type." Thus, books would be assessed by reviewers with choice minds who were able to resist pressures from publishers for a quick rave, yet who could write accessibly enough to build "a wider public for better books."[57] Bucking the trend toward journalism that had " 'Tell Me,' not 'Teach Me,' as its motto," their periodical would likewise avoid the reviewer who "uptilts his personality" and deals in gossip rather than "perception." The *Saturday Review* incorporated those intentions into its graphic design: to communicate its shift from an emphasis on "the news to opinion and to pure literature," Canby explained, it replaced the more conventional eye-catching headline running across the front page with a one-column head atop the lead article, balanced by an editorial on the other side and a poem (a symbol of the "eternal" rather than the "timely") in the middle.[58]

More precisely, Canby condemned the "waste" and "formlessness" characterizing the "easy profusion of sentiment" in a book like Dreiser's *The Three Soldiers*. His opposition to gimmickry shaped his repudiation of writers who, imitating O. Henry, strove for "speedy and evanescent effects"; his commitment to individual freedom led him to reject "formula" and "artificiality." Prizing a style that created a "sense of beauty" arising from "perfect workmanship," he attacked the prevalence of "flat prose" as a symptom of the "growing ugliness of American literature." As a model, he looked to the "skill" and "art" of figures who upheld "old categories": Edith Wharton, May Sinclair, Booth Tarkington, and Galsworthy among them. The public, for its part, needed to "learn how to do some hard reading" in place of the indiscriminate sampling to which it was accustomed.[59]

Finally, Canby steered the *Review* away from realism and literary modernism. He was particularly disturbed by what he called, with respect to William Faulkner, "sadism" in American literature—that is, the portrayal of "the abnormal, the unbalanced, the excessive." Never opposed to "modernist prophesy," Canby was visibly uncomfortable with it, relegating it to the back of the magazine. Some of his distaste verged on personal animosity: he described modernist critics as invaders and poets like Eliot and Pound as "wild men." Some of his objections were moral: although he acknowledged D. H. Lawrence's "gifts as a stylist and narrator," he also found parts of his work "as vulgar as a sparrow on a dung heap." Most important, Canby saw modernism as an assault on the "indwelling self." In his view, the virtue of books by Zona Gale and Willa Cather, for example, was that their "center of gravity" lay "within." Again calling to mind Howells, Canby contrasted those older writers with younger "expressionists" whose heroes were only "personalities shedding husk after husk of accepted belief and expected conduct, with no stopping place, no kernel in sight." In contrast to Sherman, his hopeful prediction was that morality might begin again "to mean more than morale"; his assignment as a critic was to nurture a literature of "thoughts bent inward" so as to combat the modernist view of human beings as "merely clusters of unrelated experience."[60]

Taken together, Canby's assumptions made him an unmistakable descendant of the genteel tradition. Self-consciously a transitional figure who identified himself with the "older generation," he remained, even in the 1920s and 1930s, predominantly a nineteenth-century type. This quality characterized as well his role on the Book-of-the-Month Club board. When Haas approached him about serving as chief judge, he saw the enterprise as entirely congenial to the work he was already doing. Endowing the board with the same function he assigned to the *Saturday Review*, he perfected the attitude of involvement in "two worlds at once" he had assumed at Yale; now, in a commercial context, that stance became almost literally his trademark. Although his colorlessness has made historians bypass him in favor of livelier, more iconoclastic figures, it was, in his own time, his greatest asset: it served as a source of his authority and, for Scherman, a means of garnering subscribers. Antagonistic toward business values in his demeanor as well as his writing, Canby espoused and displayed the possibility that material prosperity had not eradicated the cultured gentleman. A product of an exclusive university, he exuded erudition and respectability, upholding well-understood connections between refinement and social status. His coolness toward modernism shored up his image as a guardian of permanent values; his depiction of himself as a generalist similarly suggested a steadfastness in the face of economic and social change. Thus, his role, as he saw it, ran diametrically counter to the one in which opponents of the club's "standardizing" effect cast him.[61]

Canby's decisions as book-club judge reflected his Arnoldian mentality no less than his *Saturday Review* editorials. In retrospect, he identified Lewis's *Elmer Gantry* as one of the board's especially praiseworthy choices. With that exception, however, his list of the works he was most pleased to have selected—his personal canon, one might say—venerated older writers and established forms.[62] It included Edna Ferber's *Show Boat*, Stephen Vincent Benét's *John Brown's Body*, Marjorie Kinnan Rawlings's *The Yearling*, and Clarence Day's *Life with Father*. His responses to Thomas Wolfe's *Of Time and the River* and Faulkner's *Light in August* were more qualified: Wolfe's was "not a great novel"; Faulkner's held "terrors" and "morbidities" along with an "unsuspected tenderness." Canby's respect for workmanship appeared often: in the comment that Fitzgerald's *Tender Is the Night* was "loose, inconclusive, and occasionally careless and irrelevant"; in his remark, with respect to Cather's *Shadows on the Rock*, that the "texture of the narrative is even finer, the emergent characters more varied, the story as a whole more completely knit into an imaginative reconstruction" than her earlier work; and in his praise for a novel "woven tight like a good oriental rug."[63]

Yet Canby was more than a relic of the past. His Arnoldian inheritance notwithstanding, he coupled his plea for standards with disdain for a "dying and ineffective 'genteel tradition'"—one that merely remained lodged in a bygone era. Neither did he accept those aspects of Arnold's program that seemed conducive to the "aristocratic detachment" of a "governing class." His recognition of business priorities—his willingness, for one thing, to attach himself to Scherman's scheme—and his conviction that educators and critics ought to be responsive to the needs of the machine age represented a departure from the genteel posture of alienation. He mitigated his indictment of realism by noting that it struck a salutary blow against sentimentalism; he even encouraged "self-expressionists" and other rebels as counterweights to standardization.[64]

Moreover, Canby, like Sherman, sometimes accepted and even welcomed the trend toward standardization, rightly understood. When antagonists accused the Book-of-the-Month Club of fostering a mass mind, he pleaded guilty, taking responsibility for the type of standardizing that raised the general cultural level. "Standardize reading of the better sort, thinking of the better sort," he insisted, "and automatically you will destandardize lack of judgment and cheapness of taste." Replying to "Has America a Literary Dictatorship?," he also defended the club's willingness to recommend books that were not masterpieces on the grounds that absolute standards were a form of "literary snobbery."

In addition, Canby unintentionally fostered the connections among culture, information, and performance that he consciously resisted. First, however much the *Saturday Review* set itself up as an alternative to cultural news bulletins or gossip, it deliberately incorporated both. "Books Are News," one editorial proclaimed. One of the magazine's purposes was to present "vast quantities of accurate and indispensable facts." Another (part of a reaction against the stifling aspects of gentility) was to forge a connection to "immediate life." Thus, although Canby never shared Sherman's hunger for Isabel Paterson's ration of literary tidbits, those goals resulted in his welcoming to the pages of the *Review* some comparable efforts: William Rose Benét's "The Phoenix Nest" column, often devoted to contemporary poetry but also to information and comment, and two departments by Christopher Morley—"Trade Winds" and "The Bowling Green"—that featured news and personal revelation. Some advertising for the magazine also duplicated the Book-of-the-Month Club's emphasis on staying au courant.[65] Similarly, while Canby drew a significant distinction between personality and a "personalism" that glorified an "essentially trivial and scurrilous individualism," his occasional positive pronouncements about self-expression implied some approval of therapeutic release.

More important, as Norman Foerster well understood, the decision to limit criticism to "definition" could cancel out a commitment to standards; minimizing riskier judgments, it might simply deteriorate into a more subtle form of news. This danger was especially present in Canby's work for the Book-of-the-Month Club, where the form and "time value" of the *News* predisposed the critic to operate less as the writer's conscience than as a press agent. ("I am describing rather than criticizing *Gone With the Wind*," he told subscribers, since "readers will make their own criticisms.") Like all the articles in the *News*, Canby's contributions featured plot summary rather than comments about style, while Scherman's caveat against "damning books" permitted even less critical rigor than did the *Saturday Review*. Hence, the activity that represented the fullest expression of Canby's democratic impulse to reach a wide audience and to credit it with intelligence might also be read as the furthest retreat from the supposition that readers deserved to benefit from his trained counsel. That stance, when combined with the club's marketing strategies, abetted the depiction of the cultured person as the au courant, performing self.[66]

Institutionally, the Book-of-the-Month Club and the *Saturday Review* were at first so closely related that publishers mailed submissions for the Selecting Committee to the magazine's offices. Loveman divided her administrative time between both enterprises, while Morley joined Canby on the committee. Similarly, many of the readers who screened potential selections—Stephen Vincent Benét's wife Rosemary, Basil Davenport, Bernadine Kielty—went on to appraise the same books for the *Review*. Canby himself was at the center of this alliance until 1936, when he stepped down as editor. (He served as contributing editor for several more years.) Thereafter he focused his educational activities almost exclusively on the Book-of-the-Month Club, continuing as judge until 1954. Over the course of his tenure, he gradually lost the sense of exhilaration he had derived from his early involvement with the club. In 1930, burdened by a belief that economic and cultural collapse had rendered all his efforts futile, he suffered a breakdown. The episode suggests that his anachronistic qualities took their toll psychologically and that, unable to surrender his genteel idealism, he felt painfully out of step with the times. Slipping into a mood of nostalgia for the American past, he wrote both autobiographical volumes and studies of Thoreau and Whitman that celebrated eras and individuals with which he was more comfortable. But the 1920s—the decade when, as one observer put it, "the death of Mr. Sherman left him . . . the heir apparent to the most authoritative position of critic in the field of American literature"—remained, in Canby's memory, a "brief golden age" rich with opportunities for "the passing-on of sound values to others."[67]

The Selecting Committee: Dorothy Canfield Fisher

Canby was the most powerful member of the Book-of-the-Month Club Board of Judges, by virtue of his credentials as a critic, his appointment as chair, and his visibility as chief author of the *News*. His closest ally among the other judges was Dorothy Canfield Fisher. Fisher was, if anything, even more a voice of the past than Canby. Born in 1879 to

Flavia Camp Canfield, an artist, and James Hulme Canfield, a professor and college administrator, she was a striking blend of both her parents' interests. Under the tutelage of her mother, a free-spirited rebel who chafed at the midwestern college towns where James Canfield taught, she spent much of her childhood in Europe. As she accompanied Flavia Camp Canfield on her passionate treks from gallery to gallery, she absorbed "something of her burning conviction that masterpieces of great art are important beyond anything in the world" and something of her reverence for the cultures of France, Italy, and Spain.[68]

After completing a course of study at the Sorbonne in 1899, she enrolled at Columbia for graduate work in languages and received her Ph.D. in 1904. While the subject of her dissertation, a study of English translations of Corneille and Racine, reflected her mother's cosmopolitan influence, her initial career plans echoed her father's professional concerns. James Canfield had moved from a faculty post at the University of Kansas to chancellor of the University of Nebraska to the presidency of Ohio State and finally to the head of the Columbia University Library, a progression that exemplified, as his daughter explained it, his commitment to facilitating educational opportunity for ever-wider audiences. Of the same generation as Melvil Dewey, the inventor of modern library organization, Canfield ardently believed that the survival of American democracy depended on the existence of free public libraries in every town. That lesson, which he delivered on countless lecture tours, made a lasting impression on his daughter. Offered a teaching job at Western Reserve University but reluctant to leave her mother, who had become ill, she decided to remain in New York and accept the position of secretary and librarian of the Horace Mann School when she finished her doctoral studies.[69]

She married John Fisher in 1907 and moved with him to the Canfield family homestead in Arlington, Vermont, where she combined free-lance writing with farming. By that year she had begun selling short stories to such popular magazines as *Everybody's* and the *American Mercury*; at the same time, she undertook nonfiction projects. In particular, acting on the suggestion of the publisher William Morrow, she translated the writings of Maria Montessori into English, interviewed Montessori in Italy, and popularized the Montessori method in a book for American parents originally entitled *A Montessori Mother* (1912). Although Montessori's emphasis on individual growth converged with therapeutic ideals, Fisher saw Montessori's approach as a route to self-reliance and a way of insuring the exercise of duty necessary to the survival of democracy.

When World War I threatened to destroy the Europe of Fisher's childhood memories, she and her husband felt duty bound themselves to join the war effort by going overseas. While he served as an ambulance driver, she worked on relief projects and on publicizing the devastating effects of the conflict. Her journalistic *Home Fires in France* (1918), in the words of the Book-of-the-Month Club's 1927 brochure, "brought home to so many Americans the reality of war-time France" and "established her reputation as one of the important writers of this period."[70] Upon her return to Vermont, Fisher added her voice to the pressing discussion about whether an affluent United States could support "civilization." Articulating a viewpoint she would sustain into the 1940s, she argued that the war had revealed the precariousness of democratic institutions and exposed the inadequacies of the nation's educational system; that the bigotry rampant in the immediate postwar period had further corroded vital freedoms; and, most important, that efficient production and distribution of consumer goods, made possible by the advance of technology, required Americans to find constructive outlets for the energies they had formerly put into work. Children now, Fisher warned in 1920, are "threatened as never before by all sorts of dangers, spiritual and material; the danger to their liberty of conscience and act from un-American reaction and narrowness; to their intelligence from our lamentably imperfect system of education; to their strength and hardihood from the stifling multitude of mechanical comforts, the too-easily won, flabby, moral ease offered to the moderately well-to-do in our easy-going American civilization." If Americans gave in to the temptation to spend their newfound leisure passively absorbing material pleasures and "ready-made amusement," they invited the "dangerous degeneration of human personality," a prelude to the degeneration of American society as a whole. "Although we do not see it with the vision of the flesh as we see Valley Forge," she wrote in *Why Stop Learning?* (1927), "our country is at this moment fighting for its life, at a turning-point of its existence. It is shut up within a prison of prosperity where the older doors to spiritual and intellectual life are locked. If it cannot burst open a new door . . . many new doors . . . and fight its way to air, it will smother to death beneath its material possessions." But if Americans educated their "individual minds" for the sake of spiritual, rather than material, gain, they would enhance the quality of "national thinking" and preserve the democratic process. The choice, as she entitled one of her lectures, was to *Learn or Perish*.[71]

That prescription contained healthy doses of character, discipline, integrity, and social responsibility—virtues that made Fisher a descendant of Emerson and Norton. Like Canby, she retained a model of the "inner light," influenced in part by her grandmother's and husband's Quaker affiliation. She, too, expressed a democratic faith in the ability of every person to "shape creatively and master the raw materials of human existence"[72] and counterposed individualism to a debilitating standardization. A latter-day Jeffersonian agrarian, albeit with an overlay of sophistication acquired on her European travels, Fisher placed particular hope in nature as a source of character training. (Her 1916 child-rearing manual, *Self-Reliance*, reminded mothers that saplings were rarely far away.) Fisher's own life reflected the same mentality. Steeped in local tradition, intent on preserving what she perceived as the distinctions between Vermont's way of life and the rest of the nation's, she once traveled for two days to attend an afternoon's Book-of-the-Month Club meeting in New York, only to return home by the next train. Her letters described delight at a plentiful harvest for canning but, even when they recorded visits to the city, never expressed the pleasures of the theater or the literary social scene.[73]

Fisher's novels likewise marked her as essentially a nineteenth-century figure, although they contained enough concern with contemporary issues to rescue her from antiquarianism. Her 1921 best-seller, *The Brimming Cup*, perhaps most fully reveals her sensibility. Set first in Italy but primarily in Vermont, the novel tells the story of Marise Crittenden, housewife and mother of three; her husband, Neale, the owner of a lumber mill; and their neighbor Vincent Marks, a recent arrival from New York who falls in love with Marise and tries to liberate her from domestic drudgery and a stultifying marriage. Whereas Neale represents decency, social conscience, inner strength, and stability, Vincent embodies freedom, spontaneity, sexuality, and self-expression. Two other characters in the book magnify that contrast: Marise's unattached, sybaritic school chum Eugenia Gardner, who spends her time traveling or shopping or lolling around salons, and Vincent's housemate

Ormsby Welles, who leaves the comforts of Vermont to help eliminate discrimination against blacks in Georgia.

Faced with what appears to be the polarity between fulfillment and responsibility, Marise initially considers capitulating to the dependent, indulgent relationship Vincent offers. In the crucial chapter of the book, "Marise's Coming of Age," which consists entirely of Marise's introspective monologue concerning her dilemma, she recognizes her need for "physical excitement" and questions the sense of devoting her life to motherhood. She imagines "the endless procession of parents and children passing before her, the children so soon parents, all driven forward by what they could not understand, yearning and starving for what was not given them, all wrapped and dimmed in the twilight of their doubt and ignorance. Where were they going? And why?" But her awareness that loyalty to her best self precludes an existence free of obligations to others leads Marise to renounce Vincent's promise of intense but egocentric pleasure and to renew her admiration for Neale's quiet integrity. "She was no bound-woman," Marise decides, "bullied by the tyranny of an outgrown past, forced to revolt in order to attain the freedom without which no human decision can be taken. Neale's strong hand had opened the door to freedom and she could see . . . that freedom is not the end, but only the beginning." True fulfillment, she discovers, is, at least in her own case, inseparable from self-sacrifice. In marked contrast to Stuart Sherman's decision to "unfold leaf by leaf," Marise resolves her crisis by concluding that dependency is appropriate only for little girls, that she must "come of age" by rejecting passion for maturity. Neale's injunction that she honor what was "deepest and most living" in herself without regard for conventional dictates about duty to husband or children turns out to revivify Christian morality. In the end, maturity even pays sensual dividends: Marise discovers a new thrill in Neale's kiss, a new joy in music, a new delight in her home.[74]

Fisher's emphasis on introspection and analysis as the route to spiritual peace gave *The Brimming Cup* a Freudian tinge and signaled her acceptance of one aspect of the modern temper. Repression of conflict and failure to face one's innermost desires were emotional dodges which, according to Fisher, dead-ended in stunted growth and servility to other people's false ideals. Likewise, her refusal automatically to resort to considering Marise's problem in religious terms highlighted her divergence from the Victorian propensity for clear identification of sin and sacrament. She recognized the importance of physical satisfaction for women as well as men; she aired the notion, dear to the avant-garde and integral to the stereotype of the new woman in early-twentieth-century America, that sexual expression was the key to happiness. But if she established her modern credentials by facing sex squarely and refraining from conventional moralism, she adhered, at base, to an older outlook. Not only did she ultimately repudiate the idea that sexual repression was always harmful,[75] she never questioned, as her modernist contemporaries relentlessly did, the meaningfulness of human existence or the efficacy of personal action. For Christian commandments she substituted her own, which came to the same thing: the necessity of faithfulness to an inner self, within the bounds of devotion to others. Her forays into a post-Freudian, post-Darwinian world led her back to the safety of rules and principles, of social order and domestic tranquillity. While she gave *The Brimming Cup* a touch of cosmopolitanism—the romance of Neale and Marise's engagement in the hills above Rome, even the exotic flavor of her heroine's name—she made clear that Marise's refusal to Vincent was a rejection of "what a modern, free, European woman would do" in favor of American virtue.[76] Fisher's use of literary form revealed the same combination of new and old, and in about the same proportions. Her description of an outing to Neale's lumber mill experimented with a technique which Faulkner would later employ more skillfully in *The Sound and the Fury*: it retold the same story from different characters' vantage points in order to emphasize the subjectivity of perception. Yet her dominant mode was conventional narrative.

The impulse to enshrine vanishing values also informed Fisher's popular *The Homemaker* (1924) and *Seasoned Timber* (1939), both of which explicitly addressed twentieth-century problems. The first novel turned on a reversal of gender roles: a discontented businessman is injured in a fall and happily takes over the management of the household, while his wife, heretofore miserable at home, becomes an enthusiastic breadwinner. Although the novel ventures into feminist territory and clearly makes the point that the waste of human capacity as a result of arbitrary social restrictions is always tragic, it is important to see that Fisher's reliance on her hero's illness prevents the book from breaking entirely with traditional gender expectations. At the end of the novel, when, theoretically, Fisher might have cured her hero and then allowed him to choose to stay at home, she resorted instead to concealing his recovery from all but his doctor, who cooperates in perpetuating domesticity under false pretenses. Thus, *The Homemaker* examined issues of gender in terms that were safe from a genuine feminist perspective.

Seasoned Timber invoked the past in a different way. Written as the tide of anti-Semitism was rising in Europe, it explored the problems facing Timothy Hulme, headmaster of a struggling academy in a Vermont village, when a trustee offers to endow the school handsomely provided that it agree to exclude Jews. The triumph of Hulme over the trustee is more than the victory of American ideals over bigotry; it is the victory as well of rural virtue over urban decadence, of civilization over nouveau-riche distortions of culture. Deliberating about the offer, Hulme complains not only of the trustee's insensitivity to human values but also about his lack of taste: "Why should he take with such painful seriousness a man who was (outside the world of money) only a grotesquerie of pretentious ignorance? . . . Crumbling his bread and looking down moodily at his cooling plate of stew, the schoolteacher from the country sent his mind searching for the answer to this question." Upset that a "man totally ignorant of civilized standards and values should fancy himself an arbiter of those values," Hulme angrily sweeps a water glass from his lunch table and watches it roll on the floor unbroken. "'A brave, big city glass!,'" Fisher has Hulme muse. "'A thoroughly hard-boiled, urban glass guaranteed to have no instincts delicate enough to be breakable.'" As she courageously grappled with contemporary controversies, then, Fisher located the answers to America's dilemmas in what her biographer has called the "socially constructive" setting of Vermont—a setting that antedated the competitiveness and callousness of a society in which the businessman earned more deference than the man of learning.[77]

Fisher viewed her membership on the Book-of-the-Month Club board as her own contribution to civilization and democracy, as a means of fostering individualism and character in the face of standardization and materialism. The anecdote she repeatedly told about her decision to accept Scherman's offer reflected the same commitments that underlay her essays, novels, and way of life. As Fisher remembered it (although her biographer has cast some doubt on the sequence of events), she traveled to New York for a shopping trip during the period she was weighing Scherman's invitation. "I got myself transported to Macy's," Fisher recalled, "stepped inside and asked for the counter where sheets and pillow cases were being sold—that being my prosaic errand. The big shop was alarmingly (to my eyes) crammed with milling crowds of bargain-crazed women. . . . [A] frenzy of the purchasing mania surged five or six deep around the counter where I wanted to go." She fled from the store (deciding to order sheets by mail instead), fought crowds of shoppers on Fifth Avenue, and took refuge in Brentano's to buy her daughter a dictionary. There she found herself virtually the only customer, outnumbered by idle salespeople. The contrast between Brentano's and Macy's convinced her that it was essential to try new methods of selling books: "Evidently the distribution of books of decent quality to an adequate percentage of our population," she wrote, "is a wheel which can't be rolled forward and up hill, unless all kinds of shoulders are set to it with determination and much ingenuity." Thus, she decided to serve on the board, envisioning it as an antidote to, rather than an extension of, salesmanship. Interestingly, she said nothing about the moneymaking side of the venture, nothing about her salary as judge. As she presented it, the Book-of-the-Month Club became a nonprofit organization, a kind of mail-order public library akin to the adult education and museum outreach programs she advocated throughout her career.[78]

Similarly, when the board came under attack in 1929 in the aftermath of the Joan Lowell affair, Fisher, supplying the club's official rejoinder, dissociated it—and herself—from commercialism. "I have often thought that I, especially, must be exasperating to men immersed in the complex details of managing a big business," she wrote, "because of my rustic and countrified ignorance of such matters." In the same document, she insisted that "nothing could be farther from the facts than any statement that the business management . . . influences the choice of the judges." Instead, as her references to "decent quality" and shouldering the wheel indicate, she adhered to a conception of literary and personal integrity that perpetuated ties among culture, aesthetic standards, morality, and discipline. Of the five board members, Fisher was the most conscientious reader; her correspondence about her rating of the monthly contenders is urgent in tone and thoughtful in substance. She approached the structure and language of fiction with rigorous attention to accuracy of imagery, unity of plot, and consistency of character portrayal, condemning books that seemed "soft and arranged" while praising others exhibiting "sincerity" and "authenticity." Consequently, she did not hesitate to reject as selections novels such as Thomas B. Costain's *High Towers*, which, despite guaranteed popularity, seemed to her entirely to lack literary merit. Nor did she capitulate to the vocal minority of subscribers who protested that selections were too realistic about sex. In the mid-1940s, when a friend wrote to her complaining that the caliber of club selections had declined over the past twenty years, Fisher countered that the board had never deviated from choosing works on the basis of their "value, truth, and literary skill."[79]

Fisher's sense of her audience, and of her educational mission, is reflected in her remarks for the *News* about *Roads to Knowledge*, a collection of essays outlining scholarly disciplines for the general reader: "You will find in every one a well-informed specialist who does not think you are a helpless low-brow because you have rather vague ideas about his subject but on the contrary is delighted that you have any ideas at all, and is eager to tell you—adult to adult, with no nonsense—how to cultivate, water, prune, and feed this germ of intellectual life in your brain, till it grows into a sure fruitful source of new pleasure and vitality." Her allegiance to moral instruction and social improvement, Scherman recalled, threw her "off balance frequently in her judgments." Nonetheless, as her obituary in the *News* noted, she was, in her Book-of-the-Month Club role no less than in her career as a whole, an American "of the rarest and purest character . . . who harked back to and lent new luster to our highest pioneer traditions."[80]

Yet even more than Canby, Fisher unwittingly undermined her effort to hold the line against the deterioration of standards and the dangers of consumerism. Again, her acquiescence in furnishing only positive reports for the *Book-of-the-Month Club News* severely limited her ability to impart to the public the criteria she invoked in board meetings. More important, Fisher went further than her male counterparts in permuting her democratic outlook into a repudiation of her authority. She did so by assuming a particular, feminine version of the guise of diffident, self-effacing expert: the wife and mother as amateur critic. While Fisher maintained, rather than challenged, women's domestic sphere, and ignored the suffrage and equal-rights movements, she was always preoccupied with what might be called women's issues, not only in her books but in the way she presented herself to her audience. When, for example, she appeared on the radio program "What's Your Idea?" to promote *Our Young Folks* (1944), her assessment of the needs of American adolescents in wartime, Fisher's first words to the interviewer who asked her how she happened to write the book were "Well, I'm a mother and grandmother, so I naturally have an intense interest in the welfare of our younger generation."[81] Only secondarily did she mention her membership on the American Youth Commission of the American Council on Education, which had generated the data for her book. Taking her cue from Fisher's own self-image, Amy Loveman built the same hierarchy of activities into Fisher's citation for the Constance Lindsay Skinner Award, bestowed on women for distinguished service to literature: "Wife, mother, and grandmother too, novelist, translator, and a member of the Book-of-the-Month Club from its inception . . . , she has adorned all she has touched."

That characteristic stance—average woman first, writer second— created strikingly strong bonds between Fisher and women readers, who found in her a model and a friend. Ninety percent of her fan mail came from housewives. "I was married at eighteen," one of the most poignant letters reads, "and it was hard for me to give up or postpone some of my ambitious plans and to learn to be a good wife and mother. Your books . . . gave me many helpful ideas and encouragement." Another correspondent confessed, "I was getting awfully discouraged and bewildered over my too-full, and often monotonous days. I read and re-read every word you said and I wish I could let you know how you have heartened and encouraged me and changed my whole viewpoint. . . . My husband joins me in thanking you for this piece of missionary work that you and your pen have accomplished in our small household." To readers whom she had never met, but who confided in her their anxieties about their children's development, Fisher replied with unusual concern, often alluding to her own maternal experience. "How well I understand the feeling of failure you mention!" she consoled one correspondent. "What mother doesn't have periods of such black depression and failure of self-confidence! But you know, as well as I do, that if one grasps the essentials of child-training, success is sure, though perhaps it may not take exactly the form our short-sighted wishes would have it." The poems her admirers composed about her maternal wisdom ("The world needs women like her—strong, courageous souls /

Restorative as the Green Mountain air . . ."), the babies named for characters in her books, and the formation of the Dorothy Canfield Club of Connersville, Indiana, all testify to the sustenance and support she provided women grappling with domesticity.[82] She genuinely furnished the personal interest club advertising merely simulated.

As a basis for her role on the Book-of-the-Month Club board, however, Fisher's self-image was at odds with the critic's obligation to shape taste. Her job, she once explained to a prospective member of the board, was not to decide how a book should be "'rated' on the literary scale" but to determine "whether I myself—not as a literary person just as an American woman—have really enjoyed reading" it.[83] Similarly, she repeatedly asserted that the only reason she could serve on the board in good conscience was that she knew how frequently subscribers exercised their option to substitute their own selection for the judges'. As was true for Canby, that well-intentioned argument, while it aimed at accessibility and an active readership, eventuated in something else as well: a constriction of her audience's opportunity to acquire the aesthetic perspective and the genuine self-possession that Fisher herself exemplified.

The Selecting Committee: Morley, Broun, and White

The other three judges on the original Selecting Committee—Morley, Broun, and White—might be exonerated from the charge that they evaded the critic's responsibility to uphold standards, because they were more frankly journalistic to begin with. That is, they explicitly defined themselves as providers of news and opinion and brought to that task no coherent philosophy concerning literature and society. Moreover, they enjoyed reputations not primarily for acute aesthetic sensitivity and good taste but, rather, for astute commentary on current events, whether literary or political. Two of the three, Morley and Broun, also cemented the connection between culture and personality by exhibiting an urbanity and sophistication that served as the basis for their authority. White, by contrast, remained basically a nineteenth-century figure yet departed furthest of all the members on the board from the genteel tradition's conception of the critic's role.

Of the five initial judges, Christopher Morley is the hardest to place.

A prolific novelist, poet, and essayist whose preoccupation with books and authors earned him the label "man of letters," he was less concerned with literary values than with the literary life and was more a promoter than an educator. Morley was born in Pennsylvania in 1890, the son of an English mathematician who had come to America in 1887 to teach at Haverford College. He shared with Canby and Fisher an exposure to Quaker influences by virtue of his father's background and his own enrollment at Haverford in the class of 1906. Morley's Anglophilia, which he came by naturally, grew more pronounced during three years at Oxford as a Rhodes scholar. He published his first book of poems while in England but took a series of jobs as a journalist after returning to the United States in 1913. He brought out four collections of essays between 1918 and 1920, most of which he had written for the *Philadelphia Evening Public Ledger*. They included tributes to authors (William McFee, Rupert Brooke), excursions around Philadelphia and New York, and reflections on the commonplace objects and occurrences that revealed human foibles or suggested literary connections ("The Last Pipe," "On Filling Inkwells"). The same period saw the publication of *Parnassus on Wheels* (1917), a brief, light novel about a traveling bookseller that proclaimed the desirability of making good books accessible to ordinary people. Its sequel, *The Haunted Bookshop* (1919), used a mystery plot as a framework for literary allusions, recommendations, and remarks on the function of reading.

In 1920 Morley began writing a daily column entitled "The Bowling Green" for the *New York Evening Post*. When he moved to the *Saturday Review of Literature*, he took the column with him and continued it until 1938. "The Bowling Green" contained a mixture of poetry, parody, criticism, and gossip, with the world of books forming the principal subject matter. ("Trade Winds," a compilation of brief news items which Morley assembled in the 1920s and 1930s, was less reflective and thus less expressive of his sensibility.) Fond of seventeenth-century idioms and Latin phrases, Morley made "The Bowling Green" a showcase for puns and witticisms. His novels *Where the Blue Begins* (1922) and *Thunder on the Left* (1925), the protagonists of which were involved in book production, likewise buried Morley's philosophical concerns—especially with the importance of individualism and the benefits of reading—beneath layers of fantasy and humor. That "systematic concealment of his more serious purposes," in the phrase of his biographers

Mark Wallach and Jon Bracker, "made literature painless." The word "whimsical," Morley himself observed, was most frequently invoked to describe both his column and his fiction; "convivial," with its connotation of pleasant but not overly taxing exchange, is equally apt. Although even his friend Canby conceded that he came dangerously close to flaunting archaic style at the expense of substance, Morley escaped that charge (sometimes barely) by exhibiting a genuine passion for life. His tone, as Carl Van Doren put it, was of a man "reading old books and drinking old wine with old friends before a fire of old wood."[84]

That quality made Morley seem, in many respects, an anachronism. He resembled the country gentleman, devoted to mellow wine, fine tobacco, and excellent food along with literary classics. At worst, he was pretentious and foppish; at best, a symbol of a more gracious earlier era, when people had leisure for good conversation—and for reading. His penchant for fantasy and his ornamental style placed him at odds with the avant-garde: Malcolm Cowley, for one, recalled that his own intuitive revulsion against anyone famous for whimsy prevented him from knowing Morley as well as he did the rest of the *Saturday Review* staff.[85]

Moreover, as Canby observed in *American Estimates* (1929), Morley wrote only of "Moral Man," of characters determined not to live like "Mr. Dreiser's or Mr. Anderson's self-accommodating heroes." Morley, said Canby, in a phrase that described his own and Fisher's turn of mind as well, was "the Quaker in Literature"; he was imbued with the "inner light, which means . . . a radiant conviction of significance in the universe." Thus, Morley's evasion of the modernists' confrontation with human frailty and insignificance made his work a kind of safe harbor in the twentieth-century storm. As Canby noted, "I think that the popularity of Christopher Morley is based upon a sound instinct for joy and pathos, sentiment and beauty, in the nobler varieties of humanity, which after all have their place even in a democracy of neurotics, schizoids, morons, and the emotionally unstable."[86]

Finally, in addition to lobbying, in his work and behavior, for an older model of the self, Morley exhibited an antipathy toward business that made him seem out of step with the times. Like Canby and Fisher, whose backgrounds centered on the university, he entered literary journalism from an academic milieu and never lost his preference for the library over the marketplace. Hence, *The Haunted Bookshop* counterposed Roger Mifflin, the wise but unworldly bookseller, to Aubrey Gilbert, a naive copywriter for the Grey-Matter advertising agency who almost lets the crooks get away. In the first part of the novel, Morley contrasted advertising with the public service provided by the bookseller, who dealt not in merchandise but in the enduring "depositories of the human spirit." His "The Story of Ginger Cubes" (1922) was a more direct attack on the advertising industry, Morley labeling the piece "a business satire."[87]

Yet Morley was a good deal more at home in American consumer culture than were Canby and Fisher. His spoofs of advertising remind one of the adage "it takes one to know one," a point Earnest Elmo Calkins made when he praised the clever copy Morley wrote for some melodramas Morley helped stage in 1928 and 1929. Morley was also extremely good at publicizing the literary products of his friends or favorite authors. His essays often used descriptions of ordinary events as points of departure for references to, or full-fledged discussions of, works Morley especially liked. His "Bowling Green" column was explicitly promotional: its primary function was to draw attention to books and people Morley thought were worth knowing about. His pose as a country gentleman notwithstanding, Morley was as shrewd and effective an advertiser for literature as Maxwell Sackheim was for farm machinery. As the Book-of-the-Month Club's 1927 brochure stated, "Perhaps he has done more than any other single man to revive the memory of good old books and welcome new ones."[88]

Furthermore, "The Bowling Green" was not only promotional, it was personal, urban, and reportorial. Each of those traits connected it to the demands of American life in the 1920s, 1930s, and 1940s. Paradoxically, Morley's distinctive performance as a survivor of a more gracious era certified him as a modern personality. His mannered conduct, at times annoyingly suggestive of empty gesture, was ideally adapted to a society in which impression management was essential for success. Morley injected himself into every line of his column (and into his essays as well). "He talked exclusively," his biographers have written, "either of things that happened to him or of the people and the places that caught his fancy at a particular moment."[89]

As such, Morley surpassed Isabel Paterson as a purveyor of "inside dope." His greater influence and wider interests placed him in the same league as Don Marquis, Franklin P. Adams, Alexander Woollcott, and his fellow Book-of-the-Month Club judge Heywood Broun—writers who garnered huge audiences for their daily newspaper columns in the 1920s. In part, as Canby perceptively noticed, the popularity of the columns derived from the way they counteracted the loneliness of the urban individual. When Adams, writing as F.P.A. on the "op-ed" page of the *New York World*, described the comings and goings of his friends, he made the city that much less anonymous; when Broun, under his own name and in an intimate tone, chronicled the activities of his young son, he treated his readers as equals and confidants; when Marquis (whom Morley saw as his mentor) leavened his observations with the humorous antics of Archy the cockroach and Mehitabel the cat, he gave his column in the *New York Sun* a warmth that the rest of the newspaper lacked. Yet while the columns helped to mitigate longings for the small town, they were nevertheless unmistakably cosmopolitan. As Carl Van Doren remarked, to read them outside of New York was to miss half the points they made. Filled with references to the city's landmarks, heroes, public officials, and, in Morley's case, literary celebrities, the columns radiated the sense that it was possible—and exciting—to move deftly through the confusion of the urban scene. Their continual revelation of their authors' "untrammeled personalities," in Van Doren's phrase, made them how-to manuals for readers anxious to achieve distinctiveness for themselves.[90]

Both in spite and because of his guise as an "ancient hearty," then, Morley personified the conflation of culture with performance that formed a dominant motif in Book-of-the-Month Club advertising. Similarly, the content of his "Bowling Green" column fostered the reduction of culture to information, since that was exactly what it purported to provide. Morley was intellectually committed to the view that knowledge about writers was as valuable as insight into their works: "I suppose it is the mark of a trifling mind," he wrote, "yet I like to hear of the little particulars that surrounded those whose pens struck sparks. . . . I like to know what the author wore, how he sat, what the furniture of his desk and chamber, who cooked his meals for him, and with what appetite he approached them." On the rare occasions when he paused to define his purpose, he focused on the "duty" to keep literature alive by bringing to light the "casual memoranda, [the] marginalia" which comprised its "inside history." Those concerns were consistent with Morley's journalistic propensities, which he retained even after he

stopped identifying himself as a journalist, but they signaled a corre-
sponding rejection of the role of the critic as evaluator of meaning,
significance, and artistry. Despite Morley's commendable efforts to
generate regard for literature, moreover, his concentration on literary
trivia meshed all too well with the needs of the busy consumer for
reports from the world of books that did not interfere with business.
The same might be said for Morley's "painless" fantasies and essays.
His columns and other writings are well crafted, amusing, sometimes
uplifting, and always sincere, but they are nonetheless the intellectual
equivalent of convenience food.[91]

Thus, Morley brought to the Board of Judges an animus toward modernism and commerce coupled with a facility for advertising and a personal and literary style that represented departures from Arnoldian understandings of culture and criticism. As if to give concrete expression
to that tension, he coasted on superficial impressions (when he read the
books at all) in the first years of the club's operation but later exhibited
more of the seriousness with which Canby and Fisher approached their
responsibilities. Canby remembered him as a source of "enthusiasms,"
as did Clifton Fadiman: "Morley represented that wonderful nineteenth-
century quality, the ability to admire, and he introduced into our meetings an enthusiasm that counterbalanced the somewhat judgmatical
atmosphere." Like Canby, Morley was self-consciously a generalist in
an era of specialization. He applied his enthusiasm particularly to sea
stories, to books with a liberal political message, and, predictably, to
"whimsy, poetry and works of the imagination."[92] Yet it was Canby and
Fisher, themselves nineteenth-century to the extent that they adopted
the role of the critic as arbiter, who were supplying most of the "judgmatical atmosphere" and who make Morley stand out by contrast as the
twentieth-century adman cum journalist that he also was.

Morley's ambivalent stance becomes clearer by comparing him to his
colleague Heywood Broun, for Broun pushed Morley's personal approach to the point where it displaced literature almost entirely. A
lifelong New Yorker, Broun was born in 1888 and educated at the
Horace Mann School where, during part of his time there, Fisher was
serving as secretary and librarian. He was a member of Harvard's
famous class of 1910 but failed a course in his senior year and did not
graduate. As a reporter of sports and theatrical news for the *New York
Morning Telegraph* and the *Tribune*, he developed an idiosyncratic

style and acquired a byline, thus departing from standard journalistic practice of the time. After World War I, when he assumed his post as literary as well as drama editor of the *Tribune*, he quickly transformed the paper's thrice-weekly book column into a podium analogous to F.P.A.'s, Marquis's, and Morley's.

The process of that transformation is illuminating. At first, Broun filled the space with chatty remarks about new books, frequently relying on excerpts from readers' letters to make the job easier. That device heightened the effectiveness of the column as a force against anonymity, making it a valuable contribution to the struggle to humanize urban life, but it also represented a flight from criticism. Having certified the average reader as a literary expert equal to himself, Broun then concluded, as one of his biographers put it, that he could "skip books altogether and get away with it."[93] The result was the retitling of his column from "Books" to "Books and Things," although neither was really his focus. At most, he used books as starting points for displaying his own interests, opinions, or escapades.

That shift away from literature and toward the personal meant that, in part, Broun staked his authority not on his ability to supply the rarefied perceptions that came from specialized training but instead on his flair for communicating the down-to-earth observations that anyone might make. In the case of his famous piece "Holding a Baby," for example, he reversed his transmutation of reader into critic, changing himself from critic into average, baffled father. Yet the particular personality Broun exhibited was a more powerful source of his appeal than his affinity with ordinary readers. Even more than Morley, Broun typified the man-about-town. At first glance, it is true, he seemed an unlikely cosmopolite: his characteristic rumpled look and unassuming demeanor suggested an unwillingness to conform to a code of sophistication. Moreover, Broun retained a streak of individualism in politics that made him an updated version of the village radical. He would be temporarily fired from the *New York World* in 1927 for his defense of Sacco and Vanzetti. Even in the early 1920s, however, he made direct, honest expression of his liberal viewpoint a feature of his writing. He unhesitatingly attacked the Klan, the Red Scare, the imprisonment of Eugene Debs, censorship, and fundamentalism, earning himself a reputation as a champion of the underdog. Yet he displayed his individualism in a completely urban context. Broun's crowd was the one that gathered around the Algonquin Hotel's Round Table, where approbation depended on showy display of quick wit. Broun was often the victim, rather than the perpetrator, of the Algonquin group's repartee, yet he moved with ease in their world of late-night theater parties, junkets to night clubs, and breezy encounters with the rich and famous. More than that, he endorsed, by association, what F.P.A. and Woollcott virtually elevated into a doctrine: that survival and status depended on knowing the right people, having the right information, and being able to impress others in public. While Broun's politics made him less superficial than the foregoing formula suggests, he was, of the five members of the Book-of-the-Month Club board, the best example of the successful performing self—ill-fitting trousers and all.

Broun's outlook theoretically gave culture more accessibility than did Canby's or Fisher's, since self-expression required no training in literature; even Morley, one might argue, preserved an elitist posture in his esoteric allusions and archaic locutions. Yet, from another perspective, Morley served democracy at least by keeping his gossip centered around books. Broun did not. When he moved to the *World* (where the title of his column, "It Seems to Me," captured the triumph of the personal), he practically stopped discussing books altogether, yet—as Scherman's selection of him in 1926 shows—he continued to wear the mantle of the critic. As if to push to its logical conclusion the idea that actually coming to terms with literature mattered less than projecting an image of knowledgeability, Broun served on the Book-of-the-Month Club board without reading most of the works under consideration. Instead, he mainly left the task to his wife, the reporter and feminist Ruth Hale, presenting her reactions in the board meetings.[94]

Broun was also the most willing of all the board members to choose a book solely for its entertainment value. It was Broun who was primarily responsible for swinging the board in favor of the fraudulent *Cradle of the Deep*. As Fisher, who strongly disagreed with him, recalled: "Heywood Broun, with his good-humored, easy-going eloquences, said something like this, every time I brought this up [the book's distortion of reality], 'Oh, what's the difference? The book's good, lively reading, entertaining as the dickens.' I said that it wasn't to me, because it was so false to the premises on which it was said to be based. He pointed out that this was literary priggishness.... 'This isn't a class in English Lit. One of the things we're trying to do is to provide entertaining reading. Don't be so rigid.'"[95] Yet even though Broun's judgment of that particular book no doubt caused some of his colleagues to wonder whether they were better off when Broun took an active role or just collected his checks, his demonstration of personality made him an enormous asset as part of a marketing strategy based on apprehensions about the survival of the self.

William Allen White likewise served the club by contributing an image that had tremendous advertising value: he was the consummate symbol of small-town America. As such, White represented a way of life closer to Fisher's than to Morley's or Broun's. Yet his distance from the precepts of nineteenth-century criticism made him in a sense the most contemporary of the group. Born in 1868, White grew up on the Kansas prairie and in 1886 enrolled at the state university at Lawrence. There he took more courses from James Canfield than from any other professor, studying history, sociology, and economics under Canfield's tutelage and casting him as his political mentor (a role Canfield played for the next twenty years). White was also business manager for the campus literary magazine, an activity that foreshadowed his relationship to literature as a Book-of-the-Month Club judge.

After graduation, he held a series of jobs as a reporter, including a stint of almost four years on the *Kansas City Star*. In 1895, however, White left the attractions of the city to begin a lifelong career as owner and editor of the *Emporia Gazette*, shrewdly recognizing that he could earn more fame and exert more influence as a maverick country journalist than as an urban correspondent. Although he opposed the Populists in 1896, he came to endorse the Progressive movement and to serve as one of its chief publicists. Thus, he shared the same outlook that impelled Canby and Fisher to seek a wider audience for reading but made it far more than a backdrop for literary concerns. By the same token, except for trying his hand at fiction a couple of times, he was essentially a political writer, a critic of public policy rather than books. He helped Theodore Roosevelt launch the Bull Moose party in 1912; after World War I, he campaigned for American participation in the League of Nations. Subsequently, like Broun, he attacked both the Red Scare and the Ku Klux Klan as antithetical to the nation's ideals.

In the process, White championed small-town life, where, in his view, individualism, common sense, faith in progress, and altruism still resided despite the materialism and selfishness of the age. White himself came to represent the persistence of integrity and "sanity" in an increasingly chaotic world. His obituary for his daughter Mary, written in 1921, became a touchstone for Americans seeking reassurance that friendship, love, and innocence remained possible: F.P.A. immediately reprinted the piece in his column, Morley anthologized it later that year, and Woollcott eventually read it to his radio audience.

White performed the same function on the Book-of-the-Month Club board. He was the purest representative of character involved in the enterprise, supplying the clearest demonstration of the impulse to link culture with a vanishing model of the self. Yet, at the same time, of all the judges, he was the one most aware of and amenable to serving as a product endorser. White called the subscribers "customers" and wanted them to have their money's worth. Thus, he conceived of his job in terms of selecting those books which the rural, unsophisticated reader would find least offensive and most enjoyable. "Now if I am worth anything to you," White wrote Scherman in 1931, "it is [as] a mentor on that side of the merchandising proposition." The issue of literary quality intruded only rarely into his judgments—understandably, since he had no background in or commitment to criticism. He was more likely to pronounce a book "salable" than well wrought. On at least one occasion he threatened to resign if the board approved a novel he thought too sexually explicit, but he was less a prude than a good businessman. As he insisted to Scherman, "It seems to me we shouldn't be putting out books that baldly pander to the pornographic instincts of our subscribers. When I say shouldn't, I don't mean any moral implications in the word, but as a business proposition. . . . The list that likes that sort of thing is limited in numbers. . . . The big dollar is outside of that crowd."[96]

Although his colleagues respected and liked White as a person, his priorities distressed them in proportion to their concern with educating public taste. Canby thought White's efforts at criticism "frequently unsound"; Morley, in the words of White's biographer Walter Johnson, felt "White's judgment on books, five out of six times, was liable to be very bad." Because White frequently telegraphed his recommendations to the board in lieu of traveling to New York for the monthly meeting, the typical procedure was for the rest of the group to enjoy a good laugh over his witty, spirited missives and then for Canby to call him up and explain that he had been outnumbered. White's relative powerlessness on the board is an index of its opposition to treating culture as a commodity, as well as of its unwillingness to concede that criticism was a task anyone might perform. Yet his colleagues' failure to take White seriously behind the closed doors of the boardroom did not affect his power to portray, in the club's advertising and publications, the ordinary man as critic. White's review of Frederick Lewis Allen's *Only Yesterday*, for example, made his position clear. Implicitly identifying the book—and himself—as appropriately middlebrow, he wrote: "In reading this book the highbrow may take the pins out of his brow and let it down, and the lowbrow will feel that he has raised it up a few inches." Similarly, his name on the Board of Judges, as Johnson has noted, signified that the club was not reserved for the "'highbrow'"; it meant that life experience and common sense were qualifications enough for the evaluation of books.[97] That image of accessibility resembled Broun's. Coupled with White's refreshingly candid commercialism, it made White an effective promoter of consumer values even as he simultaneously functioned as an emblem of the past.

Summary and Postscript

Hence, the array of intellectual loyalties and individual styles on the original Book-of-the-Month Club Selecting Committee struck a highly functional balance. Canby's and Fisher's dominance as exponents of integrity, morality, and literary standards perpetuated the genteel tradition in a perhaps surprising place: at the heart of an institution inextricably tied to advertising and consumption. In light of their influence, the club appears a repository for the ideals mass society threatened to obliterate; it made the pursuit of culture a way of certifying that, despite the effects of urbanization, industrialization, bureaucratization, and specialization, some aspects of American life remained unchanged. An analogy might be found in the status accorded the home and the school, two agencies for the dissemination of culture, as those tumultuous processes got under way: both were to be refuges from the impersonal, rough-and-tumble business world outside the door. The school as citadel fell early; the growing availability and range of goods steadily implicated the home in consumption; but culture, dispensed in new forms, remained a center of resistance.[98]

At the same time, Morley and Broun made the Book-of-the-Month Club a training ground for getting ahead in a society where acquiring the right information and using it to build a personality were the ingredients of success. Their turn away from character, discipline, and duty proclaimed that the Arnoldian version of the cultured person was not only irretrievable but also irrelevant in modern America. The message they and White spoke with a louder voice than did Canby or Fisher—that culture was accessible to anyone—aided the marketing of a new product. Simultaneously, however, it also satisfied readers who clung to genteel perceptions and who, distressed by consumer priorities, took comfort in the notion that success born of self-reliance was both still available and close at hand. The tandem use of pontifical expertise and the "guarantee against dissatisfaction," of convenience and service, revealed the same adaptive mechanism. This was the "middleness" of middlebrow culture, as the Book-of-the-Month Club exemplified it: the embodiment in a single institution of competing assumptions about reading and criticism, rooted in changing historical circumstances, that accommodated a variety of needs.

At the risk of opening the Pandora's box of assessing the club's selections, it seems obligatory at least to add a postscript about the books themselves. What can be said, by way of overview, about the volumes recommended between 1926 and 1944, when the original board held sway? (Broun died in 1939 but was not immediately replaced; when White died in 1944, John P. Marquand and Clifton Fadiman filled the two openings.) Here the genteel tradition was overrepresented, in the sense that Broun's and White's withdrawal from moral and educational responsibilities went hand in hand with minimal involvement in the debates of the Selecting Committee. Thus, the monthly choices reflect Canby's and Fisher's heavy presence, Morley's "enthusiasms" to a lesser degree, and Broun's and White's detachment. Thanks largely to Canby's and Fisher's conviction that it was their job to place before the public books that met their own rigorous aesthetic standards, the club's selections in the 1920s and 1930s are better, from a literary standpoint, than today's; thanks to their animus toward modernism, which Morley also shared, they are likewise not as good as they might have been.

The actual selection procedure entailed classification of books as "A," "B," or "C," according to the reports of preliminary readers. Amy Loveman (appointed a judge herself after Fisher retired in 1951) oversaw that part of the process. The board then (in theory) read all of the "A" books and some of the "B" ones, which they were allowed to move to the "A" category. At the monthly meeting, the judges arrived at a choice for the book of the month by what Canby called "the Quaker principle of concurrence" rather than by voting.[99] That description of the process, however, omits what Fisher and Canby frankly acknowledged: that the decision rested on more than a book's intrinsic artistic merits. Although Scherman, Canby, and Fisher all made repeated statements about the danger of underestimating the intelligence of the American people, and although Scherman kept admonishing the board members to pick the books that they, as representatives of average readers, thought best, in practice the judges knew very well that they had an audience to serve whose education and taste did not match their own. As Canby explained in answer to "Has America a Literary Dictatorship?," the judges felt, on occasion, that "a subtle and symbolistic story, a poem, beautiful but obscure, an historical work of great and involved erudition, was the *best* book of the month," but they have felt that "while such a book must be placed . . . upon the recommended list, it would be folly to send it out to 40,000 readers." Thus, although the board gambled for its first selection on what Canby called "the very literary and specialized" *Lolly Willowes*, by Sylvia Townsend Warner, it was in general careful to avoid anything too esoteric or academic.[100]

Likewise, it took pains to vary the monthly offerings and to gauge the public's receptivity to a book. Fisher described the questions the judges asked themselves: "Have we, perhaps, recently sent out several books on the subject, so that a change would be desirable? Have there been indications that the subject . . . is seriously distasteful to intelligent American readers?" Except for White, the board was not so much concerned with the club's fortunes as with its impact: "[T]here is no point," Fisher remarked, in choosing a book "which most readers will not accept."[101] Finally, there was, in the first year, the element of cost. The fact that nonfiction usually sold above the three-dollar limit the club guaranteed to subscribers made for a preponderance of novels among the initial offerings, until publishers grew convinced that it was worth lowering nonfiction prices in return for a club endorsement. One element that did not directly affect the judges' choice was the opinion of Scherman and his associates. The selection of *Lolly Willowes*, Fisher recalled, was a test of management's pledge to refrain from interference, and, as promised, it kept silent, even when the book proved unpopular with subscribers. To an extent, however, the judges colluded with the business partners by internalizing their concern with retaining their audience; in addition, Scherman well knew that he had more to gain in the long run if he could vouch for the board's disinterestedness.

During the remainder of the first year, the board chose eight other novels, among them Ellen Glasgow's *The Romantic Comedians*, Edna Ferber's *Show Boat*, Esther Forbes's *O Genteel Lady!*, and Elinor Wylie's *The Orphan Angel*. Canby's remark about Elizabeth Madox Roberts's *The Time of Man* captures the flavor of those early selections (as well as his concerns about holding his audience): he called the novel "not a merely literary, not a 'high-brow' book, though it is certainly literature, and will appeal to the most exacting." Apart from the price factor, the judges predominantly picked fiction because they thought it would have the greatest attraction for readers. As William Zinsser remarked in his in-house history of the club, the mood of those first selections tended to be "poetic; the hand, very often . . . feminine." Those tendencies abated in 1927 with the selection of Lewis's *Elmer Gantry* and O. E. Rolvaag's *Giants in the Earth*. The same year, the selection of *The Heart of Emerson's Journals*, edited by Bliss Perry, demarcated the limits to which Canby's outlook appealed to subscribers: even though Canby promised that the volume made for easier reading than Emerson's essays, members who initially ordered it shipped it back "in carload lots." It was the most serious—and financially disastrous—of the club's early selections. Books by European authors frequently numbered among the choices in the late 1920s: a Galsworthy novel in 1926, H. G. Wells's *Meanwhile* the next year, Shaw's *The Intelligent Woman's Guide to Socialism and Capitalism* the year after, and in 1929 both Remarque's *All Quiet on the Western Front* and Sigrid Undset's *Kristin Lavransdatter*. From the vantage point of the mid-1930s, Scherman termed the latter "the best book our judges have ever selected."[102]

As publishers made nonfiction cheaper to the club and the Depression dampened the mood of the country, the number of novels decreased. The selections for 1931 typify the range of offerings in the early 1930s: they included Frederick Lewis Allen's *Only Yesterday* and Willa Cather's *Shadows on the Rock*, which White and Canby, respectively, had championed, along with James Truslow Adams's *The Epic of America*,

Pearl Buck's *The Good Earth*, and an anthology of *Living Philosophies*. The quality of the books remained high. Allen's and Adams's histories were solid, well researched, lively, and impressive in their relative seriousness. Cather's novel revealed her usual flair for deceptively simple narrative built on meticulously chosen imagery. Buck's book, in Malcolm Cowley's phrase, was "unjustly snooted" when it became a best-seller; as Fisher noted, it displayed the author's considerable skill at character development.[103]

Nonetheless, one has only to recall the writers whose works in the interwar period the club did not select to see how clearly the choices bear the stamp of Canby, Fisher, and Morley's resistance to experiments with form and language and to explorations of the darker side of the human condition. Canby himself, for example, identified Cather's work as part of the "summary literature of the secure and confident nineteenth century." The American "young men" Canby found indicative of "moral anarchy"—Hemingway, Wolfe, Dos Passos—are missing; so are Faulkner, Fitzgerald, Eliot, O'Neill, Sherwood Anderson. Among books by Europeans, as Cowley also pointed out, there is no Joyce, Lawrence, Yeats, or any of the other exponents of the modern tradition. Similarly, the proletarian novels of the 1930s, at least partly informed by a disillusionment with American society, are nowhere on the list. *The Grapes of Wrath*, hardly a radical critique of America, came close, Canby appreciating Steinbeck's essential conservatism, but it failed to appeal to the rest of the board. As for nonfiction, the more provocative and disturbing assessments of American life that appeared in the 1930s—the documentaries of Edmund Wilson and Theodore Dreiser, for example, or the social theory of John Dewey and Thurman Arnold—are glaringly absent, displaced by Canby's premium on balance and order as much as by the difficulty of their prose.[104]

Thus, the quality of the Book-of-the-Month Club's early selections was as mixed as the enterprise as a whole. Yet the historical interest of the venture lies not so much in what subscribers received as in the multiple anxieties and aspirations it both exploited and promised to assuage. To see the club in those terms is to arrive at a fuller understanding of its significance than the term "middlebrow" has heretofore admitted.

CLASSICS
AND
COMMERCIALS

JOHN ERSKINE
AND
"GREAT BOOKS"

In July 1915 Randolph Bourne, who had graduated from Columbia University two years earlier, contributed to the *New Republic* a sketch entitled "The Professor." Part of Bourne's call for a rebellion of youth against the genteel tradition, the essay depicted a figure who supplied his students with knowledge and inspiration but refused to commit himself openly to aesthetic or political judgments. In that tone of subtle, devastating sarcasm of which he was a master, Bourne described his subject's deepest experiences as literary ones, implicitly trivializing them as encounters that had no real consequences. Encapsulated in his study, the professor rejected the "futile babel" of "modern ideas" in favor of that serene, innocent, and, in Bourne's view, desiccated existence that the twentieth century was, he thought, eradicating none too soon.[1]

Bourne's sketch was a veiled portrait of John Erskine, poet, authority on the Elizabethan lyric, and enormously popular member of Columbia's English department. In the aftermath of "The Professor" episode,

Bourne confessed to having grown "a little bashful about visiting Columbia in the daytime" while "mine ancient enemy" was "on the warpath." The following year, however, he did not hesitate to attack Erskine in a vituperative exchange of letters, at the end of which Bourne made clear the function Erskine played for him: "I am not unconscious," he wrote, "of the way I destroy the amenities of life when I have any bearing towards you. But this is only because of my need for a personal symbol for my intellectual bêtes noires. . . . I am quite sure that I perform this same office in a limited way for you."[2]

Yet, however useful Bourne found Erskine as a foil, his analysis of him was wrong on two counts. Despite Bourne's insistence that Erskine's way of life was dying, it was the teacher, rather than his student, who remained in the public eye for the next thirty years. In the era of World War I, Erskine proposed the first full-scale "great books" curriculum to the Columbia faculty; in the 1920s he not only implemented that curriculum but became a best-selling novelist, star of the lecture circuit, and president of the Juilliard School of Music. By the mid-1940s he had somewhat faded from sight but was not nearly as obscure as Bourne, whose death in 1918 had erased him from the memories of almost everyone but the avant-garde. More important, Erskine was not the stereotype of gentility Bourne imagined but rather, like Stuart Sherman, a figure whose Arnoldian commitments competed with a desire for self-expression and experience. Incapable of going as far as Sherman in renouncing prescriptions for character, he was less comfortably ensconced in the genteel tradition than Canby or Fisher. As such, his career adds a particularly rich biographical dimension to the effort to elucidate the middlebrow perspective.

A Genteel Childhood

Born in 1879, Erskine was actually only seven years senior to Bourne. He lived in New York until he was five but spent the rest of his youth in Weehawken, New Jersey. His father, James Morrison Erskine, a scholarly man with a fondness for history and music, owned a silk factory that turned out decorative ribbons; his mother, Eliza Jane Hollingsworth Erskine, bore six children and ran the household. The genteel loyalties Bourne pilloried had their genesis in Erskine's upbringing. In

terms of manners, his family preserved a set of rituals—morning recitations, afternoon study sessions, dressing for dinner, formal meal-
time etiquette, piano recitals in the living room on leisurely afternoons—that bespoke the esteem in which it held both refinement and
decorum. As a young boy, Erskine absorbed from his father and his
"fastidious," well-read uncle William Hollingsworth the lesson that to
attain culture meant to "know good books." On Sundays Erskine and
his siblings attended Episcopal services at Grace Church, which his
father had helped to found. In his autobiography, *The Memory of
Certain Persons* (1947), he contrasted his own religious encounters with
those some of his contemporaries had recorded: whereas it was "the
fashion for American writers to describe their early contacts with
religion as intellectually stultifying and spiritually depressing," his
were "stimulating and happy." Socially, the Erskines were firmly allied
with groups accustomed to enjoying prestige and exercising leadership
in matters of taste. (In that way, his childhood was strikingly similar in
atmosphere to Henry Seidel Canby's among the old Quaker families of
Wilmington.) The Erskines' Weehawken neighbors, lined up in large
estates along the palisades, had ties to the inhabitants of the mansions
farther up the Hudson; their houses, decorated with walnut and marble, expressed their economic power. While Erskine's home and income
were somewhat more modest, he nonetheless identified his boyhood
surroundings as "aristocratic."[3]

For Erskine (as for Canby), that milieu had a number of positive
aspects. Erskine's account of his first years conveys an ineffable feeling
of belonging, of comforting stability. His aunts and uncles, for example,
including two of his mother's sisters who lived with the Erskines, were
always known by the babyish names the children had bestowed on
them, as if to enshrine within the family circle the innocence and child-
centeredness that financial security and social position permitted. The
family's daily routine and its immersion in religion buttressed his sense
of permanence. Erskine's father often told him that the beautiful and
gracious neighborhoods of the Weehawken wealthy would "always contain the homes of those who like quiet and solitude"—that, in other
words, those like the Erskines would endure against threats to their
preeminence.[4] Moreover, Erskine's father initially personified the positive features of genteel self-reliance. As a man "affectionate but slightly

reserved, always balanced and self-controlled," he seemed to embody substance and strength.[5]

By the late nineteenth century, however, it was clear that James Erskine's pronouncement about Weehawken was more wishful than prophetic. As Erskine recognized even as a child, the street on which he lived not only divided his township from the adjoining one of Union Hill but also demarcated the boundary between gentility and modern industrial America. Union Hill contained his father's factory, along with breweries and other mills; it was where the immigrants who worked for the elder Erskine lived. Before 1892 Erskine remained largely in the shelter of the past. "Perhaps the influence of all the Weehawken memories," he acknowledged, "kept me for years from observing real life, from seeing the America of the moment, which foretold the future."[6] That year, though, elements of "real life" became inescapable. In the mid-1880s James Erskine had invested in a second factory in central New York. In the economic downturn of the early 1890s, the venture proved a liability. Furthermore, changing fashions were eliminating the market for crafted ribbons and sashes. James Erskine's reaction was to pour money into the company, on the theory that his reversals were only temporary. Instead, he gradually spent most of his assets.[7]

As a witness, in adolescence, to his father's decline, Erskine acquired an impression of the human cost of commerce that cemented his allegiance to the genteel stance of alienation from the marketplace. In particular, James Erskine's predicament illustrated the fate of aesthetic impulses in the new industrial order. As Erskine explained retrospectively, "It was the artist in him who had succeeded, and when art was no longer desired in the business, he was through." Additionally, there is some evidence that Erskine connected the incursions of industrialization with the demands of women. The point is hard to document because, in his memoirs, he explicitly presented women as objects of adoration, recounting Eliza Hollingsworth Erskine's appearance at the dinner hour dressed in "flawless white" and reporting as his earliest recollection a visit to a dairy where women workers in "cool clean dresses" furnished pails of warm milk. Nevertheless, Erskine noted that his mother, the more "practical" of his parents, did not approve of his father's insistence on pursuing his artistic inclinations. In light of that disagreement about what Erskine himself called "matters of such consequence," his cameo of his mother appears retouched, as if he needed to idealize her in order to avoid acknowledging the extent to which she contributed to his father's unhappiness.[8] In any case, by the 1890s James Erskine was less a representative of genteel self-reliance than of the sensitive misfits Van Wyck Brooks portrayed as victims of the "catchpenny realities" of American capitalism.[9] The balance and self-control he displayed, it appears, hid the fact that the defeats and disappointments of business had driven his energies inward, disrupting the correspondence between outward behavior and inner self.

Yet, in the world of Erskine's childhood, that discontinuity could also arise from a different source: the genteel tradition itself. More was involved than the imposition of parlor morality Brooks especially decried. The "dignified distance between himself and others" which, in Stow Persons's words, the gentleman "scrupulously preserved" could eventuate in a debilitating isolation.[10] In an atmosphere which rewarded conformity, restraint might turn into the stifling of feeling, refinement into a retreat from creative instincts. William Hollingsworth, a man successful in business but bored and miserable because of the compliance he was expected to exhibit, epitomized the consequences of those possibilities. In language that recalls descriptions of Stuart Sherman's distance and volatility, his young nephew remarked that his "iron self-control" seemed to conceal "a furnace or boiler, which might blow up at any minute." Although it is difficult to say how much Erskine as a child ascribed his uncle's turbulence to the genteel tradition gone sour—it is in the nature of repression, after all, to keep such perceptions buried—William Hollingsworth's uneasy combination of courtliness and rebellion was a portent of his own development. "If I introduce him here at length," he apologized in *The Memory of Certain Persons*, "it is because he influenced me greatly, and in some corners of my heart I need him to explain myself."[11]

Moreover, Erskine seems to have formed early on an incipient notion that women were at least exempt from, if not responsible for, the damages that gentility, as well as business pressures, could inflict on the self. His mother and aunt hovered over William Hollingsworth, worrying about his aversion to things "too safe to be interesting." At the same time, they appeared to Erskine as models of self-actualization. Whereas the men around him smoldered with emotional potential, Eliza Hollingsworth Erskine ignited: "She was an explosive reservoir of force—and of fun."[12] One episode in particular, one may speculate, must have intensified a sense that women were the unscathed perpetrators of a genteel attempt to hamper creativity. In 1898 Erskine's piano teacher announced that he had nothing more to teach his pupil and that a great musical career awaited him if his parents would send him to study in Europe. The thought of her son as a musician was more than his mother's conventional nature could bear, and she refused. "I think I would have been a composer," Erskine wistfully wrote of the incident.[13] That decision, which, transmuted by denial, may have contributed toward his presentation of his mother as "flawless," left an aftertaste of bitterness toward women that one can detect in Erskine's writing forty years later.

Student and Teacher

Neither the challenge to genteel values the business world posed from without nor the capacity of those values to self-destruct from within, however, prevented Erskine from initially securing an education dedicated to instilling the liberal culture which marked the refined sensibility. His father sent him to Columbia Grammar School, where the idea of preparing students for "life" had not yet dislodged the nineteenth-century practice of preparing them for college by drilling them in Greek and Latin.[14] Nonetheless, the pursuit of liberal culture was growing more problematic at the school's parent institution. The rise of specialization had divided the Columbia College faculty since the late 1880s, setting the "university party" against the advocates of the liberal arts. By the time Erskine enrolled as a freshman in 1896, the specialists were in the majority, although the conflict between the two factions remained muted in the sense that the humanists continued to teach according to their point of view while their adversaries made policies in spite of them. There were enclaves, within certain departments, of genteel culture, untouched by new currents and expectations. But no one at Columbia during Erskine's undergraduate years could have failed to recognize the embattled position of those enclaves, even if, as Lionel Trilling suggested, the students on the whole were not very concerned with the college's long-range fortunes.[15] For Erskine, Columbia encompassed—and did not resolve—the dichotomy between Weehawken and Union Hill. Although not precisely the same thing, the contest between liberal study and specialization was a close enough variant of the tension between art and business as to make Columbia a stage for the second act of the drama he had begun witnessing at home.

Erskine first responded by gravitating toward the traditionalists. The composer and pianist Edward MacDowell occupied a special place in his affections. In actuality, Erskine's musical development, already thwarted by his mother, foundered under MacDowell's tutelage when MacDowell pronounced him a "good craftsman" rather than a "special talent." Yet the musician's devotion to creative expression for its own sake, without regard for either academic tradition or financial reward, made him seem the embodiment of "something ideal" and increasingly rare in the Columbia community. In that respect, MacDowell was a counterexample to James Erskine and William Hollingsworth. Erskine's description of him as an "authentic spirit" referred not only to the genuineness of his musical gifts but also to the consonance between his conduct and his nature. In the 1890s, when the mental illness that was to dominate MacDowell's last years was not much in evidence, and when his dealings with the Columbia administration were relatively untroubled, he appeared the picture not only of "energy and health" but also of self-reliance.[16]

The same qualities marked George Edward Woodberry, the poet and professor of literature to whom Erskine turned in his junior year when he began retreating from music. The greatest single influence on Erskine's career, Woodberry was born in Beverly, Massachusetts, in 1855. As a youth, he attended Emerson's last lecture and catalogued James Russell Lowell's library; in the same period, he studied at Harvard with Henry Adams and Charles Eliot Norton. Although his relations to the genteel tradition are more complex than that lineage suggests—for example, he wrote a disaffected essay on Bayard Taylor's verse—his critical categories derived essentially from Arnoldian and transcendentalist influences. Like MacDowell, Woodberry was an idealist, but in his case the term denoted a specific outlook as well as a dedication to principle: it referred to his conviction that the function of art was to illuminate the realm of the soul, which he conceived of as the primal, divine beauty common to all.[17]

In 1891, upon the recommendation of Lowell and Norton, Woodberry became a member of the English department at Columbia. From that position, he reassuringly addressed the dislocations of the late nineteenth century. For example, his lectures made the continuity of human nature the basis for literary understanding. Readers, Woodberry explained, profited most by examining literature in light of their own experience—experience which they shared with all people throughout history. In the face of ethnic diversity, class conflict, and anomie, Woodberry saw books as means of attaining what he called "the community of the soul."[18] Moreover, Woodberry's *Heart of Man*, which Erskine said "stirred" and "startled" the campus when it appeared in 1899, identified idealism as an instrument of intellectual order. The detection of universal laws and essential commonalities, Woodberry argued, organized the disparate and unsettling information that realism and science provided about the human condition. His own stance as a generalist within the university held the line against the danger that specialists would reduce knowledge to splinters, destroying faith and meaning.[19]

Woodberry's insistence that, instead of analyzing sources and symbols, individuals appropriate literature to foster "growth" and "self-development" freighted reading with a greater therapeutic function than his mentors assigned it. "Personality," he declared, "is the genius of life." Furthermore, Woodberry occasionally devalued aesthetic training in favor of business priorities. "Life is not long enough," he announced, for anyone "much occupied with many affairs" to read Shakespeare in a scholarly fashion. Similarly, his antirational bias—his democratically inspired claim that the "safest guide" to books was "the reader's instinct"—deviated from Arnoldian standards and severed the connections among cultivation, morality, and discipline.[20]

Yet, despite some kinship to modern advertisers and self-help crusaders, Woodberry largely rejected the therapeutic worldview. He commended reading not for the sake of building a malleable, other-directed self but rather to stir the "thousand susceptibilities" of the cultivated man that "never pass from his consciousness outward but are shut in his own silent world."[21] More important, Woodberry's conduct and temperament militate against the temptation to see him as primarily a purveyor of therapy in the guise of criticism. Sensitive and unworldly (Ferris Greenslet remarked that "his only outdoor sport was daydreaming"), Woodberry suggested by his visible rejection of efficiency, pragmatism, and skepticism the persistence of a romantic, confident cast of mind. Furthermore, his own life seemed to belie the need for a rehabilitation of the self. In Erskine's view, Woodberry's outstanding characteristic was unity—between belief and behavior, work and spirit. "He was the first teacher," Erskine remembered, "from whom I got the notion that the public life of the citizen is important as an expression . . . of his private aspirations, and that the business enterprises of a country cannot in the long run be separated from its essential religious or spiritual faith. Having learned from him that poetry is the flower of life but still an integral part of it, we went on to learn that all human activities are related, and—unless one is stupid or a hypocrite— must be harmonious." Erskine had seen, in his father's and uncle's cases, examples of the failure to join "business enterprises" with "spiritual faith." To be one of Woodberry's "boys" was to discover a second father, one who vindicated and realized the aspirations of the first.[22]

Woodberry's insistence on spirituality could be dismissed as tenderminded: William James observed of *Heart of Man* that the book lacked "that which our generation seems to need, the sudden word, the unmediated transition, the flash of perception that makes reasonings unnecessary."[23] For all his language about experience, Woodberry used the term as Emerson did when, in his essay of that title, he shunned "sensation" in favor of the "temperate zone . . . of thought, of spirit, of poetry." Seconding Emerson's remark that he was "content with knowing" rather than doing, Woodberry remained a poet and scholar whose encounters were mainly of the literary variety that Bourne disparaged.[24] Yet it was precisely its remoteness from a troubling present— its uncurdled gentility—that made Woodberry's outlook initially congenial to Erskine's social background, psychological requirements, and academic interests. "For boyhood," Erskine wrote (and he might have added "of a certain class and sensitivity"), "it was a thrilling vision, and in its power many who sat in Woodberry's classes have tried to live."[25]

In 1900 Erskine enrolled in the Columbia Graduate School to continue his work in English under Woodberry's direction.[26] At the same time, he began to build a reputation as a poet: Richard Watson Gilder selected Erskine's "Actaeon" as the winning entry in the *Century* magazine's 1901 poetry competition for recent college graduates. The reception of the poem, which perpetuated a vision of ideal beauty, reassuringly attested to the continuing power of Woodberry's philosophy. Similarly, Erskine's graduate training reinforced his conviction that a teaching career patterned on Woodberry's example offered a way of resisting the subordination of art to practicality. Although specialization had already placed Woodberry and his followers on the defensive, the appeal of idealism and the strength of Woodberry's popularity allowed Erskine to ignore that fact. It was as if, having conceded that his father's predicament signaled the demise of genteel culture in America at large, he turned with heightened urgency to the shelter of the university and, for a time, found what he was seeking.

Events at Columbia, however, soon challenged that institution's status as a refuge. The inauguration of Nicholas Murray Butler as president in 1902 entrenched the viewpoint of the "university" party. Butler represented everything that Woodberry was not: in place of reflective spirituality, he offered decisiveness and commitment to action. Woodberry's own circumstances were beclouded by an increasingly bitter relationship with his worldly, cynical colleague Brander Matthews. The feud between the two was more a matter of personal animosity than substantive disagreement, but whenever it spilled over into academic concerns, Butler favored Matthews. As a result, Woodberry came more and more to feel out of place at Columbia.[27]

Erskine regarded Woodberry's situation with mixed emotions; in fact, his remarks about his state of mind during 1902 and 1903 constitute a rare explicit reference to psychic conflict. Although his identification of Butler as a "supreme humanist" in "his own way" seems calculated to placate Butler (still living at the time *The Memory of Certain Persons* appeared), his subsequent expressions of confusion have a more genuine ring: "Our University would grow, its graduates would be legion, its endowment would become fabulous, its degrees would be well thought-of—but would it produce great personalities? Would there be a place on its staff for original minds? . . . On the other hand, is idealism really incompatible with practical sense? Why should not a poet like Woodberry be a man of action, competent in daily affairs? These questions, posed by swift changes at Columbia, filled my head almost as much as my studies."[28] Yet, despite such reservations, Erskine left graduate school with his image of himself as Woodberry's disciple intact. Appointed assistant professor of English at Amherst in 1903, he took up his teaching duties with the expectation that, regardless of the disturbing tendencies at Columbia, idealism would flourish in the atmosphere of the liberal arts college. The same year, he published a study of the Elizabethan lyric.

While on leave in 1904, Woodberry resigned from Columbia; a few months later MacDowell did the same, having clashed with Butler over the reorganization of the music department. Far from questioning the merits of Woodberry's case, Erskine responded to the turn of events at Columbia by helping to have Woodberry appointed a guest lecturer at Amherst for the spring of 1905, in the hope that he would stay permanently. Woodberry himself slipped into the pessimism that would characterize him until his death in 1930. As if he had awakened to the truth of James's observation, he felt increasingly at odds with the contemporary distaste for "the finer things" and depressed that he had been "passed by."[29] For Erskine, however, Woodberry's pedagogical premises remained inspiring. To his students (Bruce Barton among them), he stressed the connections between literature and life. Writing to his friend Melville Cane of his success, Erskine noted with pride, "I think you will see that I have something of a Woodberrian hold on the boys now; my work is extremely happy."[30]

Nevertheless, Erskine's cheerful identification with Woodberry masked anxieties which made his Amherst years psychologically turbulent ones. The immediate source of the turmoil was his uncertainty about his future as a poet. Henry Morton Robinson, a student of Erskine's in the 1920s and his most astute biographer, observed that reservations about his ability to meet the standard he had set in "Actaeon" began to plague Erskine after 1906. Although he eventually brought out two more volumes, self-doubt propelled him toward teaching and scholarship. Yet the crisis went deeper. As Robinson noted, Erskine's turn away from poetry resulted less from a considered judgment about his talents than from a reluctance fully to exercise his "poetic powers," as if to do so would invite an uncontrollable and isolating self-absorption. His declaration in 1907 that he would write not "for the pleasure of self-expression" but as a means of reaching "the largest possible audience" might be seen not only as a reflection of his Arnoldian sympathies but also as a flight from experience—that is, from the potentially painful unleashing of his emotions. Instead, on the one hand, Erskine remained wedded to the need for self-control shaped by his genteel upbringing. A less exuberant letter to Cane expressing the faith that it was not "unmanly" to pray for a "wise and an understanding heart" in order to "solve our own tangles" similarly revealed the power of the values with which he had been raised.[31]

Yet, on the other hand, his frustrations as a poet led him to reassess Woodberry's wraithlike spirituality. Unable, this time, to suppress the doubts he had first entertained as a graduate student, he seems to have admitted the possibility, in James's words, that "poor Woodberry" was "so high, so true, so good" yet ultimately "so ineffective."[32] His decision about his audience—which he implemented by lecturing to local women's clubs and students at Smith College—can also be read as a clue that Erskine hungered for *more* experience than Woodberry's contemplative pose provided. The same can be said of his resolve to make scholarship "creative." The social and intellectual aspects of his life in Amherst, moreover, fueled his dissatisfaction. The insular nature of a "country college" thwarted his cosmopolitan impulses; the white gloves and parlor conversation at faculty teas, while they added grace and charm to the Amherst social scene, sometimes seemed oppressive and even ridiculous. Furthermore, Amherst professors, for the most part, had few ambitions to publish research and resented anyone who did.[33] Interested in building a reputation as a scholar and concerned (if ambivalent) about being a "man of action," Erskine developed during his stint at Amherst a tension about his vocation and his genteel loyalties reminiscent of William Hollingsworth's restlessness—a tension that would reappear throughout the rest of his career. Although his writings from the period permit only speculation and inference, he appears to have broadened the questions he had formulated with respect to the future of Columbia: How could one preserve the unity Woodberry exemplified and be a "man of action" at the same time? How could one escape repression and plunge into the life that lay beyond the printed page without succumbing to the fragmentation that threatened to accompany the relinquishment of self-control?

Those dilemmas gave Erskine an affinity not only with Sherman but also—although both men would have shuddered at the comparison—with Bourne. Moreover, they were similar to the "longings for reintegrated selfhood and intense experience" Lears has described as rampant in late-nineteenth- and early-twentieth-century America.[34] Yet, although Erskine, like Sherman, resembled the antimodernists Lears has identified, he never made a thoroughgoing rejection of genteel values a prerequisite, as they did, for discovering an authentic self. Furthermore, he failed to join Bourne in attaching the search for experience to radical politics and only flirted with the prospect of therapeutic release. Erskine's way was different: to perpetuate the genteel tradition while accommodating his yearnings for freedom from restraint and control.

An invitation in 1909 to return to Columbia as associate professor in the English department promised to assuage some of Erskine's more tangible discontents. If going back to Columbia meant dealing with Butler, it also meant serving on a faculty with James Harvey Robinson, Charles Beard, John Dewey, and other distinguished scholars who made the institution in the pre–World War I period a center of extraordinary intellectual vitality. It offered as well virtually unlimited chances to extend the university's tradition of involvement with audiences outside its walls.[35]

At the height of his powers as a teacher, Erskine dazzled the Columbia undergraduates who flocked to his course on Elizabethan literature. Students like Lloyd Morris, Alfred Knopf, and Dixon Ryan Fox responded to his enthusiasm, erudition, and wit; they marveled at his analytical facility and wide-ranging interests. Yet Morris's description of him in this period suggests that Columbia could not, after all, provide Erskine with easy answers to the questions with which he seems to have grappled at Amherst. If Erskine was brilliant and dynamic in the classroom, Morris noted that he exhibited as well a reticence and detachment which some interpreted as arrogance. "The professor would have been surprised, possibly displeased," Morris remembered, "to learn how thoroughly his students discussed him; how much he puzzled and attracted them; how often he was debated in fraternity houses, at lunch counters, or over nocturnal beers in Morningside saloons." Morris's observation might be chalked up simply to student curiosity were it not for its kinship with Erskine's own regretful portraits of his father and uncle—and its contrast with his admiring depiction of Woodberry. Erskine's "aloofness" and enigmatic formality, which Bourne misinterpreted as the ivory tower intellectual's willful and conscious withdrawal from political commitment, appear instead emblems of a divided sensibility; they hint that Erskine still contended with the difficulty of giving play to his desire for engagement without forfeiting self-reliance.[36] Erskine's marriage in 1910 to Pauline Ives, a conservative, duty-bound woman of high principle and little spontaneity with whom he was increasingly unhappy, pulled him back toward genteel repression, no doubt contributing to his distant manner.[37]

Erskine's most important essay from this period, "The Moral Obligation to be Intelligent" (1913), may be interpreted, on one level, as a translation of his personal struggles into philosophical terms. His argument, on the surface, was a plea for the consideration of intelligence as a virtue along with character and goodness.[38] Erskine understood his position as an attack on conventional morality, a substitution of new virtues for "obsolete" ones. In some respects, Erskine's view of himself as iconoclast was correct. In particular, although there is no evidence that he had anything more than a passing acquaintance with his colleague John Dewey, there are marked similarities between Erskine's outlook and the challenge pragmatism was then posing to idealist philosophy: the parts of "The Moral Obligation to be Intelligent" that deplore absolute definitions of good and evil and advocate attention to an action's consequences read like a pragmatist manifesto.

Nevertheless, as Lloyd Morris pointed out, the function of intelligence, as Erskine saw it, was "to dominate experience," to harness it in order to direct activity to ideal ends. Unwilling, like the pragmatists, to follow ideas wherever they might lead without prejudging their value, Erskine conceived of intelligence as a way of creating the same situation Woodberry had promised to foster: "the infinite order, wherein man, when he enters it, shall find himself." Despite his determination to break with the past, it was the "modern world," rather than the "old" one, that, in Erskine's terms, had "got into a kind of prison." The "key to the lock," it turned out, was to substitute intelligence for character within the familiar Emersonian framework of self-reliance and "moral obligation."[39] Thus, the essay neatly juggled freedom and control, while simultaneously invoking and rejecting genteel understandings.

"A Feeling of Peace All the Time"

Erskine's response to World War I, however, revealed the continuing lure of undomesticated experience in his own life. His involvement came on the civilian side, and when the end of the war was in view.

Early in 1918, under the joint auspices of the YMCA and the army, he sailed for France to help design an educational program for American military personnel who would soon be demobilized. Assigned to *foyers* at the French front until the postwar planning could begin, he encountered firsthand the mud and the dampness of the trenches. Once he saw a nearly headless corpse dangling from an ambulance. After a few months, he moved to Paris and assumed charge of the planning commission. The following spring, having overseen the placement of American soldiers in French and British universities, he became educational director of the American University at Beaune. Within weeks, Erskine and his staff had transformed the hospital grounds there into a campus complete with a cadre of deans and streets named in honor of American colleges. The size and scope of the operation were impressive: at one point, there were close to ten thousand registered students, taught by almost eight hundred faculty members. Although several accounts have indicated that the curriculum at Beaune consisted of reading "great books," Erskine recalled that in fact the course offerings were traditional and widely varied, ranging from law to painting.[40]

Erskine reacted to his wartime activities in ways that reveal they meant more to him than simply the chance to serve the causes of education and patriotism. Until his death in 1951, he displayed pictures of the American University on the walls of his apartment and kept a folio of Beaune photographs close at hand. "Again and again," his second wife, Helen Worden, recalled, she and Erskine "looked at them together and as we looked, he described every detail of his exciting months" there. During his final illness, he made a nostalgic pilgrimage to the site of the campus, a journey he had talked about with Worden from the first day she met him. His treatment of the war occupies a radically disproportionate part of his autobiography, relegating his postwar years of public prominence to minor status in the narrative.[41] The tenaciousness of Erskine's memories—the way he sought to recapture and perpetuate them in a barrage of words and in his actions— argues that he derived from wartime service satisfactions that eluded him at other points in his life.

His letters from the front imply what those satisfactions were. Contrasting the taxing work he was doing with the "petty world" of Amherst and the prospect of "frittering myself away on small things" when he returned to Columbia, Erskine wrote his ailing mother in the spring of 1919, "I have sacrificed more in this war, I think, than some of the princes who have lost their thrones." In another letter to her, he averred, "If you were here for five minutes, you would see that this work is the moral and intellectual salvation of thousands of boys— hundreds of thousands." Constrained in those documents by his guilty awareness that his mother wanted him to return home, Erskine repeatedly proclaimed his desire only to be at her bedside. To his sister Rhoda, however, he was more candid: "The work here is enormous," he admitted. "I shall miss it if I go back."[42]

Such comments suggest that, for Erskine, World War I provided a version of the strenuous life: it was exhausting, debilitating, horrifying—yet more exhilarating than anything he had ever done before. Although Bourne actually could not have had Erskine in mind when he published his famous "The War and the Intellectuals" (1917), because Erskine had not yet joined the war effort, Bourne's description of the way the fighting assuaged the "craving for action" besetting university professors and "practitioners of literature" precisely matches Erskine's response to the conflict. Restless at Amherst, distant at Columbia, he found war a vehicle, in Bourne's phrase, for "doing something aggressive, colossal."[43] As Worden recalled, "He often said that his first trip to France in 1917 [sic] was a subconscious liberation. . . . How often he said, 'Remember to live! Be the active participant, not the onlooker!' . . . He preferred the Front. He said he found there the peace of decision, the calm that comes when you've made up your mind, when there is no turning back, when the die is cast." Nine years after the fact, a *New Yorker* profile similarly noted that the "qualities of swift and fervent living" he encountered with the army meant that "the professor in the war had a simply magnificent time." Erskine's remark in a letter home that, surrounded by war, he "had a feeling of peace all the time" corroborates the point.[44]

If he exemplified Bourne's liberated intellectual, however, his references to sacrifice make clear that he discovered in war a way of abandoning self-control that could be justified in terms of ideals of duty and self-discipline. As such, it furnished an escape from genteel repression under cover of genteel rhetoric. It was that comforting combination, one suspects, that fully accounted for Erskine's sense of peace. Similarly, his comment in his autobiography that the war passed "like a dream" encompassed several meanings: it connoted the serenity

Bourne had in mind as well as the tranquillity Erskine ascribed to Woodberry; it was both a fantasy of unity between thought and behavior and the gratification of Erskine's desire for a more intense reality.[45]

Encouraged by the students' successes at Beaune, Erskine proposed a postwar continuation of the American University in the form of a mandatory national training program run by the army for eighteen-year-old men. Explicitly, he billed the idea as a mechanism for insuring that citizens (he especially meant immigrants) receive the vocational and liberal arts instruction necessary to maintain democracy; implicitly, he addressed his own problem of vocation, envisioning a kind of educational equivalent of war which extended to peacetime the vital role he had enjoyed in France. In fact, however, his "dream" ended with the demobilization. Although his correspondence from Beaune reveals some uncertainty about whether he would actually return to Columbia, he resumed his duties in the fall of 1919 and was soon caught up in the same routines—and the same controversies—that had absorbed him before his departure.[46]

"Great Books" as Curriculum and Ideology

In particular, Erskine tackled with renewed energy an issue which he had presented to the Columbia faculty in 1916, but about which he had begun thinking as early as 1908: the problematic relationship between American civilization and the tradition of classical and European thought. Arising out of curricular concerns, this preoccupation, in its narrowest formulation, eventuated in the central achievement of his academic career, the design of an undergraduate course devoted to the study of "great books." Yet because Erskine, for over twenty years, sought through magazines and the lecture circuit an off-campus forum for many of the same ideas he articulated at Columbia, it is possible to speak more broadly as well of a "great books" ideology that Erskine propounded both within and outside of the college classroom.

As curricular reform, Erskine's "great books" proposal was a response to the widespread conviction among his contemporaries in English departments throughout the country that current undergraduates, in contrast to their predecessors, were woefully ignorant of

Western literature. In an article he wrote while still at Amherst, Erskine, reflecting Woodberry's influence, argued that the way to arrest the perceived decline was to devise courses that approached texts on their own terms, unencumbered by the baggage of scholarship and criticism. Noting that all books enshrined as "great" were at one time recent publications intended for wide audiences, Erskine urged professors of English to continue to treat them as such.[47] In fact, it was a work's susceptibility to reinterpretation by diverse readers—its capacity to function as a "mirror" of variable circumstances—that constituted Erskine's principal test of "greatness." As he put it in one of his later writings that carried his outlook beyond academia, *The Delight of Great Books* (1927), "The great books are those which . . . surprise us by remaining true even when our point of view changes. This is why we rank Homer and Virgil and Dante, Shakespeare, Chaucer, Cervantes, and Moliere so high—because they still say so much, even to peoples of an altogether foreign culture, a different past, an opposed philosophy." Such resilience, as Erskine saw it, enabled students to find joy and meaning in literature, provided their teachers would allow them simply to relate it to their own lives. Given that opportunity, they would emerge from college equipped with what "a [gentleman] should know of the recognized branches of knowledge and of the masterpieces . . . without which no education could be considered complete."[48]

To facilitate such an education, Erskine devised a list of around seventy-five works deemed "best" because they dealt with enduring human dilemmas or types. These he proposed students read in a course spanning two years. As Graff has pointed out, Erskine's "great books" curriculum was neither the first one in the United States nor solely his own invention. Nevertheless, he supplied a rationale, a system, a scope, and a commitment that distinguished his effort from its less formalized antecedents.[49] His syllabus concentrated on the Greeks in the first half-year, moving on to the Romans and Aquinas in the second semester. The third and fourth terms ranged over European history, literature, and philosophy, encompassing, among many others, Dante, Shakespeare, Voltaire, Milton, Goethe, Descartes, Mill, and Kant. Erskine's list was an obvious instance of the way in which the process of canon formation—as literary scholars have now made clear—has functioned to exclude writers who were not white males in the Western tradition. There were no women, black, or non-Western authors on the list. What is more, there were only four Americans: Josiah Royce, Santayana, William James, and Henry George. In addition, Erskine's canon entirely ignored literary modernism, although Erskine would have replied that it was premature to include such writers as Strindberg, Conrad, or Henry James.[50]

Yet the current interest in displaying those biases in the content of the "great books" program has obscured important features of its structure. Erskine's idea radically challenged a number of existing pedagogical practices. University English departments in the early twentieth century typically offered a sequence of courses organized mainly by period: a year on the Elizabethans, another on the eighteenth century, one or two more on the nineteenth century. Shakespeare usually merited separate study, and courses based on literary genres— the novel, the drama—provided alternative frameworks, but the limited focus prevailed. The standard mode of presentation was the lecture. Readings consisted exclusively of those by British and American authors, on the grounds that translations cheapened works to the point of worthlessness.[51] Even where philology competed with literary history, biography, and bibliography, the curriculum reflected the trend toward specialization, casting the professor as unveiler of linguistic mysteries, sharpening the divisions among English, foreign, and Greek and Latin texts, rewarding the acquisition of information, and discouraging the enrollment of students from other disciplines.

Erskine's sweeping survey, by contrast, implicitly legitimized the generalist. In its earliest version, his plan established similar, concurrent courses in history, philosophy, and scientific ideas. His syllabus for the first three of those courses (which he eventually modified but did not fundamentally alter) dismissed historical exegesis and philology as irrelevant, attempted interdisciplinary synthesis, cut across time and place, and accommodated translations. The format he devised was equally innovative. Although he at first retained a conventional schedule of biweekly lectures, Erskine subsequently called for small discussion groups meeting once a week under the guidance of two instructors, with each session focused on a different book. Moreover, the instructors were assigned Socratic roles: they were "not to lecture nor in any way to behave like professors" but only to keep ideas flowing by asking questions and prompting debate. In what would subsequently appear an odd convergence, given the animus between John Dewey and later

proponents of the "great books" idea, that directive resembled Deweyite pronouncements about the student-centered curriculum. In addition, Erskine suggested that the course be open to all juniors and
seniors and required for those who had not selected a major, on the
assumption that there was a body of writing with which every recipient
of a bachelor's degree ought to be acquainted.[52] Those latter two stipulations amounted to a frontal attack on the ethos of specialization,
assailing as they did its exemplar, the professorial expert, and its
curricular embodiment, the elective system.

Thus, while Richard Brodhead has observed that, at least in the case
of American literature, the promulgators of the canon in the early
twentieth century worked to "underwrite their own new cultural authority" by selecting texts so difficult as to require "expert assistance," the original "great books" ideology was predicated on precisely
the opposite idea.[53] No doubt sensing that threat to their power, many
of Erskine's colleagues objected to his plan when it came before them
for debate late in 1916. Arguing that Erskine's curriculum would perpetuate superficiality at the expense of "true scholarship," they fore-
saw the sacrifice of "real understanding" as students galloped through
the material. In addition, they were justifiably skeptical about the
merits of reading in an intellectual and historical vacuum. The faculty
nonetheless approved Erskine's scheme in principle in February 1917
but was diverted from instituting it by American entry into the war.
When Erskine left for France, the matter was in abeyance, and, by his
account, opposition persisted.[54]

In the long run, however, the war proved a boon to Erskine's campaign. Complying with a directive from the army, Columbia established
an interdisciplinary course on "War Issues" to serve student recruits.
That course in turn inspired the creation in 1919 of one devoted to "peace
issues," or, as it became known, "Contemporary Civilization." Entail-
ing discussion groups akin to those Erskine had advocated, it drew
together faculty from diverse areas in the social sciences. More important, it acknowledged the college's responsibility to furnish its undergraduates with a thorough grounding in the liberal arts. Thus, in terms
of organization and purpose, it smoothed the way for the sort of generalist venture Erskine had in mind. What is more, the sense that the war
had imperiled the heritage of the West and revealed the human capacity
for evil made educators wonder, as one of them wrote, "whether colleges

actually did make students more fit to live the life of thoughtful and effective citizens" and "to enjoy the fruits of the [human] spirit."[55]

Hence, when Erskine renewed his request to act on his idea, it was in a climate modified by precedent and enough of a change in atmosphere to win him the necessary permission. Offered in 1920 as, ironically, an elective under the rubric "General Honors," and telescoped into a single interdisciplinary seminar, the course otherwise followed Erskine's design for the next nine years. In 1934, after a brief hiatus, it was reconstituted as "Colloquium on Important Books" and offered in that form well into the 1950s. Drawing once more on Erskine's innovation, Columbia also created a lower-level humanities course in 1937 which still survives today. As is well known, other institutions, notably the University of Chicago, Harvard, and Yale, subsequently devised similar programs in "General Education"—sometimes claiming to have invented them—but Erskine's role in preparing the ground for those efforts is indisputable.[56]

As an ideology of reading, Erskine's approach to "great books" moved beyond pedagogy and curriculum to address both his own emotional requirements and the priorities of an expanding consumer culture. Most significant, perhaps, Erskine's modification of Woodberry's outlook increased the extent to which reading the classics became an instrument of self-creation, by means that might be described as both centripetal and centrifugal. That is, on the one hand, Erskine's approach drew in toward individual readers abilities and prerogatives that threatened to drift away from their control. In much the same way Sherman's reportorial stance reassigned authority from critic to audience, the primacy Erskine accorded the encounter with the text affirmed the ordinary person's capacity to understand literature. His basic message, like Woodberry's, was to trust one's own responses, or, as he put it in an unpublished manuscript that was to have introduced an "Outline of Great Books," to "get yourself a comfortable chair and a good light—and have confidence in your own mind." In a situation "unmediated" by expertise, to borrow William James's word, readers would release their "zest" and "energy," qualities which would transform literary interpretation from a passive, mechanical process into one that was "human, natural, and direct." Thus, they would obtain "training in the acquisition of experience."[57] Those phrases, too, bolstered the self by arrogating more power to the individual.

On the other hand, those who delved in "great books" would, in Erskine's resonant phrase, "free [them]selves from the prison of egotism" and take part "in the complete citizenship of mankind."[58] Woodberry's emphasis on the universality of the classics had mapped that escape route from spiritual isolation, but Erskine actually embarked on it by specifying a particular body of literature which promised to create a visible community. To locate one's own reactions in a pattern—to recognize, for example, that Hamlet's tragedy was compelling to Elizabethans and New Yorkers alike—was to augment the self by spinning it outward. In this respect, reading "great books" carried out the recommendations of "The Moral Obligation to be Intelligent" for self-discovery through a perception of "infinite order." Similarly, Erskine's hope, with regard to the curricular version of "great books," that the weekly discussion session would give students the basis for fellowship outside the classroom invested the meeting with the capacity to create not merely Woodberry's diffuse "community of the soul" but a real group of people who shared insights and interests. As Erskine later reflected, "Here would be, I believed, the true scholarly and cultural basis for human understanding and communication."[59]

Thus, Erskine's ideology encompassed self-transcendence as well as greater individualism. To shift the metaphor from modern to ancient science, it was as if Erskine imagined reading the classics as a kind of mental alchemy, whereby the reader's ample but leaden memories and feelings fused with the "golden accomplishments of the race" to produce a more complete person, one endowed with a richer understanding of life and a heightened ability to enjoy it.[60]

It is important to see that, for Erskine, that process functioned to intensify experience by adhering to a model of the self predicated on autonomy and (even though Erskine himself had devalued the word) reflective of character. If the self required more refurbishment than Woodberry had believed, it was in order to realize that ideal rather than to discard it in favor of cultivating personality. As Erskine explained in *The Delight of Great Books*, with respect to the merits of reading Sir Walter Scott: "To be steeped in his books, to be on familiar terms with the noble men and women who dwell in them, to share their courage, their zest in life, their self-reliance, their intellectual sincerity, until their outlook on life becomes our own—this would be a good protection against most of the romances which to-day it is our frailty rather than our fate to read, and against those social cure-alls which still offer to make us good and happy at low cost, with just a little rearranging of the environment."[61] In his invocation of self-reliance, his disparaging allusion to ease, and his moralistic expectations of literature, Erskine remained an heir of Emerson and Norton and a colleague of Canby and Fisher. Elsewhere, referring to the lessons of Aristotle, Erskine coupled "study" and "self-discipline" to his earlier preoccupation with "intelligence," urging that individuals apply those virtues to an examination of the wisdom of the past so as to "control" the "eternal forces of life."[62]

Similarly, to extrapolate from his later writings, even Erskine's expectation that readers would explore books socially rested on an ideal of "conversation" that owed more to Emerson than to Dale Carnegie. Although the term necessarily encompassed an element of public performance, nineteenth-century authors had typically defined that performance in terms of the revelation of inward "nobility." Surrounding "conversation" with stringent limits, they had attached restraint and lack of "egotism" to an encounter which supposedly had no goal larger than the exchange of ideas.[63] Erskine's own notion of conversational skill perpetuated those assumptions. At a time when other writers on the subject connected "conversation" with "self-assertion" and the arousal of "attraction" in order "to create an impression on the other man for social, business, or other purposes," Erskine counseled otherwise. "Conversation," he proposed, "aims at entertainment which subtly enlightens." Attainable "only so long as we remain unselfish," its "first rule" is that all voices must be kept subdued. . . . [It is] suitable for groups which are sophisticated, thoughtful and refined." Read back into Erskine's "great books" design, such language suggests that even the features of his plan that involved intellectual display remained tied to the conservation of inner resources, contradicting the imperative to win approval by donning a series of "masks."[64]

Erskine's affirmation of autonomy made him more assured and less alienated than the figures who despaired, with Howells, that the self lacked a center. (Similarly, Erskine never concluded that Protestantism was vapid and insubstantial; rather, he sustained his childhood faith throughout his life, becoming a vestryman of Trinity Church in 1916.) Yet, drawing on that part of the Emersonian legacy that celebrated growth and self-transcendence, Erskine also invested his "great books" ideology with other possibilities. His emphasis on the release of "energy" perpetuated Woodberry's attraction to therapeutic modes of self-realization. More important, Erskine's identification with the literature of earlier eras offered not merely an escape from egotism into an ultimately ego-strengthening awareness of one's part in a well-ordered human drama but also the opposite outcome: the *loss* of autonomy. By reading "great books," one might surrender to the past so completely—drown in experience so enveloping—that the self ceased to exist as a separate entity. Such impulses, present in some "anti-modernists," gave Erskine an affinity with literary modernism as well—that is, with the very texts he rejected for inclusion in his "great books" list. It was that prospect of the "continual extinction of personality," for example, that T. S. Eliot welcomed in elevating "tradition" over the "individual talent." By seeking, along with self-reliance, what Daniel Bell has called the annihilation of "finitude," Erskine thus reflected "the deepest nature of modern man."[65]

To recognize those competing views of the self in Erskine's "great books" ideology is to see his effort at canon formation not as the expression of immutable, self-evident principles but, instead, as in part a projection of the psychic tensions his historical circumstances generated. In the pliability of his outlook, one feels the inexorable weight of Erskine's own history: his genteel background and loyalties, his impatience with genteel restraints, his persistent effort—fully but only temporarily realized in France—to accommodate and conjoin both attitudes.

At the same time, Erskine's approach to "great books" supplied a comforting answer to the question of whether American consumer culture could sustain an adequate measure of "civilization." T. S. Eliot's directive that writers embrace "tradition" was feasible only if the historical record revealed that one existed. Both before and after World War I, as part of his attack on gentility, Van Wyck Brooks was among the loudest voices insisting that, in the United States, it emphatically did not. As Brooks observed in a well-known passage from "America's Coming-of-Age" (1915), American writers had no "genial middle ground of human tradition" on which to stand.[66] Although one might assume, because Brooks and Bourne together belonged to the Seven Arts coterie, that Erskine was the "ancient enemy" of both men, his postwar essays on American tradition so resembled Brooks's prewar efforts that they confound Bourne's determination to place his antagonist entirely outside the circle in which he traveled. In fact, Erskine's analysis seems derivative of Brooks's. His service in Europe had attuned him to the French reverence "for art, for scholarship, and for civilization." By contrast, Americans, having been uprooted from their original homes, lived without a life of the spirit, a sense of the "soil," or an awareness of cultural continuity. Erskine diagnosed the "cult of the contemporary" among his fellow literary critics as one symptom of that deprivation, but present-mindedness was pervasive. Emerson, Erskine's implicit model in other respects, was as guilty of it ("Why should we grope among the dry bones of the past?") as the pragmatists, whom, in this context, Erskine blamed for undermining tradition by rejecting the notion of unvarying truth.[67]

The American's disregard for history had devastating consequences for what Erskine called "taste." His statement of that conviction is worth quoting at length because it illuminates his relationship both to Brooks and company and to later figures who answered those writers' charges:

> The larger fabric of language, the racial memories to which an old country can always appeal, obviously do not exist in a land where every man is busy forgetting his past. . . . Without tradition there can be no taste, and what is worse, there can be little for taste to act upon. We have indeed some approaches, some faint hints and suggestions of a national poetry. The cartoon figure of Uncle Sam, for example, a great poet could perhaps push over into the world of art, but unless the poet soon arrives there will be few Americans left who can recognize in that gaunt figure the first Yankee, the keen, witty, audacious, and slightly melancholy type of our countrymen as they first emerged in world history.[68]

That gloomy assessment confirmed the fear that the United States would never achieve anything close to "civilization"; it implied that the nation seemed doomed to remain a bastion of clever but vulgar entrepreneurs.

Yet Brooks, Erskine, and others who addressed that prospect also provided various formulas for averting it. Brooks (along with other cultural radicals) resolved the issue of whether tradition and consumer culture could coexist by freely conceding that the two were incompatible.

They argued, instead, that true "civilization" could arise only when Americans shook off both their preoccupation with moneymaking and their loyalty to an Arnoldian insistence on "the best" in Western thought. In "Letters and Leadership" (1918), Brooks, echoing a complaint of Bourne's about "this tyranny of the 'best,'" claimed that Arnold's doctrine had permitted Americans to evade creating their own literature; it "conventionalized for them the spiritual experience of humanity, pigeon-holing it, as it were, and leaving them fancy-free to live 'for practical purposes.'" Harold Stearns, taking up the same cry, declared, "Whatever else American civilization is, it is not Anglo-Saxon." Instead, Brooks and Stearns alike placed their hopes in the creation of an American aesthetic heritage once a process of self-scrutiny had cleared away the debris of materialism.[69] Another response—that of Constance Rourke—proceeded from a similar view of America's distinctiveness but had no quarrel with the nation's practical bent. In fact, Rourke claimed, that trait had shaped an abundant basis for a unique "civilization" that only awaited discovery. Like Erskine, Rourke understood the artistic possibilities buried in the image of Uncle Sam but demonstrated that "great poets" had already arrived to incorporate that figure into their work.[70]

Erskine's approach to the reading of "great books" assuaged the same anxieties in a still different manner—one which did justify Bourne's sense of the disparity between himself and his "intellectual bete noire." His solution was simple and elegant. At exactly the moment Brooks issued "Letters and Leadership," Erskine reiterated the importance of heeding the standards Arnold had set. Moreover, instead of regarding America as exceptional, he asserted the continuity of American and European culture. Specifically, by contending that "great books" portrayed timeless, universal human situations, he permitted the conclusion that the classics of Western literature *were* the American heritage. That is, if Americans were really Romans under the skin, if they shared the same hopes and tragedies as Chaucer's pilgrims or Tennyson's knights—and if, to reverse the equation, the Greeks were like middle-class businessmen—then the troubling question of how America could reconcile art and materialism rested on a false dichotomy. All that was necessary (as Rourke also maintained) was that Americans possess the traditions that were already there. Erskine's translation of classical plots into modern language ("'Do you really mean,' [Lancelot] asks, 'that you want me to go back to my country and there marry some-body?' "), a technique he later perfected in his novels, not only fostered the self-transcendence described earlier but facilitated that comforting conflation of the United States and Europe.[71] So did Erskine's deliber-ate rejection of historical understanding as a prerequisite for critical insight. Without the bothersome intrusion of variations in time and place, Americans were free to see their own world as consonant with previous societies—and thus a "civilization" in its own right.

Erskine's vernacular style and ahistorical posture also helped him to carry out the Arnoldian mission of making tradition accessible to a wide audience. By presenting the classics in modern dress, and by emphasiz-ing the primacy of feelings rather than training, Erskine assured his readers that culture was readily at hand. His description of the "great books" course as a setting for "intimate discussion," a phrase connot-ing warmth and easy exchange, rendered the encounter unintimidating and demanding of no special skills.[72] A similar sense of accessibility resulted from his insistence on minimizing the role of the literary expert. At the same time, his willingness to *function* as an expert—to tell readers which books were classics—alleviated the effects of ex-panded book production and the specialization of knowledge in much the same way the Book-of-the-Month Club board did. Although he was never dogmatic about the titles he included, his designation of writings ranging from Aristotle to Tolstoy as "great" brought a similarity and continuity to works which had in common neither form nor subject matter nor provenance. By amalgamating them in a single, ostensibly definitive list, Erskine added another dimension to the relationship between tradition and order—not the "infinite order" here, or even the abstract organizing principles Woodberry provided, but a palpable end to intellectual chaos.

As was true for his vision of the self, the primary effect of Erskine's depiction of the vitality and accessibility of the Western tradition was to carry Arnoldian values forward well into the twentieth century. Yet Erskine's reconciliation of a consumer culture with the ideal of "civiliza-tion" was as much capable of fortifying the former as of reinvigorating the latter. It was not simply that Erskine made his audience comfort-able with their middle-class aspirations, thereby bolstering the self-congratulatory mood of the 1920s, although that was a large part of the story. Nor was it merely, as Brooks had so accurately understood, that in constructing a list of "great books" Erskine had assembled a ready-made tradition that conserved the American's time and energy for business. It was also that the list, by substituting information for aesthetics, once again increased the temptation to regard culture as a commodity. Two publishing ventures facilitated that outcome: the American Library Association's distribution in 1927, 1934, and 1935 of editions of the list as *Classics of the Western World* and the Encyclopedia Britannica's 1952 marketing of *Great Books of the Western World*, a set which Dwight Macdonald, making the same point, described in a review as "a hundred pounds of Great Books."[73]

Moreover, as Macdonald also noted, the phrase "great books," although underplayed in the initial course design and, in any event, hardly Erskine's invention, melded all too well with the propensity of advertisers to sell a product by touting it as "famous" or linking it to the testimonials of celebrities. To draw an analogy to another phenomenon of the early twentieth century, billing books as "great" could function as a literary equivalent of the star system, thrusting certain works into the spotlight as objects of pursuit and adulation on the basis of image and reputation alone. Likewise, however tightly Erskine himself clung to a different model, the social setting he devised was capable of absorbing a redefinition of conversation as an aid in winning "poise, charm, personality." Although he hardly meant to foster exchanges on the order of "Read any good books lately?," the fact that a 1936 conversation manual described Greek symposia as models of self-assertion is a reminder that Erskine's forum could serve the same end.[74]

The potential for accommodating that shift away from genteel premises was present as far back as Erskine's 1916 course proposal, which referred to furnishing "the average student with a body of cultural information, by requiring him to read certain famous books." Nevertheless, such implications, it should be stressed, were paradoxical in view of Erskine's avowed purposes. His recasting of the classics as recent publications fed the very "cult of the contemporary" he intended his advocacy of tradition to combat; the connotations of "great" undermined his attack on the proclivity of the modern magazine to be "a medium not for literature but for advertising," buying "reputations rather than writings." He also deplored the "journalistic tendency" in current books. Yet, despite his intentions, the headline introducing Erskine's *Delineator* articles revealed how susceptible his stance was to a radical revaluation of the nature and object of reading the classics. The banner proclaimed "There's Fun in Famous Books." This was a kind of literary "invasion of the body snatchers," in which the spirit of consumer culture appropriated the soul of the Arnoldian aesthetic, leaving only its outward form intact.[75]

The entanglements of genteel and consumer values in Erskine's understanding of both self and culture suggest an interpretation of the "great books" ideology, at least in its initial formulation, different from the one historians have customarily proposed in writing about its later manifestations. Its essence lay not in a one-sided assault on the dangers mass society and the fact-finding ethos of science posed to the preeminence of the refined individual, but rather in its capacity to provide familiar touchstones (self-reliance, character, Western civilization) in a changing world, while assenting to heightened demands for information, social performance, and personal growth.[76]

The debate today over the insistence of Allan Bloom and others on restricting the canon of "great books" to works by white men of European descent also makes it important to note a similar doubleness in the political ramifications of Erskine's program. Even more than Sherman and Canby, perhaps, Erskine was vulnerable to charges of elitism. To the extent that, as an academic curriculum, his plan challenged the elective system, it constituted, in Trilling's words, "a fundamental criticism of American democratic education." That is, while specialization could be construed as a type of democratization because it substituted diverse routes to education for a single body of knowledge, Erskine's innovation signaled a return to a less egalitarian policy: a fixed syllabus, handed down by the faculty and recommended for everyone regardless of aptitude, background, or vocational plans—to say nothing of gender, race, class, or ethnicity.[77]

Additionally, Erskine's assertion that immigrants ought to become familiar with "great books" barely concealed his dismay that they and their children comprised a rapidly increasing percentage of undergraduates in the postwar period. He had written to his mother in 1918, "When I see these boys [at Beaune] and realize that of the students at Columbia, many are those selfish immigrants who don't want to do anything for America, I feel as though I ought to stay here and work for the soldiers." In subsequently urging that "we [not] refuse to assume responsibility for the making of the foreign elements in the United

States into a unified nation," lest we suffer the "ignorance, the disease and the discontent which in various ways menace our society," Erskine spoke as a Weehawken Episcopalian trying to keep the Union Hill workers within bounds. Thus, he made tradition serve order in one final respect: more urgently and explicitly than Woodberry, but along lines he had laid out, Erskine employed it to dispel the threat of class conflict and social disarray. "Great books" can be considered a type of "Americanization" program, with all of the antidemocratic characteristics associated with the term: the reassertion of white Anglo-Saxon Protestant superiority, the fear that foreigners (and, in the Columbia case, particularly Jews) would undermine that superiority, and the insistence that immigrants become acculturated to an existing white middle-class mold.[78]

Yet Erskine's conscious political commitments must not be discounted. Like the Progressives to whom his interest in "Americanization" connects him, Erskine sought order in the name of preserving democracy. At least publicly, beginning in 1919 and throughout the 1920s, he urged the university to open its doors to all members of American society. That position, which ran counter to a contemporary outcry against "mass education," impelled Erskine to take a more tolerant view of the curriculum than his emphasis on the centrality of "great books" might imply. If he advocated a return to a core of humanistic study, he also urged the university's collateral involvement in providing whatever technical or other training its constituency wanted. His worry was less that the academy might become an " 'intellectual department store,' " a situation he actually welcomed, than that it might undervalue the abilities of its customers by failing to expose them to the "beauty" they were capable of perceiving. With respect to the "great books" design itself, moreover, his belief in the "resumption" of the "powers that for a while we delegated to the expert" may be seen, from one vantage point, as radically democratic.[79] The same is true of his equation of "greatness" with the ability of a book to tap every person's potential for exploring a shared human condition.

As the *New Republic* noted in a 1922 editorial on "The American College," the "abandonment of the aristocratic ideal [of culture] in fact brought about a great increase in the number of students able to enter college, while the retention of the ideal in name constituted a powerful inducement to them to do so. The college became one of those demo-

cratic institutions . . . whose function seemed to be to give exclusive-
ness to the masses."[80] Erskine's ambivalent political orientation meant
that his "great books" idea could serve that purpose as well. Both
within and outside of the classroom, his plan promised to deal equally
well with two contradictory problems: how to shore up a shaky social
structure and how to crack that structure to obtain, by firmly established means, a share of knowledge and prestige.

From Troy to Hollywood

Until the mid-1920s Erskine carried out the multiple mediations his
"great books" scheme entailed largely behind the scenes and in an
academic setting. Although he was a familiar name to lecture audiences
and readers of the *Bookman*, *Outlook*, and *North American Review*, he
exerted greatest influence in this period by teaching his "great books"
course to a group of distinguished students, notably Mortimer Adler. In
1925, however, he moved to center stage by making his debut as a
novelist.

Erskine's turn to fiction derived from several factors. Despite his
pedagogical successes, Erskine was deeply troubled in the immediate
postwar period. As Henry Morton Robinson observed, "Those who
knew him between the fortieth and forty-fifth years of his life [1919–24]
realized that he was undergoing a severe emotional crisis." Some of his
distress arose from his relationship to the university. The implementation of "great books" at Columbia had not silenced his detractors on the
faculty nor had it managed to undo the trend toward specialization.
Feeling overworked and underappreciated, especially by Butler, he
began to question once more the nature of his vocation. Robinson
contended, moreover, that Erskine suffered from the suppression of
the creative needs he had left unfulfilled in abandoning his career as a
poet. Given Erskine's recurring preoccupation with self-reliance and
experience, one might rephrase Robinson's perception in somewhat
different terms: that Erskine's impulse to escape from genteel inhibi-
tions and restore his wartime sense of wholeness and freedom was
stronger than his ideology of reading could satisfy. His repressive
marriage, now lacking any "decent friendship" and strained almost to
the breaking point, added another element to his desire for release.[81]

In consequence, Erskine's interest slackened in his scholarly research project, a biography and anthology of Milton for which Bobbs-Merrill had contracted in 1921. He found one creative outlet by resuming the study of the piano, playing five or six hours a day in the summer of 1924 to prepare for his first public symphonic concert that August. Erskine's own description of that effort as a "crash[ing] through the barriers to expression in music" suggests the psychological function the performance served—the fundamental barrier having been, one recalls, his mother's restraint on his youthful ambitions.[82] He continued to play publicly until illness made it impossible.

That fall, however, he also discovered another form of expression when, prompted by a remark in the *Odyssey* and encouraged by a friend in the publishing business, he decided to write up his speculations about what happened when Menelaos took Helen home to Sparta after the Trojan War. The result was a novel, *The Private Life of Helen of Troy*, which he offered to Bobbs-Merrill in lieu of the Milton volume. Apart from extricating him from joyless scholarship, the fictional exercise enabled him to rebel against genteel attitudes by exploring a type of experience for which academic writing had been an inadequate vehicle: sex. In the novel, he portrayed Helen as unrepentant about having run off to Troy with Paris and anxious for her daughter Hermione to marry a man who exhibited the "love of life" she valued more than propriety. In overturning genteel morality, Erskine also removed classical figures from their pedestals. His aim, he later explained, was to make readers "see that Helen, instead of being a wicked villainness, was an almost conventional illustration of American life, even in the suburbs."[83] To that end, he sat the family across the dinner table from one another and spiced their dialogue with American colloquialisms. Many of the conversations counterposed Helen's wayward behavior to the steadfastness of the younger generation, a contrast that amusingly inverted the contemporaneous indictment of the flapper and other specimens of American youth. The combination of sex, topical interest, and iconoclasm gave the book a racy, urbane tone that helped to make it a stunning success. It was the best-selling American novel for 1926 and earned Erskine far wider recognition than had "great books" alone.

Much of that recognition took the shape of heralding Erskine's metamorphosis from sober professor to free spirit. The same *New Yorker* profile which described his heady reaction to World War I, for example, concluded that in the aftermath of war he relinquished a "Victorian" sensibility for a laudably less fettered, "more vulgar" point of view. In fact, to certain readers he was unrespectably unchained. Rabbi Stephen Wise attacked *Helen of Troy* in 1927 as "a bit of semi-Lombrosian Freudism [*sic*]," the "upshot" of which was "'go to it, young people; what you need is release; standards and self-respect are incompatibles.'"[84]

Those estimates, however, misgauged the extent of Erskine's transformation. It was true that the slick satire, sexual banter, and premium on shunning convention in *Helen of Troy* carried him much further away from gentility than had even the undercurrents in his "great books" design. Erskine himself saw writing the novel as a "liberation" that permitted him a "new development in sincerity."[85] His decision in 1926 to embark on a lengthy extramarital affair with a woman writer named Adelene Pynchon meant that the liberation spilled over into his personal life as well. Yet *The Private Life of Helen of Troy* was an updated version of an old tale not merely because it used ancient protagonists but also because it recapitulated many of the themes of Erskine's earlier career. The gimmick of endowing classical characters with the argot of the 1920s was essentially an embellishment of his premise that "great books" were contemporary literature; installing Helen in the suburbs was the logical extension of his belief that a common wellspring of feeling fed American and Greek civilizations. Moreover, in keeping with the maxim that there is no such thing as bad publicity, his irreverence toward the classics nonetheless kept them in the public eye, making Agamemnon, Clytemnestra, Orestes, and Menelaos household words to thousands of readers. As a painless expedition to ancient times, the book was less an assault on the past than a device for marketing it to an audience that wanted to combine culture and "fun." *The Private Life of Helen of Troy*, Erskine's student Clifton Fadiman noted, was popular because Americans between the wars relished the gentle mockery of hallowed figures—a pursuit very different from the wholesale rejection of them.[86]

Additionally, Erskine's sexual explorations, at least on paper, veered away from a genuine frankness toward the safety the classical plot provided; like a drapery covering a Greek statue, the placement of the action in the distant past made sexuality less immediate than in the work of writers like Fitzgerald or Dos Passos.[87] Nor, it almost goes without saying, did the structure and style of the novel come anywhere near the experimentations with form and language in which Erskine's avant-garde contemporaries were engaged. Thus, the book perfectly recapitulated the same tensions between competing sets of values that animated Erskine's role generally.

In the next few years, Erskine used the formula he had invented in *Helen of Troy* to produce novels featuring such characters as Galahad, Adam and Eve, and Tristan and Isolde, all of whom he made exemplify modern mores. Simultaneously, he published extensively on "great books," for a time turned out a monthly column for the *Century*, and wrote numerous other articles. The titles of some of these read like a catalogue of Emersonian virtues: "Culture," "Taste," "Self-Reliance," "Integrity." If it misinterpreted his development, the *New Yorker* caught his stance and outlook exactly when it pronounced him "instructor in genteel sophistication to the magazine readers of America." Erskine took a leave from Columbia in 1928 to embark on a nationwide lecture tour, speaking to admiring, overflow crowds on "the moral obligation to be intelligent" and on those classics he had adapted in writing fiction. Each performance ended with a piano recital, making the occasion a dramatic demonstration of his versatility—and, consequently, of the reassuring survival of the generalist. At the same time, one can see in Erskine's "elaborate show," as he called it, the display of personality his audiences sought to emulate. Newspapers, by his own account, began referring to him as " 'the amazing Professor Erskine.' "[88]

Less enchanted, however, were his opponents within the university, several of whom now saw his novels as a further incursion against scholarship. As a result, even though he was being mentioned as a possible successor to Butler, with some misgivings he indefinitely extended his leave from Columbia at the end of the 1928 tour.[89] That summer he accepted an invitation to become the first president of the newly reorganized Juilliard School of Music. Erskine brought to that position not only his own musical talents but also the administrative skills he had developed at Beaune. In addition, his high profile and the institution's importance to New York's social and cultural scene worked to mutual advantage: Erskine was an ideal fund-raiser, and the Juilliard a good berth for someone who thrived on public trust. His philosophy as president paralleled the one he had voiced with reference to "great books." Music, he thought, ought to be accessible to and comprehensible by a broad audience, the training of which in listening and performing was as much a part of Juilliard's responsibilities as the cultivation of virtuosos.[90] That commitment to the popularization of music as well as literature drove him, beginning in the late 1920s, to speak and write on behalf of the musical amateur and, in 1935, to edit an American version of what was essentially a British "outline" book, *A Musical Companion*.

By 1930 Erskine had thus followed Sherman and Canby in adeptly reconstituting his authority outside the university. Subsequently, he added frequent radio appearances to his busy lecture schedule. Nevertheless, he continued to have difficulty sustaining in his personal life the equilibrium he achieved in his public stance. Echoing Robinson's observation about Erskine earlier in the decade, a tantalizing letter from Pynchon alludes to his "mental struggles between 1926 and 1931." Pynchon's remark may refer solely to Erskine's turbulent dealings with Columbia and with his wife, from whom he separated in 1927. Yet certain of his writings—notably the ones in which he abandoned the contrivance of the modernized ancient milieu—indicate that something else was going on: they convey a persistent anxiety about constructing a unified self. For example, his novel *Unfinished Business* (1931) featured a hero, Dick Ormer, who, at his death, is troubled by a number of unfulfilled intentions. In a fantasy that would seem an obvious representation of Erskine's own urge to join thought and behavior, Ormer, at the Golden Gates, receives a second chance at achieving a sense of integrity. Returning to earth, he revives a scheme to swindle his partner and almost rekindles a romance with a friend's wife. Afterward he reports to Saint Peter, who reiterates the lesson that, while the road to hell is paved with good intentions, completed plans—even immoral ones—mark the way to heaven. That theme, foreshadowed in Helen of Troy's injunction to live fully, and repeated in Erskine's other novels, reflected the same agitated concern with self-actualization that formed the basis for the Book-of-the-Month Club marketing campaign. It suggests that Erskine's expression in the various aspects of his career of his need to conjoin autonomy and intense experience led him only to a kind of emotional halfway house, from which he was unable to go either forward or back to a stable psychic resting place.[91]

Erskine's personal history in the 1930s and 1940s supports that hypothesis. His involvement with Helen Worden, a lively, accomplished, yet conventionally "feminine" journalist whom he met in 1931 and married after finally obtaining a divorce in 1946, offset a good deal of his malaise, so much so that some of his old friends credited the relationship with turning him into a new person. Yet he still suffered from a sense of disappointment in himself and relied on Worden for "strength and hope." Then, while on a lecture tour late in 1935, he was seriously injured in an automobile collision, suffering multiple fractures. The accident elevated his mood of self-reproach about his shortcomings.[92] Although he taught himself to play again, it also deprived him of his former agility at the piano. Faced with enormous medical bills and short of assets because of losses in the stock market crash, Erskine spent the next several months recuperating, running Juilliard, and churning out essays and fiction. One of those pieces, a vitriolic book entitled *The Influence of Women—and Its Cure*, provides the best evidence that he held women primarily accountable for genteel repression. Depicting them as parasitic and manipulative, he accused the majority of middle-class women of denying sex, side-stepping evil, reducing religion to a drug, and emasculating the fine arts—all of which might be regarded as crimes against experience.[93] One does not have to push psychology very far to see in that portrait an alternative view of the mother he remembered only in "flawless white."

In February 1937, just over a year after the accident, Erskine suffered a stroke that paralyzed his right side. Interestingly, although he might plausibly have attributed the illness to residual effects from his skull fracture, he consistently described it as a "complete crack-up of nerves" or nervous breakdown. The reason for the collapse, Erskine thought, was exhaustion from overwork. Indeed, the previous December he had announced his decision to resign the Juilliard presidency, purportedly in order to free more time for writing. Yet Erskine's own disposition to ascribe his condition to emotional causes makes it tempting to interpret the episode as at least a metaphor for, if not the direct result of, a different kind of exhaustion: the ebbing of the psychic energy he had expended for so long in both sustaining and rebelling against genteel expectations.[94]

In any event, the illness signaled the beginning of a period of Erskine's life in which the manifestations of that struggle were particularly poignant. As the discussion below will explore, his association with "great books" diminished in inverse proportion to Mortimer Adler and Robert M. Hutchins's affiliation with the idea. Moreover, on the heels of his departure from Juilliard came an unsolicited and unwelcome letter from Butler designating him emeritus professor at Columbia. Adrift from both institutions, he floundered, in part because he needed to find other sources of income but also, one suspects, because (in the Columbia case) he had lost the connection which, even though attenuated after 1927, had furnished a context against which he had defined himself. As Trilling observed, although Erskine thought the university did "nothing but check and hamper him," it "served him better than he knew," providing him with "the antagonists he needed and the subjects and the disputes that brought out his strength." To a former colleague, he admitted "a constant yearning to be teaching again."[95] More than once, he considered trying to reanchor himself at Juilliard, but a financially acceptable offer was not forthcoming. As his paralysis abated, he resumed a heavy schedule of lectures, radio broadcasts, and writing, thereby sustaining his public role. (One of his activities in 1938 was a column on "men's furnishings" for a periodical called *Heywood Broun's Nutmeg*.) Some of his novels which today appear to have few redeeming features won surprising acclaim. After ten years, however, Erskine's formula had lost some of its sparkle, and even his best-received efforts also incurred judgments like "inconsequential" and "harmless but irrelevant."[96] Thus, having chosen to stake his identity largely on his literary endeavors, Erskine had then to contend with the limitations of his talent.

Overshadowed on the educational front and fading as a novelist, Erskine turned to an additional locus for his activities: Hollywood. He spent six weeks there in 1939 as master of ceremonies for a radio variety show that included performances by the Marx Brothers. On the same trip, he gathered material for a series his friend Fulton Oursler, the editor of *Liberty*, had commissioned. He returned in the early 1940s to do other articles and to discuss adapting some of his novels to the screen. Helen Worden even thought he might construct a more permanent relationship with the film industry by succeeding Will Hays as overseer of movie morals. However comic the juxtaposition of Erskine and Groucho, the idea that they should meet is not altogether startling. Rather, in that scenario one might see the culmination of Erskine's tendency to embrace the culture of personality by facilitating literary stardom. It was a fairly short step, after all, from Helen of Troy's "private life" to "Clark Gable's Secret Wish." Yet, his fascination with celebrity notwithstanding, Erskine's encounter with Hollywood appears strained and almost pathetic. Never really comfortable with glitter, he moved about sets and stars' residences unable to shake off his Weehawken background. Distinguishing between a "screen star" and a "good actress," his *Liberty* series blamed the star system's premium on "personality" for lowering the quality of American films by requiring performers to stick to type. He thereby merely transferred an Arnoldian preoccupation with upholding standards from one art form to another.[97]

In the same period, Erskine also issued his fullest statement of his own philosophy, *The Complete Life* (1943). As a compendium of advice not only on "great books" but also on such topics as gardening, cooking, raising children, music, and art, the volume was a generalist's bible. Within that framework, Erskine's characteristic themes of experience and autonomy reasserted themselves. In the opening pages, he allied himself with an active, rather than a contemplative, life, explicitly contrasting "experience and the sideline attitude toward experience" and arguing for the former. Even more than his ideology of reading, *The Complete Life* bore traces of a therapeutic orientation: the "self-development" Erskine had in mind here contained only oblique references to the fulfillment of social or moral obligations and made growth its own reward. Yet one has only to compare the book to a contemporary advice manual such as Wiggam's *The Marks of an Educated Man* to appreciate the degree to which Erskine once again marshaled experience in the service of genteel commitments. Whereas Wiggam's concept of cultivation boiled down to mastering a series of mental "habits" that would insure practical success, Erskine's concern was with a program of study that would, echoing Emerson, increase the "power" of individuals to develop their "natural capacities." Distinguishing among opinions, information, and knowledge, Erskine urged the acquisition of the latter, although its attainment exacted "pain," because it alone derived from self-reliance. The conclusion of *The Complete Life* held out as a model an admittedly "old fashioned" conceit: the "self-made man," whose independence, genuineness, devotion to learning, and sense of responsibility for his own well-being firmly rooted him—and Erskine—in the values of an earlier age. Reviewers of the book unwittingly highlighted its anachronistic quality—its remoteness from the culture of personality—by expressing their wish that Erskine had written an autobiography instead.[98]

Nonetheless, Erskine's very preoccupation with completeness suggests the enduring incapacity of that older model to extinguish his own impulses toward a more vigorous version of experience, while it simultaneously prevented him from acting on them. As one examines his last years, the evidence of his divided sensibility mounts. He eventually produced not one autobiography but four, the titles of which are highly revealing. *My Life as a Teacher* (1948), *My Life in Music* (1950), and "My Life in Literature" (unfinished) are, taken together, a graphic representation of a fragmented (if impressively diverse) career; *The Memory of Certain Persons*, while playing to a curiosity about personality, kept the focus on others, as if to place a safe distance between his day-to-day encounters and an inner "boiler" that, like his father's and uncle's, remained hidden from sight. His letters to Worden, touching in their expression of the love and devotion he found with her, are likewise so utterly devoid of any antagonism that they point to the same buried repository of feeling, as does Worden's remark that she learned early in her marriage to Erskine never to criticize him.[99] Within *The Memory of Certain Persons*, Erskine's brand of "middleness" rose to the surface in the passages about Weehawken and Union Hill, Woodberry and Butler. Finally, always and pervasively at this time, there was the dream of Beaune—the lengthy reminiscences, the clutching of photographs and plane tickets, the actual return in 1950 under the great hardship of a second stroke—in the hope of recovering the "peace" that, one senses, his awareness of disunity obstructed.

Adler, Hutchins, and "Great Books"

By that time, Erskine's student Mortimer Adler had reshaped his teacher's lessons to fit his own concerns. Although Adler's emergence as a popularizer occurred on the chronological margins of this study, the size of his following after 1945 demands a brief analysis of the ways in which he transformed Erskine's ideas. The process of appropriation had begun in 1921, when Adler took "General Honors" with Erskine. (Two years later, together with coleader Mark Van Doren, Adler in turn taught Clifton Fadiman.)[100] In 1926 Adler approached Scott

Buchanan, a Columbia teaching fellow and assistant director of the People's Institute, a program of adult education based at Cooper Union, about the feasibility of offering "great books" seminars to the community. That fall, Adler, Fadiman, Buchanan, Richard McKeon (another Columbia instructor), and eight others led six groups modeled on "General Honors" for 134 participants.[101]

Erskine was only peripherally involved in the People's Institute undertaking—the group leaders consulted him occasionally—and was rather quickly alienated, it seems, from Adler's enthusiasms. Part of the reason for Erskine's detachment was that he and Adler were so utterly different temperamentally: Erskine, the reserved Trinity Church vestryman, must have seen in the zealous Adler, whom Fadiman dubbed a "lay Yeshiva *bucher*," the realization of many of the fears that had impelled him to embrace "great books" in the first place.[102] The next year, when the community experiment expanded and, in response, the American Library Association brought out their "great books" list, Erskine did agree to supply an introduction to it. From that point on, however, except for a short collaboration in the mid-1940s, Adler and Erskine went their separate ways.

Thanks to a grant from the Carnegie Corporation, the People's Institute venture lasted until 1928, Adler inheriting Buchanan's job. As if to accentuate both the democratic and elitist potentialities inherent in Erskine's approach, Whittaker Chambers, already a member of the Communist party, ran a group with Adler; Fadiman, en route to a brief flirtation with the party himself, likewise attributed part of the leaders' motivation to a somewhat "starry-eyed" desire to bring culture to "ordinary people." Adler, by contrast, expressed a contempt for the popularization of knowledge which, by his own later admission, did not square with either the conception of the institute or his actual activities as a popularizer.[103] In keeping with that view, Adler soon retreated from his foray into the community. Instead, in October of 1929 he described his experiences as Erskine's disciple to Robert M. Hutchins, newly appointed president of the University of Chicago; Hutchins reacted by adding Adler to his faculty.

For the next decade, Adler's activities were less an aspect of the popularization of knowledge than of innovation within the academy. He and Hutchins implemented a "General Honors" seminar at Chicago in 1930, went on to reorganize the first two years of college studies around general education courses, and, between 1936 and 1942, sought to replace the entire undergraduate curriculum with "great books" courses rooted in the classical trivium and quadrivium. Those reforms, as Mark Van Doren pointed out, were "in one sense only an extension" of Erskine's because they rested on his premise that "great books are the best teachers." As such, they replicated the weekly "unmediated" discussion format he had devised as well as the use of two Socratic instructors with divergent outlooks. Adler also preserved his mentor's animus toward specialization, adopting Erskine's policy of proceeding like "debonair amateurs." Similarly, the Chicago version of "great books" retained Erskine's insistence on the centrality of the text and, concomitantly, the superfluousness of secondary sources; like the Columbia one, it measured "greatness" as the ability to remain accessible to contemporary readers. What is more, some of Hutchins's language bespeaks an unacknowledged debt to Erskine: his repudiation of "character" in favor of "intellect" recalls Erskine's paean to intelligence, while his similar rejection of "personality" echoes the dominant element in Erskine's vision of the self.[104]

Yet Hutchins and Adler, by transforming Columbia's single course into a comprehensive "Chicago Plan," launched a more sweeping assault on the elective system than Erskine had. Moreover, they made philosophy, rather than literature, the heart of their enterprise and went even further in formalizing what had been, back in Woodberry's time, a perspective rather than a system. Thus, paradoxically, they fostered their own brand of specialization. When they argued that only logic and metaphysics based on the teachings of Aristotle and Aquinas constituted education, they accentuated the antidemocratic implications of Erskine's approach; when they castigated science as destructive to culture because it exalted facts rather than values, they withdrew whatever overtures Erskine had made to pragmatism by lobbying for "intelligence"; when Hutchins, correctly perceiving the anti-intellectual streak in Erskine's position, announced, "If we want to give our students experiences, we should go out of business" because the "place to get experiences is in life," he rescinded a central goal of Erskine's design.[105]

Those aspects of Hutchins and Adler's program provoked an outcry from colleagues who saw the two Chicago "great books" proponents as medievalist enemies of positivism, democracy, and modernity. The controversy remained largely intramural until the mid-1930s, but two events subsequently made it an object of wider attention. The first was the 1935 publication of Hutchins's *The Higher Learning in America*, which summarized his view that universities ought to prescribe a course of study ordered by metaphysical principles and employing as texts "the greatest books of the Western world." The book sold 8,500 copies and drew loud rebuttal from highly visible defenders of scientific method, vocational learning, and democratic culture, notably Alfred North Whitehead and John Dewey. The second was the establishment of St. John's College in Annapolis, Maryland, in 1937. There Adler's old friend Stringfellow Barr and his companion from the People's Institute, Scott Buchanan, presided over a curriculum which consisted solely of reading "great books." The novelty of the experiment caught the public eye; in consequence, Dewey and Hutchins's quarrel became the subject of stories in such magazines as *Fortune*. Hutchins's office began receiving a steady stream of moving requests for his book list, many from people who had never had a college education and now sought its equivalent.[106]

The effect of the Chicago–St. John's expansion and systematization of "great books" was to steal the show from Erskine. Hutchins, for example, never even mentioned him in *The Higher Learning* and rubbed salt in the wound by citing Butler's view of the classics instead. Furthermore, Erskine's own misgivings about the curriculum his former students advocated contributed to his dissociation from the movement he had started. On sufficiently good terms with Buchanan to receive an invitation to visit St. John's in 1938, he nonetheless expressed dismay at the college's attempt to "turn what was essentially a reading course into a Medieval substitute for the study of science and other non-literary subjects." Perhaps because his disaffection had hardened over time, his description in *The Memory of Certain Persons* of the Chicago and St. John's endeavors even more forcefully attested to his skepticism and bitterness; there he called them "aberrations" and declared that with them he had "no sympathy whatever."[107]

Adler, however, enjoying the fanfare, was immune to Erskine's criticism. When Simon and Schuster published his *How to Read a Book* in 1940, he carried his ideas to a general audience, thereby rededicating himself to the old People's Institute premise that the clientele for "great books" was larger than the undergraduate population.[108] Although Adler's abrasiveness adds some incongruity to the term, the values underlying that document were in certain respects as genteel as Erskine's. *How to Read a Book* defined "great books" as classics that could "elevate our spirit" by addressing timeless human problems. Its vision of the reading process stressed discipline, while an inchoate model of self-reliance lay beneath the surface of a chapter on the efficacy of self-help. Urging readers to pursue knowledge rather than information, it repudiated the aim of supplying a formula for " 'brilliant' conversation."[109]

Yet those assumptions existed within a matrix of maxims and precepts that interfered with Adler's Arnoldian message. Beginning with its title, which presumed a right and a wrong way to tackle a text, the volume reflected a rigidity that differentiated Adler from Erskine; it enjoined readers to "obey the rules," piled up distinctions (as between a "theoretical" and a "practical" book), and insisted that real reading entailed executing an elaborate sequence of fixed tasks. Even though Adler, with European fascism in mind, appended a conclusion exploring the connection between liberal education and intellectual freedom, his dictates so predominated that they largely appeared as ends in themselves. Moreover, Adler's system countermanded the genteel emphasis on aesthetics by collapsing in the face of art. As Adler readily conceded, his approach basically worked only for nonfiction. In effect, he thus relinquished to the literary modernists he disdained the genteel critic's mantle as conservator of aesthetic standards.[110]

In addition, *How to Read a Book* perpetuated and sharpened Adler's and Erskine's double-edged approach to democracy and authority. On the one hand, it registered the voice of the diffident expert. Reiterating the principle that the "great books" could be "read by every man," it depicted active readers who extracted a work's meaning with no more equipment than the text and the "power" of their own minds. On the other hand, it repeatedly portrayed "great books" classes as dramas in which deluded students, confident that they had understood the assignment, discovered that they could not answer Adler's questions and then admitted that perhaps they had not read the book after all. The effect of that conception was to enhance Adler's stature as guardian of privileged insights and to heighten the reader's nervousness about obtaining access to them.[111]

Thus, despite his explicit commitments, Adler's reduction of the reading process to the anxious mastery of a table of rules actually went beyond Erskine in feeding the predilection for equating culture with information and products; here the rules themselves became an additional commodity. Similarly, his elevation of Erskine's remarks about conversation into the notion of a "Great Conversation" among all the writers—and readers—of "great books" led him to couch many of his directives in terms of the etiquette of social performance. Some of Adler's overtures to consumer values were no doubt intentional: his title, for instance, enabled him to cash in on the popularity, in the same period, of Dale Carnegie's and others' contributions to the how-to genre. His multiple appeals worked: *How to Read a Book* topped the best-seller list when it came out and still remains in print.

In 1943 Adler renewed his pursuit of a large extracurricular following by forming a "great books" discussion seminar for prominent Chicago executives. The group, nicknamed the "Fat Man's" class, drew so much publicity that it sparked the formation of nationwide seminars totaling twenty thousand people by the end of 1946. During the next two years, that number rapidly increased fourfold, resulting in the establishment of a Great Books Foundation independent of the university to handle the surge of interest.[112]

Although no systematic studies of the members' motivations exist for this period, contemporary observers—and subsequent historians— ascribed the phenomenon to a quest for permanence and meaning in a world rendered transient and confusing by the Second World War. As was the case after 1917, Americans regarded with new appreciation the recently endangered heritage of Western civilization; they looked upon it, with relief and protective pride, as a source of "enduring truths." Even though issues of selfhood and experience had receded from Adler's rhetoric, the "great books" ideology of the late 1940s still offered Erskine's lingering promise of a self made whole through a connection to tradition. Certainly many students voiced the belief that "great books" classes provided them with "riches of the mind and heart" that they could not procure in the marketplace. Some also sought the groups' congeniality as an antidote to anonymity, finding comfort in the fact, as one promotional announcement stated, that here "you will meet your minister, banker, . . . grocery clerk, and your neighbors." Such language kept alive Erskine's communal vision and underscored his message about the accessibility of culture. It took advantage as well, one may speculate, of a nascent Cold War preoccupation with glorifying the democratic nature of American life (while it also nourished dreams of upward mobility by giving the "grocery clerk" entrée into the "banker's" milieu).[113]

These groups both fostered literature and immeasurably enriched the lives of some of their members. (The "great books" phenomenon and, in some cases, the original postwar groups still survive today.) Yet, while Adler's vigilant Aristotelianism makes the point a bit harder to see, in reality the community "great books" programs of the late 1940s were hardly the sanctuaries from the business world that some of their adherents called them. For one thing, the greater the dissemination of Adler's rules, the more dogmatic they became. A 1946 training manual asserted, for example, that "it is absolutely essential that all the participants face each other, and that they have a table of some sort in front of them to lean on."[114] Such standardization made it even easier to view Adler's technique as prefabricated culture, as the same manual's unabashed discussion of analyzing the "market" for the "product" attests. Given that phrasing, it is not surprising that Adler wound up hawking his program in a downtown Chicago department store in 1948.

Furthermore, for all the program's strengths, one might argue that, at its worst, with friends like these, literature needed no enemies. Some people joined groups, in one commentator's words, "to shine among one's fellows by a parade of new-found knowledge." More than that, Adler's disregard for aesthetics, together with the lack of context and persistent drive for relevance he adopted from Erskine, combined in some groups to engender a quality of superficiality that was at the furthest remove from the concept of culture as inward. In the absence of guidance and background, some groups degenerated into "a muddle of blind-alley arguments, profitless repetitions, irrelevant remarks, silly opinions, and fundamental misunderstandings." The "great books" advocates' rejoinder that the purpose of the undertaking was not to study works exhaustively but rather to improve one's "ability to communicate by learning how to read, speak, and listen more effectively"—objectives worthy of Dale Carnegie—only revealed the extent to which the community movement could fulfill the potential for strengthening consumer values evident in Erskine's initial design. One participant, an advertising man, took advantage of that consonance between his occupation and his reading group by providing his classmates with slogans about the assigned books: he "packaged" Aristotle's *Ethics*, for example, as "'The rich don't know how to live, but they sure know where.'"[115]

Adler and Hutchins's permutation of the "great books" idea culminated in 1952 with the publication of the Encyclopedia Britannica's fifty-four volume *Great Books of the Western World*. The idea for the project had originated with William Benton, the former advertising whiz who, as Hutchins's vice-president for public relations, had acquired the encyclopedia for the University of Chicago. Benton approached Adler in 1943 about thinking up a "special idea" to help sell a companion set of classics. Adler seized the opportunity to create his ultimate system: the Syntopicon, or "Great Ideas," an index to the texts organized according to the topics they addressed, so that a reader could, in theory, trace throughout Western history a continuous line of thought on almost three thousand subjects. The scheme additionally included introductory essays to each of the 102 chapters into which the topics fell. Theoretically a way to highlight the underlying unity of the "great conversation," the Syntopicon could also work at cross-purposes to that aim by splintering works into isolated quotations. Called a "device" and an "invention," the term itself had a technological ring that promised the ability to solve practical problems with little effort.[116]

If the Syntopicon put Adler's stamp on the set as a whole, his priorities largely determined the choice of the individual works within it as well. The story of the selection process is instructive as an instance of canon formation even more visibly reflective of special interests than Erskine's construction of the original "great books" list. Adler, Barr, and Buchanan formed the core of an advisory board over which Hutchins presided. Together, they settled on inviting Mark Van Doren and two Chicago faculty members, Clarence Faust and Joseph Schwab, to join them. It was at this point that Erskine reentered Adler's orbit: as an afterthought, they added him to the board.[117]

From the outset, the board members were in tacit agreement about four assumptions. First, they were no more willing than Erskine to acknowledge the contributions of modernism—a stance that by the late 1940s was more willful and deliberate than it had been before World War I. For example, in response to the suggestion of Wallace Brockway, the Britannica editor (on loan from Simon and Schuster) working with the board, Hutchins wrote of *Ulysses*, "It is a monument of Irish wit;

but I am not sure that this justifies its inclusion."[118] Freud, it is true, finally made it onto the list, but, because he was a writer of nonfiction, his presence dodged the issue of acknowledging the modernist aesthetic. Second, the board made no departure from Adler's emphasis on philosophy at the expense of novels, plays, and poetry; aside from the Greeks and Shakespeare, just eleven of the set's seventy-four authors were represented by writings in those categories. Third, it understood at the outset that American authors would occupy little space, although Erskine and Van Doren did labor unsuccessfully for Franklin, Emerson, Whitman, and Thoreau. The only Americans published in the set were the Founding Fathers, Melville, and William James. (Needless to say, the issue of representing women or blacks did not arise.) Fourth, in sharp contrast to modernist critics, who, as David Hollinger has described them, facilitated the canonization of the works they championed by insisting that the values they stood for had to remain elusive and mysterious in order to survive, the board had no hesitation about collectively issuing the definitive judgments that Erskine and Adler had been pronouncing for years.[119] The group also assented to two additional principles that Adler made explicit: one, that, in keeping with Erskine's bias against mediation, the texts would stand without explanatory or scholarly apparatus; the other, that, unlike the "Five-Foot Shelf," the set would include only works in their entirety. Under no circumstances was it to resemble an anthology.[120]

With so much consensus, one might conclude that *Great Books of the Western World* virtually assembled itself. Yet one controversy pervaded the deliberations throughout 1944: the question of whether, as participants in the "great conversation," all of the selections had to be thematically related to each other. Buchanan, Barr, and Van Doren approved that doctrine, which Adler called "the most important thesis we have."[121] Erskine and the others dissented, objecting that the project seemed to be endorsing a particular "philosophy of life." As Erskine queried, "Why not permit the world to use the masterpieces as it chooses, provided only that the masterpieces are read?" (In that respect, he deserves credit for anticipating the openness to diverse ways of reading that literary critics have recently explored.) To break the deadlock, Hutchins proposed the addition of new board members, among them Alexander Meiklejohn, who accepted, and Lionel Trilling, who declined. Outnumbered, Erskine lapsed into a posture that Brockway, whose sentiments Hutchins and Adler probably shared, called that of "a nice old uncle," adding, "But is that a recommendation?"[122] In the end, *Great Books of the Western World* represented exactly what Erskine had feared: a narrow, idiosyncratic embodiment of Adler's preferences.

The marketing for the set, which Benton oversaw, incorporated many of the tensions about the meaning and uses of culture that had been evident in the "great books" ideology from the start. Benton's strategies included consulting with Harry Scherman about direct-mail approaches, setting up a plan for corporate donations to nonprofit institutions, and using only an experienced book sales force. Adler, with his penchant for the limelight, was also an asset; although the two men later clashed, Benton once ventured that Adler was "America's top promotion man."[123] The key document of the campaign was an illustrated brochure. Concealing Adler's partisanship, one version assured purchasers that the board had based its selections only on the "ultimate criterion": which books were the "greatest"? Like *How to Read a Book*, the same document also disdained "intellectual ease." Allaying fears to the contrary, it told individuals that their awareness that the "best" was "hard to come by" would propel them actually to read the books. Even the primary pitch for the Syntopicon rested on an image of self-reliance: an analogue of the Book-of-the-Month Club's rhetoric of "service," it depicted the compilation as a guide to "help the reader help himself."[124] Those appeals reflected Benton's and his colleagues' belief in the continuing power of Arnoldian tenets for the set's prospective owners.

Yet the promoters were also cognizant of its audience's other needs and anxieties. At an advisory board meeting in 1944, Hutchins had impassively declared that "people would buy the books for display, and, in being sold them, would not have to be persuaded that they could understand them." Benton, schooled on Madison Avenue, went even further. Noting that "the thought of reading them [the books] would terrify many potential buyers who would perhaps fail to buy if they thought they were supposed to read them," he emphasized the attraction of the Syntopicon as a reference work supplying useful information. At one point, Benton urged the inclusion of an "index to the index"—an "Applied Course" that would point out "suitable subjects for discussion at your Christmas dinner or at Thanksgiving." Identifying with the consumer, he explained, "After all, I want to read the Great Books in order to be popular and successful—and what are the applications I would like to make of these Great Books that will help me and my child to become popular and successful?" Benton concluded, "This is actually the basic idea in Mortimer's index but it has never been expressed in this way before." Adler did not see things in quite that light; more concerned, to his credit, with the integrity of the texts, he threatened to resign if Benton carried out the "Applied Course." But Benton, as perceptive in his own way as Dwight Macdonald, was only trying to capitalize on the inherent potential of the Syntopicon to obviate reading, supply information, and serve practical ends.[125]

Even Adler was willing to exploit that potential in more subtle terms. In an interview with Clare Boothe Luce on Benton's showcase radio program "University of Chicago Round Table," he remarked that the "Great Ideas was created to save time" and explained that the reader "does not have to begin and read a whole book through, and then another book through" but could "go to the set" to learn about "taxation, government control of industry, sex, divorce," and so on. Similarly, the promotional brochure announced, "Without the Syntopicon to guide you, it would take, literally, years of reading . . . to find out what they [the "great books"] have to say." Raymond Rubicam, a veteran adman in his own right, laid bare the double nature of Benton and Adler's message when, in response to a solicitation offering him a sponsor's discount, he replied, "Great Ideas, or Syntopicon, is a fascinating idea. . . . Maybe we can just read the introductory essays in those two volumes and acquire a liberal education easily worth $500 (less 10 percent)."[126]

Great Books of the Western World made its formal debut on April 15, 1952, at a banquet for sponsors and friends in the Waldorf Astoria's Grand Ballroom. The rhetoric flowed as freely as the wine, the speakers celebrating the set's contributions to the survival of "tradition" and "Western civilization." But Erskine, who would have recognized such phrases as echoes of his own, was absent from the festivities; he had died the previous year. The incompleteness of the gathering reiterated the larger theme of his career. Erskine contributed the basis for one of the chief agencies of American middlebrow culture and indelibly colored the role of the middlebrow critic. Yet at his death he most resembled what, in describing Byron, he called the defeated romantic hero: "Failing ever to live completely, he carried with him to his grave the memory of much experience which he had yearned for, but which had escaped him."[127]

Stuart Pratt Sherman
(Courtesy of University Archives, University of Illinois at Urbana-
Champaign)

Irita Van Doren, photographed by Walter Sanders
(Courtesy of Margaret Bevans and Barbara Klaw. Copyright © Time, Inc.
Used by permission of Time, Inc.)

HENRY SEIDEL CANBY, CHAIRMAN

HEYWOOD BROUN

DOROTHY CANFIELD

CHRISTOPHER MORLEY

WILLIAM ALLEN WHITE

The best new book each month selected for you by this committee–

AND SENT TO YOU REGULARLY ON AP-
PROVAL—A UNIQUE SERVICE FOR THOSE
WHO WISH TO KEEP ABREAST OF
THE BEST NEW BOOKS AS THEY APPEAR

ERTAINLY there is nothing more satisfying, to a person who loves books, than
to keep abreast of the best new works of
our present-day writers, *as they appear.*
And, inversely, there are few things more annoy-
ing than to *miss* the outstanding books, when
everybody else of intelligence is reading, discussing
and enjoying them. Yet how frequently most of us
disappoint ourselves in this way!

Think over the last few years. How often have
interesting books appeared, widely discussed and
widely recommended, books you were really anxious
to read and fully intended to read when you "got
around to it," but which nevertheless you *missed!*
Why does this happen to you so often?

The true reason lies in your habits of book-buying.
Through carelessness, or through the driving circumstances of a busy life, you simply *overlook* obtaining books that you really want to read. Or you live
in a district remote from bookstores, where it is
impossible to get the best new books without difficulty.

This need be true no longer. A unique service has
been organized, *which will deliver to you every month,
without effort or trouble on your part,* the best book of
that month, whether fiction or non-fiction. And if
the book you receive is not one you would have
chosen yourself, *you may exchange it for a book you
prefer,* from a list of other new books that are
recommended. In this way, automatically, you keep
abreast of the best literature of the day.

These "best books" are chosen for you, *from the
books of all publishers,* by a group of unbiased critics
and writers, whose judgment as to books and
whose catholicity of taste have been demonstrated
for many years before the public. The members of
this Selecting Committee, who have agreed to perform this service, are listed above. With each book
sent there is always included some interesting comment by a member of the committee upon the book
and the author.

The price at which the books are billed to you is in
every case the publisher's retail price. There are no
extra charges for the service.

A very interesting prospectus has been prepared, explaining the many conveniences of this plan. This
prospectus will convince you of several things: that
the plan will really enable you always to "keep up"
with the best of the new books; that you will never
again, through carelessness, miss books you are anxious to read; that the recommendations of this unbiased committee will guide you in obtaining books
that are really worth-while; that there is no chance
of your purchasing books that you would not choose
to purchase anyway; and that, in spite of the many
conveniences of the plan, the cost of the books you
get is no greater than if you purchased them yourself.

Send for this prospectus, using the coupon below
or a letter. Your request will involve you in no obligation to subscribe.

BOOK-OF-THE-MONTH CLUB, INC.
218 West 40th St.   Dept. 25   New York, N. Y.

39

Advertisement for the Book-of-the-Month Club
(Time, *May 3, 1926*)

Henry Seidel Canby
(Courtesy of Yale Picture Collection, Manuscripts and Archives, Yale
University Library)

Dorothy Canfield Fisher
(Courtesy of the University of Vermont Library)

John Erskine, photographed by Pirie McDonald
(Courtesy of the Library of Congress)

Will Durant and President Gerald R. Ford
(Courtesy of the Gerald R. Ford Library)

William Lyon Phelps
(Courtesy of Yale Picture Collection, Manuscripts and Archives, Yale University Library)

Alexander Woollcott as the "Town Crier"
(Courtesy of the Columbia Broadcasting System Photo Archives)

Clifton Fadiman (standing), John Kieran, and Franklin P. Adams on
"Information, Please!"
(Courtesy of the Columbia Broadcasting System Photo Archives)

MERCHANT

OF

LIGHT

WILL DURANT
AND THE VOGUE OF
THE "OUTLINE"

"Quite possibly," the writer Henry James Forman asserted in 1935, "future historians of civilization will take account of our critical epoch by pointing to the signal appearance of popularizers of all available human knowledge from the scattered stories of the past."[1] Forman's remark alluded to the interwar period's most important nonfiction publishing trend: the vogue of the "outline." Inspired by the success in the early 1920s of the American edition of H. G. Wells's *The Outline of History*, such volumes were summaries, in a single, readable work, of the facts ostensibly comprising a given subject. Many dealt with the natural sciences, disciplines changing so rapidly that they begged for simplification of bewildering new data. Thus, J. Arthur Thomson provided an *Outline of Science* (1922), George A. Dorsey explained *Why We Behave Like Human Beings* (1925), and Paul de Kruif chronicled the discoveries of *Microbe Hunters* (1926). The humanistic fields traditionally associated with liberal culture, however, proved even more compelling. In 1922 Hendrik Willem Van Loon's *The Story of Mankind* was second in nonfiction sales only to Wells's history; five years later Will Durant, the American author most famous for "outlines," entranced the public with *The Story of Philosophy*, foreshadowing his *Story of Civilization* series (1935 to 1967). Comparable books with more limited appeal treated, for example, art, architecture, religion, psychoanalysis, and literature. Publishers of home libraries and similar compendia also capitalized on the "outline" concept.[2] Even a figure identified with the avant-garde such as Lewis Mumford rode the wave with *The Story of Utopias* (1922). Though the genre had its antecedents, the "outline" craze of the 1920s and 1930s was unprecedented in its number of titles, range of topics, and extent of sales—to say nothing of the hopes and fears it encompassed.[3]

The "outline" phenomenon resulted from a convergence of several factors. First of all, it derived from uneasiness about the specialization of knowledge. To Americans continually reminded of their ignorance by proliferating educational opportunities and new media, "outlines" promised another way to catch up culturally and to regain a unified perspective. Second, the vogue of the "outline" was a prime expression of the early-twentieth-century American's concern with sustaining an adequate level of "civilization." In their attempt to make intellectual achievement comprehensible for a broad readership, such works represented a self-conscious commitment to the idea that civilized and mass society could coexist.[4] That effort, in turn, depended on the existence of a cadre of authors who were unapologetic generalists—individuals who believed in the ability of ordinary persons to grasp what they had to say. Propelled by that faith, such writers employed a literary style that was relentlessly factual, syntactically uncomplicated, devoid of bare generalizations, confidently unambiguous, and usually more lucid than dramatic.[5] Finally, the popularity of the form reflected certain conditions in the American publishing industry during the 1920s. The strong economy of the decade not only permitted investment in big, expensive volumes, it also encouraged the redirection of power away from long-established, WASP-dominated houses toward firms headed by young, often Jewish, innovators unsqueamish about the ethos of American consumerism.[6] As "made" books, initiated by publishers rather than authors, many "outlines" were frankly products. What is more, they were the objects of advertising campaigns framed in terms of the demand for accessible information and for commodities to enhance personality.

"Outlines" thus represented the coalescence of author, publisher, and the perceptions both held of public need. In addition, the form itself entailed an inherent paradox. As John Erskine perceptively wrote in 1925, the "charm" of the "outline" was the "clarifying philosophy" it offered after "decades of thick-accumulating fact."[7] Yet philosophical overviews could also work at cross-purposes to the desire for instant mastery of presentable, up-to-the-minute data. Granting that a complete analysis would require further examples, because not all "outlines" were exactly alike, an examination of how those tensions and convergences actually informed the most popular texts and their marketing—first, briefly, in Wells's and Van Loon's early successes and then in a full case study of Durant—can begin to provide, as Forman imagined, a history of the genre adequate to its significance in the making of middlebrow culture.

The Outline of History

"For us," Will Durant observed in 1930, "the career of the outline begins with H. G. Wells."[8] By 1918 Wells, at the height of his prestige as a novelist, increasingly felt the need to focus his attention on social commentary. One of the most vocal and influential formulators of the postwar concern with the nature of civilization, Wells had come to believe that its survival depended on a world united by a common government and a sense of common mission. Trained in his youth as a teacher, he concluded that education—and particularly a knowledge of past human experience—was a prerequisite for the global perspective he sought. Thus, he proposed to the Research Committee of the League of Nations Union that it coordinate the preparation of a history textbook written for the "general intelligence." Such a work, he stipulated, ought to forgo the customary emphasis on national boundaries and the usual neutral, shapeless aggregation of names and dates; instead, he envisioned a transnational "history of mankind" that would win converts to his political ideology.[9]

To Wells's dismay, professional historians resisted the project. Encouraged by Henry Seidel Canby, however, who was also involved with the League of Nations, and by George P. Brett, the president of Macmillan Company, Wells decided to write the book himself. His qualifications for the job were ample. His outlook since the turn of the century had included an animus against specialization, which he had expressed in both essays and novels. Spurred by that conviction, he had already embraced the role of popularizer by writing about science for the uninitiated. As for historical background, his own education had included the study of evolutionary theory under T. H. Huxley, which stood him in good stead for the construction of opening chapters on prehistory and primitive societies. For additional advice and for assistance with later periods, he assembled a distinguished group of consultants, among them Ernest Barker, a historian and political scientist; Sir E. Ray Lankester, an authority on natural history; and Sir H. H. Johnston and Gilbert Murray, both versed in cultural anthropology. Their names originally appeared with Wells's on the title page of *The Outline of History* and in some early advertising.[10]

The book's larger structure and argument, however, were entirely the product of Wells's own thinking. In keeping with its underlying intention, *The Outline of History* stressed the cross-cultural elements characterizing the development of civilization. Thus, while it devoted separate chapters to certain states and individuals—Greece, Rome, Alexander the Great, Napoleon Bonaparte—it also contained thematic headings—for example, "Serfs, Slaves, Social Classes, and Free Individuals"—that rambled across five thousand years from Greece to India to China. Midway through the book, Wells announced his thesis explicitly: History revealed, and religion and science both confirmed, that "men form one universal brotherhood, that they spring from one common origin, that their individual lives, their nations and races, interbreed and blend and go on to merge again at last in one common human destiny upon this little planet amidst the stars." The "outline of history" was a tracing of the "race" from a condition "at first scattered and blind and utterly confused" to the "serenity and salvation of an ordered and coherent purpose." Self-abnegation, Wells explained, had been the key to that development: in language remarkably close to Erskine's, he declared that "to forget oneself in greater interests is to escape from a prison."[11]

Yet progress was not inevitable; in fact, forces threatening to disrupt the continuity of the "outline" were dangerously close at hand. Repeatedly, Wells claimed, societies at first governed by a "community of will" had given way to a slavish "community of faith." Modern statecraft, predicated on self-interest and conducive to blind obedience, now threatened to produce the same reversal. Exacerbating the peril was the speed of change: the "great increase and distribution of knowledge" flowed like a "swift ice-run," outpacing universal understanding. Only a "new educated and creative elite" could stave off disaster by restoring the "community of will." The task immediately ahead was thus to create that elite by accomplishing two syntheses: first, to integrate what human beings had learned and, second, to use that learning as the basis for a world polity. The future of civilization, Wells concluded, depended on the outcome of "a race between education and catastrophe."[12]

Wells's premises earned him mixed reviews when the book appeared in 1919 (England) and 1920 (the United States). At one extreme, George Bernard Shaw declared that Wells's work should replace the book of Genesis; at the other, the doctrinaire Catholic Hilaire Belloc wrote lengthy denunciations of the *Outline*'s alleged crimes against the church.[13] In between, and more typical, were the assessments of American academics allied with the orientation known as the "new history." As the discussion of Durant will set out at greater length, "new historians" championed the study of culture and society as well as politics and diplomacy; they advocated broad syntheses of the past as aids in resolving the issues of the present.[14] Wells, arriving at those tenets independently, won unmitigated praise from the distinguished Columbia University Europeanist James Harvey Robinson, a patriarch of the movement.[15] Younger "new historians" like Carl Becker also hailed the scope and ideology of the *Outline* as hallmarks of a "notable effort to enlist the experience of mankind in the service of its destiny." Yet Becker nonetheless faulted Wells for failing to take the past on its own terms—to appreciate, as Becker noted, how the "motives and interests that have produced wars and permitted politicians to flourish" actually "functioned," no matter how contemptible they appeared in retrospect. Other scholars in sympathy with Wells's synthetic aims were even harsher in their estimates of his handling of sources: Carlton J. H.

Hayes, for example, attacked both Wells's "reliance on secondary works which are elementary, prejudiced, or antiquated" and his tendency to color data with "chronic moralizings."[16]

The *Outline*'s reception among intellectuals, however, had little bearing on its fortunes with the American public. At the top of the nation's nonfiction best-seller list in 1921 and 1922, it remained popular throughout the decade, accumulating sales of nearly a half-million copies.[17] The book's popularity was predicated, first of all, on Wells's preexisting reputation. As Hayes remarked, "Anything which comes from the press under his prevailing name . . . is greedily seized upon." In addition, Hayes noted, he is "the sort of writer Americans like. He is the romanticist turned journalist. He is serious—but not too serious. He is radical—but not dangerously radical. He is scientific—because he says he is." But Wells's approach and message had their own appeal. "The book," in Hayes's words, "exactly fits the temper and fancy of our generation. The great war and its aftermath have disillusioned us and raised in our minds anxious doubts and queries—has mankind always been so bad? is there any hope of salvation?—and it is Mr. Wells who comes forward at the psychological moment and obligingly gives us . . . answers to our questions and doubts." American readers were also especially receptive to the *Outline*'s promise of perspective and order because it helped them come to terms with their postwar prominence as world leaders.[18]

Moreover, Wells's decision to write a sweeping, "plain history of life and mankind" instead of a specialized monograph satisfied the reading public's desire for unified information in a way no academic historian ever had. Wells's contribution to the contest between "education and catastrophe" was to adopt stylistic measures that made his *Outline* readily available to the "average intelligent reader." Like a good schoolmaster, he incorporated into his narrative frequent summaries of his own discussions, reminding his audience what they had read and providing glimpses of the road ahead. His diction was spare and his syntax straightforward, on the assumption that nothing ought to interfere with the comprehension of the facts. Coupled with clarity of organization and language was a high level of generalization that substituted the ring of authority for ignorance and confusion. For instance, Wells pontificated that "the true figure to represent the classical Roman attitude to science is not Lucretius, but that Roman soldier who hacked

Archimedes to death at the storming of Syracuse." Yet mingled with that unstinting assertion of expertise (a stance fueled by Wells's sense of urgency about his mission) was a self-conscious confession of the *Outline*'s limitations: the book repeatedly referred to incidents "we cannot tell here in any detail." Such demurrers went hand in hand with an intimate tone that pervaded much of the narrative. As one reviewer commented, Wells "takes the reader into his confidence and discusses with him frankly the significance of the great events of the past," as if the events chronicled "were still happening." Those strategies enhanced the approachability of the text, enabling the reader to feel a bond with both Wells and his material.[19]

Finally, the popularity of *The Outline of History* in the United States was assisted by the advertising campaign of Wells's initial American publisher, Macmillan. Founded in Britain in the 1840s, the firm originally epitomized the assumptions governing the nineteenth-century book industry: publishers best served their profession by steering clear of overt commercialism, and books by nature had a restricted market that no amount of advertising could transcend. As such, Macmillan cultivated an image of restraint and informed readers about its books through advertisements that replicated the sedate format of a catalogue. George Brett's acquisition of the American wing of the firm in 1896, however, altered those premises. One of a small group of entrepreneurs who pioneered "progressive" publishing, Brett (as his encouragement of Wells confirms) saw his role as a developer of authors. Nor did he have any qualms about functioning as a "merchandiser" who favored "hard business thinking."[20] After World War I, when the ideas he had long espoused were becoming widely accepted, he effectively brought them to bear on Wells's history.

Modest in comparison to the pitches that accompanied later "outline" ventures, the marketing effort nonetheless made generous use of three techniques. The first was the "expert" testimonial: the endorsement of newspaper columnist Dr. Frank Crane, for example, graced the initial advertisements, as did quotations from reviews. The second was the display of printing and sales figures, with the implication that, unless buyers placed orders immediately, shortages would prevent them from acquiring copies. The third theme of the campaign stressed the value of owning the *Outline* as an aid in successful social performance: not only was it "the most talked-about book of the year, which is in such demand

that the presses can hardly supply it with sufficient rapidity," but
"everybody of standing reads Wells as soon as he comes out," and "even
the non-bookish are reading this most wonderful of Histories." The
social angle in the advertising copy, as Wells himself recognized, made
the *Outline* into an item for purchase but frequently not for reading.
The book, Wells acknowledged, "was bought and stowed away. When
the topic of this H. G. Wells came up . . . , the good Anglo-Saxon world
could say: 'We know all about H. G. W. We've got an illustrated copy of
his *Outline* in the library and the Christmas before last we made it our
gift book to all our friends.'" Macmillan also sponsored a poetry contest
for the best "rhymed review" of the book to boost its sales. The
"outline" vogue—shaped by content, form, and advertising—was off
and running.[21]

The Story of Mankind

Wells's most prominent American counterpart in the early 1920s was
Hendrik Willem Van Loon. A Dutch immigrant, Van Loon graduated
from Cornell University in 1905, returned to Europe for doctoral studies in history, and from 1911 to 1922 worked as a journalist and lecturer
at various American universities. Although he wrote two historical
studies of the Netherlands, he failed to find a congenial academic post.
In the late 1910s he began revising the first of a projected twelve-
volume history of the world for children. The manuscript bounced from
publisher to publisher, finally landing on the desk of Horace Liveright.[22]

Eccentric and adventurous, Liveright departed even further than
Brett from the prevailing style of Victorian publishing. As a Jew con-
fronted with anti-Semitism in the established houses, he had struck out
on his own, free of entanglements to the "entrenched Anglo-American
literary heritage." (The same was true of B. W. Huebsch, Alfred
Knopf, and Albert Boni, who had been Harry Scherman's partner in
the Little Leather Library.) In that spirit, Liveright had joined Boni in
1917 to start the Modern Library. Liveright's open-mindedness, together with his sense that the limited vision of the older houses excluded the needs of non-Anglo-Saxons, also predisposed him toward
projects like Van Loon's. In 1920 he brought the book out as *Ancient*

Man. Thereafter, mindful of the popularity of Wells's *Outline*, he persuaded Van Loon to scrap plans for the rest of his series and instead write a one-volume world history for both children and adults.[23]

The result was *The Story of Mankind* (1921), a sprightly tour of those past events without which, in Van Loon's words, "the history of the entire human race would have been different." The book reflected the role Van Loon later ascribed to both himself and Will Durant: that of instructor-at-large in civilized values. More confident than Wells about human survival, Van Loon wrote in 1937, "I think that both Will and I have always known what we were doing. We realized that we lived in a world which had completely changed its masters. In order to save civilization from chaos, it was necessary that the new masters should know certain things which until then had been the privileged possessions of the few." Duplicating Canby and Erskine's didactic posture, Van Loon added, "We carried this necessary information to this new public and in such a form and shape that it could understand this new knowledge and enjoy it."

In *The Story of Mankind*, that curriculum translated into an emphasis on the political developments that had made the Atlantic "the centre of civilisation." The text was devoid of footnotes, parceled into brief chapters, printed in large type, and written in the simple diction befitting a juvenile audience. Those characteristics made Van Loon's book even more accessible than Wells's. His own brand of intimacy arose from a style that included direct address of the reader and a sprinkling of references to supposedly timeless practices like taking "a girl out for a walk." What the book lacked in original research—Van Loon used no primary sources—it made up in inventiveness: to describe the circumstances of Christ's crucifixion, he provided letters about it between a Roman soldier and his uncle (with no indication that they were fabricated). The same professional historians who had criticized Wells disapproved of such liberties but emphasized the reliability and wit of Van Loon's *Story* nonetheless.[24]

Added to those appeals was the phenomenon of Van Loon himself. Wells, for all his rebellion against Victorian mores, was fundamentally closer to his friend Canby's genteel demeanor. Van Loon had a streak of gentility as well: as his Connecticut neighbor Van Wyck Brooks noted, he stood for a reasonableness and faith in progress that seemed out of place in the twentieth century. Less kindly, Waldo Frank portrayed him

as an "aristocrat" unhappily surrounded by "democratic vulgarities."
Yet Van Loon's predominant quality was his participation in the culture
of personality; as Brooks put it, "his personality was more significant
than his work." He told the *New Yorker* in the mid-1930s: "I've always
been an actor. I've always stood a little apart and watched myself
perform." His interviewer added, "He says that he has played his role
so constantly that he sometimes gets mixed up and doesn't know which
Van Loon he really is." A frequenter, like Broun, of the Algonquin
Hotel dining room, he was given to grand gestures and disastrous
romantic entanglements. Those traits concealed and undermined a desire to be considered less a buffoon and more a man of letters. Nevertheless, as J. Salwyn Schapiro noted, Van Loon's personality was
"present on every page" of *The Story of Mankind*. It radiated through
the pen-and-ink sketches he drew to illustrate his narrative; it reso-
nated in the first-person voice he adopted to guide the reader from
chapter to chapter; it informed his confession, at the end of the book,
that his emphases reflected his temperament.[25]

Thus, Boni and Liveright's decision to market *The Story of Mankind*
as an object of social display was even more consonant with the nature
of the text and its author than Macmillan's use of similar enticements to
purchase Wells's *Outline*. Featuring quotations from F.P.A., Broun,
and Becker, the advertisements promised a volume "destined to be the
most talked-of book of the season"—one "big in its significance and in
the place it will fill in our reading and conversation." The publishers'
approach proved to be a self-fulfilling prophecy: Van Loon's *Story* sold
more than seventy-five thousand copies in its first edition.[26] Throughout the 1930s, as Van Loon grew more famous, his personality loomed
correspondingly larger. The title of another of his outlines, *Van Loon's
Geography* (1932), for example, unabashedly offered readers his idiosyncratic picture of the world. His self-aggrandizement culminated in
Van Loon's Lives (1942), an "outline" of biography that cast him in a
role perfectly expressive of the intertwinement of culture and public
performance: the host of a series of dinner parties at which writers such
as Erasmus, Plato, and Confucius met each other and discussed their
taste in food and ideas.

Van Loon's appropriation of the "outline" form without sustaining
Wells's political concerns was characteristic of Wells's American imitators generally, although anxiety about the fate of civilization remained a

common theme. Moreover, works capitalizing on Wells's success tended to omit the British writer's sense of his limitations. At the same time, a number of the features Van Loon's *Story* inherited from Wells's *Outline*—its emphasis on the unity of knowledge, its bold rejection of specialization, its combination of authority and intimacy, its susceptibility to being marketed as a symbol of the cultured person—continued to define the genre as American examples of it multiplied in the mid-1920s. All of those qualities, as Van Loon's reference to their common purpose implies, colored the work of the premier American "outline" writer, Will Durant.

The Making of a Popularizer

William James Durant, born in 1885, grew up in a setting decidedly different from the parlors and libraries that shaped the careers of Canby and Erskine. The son of Joseph Durant, an illiterate French-Canadian immigrant, and Marie Allors Durant, he lived first in a number of Massachusetts mill towns and eventually moved to Arlington, New Jersey. Although he later made much of his working-class origins, his father's position as superintendent in a celluloid plant made the family relatively secure economically. More salient in Durant's background than the factor of class was the impact of religion. His parents were devout Catholics, steeped in the comforts and responsibilities of their faith. That outlook dictated Durant's education, which was unusually extensive for a child of a factory worker. After attending mainly parochial elementary schools, in 1900 Durant entered St. Peter's College in Jersey City, a Jesuit academy and college. Despite some adolescent flirtations, he began preparing for the vocation that promised to realize his mother's fondest hopes for him: the priesthood. In that way, one might argue, he embarked on a course that, while distant from Yale's or Columbia's apprenticeships in gentility, offered equivalent cultural authority within his own milieu.[27]

The course, however, did not run smooth. Durant was an insatiable reader and, by the end of his sophomore year, had begun passionately exploring the holdings of the local public libraries. Among the works he discovered were those the church proscribed, notably Darwin's *The Origin of Species* and *The Descent of Man*. The encounter, reinforced by conversations with a group of intellectually inclined friends outside of St. Peter's, left him irreparably shaken and skeptical: "One night I had been reading some of this heretical literature until a single stroke of the clock aroused me into the realization that it was time for sleep. . . . Dimly I saw my faith slipping from me, saw myself left standing as if naked on some lonely shore, with the darkness falling down around me. Even more dimly I saw my whole generation, thousands and millions of youths, passing through the same ordeal." Durant's penchant for romantic self-dramatization, evident above, makes it tempting to underplay the seriousness of his crisis of faith. Certainly, by the early twentieth century, many Americans had worked out the rapprochement between religion and evolution eventually labeled religious modernism; a distinction between theistic and atheistic evolutionary theory permitted Catholics as well as Protestants to accept the idea of changes in species over time while preserving their belief in God the Creator. If nothing else, the availability of that accommodation calls into question Durant's view of his representativeness. Yet Catholic doctrine, as espoused at St. Peter's, placed Darwin himself in the atheistic category— and it was Darwin, not evolutionary theory in general, that Durant read. In that light, Durant's account seems credible, and his sense of typicality, if misplaced, at least sincere.[28]

For a time, Durant mitigated his skepticism by embracing Christian socialism. Exposed to street-corner radicals and familiar with factory conditions, he gravitated to the works of Marx. In the hope that the church might become a force against greed and exploitation, Durant rededicated himself to the priesthood. In 1909 he entered the seminary at Seton Hall, where he had been teaching high school students. There, however, he engaged less in political agitation than in reading philosophy. Convinced, finally, of the permanence of his atheism, he resigned from the seminary in 1911, staying on at Seton Hall as a lay teacher. The last chapter in his alienation came the next year, when he publicly added anthropological theories connecting sexuality and primitive worship to his repertoire of heretical doctrines. Invited to give a lecture series on the origins of religion for the Francisco Ferrer Association, an organization of New York anarchists, he discussed "The Evolution of Sex, Homosexualism, Autoeroticism, and Malthusianism"—the first three topics preoccupying him then and in his autobiography fifty-five years later. A few days later, for reasons puzzling to theologians today, he was excommunicated by the bishop of Newark.[29]

Though sentimentalized in his fictionalized autobiography *Transition* (1927), the episode caused a painful breach of Durant's relationship to his family: his mother became hysterical at the news of her son's disgrace, and his father threw him out of the house. The loss of parental approval powerfully enhanced his mixed emotions about leaving the church. As the title of his memoir suggests, he saw himself not as released from confining expectations but instead as trapped between worldviews. Durant's "middleness," as he experienced it, stemmed from his embittered conviction that industrialization and scientific discovery had forced him to renounce the familial and intellectual consolations of Catholicism without putting any other coherent perspective in its place. In a statement brimming with ambivalence about a vanished past, he lamented, "The passage from agriculture to industry, from the village to the town, and from the town to the city, has elevated science, debased art, liberated thought, ended monarchy and aristocracy, generated democracy and socialism, emancipated women, disrupted marriage, broken down the old moral code, . . . taken from us many of our most cherished religious beliefs, and given us in exchange a mechanical and fatalistic philosophy of life."

While couched primarily as a problem of faith, Durant's analysis incorporated a concern about the bounded self and a countervailing appetite for "real life" that echoed the preoccupations of Sherman and Erskine. The gravest result of the "great change," as Durant called it, was that "we are fragments of men, and nothing more." On the one hand, that consciousness made Durant envy the seminarians, who, like Woodberry, represented discipline, integrity, and inner stability; he longed for "their unity and peace of mind, the simplicity of their souls, the quiet content of their secure and limited lives." On the other hand, however, just as Erskine's vocational crisis had entailed recognizing the limitations of his mentor's outlook, Durant found himself in the throes of a "lust of knowledge and experience" that propelled him into the "chaos of the world."[30]

The quest for unity—of self as well as of knowledge—would become a recurring theme of Durant's life. So would the pursuit of experience. In addition, his departure from the seminary left Durant with the immediate practical need to find something else to do. Before examining the forms those quests took, however, it is important to note that Durant carried them out with less struggle and urgency than other middlebrow figures did. Of prime importance in Durant's case was the matter of voice, both literally and figuratively. Probably for reasons that remain buried in the unknown history of Durant's childhood, he had managed, early on, to acquire an unusually strong conviction of his power both as a speaker and a presence. While at Seton Hall, he reported, he passed soapbox agitators "in disdain" because he knew he was "a better orator myself." During the same period, if *Transition*'s fictionalized narrative is accurate, he composed "A History of English Literature," a project which assumed both a command of a subject too sweeping for less intrepid writers and an audience ready to grant him the authority to expound on it. His propensity for comparing Spinoza's excommunication with his own bespoke the same sense of self-importance. Durant's career as a paid lecturer began modestly enough when he held a course on the philosophy of Herbert Spencer at the home of his friend Timothy Cairns, charging a dozen listeners three dollars apiece to attend. Thereafter, however, he evinced no hesitation in talking about whatever topic anyone proposed he address, on the assumption that people wanted to hear him. The best evidence for Durant's high self-regard is *Transition*—not its contents so much as the fact that it exists at all. His decision, when he was barely middle-aged, to write an autobiography laden with romance and drama required a view of himself as a key figure in a riveting spectacle. That assurance, one imagines, minimized his need to offset the fragmenting consequences of his loss of faith.[31]

Even so, as he grew away from religion, Durant embarked on a number of activities that imply some anxiety about regaining a sense of wholeness. He tried some characteristic therapeutic prescriptions for reinvigoration, becoming a vegetarian and a devotee of Bernarr Macfadden's Physical Culture City in New Jersey. He also explored more fully the radicalism he had broached earlier. By 1911 his friends included Alden Freeman, a millionaire who traveled in socialist circles and championed Emma Goldman. Freeman's involvement in the Ferrer Association led to Durant's appointment as instructor at the group's school in Greenwich Village. (Freeman took Durant on a European tour in 1912, partially supported him thereafter, and eventually underwrote his graduate education.) The heady atmosphere of the protest against convention Henry May has called the "innocent rebellion," then at its height, sustained Durant for a time. In *Transition*, he had the character representing Freeman console him with a vision of a socialist church: "Never mind; . . . we too have our faith, that some day all men may be brothers." He debated revolutionary ideology with his friends, continued to lecture on topics like "free love," and applied libertarian notions to dealings with his pupils, who included the son of Margaret Sanger and the children of Konrad Bercovici. The most permanent result of his experimentation with socialism was his relationship with another of his students, Ida Kaufman, a Russian Jewish immigrant whose mother had left her father to pursue heterodoxy and sexual freedom. Durant, who nicknamed her first Puck and later Ariel, courted her over her relatives' protest and in 1913, when she was fifteen, married her. For the rest of their lives, they were collaborators, although, even after her name appeared as coauthor of their works, Ariel Durant's contributions always remained research assistance rather than writing.[32]

Yet, in the end, politics failed Durant as a replacement for the unified perspective of religion. In his first autobiography, Durant depicted himself as a victim of disillusionment, attributing to World War I the recognition that a "lust for power" underlay all forms of political behavior. Even before the war, however, other aspects of his sensibility had competed with his radical leanings. The most concrete of those was a persistent penchant for philosophy. With his energy invested in Spinoza, he made little room for Bakunin. More abstractly, his retention of a model of selfhood predicated on discipline made him unsympathetic to anarchist injunctions to "be yourself." In contrast to his later writings, where the definition of self is mainly implied (as in his portrait of the seminarians), his 1914 essay "Socialism and Anarchism" provides direct evidence that Durant's position, though mingled with other longings, was much closer to Arnoldian formulations than to paeans to self-expression. To be one's "deliberate self," he explained, meant to "rise above" the impulse to "become the slaves of our passions" and instead to act with "courageous devotion" to a moral cause. Equally at odds with at least the atheistic version of anarchism was a lingering piety his excommunication had not dissolved. Finally, Durant exhibited an optimism that led him to reject intimations of human evil but also to retreat from radical social change. Instead of tying human progress to the rise of the proletariat, he made it the inevitable outcome of the laughter of young children or the endurance of his parents' marriage. As Ariel Durant later summarized it, he had concocted, by his mid-thirties, "that sentimental, idealizing blend of love, philosophy, Christianity, and socialism which dominate[d] his spiritual chemistry" for the rest of his life.[33]

Those attributes ultimately propelled him away from radicalism as a substitute faith and from teaching young anarchists as an alternative vocation. Instead, late in 1913 he embarked on a different pursuit: the dissemination of culture. Under the auspices of Timothy Cairns, a Presbyterian minister hospitable to freethinking, Durant began lecturing to audiences of adult workers at New York's Labor Temple. Established in 1910 on the Lower East Side, Labor Temple was a project of latter-day Presbyterian Social Gospelers. By the late 1910s it was functioning as a combination of settlement house, church, and school, although the large proportion of Jews who attended its programs frustrated the evangelical ambitions of its founders. Like the People's Institute, with which, by Durant's own account, it competed in the early 1920s, Labor Temple School offered a variety of evening lectures and discussions. The 1925–26 season, for example, included presentations of one sort or another by Lewis Mumford, W. E. B. Du Bois, Stuart Chase, and Doctors Hannah and Abraham Stone. Irwin Edman, William P. Montague, and Carl and Mark Van Doren were among the Columbia University faculty members who took on additional teaching at the school. Durant, however, dominated Labor Temple's educational program. His initial course in 1914 concerned the history of philosophy from Socrates to Bergson; later, in keeping with his confidence as jack-of-all-disciplines, he added classes on music, psychology, art, poetry, and sociology. In 1921 Durant took on the directorship of the school, a position that involved soliciting contributions and recruiting instructors.[34]

Durant's success at Labor Temple was a bit more qualified than he subsequently reported. His early audiences were usually large and enthusiastic, averaging at least five hundred people. In the mid-1920s, though, just before his publication of *The Story of Philosophy* reversed his fortunes, attendance slipped to under one hundred. The decline prompted Rev. Edmund B. Chaffee, Labor Temple's director, to inquire acerbically whether Durant's lectures "can really be made to appeal once more." Those vicissitudes aside, however, Labor Temple played a crucial part in Durant's resolution of his vocational upheaval. In time, he would describe activities like those he had engaged in there in language that transparently alluded to his own struggles. He imagined "a Church" that would "make its every chapel and cathedral a citadel of adult education, bringing science and history, literature and philosophy, music and art to those too old for school, and yet young enough to learn." In that setting, "brotherhood," "truth," and "goodness" would flower. The "saints" of his church would be great writers, before whose books Durant imagined burning "candles of worship at night" and whose names he wished to string "like beads on a rosary." Despite its Catholic imagery, his characteristic piety and optimism gave that conceit more affinities with Protestant crusades for moral uplift—such as the one at Labor Temple—than with the Catholic sense of sin.[35]

If Durant's work at Labor Temple, by enabling him to become priest of a secular religion of culture, helped him to reconstruct a professional identity, however, the need for a coherent perspective and sense of self—the doctrine to accompany his pulpit—still remained. Increasingly, philosophy seemed to Durant to hold the most promise for fulfilling that need, but its mastery required entry into a different sort of cloister: the university. Thus, at the same time he was teaching at Labor Temple, he enrolled as a graduate student in philosophy at Columbia. There he continued to fashion his philosophical interests into an instrument for forging the unity he sought; he also emerged from the academy with a sharper view of his role as a generalist. Most important, through exposure to the Columbia faculty, Durant evolved a position vis-à-vis the history of American thought that added a specific intellectual dimension to his status as exemplar of "transition."

Durant and Pragmatism

Durant was at Columbia from 1913 to 1917, when he received a Ph.D. Among the men with whom he studied were Felix Adler, William P. Montague, F. J. E. Woodbridge, and John Dewey. Durant's autobiographies contain few references to his Columbia experience, nor does he appear in accounts of his mentors' careers. In part, the thinness of the historical record suggests that graduate education played a relatively peripheral role in Durant's development. He was, after all, an atypical doctoral candidate: twenty-eight years old, married, and, more to the point, already performing as a "professor" several times a week. Again, the question of voice seems important. Having found an authoritative one before he arrived at Columbia, Durant had little need for the apprenticeship aspects of graduate school. Certainly he adopted a less self-effacing posture than his teachers were accustomed to. He noted that Wendell Bush, one of the instructors at his oral examination, "frowned a bit over my self-assurance," while Felix Adler complained that "this young man thinks that he has discovered everything." It may also be that he generated so much hostility from some of the faculty that he and they both subsequently shied away from making much of the Columbia connection.[36]

Nonetheless, the product of Durant's Columbia years—his doctoral dissertation, which became his first book—reveals the unmistakable influence of Columbia philosophers, especially Dewey and Woodbridge. To understand the extent of that influence requires a short overview of the status of American philosophy at the time Durant undertook his formal training. Durant's teachers were participants in an intellectual contest that echoed tensions in American society at large. Among the competing factions were the idealists, whose views had dominated American philosophy in the late nineteenth century. George Edward Woodberry had drawn loosely on idealism to fashion his literary credo, and even the philosopher Josiah Royce sometimes equated the word with a vague moralism, but its meaning within the academy was usually more rigorous and technical. Royce and other philosophical idealists had concentrated on questions of epistemology, depicting an orderly, permanent realm of the real beyond the fragmented, temporal world of observable phenomena. The role of the philosopher, they assumed, was to build a system of thought reflective of universal principles. Their mandate from the "educated elite," in Bruce Kuklick's words, was to "perform in an almost ministerial fashion," proclaiming "the basic worth of human existence and traditional institutions" and combining "mild exhortation with a defense of fundamental verities."[37]

That set of views enabled Royce and his colleagues to focus on metaphysics rather than on social problems. As was true for Woodberry's literary version as well, philosophical idealism permitted the disregard of urban and industrial disorder by treating it as ephemeral. Darwinism could be similarly disarmed. According to David Hollinger, "the American idealists used the suprasensuous 'ultimate reality' of classical idealism as a sponge; whatever seemed threatening in their intellectual environment could be absorbed within it." Within the university, moreover, idealist philosophers performed the function of withstanding specialization; they supplied "philosophies of life" rather than solutions to technical problems. Although Santayana was unsparing in his attack on that form of gentility, the historian of Columbia's philosophy department, John H. Randall, Jr., put matters in a more favorable light: Idealism "stood in the colleges for a kind of lay spirituality, as Emerson did for the literary public. It fostered a sensitivity to cultural and spiritual values at a time when the arrogance of the newly installed scientists, to say nothing of the general atmosphere of pushing business enterprise, was tending to subordinate them in academic circles."[38]

By the turn of the century, however, the scientific developments that tested idealism's spongelike capacity had given rise to alternative outlooks, including realism and pragmatism. Both groups impatiently rejected their predecessors' concern with spiritual transcendence. The most important early pragmatist, William James, had resembled Royce in meeting his audience's desire for a wide-ranging philosophy of life. Nonetheless, James adopted an empirical, particularistic approach and championed the scientific method.[39] In those respects, pragmatism was to philosophy what Sherman, Canby, and Erskine's nemesis philology was to literary scholarship. Yet the thrust of the pragmatic approach was away from the ivory tower and down to earth: that is, toward an unsentimental scrutiny of social issues in an attempt to spur action, not metaphysical contemplation.

While some universities remained oases of the older viewpoint, Columbia in the early 1900s became a center of reaction against idealist thought. As its chair, Woodbridge, a realist, infused the philosophy department with a commitment to reconstructing the discipline. More important for Durant, however, was the presence of Dewey, who had succeeded James as pragmatism's preeminent representative.[40]

Dewey's philosophy, which he called instrumentalism, sought to obliterate a number of dualisms: between an ideal and a material world, contemplation and action, morality and science. Knowledge, he said, was "always a matter of the use that is made of experienced natural events." Convinced that the idealists' preoccupation with epistemology was fruitless, he envisioned the application of the scientific method of inquiry to the discovery of knowledge of all sorts—moral as well as cognitive. In "The Need for a Recovery of Philosophy" (1916), a key expression of Dewey's views at the time he taught Durant, he went beyond James's emphasis on the individual to insist that philosophers apply scientific procedures—"creative intelligence"—to control and change society. In addition, he replaced an emphasis on universal precepts with a genetic approach to ideas that emphasized the historical contexts in which they arose.[41]

Durant's relationship to the warring claims of idealism and pragmatism was complex. The best source for discerning his position is his dissertation, which Macmillan published in 1917 as *Philosophy and the Social Problem*. It bore the unmistakable imprint of the Columbia pragmatists; it also retained a streak of philosophical idealism. The book addressed the need to modify human greed, aggression, and evil by constructing social institutions. Its first section, "Historical Approaches," examined five philosophers—Socrates, Plato, Bacon, Spinoza, and Nietzsche—in light of the guidance each offered twentieth-century Americans dealing with that "social problem."

Durant's reading of the classical tradition was decidedly instrumentalist. The Socratic equation of intelligence and virtue, which, interestingly enough, Erskine had embraced as an alternative to the moral authority of character, held for Durant a more sweeping message: it demanded the experiential determination of communal needs and the organization of government to coordinate "adaptive activity."[42] Similarly, Plato's design of a republic ruled by philosophers was a form of "social reconstruction through intelligent control." When Durant came to discuss Francis Bacon, he expressed directly ideas Dewey would subsequently publish in *Reconstruction in Philosophy*. Both characterized Bacon as the forerunner of the experimental scientist, fearlessly delving into the unknown as part of the same search for social control that underlay the pragmatic method. As for Spinoza, Durant's favorite philosopher, his vision of a state predicated on freedom and enlightened self-interest was a model of intelligence at work in a democracy. Finally, Nietzsche, while disturbingly antidemocratic, displayed appropriate contempt for passive philosophizing and, in his conception of the superman, revealed the possibilities for human fulfillment that accompanied the liberation of the will to power.[43]

Durant's rendering of his five historical subjects in terms of pragmatic values supplied the foundation for a second section of *Philosophy and the Social Problem* entitled "Suggestions." To facilitate social reconstruction, he proposed the creation of a "Society for Social Research" composed of selected physicians and university professors. The primary task of the society was to gather information in the natural and social sciences and to issue periodic reports designed to enlighten the electorate. (The plan bore some resemblance to a newspaper scheme called "Thought News" in which Dewey had been involved in the 1890s.) By that means, Durant argued, such "merchants of light," in Bacon's phrase, would furnish Americans the advantages of government by Plato's philosopher-kings and Nietzsche's supermen while preserving Spinoza's commitments to democratic choice.

In a prophetic passage, Durant even imagined that one function of the society would be to invite a group of "the most generally and highly valued" authors to form a "Committee on Literary Awards," for the purpose of "telling the world every month, in individual instalments, their judgment on current fiction." Assenting to the redefinition of culture as news, Durant rhapsodized: "Imagine the varied judgments printed with synoptic coordination of the results as a way of fixing the standing of a book in the English literary world; and judge the stimulus that would reside in lists signed by such names."[44]

Especially to its detractors, Durant's "dream," as he called it, was the explicit expression of what a disgruntled reviewer termed "the Deweyesque brand of pragmatism." Durant himself rather glibly acknowledged his debt to Dewey in a footnote that also contained a nod to Bertrand Russell and Max Eastman.[45] Yet his plan departed from pragmatism in important, if contradictory, ways. First, Durant renounced even more completely than Dewey did the idealist penchant for abstract speculation. While Dewey's attack on what Durant breezily labeled "epistemologs" included an effort to provide the philosophical bases for the pragmatic view of knowledge, Durant had no such contributions to offer and anti-intellectually derided the entire discussion as worthless.[46] Second, however, Durant veered back toward idealism in key respects. Whereas Dewey favored scientific means to attain philosophical ends, Durant's admiration for experimental method was superimposed on the bitter posture as science's victim he had struck in the aftermath of his seminary experience. Thus, instead of joining Dewey's effort to reconcile the two disciplines, he continued to identify science with fragmentation and sustained the idealist concept of the philosopher as the figure who alone could organize knowledge. Along the same lines, Durant's tidy summary of the lessons of history for the "social problem"—"Socrates shows us how to use Bacon to reconcile Plato and Nietzsche with Spinoza"—suggested the system making of the idealists; its cheerful confidence, although directed toward a social aim, likewise echoed idealism's optimistic overtones.[47] Hence, Durant appears not so much as a thoroughgoing pragmatist but as a figure who adopted a large number of Dewey's assumptions while drawing back from precisely those aspects of pragmatism that came to terms with the modern order—that is, with uncertainty, disunity, and scientific authority. Despite his passage from seminary to university, in other words, he was (and would remain) still the embodiment of "transition."

Important in placing him as a philosopher, Durant's Columbia dissertation also contained the paradigm for his relationship to his audience. His disseminators of intelligence, although drawn from universities, were to be generalists, all of them tackling a variety of social ills irrespective of their particular fields. Moreover, Durant envisioned their reports "couched not in learned and technical language but in such phraseology as will be intelligible to the graduates of an average grammar school." In terms of social standing, the "merchants of light" were to constitute an unabashed "aristocracy." Durant revealingly interchanged that word with "priesthood," reiterating the nineteenth-century conception of the philosopher as quasi-minister and alluding to his own vocational struggle. Yet his philosopher-priests were simultaneously to serve democracy by empowering the people with the knowledge their welfare required.[48]

Durant's account of the way in which agents of the "Society for Social Research" would extend their educational activities to include working-class students was the most overt sign that his drawing of the "merchants of light" was a self-portrait. The substance and style of *Philosophy and the Social Problem*, however, implicitly communicated the same point. His decision to cover several centuries of philosophic thought and to prescribe broad reforms qualified him for membership in his own organization. As for the form of his "report," although references to class lectures and to some published sources appear in footnotes, Durant's direct address of the reader, fictive imaginings, lengthy speculative remarks, use of personae to embody competing viewpoints, and poetic cadences defied scholarly conventions in the interest of accessibility. Some passages—"We will take thought and add a cubit to our stature; we will bring intelligence to the test and call it together from the corners of the earth; we will harness the genius of the race and renew creation"—were closer to the sermons Durant had once intended to deliver than to textual analysis. Such techniques, almost flamboyant deviations from typical dissertation prose, enhanced the book's readability but in so doing marked the distance between Durant's enterprise and the specialist's efforts. Finally, by following the authoritative sketch of his plan with a chapter of possible objections entitled "The Reader Speaks," Durant struck the same political balance his democratic aristocrats attained.[49] Thus, he joined Stuart Sherman, the Book-of-the-Month Club, and the "great books" movement in mediating between elitism and democracy, though in Durant's case the result was less a tension permeating his work than a conscious espousal of a political middle way.

Philosophy and the Social Problem was largely overlooked from the moment it appeared: it sold only a hundred copies. Yet the values and assumptions it incorporated remained the basic components of Durant's thinking as he continued lecturing and laying the groundwork for his next project, *The Story of Philosophy*.[50]

The Story of The Story of Philosophy

Durant did a brief stint as instructor in the extension division at Columbia during 1917–18, but, except for a course at UCLA in 1935, his dismissal at the end of the year severed his academic affiliation permanently. The official reason for his termination was the wartime decline in enrollment; possibly his attack on Butler's repression of dissent also had something to do with it. Durant, one senses, would have preferred a continuing university tie, but he made the most of his flourishing popularity as a public lecturer. In the spring of 1917 he had embarked on his first speaking tour outside of the New York City area; he soon acquired a manager and regularly traveled the Chautauqua and women's club circuits.[51]

At the same time, he began producing a series of guides to philosophy for the maverick publisher Emanuel Haldeman-Julius. From his youth a radical and a freethinker, Haldeman-Julius was, before World War I, a drama critic, reporter, and editor for various socialist newspapers. In Greenwich Village he met Ariel Durant, who shared his Jewish immigrant background and radical sympathies. Subsequently, he migrated to Girard, Kansas, and acquired the socialist weekly *The Appeal to Reason*. In 1919 he started the business that would bring him fame and fortune: the publication of pocket-sized, cardboard-bound volumes eventually called Little Blue Books. His original intention was to create a "university in print"; hence, his first titles were classics like *The Rubaiyat of Omar Khayyam*. Part eccentric ideologue, part shrewd entrepreneur, he soon turned his "university" into a bazaar of intellectual curiosities: books of sex advice, atheist polemics, ethnic jokes, personality manuals, and practical instruction appeared alongside literature—and generally outsold it.[52]

Nicknamed "the Henry Ford of publishing," Haldeman-Julius skillfully capitalized on the clamor for culture packaged as information and compatible with business priorities. His offerings included *Facts You Should Know about the Classics, How to Get a Liberal Education*, and *Outline of U.S. History*, as well as a "one hundred best books" list. He had no qualms about abridging texts to excise "the duller portions," claiming that "for him who runs as he reads the Little Blue Book version is ample." Similarly, contending that the average American would not buy a book just because it had "stood the test of time," he routinely renamed works to give them more appeal; Theophile Gautier's *Fleece of Gold*, for example, became *The Quest for a Blonde Mistress*. Thus, he satisfied the public's desire, in his words, for "romance, adventure, fun" rather than for books too "esoteric" or "refined and highbrow." The size and feel of the volumes—they were really pamphlets—made culture seem both manageable and disposable. Yet Haldeman-Julius was probably right in contending that, because of their modest appearance, people bought Little Blue Books to read rather than to display on library shelves.[53]

In 1922 Haldeman-Julius enlisted Durant as a supplier for his popularizations. Although Durant claimed that he succumbed to Haldeman-Julius's entreaties after the publisher had anonymously attended one of his Labor Temple classes, Haldeman-Julius's recollection that Durant contacted him while on a lecture swing through Kansas seems more in keeping with the eye for the main chance Durant exhibited throughout his career. In any case, over the next three years, Durant composed eleven essays on philosophers from Plato to Dewey. Many were first printed in Haldeman-Julius's serial *Life and Letters*; all were issued as Little Blue Books.[54]

In format, the pamphlets conformed to Haldeman-Julius's standard specifications: three and a half by five inches, sixty-four pages, approximately fifteen thousand words. Consistent with his marketing principles, Haldeman-Julius retitled Durant's contributions from "guides" to "stories" because the latter word, he came to believe, "avoids any suggestion of pedantry, and emphasizes that philosophy as a whole has a story behind it which can be told in a fascinating and informative way."[55] Whatever they were called, Durant's tales of philosophy consistently sold more copies than the works of philosophers themselves, which apparently promised less "fun" and "fascination" than Durant's retellings. Haldeman-Julius also removed the taint of the "esoteric" and touted the essays' practical side by advertising them in the category of "Self-education and Self-Improvement." Yet the countervailing bow to professorial expertise was present as well: each title page identified the author as "Will Durant, Ph.D." or "Dr. Will Durant" and included a partial list of his publications and other credentials. The public responded. By Haldeman-Julius's estimates, in the early 1920s Durant's Little Blue Books sold an average of twenty-seven thousand copies annually.[56]

Their success led "the Henry Ford of publishing" to propose to Durant that they bind the pamphlets together in a single volume. In the fall of 1925, after Haldeman-Julius decided not to buy a large press for that purpose himself, he and Durant both hunted around for a firm to take on the project. Durant entered into a contract with Macmillan, but Haldeman-Julius persuaded him to cancel it and to sign instead with the fledgling house of Simon and Schuster. The next spring, *The Story of Philosophy* appeared. Almost six hundred pages long, its substantive chapters were virtually exact reproductions of the Haldeman-Julius versions. The Simon and Schuster edition included as well introductory and concluding material, an index, and a glossary. By the end of the year, it was the best-selling nonfiction book in the United States—and the epitome of the "outline" craze.[57]

A "Healing Unity of Soul" and "Mind"

What were the appeals of the text that lay between the covers, whether blue cardboard or black cloth, of the most popular American "outline"? According to Durant's publisher, Max Lincoln Schuster, the magnet was simply the fascination of philosophy itself. In any era, Schuster claimed, Durant's volume would have sold because "people are always interested in the answer to the persistent questions" of human existence.[58]

But if Americans were merely looking for surveys of traditional philosophical issues, they might have been satisfied with the "high" culture approaches to the field already available in the mid-1920s. The German scholar Friedrich Paulsen's *Introduction to Philosophy*, for example, first published in 1894, was reprinted five times between 1922 and 1930. Paulsen organized his discussion in terms of topics rather than individual thinkers: the ontological problem, the cosmological-theological problem, problems of epistemology. Ethics appeared only in a brief appendix. The sole philosopher singled out for extended, separate treatment was Kant, of some of whose theories Paulsen was a champion. His effort throughout was to take account of the impact of Darwinism and materialism on questions of faith and knowledge, conceiving of the need to reconcile science and religion as the central task of modern philosophy.[59]

Alternatively, Wilhelm Windelband's *A History of Philosophy*, translated from the German by James Tufts in 1896, located ideas in specific historical periods—for example, the philosophy of the Renaissance, the philosophy of the Enlightenment. Within those divisions, except, again, for a chapter on Kant, Windelband also focused on problems rather than people, breaking apart an individual's body of work in order to subsume pieces of it under categories like "knowledge of the outer world" or "natural right." Despite his chronological arrangement and his sensitivity to intellectual and biographical influences, in practice Windelband adduced few causal connections between a philosopher's social milieu and his writing. Yet his coverage was relatively comprehensive, emphasizing epistemology but including moral and political philosophy, and encompassing a vast period of time.[60]

If Paulsen and Windelband theoretically provided answers to "persistent questions," however, they did so by perpetuating the image of philosophy as the most difficult of the humanities. Unlike historical scholarship, for example, the abstract nature of philosophical exchange appeared to preclude much participation by lay readers. It was the "aristocrat of literature," exalted but remote.[61] Paulsen's and Windelband's homage to the majesty of their subject took the shape of erecting formidable obstacles for the uninitiated reader. Although Paulsen's book carried an endorsement by William James commending its untechnical approach, his allegiance to grappling with the legacy of nineteenth-century thought forced his audience to forgo its commonsense conclusions about reality and to confront complex and esoteric debates. With his ponderous chapters, sophisticated diction, and academic tone, Paulsen was thoroughly unsuited to anyone who "runs as he reads." Likewise, those devices of Windelband's work that announced at a glance its classroom utility—densely printed summaries of important figures, relieved only by boldface type for names demanding memorization—were equally daunting to the nonstudent.

Broadly speaking, one of the chief lures of Durant's book, as Haldeman-Julius had known and Schuster also acknowledged, was that he kept philosophy on the throne and made the expert chief courtier, while insisting that anyone could arrange a royal audience. More precisely, at a time when many Americans sought to complement or create for themselves a liberal arts education, Durant offered authoritative access to the component of that education ostensibly most abstruse. Equally important, the "persistent questions" he implicitly addressed went beyond Windelband's and Paulsen's conventional queries to encompass a set of issues particularly germane to American readers in the 1920s: Is unified knowledge possible? Is autonomy recoverable? Who were the successful personalities of the past? Given the pressures of the marketplace, what information about philosophy is essential for the busy person to know? Can affluence and civilization coexist? Assuming that the book's substance, rather than simply its marketing, contributed to its popularity, Durant's responses to those culturally generated queries more plausibly explain *The Story of Philosophy*'s attraction than his commentary on the timeless dilemmas Schuster had in mind.

The way in which the text (that is, the hardbound volume) actually worked to convey its multiple appeals is evident from the beginning. The title page, for example, contained the promise of approachability and drama attached to the word "story," along with the invocation of Durant's doctorate Haldeman-Julius had also exploited. There, too, was Durant's perceptively chosen subtitle, *The Lives and Opinions of the Greater Philosophers*, its key words tapping into wellsprings of meaning. "Lives" offered the prospect of enhancing one's image by learning from the examples of others. Although Durant's subject matter lacked the potential to join hero and reader in the bond of common consumer desire Leo Lowenthal ascribed to a rash of popular biographies in the 1940s, it could nonetheless furnish what Lowenthal called "pseudoindividualization": the chance to overcome fears of anonymity by identifying with those who stood out from the mass. "Lives" also dissociated philosophy from erudition, connecting it instead to everyday experience. "Greater," like the phrase "great books," provided the guarantee that experts had already blazed a trail through the intellectual overgrowth surrounding the bewildered novice; again, it carried the cachet of an encounter with the philosophical equivalent of the screen star—and thus promised a lesson in "being somebody." The most manipulative word in the subtitle, "Opinions," stripped philosophy of its effort to deal in fundamental truths about existence. Calling to mind the notion that everybody is entitled to an opinion, it made philosophers as fallible and expendable as anyone else. If it was vaguely anti-intellectual in this context, however, the leveling effect of the term enhanced the book's accessibility even further. By regarding philosophy simply as a matter of opinion, readers, capable of forming their own, could approach its study without fear.[62]

Three other pieces of prefatory apparatus in the first Simon and Schuster version—a foreword by Dewey, a note "to the reader," and an introduction "on the uses of philosophy"—extended that welcome and offered a preview of Durant's perspective. Giving the book his blessing, Dewey praised Durant in Arnoldian terms: he found commendable his efforts to "humanize" philosophy while adhering to sound scholarship. "This book," Durant himself declared in the note, "is not a complete history of philosophy" (a disclaimer he would rely on later to try to pacify hostile reviewers). "It is an attempt to humanize knowledge by centering the story of speculative thought around certain dominant personalities." In addition to Arnold, that language also derived, more directly, from James Harvey Robinson, whose advocacy of "the new history" had coincided with Wells's views and who had published *The Humanizing of Knowledge* in 1923. Robinson, however, while sympathetic to the role Durant assumed and to his insistence on synthesis, used "humanization" in contradistinction to the specialization of science; his book called for teachers to translate scientific discoveries into terms relevant to current social needs. In Durant's hands, "humanization" took on a somewhat different meaning. To "humanize" philosophy, as Durant employed the phrase, was to inject it with human interest rather than to emphasize its status as a humanistic discipline. The same preface repeated Durant's charges against epistemology, thereby relieving the reader of the need to deal with the esoteric "knowledge-process" at all.[63]

The book's introduction struck a more lyrical note in providing additional assurances. Its opening lines counterposed philosophy to the "mart of economic strife and gain," imputing to readers the desire, however infrequently realized, to pursue wisdom rather than wealth. Thus, Durant placed at ease even the most zealous businessmen; in the manner of Book-of-the-Month Club advertising, he credited them with good intentions while enabling them to maintain their commercial agenda. Perpetuating his distinction between science and philosophy, he went on to make clear the superiority of the latter as an instrument of "interpretive synthesis." Durant intended that argument to disarm those readers skeptical of anything that appeared useless, a defense that may have been necessary to offset the prestige of the scientist in the mid-1920s. But his message had the secondary result of calming anyone afraid that his book would prove as difficult to understand as biology or physics. His closing remarks invoked Emerson's comment that "when genius speaks to us we feel a ghostly reminiscence of having ourselves . . . had vaguely this self-same thought." Connecting himself to his readers by adopting the first person plural, Durant thus prepared them for a "story" very different from Paulsen's or Windelband's dry and difficult explorations of philosophical problems.[64]

Durant's text sustained the strategies he employed in his prefatory material. The volume contained eleven chapters, each, except for the occasional connective paragraph or change of phrase, an exact reprint of a Little Blue Book. Plato, Bacon, Spinoza, and Nietzsche, protagonists in Durant's dissertation, reappeared in the company of Aristotle, Voltaire, Kant, Schopenhauer, and Herbert Spencer. In addition, Durant included two groups of contemporary philosophers: the Europeans Bergson, Croce, and Russell and the Americans Santayana, James, and Dewey. It is useful to take stock of the individuals Durant omitted in order to see just how idiosyncratic his pantheon was. His antiepistemological bias accounted for his neglect of a number of philosophers usually considered essential—Descartes, Berkeley, Hume, Locke, and Mill—while Hegel appeared only as an afterthought in the chapter on Kant. He also left out the Scholastics on the grounds that they belonged to the study of religion, not philosophy.

The structure of each chapter was basically the same. In accordance with his announced commitment to the fascination with personality, Durant introduced his subjects with biographies that placed them in their historical settings. Sometimes he saved the details of his subjects' later years for the chapter's closing paragraphs, so that the explications of their thought became suspenseful intervals between compelling narratives. The explications themselves contained roughly chronological summaries of each figure's major works, divided into topical subsections. Except in the cases of Voltaire, Spinoza, and Dewey, Durant concluded his outlines with his own critical estimates, thus adding his "opinion" to the spectrum before the reader.

If much of Durant's rhetoric and focus appealed to contemporary concerns, the philosophical content of *The Story of Philosophy* had a more retrospective quality. As history rather than social analysis, the book evinced somewhat less affinity with instrumentalist tenets than the half-hearted pragmatism of *Philosophy and the Social Problem*. Certain pragmatic legacies in the text, however, blinded both Durant's antipragmatic adversaries and Dewey himself to that fact. It was true, as Dewey's endorsement affirmed, that the book's historical framework furnished exactly the type of explanatory dimension Dewey's genetic principles dictated. As Mortimer Adler pointed out in a thoroughly negative review, the presumption that philosophical ideas "are to be exhaustively understood . . . in terms of their origins" was (in Adler's view) just the sort of undialectical, erroneous thinking characteristic of "the pragmatic conception of philosophy." In addition, Durant's cursory attention to epistemology, which Adler also decried, reflected the pragmatists' impatience with efforts to settle in the abstract questions about knowledge and reality. As if he were following Dewey's instruction to forgo inquiries into "what or who made the world," Durant entirely eliminated Paulsen's focus on the relation between faith and science. Dewey himself appeared as a model philosopher, clear evidence of Durant's continuing allegiance to some of the premises of his graduate training.[65]

Yet Durant's account of James was far less reverential, ridiculing James's confusion of belief and truth. More broadly, Durant's early "dream" of intelligence at work dropped out of sight in *The Story of Philosophy*, replaced by merely passing allusions to twentieth-century America. Moreover, in spite of an approving reference to experimentation, Durant's dissociation of philosophy and science continued to challenge Dewey's insistence on scientific method. Thus, while Adler was certainly correct that Durant's animus toward metaphysics helped shape his choice of subjects, the pragmatic strain in *The Story of Philosophy* was not strong enough to bring Durant into line with Dewey's directive that philosophy provide moral and political direction by scientific means.[66]

In fact, assigning *The Story of Philosophy* a pervasive pragmatism grants the book much more cohesiveness than it really had. Despite its elaborate overtures to its readers, it conspicuously lacked a statement of Durant's selection principles. Conceding the influence of his intellectual commitments, one still suspects that the volume was less the outgrowth of a well-defined philosophical orientation than a pastiche of Durant's prejudices, interests, and readily assembled lecture notes. To catalogue the issues with which its sixteen thinkers dealt is to realize that the work has no center (a predictable trait, perhaps, in a book constructed from discrete pamphlets): they range from the question of the best state to the nature of science to the meaning of virtue. Even Ariel Durant noted, in *A Dual Autobiography*, that *The Story of Philosophy* was closer to what Durant himself deplored as "shredded history" than to the syntheses he extolled.[67]

Nonetheless, the book did contain a subtext that gave it a tenuous continuity, one that drew Durant closer to the idealists than the pragmatists. Ironically, given the piecemeal nature of the volume, this was his emphasis on what he elsewhere called the "healing unity of soul" and "mind" that philosophy could provide. Also present in muted form in his dissertation, the theme encompassed the same two dimensions that Erskine's "great books" design addressed: the integration of knowledge and of the self. "So much of our lives is meaningless, a self-cancelling vacillation and futility," Durant wrote in the introduction. "We want to know that the little things are little, and the big things big, before it is too late. . . . We want to be whole, to coordinate our energies by criticizing and harmonizing our desires." Without such coordination, he noted in the chapter on Aristotle, "we are all fragments of what a man might be." In place of his earlier political message, Durant's interpretations of his subjects in *The Story of Philosophy* repeatedly provided object lessons in the fulfillment of those longings.[68] No less than Erskine's list, Durant's philosophical canon took shape as a result of his history and his hopes.

Thus, as Durant here presented him, Plato exemplified the wise, disciplined union of philosophy and poetry. Aristotle's great strength was his creation of "the most marvelous and influential system of thought ever put together by any single mind." Bacon exhibited a "passion for unity," a "spirit of control," and a "desire to spread the wings of his coordinating genius over a hundred sciences." Spinoza's devotion to reason gave him an enviable serenity; together, his work and life taught that "to be ourselves we must complete ourselves." Voltaire, Durant wrote (in language that suggests his own self-concept), sought "a unifying principle by which the whole history of civilization in Europe could be woven on one thread." Even Kant, epistemologist though he was, undertook his philosophy in order to "unite the ideas of Berkeley and Hume with the feelings of Rousseau" and defined mind as "the coordination of experience." Schopenhauer, with his cranky cynicism and misanthropy, appeared as a counterexample, a "diseased" man who misunderstood the role of intellect in devising a "united and harmonious will." Spencer insisted that "the proper field and function of philosophy lies in the summation and unification of the results of science." Nietzsche, solitary and egotistical, was another counterexample, illustrating the perils of unrestrained individualism and lacking a "harmonious philosophy." Among contemporary thinkers, Croce failed to grasp the importance of "synthetic" history, but Dewey redeemed philosophy by making it "the coordination of knowledge and desire."[69]

Like the system making in his dissertation, Durant's attraction to philosophers whom he could construe as unifying knowledge highlights the affinity between him and his idealist predecessors. The syntheses he repeatedly depicted were in the same mode as idealism's absorption of disparate phenomena into a theory of an overarching mind. By envisioning philosophy as an agent of harmony and wholeness, he had more in common with Royce's "quasi-ministerial" effort to comment on the transcendent issues of life than with Dewey's emphasis on the scientific solution of concrete problems. In fact, Durant's opening paean to unity—to a sense of perspective and meaning "before it is too late"—accentuates the degree to which he transferred to philosophy the consolations of religion once he could no longer subscribe to a belief in God. To the extent that the popularity of *The Story of Philosophy* depended on its contents, those features of Durant's outlook demonstrate the vitality, outside the university, of late-nineteenth-century philosophic conceptions at the same moment Durant's academic counterparts were repudiating them. They suggest the possibility of widespread, if unspoken, discontent with what the social critic Harold Rugg called the tendency of philosophy, in the wake of the "great transition," to disregard matters of "spirit," "mood," "inner temperament," and creativity. For the bewildered American reader of the 1920s, the idealist strain in Durant's work amounted to both a protest and an accommodation: a form of resistance to technology's relentless output of disparate information and an assurance that a method for dealing with disorder was at hand.[70]

Hence, with its beckoning biographies, pragmatic debts, and idealist underpinnings, *The Story of Philosophy* recapitulated Durant's intellectual development. The last pages of the book also addressed the pressing question of how to reconcile civilization and consumer culture. There, and in a fuller discussion in the *New York Times* late in 1926, Durant provided a thoroughly reassuring assessment of the issue. Focusing on American cultural traditions (rather than, like Wells and Van Loon, on human survival), he went beyond Brooks's call for a rejection of materialism, Rourke's emphasis on an existing folk heritage, or Erskine's appropriation of European achievements. Instead, Durant argued that the American preoccupation with getting and spending was actually not a barrier to, but rather a precondition for, the creation of art. History demonstrated, he explained, that "it is in the citadels of the middle class and under the protection of bankers and business men that artists find food for their mouths and buyers for the work of their hands." Thus, American consumers ought merely to commend themselves on preparing the way for a new "age of art."[71]

Neither that theme nor the others the book addressed, however, can, by themselves, capture its essence. Perhaps the outstanding features of the volume were its style and tone. Significantly, those aspects received as much notice from reviewers as its substantive ones. Adler condemned the "vaudevillian character which informs the whole work"; Paul Weiss remarked on "a sense of humor, a lucid style and a surety born of familiarity" that combined to make the book "never ambiguous and always interesting." Chatty speculations, witty asides, and vivid anecdotes helped Durant to fulfill the pledge of the "merchant of light" to remain accessible to nonscholars. Particular stylistic habits also enlivened his narrative. His sentences were sometimes less statements than epigrams: Kant "thought out everything carefully before acting and therefore remained a bachelor all his life long"; Santayana liked "the beauty of Catholicism more than the truth of any other faith." As Ernest Sutherland Bates remarked, that practice sometimes involved the "sacrifice" of "truth" but also gave the book a sparkle analogous to (if not on the same level of sophistication as) Broun's repartee.[72]

Additionally, rhetorical questions peppered Durant's pages, prodding readers out of passivity by inviting their replies. Durant's reliance on direct address of his audience, an attribute of his dissertation, here reappeared, beginning with the enticing first sentence of chapter 1: "If you look at a map of Europe you will observe that Greece is a skeleton-like hand stretching its crooked fingers out into the Mediterranean Sea." The most subtle and pervasive of Durant's techniques for diffusing "light" was his practice of paraphrasing his sources without interpolating the usual signals—"Plato argued," "in Aristotle's words"—of the distinction between their voices and his own. By removing himself, in effect, for pages at a stretch, Durant created the illusion of a direct, unmediated immersion in philosophic thought. Through such devices, he drew readers to his material and held them spellbound as only a master storyteller could.[73]

Durant's style of expertise also expressed his message of accessibility, although it conveyed other sentiments as well. His stance incorporated a touch of diffidence, a genial admission to his audience that his knowledge was as imperfect as theirs. "[W]e must be prepared to find in these dialogues [of Plato]," he observed, "much . . . that is unintelligible except to scholars learned in the social and literary minutiae of Plato's time." Of Spinoza's word "substance," he counseled, "Eight generations have fought voluminous battles over the meaning of this term; we must not be discouraged if we fail to resolve the matter in a paragraph." Hegel's works were "masterpieces of obscurity," and Kant's so contorted that they should not be read at all. That reassuring fallibility extended to Durant's subjects as well: "No wonder," he exclaimed, "there are more errors and absurdities in Aristotle than in any other philosopher who ever wrote."[74]

Yet, as the sweep of the last remark suggests, Durant subordinated his disavowal of scholarly competence to a categoricalness that undermined his self-portrait as average reader. In the voice he had cultivated since youth, he dismissed Nietzsche's religious views with the phrase "What hilarious atheism!," introduced Spinoza by labeling him "the greatest of modern philosophers," and guided readers with such definitive signposts as "This is the key-sentence of the book, and of Francis Bacon." His "surety," as Weiss called it, manifested itself as much in what was absent as in what Durant included: no references to interpretive controversies intruded to shade his black-and-white judgments. Durant's authoritative aura also arose from his method of outlining his subjects' ideas. If his disappearance from paraphrased passages brought text and reader closer, it also blurred the line between his views and those he was summarizing. Unable to discern where Plato, for example, left off and Durant began, the reader might assign the same importance to paraphrase and commentary alike. While some might complain that Durant had thereby appropriated for himself the mantle of the "greater philosophers," the net effect was to give Durant's viewpoint the unambiguous, compelling quality which Erskine identified as the "charm" of the outline's appeal.[75]

The double nature of Durant's tone in The Story of Philosophy—his geniality and pontification—was the rhetorical embodiment of the balance he struck in his political outlook; like his plan for social reconstruction, it exhibited the tension between democratic self-effacement and elitist prescription characteristic of other middlebrow enterprises. Both aspects augmented the power of the book to assist readers troubled by the fragmentation of knowledge. Durant's "surety," moreover, exempts him from the charge that he evaded the critic's obligation to set standards. Yet the categorical note had its own disturbing reverberations. It implicitly conceded that the "busy reader," in Durant's words, had neither the time nor the need for more depth; it further assumed that Durant's function involved operating within those constraints by dispensing with anything debatable or obscure.[76] Alternative possibilities—illuminating, rather than eliminating, complexity or insisting on the responsibility of readers to fight their way through difficult material—were precluded by Durant's impatience with nuance. At the other end of the spectrum from Fisher's demurrer about being just an ordinary wife and mother, Durant's enactment of the expert's role was thus no more conducive than hers to the cultivation of readers' acumen or sensitivities.

As it made culture secondary to other pursuits, moreover, Durant's posture also helped to equate philosophical understanding with consumable information. In general, the "outline" form itself unavoidably encouraged that transformation: it promised culture condensed, subdivided, and contained. Durant's disregard for texture and controversy and his penchant for epigrams, however, packaged the ideas of his subjects even more neatly than an "outline" required. More seriously, Durant's unbuffered summaries, while they heightened the impression of philosophy's accessibility, also created the illusion of a direct encounter with the text itself—so that reading it became superfluous.

This outcome, it should be stressed, was not inevitable; in fact, the increase in sales of the Modern Library's philosophy titles in 1926 argues that Durant motivated some readers to delve into his sources. To mention Durant to practicing scholars today is to realize that an early encounter with his prose shaped many a distinguished career. Yet, for others, the danger, as Weiss put it, was that one might be "blinded by the seductive clarity and tone of finality" of the book rather than "prompted to turn to original sources." The conclusion that to read Durant was to know philosophy might in turn relieve his audience's anxieties about acquiring culture while freeing them for the more pressing practical concerns of the marketplace. By serving business values in that way, Durant was, despite his extension of Arnoldian assumptions and the boon he brought to philosophical study, a "merchant of light" in a more literal respect than he intended.[77]

A Perfect Match: Durant and Simon and Schuster

Nevertheless, it took a man who combined actual participation in the marketplace with his own brand of gentility to realize *The Story of Philosophy's* full potential to appeal to American readers in the 1920s. Max Lincoln Schuster's acquisition and advertisement of Durant's manuscript illustrates his extraordinary skill (and that of his partner, Richard L. Simon) at aligning the book industry with consumer culture while, in his words, "democratizing the publishing process."[78]

Like Liveright, Schuster was another example of the new breed of postwar publishers. Born in 1897, he was the son of an immigrant Jewish stationery store and newsstand owner. Schuster entered the School of Journalism at Columbia in 1913 and upon graduation took a series of newspaper jobs; one of his early heroes was Heywood Broun. In 1921 Schuster met Simon, whose cousin he had known at Columbia. A former salesman for Boni and Liveright, where he had "personally disposed of an incredible number of copies" of Van Loon's *The Story of Mankind*, Simon was by that year selling pianos and looking for another project. Eventually Simon and Schuster agreed to team up as publishers, and in 1924 the two announced the formation of their firm, although they had no definite prospects for their list. On their first day in business, so a famous anecdote about them goes, they hung on their office door a sign reading "Simon and Schuster, Publishers." When they returned from lunch, they discovered that a friend had dropped by and scrawled the question, "Of what?"[79]

At the beginning, they fortuitously adopted a practice that soon became their standard way of operating. Instead of waiting for manuscripts, they followed George Brett's lead by gathering ideas for books they thought would sell and arranging for authors to write them. (By the late 1930s, 80 percent of their books were the result of their instigation.) In the case of their initial project, the idea came from Simon's aunt, who suggested that compiling a volume of crossword puzzles might enable the new publishers to capitalize on a popular feature of the *New York World*. The result was *The Crossword Puzzle Book*, the first of its kind, which Simon arranged to have manufactured with a pencil attached to the binding. A well-placed advertisement in the *World* brought thousands of requests for copies. The firm quickly printed multiple editions, assembled three more volumes, and by the end of 1924 had sold more than a million books.[80]

Profits from the puzzles enabled Simon and Schuster to finance other titles, but their list in 1925 was largely a failure, and Simon's spirits were particularly low. Even so, the house's activities that year rested on assumptions it would subsequently employ successfully. Extending Brett's and Liveright's rejection of the principle that publishing remain untainted by business, Simon and Schuster were both comfortable with the notion that books were commodities that ought to be marketed like other goods. (In a 1930 memorandum, Schuster emphasized the need to "know our customers for each product we undertake to produce and distribute.") Nor did they feel bound, as earlier firms had, to protect bookstore owners by limiting the extent to which they solicited the public directly. Although by the 1920s they had plenty of company in their acceptance of commercial values, Simon and Schuster differed from their colleagues by their readier embrace of innovative merchandising techniques and their willingness to budget more money for advertising than any other trade publisher. Early in their association, Schuster made a point of stressing to Simon how much he enjoyed promotional activities.[81]

In concrete terms, the house decided on the novel tactic, in Geoffrey Hellman's words, of treating "each title as a separate business venture," advertising its books one at a time rather than grouping them in catalogue fashion. Although Simon and Schuster wrote their copy themselves (Schuster probably did the bulk of it in the early years), they turned for advice about it to proven masters of the trade: the agency of Sackheim and Scherman. To get their message across, they allocated per book five to ten times the amount of other publishers. They also stayed attuned to the market by actively surveying reader preferences through return postcards placed in their books.[82]

The house's basic principles—create a marketable commodity and sell it aggressively—were among Schuster's tenets when he signed the contract with Durant and Haldeman-Julius in 1926. Schuster was well aware of the appeal of Wells's and Van Loon's "outlines," later citing *The Outline of History* as a milestone in his own education. His initial publication plans with Simon had even called for the creation of a "Common Sense Library" of information on various subjects—such as history and psychology—for a lay audience. Thus, he appreciated the potential of Durant's work to achieve the same readership.[83]

Factors other than the profit motive, however, shaped Schuster's receptivity to *The Story of Philosophy*. At Columbia he had studied philosophy with Walter Pitkin, whose lectures had so entranced him that he had one day suggested after class that Pitkin write a survey of the great philosophers. He had also read and "loved" Durant's dissertation. Additionally, Schuster was a reader of Haldeman-Julius's magazine and had corresponded with the Kansas publisher before the two actually met. When, over lunch, Haldeman-Julius asked whether Schuster was familiar with Durant's Little Blue Books, Schuster replied that he had virtually memorized all of them. Thus, he unhesitatingly took up Haldeman-Julius's suggestion that Simon and Schuster combine Durant's studies into a book, maintaining his enthusiasm for the project even when the Columbia philosophy professor Irwin Edman advised against it.[84]

Beyond his specific interest in philosophy, Schuster was imbued with the conviction that his mission as a publisher was to widen the readership for fine literature. "We had in the back of our minds," he reminisced, "the beginning of this pattern of what I call democratizing the publishing process. . . . Without articulating it, intuitively or instinctively we were groping for this idea of better and better books for more and more people, at lower and lower prices." Schuster's sense of purpose was remarkably similar to Canby's and Erskine's. In one memorandum, he declared that he saw himself as an instructor of the public. The chief instrument for carrying out that purpose was a series Schuster called the Inner Sanctum Library of Living Literature and Basic Books, which he began conceiving in the mid-1920s and actively creating after the Second World War. The intent of the series was to make "masterpieces" and commentary about them available in a single volume, as well as to reprint editions of "world literature" and to issue "treasuries" of excerpts from great works. Combining many of the elements of the "outline"—tributes to authors by expert critics, pages of brief, separable quotations preceding selections, introductions explaining ways to approach the basic volumes—and susceptible to the same uses, the Inner Sanctum Library nonetheless aimed to inspire readers to turn from books about great writers to the writers' texts themselves. In that way, Schuster explained, he fulfilled his goal of publishing, rather than merely printing, books.[85]

Given Schuster's merchandising skill, one might be tempted to regard his idealism as merely a cover for an underlying drive to rake in the profits. Yet certain facets of his temperament argue for a less cynical interpretation of his professed commitments. He was a "loner" and a scholar, a man who, in one writer's words, was "born old." His own zeal for "cultural self-improvement" matched the intellectual ambitions of the public he sought to reach. Much more of a reader than Simon, he had an abiding love of the classics—and less interest in what he called "perishable" books. (In the 1950s he found the figures associated with the "great books" movement congenial company.) Moreover, his in-house memorandums radiate a genuine passion about his avowed goals. For example, he declared in one from 1935 about the Inner Sanctum Library, "I use my words calmly and deliberately when I state this is the most important phase of my whole publishing aspiration, and I am literally prepared to concentrate the major energies of my professional life to it."[86] The Inner Sanctum Library reflected better than anything else Schuster's genuine devotion to disseminating "the best," but Durant's book, by popularizing "great" philosophers, similarly enabled him to foster the same altruistic end.

Schuster's allegiance to that Arnoldian mission coexisted, however, with another trait that Durant's work admirably satisfied as well. He had an "incurable sense of order," as Hellman put it, or, perhaps better, a great fear of disorder. That trait compelled him to devise a system for classifying on small colored pieces of paper maxims, bits of knowledge, useful quotations, and ideas for books. A team of secretaries devoted themselves to typing and filing the snippets he stuffed into his coat pockets every day. In other words, Schuster was a kind of walking "outline" book himself and, indeed, planned one day to compile his gleanings into a "gigantic history of wisdom." His own personal style thus perfectly accorded with Durant's emphasis on unity and with the epigrammatic tendencies incipient in *The Story of Philosophy*. More generally, rather than merely a sign of eccentricity, Schuster's preoccupation with discrete facts made him at once agent and exemplar of the equation of culture with information. His reportorial cast of mind, transferred from journalism to publishing, made him as much a disciple of Broun's as of Arnold's.[87]

Similarly, Simon's well-known slogan, "Give the reader a break," to which Schuster assented, overturned at a stroke genteel precepts about the need for self-discipline and deference to expertise; it legitimated in their place not only readable typography or the provision of an index—certainly welcome improvements—but also the policy, potentially subversive of the ideal of the "best," of "steering" difficult diction into "channels more palatable for the general reader." (Two Simon and Schuster editors—Wallace Brockway, who later worked on the Britannica *Great Books* set, and Clifton Fadiman—were the principal navigators.) Those editorial decisions, in combination with his scholarly and classical bent, make it tempting to conclude that if Schuster had not existed, Durant—striking the same balance—would have had to invent him.[88]

In actuality, though, it was Schuster who invented Durant—or, at any rate, irreversibly magnified his fame as middlebrow authority—in a marketing campaign that brought together Schuster's uninhibited commercial instincts and his ideological commitments to the content of the book. As *Fortune* reported, the promotional effort for *The Story of Philosophy* "blazed with an excitement that it was impossible to escape. [Simon and Schuster] immersed themselves in the book; they swooned in its embraces, and the happy tome rewarded them with showers of gold." The Durant campaign included special incentives for bookstores that surpassed sales quotas, direct-mail solicitation of Labor Temple students, and, eventually, a money-back guarantee. Its mainstay, however, was a no-holds-barred series of advertisements directed at readers of such publications as *Books*, the *New York Times Book Review*, and the *Saturday Review of Literature*.[89]

The first advertisements were relatively small and sober in comparison to later ones and not radically different in appearance from those of other publishers who employed venturesome merchandising strategies. Even so, they managed to pack into a space at most five by ten inches more than the typical number of appeals. For example, the initial black-bordered display advertisement in the *Times* fed the desire to stay au courant by featuring the phrase "Just Published" above the title and author; appeased the need for culture made ordered, unified, and available by incorporating statements describing the book's comprehensiveness ("From Aristotle to Santayana") and comprehensibility ("each philosopher's contribution to human thought is made understandable for everyone"); made a passing bow toward the preoccupation with personality in a reference to Durant's portrayal of each of his subjects "first as a human being"; assured potential buyers that they would be getting their money's worth by specifying "octavo size, 577 pages, 21 full page illustrations"; announced a price (five dollars) sufficiently high that, in James Hart's words, it "promised edification"; invoked deference to expertise (and reaffirmed pitches to practicality, accessibility, and authoritativeness) by quoting Dewey's appraisal of the volume as "thoroughly useful, thoroughly scholarly, human and readable"; and enhanced the identity of the publishing house itself by employing the fairly rare and commercially astute device of a logo— Simon and Schuster's sower of seeds—above the firm's name and address.[90]

Subsequent copy strengthened those enticements and introduced new ones. As sales took off, advertisements featured references to the frequency of printings the book had undergone, subtly prodding readers to climb on the bandwagon. One even aimed to stimulate panic buying by referring to "patrons who have had difficulty in securing" the volume. Reminiscent of the Wells promotion, a full-page advertisement on the back cover of the *Saturday Review* touted Durant's work as "the outstanding best-seller that discriminating people are talking about." It also provided five "typical descriptive flashes from the book."[91]

Furthermore, a spate of endorsements from reviewers in addition to Dewey became, for a time, the heart of the campaign. As Schuster reported, the extensive citation of reviews with "much more space and with more emphatic typography" was a practice that distinguished the firm from its competitors; it suggests, again, Schuster's perfect attunement to the importance consumers placed on expert guidance. In the case of *The Story of Philosophy*, Schuster selected blurbs from such writers as Van Loon and from Sherman, Bates, Hansen, and other newspaper critics to assure potential buyers that they could not go wrong by purchasing the book. Many of the quotations stressed the volume's clarity and human interest. In addition, Schuster made the most of those remarks consonant with that major source of the "outline" vogue, the desire for a liberal education without the expenditure of resources traditionally necessary to attain it. Thus, he highlighted Sherman's conclusion that a week with Durant's book was "easily worth a year with the average college professor." Similarly, a full-page spread in the *New York Times Book Review* depicted the arm and hand of a man—the arm clothed in tweed, the hand holding Durant's volume— above the quotation "Enviable collegians who will have *The Story of Philosophy* as a textbook!" The rest of the advertisement went on to tout the book for college graduates and would-be graduates alike.[92]

Advertisements for *The Story of Philosophy* also exploited anxieties about the nature of American civilization. An early one, written in the form of a letter to Wells, capitalized on the same theme Sherman had sounded in his review of the book; it told Wells not to fear civilization's demise because Durant's successes proved the United States a bastion of intelligence. Later, after consulting once more with Sackheim and Scherman, Schuster decided to make that self-congratulatory message the focus of the publicity campaign; their marketing strategy, he recorded, would now be to pay homage to the nation's interest in learning. For the next few months, advertisements hailed *The Story of Philosophy*'s popularity as "a tribute to the intellectual curiosity of the American public" and as fulfilling Durant's "remarkable prediction" of an "American Renaissance."[93]

Hence, the selling of *The Story of Philosophy*, like that for the Book-of-the-Month Club and "great books," touched at various points the desires for personality development, social standing, practicality, expertise, information, self-reliance, and civilization. In visual terms, some of the advertising for Durant's volume also acquired an up-to-date, sophisticated look by presenting the printed text in the form of an inverted pyramid, an arrangement that duplicated a characteristic art deco motif.

Many of those same themes coalesced in the merchandising device that was the single most important contribution to the development of Simon and Schuster's image: the "From the Inner Sanctum" column. Schuster's copy for the column, written for the general reading public, first appeared in the *Saturday Review of Literature* on April 2, 1927. For the rest of the year, it ran sporadically there and in the *New York Times Book Review*, settling into a regular feature of both journals in March 1928. At roughly the same time, Simon's similar effort for the trade began appearing in *Publishers' Weekly*.[94]

Both versions consisted of a series of short paragraphs, usually arranged vertically down the length of the page, with each entry preceded by the house's sower logo. The heading "From the Inner Sanctum of Simon and Schuster," together with the firm's address, introduced the items, which were signed at the bottom by "Essandess." The signature is a clue to the advertisement's distinctiveness. The column format was not, in and of itself, especially innovative. Oxford University Press, for example, had already established "The Amen Corner" to present announcements about its list to booksellers; moreover, Doubleday, Page, in the words of *Publishers' Weekly*, put "personality" into its advertising as early as 1917 with a series of signed, informal talks to the public. Alfred Knopf came closest to "From the Inner Sanctum" with a compilation of publicity items it labeled "Borzoiana." Simon and Schuster, however, went furthest in deciding to construct a particular *type* of column—the witty, sophisticated cache of inside dope—and to celebrate the same kind of cosmopolitan personality that Isabel Paterson, F.P.A., Christopher Morley, and Schuster's model Heywood Broun were at that moment exhibiting noncommercially.

"Essandess" announced publication dates, trumpeted sales figures, and reported tidbits about the firm's authors; more unconventionally, it sometimes discussed its failures or strayed from Simon and Schuster books to recommend its competitors' offerings and chat about matters outside the book trade altogether. Its governing tone was what Schuster labeled "candor-carried-to-the-point-of-indiscretion," together with a note of quiet familiarity. The first column in the *Saturday Review*, for example, continued the publicity for *The Story of Philosophy* by affording a glimpse into the inner workings of the house, while endowing the persona of "Essandess" with refined taste: "One of the alluring things about an intimate column like this," it declared, "is the opportunity it affords for setting down items that are ruthlessly deleted by the cold-blooded copy-writers in the advertising department. A recent flourish for *The Story of Philosophy* began, quite fittingly, we thought, with a quotation from John Milton, but the high-pressure lads thought it didn't have sufficient 'selling punch.' Out it went, and now that we have a chance to salvage the quotation in this more private vehicle, back it goes." The Milton lines followed, together with references to the price and sales figures for Durant's volume.[95]

Perhaps the most striking aspect of that passage was its implication that "From the Inner Sanctum" was not an advertisement, as if Schuster, deeper into commercialization than most publishers, still saw some benefit in perpetuating the older dissociation of books from soap. The fiction also blurred the difference between his effort and those of the newspaper columnists. Just as significant, however, the characterization of the column as a "private vehicle" to which the reader was nonetheless admitted conveyed exactly that blend of easy participation and exclusivity irresistible for Americans eager to acquire culture while preserving its connection to prestige. In that way, it suggested the same "parable" of the "democracy of goods" Roland Marchand has detected in campaigns informing "every mother" that she could serve the breakfast cereal of the wealthy. The column's small typography, which one advertising man noted violated all the rules of good layout, may have worked to similar effect by exuding both intimacy and restraint. In addition, the column's premium on information wittily displayed was nicely adapted to readers who sought the materials out of which to fashion their own performances. The personalization of the firm—the behind-the-scenes approach, the reduction of bureaucracy to an individual—hints as well that "Essandess" functioned for Simon and Schuster the way Betty Crocker did for General Mills. As Marchand has observed, such figures not only gave businesses a more recognizable identity in the marketplace, they also won the sympathy of consumers by counteracting the faceless quality of modern life and supplying the demand for guidance. Beyond all that, "From the Inner Sanctum" was unpredictable, amusing, and delightfully well written; it even occasionally included small drawings and photographs. For those manifold reasons, it earned a devoted audience that wrote letters to "Essandess" and looked forward each week to "his" revelations.

Of course, Simon and Schuster did not restrict "From the Inner Sanctum" (or any of its other marketing strategies, for that matter) to "outline" books. Yet the column's reflection of genteel hopes and consumer values made it a particularly good medium for "outlines," which reiterated the same message. Its frequent references to Durant in the late 1920s consolidated the success that Schuster's previous copy for *The Story of Philosophy* had achieved. When, after Liveright had fallen prey to gambling and dissolution, Van Loon signed on with his old friends Dick Simon and Max Schuster, "From the Inner Sanctum" stood ready to hawk the wares of that "merchant of light." In 1928 the

Book-of-the-Month Club was using the column's format to reprint items from the *News*. By the time it served to publicize *Van Loon's Geography* (1932) and the first volume of Durant's *The Story of Civilization* (1935), there was "no more avidly read book copy being printed."[96]

Durant between Stories

The appearance of *The Story of Philosophy* fueled controversy about both Durant's merits as a philosopher and the nature of the "outline" vogue itself. Detractors such as Adler and Weiss attacked Durant's dismissal of metaphysics. Others doubted whether buyers of the book actually read it; Yale professor Charles A. Bennett noted that "the last copy of 'The Story of Philosophy' that I saw had the radio cabinet on one side of it and 'Work on Auction Bridge' on the other." Howard Mumford Jones, debating Durant in *The Forum*, connected the "outline" to consumption and the American desire for convenience. "It creates a sort of glaze of culture," Jones explained. "It is produced by our wish to buy things neatly done up in packages because they look easy to use— soap already in flakes, dishwashing preparations that foam instantaneously, coffee to be made in a cup of hot water." Jones also noted the tendency of Durant's book to discourage readers from venturing further into texts themselves. Broadly speaking, with the exception of his ongoing, though not close, relationship with Dewey, the book sealed Durant's position as an outcast from academic circles. Morris Cohen, for example, once interrupted an "interminable speech" by a visitor to one of his New School lectures with the remark that *he* was the only one "paid to waste the time of this class." Afterward, a friend chided him for his abruptness: "'Did you realize who that was?' 'That was Will Durant!' 'No . . . ,' Cohen replied, 'I didn't know. If I had known, I'd have behaved worse.'"[97]

On the other hand, the enthusiasm of prominent reviewers like Sherman enabled Durant to exercise on a national scale his disposition to speak authoritatively on a wide range of subjects. From 1926 through the late 1930s, he regularly published articles in popular periodicals on such diverse topics as "The Ten Greatest Thinkers," "The Modern Woman," "The Breakdown of Marriage," "I Want to Be Happy," "Is Our Civilization Dying?," and "One Hundred Best Books." Many were reprinted in *The Mansions of Philosophy* (1929) and *Adventures in Genius* (1931).[98]

Of all the essays in those collections, the one most revealing of Durant's underlying values was a long chapter in *The Mansions of Philosophy* entitled "The Reconstruction of Character." The title alone is enough to make the case that Durant's outlook entailed the perpetuation of the character ideal. Yet, having undertaken a more spacious treatment of the subject than his previous books permitted, Durant here added variants to the standard genteel portrait. He delineated two ideal composites, the "negative" and the "positive" character. Both sketches affirmed, directly or indirectly, Emersonian self-reliance. The "negative" figure was hungry for public approval, lacking in coordinated purpose, fearful of responsibility, and resigned to the sidelines, while its "positive" opposite, though amiable toward others, responded only to the proddings of its disciplined, unified will and spent its days in purposive action.[99]

His conception of "positive" character, however, revealed Durant's persistent streak of anti-intellectualism, distinguishing his model from the trained intelligence genteel critics had in mind. While Emerson had deplored the "bookworm" and stressed the need for "Man Thinking" to confront the world directly, he had nonetheless maintained that "action is with the scholar subordinate." Durant, by contrast, associated reading and study with his "negative" model and described his ideal as a figure who could not understand "why a man should bother with higher mathematics, or poetry, or painting, or philosophy." (In other essays in the volume, Durant hoped for his daughter that "she will not become too learned to love life, and that she will never think of books as better than friendships, or nature, or motherhood"; he also prefaced a list of book recommendations with the phrase "If you must be an intellectual. . . .") Those statements, self-deprecating in light of Durant's sense of vocation, suggest the continuing pull toward experience he had felt upon leaving the seminary.[100]

Nevertheless, beginning in the late 1920s Durant focused his energies on an activity that held him even more closely to bookish pursuits than his magazine articles did: the preparation of his massive "outline" of civilization. As early as 1904, he had begun planning a work which harnessed his drive for unity to historical interpretation. Despite his labors on *The Story of Philosophy*, he told a newspaper reporter in 1922 that his real ambition was to write a " 'complete history of the world,' " showing the " 'interdependence' " and " 'harmony' " of " 'politics, economics, art, literature, and science.' " The result, he hoped, would be to supplant "shredded history" with a view of "the past united in all its phases, as it was when it was living." That objective meant stretching his interest in individual lives to include what he later called the "biography of a civilization"; more subtly, it involved the extension of his vision of integrity from self to society. As he put it in the preface to one volume, he wished to "see and feel" the diverse "vital elements" of a civilization "not in their theoretical and scholastic isolation, but in their living interplay as the simultaneous movements of one great cultural organism, with a hundred organs and a hundred million cells, but with one body and soul."[101] The first fruits of his efforts, *Our Oriental Heritage*, appeared in 1935. By 1950 Durant had published three more installments—*The Life of Greece* (1939), *Caesar and Christ* (1944), and *The Age of Faith* (1950)—of what would eventually be his eleven-volume series *The Story of Civilization*. Thanks in part to its distribution as a Book-of-the-Month Club premium, *The Story of Civilization* set is today the work for which Durant is most often remembered.[102] Because they were not as popular initially as his first "story" and because, in terms of literary strategy and fundamental assumptions, Durant's histories largely duplicated the characteristics of his earlier "outline," they require less discussion here than their size and reputation might suggest. Even so, they instructively reveal the workings of those strategies and assumptions in their most expansive form.

The Story of Civilization

Durant's studies of the rise of civilization stood in roughly the same relation to existing scholarship as *The Story of Philosophy* had to the studies of Windelband and Paulsen. That is, although several writers had, individually or collectively, attempted overviews of the subject, no one had embarked on a venture quite like Durant's. There were already available a number of collaborative projects, notably *The Universal History of the World*, edited by J. A. Hammerton, with contributions from "one hundred and fifty of our foremost living authorities in all branches of historical knowledge." Hammerton's effort, however, was not particularly focused on cultural history, and its heavily illustrated, discrete articles gave it the appearance more of an encyclopedia than a coherent narrative. Wells's *Outline*, an obvious precedent, went to the other extreme by cramming the entire "story" into one volume, but it was similarly dependent on the research of many investigators and weighted toward Wells's political thesis. American scholars like Robinson and Beard, and also James H. Breasted, had produced highly respected syntheses on a less sweeping scale. Those works were nonetheless essentially textbooks, exhibiting the prudence (their authors might have said) of specialists who confined their chronological and geographical purviews to their areas of expertise. Thus, Durant was unique in conceiving of multiple volumes single-handedly written, centered on cultural development, aimed at the general reader, and wide in scope.[103]

At the same time, in much the way his previous writing reflected the influence of Dewey, Durant's historical undertaking, while singular in many respects, selectively borrowed from the "new history." Durant never studied with Robinson during his years at Columbia (although Ariel Durant did take a course from him), but the outlook Robinson promulgated had acquired even more influence in the 1920s than it had possessed when Wells's *Outline* appeared. Durant not only appropriated Robinson's language about the "humanizing of knowledge," he also wholeheartedly affirmed Robinson's belief that history ought to go beyond "past politics" to encompass the complete record of human cultural and intellectual achievements. Thus, *Our Oriental Heritage* began with chapters on the economic and political bases of civilization but later overrode those traditional categories to describe, where feasible for a given region, the "mental elements of civilization": letters and literature, art, philosophy, religion, science, architecture, drama, and manners. Whatever the failings of Durant's scholarship, practicing cultural historians owe him a debt of gratitude for the way in which he insisted on the legitimacy and significance of their research.[104]

To a more limited extent, Durant also assented to the ideological foundation on which the "new history" rested. As Morton White has shown, Robinson's view that the study of the past ought to provide insight into the needs of the present was equivalent to the pragmatists' demand that philosophy serve as a tool to solve current social problems. Although Durant had drawn few explicit connections to contemporary dilemmas in *The Story of Philosophy*, enough of his Deweyite training remained that, when he turned to history, he repeatedly found in ancient civilizations lessons for twentieth-century Americans. As he put it in his first volume, "It is a poor civilization from which we may not learn something to improve our own." His efforts at relevance ranged from lighthearted asides—"The women of ancient Egypt could learn very little from us in the matter of cosmetics and jewelry"—to sober acknowledgment of the importance, in 1935, of understanding Japan. The entire conception of the history of civilization as "our heritage," however, bespeaks the sense of a living past that Robinson and other "new historians" hoped to promote.[105]

To be sure, other aspects of the "new history" found no expression in *The Story of Civilization*. Robinson had urged scholars and teachers to rely heavily on original sources, both to train students in critical analysis and to enhance the vividness of the past. Durant followed the opposite practice: he confined his research almost exclusively to secondary materials. In addition, Durant rejected the implications of Robinson's view that history, as a social science, ought to employ data in accordance with scientific method. Instead of marshaling facts with a view to testing a hypothesis, Durant's "outline" was heavily anecdotal; it highlighted intriguing religious rites or exotic marriage practices for their own sake rather than for any interpretive end. Finally, Durant paid little heed to the economic or social analyses that "new" historians like Charles Beard found persuasive. His move from individual to national biography did not diminish his emphasis on personality; conceiving of historical change primarily as the product of "genius," he merely enlisted more actors in his troupe and gave them a grander stage on which to play out their roles. As in *The Story of Philosophy*, that focus on the life cycle was central to the work's appeal—it lent the text a note of friendly familiarity and provided a treasury of exemplary public performances—yet it precluded a more complex view of causality. As J. H. Plumb observed with exasperation in a review of *The Age of Louis XIV*, when "the whole rhythm and flow of history" was reduced to a "collection of personalities," the "conflicts between classes, the impact of commercial and agrarian revolutions on the structure of states" might, according to the Durants, "never have taken place."[106]

Part "new" history, part old, *The Story of Civilization* bore a more straightforward relationship to the contemporary preoccupation with the nature of both "culture" (in the anthropological sense) and "civilization." Certain volumes—*The Life of Greece, Caesar and Christ*—seem especially closely connected to other popular works of the period that pursued those concerns by comparing America to antiquity. Although they entailed much more patient, scholarly exegesis than Durant's books, Edith Hamilton's widely successful *The Greek Way* (1930) and *The Roman Way* (1932), for example, come to mind as similar exercises in self-scrutiny through classical lenses; so, for that matter, do Erskine's mythologically based novels.

In any case, Durant's conclusions about what he saw through those lenses appeared to allay, once and for all, qualms about whether a consumer society could also be a viable civilization. By identifying both Eastern and Western history as America's birthright—noting that the Orient was home to America's "real founders," depicting Sumerian business contracts as antecedents to American ones, or demonstrating the survival of Roman ideas of the state—Durant pointed to the inescapable conclusion that American roots were strong and ancient. (Erskine, in pursuing that line of reasoning, had kept his sights only on the West; Durant, so to speak, treated the entire world as his oyster.) The sheer bulk of his "outline" (each volume averaged around seven hundred pages) made an impressive retort to the argument that Americans lacked spiritual resources. As Cullen Murphy aptly put it in a brief but extraordinarily perceptive recent commentary on Durant, the books, occupying "places of prominence in the nation's living rooms and dens," were "visible affirmations that civilization itself" was "no stranger to the neighborhood."[107]

If, however, doubt chanced to permeate that bulwark, Durant's characteristic optimism, here infused into his overarching philosophy of history, could supply a second line of defense. According to Durant, the course of civilization was, despite reverses, upward. Although he added drama to his tale by insisting that civilization was precariously erected on top of a "volcano" of "barbarism, superstition, and ignorance," his "story" always had a happy ending. History's most important lesson, Durant implied, was not to be discouraged by present woes but to trust to the future. "Every chaos," he wrote, "is a transition"

preceding a "rebirth." His stress on biography contributed to his up-
beat message by underscoring his belief in the unflagging power of
individual action.[108]

To be fair, Durant occasionally speculated that ancient achievements
might have been humankind's "finest." More important, his resentment of the civilizing process, earlier evident in his reaction to his loss
of faith, occasionally broke through the placid surface of his melioristic
tale. At such moments, his longing for experience became attached not
only to anti-intellectual sentiments but also to an ideal of primitive
abandon: "As civilization develops," he argued in *The Life of Greece*,
"action gives way to thought, achievement to imagination, directness to
subtlety, expression to concealment . . . ; the unity of character common
to animals and primitive men passes away. . . . Few nations have been
able to reach intellectual refinement and esthetic sensitivity without
sacrificing so much in virility and unity that their wealth presents an
irresistible temptation to impecunious barbarians."[109] Yet Durant's
impulses to side with the invading hordes were, for the most part,
submerged by his faith in progress. His predominant optimism cleared
the way to regard the United States, complete with its materialism, not
only as a true civilization but also as the latest—and thus the highest—
manifestation of human possibility. In addition, his "positive thinking"
could provide special comfort during the discouraging days of the Depression, when his first two historical volumes appeared. To judge from
reviews, his outlook also offered sustenance as the outbreak of war in
Europe made Americans wonder whether their democracy, too, would
undergo a decline and fall. The self-help prophet Emile Coué told
anxious Americans in the 1920s that "every day, in every way" they
were "getting better and better"; *The Story of Civilization* made Durant the Coué of culture.

To turn from content to form, Durant's historical "outline" polished
many of the techniques on which he had relied in *The Story of Philosophy*. In Murphy's words, he "perfected a glib, equable, didactic style
of exposition that is virtually without peer in the modern hardcover
trade." The glibness particularly came across in Durant's epigrammatic phrasings, which were even more plentiful than in his earlier
work and which voiced even bolder generalizations. "Barbarism is like
the jungle; it never admits its defeat," he declared. Likewise, "eternal
vigilance is the price of civilization" because "it is in the nature of

governments to degenerate." The potential of those maxims to satisfy the desire for quick, presentable information existed in tension with the aim of synthesis; what began as an effort to attain a unified perspective was in actuality an unstable compound on the verge of decomposing into a collection of "quotable quotes." Moreover, Durant (perhaps guided by his publishers) exacerbated the tension between unity and fragmentation by building into *The Story of Civilization* a device that encouraged readers to skip large chunks of it: the use of reduced type for "technical" passages deemed "difficult" or "dull." In "A Note on the Use of This Book," Durant also admonished his audience to avoid boredom by not attempting "more than a chapter at a time." Such instant abridgment and time management tended to shatter not only the integrity of the text but also the genteel premium on self-discipline.[110]

Furthermore, as Murphy noticed, Durant's maxims here performed the additional function of "distilling" history into "orderly rules"; thus, the device reinforced Durant's optimism and enhanced his stature by casting him as a lawgiver. At the same time, his commitment, as a "merchant of light," not to intimidate the general reader led him to proffer his familiar tincture of geniality, humor, and self-effacement. Murphy beautifully summarized the effects of Durant's long-cultivated dual authorial voices: "Occasionally Durant confessed ignorance, but always wearily, as if what he couldn't establish was in any case irrelevant. 'We do not know which of the many roads to decay Crete chose,' he allowed; 'perhaps she took them all.' He donned humility in a way that left all but himself decked in its raiments. . . . From time to time he slyly asserted his authority by casting the reader abruptly overboard— 'Recall the situation of Italy in 1494'—and then throwing him a life preserver."[111]

Durant also engaged in the lyricism, the romantic flights, the flair for dramatic effect, and the "intimate" tone, as the historian Garrett Mattingly called it, that made his "stories" so engrossing. Writing of Augustus's last days, for example, he reflected: "Perhaps it had been wiser to die like Antony, at the peak of life and in the arms of love. How sadly pleasant must have seemed, in retrospect, the days when Julia and Agrippa were happy, and grandchildren frolicked on the palace floor." Thick with ostensibly universal emotions, such language, in the words of Norman Cousins, "enabled people to add thousands of years to their natural lifetimes through a sense of direct participation in the past."

Like the communal ties Erskine hoped reading "great books" would prompt, the feelings of kinship Durant's style evoked could counteract anonymity and affirm an entity outside the fragmented self. Perhaps that is why both Mattingly and Murphy, though two of Durant's severest critics, almost gratefully ascribed to his histories the ability to survive the descent of a modern dark age.[112]

If it successfully brought his audience and his material closer together, however, *The Story of Civilization* widened the breach between Durant and the academy. Some professional historians, of course, championed the books. Others were too quickly dismissive: when Breasted compiled a list of Durant's supposed omissions and errors of fact, Durant effectively made him look like a careless reader. Yet he could not as handily refute other specialists' detection of factual errors, nor could he defend himself against their other damaging charge: his unscholarly handling of sources. "His bibliography and notes," one reviewer put it, "show how often he has relied upon the unreliable and neglected the unneglectable." Whether out of blindness or egotism, Durant never quite understood this accusation; he repeatedly replied that his aim was not to engage in original research but to write synthetically. The point, however, was not that he had solely depended on secondary materials but, rather, that he had not subjected those materials to the critical scrutiny that was one of the scholar's chief obligations. As Mattingly wrote with respect to Durant's sixth volume, *The Reformation*, "In the field of universal history, where nobody can be expected to do all that work [of primary research] himself, it [scholarship] means, at the least, some discrimination as to the scholarly merits of the secondary works used, and some effort to keep abreast of the latest findings of the specialists. In this sense, there is not the slightest taint of scholarship about this volume." Plumb's review, which the Durants (by then officially coauthors) considered most devastating of all, said the same thing with more venom and caught as well the connection between the focus on personality and consumer values: "No effort is called for: like a television series, it doesn't matter much at which episode you start. The result is like cheese spread—good color, little taste, easy to use, boring in bulk, and infinitely remote from the true product. . . . The Durants ignore almost completely and in the most astonishing way the work of professional scholars." To this, the Durants could make only the feeble rejoinder that they were "more interested in persons than in things" and had ignored recent monographs because younger scholars "add little to the standard authorities." Fostering bitterness on both sides, Durant's most elaborate attempt to function as a "merchant of light" thus only increased the need for mediation between the academy and the public that had helped to create the "outline" vogue in the first place.[113]

Selling Civilization

Although a more restrained effort, Simon and Schuster's marketing of the first three volumes of *The Story of Civilization* drew, in varying degrees, on all of the strategies the firm had used so successfully with *The Story of Philosophy*. The general theme of the campaign for the early part of the series was that Durant's histories were "better than *The Story of Philosophy*," a slogan designed to recapture the audience for his previous work. Reworking the appeal to the desire for social acceptance, much of the copy ignored the content of the books in favor of an emphasis on the growing crowd of Durant fans. In addition, endorsements from experts—Van Loon, Harry Elmer Barnes, Harry Hansen—as well as from readers were still prominent selling points.[114]

One other type of advertisement, however, distinguished the marketing of *The Story of Civilization* from that of Durant's first "outline." This was Schuster's famous "windswept" copy—so called because of its wordy, florid, uninhibited quality. Schuster had invented the technique in the 1920s but, in terms of Durant's works, first used it to full effect to promote *The Life of Greece* and subsequently employed it for *Caesar and Christ*. "Tonight I will open to the first page of *The Life of Greece*," one such advertisement read, "and tonight, in my own armchair and under my own reading lamp, I shall instantly be transported through thousands of years and miles to the glory that was Greece. Before my astonished eyes will unfold a civilization so like my own that I shall come to realize the mists of history to be a thin veil indeed between two kindred cultures. . . . In Crete, 2,000 B.C. I shall find the same fashion of feminine slenderness as today. I shall discover only minor differences between the Solonian and the Roosevelt revolutions. . . . But, best of all, tonight before my eyes will come alive a mighty upsurge of the human spirit such as no other age can boast." That pitch made more explicit than Durant's text did the links between American and past civilizations. Another indication of Schuster's merchandising savvy, it also relied on first person verbs and homey references to create an intimate tone similar to that of "From the Inner Sanctum." Here, though, the promise that Durant's product would confer "adventure, mystery, and romance" gave the text of the advertisement additional force. It helped to enact what Neil Harris has termed "the drama of consumer desire": the endowment of the purchasing act itself with the power to substitute unique experience for standardization, alluring excitement for tedium and anonymity. Schuster's role as stage manager in that drama completed his rejection of genteel prohibitions about book advertising. In that additional regard, the story of *The Story of Civilization* was a tale of the culture of consumption.[115]

The End of the Story

Durant kept publishing his "outline" of civilization at regular intervals until 1975. By the time he died in 1981, the disjuncture between his reputation among academics and his standing with the public had grown even more pronounced than it had been before 1950. In his final years, he not only incurred the disparagement of Mattingly and Plumb but also received the Medal of Freedom from President Gerald Ford. When Murphy, commemorating the centenary of Durant's birth, suggested that few people, if any, had actually finished even a single volume of *The Story of Civilization*, one of Durant's champions among the reading public shot back that her book discussion group had not only studied the entire series but was "ready to start over again."[116]

Yet the longevity of Durant's "outline" was exceptional. Although Van Loon produced *The Arts* in 1937 and his popular *Lives* as late as 1942, the vogue reached its peak in the late 1920s, tapered off in the 1930s, and (except in pockets like the aforementioned discussion group) did not survive the Second World War. Part of the explanation for its disappearance, one may surmise, was the expansion of higher education in the postwar era. Instead of turning to "outlines" in order to offset their awareness of having missed out on college, Americans could, in unprecedented numbers, now take courses on philosophy or history at proliferating campuses. Similarly, the availability of cheaper editions of texts themselves (while it may have heightened the sense of an unending flow of print) supplanted some of the need for summary volumes. This phenomenon had begun before the war; the Modern Library, for example, which Liveright had sold to Bennett Cerf in 1925, had shifted its contents away from avant-garde writings toward making "the world's best books" more affordable. The postwar "paperback revolution," however, accelerated the trend. In short, for people who still clung to an ideal of liberal culture, there were ways to get it other than in "outline" form.[117]

At the same time, the persistent belief of the "merchants of light" in a generalist orientation made their wares, by mid-century, somewhat obsolete. The inexorable tide of specialization, coupled with the academization of American intellectual life, further eroded the role Durant and his cohorts had managed to preserve in the 1920s and 1930s. For college graduates and nongraduates alike, the idea that an "outline" could adequately cover a subject they had forgotten or missed seemed, one imagines, increasingly untenable; so did the practice of investing authority in a figure disconnected from a university. Durant still thought in the late 1970s that there was a place among "intelligent high school graduates" for his unspecialized approach, but that conception was far narrower than the tweedy image Simon and Schuster had invoked in selling his work to "collegians" and "discriminating general readers." Even so, the "story" Durant and his fellow popularizers told remains vital for another reason: as a source of insight into that moment when it still seemed possible not only to synthesize knowledge but also to unify the self—and to affirm, in the process, the existence of civilization in the United States.[118]

INFORMATION, PLEASE !

BOOK PROGRAMS
ON COMMERCIAL
RADIO

On March 24, 1935, radio listeners tuned to "An American Fireside" (significantly subtitled "A Half Hour of Civilization") heard Christopher Morley, Amy Loveman, and Henry Seidel Canby pretend to gather in the offices of the *Saturday Review of Literature* to collaborate on the forthcoming spring book number. "What is it, Amy, a critical essay?" Morley asked Loveman about a featured article on Thomas Wolfe. "No," she replied reassuringly, "it's a personal sketch." Loveman also announced the "important books for next week," quoted from a reader's letter ribbing "Bill" Benét, and exchanged lighthearted remarks with "Henry." The dialogue, which Morley wrote, made the editorial staff come alive, turning them (at least for a few moments) into personalities. "Amy—oh please, please," Canby remarked at one point, with what seems as much vivacity as he ever mustered, "you're breaking my heart."

That broadcast, which could also gratify the desire for a behind-the-scenes look at the world of book reviewing, was apparently a one-time effort rather than an ongoing attempt to promote the magazine. As such, it resembled numerous other occasional radio appearances by the

makers of middlebrow culture. Canby, for example, observing a publi-
cation-day ritual of the late 1940s, discussed his memoirs on Mary
Margaret McBride's popular interview show and plugged his biography
of Thoreau on "Adventure in Reading." Broun briefly conducted an
interview series himself in 1930–31, querying Morley and Van Loon,
among others, about their recent work; he also visited variety shows,
debated political issues on the air, and in 1937 delivered regular observations about current events. Fisher's radio presentations included
both her aforementioned one on youth and another entitled "Reading—
A Family Adventure," as well as broadcasts to schoolchildren. Durant
addressed "The Problem of Marriage" and gave interviews about his
books. Irita Van Doren assessed recent historical fiction on a 1939
episode of "Let's Talk It Over"; the next year, she was a frequent
panelist on "The Author Meets the Critics." Adler, as has been noted,
spoke on behalf of the Britannica set. Such uses of radio did not so much
expand or divert the careers of those individuals as transmit their
previously established roles.[1]

Other middlebrow figures employed the medium for more sustained
ventures, with proportionately greater impact on their reputations.
Erskine's transmissions from Hollywood fall into this category. In addition, Erskine hobnobbed with Mary Margaret McBride and, on "Kraft
Music Hall," with Bing Crosby. He also appeared on "The Lively Arts"
and made a number of speeches on the air. In the early 1940s, Erskine
participated in "Sunday Evening at Fannie Hurst's," discussing literature over coffee with the novelist and her "friends." Similarly, Carl Van
Doren became familiar to audiences not only for visits to the McBride
show but also as master of ceremonies on a weekly book-review program over the Mutual network in 1939. In 1943–44 he was commentator
on "American Scriptures," a series of historical and literary talks heard
during intermissions of New York Philharmonic concerts. The next
season, he frequently introduced dramatizations of novels on NBC; in
1947 he was part of ABC's "World Security Workshop" series. Van
Doren's brother Mark appeared weekly in 1940 and 1941 on the discussion program "Invitation to Learning," an outgrowth of his commitment to Erskine's "great books" concept. Another Erskine student,
Clifton Fadiman, won nationwide fame as master of ceremonies on the
popular quiz show "Information, Please!."[2]

Whether single contributions or ongoing programs, such talks, interviews, roundtables, and quizzes were part of an array of broadcasts on commercial stations in the 1930s and 1940s that concentrated on books and authors or depended at least in part on literary material. The gamut included didactic addresses on the classics as well as variety hours that barely made room for reviews of recently published works. (The terms "book" or "literary" shows, for want of better phrases, hereinafter designate that disparate body of material.) The range of formats, moreover, expressed a range of values. As Simon Frith has perceptively noted with respect to the BBC, the poles of the axis were *not* entertainment versus serious listening or "public service." All book shows strove, one way or another, to entertain as well as enlighten. Nonetheless, they constituted a particular *kind* of amusement that, to varying extents, mingled ideals of character and liberal learning with elements of fantasy, "fun," and the veneration of personality. Like other middlebrow forms, such programs also oscillated between the association of literature with privilege and with accessibility, featuring experts who projected both superiority and kinship to the average reader.[3]

Moreover, certain aspects of the medium literally amplified that set of tensions, making radio an especially good instrument with which to discern the middlebrow blend. First, the essence of the radio show was performance; its "star," even if merely a book reviewer, was, if only while on the air, inevitably a social self. Second, the constraints of time and the juxtaposition of unrelated programs tended to reduce book broadcasts to discrete packages of knowledge, as if they were aural "outlines." One listener, making the connection to consumerism, objected, "Busy as the average American is, he or she has not yet reached the point where either education or entertainment is absorbed in the five-minute installment plan . . . yet the originators of the present style in radio programs multiply [the five-minute period] indefinitely." Such protests, however, were in vain. Indeed, *Radio Guide* magazine's "Listen . . . and Learn" column touted that "style" as one of the medium's advantages: "'Fifteen minutes a day' won't do it . . . but thirty minutes will help. . . . Let's get excited about learning. Radio's capsule classroom is the busy person's best way."[4]

Third, the fact that, thanks to the omnipresence of radio, literary guidance was now as free as the air itself forcefully declared that culture was no longer the exclusive possession of an elite. Along the same lines, the quality of intimacy radio possessed—its apparent ability to offer anyone a private encounter with a famous person—encouraged the idea that speaker and audience were meeting as equals. Fourth, the prospect that dissatisfied listeners could assert their opinions simply by twisting the dial presented a forceful challenge to the power of the expert. "As soon as he buys his set," one observer noted, the member of the radio audience "becomes a critic, tuning out this, tuning in that, preferring, disliking. . . . What he says is law." As John Erskine put it, "Radio is the easiest of all the arts to walk out on." That fact underscored the precarious status of the literary authority in a "business civilization."[5]

At the same time, however, radio's intimate properties could actually perpetuate genteel homage to critical preeminence. As Frith has pointed out in the British context, the essence of "light entertainment" was its development of a tone distinct from the noise and disorder of the music hall. By featuring a reviewer who adopted a professorial or even aristocratic pose, and by exuding balance and restraint, what many radio book programs offered was a private lesson in deference. The simulation of personal contact with a well-known speaker might elicit, along with a sense that listener and performer were both ordinary people, an equally strong feeling of indebtedness to the distinguished visitor who had graced one's home. As the writer Constance Lindsay Skinner phrased it in a 1929 article lamenting the impact of radio on reading, the broadcaster's voice "comes to you not as the platform speaker's to one of a mob, but as if you alone were the object of his solicitude. It enters upon your solitary hours as companionably as spirits rap on the walls of the elect. . . . This personal attention upbuilds your ego. . . . You respond gratefully with a whole-hearted endorsement of whatever the voices tell you." The access to culture radio offered was thus, in Frith's words, "access to a community, a language, a set of radio manners" structured "through an authority."[6]

The discussion which follows aims, first, to delineate the spectrum, in terms of content, along which book broadcasts fell by surveying the types of shows on the air. It is more descriptive than the preceding chapters because no other account of the development of radio has supplied such an overview. Historians have only recently turned from chronicling the technical, institutional, and legal growth of the medium to an investigation of programming. In embarking on that enterprise, they have focused, logically enough, on the most popular sorts of shows: comedy, news, and soap operas. Yet book programs and other less flashy staples of airtime—concerts, health talks, advice to home-makers—require attention if the goal is to take the full measure of the offerings available to the American audience.

Second, this discussion strives to display the range of attitudes liter-ary broadcasts entailed by treating representative examples as texts. Here, again, the objective is to fill a need scholars have usually ne-glected. The studies which have begun to chart programming typically contain strikingly few quotations of what was actually said on the air. In contrast, the following analysis heeds, wherever possible, the pace and mood of a show as well as its language. To some extent, that practice makes a virtue of necessity: although records of a station's, network's, or sponsor's decisions surrounding the creation, production, and can-cellation of book programs would tell a vital part of their history, they are largely missing; so are systematic surveys of audience response to most literary shows. Yet the focus on textual interpretation is also adopted in the belief that a radio broadcast can and, indeed, must be explicated like any other document if the intent is to understand the preoccupations of the culture which generated it.[7]

The Vision—and Reality—of Educational Radio

The history of book programs unfolded against the backdrop of educa-tional radio. The term describes the movement, beginning in the early 1920s, to allocate the airwaves for exclusively instructional, noncom-mercial purposes. When broadcasting expanded after World War I from haphazard transmissions by wirelesses in garages to the establishment of licensed stations, the nature of programming was open to experimen-tation. Pittsburgh's pioneer station KDKA, which the Westinghouse Corporation had started in 1920 to promote its radio equipment, began playing recorded music and arranging live concerts almost as an after-thought. As such efforts multiplied, educators saw the potential radio held for fostering their own interests and quickly moved to found stations dedicated solely to the dissemination of knowledge. Second-arily, they sought airtime on nascent commercial frequencies.

By January 1923 seventy-two universities, colleges, and schools had obtained broadcasting licenses. Many educational institutions, regarding the medium as an arm of university extension divisions, gave listeners the opportunity to pay tuition and receive degree credit for courses they "took" on the air. They also paraded a procession of faculty members before the microphone, offering, as Daniel Czitrom reports, dramatic readings and talks on "nearly every imaginable topic." In addition, educators targeted the primary and secondary school audiences, broadcasting to classrooms on both commercial and noncommercial channels during selected daytime hours. Those ventures, located throughout the country, met with varying success. In 1924–25, for example, Chicago's "Little Red Schoolhouse of Radio" reached twenty-seven thousand children with lessons in numerous subjects but then lost its director, ran out of money, and was discontinued. Three years later, however, Ohio State University's station WEAO joined forces with Cincinnati's WLW to broadcast "The Ohio School of the Air." The "school" provided a weekly "dramatization of literature for high schools" and in 1929 added lectures on "Literature by Living Writers," including one by Fisher. The University of Wisconsin's School of the Air, begun in 1931 on WHA, presented a similar curriculum; among its features was a "Radio Reading Club" for schoolchildren and a series entitled "Invitation to Reading," narrated by a campus professor and designed to "broaden the student's 'reading horizon.'"[8]

Predicated on a concept of radio as an aid to formal study, the structure of most such programs rested on a conventional pedagogical model. Casting the speaker as learned authority, their creators assumed an audience of dutifully attentive pupils seated in rows of an imaginary classroom. In terms of tone, early educational radio shows (except for the "dramalogs") did not do much more than replicate the standard techniques of the professional teacher; at most, they strove for warmth and intimacy by cultivating "smiling voices" or incorporated opening musical selections to "establish an appreciation atmosphere" for the lesson which followed. Yet they had the unintended consequence of attracting a sizable number of nonstudents: "home listeners" (mainly mothers curious about what their children were learning); restaurant and store employees who caught the broadcasts when business was slow; travelers who tuned in from their cars; people marooned in hotels. Schools of the air catered to their wider following by distributing printed lessons and announcing program information in the press.[9]

Those developments encouraged proponents of educational radio to think of the medium as an instrument of social reconstruction. Influenced, in some cases, by Dewey's view of communication as a source of reform, they also shared their contemporaries' concern with safeguarding and unifying civilization. Embellishing the classroom model, Ray Lyman Wilbur, secretary of the interior under Hoover, declared, "The radio seems to make it possible to turn the whole world into a single schoolroom." Similarly, Joy Elmer Morgan, chair of the National Committee on Education by Radio, argued in 1930 that the medium's particular strength lay in its capacity to improve the "quality of thinking among the masses" by exposing millions of people—adults and children alike—to the finest intellects humankind had produced. "Who can estimate the motivating and inspiring force of some future occasion when the entire race will listen to one of its brilliant scientists as he explains some great truth?" Morgan queried. "A world language is as certain as tomorrow's sun. It will be the language of the best radio programs." Four years later, against the backdrop of what he saw as worsening cultural as well as economic depression, Morgan emphasized even more strongly the desirability of a "national culture" and called, in the vocabulary of the New Deal, for "planning" and government regulation to secure the "enlightenment" radio could foster.[10]

Such dreams of unity coexisted with fears that radio's ability to spread a message universally would make it an agent of that other preoccupation of the 1920s and 1930s: standardization. Thanks to broadcasting, one writer prophesied in 1922, one "great mind" would shape "men" into "a common, uniform, subservient mediocrity."[11] Yet, with respect to educational programs, such worries were unfounded, to say the least. In fact, the prospect that educators would realize their grandiose hopes had begun fading even as they were formulating them. In 1922 American Telephone and Telegraph Company's station WEAF started selling airtime to anyone who wanted to sponsor a commercial program. Within a few years, privately owned stations financed by advertising threatened to shut educational stations out of the competition for available channels. The rise of network broadcasting in the late 1920s consolidated the power of commercial radio by providing advertisers with a national market. As a result, numerous college and university stations were either forced to share time with their arch-rivals or to give up completely. A 1930 Supreme Court ruling that denied educational stations any special standing made matters worse. By 1933 only twenty-four remained on the air. (The story of their continuing efforts, together with the instructional activities of shortwave and FM stations, will not be pursued here.) The failure in 1934 of a bill to appropriate 25 percent of all programming for educational and nonprofit purposes guaranteed the dominance of private enterprise.[12]

Even so, the lingering conception of radio as an agent of refinement at first prompted advertisers to limit their activities to sponsorship rather than direct pitches for products.[13] Moreover, the emergent networks, recognizing the need to uphold a semblance of the educators' ideals, mounted a number of "sustaining" or unsponsored programs of a "serious" nature: talks, classical music concerts, public affairs presentations. The commercial stations also retained some responsibility for school broadcasts. In 1928 the recently formed National Broadcasting Company offered the first network program for classroom use—the conductor Walter Damrosch's famous lessons in music appreciation. The next year, the Columbia Broadcasting System planned its American School of the Air, which included the dramatization of literature. Later, when NBC opposed the 25 percent for education idea, it made sure simultaneously to promote its commitment to "cultural" programs which "move distinctly toward a raising of the level of taste and thought." In 1937, when James Rowland Angell retired as president of Yale, NBC hired him as an adviser on educational broadcasts.[14]

Such efforts, however, came to occupy an increasingly tenuous position in the networks' priorities. Before a scheduled meeting between Angell and the BBC's Sir John Reith, NBC's vice-president for programming, John F. Royal, took pains to tutor Angell in the "weaknesses" of the BBC's use of government-supported radio for the diffusion of knowledge. Publicly, the network also reminded Americans that too much "talk would suffocate any radio audience." One of NBC's promotional documents quoted Hilda Matheson, a BBC official, in support of its supposedly more democratic approach: "I doubt if it is yet realized by the average educated person that the key to successful broadcasting is personality,—and personality as seen not from the point of view of the sophisticated listener but from the point of view of the average man and woman, *who is suspicious of any trace of superiority and of anything that sounds highbrow and of any attempt at uplift or education*" (emphasis in original). Only by insuring that the majority of programs entertained the "masses," the network explained, could radio "hope to stimulate culture."[15]

Those high-minded justifications for minimizing "talk," however, hardly represented the full explanation for the status of educational shows as network radio evolved. In the late 1920s, after a period of caution, advertisers had begun wholeheartedly exploiting the medium's capacity for intimate persuasion. As testimonials and slogans proved profitable, sustaining shows became liabilities. "The fatality," Gilbert Seldes noted in the case of CBS, "was that a half-hour of education broke the mood of the morning program schedule, which was primarily the mood of the daytime serial; sponsors who wanted to buy a block of quarter-hours, letting the audience flow from one to the other, could not tolerate this dam in the stream. . . . 'The School of the Air' shifted to late afternoon, and a philosophical explanation was issued to prove that this was more advantageous. Presently the programs were shifted off the air entirely." By the late 1930s tensions between NBC and the Carnegie Institute's National Advisory Council on Radio in Education ran especially high. The use of radio profits to pay for television development in the 1940s constituted an added pressure to avoid non-money-makers. The Communications Act of 1934 prevented the total elimination of such efforts by requiring as a condition of licensing that stations demonstrate service to the "public interest." Yet the legislation was ambiguous and easy to subvert. As one writer complained when the triumph of commercialization was becoming evident, "Now we know definitely what we have got in radio—just another disintegrating toy. Just another medium—like the newspapers, the magazines, the billboards, and the mail box—for advertisers to use in pestering us."[16]

More unfortunate (from the educators' standpoint), the radio audience collaborated with those priorities. By 1939, when the sociologist Paul F. Lazarsfeld tabulated the preferences of Buffalo residents, he concluded that, while the average middle- or upper-income listener played the radio slightly more than 20 hours a week and the average working-class listener around 23.5 hours a week, the first group tuned into "serious broadcasts" an average of 12.4 minutes a week and the second group only 6.7 minutes. Lazarsfeld's survey of listening among Book-of-the-Month Club members, reported in *Radio and the Printed Page* (1940), was similarly discouraging. Instead of proving that radio augmented the knowledge of people with little exposure to print, it demonstrated that the largest audience for educational programs consisted of avid readers—arguably the population that needed them least. In general, Lazarsfeld observed, as one moved down the scale of what he termed "cultural levels," based on either income or education, the amount of "serious listening" declined. Assuredly, radio and learning were not incompatible: the medium did not apparently decrease reading in American society as a whole and, for some groups, actually spurred "follow-up" book acquisition. Yet the most popular program among middle-class listeners in 1937–38, for instance, was "Major Bowes," an hour not of "great truth" but of hog calling and amateur tryouts. Lazarsfeld and Harry Field's later study *The People Look at Radio* (1946) even noted that most listeners did not object to advertisements.[17]

For educational broadcasters, those conclusions raised questions of voice and tone. As Lazarsfeld put it, with particular reference to discussions of books, should reviewers assume that their "quiet comments can compete with the sort of delivery the listener is used to hearing," or should they "try to keep pace with the lingo of current advertising?" Some champions of education by radio gave unequivocally negative answers to those queries. One book columnist, for example, offered this embittered parody: "Good evening, ladies and gentlemen. You are about to hear a half hour of sweet and hot jazz played by the Book-of-the-Week Blue Symphonists. And if you wonder why the boys seem pepped up tonight, . . . [it is] because they all have read Millicent Pashim's latest romance, *She Got Out and Walked*. And after you have heard . . . this Book-of-the-Week hour, take my tip and walk (heh heh)— do not run—to the nearest bookstore and get your copy of *She Got Out and Walked*." The writer James Rorty summarized the disillusionment of those who left the field in disgust. "Do you imagine for a moment," he asked in dismay, "that education can permanently function as an appendage of toothpaste-and-cigarette-sponsored jazz and vaudeville?" Lazarsfeld and Field's own conclusion was only slightly less disheartening. At best, they counseled, the broadcaster could adopt a style "slightly above what the masses want. In this way, he may contribute to a systematic rise in the general cultural level without defeating the educational goal by driving the audience away."[18]

Yet the commercialization of radio did not deter everyone who hoped radio would serve a pedagogical function. Some educators continued to approximate conventional instruction on for-profit stations while accepting a status frankly subordinate to that of the comedian or the crooner. Others accepted the necessity of sounding more like advertisers than instructors. Still others went even further, relinquishing the vision of the extended classroom for roles on programs that supplied knowledge in other guises. When Lazarsfeld remarked in his first radio study that professors "obviously feel" that a "how to get along" program or a "quiz contest" is "beneath their dignity," he overlooked the fact that many had participated in precisely those types of shows. John Erskine even welcomed the opportunity to create "new art forms" for teaching, urging educators to create a "radio personality" and to present "scholarship as information" made "as fascinating as possible." Deliberately addressing the general listener the school broadcasts reached by accident, the figures who followed Erskine's advice enjoyed greater popularity and influence than their more didactic colleagues. For example, when a sample of 745 high school students replied to the question "What are the programs from which you can learn something?," 28.6 percent mentioned quizzes and 5.1 percent singled out "popularized information," as against .7 percent for "straight education."[19]

Whether in terms of format or scheduling, book broadcasts on commercial stations between 1922 and 1950 all signified some compromise between educational ideals and the realities of the marketplace. As such, they belonged to a region of early radio located somewhere between "Amos 'n' Andy" and the "Wisconsin School of the Air," between Morgan's elation and Rorty's despair. On that ground, English professors joined writers, critics, editors, bookstore proprietors, and self-styled literary authorities in an unprecedented effort to employ spoken language in the service of the printed word.

Toward the Conversation in the Living Room

One of the first book programs that departed from the classroom model was Edgar White Burrill's weekly "Literary Vespers." On the air in 1922, the broadcast repeated talks Burrill delivered before live audiences in New York's Town Hall. Its primary purpose, in Burrill's own

words, was to present "the choice passages of the world's best literature." A Protestant minister, Burrill retained as his underlying aim
"stimulation" toward the "reading of books that will build character"
and echoed Arnoldian sentiments about the "best"; the program's title
even connected reading with religious devotion. The "keynote," Burrill
wrote, "is inspiration rather than mere information; not facts alone, but
high ideals." To achieve that goal, however, he consciously rejected
"the academic atmosphere associated with college and university
courses" in favor of an emphasis on what he called "the basic human
values of books." Specifically, he avoided discussions of authors, remarks about literary influence, or, most tellingly, criticism, instead
reciting excerpts from texts and then linking them to "current events."
Justified in terms of supplying a connection between "literature and
life," Burrill's approach could actually sabotage "inspiration" and subvert the character ideal: it intentionally transformed culture into what
he called "news items" and, as he put it, served the needs of "busy"
consumers. In that way, however, Burrill saw himself as satisfying
listeners impatient with "mediocre efforts" and ready to indicate their
displeasure by turning the dial. In all those respects—its dualistic
premises, its accommodation of consumerism, its empowerment of the
audience—"Literary Vespers" sounded themes that would recur on
later, more widely disseminated book shows.[20]

While Burrill concentrated on reading passages aloud, some commercial stations in the 1920s offered book reviews. Necessarily local in
reach before the rise of networks, such broadcasts sometimes reflected
parochial interests as well. In 1925, for example, the manager of the
Doubleday, Page bookshop in Springfield, Massachusetts, gave semi-
weekly talks in what *Radio Broadcast* called a "pleasantly different
fashion." As the magazine phrased it, "instead of critically discussing a
book that many of his hearers have not read," the speaker "attempt[ed]
to give the facts about each book which are calculated to inspire interest
in reading it." As such, he engaged less in reviewing than in trying to
create traffic to his store. In fact, he anticipated precisely the recommendation *Publishers' Weekly* made a few years later to exploit the
advertising value of the medium by "stressing the bookshop in radio
reviews."[21]

Another commentator of the 1920s, Oliver M. Sayler, was more
cosmopolitan. His "Footlight and Lamplight" program, broadcast from

New York, appears to be the first of several which combined remarks about the theater with an assessment of recently published books. Sayler, whom *Radio Broadcast* dubbed "by far the best of the radio book reviewers," mingled "sound criticism with an entertaining manner of presentation." Of James Branch Cabell's *The Silver Stallion*, for example, he declared: "Five times I tried to get started on this book and stopped. I gritted my teeth and went at it. Fifty or so pages and I was so wrapped up in the thing that you couldn't have torn it from me. And so, if you are awarded *The Silver Stallion* at your next bridge party, don't get discouraged." In those statements, part of the "entertainment" derived from Sayler's self-parodying presentation of himself as beleaguered reader; that posture, along with the reference to bridge, grounded his appeal in his acknowledgment of human foibles and ordinary pastimes rather than in his intellectual credentials.[22]

Something of the same disarming approach characterized the most successful of the local reviewers, Joseph Henry Jackson. A newspaper critic and travel writer, Jackson began his "Reader's Guide" series (later titled "Bookman's Notebook") in San Francisco in 1924; the program was eventually aired nationally on NBC. Although his voice sounded "patriarchal," Jackson replaced the classroom approach with a homier conceit: the "conversation" in the "living room." His basic principle, he reported, was to remember that "you are not talking to a 'vast audience.' You are talking, at most, to two or three people, sitting in their living room. . . . Speak exactly as you would if you were in that living room, telling those people why you liked a book that one of them happened to ask you about. And don't forget, you wouldn't be there if you didn't like those people and they didn't like you; and you wouldn't be telling them about a book unless they were the kind who wanted to hear about it."[23]

Jackson's vision of addressing easy chairs rather than rows of desks— a sense of role he shared with his less famous counterparts in other localities—alluded to radio's special ability to generate an illusion of intimacy: in this case, the fantasy that the critic was physically situated in one's home, among one's family and friends. That image could trigger a number of associations. The living room, Karen Halttunen has proposed, was a domestic representation of the culture of personality. In place of the restraint of the parlor, it celebrated the virtues of charm and self-expression.[24] Arguably, the substitution of the "personal touch" in home decorating for furnishings which conformed to formal codes of propriety was the material analogue of the drift away from Arnoldian strictures toward a definition of culture tied to self-expression. Certainly the idea of a critic comfortably installed in the "heart" of the household betokened the accessibility of literature.

The term "conversation," moreover, excluded didactic explication. As the Chicago-area reviewer Howard Vincent O'Brien advised, a "politely deferential conversation technique" could woo an audience that, he implied, was in no mood to defer in return. O'Brien imagined himself as "intruding into countless private homes," a position that demanded he "behave as though he were being casually introduced to the family and asked to enter into a discussion about books." Similarly, in a 1931 article entitled "Fatal to Review: How Does One Review Books over the Air?," Harry Salpeter recommended a conversational approach that required the critic to be a "glittering dragon fly" rather than a "mole," an actor who emphasized his own personal qualities and that of the author under discussion rather than a scholar who evaluated the form or content of the book. Both Salpeter and O'Brien agreed that, in the latter's words, reviewing "is entirely a matter of creating personality. One cannot afford a negative attitude. One must like the books."[25]

Nonetheless, the ideal of a "conversation" involved the same complexities here as in Erskine's "great books" design. Susceptible to serving the goal of successful public performance, it still potentially encompassed an etiquette of self-discipline, a subdued tone, and a set of external standards; it could, in other words, suggest the display of cultivated taste and refined character. Thus, the mood of Jackson's program, and others which strove for the same effect, might best be described as self-assertion bounded by genteel decorum and sensibility. As such, the image of the "conversation in the living room" can serve as an emblem of the broadcasts' capacity, augmented by the attributes of radio itself, to mediate between two sets of values.

In addition, in the hands of the book trade, the conversational conceit represented an alternative not only to a classroom approach but also to a more blatant sales pitch. A description of the local radio talks of Richard G. Montgomery, a Portland bookseller who began reviewing in 1925, makes the connection clear: "The Montgomery book talks have personality," *Publishers' Weekly* noted. "There is in them a conversational quality, an informal, discursive element that gives the Sunday evening broadcast the atmosphere of a pleasant visit with a friend who always has something to talk about. People know that they are listening to a man whose job it is to sell books, but they are able to lose track of this fact entirely while Dick Montgomery talks to them, and herein lies one of the reasons why his program does sell books."[26]

The full force of the "conversation in the living room" as a marketing strategy appeared in a 1929 radio advertisement for the Literary Guild, heard over New York station WABC. As Marchand has noted, print advertisers had come by this time to appreciate the appeal of the "overheard conversation" as a technique for capturing the reader's interest. Radio commercials which furnished the "initial titillation of eavesdropping" could be even more effective, since they involved the listener's assent to the role of the host's "unwitting accomplice."[27] Capitalizing on that advantage of radio, as well as on the medium's affinity for making drama come alive, the guild created a conversational skit to publicize its monthly selection. (It is unclear how many programs they did; in the one surviving script, the book is Ring Lardner's *Round-Up*.) "At the invitation of the Literary Guild," the announcer began, "we are going to place our microphone in the living room of an average American home." In the vignette which followed, Grace, a friend, arrives at the door of Ann and John Livingwell and their son Joe. She is carrying the Lardner volume. After a gracious exchange of pleasantries, during which Joe loses Grace's place in the book, the group decides to have Joe read them all Lardner's "Haircut." The "reading" permits a dramatization of the plot, along with two barbershop quartet numbers. The action returns to the living room for conversation about the guild's previous selections, including this dialogue: "Joe: 'Seems to me you can hardly mention a well known book success that they didn't sponsor.' Grace: 'Well, if you read the Guild books you can depend on reading the best.'" At the conclusion of the story, the announcer reappears with a more direct pitch, encouraging listeners to send for information about guild membership.[28]

In constructing that scenario, the Literary Guild broadcast exhibited a nascent version of the interweaving of program and advertisement that radio developed in this period: the entertainment was the ad, and vice versa. Specifically, it blended the depiction of self-expression and refined exchange with the identification of a commodity that promised to supply both. More than that, however, by adopting the setting of the home, the guild program almost overtly conveyed the announcement that Frith has attributed to comparable BBC broadcasts: "The message was that [the radio performer] was honoured to enter your home; the assumption was that your home was a particular kind of place; the promise was that if it wasn't . . . , [the radio show], by entering, could make it so." To be privy to Ann, John, Joe, and Grace's "conversation in the living room" was to declare that you, too, were "living well." The conversational image, with its complex of ambivalent values and commercial potential, would reappear in various forms on radio book programs throughout the 1930s and 1940s.[29]

Swift's Premium Ham

The power and prototypicality of their appeals notwithstanding, however, the book broadcasts of the 1920s were, in comparison to network efforts later on, largely the province of obscure reviewers with relatively limited influence. That situation changed in the mid-1930s, when figures with national reputations began discussing literature on the air. Among them was William Lyon Phelps, who brought his prestige as Lampson Professor of English at Yale University to a series of appearances on Sigmund Romberg's "Swift Hour" variety program in 1934 and 1935. In so doing he gave elements of the 1920s broadcasts— Burrill's interpretations of culture and expertise, Sayler's human touch, and Jackson's genteel intimacy—his own inimitable stamp.

"Billy" Phelps, wrote the columnist Lucius Beebe in 1939, "has probably done more than any living figure to inculcate the American mind with reverence for the written and spoken word. For nearly four decades he has been the nation's most popular lecturer on literature." Born in New Haven in 1865, Phelps graduated from Yale in 1887. Four years later he completed a Ph.D. at Harvard, writing a conventional dissertation on *The Beginnings of the English Romantic Movement*. In 1892 he embarked on a forty-one-year career as a member of the Yale faculty. Beginning in 1895, he also ventured outside academia to address women's clubs, Chautauqua gatherings, and lecture series on literary topics. In addition, he wrote frequently for magazines: his column "As I Like It" ran monthly in *Scribner's* from 1922 to 1936; he did book reviews for the *Rotarian* beginning in 1933; and he often contributed to the *Ladies' Home Journal* and the *Delineator*. Many of those pieces found their way into the collections of essays he published at regular intervals. For a time, he also produced a daily newspaper column. By the early 1920s Phelps had surpassed Erskine and others on the lecture circuit in terms of audience size, drawing up to two thousand people at a performance. His fame, the journalist Joseph J. Reilly noted, amounted to "a peculiarly personal triumph." Even those who had never heard him lecture regarded him, in Reilly's words, as "nothing less than an intimate personal friend." His wide acceptance as guide and mentor prompted Edward Bok, the editor of the *Ladies' Home Journal*, to introduce a sketch of Phelps in 1925 with the caption "Nobody has ever said it until Billy Phelps says it."[30]

Inclined to favor canonical British writers and their unrebellious descendants, Phelps frankly admitted his antipathy to modernism and deliberately ignored the movement, during the Depression, for "proletarian literature." His demeanor—he exuded conservatism, erudition, and firsthand acquaintance with literary celebrities—partially sustained a view of culture as the possession of an educated minority. As a critic, he often tinted his literary judgments with moralism: "Their pictures of slime," he wrote of "some of our modern writers" in *Appreciation* (1932), "are of little value because there is no suggestion that there ought to be, as of course there is, a higher level of character and environment."[31]

Yet, especially in his younger years, Phelps was also an innovator and an iconoclast, shocking the university community early in his career by adding the study of contemporary fiction to the curriculum. His courses on modern drama and poetry delighted generations of undergraduates, some of whom owed to Phelps their eligibility for the football team. He introduced his students to Ibsen and Tolstoy as well as Shakespeare, Tennyson, and Browning and welcomed the poetic experiments of Amy Lowell and the satire of Sinclair Lewis. He also exhibited a cheery outlook, passion for sports, and open-mindedness toward almost anything between covers. Oswald Garrison Villard remarked that he was "the most easily pleased book reviewer in America"; Carl Van Doren called him "a literary tea taster greeting each new spoonful with uncensored approbation." Those attributes countermanded the more sober and rigorous aspects of the genteel tradition.[32]

Upon his retirement from Yale in 1933, Phelps embarked on a number of radio talks. At the urging of a former student, these included a stint as narrator and master of ceremonies on the CBS "Voice of America" series, sponsored by the Underwood Typewriter Company. The role permitted him to address such subjects as "good reading" and "courage." Thereafter, Phelps signed on with the "Swift Hour." On Saturday evenings at eight o'clock, listeners who tuned into the NBC network could hear Phelps and Romberg, the conductor and composer of such operettas as *The Student Prince*, broadcasting over station WEAF, New York. By December 1934 the success of the collaboration merited an item in *Newsweek*: "More than sixteen percent of America's radio sets were dialed" to the show, which "led a field of six new hour programs in the race for popularity" and lagged "only two points behind the older program of Armour," Swift's competitor. Because recordings of them have survived, Phelps's "Swift Hour" appearances provide unusually full documentation of the tensions that could govern the role of tastemaker of the airwaves.[33]

Billed as "an hour of melody, drama (or anecdote) and song," the "Swift Hour" characteristically opened with the announcement that the program featured the music of Romberg, followed by a few bars of theme song. Then came the initial introduction of Phelps, first formally—as "Professor William Lyon Phelps"—and second, as if to humanize and demystify him, by way of some complimentary, descriptive phrase preceding his nickname: "the genial, informative Billy Phelps of Yale," "the friendly and engaging Billy Phelps of Yale," "the beloved," "the ever-popular," etc. Such designations, which always incorporated a reference to Yale, carried a double message. They certified Phelps as a representative of the best education America had to offer, thus perpetuating the extended classroom motif, while at the same time suggesting that (like Sayler before him) he was just a "regular guy" akin to the average listener. The *American Mercury* writer John Bakeless sarcastically noticed the first of those appeals when he wrote that "the Phelpsian outpourings . . . spout from a pundit of a famous university, and are therefore fondly believed to be the final dictum of infallible literary taste in circulating libraries and women's clubs from Eastport, Keokuk, and Dubuque, to San Pedro and Walla Walla"; Reilly highlighted the second attribute when he cited the story that Phelps re-

sponded to the question "Which would you rather do, discover a beautiful poem or see Yale defeat Harvard on the gridiron?" with the answer
"I never smashed my hat over a beautiful poem."[34]

Subsequent exchanges typically called upon the "professor," who
responded with a brief comment either hinting at his topic for the
evening or revealing that he was indeed unintimidating. "If I were now
given the opportunity to spend every day for the next five hundred
years with an invariable program of work every morning, golf every
afternoon, and social entertainment every evening," he declared on
one broadcast, "I should accept with alacrity." He then proclaimed that
the culture he purveyed was compatible with amusement, conveying a
familiarity with his audience that overrode his professorial stature: "I
know we're going to have a most entertaining hour together." Expressing the solicitousness O'Brien had recommended, that remark in
effect gave Phelps's listeners credit for satisfying the desire for social
activity he had voiced a moment earlier.

Having thus amalgamated both cultivation and informality, authority
and deference (or at least equality), the "Swift Hour" quickly proceeded to its first musical selection. This was generally a Romberg
arrangement of a well-known piece such as "The Merry Widow." Although the order of presentation varied somewhat, the next segment
was most often a commercial, the content of which strikingly paralleled
the message of Phelps's portions of the program. Stressing Swift's fifty-
year record of "service," "responsibility," "quality," "dependability,"
and "fairness," attributes which implied stability and selflessness in a
time of economic distress, the advertisements also portrayed the company as an upholder of standards. The "Swift Hour," one commercial
proclaimed, was designed to "entertain you and help you in the selection of fine foods for your table," including the choice of such food
"classics" of New England as lard. Another stated that Swift was
engaged in balancing new methods of preparing products against venerable old ways (just as Phelps, later in the program, balanced references to the literary canon against recommendations of contemporary
fiction). In fact, Phelps identified himself with his sponsor to the extent
that he supplanted the announcer on at least one commercial, hailing
not books but "foods distinguished by their excellence" and extending
"on behalf of Mr. Romberg, myself, and the entire cast heartiest con-
gratulations" on the occasion of the company's jubilee.[35]

Such advertisements constituted a more sophisticated use of the device the Literary Guild's "conversation" had exploited: the blurring of the boundary between sales talk and program content. If, as Marchand has shown, that technique permitted advertisers "to preserve radio's aura of refinement and its mood of relaxed entertainment," it here attached refinement to Swift and Company as well.[36] By functioning as Swift's "premium ham," Phelps implicitly addressed the issue of the nature of civilization in a consumer society: Repudiating the image of American businessmen as "boobs" and Babbitts, he conspired to suggest that culture and business were parts of the same enterprise— that sponsor and professor alike were interested only in improving taste in both senses of the word.

The affinity between selling ham and discussing literature eased the transition from one to the other when, following another interlude of Romberg arrangements, the announcer called on Phelps for his weekly commentary. For five minutes, Phelps spoke about books, movies, the theater, or his philosophy of life, bringing to each topic a blend of fact, opinion, and personal anecdote. On February 23, 1935, for example, he praised Thornton Wilder's *Heaven's My Destination* and thanked Wilder for writing short books, flipped abruptly to a story concerning James Hilton and dubbed him a worthy replacement for Hardy and Conrad, quickly described Pearl Buck's life, identified the "greatest biography" of the season, issued decisive verdicts on current Broadway performances, and pronounced the film *David Copperfield* "the best picture I ever saw"—made from "the best novel in the English language." His March 16, 1935, address on "Youth" similarly evolved from an approving sermon on youthful idealism to references to Ibsen, Homer, the Egyptians, and a young Yale graduate. Many of his remarks, like Durant's, drew on what seems an unlimited stock of one-liners: "If the whole world played golf and tennis we might not have had the world war"; Jesus was "the most interesting person in history"; "the most fascinating thing about life is mystery."

The effect of Phelps's combination of gossip, homily, and criticism was, like Erskine's re-creation of Helen of Troy in suburbia, to place literature on the same level as everyday experience. When, for example, in his March 23, 1935, talk, "The Art of Living Together," Phelps cited Turgenev's statement that he would give all his art "if there were one woman who cared whether he came home to dinner," he tacitly assured the audience that their activities were as valuable as a great writer's.[37] Moving on to Hawthorne, whom he called, in passing, "the greatest literary artist in American history," Phelps connected a description of the author's wife to a general discussion of marriage: that it could be a blissful state for "many people, rich and poor, educated and uneducated," and that it was "a success within the reach of the average man." Those juxtapositions reiterated his message that the same was true for culture.

On another broadcast, Phelps made that understanding explicit, in terms that incontrovertibly shifted the *meaning* of culture away from the building of character toward the development of personality. After prescribing a rule for happiness ("Take nothing for granted"), he asserted that the greatest books—the Bible and Shakespeare—were still the "best sellers." That statement, like the pats on the back Simon and Schuster incorporated into advertisements for Durant, at once accepted the legitimacy of commercialism and calmed fears that the marketplace had destroyed artistic standards. Phelps's next remark, however, contained his main point—indeed, it can serve as his credo: "The entire intellectual wealth of mankind is within reach of every humble person," he declared. "You've got a mind. Why not cultivate it? Not every person can become a personage, but every person can become a personality." As the texts he singled out made clear, the means of "cultivation" was still in large measure reading the recognized masterpieces of Western civilization. Yet the goal of such reading, Phelps intimated, was not primarily to fulfill a moral duty or to train mental powers—or even to develop individual abilities—but instead to prevent oneself from "boring others."[38] As was true for Durant, Phelps's epigrammatic style and quick doses of information supported that end by condensing culture into a form capable of enhancing public performance.

Phelps's double-edged assumptions about expertise and culture pervaded more than his radio appearances. In an advertisement for Eliot's "Five-Foot Shelf" a few years before he went on the air, Phelps had averred, "A well-read man is always an interesting man." His "As I Like It" columns, which (in another embodiment of the conversational ideal) he described not as reviews or guides but as "causeries," gave as much weight to items of literary and linguistic curiosity submitted by readers as to Phelps's own evaluations. ("Perhaps at their best in entertainment and information," declared one blurb for a compilation of the columns.) Similarly, his creation of the "Ignoble Prize," for which he and his *Scribner's* audience proposed as recipients those famous authors whom they found boring or incomprehensible, lent the weight of an authoritative column to Phelps's confession of the prejudices and weaknesses of the "average man." Like the broadcasts, the columns also dispensed culture as news, joining capsule notices of recent books to brief remarks on literary matters and averaging thirty topics in the space of eight pages. Finally, in print as well as on broadcasts, Phelps made "happiness" the goal of a college education and identified entrance into "a world of thought and art and culture" with making "a larger personality." His *Autobiography with Letters* (1929) reflected his own effort to construct an interesting self. Opening with an introduction on ways to achieve happiness, it skidded from a description of Phelps's boyhood to an "interlude on cats" that emphasized his idiosyncrasies, rather than furnishing the chronological narrative one might have expected.[39]

The medium of radio, however, added special force to Phelps's stance as both "personage" and "personality." First, its ability to engender what Hadley Cantril and Gordon W. Allport called a "feeling of personal involvement in the events of the outside world" from which the audience "would otherwise be excluded" could engender, in this case, the impression of studying not just in any classroom but at an elite university.[40] Phelps, the announcer declared on one show, was "this program's personal don," suggesting that he took an individual interest in his listeners and considered them no less his students than those he taught at Yale. Phelps was well aware of the appeal of that fantasy and made the most of it. For example, he commented at the beginning of his broadcast for February 9, 1935, "When I come to these weekly Swift reunions I feel as if I were attending a class reunion with many of my former pupils," who, he observed, "don't seem a day older than last time." That remark not only turned Phelps's listeners into honorary Yalies; by mentioning their appearance, it compensated for the loss of face-to-face contact that radio necessarily involved. Although the fiction of the "personal don" suggested the democratization of an Ivy League education, it was also capable, as Skinner remarked, of exacting from the audience a more gratefully submissive response than the printed word or lecture hall address might prompt. Phelps's characteristic sign-off, "Now I must take my train to New Haven," by reminding listeners of his prestigious affiliation and playing on their knowledge of Yale's location, likewise emphasized the connection between culture and social status and made the audience "insiders." Phelps's upper-class accent and modulated pitch contributed to the same result.

At the same time, both the tone and style Phelps adopted could work to a somewhat different effect. Despite the classroom metaphor, his delivery was closer to the conversational model than to pedagogy, its warmth confirming his "friendly" image. Moreover, the time constraints radio necessarily imposed dictated that Phelps rely on concise pronouncements and homilies even more than he did in print, and that he do so at a rapid pace. Thus, on an early 1935 broadcast, for example, he rendered his list of "best books" of the preceding year so quickly that no listener could easily take notes on individual titles. Similarly, his theater reviews were often single, isolated sentences: "I think the best new play of the season is *Merrily We Roll Along*."[41] As such, Phelps's sprightly manner reinforced his turn away from genteel critical intentions. On the air, his lists and epigrams functioned not to provide literary analysis or aesthetic instruction but to create in listeners the sense that they were culturally "in the know." Given that fact, Phelps's effort to accommodate an old lesson—the importance of reading good books—to a new medium threatened to subvert his entire mission. That is, while "Turns with a Bookworm," the *Book-of-the-Month Club News*, the Syntopicon, or the "outline" permitted the conclusion that one might become refined by reading *about* books rather than by reading the books themselves, radio legitimated acquiring culture by hearing the news and discarding print altogether.

Finally, the context in which Phelps's talks appeared—the Romberg variety hour—buttressed the idea that culture, while accessible, was also a matter not of training but of accumulation. In general, variety shows exemplified radio's ability to thwart boredom and indulge an audience's desire for change while offering what Gilbert Seldes has called the "triumph of format." Seldes's argument—that, to cope with the need to create large numbers of programs, broadcasters relied on fixed "packaging" and made the content of any given show forgettable—seems applicable to the throwaway quality of much of Phelps's monologue. More specifically, however, Romberg's version of the variety format furnished an analogue to Phelps's treatment of literature, echoing and reinforcing his approach. His presentation of bits of opera, dramatic sketches, snippets of musical history, and "light classics" elaborated on Phelps's implication that the mastery of titles and aphorisms added up to a cultural education—while simultaneously removing the barriers to such mastery. On one broadcast, for example, the composer offered a rendition of "Ave Maria" reworded to make it fit into the plot of an operetta based on Schubert's life, after which he supplied the original version. By that device, he translated Schubert's song into contemporary idiom (Erskine again comes to mind) and then eased listeners into the real thing. Phelps himself often played the role of mediator between audience and music, as if to assure everyone that no formidable obstacles lay ahead. After depicting the colorful atmosphere of the Latin Quarter, for instance, he declared that the orchestra would play an excerpt from *La Bohème* "under Mr. Romberg's baton and with my own personal blessing."[42]

The fifteen-minute dramas that regularly comprised a segment of the Romberg program's last half hour had the same disarming effect. As vehicles for more musical performances, they linked Haydn, Wagner, or Romberg himself with love stories, mysteries, or historical skits, thereby removing culture from a rarefied atmosphere and associating it, as Phelps had, with human emotions. The juxtaposition of the musical selections in the remainder of the show also reiterated something of Phelps's relatively indiscriminate critical outlook. On the February 9, 1935, broadcast, for example, the orchestra played the overture to *Die Fledermaus* and Romberg's "Like a Star in the Night" in quick succession and gave as much time to the "Swift Anniversary March" as to the selection from Wagner which preceded it, as if all those pieces were of the same quality and significance.

Molded by the limitations and opportunities of radio, the "Swift Hour" as a whole thus declared that, although time-honored standards still applied, culture might be attained by tuning in next week. Yet it also left ample room for the conviction that "business civilization" was civilization enough. Those conclusions, one imagines, might be especially comforting in the midst of the Depression, when both traditional priorities and new roads to success held the heightened promise of fending off psychological upheaval and economic disaster. Phelps's own term for what he offered—"appreciation"—provides the best summary of his appeal. To appreciate culture, he implied, was to under-stand that it was good for you, to pay homage to experts who guarded the heritage of Western civilization, to acknowledge aesthetic judg-ments and standards, to make a limited commitment of time and energy to the improvement of personality, to grace your home with the voice of refinement—and then to move on to activities more central to twen-tieth-century American life.

Even so, Phelps's tenure as the "personal don" of the "Swift Hour" ended in the spring of 1935. Because he went on to other appearances on the air, it would be wrong automatically to assume that he was a casualty of negative audience response. In fact, the existing evidence, while impressionistic, points to the opposite conclusion. For example, one listener, a "workman," expressed gratitude to Phelps for bringing him, "through a radio program, an understanding of music such as he had never had before." Similarly, a bookseller, overwhelmed by the demand Phelps triggered when he urged people to acquire "the one hundred best books," announced the desire to "wring his neck" if he ever created such a stir on the air again.[43] In 1938 Phelps was still sufficiently popular to be used as the intermission speaker on an NBC Symphony broadcast. Nonetheless, the shape the show took after his departure symbolizes a resolution of the tensions his role encompassed in favor of listeners impatient even with the vestiges of gentility. On the September 10, 1935, broadcast, Deems Taylor, himself a well-known cultural authority, replaced Phelps as cohost of the "Swift Hour," but the program's fictive setting was neither classroom nor living room. Instead, Taylor played a guest at an "informal party" in the studio at which the chorus, dubbed "Mr. Romberg's young people," exhibited the charm, gaiety—and personality—of a carefree bunch of kids.[44]

The Town Crier

The disappearance of Phelps's imaginary Yale lecture hall left as the preeminent American radio commentator on books a man who, in time, became "a legend" and a "national institution": Alexander Woollcott. Born in 1887 to an unconventional family with roots in an upstate New York Fourierite community, Woollcott was a bookish child who, by the time he was in high school, had developed an interest in journalism and the theater. As an undergraduate at Hamilton College, he edited and wrote stories for the literary magazine, while earning some notoriety in campus plays. He was hired as a cub reporter at the *New York Times* in 1909 and five years later became the newspaper's drama critic. His "stagestruck" reviews, which defied custom by evincing his personal involvement with actors and playwrights, quickly earned him a loyal following. At the same time, his honesty in "slashing" productions he found inferior made him a controversial celebrity. After wartime work on the army publication *Stars and Stripes*, where his colleagues included F.P.A. and eventual *New Yorker* editor Harold Ross, he resumed his watch on the Broadway scene. A few years later Woollcott left the *Times* for the *New York Herald* and then for the *Sun*. In 1925 he took over the drama desk at the *World* from his friend Heywood Broun. Those positions made Woollcott one of the two or three most powerful theater critics in New York.[45]

Like Broun, whose sensibility so resembled his own that, for a period, the two habitually shared a hotel room from which they issued their opening night reviews, he acquired a distinctive public image by the early 1920s. It was Woollcott who had originally invited Broun to lunch at what became the Algonquin Round Table and Woollcott who remained a chief purveyor of sparkling quips and pithy, if outrageous, pronouncements. According to his biographer, his well-publicized antics and venomous humor hid a sexually ambivalent, shy, and sensitive inner man. That observation, strikingly similar to descriptions of Hendrik Van Loon, corroborates the fragmentation of self at the heart of the culture of personality. The title of one of Woollcott's essay collections, *Going to Pieces*, most concisely captures his pun-laden brand of wit and the painful self-concept it concealed. Yet most people never glimpsed the insecure, lonely figure underneath the opera cape with which he draped his enormous body. They saw only Woollcott the man-about-town—the master of the prerequisites for success in modern America.[46]

In 1924 Woollcott made a single appearance on radio, narrating the story of an American naval hero. Five years later, on New York's station WOR, he did twenty-six weeks of sponsored broadcasts. As host of what was essentially a variety hour, he adopted the persona that he would retain for the rest of his career: the "Town Crier." Stars like Clifton Webb, Fred Allen, and Libby Holman joined him on the show, to which Woollcott himself contributed book reviews and historical anecdotes along with his assessments of the theater. The next season, on the CBS affiliate WABC, he embarked on "The Early Bookworm," the first attempt at a nationwide book-review program. As *Publishers' Weekly* reported, the broadcast had a number of aspects in its favor: Woollcott's reputation; a station with a hook-up to thirty-three affiliates; a time slot (7:45 to 8:00 in the evening) at which people "are not especially looking for dance music and might like to turn to book gossip"; and the backing of the American Book Bindery and ten publishers (including Simon and Schuster, Macmillan, Knopf, and E. P. Dutton).[47]

The latter element dictated the four titles Woollcott discussed on each program. Although he was free to select among them, he was restricted to reviewing new works issued by the program's sponsors. The promotional tie-in was explicit and aggressive. The bindery company supplied booksellers with posters they could use to display each broadcast's featured titles. Additionally, it printed a thirty-two-page booklet of "interesting and personal material about authors" known as "Radio Book Chat." Distributed to both listeners and bookstore owners, the pamphlet also announced a contest for the best review of any of the books Woollcott mentioned on the air. The emphasis on gossip, the conceit of the "chat," the competition to stand out from the crowd, and the promise of foreknowledge implicit in its title indicate the extent to which the content and marketing of "The Early Bookworm" expressed and augmented Woollcott's stature as exemplar of personality.

In 1933 Woollcott returned to the microphone as the "Town Crier." This time he was unencumbered by the publishers' constraints: CBS initially placed the program on a sustaining basis; later it was sponsored by Cream of Wheat. The twice-weekly, fifteen-minute show reached a network of eighty stations. Coupled with a monthly review for *Mc-Call's*, it made Woollcott as influential a critic of books as he had been of drama. "Within a few months," *Literary Digest* reported, "his voice was familiar to every one in America who owned a radio, and he had only to mention that he had gone 'quietly mad' over a book to have the country go mad too." His enthusiasm over *Goodbye, Mr. Chips*, for example, skyrocketed it to the top of the best-seller lists. As his biographer noted, "For a single performer on what was basically an intellectual program, [his Crossley ratings] were very high, say 6 as against 40 for someone like Jack Benny. A rating of 6 was very comfortable in

1933." At the height of his popularity, Woollcott once invited his listeners to help Theodore Roosevelt, Jr., compile a poetry anthology; Roosevelt received forty thousand submissions.[48]

Even cornier than Broun, and initially less political, Woollcott appealed in part because of his skillful blend of nostalgia, sentimentality, and hope. In the midst of the Depression, his biographer argued, he used books as mirrors to show "the American people moments of their greatness, moments of sadness, moments of beauty." That emotional predisposition earned Woollcott the contempt of observers like Louis Kronenberger and Bennett Cerf because it led him, in their view, to champion "second-rate" works outside their concept of the canon. As Kronenberger phrased it, "Woollcott is no friend of difficult and stodgy classics: he is skeptical of their worth, or at least of their readability, and prefers the readier laughter and tears of writers not in the pantheon." Two somewhat less vituperative images perhaps best characterize his approach to literature: John Chamberlain's remark that Woollcott was not so much a critic as an "intellectual crooner" and Malcolm Cowley and Canby's judgment that Woollcott had succeeded Christopher Morley as a "caresser of books."[49]

Although Kronenberger's comment rightly presupposed that Woollcott possessed a set of critical principles, both Chamberlain's observation and Cowley and Canby's remark highlight the extent to which Woollcott's style made those criteria irrelevant, in the sense that he kept his evaluative statements to a minimum. In that way, his role as a book reviewer reflected, in exaggerated form, many of the same assumptions that governed the "Swift Hour." A close examination of Woollcott's columns and broadcasts in light of Phelps's—whom Kronenberger dubbed "Mr. Woollcott's immediate predecessor in the land"—provides a more precise understanding of his approach. Superficially, it is true, the two figures make an odd pair. As Kronenberger noted, Woollcott focused almost exclusively on contemporary works, whereas Phelps kept up some effort to promote the classics. In addition, Woollcott was a living reproach to the part of Phelps that clung to genteel manners and moralism. Woollcott was also smarter and funnier than Phelps and much nastier in temperament; he was as famous for insults as Phelps was for homilies. Yet the contrast is not as stark as it first appears: Phelps once rocked staid Yale himself by parading around the campus dressed as Sarah Bernhardt, and his penchant for bad puns made him a kind of failed Algonquin wit, while Woollcott, however misguided his taste, retained an integrity about it that his detractors could not gainsay.[50]

More important, however, Woollcott magnified Phelps's tendency to portray the cultured person as well informed as opposed to well read. His *McCall's* columns, in which he referred to himself as "your correspondent," epitomized his reportorial stance by appearing under the headings "What's Going on in the World" or "What's Going on This Month." In that respect, the name "Town Crier" was the analogue of the *Book-of-the-Month Club News* and of Stuart Sherman's determination to chronicle "what is going on." "I know it's my job," Woollcott declared on the October 6, 1933, show, "to tell you the news as I note it in the passing crowd, to talk of people I've seen, plays I've attended, books I've just read, jokes I've just heard." That broad mandate conspicuously excluded the pedagogical orientation that the fiction of the "personal don" had at least loosely perpetuated. Instead, even more than Phelps, Woollcott couched his recommendations in a form stripped of judgment and comprehensible at a glance, or in a moment's casual listening.[51]

In practical terms, Woollcott's version of the reduction of criticism to headlines meant that he devoted only a small percentage of a typical column or broadcast to a discussion of books. For instance, in *McCall's* for December 1931, he alerted readers to Pearl Buck's latest work by telling them to "put in your order for the nobly imagined novel *The Good Earth*—it is, I suppose, the book of the year." Such a directive, with its omission of any details about the style and substance of the book, let alone the author's name, was even more cursory than Phelps's pronouncements. As was true for Phelps, radio heightened the effect of giving such short shrift to literary values by eliminating the possibility of lingering over the page. Rather, the "Town Crier" program entailed quick, unpredictable movement from Woollcott's monologue to musical selections, blurring the difference between cultural commentary (such as it was) and other forms of entertainment. The book portion of the October 6, 1933, show was typical: apart from three passing references to other works, it consisted solely of Woollcott's saying that he had recently "enjoyed" the new book from England called *Brazilian Adventure,* by Peter Fleming. Following this announcement, at the point at which one might have expected further appraisal of the book, Woollcott merely cued in the next orchestral number.[52]

Thus, Woollcott offered book reviews without the reviews—and almost without the books. To fill the vacuum, he furnished himself, in the form of a revealing anecdote or other display of personal style. His discussion of A. J. Cronin's *Hatter's Castle*, for example, primarily consisted of a narrative of his own boyhood acquaintance with a friend's tyrannical father. Woollcott concluded his remarks with the warning that he did mean to "mislead" readers into thinking that he regarded the novel as the "book of books." That disclaimer, after many paragraphs of reminiscence, transformed *Hatter's Castle* into simply an occasion for comments about Woollcott's experiences and memories. In other words, Woollcott not only exemplified personality, he also made it the determinant of his critical orientation. As John Mason Brown remarked, "Though admirably equipped to think, Woollcott preferred to feel. Ideas did not interest him as much as people. He rejoiced in personalities, and left principles alone."[53]

Woollcott's displacement of ideas pushed to its logical conclusion Phelps's intimation that the object of reading was to make oneself more interesting. For the person who was *already* interesting, Woollcott suggested in print and by his own behavior, books became superfluous—or, at most, peripheral. That formulation surpassed Phelps's in transmitting the view that culture was accessible; in fact, it represented the extreme end of a continuum that stretched from Canby to Erskine to Durant to Broun. Personality, which presumably existed for everyone in unlimited supply, became, by itself, the sign of the cultured individual. If, by devaluing the classics and paring reviews down to bulletins, Woollcott further loosened the moorings of genteel criticism, his almost total identification of personality and culture threatened to sever those worn and unraveling ties altogether.

Certain of Woollcott's techniques on the air accelerated his drift away from Arnoldian precepts. Although they made no explicit use of the "conversation in the living room" image, his "Town Crier" broadcasts approximated that ideal, treating listeners as friends. The October 6, 1933, program began with Woollcott's request that the audience "go with him" on a journey through time and continued with a series of engaging imperatives: "Come on," "Let's look around us," etc. The device permitted Woollcott to simulate not only a return to the past but also the sense of meeting each listener privately and on a footing equal to his own. Another of his strategies, which became virtually his trademark, involved talking about people without immediately naming them, saving their identities for a climactic revelation. By forcing his listeners to ransack their brains in an effort to guess his subject, he further transformed them into his collaborators. Woollcott used the tactic in his essays in *While Rome Burns* (1934) and *Long, Long Ago* (1943) as well, but it was especially effective—if also maddening—on radio because no opportunity existed to disengage from the partnership by skipping to the end of the text.[54]

Yet Woollcott's message that, to twist a phrase of Ruth Benedict's, culture was personality writ large was not a purely democratic one. Woollcott, after all, was not just any personality but rather the member of a coterie as exclusive, in its own way, as Phelps's Yale. His popularity stemmed not only from his suggestion that anyone might emulate his style but also, paradoxically, from his representation that, in so doing, they would differentiate themselves from everyone else. As James Gaines put it, part of Woollcott's appeal was his "ability to convey a sense of in-ness."[55] The same punch-line disclosures that fostered egalitarian participation were also a kind of admission to Woollcott's own "inner sanctum." His designation of his radio audience as "eavesdroppers," together with his habit of namedropping, accomplished that end as well. Along with his assurance of approachability, then, Woollcott preserved, albeit in modified form, the understanding that culture belonged only to a privileged minority.

True, Woollcott jettisoned the classics and substituted sophistication for education as the prerequisite for entering the ranks of the elect. More implicated in consumerism than Phelps, he did commercials for cars and cigarettes and train tickets; he even endorsed products he did not actually use. The tone he adopted answered with a resounding "yes" Lazarsfeld's query about whether reviewers should compete with advertisers by mimicking their delivery. (Given Marchand's and Herman Hettinger's argument that, because of its gentle intimacy, crooning became a particularly persuasive marketing technique, Chamberlain's remark about Woollcott's "intellectual crooning" appears even more apt.) Yet Woollcott, by selling himself as part of an enviable inner circle, joined Phelps in shoring up the idea that familiarity with literature was a desirable and hard-won characteristic, that knowledge about books and the arts remained a concomitant of social status. What is more, for all his emphasis on being au courant, Woollcott retained an elegance, both in his writing style and his manner, that echoed his genteel predecessors. Woollcott's "wit, his air of omniscience, his imperturbable poise, and most of all the beauty of his fastidious prose," the *Yale Review* noted, "relate him to certain English writers who adorned the last age of literary style." Yearning for "some golden American day . . . that comes not back again," he "manages to be up-to-date in a charmingly old fashioned way." That persistent trait is why, for all his rocking of the boat, Woollcott's moorings to the genteel tradition nevertheless remained intact.[56]

As one might predict, moreover, Woollcott's approach to his role as expert exhibited a parallel duality. On the one hand, he often referred to his *McCall's* columns in terms that stressed his authority: he called them "pastoral letters," "booksy gospels," "prescriptions." His famous opening line on the air, "This is Woollcott speaking," asserted that he was a force to be reckoned with. His "sterner critics," *Newsweek* noted, found that simple statement "as diffident as a fanfare of trumpets."[57] By entirely staking his expertise on personality, rather than on some specific training or recognized set of credentials, Woollcott was in some respects capable of compelling greater obeisance than a figure like Erskine or "Dr. Will Durant." He resembled a dictator whose orders demanded compliance just because he said so.

On the other hand, Woollcott made the revealing observation that he thought of himself as what Carl Van Doren had considered Phelps: "taster-at-large" to the American public. That notion not only reinforced Woollcott's (and Phelps's) smorgasbord attitude toward culture, it also unmistakably implied that he served at the behest of his audience—a circumstance that radio endowed with greater reality. The same subordinate pose appeared in Woollcott's *McCall's* column for October 1931, in which he called upon his readers to identify the best books in English published since 1911 and send the list to him. His repeated description of himself in metaphorical terms—as pastor, physician, correspondent, as well as "taster," but never as critic—suggests the need to scramble under the cover of some other profession, as if he were uneasy about openly asserting his right to pass literary judgments. Similarly, his frequent self-deprecating remarks signified a complete reversal of the assumptions underlying genteel criticism. "Wait a minute, wait a minute," he interrupted the narrator on the January 27, 1935, "Town Crier" show, "I'm not ready—and now, this is Woollcott collecting his wit." Such jibes were vehicles for humor and inside information and had as much to do with Woollcott's insecurities as anything, but they had even more potential to undermine his authoritative position than Fisher's wife-and-mother comments. This was the underside of stressing personality: Phelps, too, brought both pontification and humility to the air, but Woollcott's greater emphasis on himself introduced correspondingly deeper strains into his role, for while he might be lauded as a presence, he might also be dismissed, when convenient, as an affable but unimportant eccentric.[58]

In effect, that is what happened in the long run. In the fall of 1935 Woollcott got into a political dispute with his sponsor and their advertising agency; courageously, he refused to comply with Cream of Wheat's demand that he avoid attacking Hitler and Mussolini, and he gave up his contract. He returned to radio in 1936 on behalf of Roosevelt's presidential campaign. The following year he was back on CBS as the "Town Crier," broadcasting twice a week in the early evening under the sponsorship of the Granger Pipe Tobacco Company. By then his "range of enthusiasms" had widened, prompting discussions on the air not only of books but of topics as diverse as English usage, Seeing Eye Dogs (his favorite charity), Mary White, and his friend Harpo Marx. As fascism grew more menacing, Woollcott became a more vocal partisan of democracy. He also served, along with Clifton Fadiman and Carl Van Doren, as a judge of the Reader's Club, selecting books of "classic interest" for cheap reprints.

Even so, the 1939 debut of *The Man Who Came to Dinner*, a comedy transparently about Woollcott's outrageous behavior, made him, more than ever, preeminently a personality. In his last years the image of Woollcott the bon vivant was at odds with reality: he quarreled with friends, experienced failing health, and saw much of his inner circle disappear. Within a short time of his death in 1943, he was largely forgotten—remembered, if at all, only as the model for the main character in a zany play. Few recalled that, at the peak of his career on radio, Woollcott had attracted what his biographer estimated as "the largest audience of any critic in history."[59]

Innovations of the Late 1930s and Early 1940s

Although Woollcott, like Phelps, adopted the variety-hour format, his "Town Crier" show remained essentially a discussion program, providing commentary about books and authors as well as whatever else caught Woollcott's fancy. By the early 1940s the number of broadcasts that could be classified, with Woollcott's, as book talks had proliferated. The Book-of-the-Month Club sponsored interviews with authors about their favorite reading. In 1941 its publicity director, Edwin Seaver, himself a radio reviewer over *New York Times* station WQXR, also made scripts on "Books and Authors" available to stations around the country. One-time shows included "The Ten Best Non-Fiction Books of 1937," on which the writer Carl Carmer presented a list selected by Canby, Loveman, and others.[60] The NBC roster for 1940 included "The Best Books of the Month." Local efforts such as "The Reader's Almanac," a New York–area interview show that began in 1937 and lasted more than thirteen years, remained on the air alongside nationwide programming. Broadcasts during school hours continued to recommend stories for children.[61] Daytime offerings also included several shows that, while not primarily about books, often contained a literary element; beginning in 1937, for example, Ed (later with Pegeen) Fitzgerald added author interviews or short summaries of new volumes to daily humorous commentaries. Similarly, reviews and interviews increasingly supplemented household hints on morning and afternoon women's programs. When Lazarsfeld tabulated the responses of about two hundred stations to a survey inquiring whether they were broadcasting "some kind of literary comment," he counted 146 that did so at "regular or irregular intervals."[62]

Many such efforts, however—especially those entirely devoted to books—were as evanescent as the radio wave itself. Of all "radio ephemera," *Time* magazine reported in 1938, "none is more ephemeral than the studio book critic." As Phelps's experience demonstrated, network performers did not always fare much better; Carl Van Doren's review show, too, apparently lasted less than a season. One explanation for the turnover was obviously the set of commercial priorities Seldes noted, since most book talks were sustaining programs easily "bumped" for more lucrative enterprises. Compounding the matter was the fact that publishers, who logically might have stepped in as sponsors for such efforts, remained unconvinced throughout the 1940s that the medium promised enough favorable publicity to warrant buying radio advertising or distributing review copies to broadcasters. Acknowledging Woollcott's demonstrable impact on sales, they nonetheless insisted that "books were different" from other merchandise because it was impossible to build brand loyalty. Consumers, they also argued, only followed the guidance of reviewers they judged unprejudiced, a quality critics in the pay of a publishing house could hardly exhibit.[63]

Even so, publishers might have risked some investment (as did the consortium originally underwriting Woollcott) had they believed sponsored programs could couch their recommendations in a form that would "please the listeners." That became more problematic, however, as radio music and comedy grew more enticing. "Of all radio program forms," wrote Judith C. Waller, director of public service for NBC's Central Division, in 1946, "the radio talk is the hardest to write, to give, and to make interesting and acceptable to the listening public. The first inclination of almost everyone, in turning on the radio and finding someone talking, is to switch the dial immediately until a musical program is found. That is done almost as unconsciously as breathing."[64]

In that context, four initially unsponsored book talks originating in the late 1930s and early 1940s are especially noteworthy because, although not as popular as Woollcott's show, they were ambitious, nationwide undertakings that attracted considerable attention from contemporary observers and relatively sizable audiences. One, Edward Weeks's "The Human Side of Literature" (also called "Meet Mr. Weeks" or "Meet Edward Weeks"), drew deliberately on Woollcott's example, and implicitly on Phelps's, to foster a variant on the "conversation in the living room." Another, the panel show "The Author Meets the Critics," exemplified the search for a pleasing format by coming as close as possible to turning literary criticism into a prize contest. Two others, John Towner Frederick's "Of Men and Books" and the panel discussion "Invitation to Learning," incorporated elements of "conversation" but at least attempted to reiterate the importance of reading as well as hearing about books.

The editor of the *Atlantic Monthly*, Weeks had, as a young man, encountered both the genteel tradition and the literary rebellion against it. A volunteer ambulance driver in World War I under the command of Dorothy Canfield Fisher's husband, he studied English at Harvard after the war with John Livingston Lowes and Phelps's counterpart, Charles Townsend Copeland. Drawn to the literary circle that clustered around the poet Robert Hillyer, he made friends with Malcolm Cowley, John Dos Passos, and other burgeoning writers. In 1923, following a fellowship to Cambridge, England, he moved to Greenwich Village, where he worked with Richard Simon as a salesman for Boni and Liveright. Returning to Boston, he joined the staff of the *Atlantic* at a time when it still thrived on what H. L. Mencken disparaged as the prose of "refined" American authors who wrote "chastely" and "elegantly." On Simon's advice, Weeks began editing *Atlantic* books in 1928, including such best-sellers as Charles Nordhoff and James Norman Hall's *Mutiny on the Bounty*. He also continued his affiliation with the magazine by writing a book-review column. No fan of the "inbred, introverted short stories" produced by the avant-garde, he saw himself, when he took over the editorship of the monthly in 1938, as serving an audience with a taste for the "genuine." Like his genteel forebears, he defined his purpose in educational terms, operating on the assumption that "editing up" would contribute to the "public good." Yet he also strove to "personalize" a magazine that he thought had grown "dreary" and "too scholarly." His view of the *Atlantic*, he once explained, was that it should be "the means of reconciling the old and the new." In practice, that meant perpetuating the journal's commitment to serious essays and poetry while meeting the competition from "news and picture magazines" by increasing the number of contributors per issue, condensing articles, and serializing fiction.[65]

Throughout the 1930s Weeks was also in demand as a lecturer who brought a "charming" manner and "excellent delivery" to remarks about reading. Thus, he was a logical choice when, at the end of the decade, NBC decided to search for a figure who would do for it what Woollcott had done for CBS. The network had received "a steady if small stream of requests for book programs" but was determined, as

Lazarsfeld reported, to design a series "so that it would not, like earlier radio efforts, become a 'flop.'" (The initial plan was to mimic the successful "America's Town Meeting of the Air" by having Weeks entertain questions from the floor at the end of the broadcast.) Weeks had his own commercial agenda: he hoped appearing on the air would help him to "drum up fresh interest" in the *Atlantic* "without spending money." Specifically, the show promised to boost circulation by "personalizing" Weeks himself. As the *Atlantic* stockholder and advertising man Arthur Kudner responded when Weeks told him about plans for the program: "Great! That's just what we need, better even than the lectures. I want you to be recognized. People have got to know that you're the new *Atlantic*!"[66]

Before accepting NBC's offer, Weeks sought guidance from Woollcott, who went over the topics Weeks had identified and coached him on presentation. The conversational model was at the core of Woollcott's advice. "[I]s there a book that will help me write my scripts?" Weeks asked. "No," Woollcott replied. "And you don't write them: you make notes and then talk aloud to someone with good ears and repeat until it sounds like talk. The curse of radio is professors who read."[67]

Those goals and assumptions coalesced with Weeks's background to shape the thirty-minute program that went on the air over the NBC Red network on October 17, 1939. The setting of the venture was promising: the audience was live and in the same Radio City studio that had just been occupied by the popular quiz show "Information, Please!." In terms of content, "The Human Side of Literature" operated from the premise that the successful program would not discuss "books as such." Instead, no doubt reflecting Woollcott's approach, it offered the "conversation of a recognized editor" about authors' "little quirks of character," literary perspectives on current events, or "historical tidbits." Each broadcast also included an interview with a famous writer such as André Maurois, Sherwood Anderson, or Archibald MacLeish. As intended, the emphasis was on literary personalities, including Weeks's own (hence the imperative to "meet" him); in fact, the phrase "the human side of literature" is strikingly close to Durant's mission of "humanization" and its attendant message of accessibility. Dropping reviews entirely, the broadcast did not even pretend that culture required reading books themselves. At the same time, however, Weeks's Harvard connection, his role as the heir of Charles Eliot Norton and James Russell Lowell, and his emphasis on older as well as recent works gave "meeting Mr. Weeks" something of the same aura that Phelps's Yale association and loyalty to the classics had created.[68]

An article about the show in *Radio Guide* highlighted Weeks's capacity to combine intimacy and authority, the writer explicitly casting the listener as a participant in Weeks's "conversation": "You hold out your hand reservedly and say 'How do you do' in a stiff sort of way, because this is Edward Weeks, editor of one of our uppercrust magazines, . . . and you naturally expect him to be—well, intellectual and far above the rank and file. . . . Then he starts talking and his accents aren't nearly as Harvardish as you had expected, and the things he talks about are things you always wanted to know anyway about people who write books. . . . You find you aren't listening to a cold book-review at all. You're going on a real journey of adventure and exploration with a guide who knows his way around. . . . [So] forget your fears and this Tuesday night meet Mr. Weeks!"[69]

One extant recording of the show, the November 12, 1940, broadcast, illustrates the tactics Weeks employed to achieve that result. Many of his devices were similar to the ones Woollcott used to create an atmosphere of drama and acknowledge his listeners' prerogatives. Discussing Christopher Marlowe, for example, Weeks simulated a voyage, with the audience in tow, to a seventeenth-century tavern ("Watch out! There goes the table!"). He routinely incorporated remarks like "You know what happened" or "You remember the story" and asked "What do *you* think?" as listeners "overheard" a meeting of the Confederate cabinet. Yet he accompanied those egalitarian overtures with an accent that, if not overly "Harvardish," still conveyed prestige and refinement.[70]

Even so, for reasons that remain murky, Weeks's ability to embody that combination did not, in the long run, provide NBC with a success equal to the "Town Crier." Perhaps Weeks's less cheerful, more reserved temperament could not compete with Woollcott's theatricality; perhaps, given the "strong" fan mail he received (including endorsements from Van Loon, Dixon Wecter, and Felix Frankfurter), factors other than audience response entered the picture. In any event, the program went off the air in the spring of 1941.[71]

A year or so earlier, however, two Albany radio entrepreneurs, R. J. Lewis, Jr., and Martin Stone, had launched a book-review show less dependent on the appeal of an individual critic. Their unrehearsed panel show "Speaking of Books," broadcast over the powerful Schenectady, New York, station WGY, devoted fifteen minutes to reviewers' comments about a new book, followed by fifteen more minutes of exchange with the author. At the conclusion of the program, critics declared whether they recommended the book. The announcer then offered listeners prizes—free Book-of-the-Month Club subscriptions—for the best letters on "Why I am (or am not) going to read the book discussed on tonight's program." This gimmick, which, accompanied by bells to keep time, turned the experts' performance into a competition, generated enough novelty and tension to overcome the liabilities of the talk format. "Speaking of Books" quickly acquired numerous regional fans.[72]

By 1942 the producers had given up the idea of including an "average reader" and a "humorist" on the panel in favor of regular appearances by such figures as Irita Van Doren and Lewis Gannett. Van Doren, introduced on one episode as "easily" the "most popular woman about books," began by summarizing the book under discussion "just as if we hadn't read it." Her queries to authors such as Jan Valtin and Margaret Leech focused on the accuracy of their historical narratives but were typically favorable or at least conciliatory. One index of the show's initial tone was that it was suitable for broadcast to a convention of librarians; early transcripts also appeared in a library journal.[73]

Retitled "The Author Meets the Critics," the program began broadcasting live over a local Manhattan station in 1943; in 1945 the Book-of-the-Month Club became, for a time, its official sponsor; after bouncing around a bit, the show finally landed on NBC in 1947. In the course of those changes, "The Author Meets the Critics" acquired not only new personnel but also a somewhat more trenchant (and even vicious) atmosphere. Gannett and Van Doren gave way to a permanent moderator, John K. M. McCaffery. Billed as a "literary tug of war," the show by 1946 featured two critics, one pro and one con, as well as the author. The audience "sat as judge" on their performances—significantly, without having read the book. Guests included Canby, whose role seems to have been defending the "book of the month," as well as reviewers like Bennett Cerf, Harry Hansen, and Dorothy Thompson. Dialogue often contained as much acerbity as Woollcott's had, delivered at a pace that, like Phelps's, precluded extended analysis. For example,

Fannie Hurst instructed her critics to "crawl back in the wall" where they came from; McCaffery asked Canby how the club could "possibly have picked such an inconsequential book as this." Zeroing in on the way in which the transformation of reviewing into a sparring match caught the tenor of the culture of personality, McCaffery also queried: "If the humor of insult goes out of fashion, Mr. Cerf, what will happen to this program?" The contest element had the additional advantage of fitting nicely with the Book-of-the-Month Club's standard marketing strategy; by asking listeners, "Do you or do you not intend to read" the book discussed, the announcer effectively prepared them to turn to the club for assistance when they defaulted on their plans.[74]

In 1946 the program received between six hundred and a thousand fan letters per week. The same year the Literary Guild, seeking to duplicate its rival's success, underwrote "Books on Trial," a show identical to "The Author Meets the Critics" except for its inclusion of dramatized scenes from the book under consideration. Although the guild pulled out of the venture when Stone sued his alleged imitators for pirating his format, Sterling North continued to host "Books on Trial" in the New York area. "The Author Meets the Critics" had its ups and downs on network radio but moved to NBC television in 1947, where it was sponsored by General Foods. Three years later it aired simultaneously on both media—the only book show of the period to do so.[75]

"The Human Side of Literature" and "The Author Meets the Critics" continued, in the words of one radio columnist, to replace "the book critics of old" with "literary wits."[76] Two roughly contemporaneous innovations, however—again, one featuring an individual and one a panel—represented something of an opposing trend. The first counterweight was Frederick's "Of Men and Books." As an undergraduate at the University of Iowa before World War I, Frederick had founded a regional literary magazine, *The Midland*. Following a series of teaching positions elsewhere, he returned to the Iowa campus in the early 1920s as a member of the English department. Under his editorship, *The Midland* became a distinguished national outlet for new writing. In the late 1930s, after attempts to expand the magazine failed, Frederick combined an academic appointment at Northwestern University with an effort to build, through broadcasting, an off-campus audience for reading. In the fall of 1937 he became a radio reviewer on "The Northwestern University Bookshelf," which another faculty member had started earlier that year. The fifteen-minute program, initially under the auspices of the University Broadcasting Council (a coalition of Northwestern, the University of Chicago, and DePaul University with some backing from the Rockefeller and Carnegie Foundations) was heard on midwestern and southwestern CBS affiliates until May 1938, when it received a national hook-up and a new title: "Of Men and Books." First slated on late Tuesday afternoons, in 1941 it was carried on Saturdays around noon over more than fifty stations.[77]

The time slots for Frederick's offering—during the day rather than in "prime time"—are an index of the networks' capacity to absorb a limited number of "purely cultural broadcasts" as long as they did not interfere with more lucrative programming.[78] In fact, more than any other book critic on commercial stations in the 1930s and 1940s, Frederick retained an allegiance to the vision of educational radio. Although the name of the show partially suggested the same emphasis on literary personalities Weeks provided, Frederick's intentions, as he phrased them, were rather different. The "permanent aim of this program," he stated on an October 1939 broadcast, was to present "informal, honest radio discussions" that "may contribute to the increased enjoyment and understanding of good books," on the assumption that "reading is an important part of living." Frederick told his listeners that he thought of the microphone as "just another way of talking with friendly people about subjects of common interest." The show's announcer similarly invoked the "conversation" image. Frederick also declared that "the fundamental idea of education is changing"—that specialization was giving way to the broad, lifelong learning that steady reading could furnish. Yet he provided those assurances of accessibility without abandoning an essentially professorial posture. On the air, he identified himself as a "teacher and professor" as well as a writer and spoke of the "opportunity and obligation" those roles entailed. Underscoring the classroom atmosphere of the program, in 1940 Frederick gave the broadcasts as a two-credit course to his Northwestern students and supplied home listeners with manuals of study so that they could "participate" as well.[79]

In keeping with his sense of purpose, Frederick made a point of rejecting much of the cult of the best-seller. While the program was exclusively devoted to reviews of newly published work and concluded with the *Herald Tribune*'s survey of the week's most popular titles, it made what *Radio Guide* called "a very unusual claim to distinction": at least half the books Frederick reviewed never approached best-seller status. "'That doesn't mean they aren't worthwhile reading,'" Frederick explained. "'On the contrary, they frequently are of greater literary merit than works that sell by the hundreds and thousands. But they weren't written by popular authors, or as well publicized. . . . That's why I review them. I want my listeners to become acquainted with authors of really important books.'" Frederick (like Durant and others) also tied reading to the concern with the survival of American civilization—which, given the international tensions of the late 1930s, he saw as under threat not from consumerism but from imminent world war. His specific goal for the fall of 1939 was to discuss books that would help his audience "to renew and define our appreciation of American life." Guests (for example, Librarian of Congress Archibald MacLeish and Mark Van Doren) occasionally appeared on the program to reinforce the same objectives.[80]

Frederick did his share of list making: *Publishers' Weekly* reported in 1939 that he expected to fill ten thousand requests for copies of his recommendations for Christmas gifts. Booksellers welcomed the contribution of the program to commercial ends; in a CBS survey that same year, ninety out of a hundred bookstores reported that Frederick helped to generate sales. Yet Frederick's distribution, as well, of his criteria for assessing books suggests the degree to which he attempted to adhere to the position that news about books was no substitute for reading them. In fact, to judge from the December 26, 1939, broadcast, the heart of his appeal seems to have been his conferral upon his audience of a special identity they and he shared as "readers of American books, as persons thinking and talking about literature, about journalism, and about the printed word." By certifying his listeners as serious readers, in other words, he may have bestowed upon them the sense that they were more cultured even than Woollcott's "insiders."[81]

Frederick's stance earned him about a thousand letters a month, a number which, though small in comparison to Woollcott's drawing power, CBS called "an unusual mail response" to a show on which "nothing is given away free." In some cities, reading groups gathered to hear Frederick's remarks. "Of Men and Books" remained on the air with Frederick as host until 1944, when the critic John Mason Brown took it over. The next year, one observer complained that the show's new host, Russell Maloney, "strains too hard for humor." The network assumed tighter control of the show in 1947, empowering producer Leon Levine to select reviewers from the ranks of CBS's staff; by 1949 it was off the air.[82]

While Frederick's effort on behalf of recent writing kept the extended classroom alive, the fourth important new program of the late 1930s and early 1940s—"Invitation to Learning"—largely returned "conversation" to the service of genteel values. The brainchild of Stringfellow Barr, who had exported Erskine's curriculum to St. John's College, the program brought "great books" to radio. In the spring of 1940 Barr suggested to Lyman Bryson, moderator of the current-events forum "The People's Platform," chair of CBS's Adult Education Board, and eventual director of educational activities for the network, the possibility of reproducing the St. John's experience on the air. While Bryson handled the administrative aspects of the show, Barr thought of its name and decided on its format. Eliminating Erskine's class of novices, he constructed a panel of critics instead. Nonetheless, the initial design for the half-hour program, in which Scott Buchanan also had a hand, remained somewhat faithful to Erskine's intentions by envisioning as panelists "seasoned amateurs" whose authority derived from their speculative powers rather than their scholarly accomplishments. The first broadcast on May 26 presented Barr, Huntington Cairns, Andrew Chiappe, and Helen Hull Miller discussing the United States Constitution. Throughout the summer, in keeping with Barr and Buchanan's idea that the same individuals ought to "pass the books through their minds" each week, Cairns, a Treasury Department attorney and economist who doubled as a newspaper book reviewer, continued the experiment with Barr and Chiappe, a Columbia English instructor.[83]

In late September Barr was summarily fired by Levine, at that time CBS's director of discussion broadcasts. As Bryson recalled the dispute, "There was disagreement as to what was interesting to the public, disagreement as to how much discussion of books of the very highest importance, which have always been the material of the show, could be made interesting to the public—at any rate, it was the old struggle between the scholar and the showman and the showman naturally had to win."[84] The network's dissatisfaction with Barr's conception of the program was not immediately evident, however, even to the participants who replaced him and Chiappe: Mark Van Doren and the poet Allen Tate. "Quite without sparkle," *Time* reported, Cairns, Van Doren, and Tate examined the classics at a "pedestrian classroom pace," trying "earnestly" to "enliven their performance with modern applications" of their subjects. By the end of October, to the surprise of everyone involved, "Invitation to Learning" had earned an estimated following of a million listeners. CBS responded by putting the show on a regular basis, scheduling it on Sunday afternoons following broadcasts of the New York Philharmonic orchestra.[85]

In terms of content, the first year of "Invitation to Learning" offered explorations of "great books" in ten categories, ranging from politics, ethics, and religion to fiction and autobiography. Within that framework, Greek and Roman authors appeared most frequently, supplemented by such figures as Montaigne, Rousseau, Shakespeare, and Milton. The only gesture toward modernism was a program devoted to Proust; the only American treated was Henry Adams. To judge from published transcripts of the show, which was unscripted and, except for a brief warm-up, unrehearsed, the panelists concentrated on identifying the thesis of the text under discussion and on clarifying its key terms. The session on Aristotle's *Politics*, for example, defined Aristotle's six forms of government, while the one on Tolstoy's *War and Peace* included an effort to specify the theme of the novel. Contemporary parallels usually entailed allusions to foreign affairs, a trend that accelerated in the show's second season when American entry into World War II gave the issue of civilization's survival more immediacy. "Great books," both the network and Van Doren explained, were the "things of lasting value" for which the nation was fighting.[86]

Those emphases (like Adler's agenda for "great books" reading groups) precluded much attention to aesthetic issues, literary history, or, apart from the brief quotation that concluded each program, the language of the text itself. Ironically, moreover, given the program's ostensible political importance, the focus on discerning basic arguments often backfired into triviality or inconclusiveness. The discussion of Montaigne's *Essays*, for instance, ended with this pointless dialogue: "Cairns: Do you go as far as Montaigne does in insisting that the education of the young is the most difficult and important branch of human knowledge? Van Doren: Education is not a branch of knowledge. Cairns: Montaigne seemed to think it was. . . . That is the point as I understand it. Van Doren: I agree with him that education is very important."[87]

Even so, Van Doren and Tate for the most part shunned oversimplification. (Cairns was more prone to it.) As a *New York Times* reviewer admiringly stated: "There is no appeal here to the seekers after 'popularizations' and 'digests' and other short cuts to an illusion of culture. This is the real thing." Moreover, the program entirely avoided an overt preoccupation with the cultivation of personality, rejecting Phelps's news bulletins or Woollcott's name-dropping in favor of an uncompromising commitment to the elucidation of ideas. Tate was especially impressive. On several broadcasts, he displayed his capacity for subtle, imaginative explication; one of his characteristic contributions was to provide symbolic readings of passages Cairns took literally. In the words of his biographer, he thereby "gave to the nation an example of a mind that never descended to jargon and never offered some substitute for intellectual responsibility."[88]

In terms of tone, the early broadcasts of "Invitation to Learning" represented the most explicit attempt in the interwar period to endow the discussion of books on the air with the genteel connotations the term "conversation" encompassed. To be sure, gentility did not preclude controversy; in fact, Cairns, as moderator, encouraged it by routinely asking his fellow panelists if they agreed with one another. Often he got more than he bargained for: as the exchange cited above reveals, Van Doren and Tate showed little patience with Cairns's remarks, barely tolerating his dissent from their own more sophisticated interpretations. Sometimes their responses (however well deserved) were caustic and abrupt. When Cairns, for example, declared, "After Aristotle, as you know, ethics and politics separated," Tate patronizingly replied, "I didn't know they did, Mr. Cairns." Yet, despite the undercurrent of acrimony, the surface of the early "Invitation to Learning" show stayed temperate and restrained, as if the participants were following Erskine's etiquette about conversational form. Addressing each other as "Mr.," Cairns, Tate, and Van Doren spoke, as one writer noted, "pleasantly, easily, politely." In so doing, they consciously replicated the atmosphere not, in this case, of a living room but rather of "Mr. Cairns's library in Washington." Despite *Time*'s classroom analogy, their purpose, as they conceived it, was to furnish contemplative dialogues conveying a "sense of proportion" about a book's themes instead of fact-filled lectures. In that way, they thought of themselves as counteracting, in Tate's phrase, the "specialization of knowledge and interest in 'practicality' that make for the decline of conversation."[89]

Yet, interestingly, "Invitation to Learning" deviated from other radio book "conversations" by deliberately excluding its listeners from even the illusion of participation. In place of Woollcott's "Let's go" or Phelps's simulated "reunions," the discussants remained self-contained and remote. As the creators of the Literary Guild program and other advertisers had known by the late 1920s, however, the resulting effect could be as attractive in its own way as the illusion of intimacy. "It is as an overheard conversation," Van Doren wrote, "that 'Invitation to Learning' has gained its audience. . . . The three men address only one another, endeavoring to interest and convince themselves first of all. He who wishes may overhear; and it is clear that his wish alone will decide the matter. As he is not being addressed, so he is not being urged or belabored; he is free from the sense of being used."[90] In other words, to the extent that its participants carried out Erskine's directive not "in any way to behave like professors," the program affirmed its audience's independence and power. "Invitation to Learning"'s presentation of a group of critics talking only among themselves was thus as much a mediation between the desire for expert guidance and the preservation of listeners' prerogatives as Phelps's or Woollcott's strategies of self-effacement.

Whether or not the eavesdroppers exercised those prerogatives by forming their own judgments was another matter. The greatest strength of the 1940–41 programs—their fidelity to textual analysis— meant that listeners unfamiliar with the book under discussion heard "Invitation to Learning" without understanding it. This was no doubt unavoidable, and its consequences were not necessarily negative. As Van Doren recounted: "[A] restaurant keeper in a little Illinois town told some one of my acquaintance that this was his favorite program in spite of the fact that it was over his head. What he liked was the compliment paid to him in the refusal to explain and water down. The matter sounded important, as in fact he knew it was." At best, the appearance of significance gave the broadcast's followers a greater desire to stretch their own minds, spurring them to pursue the bibliographies the volumes of published transcripts contained. The fact that libraries and booksellers reported increased requests for the works treated on the air demonstrates that many listeners took the program's expectation of further study seriously. Yet, significantly, others pleaded for the critics to spend more time summarizing plots and arguments, as if they wished the program to serve not as an "invitation" to culture but as culture itself. (In a sense, Van Doren complied with this demand by issuing one-paragraph summaries of each featured text in the "Listener's Guide" obtainable from CBS.) For members of the audience unfamiliar with the broadcast's subject matter, the encounter with an "important sound" or the "plain fascination," as one observer put it, in the "clever play of good minds" may have constituted the entire impact of the show.[91]

In fact, the evolution of "Invitation to Learning" after its initial season entailed a gradual acceptance, and even defense, of the program's potential to replace, rather than to stimulate, reading "great books." At the same time, and perhaps for that reason, the series exhibited a remarkable tenacity, surviving, unsponsored, through the 1950s as perhaps the most unabashedly intellectual undertaking on commercial radio. The second half of the first year was more tumultuous than the transcripts reveal. By January of 1941 Van Doren and Tate had concluded that Cairns's amateurism was less "seasoned" than incompetent. "I offered Joe [Joseph Wood Krutch] the innocent theory," Van Doren wrote Tate, "that HC deliberately talks like a dope in order to provide differences." Tate, convinced that the dopiness was real, disabused Van Doren of that idea, and the two decided to present a united front to CBS. In the meantime, rumor had it that Barr, presumably still smarting from his dismissal, was lobbying the network to replace Tate as well as Cairns. For his part, Van Doren, unhappy about the "idiotic spectacle" of some of the program's guest panelists, urged Cairns to find suitable participants before the show "kills itself." Added to those pressures was the fact that Levine and other executives engaged in what Tate called "backstairs intrigue" and constant "interference" in the broadcast. In August CBS told Tate that he would make only occasional appearances on the show. Yet the immediate result of this situation was actually in the direction of more scholarly rigor: at the beginning of the second season, CBS made Van Doren chair of "Invitation to Learning" and agreed to give him some power over the choice of books and participants.[92]

The arrangement, however, could not survive the network executives' perception that the show required a different structure. In the fall of 1942 Levine, probably collaborating with Bryson, proposed to divide the program's subject matter into "fields," each presided over by a variety of authorities. As Van Doren complained to Buchanan, this scheme "quite killed the idea" of generalist speculation on which the "great books" approach rested. In its place, he told Tate, the broadcast glorified "'experts' and stunt men"—that is, specialization and celebrity. Van Doren's opposition to CBS's plan was his downfall: late in October the network fired him. ("This will be good for Mark," Tate commented afterwards, "because the program was bad for him. It developed in him the small fraction of Van Dorenism which he shares with Carl.") Subsequently, "Invitation to Learning" modified its content as well as its personnel. The 1944 season, for example, while continuing to emphasize the classics, included a discussion of Stephen Vincent Benét. Around the same time, the show adopted a topical orientation that supposedly heightened its relevance to contemporary concerns like "Man and His Government."[93]

Following World War II, Bryson, who had been active behind the scenes since the program's inception, emerged to preside over the group of rotating specialists. Heralded for his "personal warmth" and "enthusiasm," Bryson saw himself not as a reflective intellectual but as coordinator of his guests' performances; although "conversation" remained the show's motif, Bryson likened his role to that of "orchestra leader." Employing a "system of signs and gestures" to prevent the exchange from becoming "too bookish or professional," he often rephrased discussants' remarks he thought too esoteric. Yet Bryson's tendency, as one commentator noted, "to steer the talk away from the ivory halls and into the street" coexisted with his express conviction that hearing about "great books" might constitute adequate exposure to them. "In the series of books we are now doing," Bryson averred in 1947, "there are at least three that we are compelled to describe as unreadable for the average intelligent man. . . . [Yet] we can truthfully say that even those who do not want to go to the trouble of reading them . . . might at least want to know what interpreters can say about them." The "ordinary fellow," he similarly noted, might not read certain difficult books but "would like to hear about [them] if explained in the right way." If Tate and Van Doren inadvertently created the opportunity to equate culture with an "important sound," Bryson's premium on explanations delivered with "bargain-basement simplicity" involved its own costs. In addition, Bryson's efforts to shift the program toward greater accessibility entailed an increased reliance on recent writing and a flashier use of "experts": among "Invitation to Learning"'s offerings in 1947, for example, were a discussion of Dreiser's insights into "The Pursuit of Happiness" and Herbert Hoover's appearance to "extol the virtues of fishing."[94]

What is more, Bryson's permutation of "Invitation to Learning" (as well as Cairns's and Van Doren's) courted the same danger of commodification that marked print versions of the "great books" approach. Thus, Max Schuster, with characteristic quantitative imagery, called the program "C.Q.," or "Civilization Quotient." No doubt it was that sort of response, together with Bryson's posture, that drove one unidentified scholar to label the broadcast "Imitation of Learning." Yet, real or artificial, the program, even in its later version, at least succeeded in widening the audience for serious ideas rather than flamboyant personalities: its ratings, Bryson noted in 1947, were consistently as high as a number of popular commercial programs. However qualified, that was no small accomplishment.[95]

The Emergence of the Quiz

From the outbreak of World War II through the end of the 1940s, new local and network book discussions continued to emerge along the axis the prewar programs had defined. Armed Forces Radio broadcasts included book reviews and "Invitation to Learning." The Council on Books in Wartime organized domestic efforts to talk about war-related volumes on the air. In the New York area, discussion programs included "Author's Round Table," while interview shows remained popular. On another local New York program of the same period, "Conversation at 8," Thomas Sugrue queried writers about their latest work. Nonbook talk shows with literary aspects also flourished.[96] Mary Margaret McBride, on the air until 1954, had numerous counterparts—Bessie Beatty, Martha Deane, Nancy Craig—throughout the 1940s, both on other New York stations and in cities around the country.[97]

On an intersecting axis lay one other talk show of note: Hendrik Van Loon's reflections on history and current events. In 1932 Van Loon had volunteered to do a weekly half-hour history talk on WEVD, a New

York station founded by socialists (including Broun) and named for Eugene Debs. He launched the "WEVD University of the Air" in 1933, organizing a "faculty" that included John Dewey and overseeing a curriculum that consisted of five half-hour programs per week. His success ultimately led NBC to sign Van Loon up for six months of twice-weekly appearances in 1935. After one hiatus to complete *The Arts* and another the network imposed to quell controversy, he became, from 1938 until his death in 1944, a familiar presence on the air. If the original WEVD undertaking had included literary study, however, Van Loon's own programs had virtually nothing to do with books. Instead, they consisted of historical allusions and philosophical musings mustered in the service of Van Loon's political opinions, which grew more pointedly anti-Fascist as the Nazis overran his Dutch homeland. (He took a similar position on behalf of democracy as guest on Carmer's "Ten Best" awards program.) Even so, two of *Radio Guide*'s remarks about Van Loon's broadcasts implicitly connected them to his role as purveyor of "outlines": an announcement urging the audience to "Hear Philosophy as News" and the identification of Van Loon as "perhaps the most cultured man of our day." Surveying Van Loon's fan mail, one NBC official reported that "listeners are surprised that a man of Van Loon's intelligence should be on the radio" and traced his popularity in part to curiosity about the voice of the man whose works so many had read.[98]

As talk programs developed throughout the 1930s and 1940s, however, several additional formats arose that belonged to a different plane entirely. While still related to literature, most of these made little or no attempt at criticism or discussion. In 1938, for example, the NBC Blue network aired "Adventure in Reading," written by Helen Walpole and Margaret Lee. Although it entailed some interviews, such as the one with Canby, the series primarily consisted of plays about episodes in the lives of American writers like Louisa May Alcott. Perpetuating the "dramalogs" of the early school broadcasts, "Adventure in Reading," too, was designed for school listeners. At the same time, CBS carried "Treasures Next Door," a dramatization for schoolchildren prepared by the federal Office of Education.[99] Those programs coexisted with other dramatizations that, on the loosest definition of the term, might be considered book shows as well: performances of Shakespeare, Orson Welles starring in *Dracula*, and the renowned Columbia Workshop and Studio One productions of serious writing, for example.

One of the most ambitious series of book dramatizations did provide some critical commentary. Beginning in 1944, the "NBC University of the Air" sought to go beyond giving listeners merely "a *taste* of the quality" of the "classics" by serializing enactments of "the world's great novels," some introduced by Weeks and Carl and Mark Van Doren. The show subsequently evolved into "NBC University Theatre," complete with an advisory council to identify the canon of works appropriate for broadcast. (Characteristically, Lionel Trilling briefly served on the council but resigned because of writing and teaching commitments, while Clifton Fadiman remained to supply guidance and frequent appearances as commentator.) In 1948 "NBC University Theatre" drew more than six million listeners, many of whom earned college credit in connection with the program. Eventually, it was presented on Sunday afternoons, a time slot that invited the audience to make tuning in an extension of church attendance.[100]

Still other programs resembled Burrill's early effort by featuring recitations rather than commentary. Some shows, such as the Mutual network's "A Book a Week," condensed and serialized novels. Poetry had its own folksy, self-styled "ambassador," Ted Malone. Malone, whose real name was Frank Alden Russell, started broadcasting "Between the Bookends" on the NBC Blue network in 1938. Tapping the same vein of sentimentality Woollcott had mined, Malone interspersed reading light verse with organ music and literary talk. A master of the simulated intimate encounter, he opened one show as follows: "May I come in? I see you are alone. Now I'll just take this rocker here by the radio and chat awhile. . . . What lovely new curtains." The technique earned him thousands of fan letters, which influenced the network to reverse its decision to cancel the program in the spring of 1939. "Can't you help us get Ted [Malone] back," a woman wrote to *Radio Guide* during the brief period when he was off the air, "and get more of the type of thing which gives us so much emotional lift as well as education and entertainment?" According to one account, such listeners were as interested in Malone himself as in literature. Occasional guests on the program included Carl Van Doren, who, along with Mark Sullivan and Norman Thomas, stepped "into your living room" (as Malone put it) to discuss the subject of his recent biography, Benjamin Franklin. By the early 1940s the program had acquired an almost frivolous tone, with

Malone a more blatantly absentminded host "coming over" to his listeners' homes to play "I'm Forever Blowing Bubbles."[101]

Another Malone enterprise, "Pilgrimage of Poetry," began in 1939 on NBC. In an effort to bolster the educational content of the program, Malone enlisted college English teachers to help select the authors to be covered. He also secured promotional assistance from the Library of Congress Poetry Division, which named Malone "The Voice of Poetry." The aim of the program, one memorandum about it to network executives declared, was to "make the mass of the people poetry conscious." In this, it may have succeeded. Yet consciousness was different from understanding. "Making no attempt to be critical or to enter into erudite literary discussion," as *Radio Guide* wrote of the show, Malone emphasized not the work of famous poets but rather the locus of their personalities—their homes. After depicting Poe's rocking chair, complete with sound effects, for example, he read selected lines from "The Raven." Promising his listeners an "adventure" and an encounter with "genius," he even offered to authenticate their brush with culture by registering their names as visitors to the sites he featured.[102]

Among programs that treated books but departed from reviewing or analyzing them, however, the most captivating and innovative format to develop as radio came of age was the quiz show. Spelling bees, parlor games, and volumes of queries about literature had all furnished nineteenth-century Americans the opportunity to amuse themselves by guessing the answers to questions.[103] In the 1920s, however, the demand for quiz books reached craze proportions. For example, Justin Spafford and Lucien Esty's *Ask Me Another* (1927), which contained around fifty tests of both general knowledge and particular subjects, sold more than one hundred thousand copies in its first month.[104] *Ask Me Another* was especially popular because it enabled purchasers to compare their own scores with those of celebrities who had taken the tests prior to publication—Phelps and Dewey among them. Numerous other less unusual collections of quizzes, though, appeared about the same time, with titles like *I Ought to Know That, Guess Again*, and *Answer This One*.[105]

In the 1930s quizzes arrived on radio. Among the initial quiz programs was a Washington newspaperman's 1935 creation of a local question bee entitled "Professor Quiz's Night School of the Air." Eventually picked up by CBS, it was the first example of the format to receive a national hook-up. Edward (Jim) MacWilliams, a veteran vaudeville actor, originally starred in the show, awarding ten dollars to members of the studio audience who correctly answered questions submitted by listeners. Variations on that formula, which had affinities with the amateur hour, quickly proliferated. When MacWilliams went to NBC, he transformed the program into "Uncle Jim's Question Bee"; later he appeared as well on the Colgate "Ask-It-Basket."[106] CBS kept its own version of "Professor Quiz" alive, featuring what the *Literary Digest* called a "two-hundred pound question asker" whose anonymity ("Quiz" was his surname) was part of the show's mystique.[107] By the late 1930s "Dr. I. Q.," introduced as "that genial master of wit and information," was turning his "assistants" loose in the audience to find contestants ("I have a lady in the balcony, Doctor"). For the right responses to queries about current events and the like, the "doctor" passed out silver dollars. Some quizzes, such as "True or False" and "Spelling Bee," both NBC offerings, relied on teams, occasionally pitting famous as well as ordinary citizens against each other. (A panel show such as "The Author Meets the Critics" overlapped with that version of the quiz format.) In 1940 Louis Cowan, later the inventor of big-money television quizzes, created "Quiz Kids," featuring a panel of young "geniuses." The program, which until 1954 captured many a child's dream and a parent's ambitions, received eight million questions from listeners during its first two years.[108]

Many quiz shows, of course, had little or nothing to do with books, literature, or liberal studies. The lucrative "Pot O' Gold" was purely a giveaway program, demanding only that winners answer their telephones. "Kay Kyser's Kollege of Musical Knowledge," on which Cowan also collaborated, typified the musical quiz. Some quizzes concentrated on sports or geography; others tested the audience's memory. Still others, like "Truth or Consequences" or "Take It or Leave It," were as much comedy or variety shows as quiz games. The same was true of spoofs like "It Pays to Be Ignorant."[109] Yet virtually all quizzes, to one degree or another, drew on a familiar set of tensions about culture and expertise. More explicitly, perhaps, than any other artifact of the early and mid-twentieth century, radio quiz programs (and their counterparts in print) revealed frank acceptance of the premise that, in modern America, culture entailed the acquisition and display of information.

"Necessarily," one article about the phenomenon reported, "the facts are unorganized, but followers of the mass appeal quiz shows prefer interesting factual tidbits and many of them admit that they store them up for conversational purposes." The reward of cash or other prizes affirmed the connection between the mastery of data and the achievement of economic success. Quizzes permitted participants a way to measure and improve their ability to make it on those terms—to become, in effect, experts themselves. At the same time, however, they enabled contestants, directly or indirectly, to challenge the authorities who symbolized and enforced the demand for specialized knowledge.[110]

A 1940 "gratification study" in Lazarsfeld's *Radio and the Printed Page* makes it possible, for once, to rely on more than inference to discern those tensions. Surveying listeners to "Professor Quiz," the study reported that, on the one hand, many respondents stressed the program's educational function. One woman, a typist, declared that, without the show, "she would 'not know what books to pick' even if she wanted to read." The uses respondents made of the show reflects the extent to which, again, the redefinition of culture as information served the development of personality. Part of the appeal of the program, Lazarsfeld noted, was its promise to "increase one's popularity and status in the eyes of one's neighbors or customers" and make one a "better social entertainer." It also relieved listeners, as Lazarsfeld put it, of the responsibility of "having any standards of judgment of [their] own" and assuaged their "guilt" about self-improvement "without any effort on their part." Nonetheless, those gains rested on the audience's assent to the same deferential relationship genteel critics had preserved.

On the other hand, Lazarsfeld's interviews also revealed that "Professor Quiz" supplied a different, and contradictory, "gratification." The respondents, all but one of whom had high school diplomas at most, emphasized that the show allowed them to compete with, and defeat, those with more formal education. "You don't have to be a college graduate," remarked one subject in the study, "but being well-read and interested in world affairs and reading newspapers makes you able to answer the questions." Listeners derived satisfaction not from choosing the contestant most likely to win but from identifying with the person "like myself" and egging that player on to victory over the "college man." As Lazarsfeld concluded, "There is an almost hysterical stress on 'the average man' and what the average man knows and can do, and how he can beat 'the others.' "[111] This finding lends itself to two interpretations. First, particularly given Lazarsfeld's choice of the word "hysterical," it may be seen as a form of protesting too much—as an admission of the expert's deservedly greater respect and standing. Second, however, it must be taken at face value. The resentment Lazarsfeld's respondents voiced toward college graduates suggests that, even if anxious for guidance in the quest for success, the "Professor Quiz" audience also questioned altogether the need for the culture experts represented. To listeners already confident of their own power in the marketplace, "stumping" experts might become a means not of emulating them but of repudiating their authority as irrelevant.

If the tensions the "Professor Quiz" survey uncovered were only minimally applicable to a competition on which the participants came from the audience and the questions steered away from literature, they were magnified on the contest that, more than any other popular, nationally broadcast quiz, might be considered a book broadcast: "Information, Please!."[112] The show was the idea of Dan Golenpaul, whose previous radio creations had included Broun's program of interviews with authors. Its most distinctive feature was its use of professional experts—recognized writers, critics, and other celebrities—rather than amateur ones. Phelps, Woollcott, and Van Loon were all occasional panel members. Program regulars included F.P.A. and sports editor John Kieran, with frequent appearances by Oscar Levant and science teacher Bernard Jaffee.[113]

In the role of master of ceremonies, Clifton Fadiman virtually personified middlebrow culture. Fadiman, whose previous radio experience had included book reviewing, had left Simon and Schuster in 1933 to become book critic for the *New Yorker*. Until he resigned that job in 1943, his sober, judicious appraisals of new writing reflected the breadth of knowledge and verbal facility he had displayed ever since his days as Erskine's and Mark Van Doren's student. Yet he appealed to Golenpaul because he was as "witty" as he was "knowledgeable," projecting a worldly "professorial manner" without the deadening qualities Golenpaul ascribed to actual professors. It was this pleasantly but harmlessly cultivated Fadiman, a Fadiman who was both intellectual and man-next-door, who oversaw the debut of "Information, Please!" on May 17, 1938.[114]

The first broadcast opened with a pair of attention-getting exchanges between an awed questioner and a nonchalant authority. "Amazing!" exclaimed the questioner when the expert correctly answered his query. "Elementary," came the expert's reply. "Yes, folks," the narrator (Milton Cross) continued, "during the next half hour the public asks amazing questions, and a group of experts assembled here are supposed to make them elementary." That comment revered the panel members for the valuable mediation they could provide, preserving their elevated status as guides. Fadiman's deliberate practice of addressing participants by their surnames rested on his supposition that the audience shared and required such reverence: "We called each other Mister . . . ," he recalled. "People . . . liked it. They *wanted* to feel a certain distance between themselves and the panel. The experts really *were* experts, demonstrably superior men. The audience liked to have the experts' dignity marked by the emblematic use, often humorous of course, of the formal mode of address."[115]

Like the "Professor Quiz" study, however, the narrator's introductory remarks also embodied a countervailing attitude toward expertise. "We present tonight the first in a series of programs . . . ," he announced, "in which you, the very much-quizzed public, will quiz the professors. Yes, the worm turns, and now the experts will have to know the answers to your questions or else." Or else what? *Radio Guide* noted the satisfactions for listeners when contestants faltered: "It's the know-it-alls, the wise men, who must take the witness stand and squirm shame-facedly when they don't know the answer, while John Q. Fan, out there in the studio audience, rocks with laughter. . . . Weren't the 'Information, Please' experts supposed to be wizards, or, at least, near-wizards? And when one of them stumbled over a question, guessed wrong, or tossed up his hands and quit, you could almost hear the happy chortling of radio fans the country over." Although the laughter had an element of relief ("Boy, I'm glad *I'm* not up there in his shoes"), it rang as well with the sound of money: "Or else," the narrator continued, "you win five dollars." As if to symbolize the ascendancy of commercialism over culture, the experts' downfall came complete with appropriate sound effects—the ringing of a cash register bell each time a panel member missed a question.[116]

Fadiman's preface to a 1939 collection of broadcast transcripts explicitly captured the show's ambivalence toward expertise. " 'Informa-

tion, Please!,'" he declared, "was created to give the public an opportunity to stump the experts." Returning the quiz to its status as parlor
game, he elaborated: "Every home may not have a professional expert
on hand, but we are sure you will find many in your own family or
among your friends who will be glad to play the part. As a matter of
fact, you don't have to be an expert to play 'Information, Please!' Very
few of the questions are tricky or specialized. The majority have been
selected for their general interest and appeal." Similarly, he remarked
elsewhere that the program exhibited the "wit," "erudition," and
"mental agility" of its participants while aiming to be "genuinely informal and friendly." On the air, Fadiman translated the program's double
message into dialogue that alternately touted and sabotaged the contestants' credentials, typically mixing respectfulness and satire. He
observed after welcoming the evening's players, for instance, "Here
they sit, these four towering intellects. On their faces is a look of
confidence, which I believe to be entirely false." Such banter both
permitted the audience a laugh at the panel's expense and set contestants up for impressively quick comebacks.[117]

Within the framework of stumping the experts, "Information,
Please!" incorporated a range of additional messages. In language that
strikingly connects it to other book programs, Gilbert Seldes called the
show "essentially more a conversation than a quiz." Fadiman's retrospective description of the tone his role required reveals the extent to
which he purported to sustain the genteel connotations "conversation"
could carry. The successful master of ceremonies, he asserted, must
have "class"—that is, "at least a moderate amount of mental cultivation." In other words, Fadiman explained, "his manner, choice of
words, intonation [must] appear to suggest some connection with a
world that, oddly enough, is supposed to have nothing to do with mass
entertainment. The presumably non-intellectual pop audience seems to
like an occasional suggestion of intellectual good manners."[118] Although light years away, in level of sophistication, from the Literary
Guild's living-room tableau, "Information, Please!" thus offered the
same opportunity to declare one's home a center of refinement and
distinctiveness.

The intellectual content of the program also paid some homage to
liberal, and especially literary, study. It was primarily this quality of
the show, in fact, that permits its classification as a book broadcast. As

Canby observed in April 1940, when the *Saturday Review* gave the quiz its award "For Distinguished Service to American Literature": "The questions and answers which radiate from this room every week have sent thousands to useful reference volumes; they have brought to life good books long unopened; the wit and erudition in this hour have electrified the minds of thousands listening in." The program, he added, "has precipitated an enthusiasm in and curiosity about books and authors without parallel in the history of radio."[119]

Only a year earlier, the same journal had complained that the intelligence of the panel was wasted on trick questions which approached "the level of inanity." It may be that the editorial itself prompted Golenpaul to make the show more intellectually serious thereafter. Nonetheless, the intrinsic nature of the program—the premium on what the "College Bowl" quiz of the 1960s would label "quick recall of specific fact"—necessarily limited the extent to which it could supply anything other than culture recast as data. Moreover, the educational feature of the broadcast always competed with another of its appeals: the display of personality. F.P.A., after all, was as much the exemplar of sophistication on the air as in print; Levant even symbolized the glamour of Hollywood. If the tenor of the conversation the group conducted was the polite one of the parlor, its style belonged to the theater and the Algonquin Hotel dining room. The initial resistance of sponsors to a show they feared might be "too highbrow for general consumption" partly accounts for the program's subsequently greater emphasis on performance. Network executive Phillips Carlin cautioned Golenpaul in 1938 that, despite the need to "get ready for the commercial and make the programme popular," he should be careful not to "get it in the same group with all the other question and answer shows." Yet by 1942 John K. Hutchens reported that "Information, Please!," bowing slightly to commercial pressures, had increased "its entertainment value by stressing the personalities on its board of experts. They don't just answer questions now, as they did at first. They put on a show."[120]

This facet of the broadcast bothered even some of the representatives of personality themselves. Writing to a friend, Van Loon complained, "When, after six years of the University of the Air and six years of independent yodeling on the air, I attend one performance of 'Information, Please,' which is so hopelessly cheap I feel ashamed of myself, I get endless letters telling me how brilliant I am." Though he reveled more than Van Loon did in the program's theatricality, F.P.A. offered a similar analysis of the quiz's actual contribution to education: "What educational value is in the fact that Judge James Garret Wallace and I can sing the words and music of 'She's More to be Pitied than Censured'? . . . Time to wake up, America, and stump the experts. Experts, my grandmother's left hind hat!"[121]

None of this is to suggest that the show itself was not immensely enjoyable and amusing, alive with a brilliance seldom found on the air today. Some of its dialogue is deservedly famous: When the correspondent John Gunther correctly named the shah of Persia, Fadiman queried, "Are you shah, Mr. Gunther?" Came Gunther's retort: "Sultanly."[122] Yet, writing from the perspective of the 1950s, Fadiman noted the losses the success of "Information, Please!" masked—especially the reality beneath the program's semblance of refined exchange. "Breakfast programs, forums, interviews, 'panel' shows (as a small-time sinner myself, I'm particularly sensitive on this point), teams of radio comedians, ad-lib quiz shows—all pour out an endless stream of what passes as conversation." Such formats created an "overavailability" of both "authority" and "timely information" which turned discussion into "a kind of game of quotations." In contrast to Seldes, Fadiman generalized: "Air-wave talk is not really conversation at all"; because "the average mass communicator" is, "unavoidably, a departure from himself, talking wholesale to millions, he is not in a position to produce the personal, retail stuff called conversation."[123]

Moreover, Fadiman's distinction between the genuine display of personality and the illusion of the personal stopped short of recognizing the further difference between self-expression and the exercise of aesthetic judgment. Some of Fadiman's other activities in the same period he appeared on "Information, Please!" contributed to the underavailability of authority at the expense of cultivating that judgment. His 1941 collection *Reading I've Liked* made him a master of ceremonies on paper, figuratively extending his quiz show stint to the coordination of "guest appearances" in a volume of selections from writers around the world. As the title implies, Fadiman replaced literary standards with feelings, describing himself in the preface not as a critic but as a "reading enthusiast." A few pages later he distinguished the "art" of criticism from the "business" of book reviewing and allied himself with the latter pursuit. ("I'm a business man, not an esthete," he proudly announced in a 1943 *Time* interview.) Rejecting the idea that the classics were necessarily the best books, he named "magic" and "personality" the attributes of those works that withstood rereading. Thus, *Reading I've Liked* represented one more effort to adjust the definition of culture to modern needs, one more flight from evaluative criticism toward "the most informal kind of personal annotation." Fadiman maintained that unassuming, weightless posture even while functioning, in practice, as an expert—as lecturer, essayist, and, after 1944, as a member of the Book-of-the-Month Club board.[124]

The Decline of Attention

As Fadiman's rueful reference to himself as a "small-time sinner" suggests, he was not unaware of the tensions his career encompassed. In fact, Fadiman's inventory of his accomplishments at age fifty, written for the preface to his collection *Party of One*, is, as far as it goes, a remarkably apt description of the role that, with respect to radio, had evolved from Burrill and Jackson to Phelps and Woollcott to Weeks, Frederick, and Mark Van Doren. Calling himself a "middleman" of "thought and opinion," Fadiman remarked, "I have been a kind of pitchman-professor, selling ideas, often other men's, at marked-down figures, which are easier to pay than the full price of complete intellectual concentration." His "mental brokerage business," unabashedly tied to consumption in both metaphor and reality, was a strategy, Fadiman thought, for preserving literacy and respect for intellect among the "intermediate class" that was "in danger of becoming the Forgotten Public."[125]

The trouble was that Fadiman's bargain depended on readers and listeners who, retaining some allegiance to older ideals of character and culture, at least prized marked-down ideas. Striking that bargain on a widespread basis grew increasingly difficult after 1950. The publishing industry, mirroring the triumph of specialization, gradually abandoned most efforts to target thoughtful books to a broad audience. The rise of television heightened Americans' preoccupation with celebrity and further devalued the idea that acquiring knowledge required patient, disciplined training. At the same time, the quest for self-realization through consumption hardened into a virtual science of "impression

management." Fadiman himself summarized those trends in a perceptive essay entitled "The Decline of Attention." Modern American culture, he observed, engendered "producers and consumers" rather than
"rational men" with humanistic values. Impatient with nonutilitarian
pursuits, the reading public became a " 'consuming public' that must be
sold words and thoughts." As a result, writers characteristically strove
to "please" rather than to make demands on their audiences, portray-
ing themselves as "equal" but not "superior" to their readers. Likewise, American journalists relied on a number of devices that "*attract*
the attention without actually *engaging* it." Among these, Fadiman
again noted "the emphasis on 'personalities' as well as the avoidance of
personality." Other symptoms of "the decline of attention" included
the "exploitation of the 'column' as against the discursive essay," the
"featuring of headlines" akin to advertising, "the often remarkable
ingenuity displayed in 'packaging,' an almost religious veneration for
the 'fact' (to be 'well informed' is our substitute for the capacity to
reflect)," and "the rapid alternation of appeals (known as 'balance,' or
something for everybody)."[126]

Fadiman and others did make some attempt to adapt the "pitchman-
professor" role to those discouraging conditions. Although "Information, Please!" went off the air in 1952 after failing to make a transition
to television, Fadiman returned to radio in 1954 as host of a program
that, while not exclusively devoted to books, explicitly resuscitated the
conversational ideal as Erskine had understood it. In fact, the broadcast (another Louis Cowan production) was called "Conversation."
Guests (Seldes, Norman Cousins, and Jacques Barzun among them)
deliberately minimized their impulses to trade information, anecdotes,
or personal experiences. Instead, they offered their listeners an intimate encounter with "people thinking" in a "quiet, well-mannered"
way. The show's audience, Fadiman reported, appeared to be "fed up
with facts" and tired of keeping up with "the latest gossip, book, play,
or 'personality.'" In that sense, coming at the end of the medium's
heyday, "Conversation" (along with "Invitation to Learning") represented the fullest development of the genteel strain in radio book
programming. Similarly, while instrumental in fostering "the decline of
attention," the development of television also rekindled the movement
for educational broadcasting and led to the creation, on the new com-

mercial networks, of some book shows less frivolous than "The Author Meets the Critics." These included numerous local programs featuring book reviews and children's literature. Of special note were the early "anthologies," which presented high quality enactments of contemporary writing. One of these, Philco Television Playhouse, initially dramatized works chosen in cooperation with the Book-of-the-Month Club.[127]

If those efforts preserved opportunities for the survival of the genteel tradition into the 1950s, however, another television broadcast from the same period may be read as a commentary on its tenuous position as consumer values grew ever more dominant. This was the appearance in November 1956 of Mark Van Doren's son Charles on the quiz show "Twenty-One," a big-money contest that had none of the conversational features of "Information, Please!." Van Doren's tale of woe provides a poignant postscript to the history of the making of middlebrow culture.

Well acquainted since childhood with Adler and Fadiman, the younger Van Doren had attended St. John's College. Thereafter, however, he had experienced difficulty choosing a profession: he tried acting, mathematics, doctoral study in literature, and fiction writing before taking a job as a researcher for Fadiman. His parents' successes and expectations cast a long shadow, as Mark Van Doren himself understood. ("Mama and I have been saying tonight," the elder Van Doren wrote his son in 1952, "that you very rightly recognize your need of getting free of us.") Nonetheless, Charles eventually became an instructor in English at Columbia. Soon thereafter, at the urging of a friend, he tried out for "Twenty-One." Instantly, Van Doren became a celebrity. Tall, attractive, and engaging, he projected an Ivy League image that contrasted sharply with the background of his first opponent, Herbert Stempel, a Jewish graduate of the City College of New York. Entranced by the "weekly visits" of such a "likable friend," fans sent Van Doren two thousand letters per week. On February 11, 1957, he appeared on the cover of *Time*.[128]

Van Doren's fame continued until March 1957, when, having amassed $129,000, he lost to an attorney named Vivienne Nearing. Congressional investigations subsequently revealed that not only his defeat but also Van Doren's victories had been "rigged." Justifying his actions on the grounds that his success was "having such a good effect on the national attitude to teachers, education, and the intellectual life," Van Doren had agreed to memorize the answers to the quiz.[129]

What is most interesting about the deception is not so much its moral as its symbolic dimension. The son of a man who, to a significant extent, perpetuated gentility, Van Doren captured the admiration of the public by exhibiting the mastery of information, earning money, and re-defining culture as performance. As he himself explained shortly after the scandal broke, "I've been acting a part, a role, not just the last few years—I've been acting a role for ten or fifteen years, maybe all my life." From that perspective, Van Doren appears less dishonest than lost—an uneasy, floundering figure whose outward resemblance to an Emersonian man of letters concealed his inability to sustain that tradition in post–World War II America.[130]

Although book programs remain on the air today—largely relegated to public broadcasting—Van Doren's capitulation was a portent of the limited hopes they have come to entail. By now the whir of the "wheel of fortune" has virtually drowned out the sound of both the extended classroom and the "conversation in the living room." The continuing "decline of attention" has diminished other expressions of the mid-dlebrow critic's aspirations as well. Stuart Pratt Sherman's observa-tion, before the founding of *Books*, that the United States lacked a forum for serious generalist reviewing is equally true at present. While academic journals and publications such as the *New York Review of Books* serve what Sherman termed "the damned professor," assess-ments of books in the daily press are overshadowed by reviews of movies and television. The Book-of-the-Month Club and its numerous imitators have increased the range of choice available to subscribers, yet the virtual disappearance of the Board of Judges from Book-of-the-Month Club advertising and the recent shake-up of board composition by the club's owners, Time Warner, suggest the subordination of the judges' authority to commercial considerations. Although the club's in-house editors shy away from "trash" in evaluating possible selections, Dorothy Canfield Fisher's criteria of "value, truth, and literary skill" are secondary to a search for the engaging "personality" and interest-ing story line.[131]

Meanwhile, the "great books" movement has ossified at the point where John Erskine's initial vision of character and community gave way to Mortimer Adler's system—the only difference being that a new edition of *Great Books of the Western World* issued in the fall of 1990 excludes people of color and most women deliberately rather than unthinkingly.[132] Durant's *Story of Civilization*, in the brightly colored jackets of the Book-of-the-Month Club edition, remains in print, yet it often seems merely part of the "wall unit" on which it sits unread. Given the widespread disregard for the possession of liberal learning, the popularizers of the 1920s and 1930s, whose ranks Durant joined in the aftermath of his religious crisis, appear themselves apostles of a shattered faith. More broadly, while the market remains capable of disseminating the importance of reading—not long ago a cereal box urged breakfast eaters to discover the world of books and libraries—its capacity to subvert genuine understanding and autonomy survives and flourishes as well. The stakes in what H. G. Wells called the "race between education and catastrophe" currently seem higher than ever. While recognizing the drawbacks and limitations of the middlebrow perspective, one might thus hope to recover the moral and aesthetic commitments which the makers of middlebrow culture at their best tried to diffuse.

NOTES

INTRODUCTION

1. Canby, *American Memoir*, p. 264; Fisher, *Why Stop Learning?*, p. 257.

2. Lawrence W. Levine, *Highbrow/Lowbrow*, pp. 221–22; Brooks, "America's Coming-of-Age," pp. 15–35; Widdemer, "Message and Middlebrow," pp. 433–34.

3. Woolf, "Middlebrow," pp. 180–84; Greenberg, "State of American Writing," p. 879.

4. Lynes, "Highbrow, Lowbrow, Middlebrow," pp. 19–28.

5. "High-Brow, Low-Brow, Middle-Brow," pp. 99–102; Sargeant, "In Defense of the High-Brow," p. 102.

6. Dwight Macdonald, "Masscult and Midcult: II," pp. 592, 595–605, 615, 618, 626, 628.

7. The most important exception to the neglect of middlebrow forms is the compelling work of Janice Radway on the Book-of-the-Month Club, which seeks to rescue the club from the scorn of intellectuals by arguing that its criteria for book selection are no less valuable to its readers than those governing academic criticism. See Radway, "Book-of-the-Month Club," pp. 259–84. See also Graff, *Professing Literature*, pp. 91–97, 110–12, 133–36.

8. Hawley, *Great War*, p. 166. For a survey of trends in "high" culture during the early twentieth century, see Lewis Perry, *Intellectual Life*, pp. 318–417. On popular amusement, see, for example, Kasson, *Amusing the Million*.

9. Lawrence W. Levine, *Highbrow/Lowbrow*; David D. Hall, *Worlds of Wonder*. See also Weber, "Wagner, Wagnerism, and Musical Idealism," pp. 28–71.

10. Santayana, "Genteel Tradition in American Philosophy," in *Genteel Tradition*, p. 43; Brooks, "America's Coming-of-Age," p. 41 and passim; Brooks, "On Creating a Usable Past," p. 220; Cowley, *After the Genteel Tradition*.

Kenneth Cmiel has recently noted that the word "genteel" had slowly begun to acquire negative connotations a half-century before Brooks attacked the "genteel tradition." See Cmiel, *Democratic Eloquence*, pp. 131–32. Yet "genteel" was resilient enough that, as late as 1926, Katharine Fullerton Gerould could speak sympathetically of "the plight of the genteel" and connect the persistence of gentility to the preservation of "civilization." Gerould, "Plight of the Genteel," pp. 310–19.

11. May, *American Innocence*, pp. vii–xii, 333, and passim; Kasson, *Amusing the Million*, p. 6; Garrison, *Apostles of Culture*, p. 14.

12. O'Brien, "Becoming Noncanonical," p. 241. For examples of studies which explore the changing nature of the canon, see, in addition to the works of Graff and Radway cited above, Tompkins, *Sensational Designs*; Brodhead, *School of Hawthorne*; and the essays in Showalter, *New Feminist Criticism*.

13. The quotation is from Lillian Robinson, "Treason Our Text: Feminist Challenges to the Literary Canon," in Showalter, *New Feminist Criticism*, p. 106. See also Tompkins, *Sensational Designs*, p. 30.

14. Matthiessen, *Responsibilities of the Critic*, pp. 6–10, 14, 17, 18, 183. For a different view of Matthiessen's politics, see Cain, *F. O. Matthiessen*.

15. Cady, *Gentleman in America*, p. 25.

CHAPTER I

1. Mabie, "Mr. Mabie's Answers," p. 26.

2. Bushman, "American High-Style," pp. 355–56, 359.

3. Ibid., pp. 352, 358, 364, 374–75; Bender, *New York Intellect*, pp. 37, 39.

4. Bender, *New York Intellect*, p. 41; Williams, *Culture and Society*, pp. 34–38.

5. Bender, *New York Intellect*, pp. 66, 121; Kasson, *Rudeness and Civility*, p. 57; Story, "Class and Culture," p. 185; Lewis Perry, *Intellectual Life*, p. 179; Persons, *Decline of American Gentility*, p. 132.

6. Kasson, *Rudeness and Civility*, pp. 43, 70–111.

7. Susman, "'Personality' and the Making of Twentieth-Century Culture," in *Culture as History*, pp. 271–85; Bledstein, *Culture of Professionalism*, p. 146; Halttunen, *Confidence Men*, pp. 49–50; Riesman with Glazer and Denney, *Lonely Crowd*, pp. xxvii, 16, 24, 242, 250.

8. Persons, *Decline of American Gentility*, pp. 39–41, 43; Halttunen, *Confidence Men*, p. 63; Cady, *Gentleman in America*, pp. 52–67. On women and "polite culture," see Lewis Perry, *Intellectual Life*, pp. 251–52; Persons, *Decline of American Gentility*, pp. 87, 91; and Trachtenberg, *Incorporation of America*, p. 146.

9. Bushman, "American High-Style," p. 362; Stevenson, *Scholarly Means*, p. 127; Kasson, *Rudeness and Civility*, pp. 169, 257–58.

10. Kasson, *Rudeness and Civility*, p. 96; Cmiel, *Democratic Eloquence*, pp. 66–70, 90–91.

11. Howe, *Unitarian Conscience*, pp. 61, 108, 116–17.

12. Channing, *Self-Culture*, pp. 26, 29, 37, 39, 46, 55.

13. Howe, *Unitarian Conscience*, pp. 63, 188, 190, 201.

14. Ibid., pp. 176, 178, 181, 187.

15. Ibid., pp. 181–87, 203.

16. Stevenson, *Scholarly Means*, pp. 50, 55, 58, 61, 118, 120, 126.

17. Ibid., pp. 24–26, 64–65, 121–23.

18. Emerson, "Progress of Culture," in *Works*, 8:206; Emerson, "Human Culture," in *Early Lectures*, p. 267; Emerson, "Character," in *Works*, 10:103.

19. Emerson, "Aristocracy," in *Works*, 10:66–67; David Robinson, *Apostle of Culture*, p. 99; Emerson, "Progress of Culture," 8:216; Paul, *Emerson's Angle of Vision*, pp. 157, 173; Emerson, "Human Culture," in *Early Lectures*, p. 264.

20. David Robinson, *Apostle of Culture*, pp. 66, 89, 155; Emerson, "Human Culture," in *Early Lectures*, p. 216.

21. Emerson, "Human Culture," in *Early Lectures*, pp. 215, 218, 256, 258, 260; David Robinson, *Apostle of Culture*, p. 215; Paul, *Emerson's Angle of Vision*, p. 133.

22. Emerson, "Self-Reliance," in *Works*, 2:52; Emerson, "American Scholar," in *Works*, 1:90; Emerson, "Books," in *Works*, 7:210.

23. Trachtenberg, *Incorporation of America*, p. 156; Emerson, "Books," in *Works*, 7:188, 198; David Robinson, *Apostle of Culture*, pp. 177–78.

24. Bender, *New York Intellect*, pp. 213–15; Howe, *Unitarian Conscience*, p. 11; Tomsich, *Genteel Endeavor*, p. 35; *Letters of Charles Eliot Norton*, 1:218, 2:43, 140.

25. David D. Hall, "Victorian Connection," pp. 561–74. Although the network of personal relationships eventually disintegrated, many commonalities remained between British and American approaches to culture. For example, late-nineteenth-century British periodicals such as the *Bookman* featured the same emphasis on "appreciation" and bookish "small talk" that characterized the American magazine of the same title; later the development of BBC cultural broadcasts paralleled the activities of American advocates of educational radio. Similarly, the volume that inspired Will Durant's "stories," H. G. Wells's *Outline of History*, was from England. As John Gross noted of the British case, between 1880 and 1914 "a large middle-brow public . . . asked to be painlessly instructed in what might be termed the folklore of literature; and there were plenty of instructors happy to come forward and satisfy the demand." John Gross, *Man of Letters*, p. 200. In the United States, however, those commonalities eventuated by the interwar period in institutions and commodities that were, at least initially, uniquely American in form or scale. For example, the American penchant for making lists of "great books" was not replicated to the same extent in England. As Gross put it, "In America, where they order these matters more spectacularly, the pursuit of Greatness led on to President Eliot's Harvard Classics—the Five-Foot Shelf of culture—and then, in the fullness of time, to the Chicago Great Books. . . . But no comparable chimera has ever been dreamed up over here." John Gross, *Man of Letters*, p. 197. Similarly, the Book-of-the Month Club, the expansion of the "outline" genre to craze proportions, and the literary broadcast on commercial radio were distinctly American developments.

26. Norton, review of *Divina Commedia*, p. 628; Veysey, *American University*, pp. 223–24; *Letters of Charles Eliot Norton*, 2:47.

27. *Letters of Charles Eliot Norton*, 2:282, 376; Vanderbilt, *Charles Eliot Norton*, p. 182; Lowell, "Criticism and Culture," p. 516.

28. David D. Hall, "Victorian Connection," p. 570; Trachtenberg, *Incorporation of America*, p. 157; Vanderbilt, *Charles Eliot Norton*, p. 264; Higginson, "Plea for Culture," p. 30; Godkin, "Chromo-Civilization," p. 202; Norton, "Notices of Gillett's Huss," pp. 270–71; *Letters of Charles Eliot Norton*, 2:230; Aaron, "Informal Letter," p. 29.

29. Green, *Problem of Boston*, pp. 125–26; Higginson, "Literature as an Art," pp. 745–54; Norton, "Notices of Gillett's Huss," p. 270; Lowell, "Criticism and Culture," p. 516; Higginson, "Plea for Culture," p. 33.

30. David D. Hall, "Victorian Connection," p. 570; Vanderbilt, *Charles Eliot Norton*, p. 88; *Letters of Charles Eliot Norton*, 2:199; Norton, "Notices of Gillett's Huss," p. 270; Lowell, "Criticism and Culture," p. 516.

31. Norton, "Paradise of Mediocrities," pp. 43–44; Norton, "Notices of Gillett's Huss," p. 273; Godkin, "Organization of Culture," p. 488.

32. David D. Hall, "Higher Journalism," p. 15; Raleigh, *Matthew Arnold*, pp. 31, 61–62; Arnold, *Culture and Anarchy*, pp. 6, 49, 54, 95, 103, 107. James is quoted in Lawrence W. Levine, *Highbrow/Lowbrow*, p. 223.

33. Arnold, *Culture and Anarchy*, pp. 70, 163, 179.

34. David D. Hall, "Victorian Connection," p. 570.

35. Lawrence W. Levine, *Highbrow/Lowbrow*, pp. 23–30 and passim. See also DiMaggio, "Cultural Entrepreneurship" and "Cultural Entrepreneurship, Part II."

36. Lewis Perry, *Intellectual Life*, p. 180; Lawrence W. Levine, *Highbrow/Lowbrow*, pp. 25, 32, 115–32; Kasson, *Rudeness and Civility*, pp. 215–56; Bushman, "American High-Style," p. 374.

37. Lehmann-Haupt, Wroth, and Silver, *Book in America*, pp. 63–90, 119–36; David D. Hall, "Uses of Literacy," pp. 1–47; Tebbel, *History of Book Publishing*, 1:203–30; Kasson, *Rudeness and Civility*, pp. 37–47.

38. Channing, *Self-Culture*, pp. 66–67; David D. Hall, "Uses of Literacy," pp. 46–47.

39. Mott, *History of American Magazines*, 3:6–9, 4:11–12; Shove, *Cheap Book Production*, pp. 49–50, 58, and passim; Tebbel, *History of Book Publishing*, 1:238, 2:511–34; Lehmann-Haupt, Wroth, and Silver, *Book in America*, p. 198; Bledstein, *Culture of Professionalism*, pp. 65–79.

40. Kasson, *Rudeness and Civility*, p. 5.

41. Bledstein, *Culture of Professionalism*, p. 78.

42. Lowell, "Five Indispensable Authors," pp. 223; Godkin, "Chromo-Civilization," pp. 201, 204.

43. Porter, *Books and Reading*, pp. 31–33, 97–100, and passim.

44. Veysey, *American University*, pp. 88, 91, and passim; Charles W. Eliot,

"New Definition," pp. 3806–11; Bledstein, *Culture of Professionalism*, pp. 127, 129–58, 172, 259–68, 325.

45. Veysey, *American University*, pp. 194–95, 216.

46. Scott, "Popular Lecture," pp. 791–809; Bode, *American Lyceum*, pp. 48, 124, 137, 240–41; Bender, *New York Intellect*, pp. 79–80, 172. The same preference for knowledge in "popular and useful" form dominated the Concord (Mass.) Social Library, the members of which were instrumental in starting the Concord Lyceum. See Robert A. Gross, "Much Instruction," pp. 166–67.

47. Cayton, "Making of an American Prophet," pp. 597–620.

48. Scott, "Popular Lecture," pp. 794, 799, 801–2.

49. Kasson, *Amusing the Million*, pp. 5–9; Wiebe, *Search for Order*, pp. 50, 57; Lawrence W. Levine, *Highbrow/Lowbrow*, pp. 176–77.

50. Lears, *No Place of Grace*, pp. 34–35; Lears, "From Salvation to Self-Realization," pp. 7–8.

51. Lears, "From Salvation to Self-Realization," pp. 15–25; Hofstadter, *Anti-Intellectualism*, p. 404; Susman, *Culture as History*, pp. 276–84.

Richard Sennett makes a somewhat different argument, postulating the replacement of an eighteenth-century vision of "natural character" by a nineteenth-century culture of personality, in which outward appearance is a "direct expression of the 'inner' self." Yet Sennett's and Riesman's divergent scenarios eventuate in much the same outcome: a modern self consisting entirely of "masks" and a concomitant impoverishment of human life—what Sennett identified as a loss of "civility," genuine "sociability," and the capacity for "play." At the same time, one should note that while Riesman thought autonomy easier to attain in an inner-directed society, he remained hopeful that what he saw as the liberating aspects of industrial production would permit "an organic development of autonomy out of other-direction." See Sennett, *Fall of Public Man*, pp. 153, 259–68, 308–11, 313–27, 337–39, and Riesman with Glazer and Denney, *Lonely Crowd*, pp. 242, 260–61, 269, 291.

52. Fitzgerald, *Great Gatsby*, p. 2; Fox, "Character and Personality"; Blake, "Young Intellectuals," pp. 510–31; Blake, *Beloved Community*, pp. 120, 132–43, and passim; Westbrook, *John Dewey*, pp. 151–66; Whitman, "Democratic Vistas," p. 962.

53. This argument rests on a distinction between the American economy prior to the late nineteenth century, when middle-class consumers undeniably purchased a range of household furnishings, clothing, and other commodities, and the emergence thereafter of an infrastructure—corporate organization, efficient, large-scale distribution networks for an unprecedented variety of goods, specialized advertisers, and so forth—that shifted American values toward a pervasive quest for material comfort. Kathy Peiss usefully summarizes that distinction in her "Comment: Consumer Culture in Historical Perspective." For two helpful discussions of the debate about when American consumer culture emerged, both of which basically uphold Peiss's distinction,

see Horowitz, *Morality of Spending*, pp. xxiv–xxix, and the essay on which Peiss was commenting: Agnew, "Coming Up for Air." See also Strasser, *Satisfaction Guaranteed*, especially pp. 16–19, 26, 89–91.

54. Lears, "From Salvation to Self-Realization," pp. 15, 17–27; Lears, *No Place of Grace*, p. 37; Halttunen, *Confidence Men*, pp. 207–8; Lasch, *Culture of Narcissism*, pp. 52–70; Susman, *Culture as History*, p. 280. See also Gilkeson, *Middle-Class Providence*, pp. 300–309, 334–36.

55. Halttunen, *Confidence Men*, p. 54; Cayton, "Making of an American Prophet," p. 618; Kasson, *Rudeness and Civility*, pp. 257–60.

56. Higham, "Matrix of Specialization," pp. 3–18; David Robinson, *Apostle of Culture*, pp. 611–13; Ford, "Fad of Imitation Culture," pp. 153–57.

57. Lawrence W. Levine, *Highbrow/Lowbrow*, pp. 203, 219–21; Trachtenberg, *Incorporation of America*, p. 147.

58. Lawrence W. Levine, *Highbrow/Lowbrow*, pp. 206–7; David D. Hall, "Victorian Connection," p. 574.

59. Green, *Problem of Boston*, pp. 142–63.

60. Hugh Hawkins, *Between Harvard and America*, pp. 148, 151, 165, 203; Charles W. Eliot, *Harvard Classics*, 50:3–4, 7, 10.

61. Hugh Hawkins, *Between Harvard and America*, between pp. 180 and 181; Bledstein, *Culture of Professionalism*, p. 78.

62. See, for example, Chase, "Our Lock-Step Culture," pp. 238–42; Russell, "Take Them or Leave Them," pp. 168–77; Sprague, "Chain-Store Mind," pp. 356–66.

63. Wiggam, *Marks of an Educated Man*, pp. 75–100; advertisements for "Dr. Eliot's Five-Foot Shelf of Books," *New York Times Book Review*, Nov. 16, 1924, p. 15; *New York Herald Tribune Books*, Oct. 19, 1924, p. 16; Dec. 7, 1924, p. 24; and Feb. 14, 1932, p. 24; advertisement for *Emerson's Complete Writings*, *New York Herald Tribune Books*, Sept. 8, 1929, p. 32; Martin, *Meaning of a Liberal Education*, p. 14. The phrase "impression management" is from Goffman, *Presentation of Self*, pp. 208–38.

64. James Truslow Adams, *Our Business Civilization*, pp. 35, 169; Curti, *Growth of American Thought*, p. 689; David O. Levine, *American College*, pp. 45–67.

65. Lewis, *Babbitt*, p. 212.

66. Angoff, "Culture at Cut Rates," pp. 18–19; James Steel Smith, "Day of the Popularizers," pp. 297–309; Lehmann-Haupt, Wroth, and Silver, *Book in America*, p. 320; Cheney, *Economic Survey*, pp. 44, 53–58, 121.

67. Peter Dobkin Hall, *Organization of American Culture*, p. 3; Wiebe, *Segmented Society*, pp. 61, 70–71; Wiebe, *Search for Order*, p. 262.

68. James Truslow Adams, *Our Business Civilization*, pp. 20–21, 31; Susman, *Culture as History*, p. 107; Stearns, *Civilization*; Duffus, *Books*; Gray and Monroe, *Reading Interests*, pp. 3, 259–74; Waples and Tyler, *What People Want to Read About*, pp. 1–7; Cheney, *Economic Survey*, pp. 104, 209, 329.

CHAPTER 2

1. Hardwick, "Decline of Book Reviewing," pp. 140–41, 143.

2. "Two Views of the Reviews," pp. 6, 8. More reactions to Hardwick's essays appeared in a subsequent issue of *Harper's*. See "Reading and Reviewing," pp. 8, 10.

3. For an essay of the same title that appeared just prior to Hardwick's, see Wagner, "Decline of Book Reviewing," pp. 23–36. See also Nobile, *Intellectual Skywriting*, p. 18, and the following essays in the *Daedalus* issue on "The American Reading Public" (*Daedalus* 92 [Winter 1963]): Best, "In Books," pp. 30–32; Peyre, "What Is Wrong?," pp. 128–44; and Hollander, "Some Animadversions," pp. 145–54.

4. Florin L. McDonald, "Book Reviewing," p. 50; Hyman, *Armed Vision*, pp. 7–8. Hyman actually distinguishes among reviewing, criticism, and aesthetics, but he recognizes the possibility that some reviews can contain both of the latter.

5. Charvat, *Profession of Authorship*, pp. 168–87; Cortissoz, *New York Tribune*, p. 36; Nevins, *Evening Post*, p. 407; Kluger, *The Paper*, pp. 16, 59–63; Baehr, *New York Tribune*, p. 127.

6. Nevins, *Evening Post*, pp. 407, 409–10.

7. Nadal, "Newspaper Literary Criticism," pp. 312–17; Nevins, *Evening Post*, p. 416.

8. David D. Hall, "Higher Journalism"; Brownell, "Nation," pp. 42–44. Bagehot is cited in Houghton, *Victorian Frame of Mind*, pp. 104–5.

9. Nevins, *Evening Post*, pp. 267–68, 436, 448, 553–54.

10. "Varieties of Book Reviewing," p. 8.

11. Florin L. McDonald, "Book Reviewing," p. 35; Rascoe, *Before I Forget*, pp. 323–24; Davis, *History of the New York Times*, p. 214; Berger, *Story of the New York Times*, p. 558.

12. Bliss Perry, "Literary Criticism," p. 642; "Book Reviewing a la Mode," pp. 139–40.

13. "Up-to-Date Book Reviewing," pp. 3096–99; Cowley and Canby, "Creating an Audience," pp. 1125–26; Canby, *Definitions*, pp. 186–91; Bliss Perry, "American Reviewer," p. 4; "Varieties of Book Reviewing," p. 8.

14. Hansen, "Book Reviews," p. 128; Cowley and Canby, "Creating an Audience," p. 1123; Florin L. McDonald, "Book Reviewing," p. 12. Other daily book reviewers in the interwar period included Laurence Stallings, Hansen's predecessor at the *New York World*, William Soskin at the *New York American*, and Lewis Gannett at the *New York Herald Tribune*. Some columns, such as Hansen's and Soskin's, were syndicated around the country. The *New York Times* lagged behind its competitors, however, waiting until 1933 to start a daily signed review. Hansen, "Book Reviews," p. 128. In McDonald's survey, the remaining 7 percent listed "to create new interest" as their top priority.

15. Kluger, *The Paper*, p. 346; Berger, *Story of the New York Times*, p. 559. A major shift in the tenor of the *Times Book Review* did not occur until 1971, when editor John Leonard set about "upping literary standards" and "depreciating the book-as-news line." Nobile, *Intellectual Skywriting*, pp. 269–70.

16. The name was changed to the *Weekly Book Review* in 1943 and to the *Book Review* in 1949.

17. Canby, "Books Are News," p. 1.

18. Ruland, *Rediscovery*, p. 57. See also Zeitlin and Woodbridge, *Life and Letters of Stuart P. Sherman*, 1:vii (hereafter cited as ZW).

19. Carson, "Mr. Stuart Sherman," pp. 389–96; Raleigh, *Matthew Arnold*, pp. 158–89; Ruland, *Rediscovery*, pp. 60–61, 88–90, 95–96; Spiller, "Battle of the Books," pp. 1152–53.

20. Canby is quoted in an advertisement for the Zeitlin and Woodbridge biography. See *New York Herald Tribune Books*, Oct. 6, 1929, p. 11 (hereafter cited as *Books*).

21. ZW, 1:1–50, 75–76, 98.

22. Nevin, *Irving Babbitt*, p. 14; Graff, *Professing Literature*, pp. 67–72; Sherman, *Shaping Men and Women*, pp. 68, 81.

23. ZW, 1:117.

24. Hoeveler, *New Humanism*, p. 32; Ruland, *Rediscovery*, pp. 14–20.

25. Hoeveler, *New Humanism*, pp. 40, 67.

26. Ibid., pp. 61–62; Mencken, "Motive of the Critic," p. 250; Murry, "Critical Credo," p. 251; Ruland, *Rediscovery*, pp. 23–56.

27. Ruland, *Rediscovery*, p. 61.

28. Babbitt, *Literature*, pp. 31, 80, 105, and passim.

29. Santayana, "Genteel Tradition at Bay," in *Genteel Tradition*, pp. 153–96; Ruland, *Rediscovery*, pp. 12, 26; Hoeveler, *New Humanism*, p. 33; Nevin, *Irving Babbitt*, p. 84.

30. ZW, 1:127, 152.

31. Sherman, *Shaping Men and Women*, pp. 39, 43–44.

32. ZW, 1:175–76, 179, 182; Sherman, "George Moore," pp. 385–88.

33. Sherman, "Education by the People," pp. 461–64; ZW, 1:221–26, 241; Ruland, *Rediscovery*, pp. 63, 77, 80.

34. ZW, 1:142–43, 147–48, 155, 160.

35. Ibid., 1:165, 265; Carl Van Doren, "Stuart Sherman," p. 2.

36. ZW, 1:160–61.

37. Ibid., 1:234–36.

38. Ibid., 1:203–4.

39. Ibid., 1:297, 299; Sherman, *Matthew Arnold*, pp. 4, 10, 18.

40. Sherman, *Matthew Arnold*, pp. 147, 152, 154, 174.

41. Ibid., pp. 70, 159, 168, 185; Babbitt, "Matthew Arnold," p. 118.

42. Sherman, *Matthew Arnold*, pp. 227–28; ZW, 1:297.

43. Sherman, *On Contemporary Literature*, pp. 17, 85–101; Ruland, *Rediscovery*, p. 154.

44. Rascoe, *Before I Forget*, p. 262; Boyd, "Ku Klux Kriticism," pp. 723–24; Carl Van Doren, *Many Minds*, pp. 67–82; Carl Van Doren to Sherman, Sept. 7, 1920, Jan. 31, 1922, and Aug. 6, 1923, Stuart Pratt Sherman Papers, University Archives, University of Illinois at Urbana-Champaign, Urbana, Ill.; ZW, 1:333–40.

45. Sherman, *Americans*, pp. 2, 13–14, 98; Sherman, *Genius*, p. 28; Sherman, *Points of View*, p. 215; ZW, 1:259; Ruland, *Rediscovery*, pp. 85–86, 89.

46. ZW, 2:521–22.

47. Ibid., 1:345, 367; Ruland, *Rediscovery*, pp. 56, 70, 92; Lasch, *New Radicalism*, pp. 99–103 and passim.

48. ZW, 1:346, 2:407, 410, 420, 467.

49. Ibid., 2:393, 399. The word recurred in an exchange with Babbitt about Sherman's treatment of George Sand in which Babbitt, in predictable New Humanist fashion, remarked, "You end on the note of *love*, whereas my final stress is on *will*, the type of will that can alone raise one above the naturalistic level." Ibid., 2:515.

50. Ibid., 2:590–96.

51. Ibid., 2:592; Sherman, "Shifting Centre of Morality," in *Genius*, pp. 100, 102–3; Carson, "Mr. Stuart Sherman," p. 393.

52. ZW, 2:501.

53. Ibid., 1:346, 367.

54. Ibid., 2:477.

55. Sherman, *My Dear Cornelia*, pp. 54, 89–90; ZW, 2:612, 620.

56. ZW, 2:633.

57. Rascoe, *We Were Interrupted*, p. 122.

58. Kluger, *The Paper*, p. 286; Royal Cortissoz to Geoffrey Parsons, Jan. 6, 1923, Reid Family Papers, Series D (Helen Rogers Reid), Box D13, Library of Congress, Washington, D.C.; Helen Rogers Reid to John Macrae, Apr. 4, 1924, Box D15, Reid Family Papers.

59. Rascoe, *We Were Interrupted*, p. 151; Kluger, *The Paper*, p. 201; Royal Cortissoz to Geoffrey Parsons, Jan. 6, 1923, Reid Family Papers.

60. Brichford, "Notes from the Archives." I am grateful to Mr. Brichford for sending me this item. See also ZW, 2:643–48. There is as well the hint, in some correspondence in Carl Van Doren's papers, that a romantic entanglement drew Sherman away from Urbana. See Frederick P. N. McDowell to Carl Van Doren, Feb. 1, 1949, Box 19, Folder 2, Carl Van Doren Papers, Rare Books and Special Collections, Princeton University, Princeton, N.J. Even so, although one has the impression that his marriage was not a source of passion, there is no concrete evidence of another involvement.

61. Carson, "Van Doren, Irita Bradford," pp. 704–6; "Van Doren, Irita Bradford," pp. 881–82; Kluger, *The Paper*, p. 323; William Peterfield Trent to Irita Van Doren, Oct. 19, 1916, Box 9, Irita Van Doren Papers, Library of Congress, Washington, D.C. Irita Van Doren's role in the *Cambridge History* is omitted from Kermit Vanderbilt, *American Literature and the Academy: The*

Roots, Growth, and Maturity of a Profession (Philadelphia: University of Pennsylvania Press, 1986).

62. ZW, 1:379, 2:645.

63. Ibid., 2:595.

64. Ibid., 2:673, 674, 677, 678.

65. Ruland, *Rediscovery*, p. 88; ZW, 2:654, 679, 681, 686.

66. ZW, 2:683, 685.

67. Ibid., 2:682, 686.

68. Ibid., 2:673; Stuart P. Sherman to Irita Van Doren, May 23, 1924, Box 8, Irita Van Doren Papers.

69. Sherman, "Indifferent? No!," p. 2. The characterization of Sherman is from an advertisement for *Books* in the same issue. *Books*, Sept. 21, 1924, p. 18. See also Arnold, "Function of Criticism," p. 18.

70. Ruland, *Rediscovery*, p. 72; Sherman, "Style," p. 2, and "Recognizing One of Our Contemporaries," p. 1.

71. See Sherman, "Vanity Fair," p. 1; "Mark Twain's Last Phase," p. 1; "Miss Sinclair," p. 1; "Irish Epicure Caviare," p. 2; "R.L.S. Encounters," p. 3; "'Modern' Soul," p. 2; "Supermen," p. 1; "Lawrence Cultivates His Beard," p. 3; "Anatole France," p. 3; and "O Brave Sea Captain," p. 3.

72. Sherman, "Five Years," p. 1, and "Miss Sinclair," p. 1.

73. Sherman, "Anatole France," p. 3; "Farewell," p. 3; and "Sick Man's Vision," p. 3.

74. Sherman, *Critical Woodcuts*, pp. xii–xiii, and "Here Is a Novelist," p. 1.

75. Advertisement for "Dr. Eliot's Five-Foot Shelf of Books," *Books*, Nov. 16, 1924, p. 16; advertisement for *Books*, *Books*, July 8, 1928, p. 16; Hardwick, "Decline of Book Reviewing," p. 143.

76. Sherman, *Critical Woodcuts*, p. xiii; Foerster, *Towards Standards*, p. 86; Sherman, "Philosophy," p. 1; Sherman, "What People Want," p. 1.

77. "Man in the Street Protests," p. 12.

78. Sherman, "Here Is a Novelist," p. 1; Sherman, *Critical Woodcuts*, pp. 10–11, 25; Sherman, "Uncommon Essayist," p. 1; Brooks, "Evolution of a Critic," p. 5.

79. Sherman, "Uncommon Essayist," p. 4; Sherman, "Don Marquis," p. 2; ZW, 2:711; Sherman, "Here Is a Novelist," p. 1; Sherman, "'Big' Novels," p. 1.

80. Edmund Wilson, "All-Star Literary Vaudeville," p. 158.

81. Sherman, "Lawrence Cultivates His Beard," p. 1, and "Man against the Sky," p. 1.

82. ZW, 2:683–84, 718–19.

83. Sherman, "Philosophy," p. 1, and "Finding the Intelligent Public," p. 1783.

84. Sherman, "What Transforms Life," p. 2; "Middle Class Strategy," p. 2; and "Speaking to Successful Executives and Business Men Only on the Literary Profession," in *Emotional Discovery of America*, p. 128.

85. Sherman, "Man against the Sky," p. 3; Carl Van Doren, "Stuart Sherman," p. 1.

86. ZW, 2:697, 699, 700, 753.

87. Ibid., 2:688, 696, 736, 771–72.

88. Ibid., 2:691, 699, 763; Sherman, "Miss Sinclair," p. 1.

89. Sherman, *Letters*, pp. vii–viii.

90. Stuart P. Sherman to Irita Van Doren, Mar. 5, 1923, and Aug. 27, 1923, Box 8, Irita Van Doren Papers. The theme of the "metropolitan type" also informed Sherman's glib "Interview with a New Comer to New York," in *Shaping Men and Women*, pp. 87–117. The first year's "letters" were published as a book in 1925.

91. Sherman, *Letters*, p. 157; Sherman, "New Letters to a Lady in the Country," *Books*, June 6, 1926, p. 10.

92. Sherman, *Letters*, p. 108; ZW, 2:747.

93. Rascoe had also had a "revelatory page"—"Bookman's Day Book"—during his tenure as editor. For reactions of readers who missed it, see *Books*, Oct. 12, 1924, p. 13, and June 21, 1925, p. 12.

94. Bush, "Pale-Eyed Priests," p. 700; Paterson, "Up to the Minute," p. 6; Paterson, "Turns with a Bookworm," Sept. 5, 1926, p. 15, and Oct. 19, 1924, p. 12. The ellipses are Paterson's.

95. Sherman, "Letter to a Lady in the Country," *Books*, Mar. 28, 1926, p. 8.

96. Paterson, "Turns with a Bookworm," Jan. 3, 1926, p. 17; "'Books' Covers the World of Books," p. 1341. The *Bookman*'s replacement in 1918 of its long-standing feature "Chronicle and Comment" with "The Gossip Shop" capitalized on the same appeal. The difference, however, was that Paterson herself became a distinctive personality and infused her column with glimpses of her own activities and responses. Comparable features in other journals included Carl Van Doren's contributions to the *Nation*'s "In the Driftway" as well as Christopher Morley's and William Rose Benét's columns in the *Saturday Review of Literature*, discussed in chapter 2. Christopher P. Wilson has also ascribed a similar emphasis on "inside dope" to the new breed of editors who by the same period had transformed the popular magazine from a genteel domain into an embodiment of consumer values. See Christopher P. Wilson, "The Rhetoric of Consumption," pp. 39–64.

97. Sheldon Cheney to Irita Van Doren, Dec. 12, 1934, Box 2, Irita Van Doren Papers.

98. One exception was Gertrude Stein, whose *Making of Americans* and *Autobiography of Alice B. Toklas* received front-page reviews on Jan. 26, 1927, and Sept. 3, 1933, respectively.

99. Wolf, "In Our Time," p. 3; Newman, "One of the Wistful Young Men," p. 4; Snow, "Literalist of the Imagination," p. 3. Stribling's novel was also a Book-of-the-Month Club selection.

100. James Truslow Adams, "Reviewing in America," p. 583.

101. Irita Van Doren to Jacob Zeitlin, Sept. 22, 1926, Box 10, Irita Van Doren Papers.

102. Irita Van Doren to H. K. Norton, Sept. 16, 1926, Box 7, Irita Van Doren Papers.

103. Irita Van Doren to Harry Scherman, June 10, 1963, Box 8, Irita Van Doren Papers; Mark Van Doren, "Irita Van Doren," (1968), p. 9, Allan Nevins Papers, Rare Book and Manuscript Library, Columbia University, New York, N.Y.; Kluger, *The Paper*, p. 286. It must be noted that Mark Van Doren's wife, Dorothy Graffe, remained a writer throughout her marriage. On the other hand, Carl Van Doren was a more egocentric personality.

104. Mark Van Doren, "Irita Van Doren," pp. 1, 3, 5–6; "Irita Van Doren, Editor of Books," p. 37; Cowley, *And I Worked at the Writer's Trade*, p. 63; Kluger, *The Paper*, p. 324.

105. Kluger, *The Paper*, p. 324.

106. Ibid.; Cowley, *And I Worked at the Writer's Trade*, p. 63; "'Books' Covers the World of Books," p. 1339; Irita Van Doren, untitled, undated radio address, Box 13, Irita Van Doren Papers, pp. 4–5, 12.

107. Irita Van Doren, radio address, pp. 9, 12.

108. Mary Ross, "Dos Passos," p. 5; Gregory, "Criticism," p. 16; Redman, "Old Wine," p. 10; Colum, "Literature or Propaganda," pp. 1–2; Edmund Wilson, "Critics of the Middle Class," p. 6; Freeman, introduction to *Proletarian Literature*, p. 9.

109. Foerster, *Towards Standards*, pp. 92, 102–3; Bodenheim, "Criticism in America," p. 802.

110. Becker had taken over *Books*'s children's literature page in 1932.

111. May Lamberton Becker, "Reader's Guide," Sept. 10, 1933, p. 21; Sept. 17, 1933, p. 21; Sept. 24, 1933, p. 25.

112. Ibid., Sept. 24, 1933, p. 25, and Oct. 1, 1933, p. 20; May Lamberton Becker, "Choir Invisible," p. 73; "'Books' Covers the World of Books," p. 1340.

113. "'Books' Covers the World of Books," p. 1342; Ishbel Ross, *Ladies of the Press*, p. 404.

114. "'Books' Covers the World of Books," p. 1346; headlines in *Books*, Jan. 22, 1933, pp. 1, 5; Bromfield, "Gertrude Stein," pp. 1–2; Beatrice Burton Morgan to Irita Van Doren, Dec. 5, 1934, Box 6, Irita Van Doren Papers.

115. The circulation of the *Herald Tribune* as a whole in 1934 was 350,000, up from 275,312 in 1925. See Baehr, *New York Tribune*, pp. 383–84.

116. "'Books' Covers the World of Books," p. 1344; Royal Cortissoz to Helen Rogers Reid, Nov. 4, 1926, Box D19, Reid Family Papers.

117. John Macrae to Helen Rogers Reid, Sept. 12, 1924, Box D15, Reid Family Papers; David L. Chambers to Helen Rogers Reid, Mar. 2, 1935, Box D30, Reid Family Papers; Helen Rogers Reid to David L. Chambers, Feb. 28, 1938, Bobbs-Merrill File, Reid Family Papers; Rascoe, *Before I Forget*, p. 349.

118. Orrick, "Reviewers, Reviewing, and Book Promotion," p. 2632; Adams, "Reviewing in America," pp. 582–83; Canby, "Blurbing," p. 308.

119. Ezra Pound to Irita Van Doren, Dec. 14, 1931(?), Box 7, Irita Van Doren Papers; Ludwig Lewisohn to Irita Van Doren, Jan. 6, 1936, Box 6, Irita Van Doren Papers.

120. Gannett, "A Quarter Century," p. 5.

121. Richard Kluger, "Notes on Geoffrey Parsons Memos, Sept. 1, 1952, and Aug. 31, 1955," in "Irita Van Doren," p. 3, Richard Kluger Papers, Box 14, Folder 326, Manuscripts and Archives, Yale University, New Haven, Conn.

122. Ibid.; ZW, 2:773; Kluger, *The Paper*, p. 682.

CHAPTER 3

1. Foerster, *Towards Standards*, p. 93.

2. Lee, *Hidden Public*, pp. 20–23. Lee's book is a useful, though virtually in-house, business history of the club. See also "The Reminiscences of Harry Scherman," interview by Louis M. Starr, 1955, Columbia University Oral History Collection, Butler Library, Columbia University, New York, N.Y., pp. 1–38 (hereafter cited as Scherman, COHC).

3. Scherman, COHC, p. 38.

4. Duffus, *Books*, pp. 85–89; Lehmann-Haupt, Wroth, and Silver, *Book in America*, pp. 381–83; Lee, *Hidden Public*, pp. 14–18, 30–43.

5. The Literary Guild was the Book-of-the-Month Club's chief competitor, although the club remained the larger of the two operations until World War II. More willing to emphasize bargains and less flexible about exchanges, the Literary Guild nevertheless at first resembled the club in structure and in general approach. Carl Van Doren initially presided over its selecting committee. In 1934, however, Nelson Doubleday purchased all the guild's stock and started screening publishers' submissions for the judges; three years later the guild eliminated judges altogether and began concentrating on selling popular fiction to an audience presumed to be less sophisticated than the club's. Spiller et al., *Literary History*, pp. 1267–68; Madison, *Book Publishing*, pp. 289–90; Duffus, *Books*, pp. 90–91.

6. "New Battle of the Books," p. 27; Lee, *Hidden Public*, pp. 45–59; "Daniel among the Lions," p. 615; "Has America a Literary Dictatorship?," pp. 191–99; Whipple, "Books on the Belt," pp. 182–83.

7. Lee, *Hidden Public*, pp. 206–7.

8. "Book Clubs," pp. 420–21; Lee, *Hidden Public*, pp. 153–54, 202–3; Scherman, "What the Record Means."

9. Canby, *Definitions*, p. 227.

10. Lee, *Hidden Public*, pp. 138, 149. The club did not develop sophisticated analyses of its audience until the late 1930s, when George Gallup conducted his first survey of the membership. (Gallup later became a director of the club.) Scherman's impression, in the club's early period, was that the "most representative type" of member was a middle-aged, married college graduate who had

drifted away from intellectual pursuits. He also singled out a "good-sized proportion" of "girls, secretaries, career girls," who, Scherman added, were "awfully good readers." By the 1940s women outnumbered male subscribers two to one, although women sometimes registered subscriptions for the entire family. Scherman, COHC, pp. 118–19; Zinsser, *Revolution*, p. 12.

11. Sackheim, *My First Sixty Years*, pp. 54, 78.

12. Lears, "From Salvation to Self-Realization," pp. 1–38.

13. Lee, *Hidden Public*, p. 134.

14. Reprinted in Sackheim, *My First Sixty Years*, p. 118; Scherman, COHC, pp. 117–18, 120.

15. Advertisement for the Book-of-the-Month Club, *New York Times Book Review*, Jan. 30, 1927, p. 19.

16. "The Book-of-the-Month Club," pp. 2–3, 5 (hereafter cited as BOMC, 1927 brochure).

17. BOMC, 1927 brochure, p. 2; Lee, *Hidden Public*, p. 136; advertisement for *The Elbert Hubbard Scrap Book*, *New York Times Book Review*, Jan. 23, 1927, p. 32.

18. Lee, *Hidden Public*, pp. 28, 37, 135; Sackheim, *My First Sixty Years*, pp. 119–20.

19. BOMC, 1927 brochure, pp. 11, 16.

20. Marchand, *Advertising the American Dream*, pp. 341–47.

21. "Has America a Literary Dictatorship?," pp. 195–96; Radway, "Scandal of the Middlebrow."

22. Lee, *Hidden Public*, p. 57. For features of the *Book-of-the-Month Club News*, see, for example, Dec. 1943, Mar. 1936, June 1940, Jan. 1944.

23. Scherman, COHC, pp. 100–101; "The Reminiscences of Clifton Fadiman," interview by Louis M. Starr, 1955, Columbia University Oral History Collection, Butler Library, Columbia University, New York, N.Y., pp. 33–34.

24. Swan, "How the Book-of-the-Month Club Has Thrived," p. 58.

25. Hawley, *Great War*, pp. 165–69; Scott, "Popular Lecture," p. 802; Scherman, COHC, p. 38.

26. Calkins, *Business the Civilizer*, pp. 153–65.

27. BOMC, 1927 brochure, p. 16; Duffus, *Books*, p. 93; Susman, *Culture as History*, pp. 220–21; Lee, *Hidden Public*, p. 138.

28. Advertisement for the Book-of-the-Month Club, *New York Times Book Review*, Jan. 20, 1935, p. 20; Hawley, *Great War*, pp. 165–69. The Literary Guild's advertisements similarly promised subscribers "prestige" and inclusion in "the talk of the day." See Sackheim, "Why the Book Clubs Are Successful," p. 68.

29. Advertisement for the Literary Guild, *Books*, Apr. 1, 1928, p. 11; for example, *Book-of-the-Month Club News*, Apr. 1928, which offered Stephen Crane's *The Red Badge of Courage* as an alternate selection; Dorothy Canfield Fisher to Ada McCormick, June 19, 1945, Box 16, Folder 6, Dorothy Canfield Fisher Papers, Special Collections, University of Vermont, Burlington, Vt.

30. Martin, *Meaning of a Liberal Education*, pp. 13–14.

31. Advertisement for the Book-of-the-Month Club, *Books*, Nov. 16, 1924, p. 16; Lee, *Hidden Public*, p. 136.

32. Schudson, *Advertising*, pp. 199–200.

33. Lee, *Hidden Public*, p. 135; Sackheim, *My First Sixty Years*, p. 118. In terms which must have made Eliot cringe, a 1920 "Five-Foot Shelf" advertisement likewise promised buyers "the pleasant path to a liberal education," which readers could follow "in pleasant moments of spare time." *Outlook*, Sept. 1, 1920, p. 41.

34. BOMC, 1927 brochure, pp. 2, 3, 20.

35. Sackheim, *My First Sixty Years*, p. 118; BOMC, 1927 brochure, p. 9; *Book-of-the Month Club News*, Nov. 1927 and Jan. 1930. The bargain book was Charles A. and Mary R. Beard's *The Rise of American Civilization*.

36. Marchand, *Advertising the American Dream*, p. 352.

37. BOMC, 1927 brochure, p. 16; Heald, "Business Thought," pp. 126–29.

38. Gilkeson, *Middle-Class Providence*, pp. 163–74; Harris, "Lay Mastery in America." On women's clubs, see Blair, *Clubwoman as Feminist*.

39. Marchand, *Advertising the American Dream*, pp. 353–59; *Book-of-the-Month Club News*, Apr. 1949 and Dec. 1949; Lee, *Hidden Public*, p. 131.

40. Advertisements for the Book-of-the-Month Club, *New York Times Book Review*, Jan. 20, 1935, p. 20, and Jan. 17, 1937, p. 28; Scherman, COHC, pp. 127, 297; Lee, *Hidden Public*, pp. 39, 62–63, 137; Whipple, "Books on the Belt," p. 182.

41. Canby, *American Memoir*, pp. 10, 51, 75–77; Canby, *Seven Years' Harvest*, p. 131.

42. Canby, *American Memoir*, pp. 13, 45, 51, 61, 110, and passim.

43. Ibid., pp. 189–90.

44. Ibid., pp. 195, 223–24, 228, 231, 251–52.

45. Ibid., p. 206.

46. Graff, *Professing Literature*, pp. 91, 96; Veysey, "Plural Organized Worlds," p. 88.

47. Canby, *American Memoir*, pp. 271, 273, 275. He did maintain his ties to Yale by teaching occasional courses in writing and criticism.

48. Ibid., pp. 275, 276, 287; Canby, *Definitions*, pp. 200–201, 294–302.

49. Canby, *Definitions*, pp. 187–94; Canby, *American Memoir*, pp. 270–71.

50. Canby, *Definitions (Second Series)*, pp. 130–31. See also Canby, *Seven Years' Harvest*, pp. 154–59.

51. Canby, *Everyday Americans*, pp. 171–72; Canby, *Definitions*, p. 171; Canby, *Definitions (Second Series)*, pp. 137–38; Canby, *College Sons*, p. 131; Canby, "Thoreau," p. 113.

52. Canby, *Everyday Americans*, p. 172; Canby, *Definitions*, pp. 138–39, 144–45; Canby, *Definitions (Second Series)*, pp. 152–53.

53. Canby, *College Sons*, pp. 126, 128, 131, and passim.

54. Canby, *American Memoir*, p. 275; Canby, *Definitions*, pp. 177, 180–81;

Canby, *Everyday Americans*, pp. 172–73; Canby, *Seven Years' Harvest*, pp. 282–83.

55. Canby, *Definitions*, pp. 165–66; Canby, *Definitions (Second Series)*, pp. 6, 9, 13, 16, 28–29.

56. Canby, *Definitions (Second Series)*, pp. 29–30. In *American Memoir*, Canby himself lumped together the outlooks of the *Literary Review* and the *Saturday Review of Literature*, saying that "history will not be falsified" by treating them as a single entity (p. 278). The discussion which follows does the same. Similarly, although Canby, Morley, and Loveman obviously held independent opinions, they saw themselves as representing "but a single philosophy of good writing and practicable art." See Canby et al., *Saturday Papers*, p. iii.

57. Canby, *Seven Years' Harvest*, pp. 85, 302–3; Canby, *Definitions (Second Series)*, pp. 43, 221; Canby, *American Memoir*, p. 277.

58. Canby, *Seven Years' Harvest*, p. 76; Canby et al., *Saturday Papers*, pp. 101–2; Canby, *American Memoir*, p. 273.

59. Canby, *Definitions*, pp. 22, 37, 160, 162, 167–70, 249–53; Canby, Benét, and Loveman, *Saturday Papers*, pp. 40–41; Canby, *Seven Years' Harvest*, p. 173.

60. Canby, *Seven Years' Harvest*, pp. 55, 79, 82; Canby, *American Memoir*, p. 286–88; Canby, *Definitions (Second Series)*, pp. 12, 19, 22, 26, 28.

61. Canby, *American Memoir*, p. 359.

62. Although he had endorsed *Elmer Gantry* as a selection, Canby nonetheless wrote in *Seven Years' Harvest* that, in the book, "sheer hate" had "lifted" Lewis to a "bad eminence of denunciation" (pp. 133–34). In general, with respect to subject, he was partial to nature books and to expressions of liberal social policy. Scherman, COHC, p. 95; "The Reminiscences of Henry Seidel Canby," interview by Louis M. Starr, 1955, Columbia University Oral History Collection, Butler Library, Columbia University, New York, N.Y., p. 375.

63. Silverman, *Book of the Month*, pp. 28, 57, 74; *Book-of-the-Month Club News*, July 1931 and Oct. 1926.

64. Canby, *Seven Years' Harvest*, pp. 117, 183, 303; Canby, *Definitions (Second Series)*, p. 142.

65. Canby, "Standardization," p. 573; Canby, "In Answer," p. 444; Canby, "Books Are News," p. 521; Canby, *Definitions*, p. 194; Canby, *American Memoir*, p. 273; advertisement for the *Saturday Review of Literature*, *Books*, May 1, 1927, p. 13.

66. Canby, *Seven Years' Harvest*, p. 297; Silverman, *Book of the Month*, p. 45.

67. "The Reminiscences of Amy Loveman," interview by Louis M. Starr, 1955, Columbia University Oral History Collection, Butler Library, Columbia University, New York, N.Y., p. 533; Canby, *American Memoir*, pp. 275, 383, and 249–420 passim; "Has America a Literary Dictatorship?," pp. 195–96.

68. Fisher was born Dorothea Frances Canfield. After her marriage, she wrote nonfiction under the name "Dorothy Canfield Fisher." She used "Dorothy Canfield" for her fictional writings and in her role as Book-of-the-Month

Club judge. I have, however, referred to her throughout by her married name because that is the way scholars and archivists now usually identify her. On her attitudes toward art and Europe, see Fisher, "What My Mother Taught Me," p. xviii.

69. Washington, *Dorothy Canfield Fisher*, pp. 3–43.

70. BOMC, 1927 brochure, p. 8.

71. Fisher, "What Makes It Worth While," p. 8; Fisher, *Our Young Folks*, pp. 254, 271; Fisher, *Why Stop Learning?*, p. 28.

72. Fisher, "Teen Age Children"; Fisher, *Our Young Folks*, p. 271.

73. Fisher, *Self-Reliance*, p. 103; Fisher, *Vermont Tradition*, p. 12; Fisher, *Memories of Arlington*, pp. 3–29.

74. Canfield (Fisher), *Brimming Cup*, pp. 344, 353, 356.

75. "Personally," Fisher wrote to a member of the *Woman's Day* staff in 1945, "I think a considerable amount of nonsense is talked about that ["sex-fulfillment"], and I don't think it plays such a large part in human life as moderns excited by the recent freedom really to say something about sex, seem to feel." Fisher to Miss Souvaine, May 23, 1945, Box 18, Folder 3, Fisher Papers.

76. Fisher, *Brimming Cup*, p. 350.

77. Canfield (Fisher), *Seasoned Timber*, pp. 156–57; Washington, *Dorothy Canfield Fisher*, p. 229.

78. Fisher, "Book Clubs," p. 9.

79. *Book-of-the-Month Club News*, June 1929; Fisher to Scherman, Jan. 3, 1941, Box 3, Folder 2; Fisher to Scherman, undated telegram, Box 23, Folder 7; Fisher to Meredith Wood, June 27, 1947, Box 24, Folder 1; Fisher to Amy Loveman, Sept. 8, 1948, Box 24, Folder 2; Fisher to Ada McCormick, Aug. 1, 1946, Box 16, Folder 6, Fisher Papers.

80. *Book-of-the-Month Club News*, Apr. 1932; Scherman, COHC, pp. 93–94; *Dorothy Canfield Fisher: In Memoriam*, p. 1.

81. Dorothy Canfield Fisher, "What's Your Idea?," broadcast, Mar. 17, 1944, recording in Fisher Papers.

82. Dorothy W. Bowes to Fisher, Jan. 15, 1947, Box 8, Folder 30; Louise G. Myers to Fisher, n.d., Box 8, Folder 30; Fisher to Mrs. W. W. Smith, Apr. 1, 1916, Box 18, Folder 3. The undated poem is by Dorothy Ann Gardyne, Box 10, Folder 4. All in Fisher Papers.

83. Fisher to Mr. [E. B.?] White, Aug. 15, 1943, Box 23, Folder 9, Fisher Papers.

84. Wallach and Bracker, *Christopher Morley*, p. 34; "Morley, Christopher," pp. 986–87; Canby, *American Estimates*, p. 62; Carl Van Doren, "Day In and Day Out," p. 311.

85. Cowley, "Dr. Canby and His Team," pp. 55.

86. Canby, *American Estimates*, pp. 66–67.

87. Morley, *Haunted Bookshop*, p. 52; *Christopher Morley*, p. 16.

88. BOMC, 1927 brochure, p. 10.

89. Wallach and Bracker, *Christopher Morley*, p. 32.

90. Cowley and Canby, "Creating an Audience," p. 1130; Carl Van Doren, "Day In and Day Out," p. 310.

91. Canby, *American Estimates*, p. 64; Morley, *Forty-Four Essays*, p. 166; Morley, *Ex Libris Carissimus*, p. 53; Wallach and Bracker, *Christopher Morley*, p. 32.

92. Canby, *American Memoir*, p. 359; Fadiman quoted in Zinsser, *Revolution*, p. 6.

93. Kramer, *Heywood Broun*, p. 92; O'Connor, *Heywood Broun*, pp. 15–43, 66–71.

94. Broun, *Whose Little Boy Are You?*, pp. 77–78; Scherman, COHC, p. 106.

95. Fisher to Meredith Wood, Jan. 16, 1945, Box 22, Folder 11, Fisher Papers.

96. BOMC, 1927 brochure, p. 12; White to Scherman, Jan. 28, 1931, Series C, William Allen White Papers, Library of Congress, Washington, D.C.; Walter Johnson, *William Allen White's America*, p. 500; Zinsser, *Revolution*, p. 6. For a recent study of White, see Griffith, *Home Town News*.

97. Walter Johnson, *William Allen White's America*, pp. 495–96; *Book-of-the-Month Club News*, Dec. 1931.

98. Trachtenberg, *Incorporation of America*, pp. 145–47.

99. Canby, *American Memoir*, p. 362.

100. Canby, "In Answer," pp. 444–45; Canby, *American Memoir*, p. 358.

101. Lee, *Hidden Public*, p. 121; Fisher, "Book Clubs," p. 14.

102. *Book-of-the-Month Club News*, Oct. 1926 and May 1934; Zinsser, *Revolution*, pp. 2, 7.

103. Lee, *Hidden Public*, p. 203.

104. Ibid.; Canby, "Fiction Sums Up," p. 1212; Canby, *American Memoir*, p. 344.

CHAPTER 4

1. Bourne, "The Professor," pp. 91–97.

2. *Letters of Randolph Bourne*, pp. 55–56, 136–38, 143, 188, 290–91, 340, 367–69.

3. Erskine, *The Memory*, pp. 14, 18, 21, 43–46, 51.

4. Ibid., p. 23.

5. Persons, *Decline of American Gentility*, pp. 3, 6–7, 55; Bledstein, *Culture of Professionalism*, p. 146.

6. Erskine, *The Memory*, pp. 21, 23.

7. Ibid., pp. 47–48.

8. Ibid., pp. 10, 45, 48.

9. Brooks, "America's Coming-of-Age," p. 17.

10. Persons, *Decline of American Gentility*, p. 43

11. Erskine, *The Memory*, p. 14.

12. Ibid., pp. 12, 14.

13. Erskine, *My Life in Music*, p. 9.

14. Erskine, *The Memory*, pp. 63, 67.

15. Trilling, "Van Amringe and Keppel Eras," pp. 19, 21.

16. Erskine, *The Memory*, pp. 72–79; Erskine, *My Life in Music*, pp. 10–16; Erskine, "MacDowell, Edward," pp. 24–27.

17. Spingarn, "Woodberry, George Edward," pp. 478–81.

18. Woodberry, *Appreciation of Literature*, p. 2; Woodberry, *Heart of Man*, p. 209.

19. Erskine, *The Memory*, p. 94; Woodberry, *Heart of Man*, pp. 121, 170.

20. Woodberry, *Appreciation of Literature*, pp. 90, 107, 175, 193; Lewis Perry, *Intellectual Life*, p. 311.

21. Woodberry, *Appreciation of Literature*, p. 53.

22. Greenslet, *Under the Bridge*, p. 51; Erskine, *The Memory*, pp. 93–94; Trilling, "Van Amringe and Keppel Eras," p. 25.

23. William James to Mrs. Henry Whitman, *Letters of William James*, 2:89.

24. Whicher, *Selections from Ralph Waldo Emerson*, pp. 263–74.

25. Erskine, *The Memory*, p. 94.

26. Because Woodberry, in keeping with his generalist orientation, had been reappointed in comparative literature, Thomas R. Price became Erskine's official supervisor.

27. Erskine, *The Memory*, pp. 101, 150–51; Morris, *Threshold*, pp. 81–84; Trilling, "Van Amringe and Keppel Eras," p. 24; Veysey, *American University*, pp. 426–27.

28. Erskine, *The Memory*, pp. 110–11.

29. Ibid., p. 151; Spingarn, "Woodberry, George Edward," p. 480.

30. Erskine, *My Life as a Teacher*, p. 33; Erskine to Melville Cane, Apr. 15, 1907, Catalogued Correspondence, John Erskine Papers, Rare Book and Manuscript Library, Columbia University, New York, N.Y.

31. Henry Morton Robinson, "John Erskine," p. 9; Erskine, *The Memory*, p. 182; Erskine to Cane, Oct. 3, 1906, Catalogued Correspondence, Erskine Papers.

32. William James to Mrs. Henry Whitman, *Letters of William James*, 2:89.

33. Erskine, *My Life as a Teacher*, pp. 32–49.

34. Lears, "From Salvation to Self-Realization," p. 17; Lasch, *New Radicalism*, pp. 69–103; Blake, *Beloved Community*, pp. 63–75.

35. Morris, *Threshold*, p. 80.

36. Ibid., pp. 85–86.

37. "Helen Worden Erskine and Melville Cane," Erskine Biographical File, Box 6, Folder Columbia 1900, pp. 11–12, Erskine Papers.

38. Displeased by Theodore Roosevelt's presence at Butler's inauguration,

Erskine may well have been responding to Roosevelt's habit during this time of labeling character, rather than intellect, the essential ingredient of civilization. Hofstadter, *Anti-Intellectualism*, pp. 207–8.

39. Erskine, *Moral Obligation*, pp. 3, 12, 18, 24–25, 31; Morris, *Threshhold*, p. 88.

40. Erskine wrote to Scott Buchanan about an article Buchanan did on the history of the "great books" movement: "I was amused to see the legend of the A.E.F. University in Beaune growing steadily, and how like all legends it gets badly twisted. You seem to make the reading list the core of the army enterprise, though as far as my memory now serves, we had no selected reading list at Beaune." Erskine to Buchanan, Dec. 27, 1938, Box G-K, Folder "Great Books," Arranged Correspondence, Erskine Papers; Erskine, *The Memory*, p. 253; Graff, *Professing Literature*, p. 133.

41. "The Reminiscences of Helen Worden Erskine," interview by Joan Pring, 1957, Columbia University Oral History Project, Butler Library, Columbia University, New York, N.Y., p. 161 (hereafter cited as Erskine, COHC); Erskine, *My Life in Music*, p. 113; Erskine, *The Memory*, pp. 256–337.

42. John Erskine to Eliza Hollingsworth Erskine, Feb. 23, 1919, and Sept. 7, 1918, Box 1, 1975 Addition, Erskine Papers; John Erskine to Rhoda Erskine, July 16, 1918, Box 2, 1975 Addition, Erskine Papers.

43. Bourne, "War and the Intellectuals," pp. 3, 11.

44. Erskine, COHC, p. 113; Helen Huntington Smith, "Professor's Progress," p. 28; John Erskine to Eliza Hollingsworth Erskine, Mar. 18, 1918, Box 1, 1975 Addition, Erskine Papers.

45. Erskine, *The Memory*, p. 329.

46. Erskine, *Democracy and Ideals*, pp. 118–32; John Erskine to Eliza Hollingsworth Erskine, Feb. 23, 1919, Box 1, 1975 Addition, Erskine Papers.

47. "Preliminary Report," p. 3; Erskine, "Teaching of Literature," pp. 202–5.

48. Erskine, *Delight of Great Books*, pp. 21–22; "Abstract of the Discussion," p. 1.

49. Graff, *Professing Literature*, pp. 133–36. Graff notes that—in addition to Woodberry—William Lyon Phelps, Bliss Perry, and Charles Mills Gayley all contributed to the "great books" concept and that Gayley initiated a course with that title at Berkeley in 1901. One should add that Mortimer Adler did not invent the phrase "great books" either—despite his claim that it came to him in discussions with Robert Maynard Hutchins "at the end of the twenties." Perhaps Adler can be credited with devising (or, certainly, popularizing) the phrase "great books course." See Adler, *Philosopher-at-Large*, p. 55.

50. "Preliminary Report," pp. 4–6; Moorhead, "Great Books Movement," pp. 688–89; Hollinger, "Canon and Its Keepers," pp. 74–91.

51. Erskine, "English in the College Course," pp. 340–47.

52. Erskine, *My Life as a Teacher*, p. 170; "Preliminary Report," p. 3.

53. Brodhead, *School of Hawthorne*, p. 5.

54. William W. Lawrence to Dean Frederick Keppel, Feb. 9, 1917, Box C, Arranged Correspondence, Erskine Papers; Erskine, *My Life as a Teacher*, p. 168; Erskine, "General Honors at Columbia," p. 13. Erskine's own memories of the sequence of events are at odds with the incomplete college records.

55. Coss, introduction to *Five College Plans*, pp. 2–3.

56. Trilling, "Van Amringe and Keppel Eras," pp. 44–47; Justus Buchler, "Reconstruction in the Liberal Arts," in *A History of Columbia College on Morningside*, pp. 48–54; Allen, *Romance of Commerce*, pp. 81–99; Barzun, *Teacher in America*, pp. 154–59.

57. Erskine, "Outline of Great Books," p. 4, Uncatalogued Manuscripts, Helen Worden Erskine Papers, Rare Book and Manuscript Library, Columbia University, New York, N.Y.; Erskine, "Teaching of Literature," p. 203; Erskine, "My Life in Literature," p. 260, Uncatalogued Manuscripts, Helen Worden Erskine Papers.

58. Erskine, *Prohibition and Christianity*, p. 250.

59. Erskine, *The Memory*, p. 343.

60. Erskine, *Prohibition and Christianity*, p. 255.

61. Erskine, *Delight of Great Books*, p. 200.

62. Erskine, *Democracy and Ideals*, pp. 82–83.

63. Leland, *Art of Conversation*, p. 47.

64. Wright, *Art of Conversation*, pp. 23, 38–40, 44–45; Erskine, *Complete Life*, pp. 145, 147; Erskine, *Prohibition and Christianity*, pp. 215–18.

65. T. S. Eliot, "Tradition and the Individual Talent," pp. 13–22; Bell, "Beyond Modernism," pp. 214, 219.

66. Brooks, "America's Coming-of-Age," p. 57.

67. Erskine, *Democracy and Ideals*, pp. 42–44, 49–53, 62–63, 71.

68. Ibid., p. 56.

69. Brooks, "Letters and Leadership," in *Three Essays on America*, p. 135; Bourne, "Our Cultural Humility," p. 39; Stearns, *Civilization*, p. vii; Blake, *Beloved Community*, pp. 99–121.

70. Rourke, *American Humor*, pp. 3–32.

71. Erskine, *Delight of Great Books*, p. 66.

72. Erskine, *My Life as a Teacher*, p. 169.

73. Dwight Macdonald, "Book-of-the-Millennium Club," p. 171.

74. Erskine, *My Life as a Teacher*, p. 169; Wright, *Art of Conversation*, pp. 117–19. On the "star system," see Boorstin, *The Image*, pp. 57, 154–68.

75. "Preliminary Report," p. 4; Erskine, *American Character*, pp. 161–208; Erskine, "Spotlight or Fame?," pp. 449–51; Erskine, "Literature," p. 420. The inclusion of Erskine's "Literature" essay in *Century of Progress*, one of a series Charles A. Beard edited in order to grapple with the meaning of American civilization, symbolizes Erskine's involvement in that debate. Erskine, "There's Fun in Famous Books," pp. 14–15.

76. Allen, *Romance of Commerce*, pp. 86–91. The idea that the impetus behind the later "great books" movement consisted solely of a rejection of

"modern culture" has made its way into at least one American history text-book. See the discussion by Robert H. Wiebe in Bailyn et al., *Great Republic*, p. 1151.

77. Trilling is quoted in Bell, *General Education*, p. 15; "American College," p. 208.

78. John Erskine to Eliza Hollingsworth Erskine, May 5, 1918, Box 1, 1975 Addition, Erskine Papers; Erskine, *Democracy and Ideals*, pp. 128–29; Bell, *General Education*, p. 14.

79. Erskine, *Democracy and Ideals*, pp. 110, 133–52; Erskine, *Prohibition and Christianity*, pp. 236–42; Erskine, "Twilight of the Specialist," p. 231.

80. "American College," p. 208.

81. Henry Morton Robinson, "John Erskine," p. 9; Erskine, COHC, pp. 146–47; Erskine, *My Life in Music*, p. 163; John Erskine to Hugh Guiler, Dec. 9, 1930, Box 10, Folder Anais Nin–Hugh Guiler, Biographical File, Erskine Papers.

82. Erskine, *The Memory*, p. 347.

83. Erskine, *Private Life*, pp. 70–76; Erskine, "My Life in Literature," p. 29.

84. Helen Huntington Smith, "Professor's Progress," p. 28; "Helen and Galahad under Fire," p. 26.

85. Erskine, "My Life in Literature," p. 32.

86. Clifton Fadiman, interview with author, Apr. 1984, Santa Barbara, Calif.

87. Erskine was somewhat aware of this, admitting that he had set his stories in the past "to make it easier for Mrs. Grundy." Erskine, *Complete Life*, p. 303.

88. Erskine, *My Life as a Teacher*, pp. 206–11; Erskine, *My Life in Music*, pp. 81–82, 110.

89. Erskine, *My Life in Music*, p. 163; Erskine, *My Life as a Teacher*, p. 209; Henry Morton Robinson, "John Erskine," p. 10.

90. Erskine, "Adult Education in Music," pp. 647–53.

91. Adelene Pynchon to Fulton Oursler, Aug. 21, 1951, Box 4, Folder Adelene [Atwater] Pynchon, Biographical File, Erskine Papers; Erskine, *Unfinished Business*.

92. Erskine, COHC, p. 121; John Erskine to Helen Worden, May 12, 1933, May 16, 1933, Uncatalogued Correspondence, Helen Worden Erskine Papers; Erskine, *My Life in Music*, pp. 162–63.

93. Erskine, *Influence of Women*, pp. 18–19, 87, 112–13.

94. John Erskine to Curtis Walker, Dec. 15, 1937, Uncatalogued Correspondence, Helen Worden Erskine Papers; Erskine, *The Memory*, p. 402; Erskine, *My Life in Music*, pp. 176–80. He did make a connection between the accident and a second stroke in 1949. *My Life in Music*, p. 269.

95. Erskine, *My Life in Music*, p. 173; Trilling, "Van Amringe and Keppel Eras," p. 28; John Erskine to F. J. E. Woodbridge, Sept. 28, 1937, Box 5, 1975 Addition, Erskine Papers.

96. Fadiman, "Two Lives," pp. 81–82; "Democracy's Poet," p. 57; Theodore Purdy, "Snows of Yesteryear," p. 11.

97. Helen Worden to John Erskine, n.d., Folder H. W. Erskine—Letters to John Erskine, Helen Worden Erskine Papers; Erskine, "Mickey Mouse," p. 11; Erskine, "Why Films Have So Many Authors," p. 13; Erskine, "Hollywood Stars," pp. 14–15; Erskine, "Clark Gable's Secret Wish," p. 14.

98. Erskine, *Complete Life*, pp. 3, 11–12, 336–38; Roberts, "Personal Preferences," p. 8; Sugrue, "Civilized Man's Guide," p. 9.

99. For example, John Erskine to Helen Worden Erskine, July 5, 1946, Uncatalogued Correspondence, Helen Worden Erskine Papers; Erskine, COHC, p. 128.

100. Allen, *Romance of Commerce*, p. 86. Others associated with the course in its first year, either as instructors or students, included Jacques Barzun, Lionel Trilling, Irwin Edman, Rexford Tugwell, and Raymond Weaver. In their subsequent careers, some of those figures (the literary critics Weaver and Trilling) remained largely identified with "high" culture, but, in addition to Fadiman and Adler, Edman followed Erskine's lead as a popularizer, while Barzun and, to an extent, Van Doren combined academic stature with efforts to reach a wide audience.

101. Moorhead, "Great Books Movement," p. 122.

102. Fadiman interview.

103. Ibid.; Adler, *Philosopher-at-Large*, pp. 106–7.

104. Allen, *Romance of Commerce*, pp. 83–85; Mark Van Doren, *Autobiography*, p. 175; Adler, *Philosopher-at-Large*, pp. 56, 58; Hutchins, *Higher Learning*, pp. 67–78; Hutchins, *No Friendly Voice*, pp. 29–30. For a biography of Hutchins, see Ashmore, *Unseasonable Truths*.

105. Mark Van Doren, *Autobiography*, p. 175; Hutchins, *No Friendly Voice*, p. 38.

106. Allen, *Romance of Commerce*, pp. 85–86, 88, 92–93; Adler, *Philosopher-at-Large*, pp. 177–78; for example, Joseph G. Becht to Robert Maynard Hutchins, Dec. 28, 1938; Paul Dunaway to Robert Maynard Hutchins, June 23, 1944, Robert M. Hutchins Papers, University Archives, University of Chicago.

107. Scott Buchanan to John Erskine, Dec. 16, 1938, and John Erskine to Robert E. Spiller, Mar. 5, 1942, Box G-K, Arranged Correspondence, Erskine Papers; John Erskine to John S. Kieffer, Dec. 29, 1948, Miscellaneous Additions, Erskine Papers; Erskine, *The Memory*, p. 343.

108. Adler had kept the idea alive in the 1930s by leading occasional alumni discussion groups and, at the end of the decade, by having Chicago's extension division offer a "great books" seminar. Allen, *Romance of Commerce*, p. 99.

109. Adler, *How to Read a Book*, pp. 35, 101–16, 328–35, 354–57.

110. Ibid., pp. 102–10, 138, 147–53, 266–68; Hollinger, "Canon and Its Keepers," pp. 85–86.

111. Adler, *How to Read a Book*, pp. 27, 62, 199.

112. Ibid., p. 236; Allen, *Romance of Commerce*, p. 106.

113. Redman, "No: Not without Socrates," pp. 32, 34; Allen, *Romance of Commerce*, p. 106; John D. Hill, "Business Man Views the Classics," p. 167.

114. "Manual for Discussion Leaders," pp. 131, 137, Box 17, Folder 5, Hutchins Papers.

115. Redman, "No: Not without Socrates," pp. 33, 35; "Manual for Discussion Leaders," p. 126; Mayer, "Great Books," p. 8.

116. Adler, *Philosopher-at-Large*, pp. 237–38; "The University of Chicago Roundtable: The Great Ideas" (no. 637, June 11, 1950), p. 1, Box 35, Folder 2, Presidents' Papers ca. 1925–45, University Archives, University of Chicago.

117. "Memo on the Britannica Project," Box 12, Folder 2, Presidents' Papers.

118. Robert Maynard Hutchins to Wallace Brockway, Oct. 3, 1945, Box 34, Folder 6, Presidents' Papers.

119. Hollinger, "Canon and Its Keepers," p. 64.

120. This remained one of Adler's inviolable principles, even though, in practice, the community reading groups routinely read excerpts in order to accommodate their busy schedules. Redman, "No: Not without Socrates," p. 33; "Manual for Discussion Leaders," p. 126.

121. "Report of the Encyclopedia Britannica Great Books Advisory Board meeting, Aug. 30, 1944," p. 3, Box 34, Folder 5, Presidents' Papers. Buchanan later rejected the doctrine. Adler, *Philosopher-at-Large*, p. 251.

122. John Erskine to Robert Maynard Hutchins, Feb. 29, 1944, Box 34, Folder 5, Presidents' Papers; Lionel Trilling to Robert Maynard Hutchins, Sept. 19, 1944, Presidents' Papers; Wallace Brockway to Robert Maynard Hutchins, Apr. 19, 1945, Box 34, Folder 6, Presidents' Papers. Trilling refused out of misgivings about the esoteric, unedited nature of the set and about the board itself.

123. William Benton to Mortimer J. Adler, Sept. 19, 1946, Presidents' Papers.

124. "The Wisdom of Thirty Centuries," pp. 4, 7–8, Box 12, Folder 3, Presidents' Papers. This appears to be a near-final draft of the brochure.

125. "Report of the Encyclopedia Britannica Great Books Advisory Board meeting, Aug. 30, 1944," p. 13; William Benton to Robert Maynard Hutchins, Oct. 18, 1949, Box 35, Folder 1, Presidents' Papers; Mortimer J. Adler to Robert M. Hutchins, Oct. 22, 1949, Presidents' Papers.

126. "The University of Chicago Round Table: The Great Ideas," pp. 1, 6–7; "The Wisdom of Thirty Centuries," p. 21; Raymond Rubicam to Robert Maynard Hutchins, Apr. 24, 1950, Box 11, Folder 3, Presidents' Papers.

127. Adler, *Philosopher-at-Large*, p. 216; Erskine, *Delight of Great Books*, p. 220.

CHAPTER 5

1. Forman, "Will Durant," p. 3.

2. Vanguard Press, for example, issued a five-volume set of summaries

entitled *Educational Outline Library* in 1926. See the advertisement for it in the *New York Times Book Review*, Nov. 7, 1926, p. 33.

3. Tebbel, *History of Book Publishing*, 3:33–34; James D. Hart, *Popular Book*, pp. 238–39; Mott, *Golden Multitudes*, pp. 242–43.

4. Susman, *Culture as History*, p. 107.

5. James Steel Smith, "Day of the Popularizers," pp. 297–309.

6. Gilmer, *Horace Liveright*, pp. 8–10.

7. Erskine, "Outlines," pp. 29–32.

8. Durant, "In Defense of Outlines," p. 10.

9. Wells, *Experiment in Autobiography*, pp. 612–22; David C. Smith, *H. G. Wells*, pp. 245–58; Wagar, *H. G. Wells*.

10. Tebbel, *History of Book Publishing*, 3:33–34; Henry Seidel Canby to H. G. Wells, July 16, 1918, Gedge Fiske & Co. Correspondence, H. G. Wells Papers, Rare Book Room, University of Illinois at Urbana-Champaign, Urbana, Ill.; Wagar, *H. G. Wells*, pp. 156–57; Wells, *Outline*, p. iii.

11. Wells, *Outline*, pp. 196–214, 252–353, 362, 507, 892–921.

12. Ibid., pp. 765, 929, 1100; Wagar, *H. G. Wells*, p. 84; Mackenzie, *H. G. Wells*, p. 323.

13. Wagar, *H. G. Wells*, p. 145; Belloc, *Companion to "Outline of History."*

14. White, *Social Thought*, pp. 47–58 and passim; Hendricks, *James Harvey Robinson*, p. 42.

15. Robinson approvingly cited Wells in his *Mind in the Making*, a book which urged the popularization of knowledge in order to foster intelligence. James Harvey Robinson, *Mind in the Making*, p. 28.

16. Carl Becker, *Everyman His Own Historian*, pp. 182, 190; Hayes, "Other-Worldly Mr. Wells," pp. 19–20.

17. Tebbel, *History of Book Publishing*, 3:33–34; James D. Hart, *Popular Book*, p. 238; David C. Smith, *H. G. Wells*, p. 251. A "definitive" edition appeared in 1924 and a fifth revision in 1931.

18. Hayes, "Other-Worldly Mr. Wells," p. 18; Wagar, *H. G. Wells*, p. 40.

19. Wells, *Outline*, pp. v, 462–63, 467, 494. Resembling the Book-of-the-Month Club, Schapiro used the phrase "average intelligent person" in "Mr. Wells Discovers the Past," p. 224; see also pp. 225–31.

20. Charles Morgan, *House of Macmillan*, pp. 145–47, 163–64; Madison, *Book Publishing*, pp. 157–58; Christopher P. Wilson, *Labor of Words*, pp. 76–77.

21. Advertisements for *The Outline of History*, *New York Times Book Review and Magazine*, Nov. 21, 1920, p. 23; Nov. 28, 1920, p. 22; and Dec. 26, 1920, p. 23; Wagar, *H. G. Wells*, p. 147.

22. Because of his penchant for perpetuating myths about himself, most biographical accounts of Van Loon are inaccurate. The exceptions are Gerard Willem Van Loon, *Story of Hendrik Willem Van Loon*, and Filler, "Van Loon, Hendrik Willem," pp. 789–91.

Similarly, how Van Loon came to publish with Boni and Liveright is open to dispute. Waldo Frank claimed that he introduced Van Loon to Liveright, but Boni thought he met Van Loon first and subsequently got him together with his partner. Margaret Naumberg, who was married to Frank at the time, remembered that *she* introduced Van Loon to Liveright. In any case, it was Liveright who decided to take a chance on Van Loon's project. See Folders 1, 2, and 5, Box 65, Series 9, Hendrik Willem Van Loon Papers, University Archives, Cornell University, Ithaca, N.Y.

23. Gilmer, *Horace Liveright*, pp. 1–33.

24. Van Loon, *Story of Mankind*, pp. 119–23, 192, 239, 449; Van Loon, introduction to *What Is Civilization?*, pp. 1–15; Van Loon, *How I Came To Publish*, p. 8; Schapiro, "History Wise and Witty," p. 759; Beard, "Story of Mankind," p. 105.

25. Wagar, *H. G. Wells*, pp. 270–71; Brooks, *Days of the Phoenix*, pp. 127–40; "Search-Light" [Waldo Frank], "Poor Little Rich Boy," pp. 19–20; Case, *Tales of a Wayward Inn*, pp. 71–77; Boyer, "Story of Everything—II," p. 25; Boyer, "Story of Everything—I," p. 26; Gerard Willem Van Loon, *Story of Hendrik Willem Van Loon*, p. 364; Schapiro, "History Wise and Witty," p. 760; Van Loon, *Story of Mankind*, pp. 197, 446–51.

26. Advertisement for *The Story of Mankind*, *New York Times Book Review and Magazine*, Dec. 4, 1921, p. 8; Tebbel, *History of Book Publishing*, 3:34.

27. Durant and Durant, *Autobiography*, pp. 28–35; Karsner, *Sixteen Authors to One*, pp. 224; Durant, *Transition*, pp. 6–8.

28. Durant, *Transition*, p. 63; "Evolution," pp. 654–69; Schroth, "Excommunication," p. 10.

29. Durant, *Transition*, p. 122; Durant and Durant, *Autobiography*, pp. 35–39. Durant misdates as 1908 the year he entered the seminary. Schroth, "Excommunication," pp. 14–21.

30. Durant, *Transition*, pp. 145, 148, 162–76; Durant, *Mansions*, pp. vii–viii.

31. Durant, *Transition*, pp. 77, 136–37; Durant and Durant, *Autobiography*, p. 38.

32. Durant and Durant, *Autobiography*, pp. 37–54; Durant, *Transition*, p. 160; May, *End of American Innocence*, pp. 219–329; Schroth, "Excommunication," footnotes, p. 4.

33. Durant, *Transition*, pp. 196, 317, 350–51; Durant, *Socialism and Anarchism*, pp. 19–22; Durant and Durant, *Autobiography*, p. 87. I am indebted to George Cotkin for calling the 1914 essay to my attention and sending me a copy.

34. Durant and Durant, *Autobiography*, pp. 58–59, 78, 90, 111; Will Durant to Rev. Edmund B. Chaffee, Aug. 4, 1921, Series 1, Box 2, Folder 1921 Durant Correspondence, Edmund B. Chaffee Papers, George Arents Research Library, Syracuse University, Syracuse, N.Y.; 1925–26 Labor Temple Fall Schedule, Series 1, Box 7, Folder 1925 August–September Durant Correspondence, Chaffee Papers.

35. Rev. Edmund B. Chaffee to Will Durant, Apr. 30, 1926, Series 1, Box 9,

Folder Durant Correspondence, Chaffee Papers; Durant, *Mansions*, p. 42; Durant, *Adventures in Genius*, p. 51.

36. Durant and Durant, *Autobiography*, pp. 67, 73–74; Randall, "Department of Philosophy," pp. 108–29. As noted below, Dewey remained involved enough with Durant to write a preface to *The Story of Philosophy*, but Dewey commonly endorsed books for a variety of authors without maintaining personal ties to them.

37. May, *End of American Innocence*, p. 14; Hollinger, *Morris R. Cohen*, pp. 47–48; Kuklick, *Rise of American Philosophy*, p. 306 and passim.

38. Hollinger, *Morris R. Cohen*, p. 47; Santayana, *Genteel Tradition*, pp. 38–64; Randall, "Department of Philosophy," p. 114.

39. Hollinger, *Morris R. Cohen*, pp. 45–47; Kuklick, *Rise of American Philosophy*, p. 291; Brodbeck, "Philosophy in America," pp. 3–94.

40. Daniel J. Wilson, "Science and the Crisis of Confidence"; Delaney, *Mind and Nature*, pp. 1–3, 5–7, 91–144; William Frank Jones, *Nature and Natural Science*; Randall, "Department of Philosophy," p. 117.

41. White, *Social Thought in America*, pp. 128–46, 188–90, and passim; White, *Science and Sentiment*, pp. 269–74; Dewey, "The Need for a Recovery of Philosophy," in Sidorsky, *John Dewey*, pp. 70–95; Dewey, *Reconstruction in Philosophy*, pp. 1–27, 105. The best account of Dewey's thought is Westbrook, *John Dewey*.

42. Durant, *Social Problem*, p. 32. Despite the similarity of their language, there is no evidence that Durant and Erskine knew each other at Columbia.

43. Durant, *Social Problem*, pp. 36, 70–79, 112–15, 165; Dewey, *Reconstruction in Philosophy*, pp. 32–37.

44. Durant, *Social Problem*, pp. 235–41.

45. "Notes," p. 490; Durant, *Social Problem*, pp. 212–13.

46. White, *Social Thought in America*, pp. 199–201; Brodbeck, "Philosophy in America," pp. 53–54; Delaney, *Mind and Nature*, pp. 3, 113.

47. Durant, *Social Problem*, pp. 222, 269–70.

48. Ibid., pp. 234, 251.

49. Ibid., pp. 185–88, for example, and p. 127.

50. Durant and Durant, *Autobiography*, p. 72.

51. Ibid., pp. 75–76, 78.

52. Herder, "Haldeman-Julius," pp. 881–91; Cothran, "Little Blue Book Man"; Haldeman-Julius, *First Hundred Million*; McConnell, "E. Haldeman-Julius," pp. 59–79.

53. Haldeman-Julius, *First Hundred Million*, pp. 118, 119, 125, 161, 194.

54. Durant and Durant, *Autobiography*, p. 95; Haldeman-Julius, *Second Twenty-Five Years*, pp. 19–20; Mordell, *World of Haldeman-Julius*, pp. 31–35. I am grateful to Gene DeGruson, curator of the Haldeman-Julius Collection at Pittsburg State University, Pittsburg, Kans., for pointing out the material in *Life and Letters*.

55. Haldeman-Julius, *First Hundred Million*, pp. 4, 158, 223. Haldeman-Julius credited retitling for the jump in sales of Durant's essay on Nietzsche. Originally called "Nietzsche: Who He Was and What He Stood For," it was selling "barely the necessary 10,000 copies annually" until 1927, when, as "The Story of Nietzsche's Philosophy," it sold 45,000. Haldeman-Julius, *First Hundred Million*, p. 177. By that time, however, sales were no doubt reflecting the popularity of *The Story of Philosophy* (1926).

56. Haldeman-Julius, *First Hundred Million*, pp. 101, 107, 322.

57. Haldeman-Julius, *Second Twenty-Five Years*, pp. 33–35; Durant and Durant, *Autobiography*, pp. 101–2.

58. "The Reminiscences of Max Lincoln Schuster," interview by Louis Starr and Neil Gold, 1956 and 1964, Columbia University Oral History Collection, Butler Library, Columbia University, New York, N.Y., p. 77 (hereafter cited as Schuster, COHC).

59. Paulsen, *Introduction to Philosophy*, pp. xiii, 414.

60. Windelband, *History of Philosophy*.

61. Veysey, "Plural Organized Worlds," pp. 78–80; Hinshaw, "Philosophy," pp. 6, 18.

62. Durant, *Story of Philosophy*, p. i; Lowenthal, "Triumph of Mass Idols," pp. 203–35; Boorstin, *The Image*, pp. 154–68; Susman, *Culture as History*, p. 277.

63. Durant, *Story of Philosophy*, p. xiii; James Harvey Robinson, *Humanizing of Knowledge*, pp. 75, 183. I am indebted to Gene DeGruson for a copy of the hard-to-find Dewey preface.

64. Durant, *Story of Philosophy*, pp. 1, 5.

65. Adler, "Sleight of Hand," p. 298–99; Dewey, "Influence of Darwinism," in Sidorsky, *John Dewey*, p. 20; Durant, *Story of Philosophy*, pp. 565–75.

66. Durant, *Story of Philosophy*, pp. 564–65, 573. James Steel Smith mistakenly argued that the volume's relevance to its readers lay in its explicit comparison of classical philosophical dilemmas and modern American problems. Actually, the passage he cites as typical of that comparison is the only one of its kind in the book. James Steel Smith, "Day of the Popularizers," p. 305; Durant, *Story of Philosophy*, p. 22.

67. Durant and Durant, *Autobiography*, p. 95; Durant, *Story of Philosophy*, p. 516.

68. Durant, "Failure of Philosophy," p. 90; Durant, *Story of Philosophy*, pp. 1, 102.

69. Durant, *Story of Philosophy*, pp. 20, 104, 156–57, 201, 242, 284, 295, 373, 379, 397, 481, 516–17, 570.

70. Hollinger, *Morris R. Cohen*, p. 47; Rugg, "Artist and the Great Transition," p. 187.

71. Durant, *Story of Philosophy*, pp. 576–77; Durant, "America's Age of Art," p. 20.

72. Adler, "Sleight of Hand," p. 298; Weiss, "Human, All Too Human,"

p. 286; Durant, *Story of Philosophy*, pp. 288, 333, 543; Bates, "Beauty of Philosophy," p. 899.

73. Durant, *Story of Philosophy*, p. 7, and, for example, pp. 49, 96–97.

74. Ibid., pp. 21, 65, 188, 277, 321.

75. Ibid., pp. 151, 164, 452.

76. Ibid., p. 66.

77. Neavill, "Modern Library Series," pp. 247–48; Weiss, "Human, All Too Human," p. 286.

78. Schuster, COHC, p. 58.

79. Ibid., pp. 2–69; Hellman, "Part II," p. 24; Schwed, *Turning the Pages*, p. 1.

80. Schuster, COHC, p. 69; Hellman, "Part I," p. 24; Madison, *Book Publishing*, pp. 346–54; Lehmann-Haupt, Wroth, and Silver, *Book in America*, pp. 343–44; Schwed, *Turning the Pages*, pp. 1–16.

81. Richard L. Simon to Henry Morton Robinson, Mar. 11, 1925, Catalogued Correspondence, Henry Morton Robinson Papers, Rare Book and Manuscript Library, Columbia University, New York, N.Y.; "ABC Plan for a Million Registered Book Readers," Production Files, Box 1, Max Lincoln Schuster Papers, Rare Book and Manuscript Library, Columbia University, New York, N.Y.; Max Lincoln Schuster to Richard L. Simon, May 24, 1931, Catalogued Correspondence, Richard L. Simon Papers, Rare Book and Manuscript Library, Columbia University, New York, N.Y. I was unable to examine the bulk of the Schuster Papers because of restrictions on its use. See also Hellman, "Part I," p. 22.

82. Hellman, "Part II," p. 28; Schwed, *Turning the Pages*, p. 96; Max Lincoln Schuster, diary entry, Dec. 27, 1926, Catalogued Correspondence, Simon Papers; Richard L. Simon, diary notes, 1924, Max Lincoln Schuster File, Catalogued Correspondence, Simon Papers. Knopf also used return postcards, but Simon and Schuster made the most of their responses by quoting readers' reactions in their advertisements. See Simon, "About Those Essandess Cards," pp. 1676–77.

83. Schuster, COHC, p. 39; "Book Publishing Plans," Box 25, Simon Papers.

84. Schuster, COHC, pp. 24, 72–75, 96, 152.

85. Ibid., p. 58; "An Editorial Research Report on The Inner Sanctum Library of Living Literature and Basic Books," (1946), Box 35, Simon Papers; Max Lincoln Schuster, "Memo to QH, etc., *re* The Inner Sanctum Library of Basic Books," June 21, 1935, and "Plan for Inner Sanctum Library of Basic Books," Folder "Miscellaneous," Production Files, Box 1, Schuster Papers; Max Lincoln Schuster to Jacques Barzun, Feb. 9, 1949, Catalogued Correspondence, Jacques Barzun Papers, Rare Book and Manuscript Library, Columbia University, New York, N.Y.

86. Schwed, *Turning the Pages*, p. 55; "20,000 Per Cent Increase," p. 51; Max Lincoln Schuster, "Memo to CPF *re* ABC Plan," Nov. 9, 1930, Production Files, Box 1, Schuster Papers; Schuster, "Memo to QH, etc."

87. Hellman, "Part I," pp. 22–23; Schwed, *Turning the Pages*, p. 46. Lewis Gannett once remarked to Schuster, "You have been, you are, you always will be, a newspaperman in the publishing business." Quoted in "Max Lincoln Schuster," p. 38.

88. Schwed, *Turning the Pages*, pp. 48–51, 55–62, 148, 182–83.

89. "20,000 Per Cent Increase," p. 100; "In the Book Market," p. 2036; Schuster, "Memo to CPF"; for example, *New York Times Book Review*, Dec. 4, 1927, p. 35.

90. Advertisement for *The Story of Philosophy*, *New York Times Book Review*, June 13, 1926, p. 25; James D. Hart, *Popular Book*, p. 239.

91. Advertisements for *The Story of Philosophy*, *New York Times Book Review*, July 4, 1926, p. 19, and *Saturday Review of Literature*, July 3, 1926, p. 912. See also *Books*, July 25, 1926, p. 16.

92. Schuster, COHC, pp. 90–91; advertisements for *The Story of Philosophy*, *New York Times Book Review*, July 4, 1926, p. 19; July 11, 1926, p. 16; and Aug. 22, 1926, p. 11.

93. Max Lincoln Schuster, diary entry, Dec. 27. 1926, Catalogued Correspondence, Simon Papers; advertisements for *The Story of Philosophy*, *New York Times Book Review*, Aug. 1, 1926, p. 21; Jan. 23, 1927, p. 15; and Feb. 27, 1927, p. 17.

94. Advertisement for *The Story of Philosophy*, *New York Times Book Review*, Nov. 13, 1927, p. 21; "From the Inner Sanctum," *Saturday Review of Literature*, Apr. 2, 1927, p. 708.

95. "From the Inner Sanctum," *Saturday Review of Literature*, Mar. 3, 1928, p. 660, and Apr. 2, 1927, p. 708.

96. Marchand, *Advertising the American Dream*, pp. 217–22, 349–59; Sussman, "See the Pretty Birdie," p. 195.

97. Bennett, "Philosophy Comes to Main Street," p. 667; Howard Mumford Jones, "Cult of Short-Cut Culture," p. 7; Rosenfield, *Portrait of a Philosopher*, pp. 143–44. Some years later, Canby assessed the "outline" vogue by condemning the "carelessness of popularizers," but he applauded the "man of life and courage" who offered an alternative to the "rigid specialists." Canby, "Popularizers," p. 349.

98. For example, Durant, "Ten Greatest Thinkers," pp. 7–9, 103–4, 106, 108, 110; "Modern Woman," pp. 418–29; "Breakdown of Marriage," pp. 4, 94, 97–98, 112; "I Want to Be Happy," pp. 80, 214–16; "Is Our Civilization Dying?," pp. 8–9, 77–78, 81–82; "One Hundred Best Books," pp. 26–28, 109, 112, 115–16, 118.

99. Durant, *Mansions*, pp. 255–78.

100. Emerson, "American Scholar," in *Works*, 1:91, 95; Durant, *Mansions*, pp. 254, 265, 642.

101. Durant and Durant, *Autobiography*, pp. 95, 207; Durant, *Mansions*, p. 351; Durant, *The Life of Greece*, p. vii.

102. Cullen Murphy estimated in 1985 that the Book-of-the-Month Club had

distributed at least 500,000 complete editions. Murphy, "Venerable Will," pp. 22, 24.

103. Hammerton, *Universal History*, 1:iii; James Harvey Robinson, *History of Western Europe*; Robinson and Beard, *Outlines of European History*.

104. Durant and Durant, *Autobiography*, pp. 67–68; Hendricks, *James Harvey Robinson*, p. 42; Durant, *Our Oriental Heritage*, p. xii.

105. White, *Social Thought in America*, pp. 47–58; Hendricks, *James Harvey Robinson*, p. 38; Durant, *Our Oriental Heritage*, pp. 127, 170.

106. Hendricks, *James Harvey Robinson*, pp. 39–40; Durant, *Adventures in Genius*, p. xvi; Plumb, "Some Personalities," pp. 3, 44.

107. Durant, *Our Oriental Heritage*, pp. 116, 934–38; Murphy, "Venerable Will," p. 22.

108. Murphy, "Venerable Will," p. 22; Durant, *Our Oriental Heritage*, pp. 67, 459, 823.

109. Durant, *Our Oriental Heritage*, p. 43; Durant, *The Life of Greece*, p. 470.

110. Murphy, "Venerable Will," pp. 22, 24; Durant, *Our Oriental Heritage*, pp. x, 265, 463.

111. Murphy, "Venerable Will," p. 24.

112. Mattingly, "Storytelling Historian," p. 20; Durant, *Caesar and Christ*, p. 232; Cousins, "Birthday Party," p. 4.

113. Durant and Durant, *Autobiography*, pp. 362–63; Breasted, "Interpreting the Orient," pp. 3–4, 14–15; Durant, "Letter to the Editor," pp. 9, 18; Brown, "Synthesis by Will Durant," p. 307; Mattingly, "Storytelling Historian," p. 20; Plumb, "Some Personalities," p. 3; Durant and Durant, "Durant History," pp. 36–37.

114. "From the Inner Sanctum," *Saturday Review of Literature*, July 20, 1935, p. 21, and Feb. 29, 1936, p. 21. *Our Oriental Heritage* was actually advertised by its series title, taking advantage of the interest in civilization. See advertisements for it in *New York Times Book Review*, Aug. 18, 1935, p. 12; Oct. 6, 1935, p. 19; and Nov. 17, 1935, p. 27.

115. Schwed, *Turning the Pages*, p. 94; advertisement for *The Life of Greece*, *New York Times Book Review*, Dec. 17, 1939, p. 11; Harris, "Drama of Consumer Desire," pp. 192–212.

116. Murphy, "Venerable Will," p. 22; Sylvia Spector Lamont, letter to the editor, *Atlantic*, Feb. 1986, p. 12.

117. Neavill, "Modern Library Series," pp. 243, 246.

118. Baker, "Will and Ariel Durant," p. 6; advertisements for *The Story of Philosophy*, *New York Times Book Review*, Aug. 22, 1926, p. 11, and *Saturday Review of Literature*, July 3, 1926, p. 912.

CHAPTER 6

1. "An American Fireside," Mar. 24, 1935, Motion Picture, Broadcasting, and Recorded Sound Division, Library of Congress, Washington, D.C. (hereaf-

ter cited as LC). "Mary Margaret McBride," July 2, 1947, LC, and "Listening to Learn," *Radio Guide*, Dec. 1, 1939, p. 17 (Canby). "The Reminiscences of Dan Golenpaul," interview by Neil Gold, 1964, Columbia University Oral History Collection, Butler Library, Columbia University, New York, N.Y., pp. 26–29 (hereafter cited as Golenpaul, COHC); "Views of Roosevelt and Thomas Debated," p. 10; "The Rudy Vallee Program," Nov. 2, 1933, LC; "Broun: Auto-Accessory Boys Make Room for Big News Man," p. 30 (Broun). "Reading—A Family Adventure," May 23, 1950, and broadcast for the Children's Book Council, May 26, 1950, Fisher Papers; Darrow, *Radio*, p. 44 (Fisher). "Radio Broadcasts Sell Books for Gill," p. 2473; McBride, *Out of the Air*, pp. 348–49; Margaret Cuthbert to Will Durant, Sept. 15, 1932, and Sept. 30, 1932, Box 9, Folder 21, and Script File, National Broadcasting Company Records, State Historical Society of Wisconsin, Madison, Wis. (hereafter cited as NBC Records) (Durant). "Let's Talk It Over," Mar. 24, 1939, LC; "Author-Critic Radio Program in New York," p. 2424 (Irita Van Doren).

2. Barnouw, *Golden Web*, p. 93; "Mary Margaret McBride," Oct. 17, 1945, LC; "Coming Events," p. 3; "Columbia University Alumni Day Dinner," Feb. 11, 1932, LC; "Columbia University Discussion Council," Mar. 18, 1939, LC; Morrison, *Chautauqua*, pp. 134–35; "Sunday Evening at Fannie Hurst's," ca. 1943, LC; John Erskine to Franklin Dunham, Sept. 13, 1934, Box 26, Folder 19, NBC Records (Erskine). "WOR Starts Radio Book Program," p. 1921; Kaplan, *Radio and Poetry*, p. 48; "Council's 'Words at War' Program Gets Commercial Sponsor," p. 32; list of commentators for "The World's Great Novels," Box 336, Folder 2, NBC Records (Carl Van Doren). Mark Van Doren, *Autobiography*, pp. 257–58 (Mark Van Doren). Kenneth W. Purdy, "Bright Young Man," p. 4 (Fadiman).

3. Frith, "Pleasures of the Hearth," pp. 101–23. In using the blanket terms "book" or "literary" programs, I am following the practice of the reference work *The Literary Marketplace*, which, beginning in 1940, listed book broadcasts, noting that some are "programs which deal with books; some are real critics, others are reviewers, some merely give informal chats." *Literary Marketplace*, 1940, p. 51.

4. Covert, "'We May Hear Too Much,'" p. 208; Seldes, *Great Audience*, p. 124; "How to Avoid the Mental Draft," p. 10.

5. Frith, "Pleasures of the Hearth," p. 121; Sullivan, "Will Radio Make the People the Government?," p. 23; Goldsmith and Lescarboura, *This Thing Called Broadcasting*, p. 104; *Broadcasting*, vol. 1, *To All Homes* (New York: National Broadcasting Co., 1935), p. 70, in Box 8, E. P. H. James Papers, State Historical Society of Wisconsin, Madison, Wis.

6. Frith, "Pleasures of the Hearth," pp. 112, 121–22; Skinner, "What the Well-Dressed Women are Reading," pp. 433–34.

7. The annual volumes of *The Literary Marketplace*, cited above, catalog book programs on the air in the 1940s, but no such compilation exists for the 1920s and 1930s. For a listing of network programs generally, see Summers,

Thirty-Year History. For the content of programs, see J. Fred MacDonald, *Don't Touch That Dial*, and Wertheim, *Radio Comedy*.

8. Barnouw, *Tower in Babel*, pp. 97–98, 173–75, 272–75; Czitrom, *Media and the American Mind*, p. 72; Darrow, *Radio*, pp. 19–20, 38, 42–44; Kaplan, *Radio and Poetry*, pp. 173, 215.

9. Darrow, *Radio*, pp. 115, 166, 223–38.

10. Ibid., pp. vii, 64–65; Czitrom, *Media and the American Mind*, pp. 102–12; Joy Elmer Morgan, "Radio and Education," pp. 71–72, and "National Culture," pp. 26–31. See also Douglas, *Inventing American Broadcasting*, pp. 303–14.

11. Joseph K. Hart, "Radiating Culture," p. 949; Mix, "Is Radio Standardizing the American Mind?," pp. 48–50.

12. Morris, *Not So Long Ago*, pp. 447–48, 450; Barnouw, *Tower in Babel*, p. 271; Barnouw, *Golden Web*, pp. 22–36; Banning, *Commercial Broadcasting Pioneer*, pp. 108–10, 118–20, 152–55, 259–63. The National Broadcasting Company was quick to publicize the opposition of both John Erskine and William Lyon Phelps to the proposed 25 percent reservation. See *Broadcasting*, vol. 2, *Music—Literature—Drama—Art* (New York: National Broadcasting Co., 1935), pp. 72–73, in Box 8, E. P. H. James Papers.

13. Marchand, *Advertising the American Dream*, pp. 89–92.

14. Morris, *Not So Long Ago*, p. 451; Barnouw, *Golden Web*, p. 71; *Broadcasting*, 1:33; James R. Angell to John F. Royal, Nov. 12, 1938, Box 93, Folder 57, NBC Records.

15. John F. Royal to Fred B. Bate, Oct. 5, 1937, and Bate to Royal, Oct. 21, 1937, Box 92, Folder 64, NBC Records; *Broadcasting*, 1:9–10, 12, 48; *Broadcasting*, 2:32. NBC also quoted Sir John Reith, director general of the BBC, on the danger of transmitting a "pontifical attitude" in radio education. *Broadcasting*, 1:11. The American network's use of Reith, however, distorted his strong commitment to "uplift." For a discussion of the tension between Reith's position and more "egalitarian" impulses during the 1930s, see LeMahieu, *Culture for Democracy*, pp. 290–91. On the BBC, see Briggs, *History of Broadcasting*.

16. Marchand, *Advertising the American Dream*, pp. 92–110; Seldes, *Great Audience*, p. 123; John F. Royal to Lenox R. Lohr, Sept. 18, 1937, Box 108, Folder 14, NBC Records; John F. Royal to David Sarnoff, Feb. 9, 1937, Box 108, Folder 9, NBC Records; Barnouw, *Golden Web*, pp. 29–36, 244–45; Woodford, "Radio—A Blessing or a Curse?," p. 169.

17. Lazarsfeld, *Radio and the Printed Page*, pp. 31–44. Lazarsfeld's findings were meant to allay the fears of publishers, librarians, and educators who, beginning in the early 1920s, worried that radio deterred people from reading. A short story from 1925 about a man who turns bookcases into radio cabinets, pronouncing them the furniture of the future, suggests some basis for those concerns. Ordway, "Books in the Air," p. 1153, 1284–87. Yet, as the *Saturday Review* noted in the mid-1930s (reversing its earlier skepticism), radio was just

as likely to win a new audience for literature. "Mobilizing Readers," p. 81. See also Lazarsfeld and Field, *People Look at Radio*, pp. 13–37.

18. Lazarsfeld, *Radio and the Printed Page*, p. 285; Rorty, "Free Air," p. 281; Lazarsfeld and Field, *People Look at Radio*, p. 73.

19. Lazarsfeld, *Radio and the Printed Page*, pp. 54, 93; Erskine, "Future of Broadcasting," pp. 150–53. Ironically, John F. Royal once commanded production personnel to tone down John Erskine's yelling on the air. See Royal to Wm. S. Rainey, Jan. 9, 1934, Box 26, Folder 19, NBC Records. See also Frank Ernest Hill, *Listen and Learn*, pp. 134–35.

20. Burrill, "Broadcasting," pp. 54–56.

21. "Broadcast Miscellany," Sept. 1925, p. 637; "Stress the Bookshop in Radio Reviews," pp. 2521–22.

22. "Broadcast Miscellany," Jan. 1927, p. 275.

23. "Jackson, Joseph Henry," pp. 710–11; "Hardy Perennial," p. 43; Bramble, "Selling Books by Radio," pp. 1772–74; Jackson, "Radio and Reading," pp. 2000–2004, and "Technique of Radio Book Reviews," p. 1891; "Person to Person," p. 19.

24. Halttunen, "From Parlor to Living Room," pp. 157–89.

25. "Radio Reviews Sell Books," pp. 1252–54; Salpeter, "Fatal to Review," pp. 2417–19.

26. Carr, "Fifteen Years of Radio Reviewing," p. 930.

27. As Marchand reports, the J. Walter Thompson advertising agency pioneered this technique in 1929 on crooner Rudy Vallee's variety show, when Vallee "listened" to a nightclub conversation about Fleischmann's yeast. Marchand, *Advertising the American Dream*, p. 106.

28. Script for "Round-Up," Literary Guild of America, May 7, 1929, Container 7, Columbia Broadcasting System Script Collection, Manuscript Division, Library of Congress, Washington, D.C. The Literary Guild's subsidiary for children's books, the Junior Guild, also broadcast a weekly program in 1930 on which a figure named "Guild Junior" dramatized "characters from popular juvenile books." "Junior Guild Broadcasts," p. 30.

29. Frith, "Pleasures of the Hearth," p. 122.

30. Beebe, "Billy Phelps of Yale," p. 29; Phelps, *Autobiography with Letters*; Reilly, "'Billy' Phelps of Yale," pp. 376–78; Bok, "Nobody Has Ever Said It," p. 18. For the size of Phelps's audience, see a letter from him to Mr. Pratt of Houghton Mifflin Company, Mar. 20, 1922, Phelps Papers, Houghton Library, Harvard University, Cambridge, Mass.

31. Phelps, *Appreciation*, p. 33.

32. Villard is quoted in "Detours of Billy Phelps," p. 44. See also Lewis, "William Lyon Phelps," pp. 3–4; Edgar Johnson, "Brother Cheeryble," pp. 53–54; Canby, "William Lyon Phelps," p. 12; Carl Van Doren, "Literary Spotlight," p. 357. As a Yale undergraduate, Dwight Macdonald wrote a scathing attack on Phelps and other "romantic lecturers" on the faculty, calling "ridiculous and distasteful" the "injection of the teacher's personality into every

phrase, every word uttered on the platform" and charging that instructors such as Phelps appealed to "precisely that element of the class who have no business to be in college." See Macdonald, "Romantic Lecturers," pp. 1–2. I am indebted to Robert Westbrook for telling me about Macdonald's essay and giving me a copy.

33. Kaufman, "Backstage in Broadcasting," p. 485; "Romberg," p. 28.

34. "The Swift Hour," Feb. 9, 1935, Feb. 16, 1935, Oct. 27, 1934, Mar. 16, 1935, and undated fragments, LC; Bakeless, "William Lyon Phelps," p. 268; Reilly, "'Billy' Phelps of Yale," p. 378.

35. "The Swift Hour," Feb. 2, 1935, Feb. 9, 1935, and undated fragment, LC.

36. Marchand, *Advertising the American Dream*, p. 105.

37. His comment especially complimented women, who, in light of the emphasis on food selection and household management in the program's commercials, appear to have been assumed to comprise the majority of the listeners to the "Swift Hour."

38. "The Swift Hour," Oct. 27, 1934, LC.

39. Advertisement for "Dr. Eliot's Five-Foot Shelf of Books," *Books*, Feb. 16, 1930, p. 17; Phelps, *As I Like It*, pp. 85–87, 145–52, and passim; advertisement for *As I Like It*, *Books*, June 27, 1926, p. 16; Phelps, *Yearbook*, p. 203; Phelps, *Autobiography with Letters*, pp. xvii–xxiii, 28–37.

40. Cantril and Allport, *Psychology of Radio*, p. 260.

41. "The Swift Hour," Feb. 23, 1935, LC.

42. Seldes, *Great Audience*, pp. 109–13; "The Swift Hour," undated fragment and Jan. 5, 1935, LC.

43. Barber, *Fellow of Infinite Jest*, p. 158; Lazarsfeld, *Radio and the Printed Page*, p. 298; Margaret O'Connor to Ernest LaPrade, Mar. 17, 1938, Box 108, Folder 20, NBC Records.

44. Taylor was perfect for this role. As he declared in 1934 about his radio opera presentations, "Now please don't be alarmed; we're not trying to educate anybody. On the contrary, we hope to prove that no one needs any special training in order to enjoy grand opera." See "Opera," p. 33. On the "Swift Studio Party," see J. K. Mason to David McKay, Oct. 5, 1935, Box 41, Folder 71, NBC Records.

45. Hoyt, *Alexander Woollcott*, pp. 24–33, 66–68, 77. See also Samuel Hopkins Adams, *A. Woollcott*.

46. Hoyt, *Alexander Woollcott*, pp. 132, 134, 171; Gaines, *Wit's End*.

47. Hoyt, *Alexander Woollcott*, p. 208; "Tune in on 'The Early Bookworm,'" pp. 1038–39.

48. Hoyt, *Alexander Woollcott*, pp. 216, 246, 303; "Four Best-Selling Personalities," p. 28; Benn Hall, "Radio Outlets," p. 926.

49. Hoyt, *Alexander Woollcott*, pp. 261–68; Kronenberger, "Down with Woollcott," pp. 720–21; Cowley and Canby, "Creating an Audience," p. 1132. Chamberlain is quoted in Hoyt, *Alexander Woollcott*, p. 264.

50. Kronenberger, "Down with Woollcott," pp. 720–21; Hoyt, *Alexander Woollcott*, p. 247.

51. "Town Crier," Oct. 6, 1933, Museum of Broadcasting Collection, New York, N.Y. (hereafter cited as MB).

52. Woollcott, "Reading and Writing," Dec. 1931, p. 53; "Town Crier," Oct. 6, 1933, MB.

53. Woollcott, "Reading and Writing," Dec. 1931, p. 53; John Mason Brown, Introduction to *The Portable Woollcott*, pp. xi, xxi–xxii.

54. Winterich, "This Is Woollcott . . . ," p. 505; "Town Crier," Oct. 6, 1933, MB.

55. Gaines, *Wit's End*, pp. 47–48.

56. Hoyt, *Alexander Woollcott*, pp. 276–77, 290; Marchand, *Advertising the American Dream*, p. 108.

57. See, for example, Woollcott, "Reading and Writing," Sept. 1931, p. 41; "Town Crier," p. 63.

58. Woollcott, "Books," p. 56; Woollcott, "Reading and Writing," Oct. 1931, p. 138; "Town Crier," Jan. 27, 1935, MB.

59. Hoyt, *Alexander Woollcott*, pp. 266, 293, 321.

60. Lazarsfeld, *Radio and the Printed Page*, p. 287; "Seaver Starts Book-of-the-Month Radio Service," p. 1301; "Book-of-the-Month Radio Scripts Popular," pp. 86–87. Two hundred thirty-one stations reported using the scripts in part; 171 used them in their entirety. In the late 1940s Seaver was succeeded by his assistant, Robin McKown. See also "The Ten Best Non-Fiction Books of 1937," Jan. 14, 1938, LC.

61. The children's shows included "The Battle of Books," a quiz program written by Ruth Hetzel Harshaw and Dilla MacBean and broadcast to elementary-school children in the Chicago public schools. Later, Harshaw also did "The Hobby Horse Presents," an interview program sponsored by the "Educational Service Bureau" of the Carson Pirie Scott department store that featured children's authors. The program was tied in with monthly authors' luncheons at the store, and autograph parties followed broadcasts. Ruth Hetzel Harshaw Papers, Manuscript Division, Library of Congress, Washington, D.C. See also "Department Store Methods," p. 2484.

Librarians' and teachers' groups were another source of children's programs. See "Radio Stories from Children's Books," p. 871, and "Broadcasting on Children's Reading," p. 32. In 1943 Boston students also reviewed books on the air as part of a program established by local publishers, booksellers, and the *Boston Herald*. "Boston Herald Junior Reviewers," p. 1644.

62. "Ed Fitzgerald's Broadcasts Sell Books," pp. 1658–69; Levinthal, "Daytime Radio Programs," pp. 2448–52; Lazarsfeld, *Radio and the Printed Page*, p. 280.

63. "Hardy Perennial," p. 43; Lazarsfeld, *Radio and the Printed Page*, pp. 284–85; "Books Are Different," p. 531; Benn Hall, "Radio Outlets," pp. 926, 931; Levinthal, "Daytime Radio Programs," p. 2448. Two exceptions

were E. P. Dutton, which presented an informal book talk in the mid-1940s, and Doubleday, which sponsored the "Doubleday Book Concert," offering "good music and news about books," in 1947. Both shows were on the *New York Times* station WQXR, the intellectual level of the audience thus making for a relatively safe investment. See "E. P. Dutton Starts Radio Program," pp. 1597–98, and "Doubleday Book Shops Put on Radio Program," p. 2169. In 1946 the Book-of-the-Month Club also sponsored "Let's Go to the Opera," giving away free copies of an opera "outline" to earn publicity for itself. But the venture was nonetheless considered an experiment. See "Recent Experiments," pp. 47–48. Additionally, in 1934 the National Association of Book Publishers, along with the National Home Library Foundation, supported "The American Fireside" hour on NBC, the show on which the *Saturday Review* staff appeared in 1935. "Fireside Hour," p. 1917.

64. Stuart Hawkins, "Broadcasting and Literature," pp. 127–28; Waller, *Radio*, p. 176.

65. Weeks, *In Friendly Candor*, pp. 56, 262, 287, 290, and passim; Weeks, *My Green Age*, p. 318; Warren, "'Weeks'—of the *Atlantic*," pp. 448–51. Weeks took as heartening signs of the American public's receptivity to his efforts the spread of "great books" discussion groups and the popularity of a new version of *The Outline of History*. Weeks, *In Friendly Candor*, pp. 265, 290. For the role the *Atlantic Monthly* played among "women who wanted to warn people they were cultured," see Rascoe, *Before I Forget*, p. 321.

66. Warren, "'Weeks'—of the *Atlantic*," p. 449; Lazarsfeld, *Radio and the Printed Page*, p. 279; Memo to John F. Royal, June 21, 1939, Box 94, Folder 60, NBC Records; L. H. Titterton to E. A. Weeks, Apr. 17, 1939, and Weeks to Titterton, Apr. 21, 1939, Box 70, Folder 38, NBC Records; James R. Angell to John F. Royal, May 25, 1939, Box 70, Folder 38, NBC Records; Weeks, *Writers and Friends*, p. 19; Weeks, *My Green Age*, p. 324.

67. Weeks, *Writers and Friends*, p. 20.

68. Thomas, "Meet Mr. Weeks," p. 26; Lazarsfeld, *Radio and the Printed Page*, p. 279.

69. Thomas, "Meet Mr. Weeks," p. 26.

70. "Meet Edward Weeks," Nov. 12, 1940, LC.

71. Weeks, *Writers and Friends*, pp. 20–24.

72. "'Speaking of Books' Radio Program," p. 2298–99; "Amateur Meets an Audience," p. 72.

73. "Jan Valtin Explains," pp. 213–14. See also "Wartime Washington," pp. 521–28; "Century of Thrills and Chills," pp. 638–44; "They Stopped Hitler," pp. 285–91; and "There Is No Formula to Life," pp. 609–15.

74. "Amateur Meets an Audience," p. 72; "Author Talks Back," p. 61; "The Author Meets the Critics," Feb. 19, 1945, LC.

75. "Author Talks Back," p. 61; "Stone, Producer of 'Author Meets the Critics,'" p. 3019; "Literary Guild Drops Books," p. 290; Miller, "Your Regular Moderator," pp. 40–45; "Author Meets Network," p. 52. Another New York

spin-off, the short-lived "Balancing the Books," used amateur reviewers. "Amateur Critics Meet Authors," p. 2042. The NBC Records at the State Historical Society of Wisconsin contain a large number of "The Author Meets the Critics" broadcasts from 1947–50.

76. "Radio Notes," Apr. 17, 1948, p. 1690.

77. "Frederick, John T(owner)," pp. 309–11; Waller, *Radio*, p. 315; "Radio Reviewer's Christmas List," p. 2186.

78. In the late 1940s, when Frederick was no longer host, the program was suspended for the football and holiday seasons, returning to the air in January. "Radio Notes," Sept. 13, 1947, p. 1158, and Jan. 17, 1948, p. 217.

79. "Of Men and Books," transcript, Oct. 10 and 15, 1939, p. 4, University Archives, Northwestern University, Evanston, Ill.; "Of Men and Books," Dec. 26, 1939, LC; "Listening to Learn," Feb. 16, 1940, p. 17. Transcripts appear as well in *Northwestern University on the Air*, vols. 1–3 (Evanston, Ill.: Northwestern University, 1941–44).

80. "Listening to Learn," Nov. 17, 1939, p. 15; "Of Men and Books," transcript, Oct. 10 and 15, 1939, p. 4; "Of Men and Books," Dec. 26, 1939, LC; "Of Men and Books," Dec. 27, 1941, *Northwestern University on the Air*, 1:5.

81. "Radio Reviewer's Christmas List," p. 2186; "Of Men and Books," Dec. 26, 1939, LC.

82. "Radio Reviewer's Christmas List," p. 2186; "Of Men and Books," CBS Script Collection; "Radio Notes," Apr. 17, 1948, p. 1690; "Leon Levine Will Produce," p. 434.

83. "The Reminiscences of Lyman L. Bryson," interview by Frank Ernest Hill, 1951, Columbia University Oral History Collection, Butler Library, Columbia University, New York, N.Y., pp. 161–63 (hereafter cited as Bryson, COHC); Mark Van Doren, *Autobiography*, pp. 257–58; Sproul, "Dialing Civilization," p. 20; Kaplan, *Radio and Poetry*, p. 220.

84. Bryson, COHC, p. 162. Bryson reported that Barr also did not get along with Douglas Coulter, another executive in CBS's program department. Bryson, COHC, p. 161.

85. Mark Van Doren to Scott Buchanan, Sept. 30, 1940, in *Selected Letters of Mark Van Doren*, pp. 143–44; "How to Make People Read," p. 58.

86. Cairns, Tate, and Van Doren, *Invitation to Learning*, pp. 3–18, 162, and passim; Mark Van Doren, *New Invitation to Learning*; Mark Van Doren, "Listener's Guide," pp. 3–4.

87. Cairns, Tate, and Van Doren, *Invitation to Learning*, p. 80.

88. "Twenty-Seven Great Books," p. 6; Squires, *Allen Tate*, p. 155; Cairns, Tate, and Van Doren, *Invitation to Learning*, pp. 185–97.

89. Cairns, Tate, and Van Doren, *Invitation to Learning*, pp. xiii–xviii, 63; Stevens, "Scholars Discourse," p. 14.

90. Mark Van Doren, "High in the Air," IX, p. 12.

91. Ibid.; Stevens, "Scholars Discourse," p. 14.

92. Mark Van Doren to Allen Tate, Jan. 9, 1941; Mark Van Doren to Hunt-

ington Cairns, May 29, 1941; Mark Van Doren to Allen Tate and Huntington Cairns, Sept. 30, 1941, in *Selected Letters of Mark Van Doren*, pp. 145, 147, 149.

93. Mark Van Doren to Scott Buchanan, Oct. 20, 1942; Mark Van Doren to Allen Tate, Oct. 27, 1942, in *Selected Letters of Mark Van Doren*, pp. 154–55; Lohman, "Radio Row," Sept. 29, 1946, II, p. 9.

94. Sproul, "Dialing Civilization," p. 20; Deitch, "About 'Invitation to Learning,'" II, p. 9; Bryson, "Highbrow Experiment," p. 9; Lohman, "Radio Row," Feb. 2, 1947, II, p. 11; "Hoover Reveals Presidents Fish," p. 1.

95. Sproul, "Dialing Civilization," p. 19; Bryson, "Highbrow Experiment," p. 9. Bryson reported that the " 'Pulse of New York' figures have been as high as 3.5, which is a high rating for any show that is on the air at noon on Sundays." He added that "Hooper averages for the country run lower but they also get up occasionally to three or more." He also noted that the program was heard "in about 21 per cent of the A and B, the top level homes" on a "roughly reliable socio-economic scale."

96. Benn Hall, "Radio Outlets," p. 931; "Books on Radio Programs," Oct. 15, 1949, p. 1725; "Radio Notes," Apr. 17, 1948, p. 1690. LC has representative Armed Forces Radio broadcasts, including "Invitation to Learning." Sugrue's program began in 1946 on WINS, turned into a book interview show the next year, and subsequently moved from Saturday night to a Sunday morning time slot. "Radio Notes," Nov. 1, 1947, p. 2161. Other local examples included the "book review and literary chitchat" broadcast over station WBML, Macon, Ga., in 1947; KGO San Francisco's "Book Time," a new review program of 1948; and a similar combination of reviews and literary gossip launched in Denver the same year. See "Radio Notes," Dec. 6, 1947, p. 2533; "Books on Forthcoming Radio Programs," p. 139; and "Books and Radio," p. 2607.

97. McBride, *Out of the Air*, p. 367; "Beatty Radio Program," pp. 266–67.

98. Gerard Willem Van Loon, *Story of Hendrik Willem Van Loon*, pp. 270, 309, 312, 336–37; "Recommended Programs," p. 11; "Designed for Listening," p. 9. See also Hendrik Willem Van Loon, *Air-storming*, a collection of broadcast transcripts. About the book, NBC vice-president John F. Royal declared, "To my knowledge, this is the first time in the history of radio in this country or elsewhere that a publisher has solicited a series of radio talks to publish in book form." Royal to Richard C. Patterson, Jr., Nov. 9, 1935, Box 42, Folder 40, NBC Records. Recordings of several Van Loon broadcasts from the late 1930s and early 1940s are in the Van Loon Collection at Cornell University. On Van Loon's popularity, see Margaret Cuthbert to John F. Royal, June 10, 1935, Box 42, Folder 40, NBC Records. Correspondence from 1936 and 1937 that reveals Van Loon's volatility as a performer is also in the NBC Records, especially Box 57, Folder 57.

99. "Adventure in Reading," May 16, 1938, LC; "Treasures Next Door," CBS Script Collection; "Innovation in Broadcast of 'Great Novels' Series," Dec. 1944, Box 220, Folder 42, NBC Records. In addition, Boston booksellers sponsored "Book Theatre." Philadelphia's WFIL had a similar dramatization

for children, "The Magic of Books." In Chicago Ruth Harshaw continued her activities in children's broadcasting by hosting "Carnival of Books," beginning in 1949; recordings of some broadcasts are in the Library of Congress. Nationally, the Junior League made dramatic scripts entitled "Books Bring Adventure" available to local stations in the mid-1940s. See Lazarsfeld, *Radio and the Printed Page*, p. 286; "Radio Notes," Oct. 4, 1947, p. 1782; "Gloria Chandler Recordings," p. 2219.

100. "Mercury Theater of the Air," July 11, 1938, LC. In 1939 Welles was also associated with the Campbell Playhouse, which, in the fashion of the Book-of-the-Month Club, used a jury to pick a book suitable for dramatization. "Orson Welles Begins Radio Book Series," p. 956. The handbook accompanying "The World's Great Novels" for 1944–45, written by Herbert Gorman, is in Box 336, Folder 2, NBC Records. There is a great deal of material on "NBC University Theatre" in the NBC Records, primarily in the papers of Margaret Cuthbert, the network official responsible for the show. On the advisory council, see Lionel Trilling to Margaret Cuthbert, Mar. 28, 1949, Box 335, Folder 26; memos from Fadiman in Box 335, Folder 24; and Margaret Cuthbert to Dr. Harvey C. Webster, Aug. 9, 1948, Box 335, Folder 23, NBC Records. Amy Loveman also served on the council, and Canby was a commentator for the dramatization of *Huckleberry Finn*. In 1950 the *Saturday Review of Literature* had a tie-in to "NBC Theatre": each week it ran an article "re-evaluating" the novel dramatized on the air. See "SRL Series Ties In," pp. 1389–90.

101. Lazarsfeld, *Radio and the Printed Page*, p. 291; Kaplan, *Radio and Poetry*, p. 207; "Voice of the Listener," p. 19; "So You Want to Dream?," p. 20; "Between the Bookends," Dec. 11, 1938, and Jan. 19, 1942, LC; "Listening to Learn," Oct. 27, 1939, p. 14; Phillips Carlin to James R. Angell, Apr. 25, 1939, Box 66, Folder 44, NBC Records. Another show of the early 1940s that offered readings of sentimental poetry was "Tony Won's Scrapbook," broadcast on NBC. The Oct. 5, Dec. 2, Dec. 9, and Dec. 25, 1941, broadcasts are at LC.

102. Memo beginning "What Has Been Done," Box 66, Folder 44, NBC Records; Blevins Davis to James Rowland Angell, Apr. 6, 1939, Box 66, Folder 44, NBC Records; "Join Ted Malone's 'Pilgrimage of Poetry,'" pp. 24–26; "Pilgrimage of Poetry," Oct. 29, 1939, and Apr. 7, 1940, LC.

103. For an early example, see Killikelly, *Curious Questions in History*.

104. Three months later, following the publication of a companion volume, sales of the two books totaled approximately 250,000 copies. Harris, "Lay Mastery in America," p. 27.

105. Braley, *I Ought to Know That*; Monahan and Davis, *Guess Again*; Adams [F.P.A.] and Hansen, *Answer This One*.

106. Hutchens, "Who Thought Up the Quiz Show?," pp. 12–13, 31; J. Fred MacDonald, *Don't Touch That Dial*, pp. 48–50; "Jim M'Williams," p. 15.

107. "Q. & A.," p. 32. *Radio Guide* implied that a Dr. Craig Earle was the professor, identifying him as "one of the first to bring the quiz program to national radio fame." "Listening to Learn," June 27, 1939, p. 40.

108. Hutchens, "Who Thought Up the Quiz Show?," p. 31; Harris, "Lay Mastery in America," pp. 25–26. See also Feldman, *Whatever Happened to the Quiz Kids?*. Representative recordings of quiz programs in the Library of Congress collection include, in addition to the "Information, Please!" broadcasts cited below, "Dr. I. Q.," Dec. 8, 1941; "True or False," June 9, 1941, and Dec. 8, 1941; "The Colgate Askit Baskit," Sept. 21, 1939; "Uncle Jim's Question Bee," Feb. 19, 1938; "Quiz Kids," June 11, 1941; "Treasure Chest," June 25, 1940, and Dec. 24, 1940; "Battle of the Sexes," Mar. 19, 1940; and "Pot 'O Gold," Apr. 23, 1940.

109. "Get in the Quiz Game," p. 8; Hutchens, "Who Thought Up the Quiz Show?," p. 12; "Ignorance Loves Company," p. 64.

110. Hutchens, "Who Thought Up the Quiz Show?," p. 12.

111. Lazarsfeld, *Radio and the Printed Page*, pp. 67–81.

112. The most book-oriented quiz of all was probably "Let's Balance the Books," which Louis Untermeyer hosted in 1947 and 1948 over WNEW, New York, with sponsorship from the *Saturday Review*. The show subjected three authors or critics to listeners' questions about old or new books. It never gained the following that "Information, Please!" enjoyed, however. "Saturday Review and WNEW," p. 2113. Neither did "Author, Author," a short-story quiz of the late 1930s on the Mutual network. Lazarsfeld, *Radio and the Printed Page*, p. 279.

113. Golenpaul, COHC, p. 26; "Danger: Brains at Work," pp. 1, 14, 19; Kenneth W. Purdy, "Bright Young Man," p. 4; Hutchens, "Who Thought Up the Quiz Show?," p. 12.

114. Lazarsfeld, *Radio and the Printed Page*, p. 285; Mark Van Doren, "Jewish Students," p. 265; Golenpaul, COHC, pp. 110, 129. For Fadiman's career generally, see especially Katz, "Afternoon with Clifton Fadiman," pp. 30–32, 57; Fadiman interview.

115. "Information, Please!," May 17, 1938, LC; Fadiman, *Party of One*, pp. 295, 306.

116. "Danger: Brains at Work," p. 1.

117. Golenpaul, *Information, Please!*, pp. vi, 5.

118. Seldes, *Great Audience*, p. 112; Fadiman, *Party of One*, p. 301.

119. Cousins, "S.R.L. Award," p. 12. See also "Medal of Merit," p. 2.

120. "Information, Please, Yes," p. 8; Phillips Carlin to Dan Golenpaul, Oct. 14, 1936, Box 61, Folder 66, NBC Records; Hutchens, "Who Thought Up the Quiz Show?," p. 31.

121. Gerard Willem Van Loon, *Story of Hendrik Willem Van Loon*, p. 336; Franklin P. Adams, "Inside 'Information, Please!,'" p. 257.

122. Kenneth W. Purdy, "Bright Young Man," p. 1.

123. Fadiman, *Party of One*, pp. 254–55.

124. Fadiman, *Reading I've Liked*, pp. xiv, xxxvii–xxxviii, lviii–lxi; "Fadiman Quits," p. 46.

125. Fadiman, *Party of One*, pp. 23–26.

372 | NOTES TO PAGES 326-29

126. Coser, Kadushin, and Powell, *Books*, pp. 41–50; Fadiman, *Party of One*, pp. 359–60, 363.

127. Fadiman, *Any Number Can Play*, pp. 45–46; Gordon, *Educational Television*, pp. 1–16, 29–49; Barnouw, *Image Empire*, pp. 25–28; "Philco Television Playhouse," pp. 661–62.

128. Mark Van Doren to Charles Van Doren, July 23, 1952, in *Selected Letters of Mark Van Doren*, p. 194; Anderson, *Television Fraud*, pp. 53–54, 70; *Time*, Feb. 11, 1957 cover; Goldman, *Crucial Decade*, pp. 316–24.

129. Anderson, *Television Fraud*, p. 70. See also Tedlow, "Intellect on Television," pp. 483–95.

130. Anderson, *Television Fraud*, p. 148. For Mark Van Doren's reaction to the episode, see Mark Van Doren to Joseph Wood and Marcelle Krutch, Nov. 21, 1959; Mark Van Doren to Margaret Clark, Nov. 29, 1959; and Mark Van Doren to Thomas Merton, Jan. 26, 1962, in *Selected Letters of Mark Van Doren*, pp. 226–27, 234.

131. Radway, "Book-of-the-Month Club," p. 273.

132. Alterman, "Not So Great," pp. 584–85.

BIBLIOGRAPHY

MANUSCRIPT AND RECORDED SOUND
COLLECTIONS CITED

Burlington, Vt.
  Special Collections, University of Vermont
    Dorothy Canfield Fisher Papers
Cambridge, Mass.
  Houghton Library, Harvard University
    William Lyon Phelps Papers
Chicago, Ill.
  University Archives, University of Chicago
    Robert M. Hutchins Papers
    Presidents' Papers
Evanston, Ill.
  University Archives, Northwestern University
    "Of Men and Books" Transcripts
Ithaca, N.Y.
  University Archives, Cornell University
    Hendrik Willem Van Loon Papers
Madison, Wis.
  State Historical Society of Wisconsin
    E. P. H. James Papers
    National Broadcasting Company Records
New Haven, Conn.
  Manuscripts and Archives, Yale University
    Richard Kluger Papers
New York, N.Y.
  Museum of Broadcasting Collection
  Oral History Collection, Butler Library, Columbia University
  Rare Book and Manuscript Library, Columbia University
    Jacques Barzun Papers
    Helen Worden Erskine Papers
    John Erskine Papers
    Allan Nevins Papers
    Henry Morton Robinson Papers

Max Lincoln Schuster Papers
Richard L. Simon Papers
Princeton, N.J.
   Rare Books and Special Collections, Princeton University
      Carl Van Doren Papers
Syracuse, N.Y.
   George Arents Research Library, Syracuse University
      Edmund B. Chaffee Papers
Urbana, Ill.
   University Archives, University of Illinois at Urbana-Champaign
      Stuart Pratt Sherman Papers
   Rare Book Room, University of Illinois at Urbana-Champaign
      H. G. Wells Papers
Washington, D.C.
   Manuscript Division, Library of Congress
      Columbia Broadcasting System Script Collection
      Ruth Hetzel Harshaw Papers
      Reid Family Papers
      Irita Van Doren Papers
      William Allen White Papers
   Motion Picture, Broadcasting, and Recorded Sound Division, Library of
   Congress

PUBLISHED WORKS CITED

Aaron, Daniel. "An Informal Letter to the Editor." *Daedalus* 112 (Winter 1983): 27–33.

"Abstract of the Discussion at the February Meeting of the College Faculty." *Columbia College Gazette*, May 1917, pp. 1–4.

Adams, Franklin P. "Inside 'Information, Please!'" *Harper's*, Feb. 1942, pp. 252–57.

Adams, Franklin P. [F.P.A.], and Harry Hansen, comps. *Answer This One: Questions for Everybody*. New York: E. J. Cole, 1927.

Adams, James Truslow. *Our Business Civilization: Some Aspects of American Culture*. New York: Albert and Charles Boni, 1929.

———. "Reviewing in America." *Saturday Review of Literature*, Feb. 7, 1931, pp. 582–83.

Adams, Samuel Hopkins. *A. Woollcott: His Life and His World*. New York: Reynal and Hitchcock, 1945.

Adler, Mortimer J. *How to Read a Book: The Art of Getting a Liberal Education*. New York: Simon and Schuster, 1940.

———. *Philosopher-at-Large: An Intellectual Autobiography*. New York: Macmillan, 1977.

——. "Sleight of Hand." *Nation*, Sept. 29, 1926, pp. 298–99.

Agnew, Jean-Christophe. "Coming Up for Air: Consumer Culture in Historical Perspective." *Intellectual History Newsletter* 12 (1990): 3–21.

Allen, James Sloan. *The Romance of Commerce and Culture*. Chicago: University of Chicago Press, 1983.

Alterman, Eric. "Not So Great." *Nation*, Nov. 19, 1990, pp. 584–85.

"Amateur Critics Meet Authors on New Radio Program." *Publishers' Weekly*, Nov. 3, 1945, p. 2042.

"Amateur Meets an Audience." *Time*, June 2, 1947, p. 72.

"The American College." *New Republic*, Oct. 25, 1922, pp. 208–9.

Anderson, Kent. *Television Fraud: The History and Implications of the Quiz Show Scandals*. Westport, Conn.: Greenwood Press, 1978.

Angoff, Charles. "Culture at Cut Rates." *New Republic*, Aug. 15, 1955, pp. 18–19.

Arnold, Matthew. *Culture and Anarchy*. Edited by J. Dover Wilson. Cambridge: Cambridge University Press, 1969.

——. "The Function of Criticism at the Present Time." In *Essays in Criticism*, pp. 1–41. New York: Macmillan, 1883.

Ashmore, Harry S. *Unseasonable Truths: The Life of Robert Maynard Hutchins*. Boston: Little, Brown, 1989.

"Author-Critic Radio Program in New York." *Publishers' Weekly*, Dec. 19, 1942, p. 2424.

"Author Meets Network." *Newsweek*, July 12, 1948, p. 52.

"Author Talks Back." *Newsweek*, Apr. 1, 1946, p. 61.

Babbitt, Irving. *Literature and the American College*. Boston: Houghton Mifflin, 1908.

——. "Matthew Arnold." *Nation*, Aug. 2, 1917, pp. 117–21.

Baehr, Harry W., Jr. *The New York Tribune since the Civil War*. New York: Dodd, Mead, 1936.

Bailyn, Bernard, David Brion Davis, David Herbert Donald, John L. Thomas, Robert H. Wiebe, and Gordon S. Wood. *The Great Republic*. Lexington, Mass.: D. C. Heath, 1977.

Bakeless, John. "William Lyon Phelps, Book-Booster." *American Mercury*, Nov. 1935, pp. 265–72.

Baker, John F. "Will and Ariel Durant." *Publishers Weekly*, Nov. 24, 1975, pp. 6–7.

Banning, William Peck. *Commercial Broadcasting Pioneer: The WEAF Experiment*. Cambridge: Harvard University Press, 1946.

Barber, Florence Holladay. *Fellow of Infinite Jest*. New Haven: Payne and Lane Printers, 1939.

Barnouw, Erik. *The Golden Web: A History of Broadcasting in the United States*. Vol. 2, *1933 to 1953*. New York: Oxford University Press, 1968.

——. *The Image Empire: A History of Broadcasting in the United States*. Vol. 3, *From 1953*. New York: Oxford University Press, 1970.

————. *A Tower in Babel: A History of Broadcasting in the United States.* Vol. 1, *To 1933.* New York: Oxford University Press, 1961.

Barzun, Jacques. *Teacher in America.* Boston: Little, Brown, 1945.

Bates, Ernest Sutherland. "The Beauty of Philosophy." *Saturday Review of Literature,* July 3, 1926, p. 899.

Beard, Charles A. "The Story of Mankind." *New Republic,* Dec. 21, 1921, p. 105.

"Beatty Radio Program Covers Many Books." *Publishers' Weekly,* July 24, 1943, pp. 266–67.

Becker, Carl. *Everyman His Own Historian: Essays on History and Politics.* New York: Appleton-Century-Crofts, 1935.

Becker, May Lamberton. "The Choir Invisible of the Reader's Guide." *New York Herald Tribune Books,* Sept. 25, 1949, pp. 73–74.

————. "Reader's Guide." *New York Herald Tribune Books,* Sept. 10, 1933, p. 21; Sept. 17, 1933, p. 21; Sept. 24, 1933, p. 25; Oct. 1, 1933, p. 20.

Beebe, Lucius. "Billy Phelps of Yale." *Reader's Digest,* Feb. 1939, pp. 29–33.

Bell, Daniel. "Beyond Modernism, Beyond Self." In *Art, Politics and Will: Essays in Honor of Lionel Trilling,* edited by Quentin Anderson, Stephen Donadio, and Steven Marcus, pp. 213–53. New York: Basic Books, 1977.

————. *The Reforming of General Education: The Columbia College Experience in Its National Setting.* New York: Columbia University Press, 1966.

Belloc, Hilaire. *A Companion to Mr. Wells's "Outline of History."* San Francisco: Ecclesiastical Supply Association, 1927.

Bender, Thomas. *New York Intellect.* New York: Knopf, 1987.

Bennett, Charles A. "Philosophy Comes to Main Street." *Independent,* Dec. 11, 1926, pp. 667–68.

Berger, Meyer. *The Story of the New York Times, 1851–1951.* New York: Simon and Schuster, 1951.

Best, Marshall A. "In Books, They Call It Revolution." *Daedalus* 92 (Winter 1963): 30–41.

Blair, Karen J. *The Clubwoman as Feminist: True Womanhood Redefined, 1868–1914.* New York: Holmes and Meier, 1980.

Blake, Casey Nelson. *Beloved Community: The Cultural Criticism of Randolph Bourne, Van Wyck Brooks, Waldo Frank, and Lewis Mumford.* Chapel Hill: University of North Carolina Press, 1990.

————. "The Young Intellectuals and the Culture of Personality." *American Literary History* 1 (Fall 1989): 510–31.

Bledstein, Burton. *The Culture of Professionalism: The Middle Class and the Development of Higher Education in America.* New York: Norton, 1976.

Bode, Carl. *The American Lyceum: Town Meeting of the Mind.* New York: Oxford University Press, 1956.

Bodenheim, Maxwell. "Criticism in America." *Saturday Review of Literature*, June 6, 1925, pp. 801–2.

Bok, Edward W. "Nobody Has Ever Said It until Billy Phelps Says It." *Ladies' Home Journal*, Feb. 1925, p. 18.

"The Book Clubs." *New Republic*, Sept. 30, 1946, pp. 420–21.

"The Book-of-the-Month Club." New York: Book-of-the-Month Club, 1927.

Book-of-the-Month Club News, Oct. 1926, Nov. 1927, June 1929, Jan. 1930, July 1931, Dec. 1931, Apr. 1932, May 1934, Apr. 1949, Dec. 1949.

"Book-of-the-Month Radio Scripts Popular." *Publishers' Weekly*, July 12, 1941, pp. 86–87.

"Book Reviewing à la Mode." *Nation*, Aug. 17, 1911, pp. 139–40.

"Books and Radio." *Publishers' Weekly*, June 26, 1948, p. 2607.

"Books Are Different." *Publishers' Weekly*, Aug. 5, 1933, p. 531.

"'Books' Covers the World of Books." *Publishers' Weekly*. Sept. 30, 1939, pp. 1338–47.

"Books on Forthcoming Radio Programs." *Publishers' Weekly*, Jan. 10, 1948, p. 139.

"Books on Radio Programs." *Publishers' Weekly*, Oct. 15, 1949, p. 1725.

Boorstin, Daniel J. *The Image: A Guide to Pseudo-Events in America*. New York: Harper Colophon Books, 1964.

"Boston Herald Junior Reviewers Meet Success on Radio." *Publishers' Weekly*, Apr. 24, 1943, p. 1644.

Bourne, Randolph. *The Letters of Randolph Bourne: A Comprehensive Edition*. Edited by Eric J. Sandeen. Troy, N.Y.: Whitston Publishing, 1981.

———. "Our Cultural Humility" and "The Professor." In *History of a Literary Radical and Other Essays*, edited by Van Wyck Brooks, pp. 31–43, 91–97. New York: B. W. Huebsch, 1920.

———. "The War and the Intellectuals." In *The War and the Intellectuals: Collected Essays, 1915–1919*, edited by Carl Resek, pp. 3–14. New York: Harper Torchbooks, 1964.

Boyd, Ernest. "Ku Klux Kriticism." *Nation*, June 20, 1923, pp. 723–24.

Boyer, Richard O. "The Story of Everything—I." *New Yorker*, Mar. 20, 1943, pp. 24–28.

———. "The Story of Everything—II." *New Yorker*, Mar. 27, 1943, pp. 24–36.

Braley, Berton. *I Ought to Know That*. New York: Appleton, 1927.

Bramble, David. "Selling Books by Radio." *Publishers' Weekly*, Nov. 5, 1932, pp. 1772–74.

Breasted, James H. "Interpreting the Orient." *Saturday Review of Literature*, July 13, 1935, pp. 3–4, 14–15.

Brichford, Maynard. "Notes from the Archives." *Laputa Gazette and Faculty News*, University of Illinois at Urbana-Champaign, Mar. 20, 1969.

Briggs, Asa. *The History of Broadcasting in the United Kingdom.* 4 vols. London: Oxford University Press, 1961–79.

"Broadcasting on Children's Reading." *Publishers' Weekly*, July 6, 1940, p. 32.

"Broadcast Miscellany." *Radio Broadcast*, Sept. 1925, pp. 637–38, and Jan. 1927, p. 275.

Brodbeck, May. "Philosophy in America, 1900–1950." In *American Non-Fiction, 1900–1950*, by May Brodbeck, James Gray, and Walter Metzger, pp. 3–94. Chicago: Henry Regnery, 1952.

Brodhead, Richard H. *The School of Hawthorne.* New York: Oxford University Press, 1986.

Bromfield, Louis. "Gertrude Stein, Experimenter with Words." *New York Herald Tribune Books*, Sept. 3, 1933, pp. 1–2.

Brooks, Van Wyck. "America's Coming-of-Age." In *Three Essays on America*, pp. 13–112. New York: E. P. Dutton, 1934.

———. *Days of the Phoenix: The Nineteen Twenties I Remember.* New York: Dutton, 1957.

———. "The Evolution of a Critic." *New York Herald Tribune Books*, Apr. 18, 1926, p. 5.

———. "Letters and Leadership." In *Three Essays on America*, pp. 113–90. New York: E. P. Dutton, 1934.

———. "On Creating a Usable Past." In *Van Wyck Brooks: The Early Years: A Selection from His Works, 1908–1921*, edited by Claire Sprague, pp. 219–26. New York: Harper Torchbooks, 1968.

"Broun: Auto-Accessory Boys Make Room for Big News Man." *Newsweek*, Feb. 20, 1937, p. 30.

Broun, Heywood Hale. *Whose Little Boy Are You?: A Memoir of the Broun Family.* New York: St. Martin's/Marek, 1983.

Brown, John Mason. Introduction to *The Portable Woollcott*, selected by Joseph Hennessey. New York: Viking, 1946.

Brown, W. Norman. "Synthesis by Will Durant." *Nation*, Sept. 11, 1935, p. 307.

Brownell, W. C. "The 'Nation' from the Inside." *Nation*, July 8, 1918, pp. 42–44.

Bryson, Lyman. "A Highbrow Experiment." *New York Times*, Nov. 9, 1947, II, p. 9.

Burrill, Edgar White. "Broadcasting the World's Best Literature." *Radio Broadcast*, Dec. 1922, pp. 54–56.

Bush, Douglas. "Pale-Eyed Priests and Happy Journalists." *Bookman*, Nov. 1932, pp. 699–702.

Bushman, Richard L. "American High-Style and Vernacular Cultures." In *Colonial British America: Essays in the New History of the Early Modern Era*, edited by Jack P. Greene and J. R. Pole, pp. 345–83. Baltimore: Johns Hopkins University Press, 1984.

Cady, Edwin Harrison. *The Gentleman in America: A Literary Study in American Culture*. Syracuse: Syracuse University Press, 1949.

Cain, William E. *F. O. Matthiessen and the Politics of Criticism*. Madison: University of Wisconsin Press, 1988.

Cairns, Huntington, Allen Tate, and Mark Van Doren. *Invitation to Learning*. New York: New Home Library, 1942.

Calkins, Earnest Elmo. *Business the Civilizer*. Boston: Little, Brown, 1928.

Canby, Henry Seidel. *American Estimates*. London: Jonathan Cape, 1929.

————. *American Memoir*. Boston: Houghton Mifflin, 1947.

————. "Blurbing." *Saturday Review of Literature*, Nov. 24, 1934, p. 308.

————. "Books Are News." *Saturday Review of Literature*, Jan. 30, 1926, p. 521.

————. *College Sons and College Fathers*. New York: Harper and Brothers, 1915.

————. *Definitions: Essays in Contemporary Criticism*. New York: Harcourt, Brace, 1922.

————. *Definitions: Essays in Contemporary Criticism (Second Series)*. New York: Harcourt, Brace, 1924.

————. *Everyday Americans*. New York: Century, 1920.

————. "Fiction Sums Up a Century." In *Literary History of the United States*, 3d ed., edited by Robert E. Spiller, Willard Thorp, Thomas H. Johnson, Henry Seidel Canby, and Richard Ludwig, pp. 1208–36. New York: Macmillan, 1963.

————. "In Answer to 'Has America a Literary Dictatorship?'" *Bookman*, June 1927, pp. 444–45.

————. "Popularizers." *Saturday Review of Literature*, Dec. 31, 1932, p. 349.

————. *Seven Years' Harvest: Notes on Contemporary Literature*. New York: Farrar and Rinehart, 1936.

————. "Standardization." *Saturday Review of Literature*, Feb. 12, 1927, p. 573.

————. "Thoreau and the Machine Age." In *Aspects of the Social History of America*, by Theodore Sizer, Andrew C. McLaughlin, Dixon Ryan Fox, and Henry Seidel Canby, pp. 93–115. Chapel Hill: University of North Carolina Press, 1931.

————. "William Lyon Phelps." *Saturday Review of Literature*, Sept. 4, 1943, p. 12.

Canby, Henry Seidel, William Rose Benét, and Amy Loveman. *Saturday Papers*. New York: Macmillan, 1921.

Cantril, Hadley, and Gordon W. Allport. *The Psychology of Radio*. New York: Harper and Brothers, 1935.

Carr, Mary Jane. "Fifteen Years of Radio Reviewing." *Publishers' Weekly*, Sept. 14, 1940, p. 930.

Carson, Gerald. "Mr. Stuart Sherman Discovers Aphrodite Pandemos." *Bookman*, June 1926, pp. 389–96.

———. "Van Doren, Irita Bradford." In *Notable American Women: The Modern Period*, edited by Barbara Sicherman and Carol Hurd Green, with Ilene Kantrov and Harriette Walker, pp. 704–6. Cambridge: Harvard University Press, 1980.

Case, Frank. *Tales of a Wayward Inn*. New York: Garden City Publishing, 1940.

Cayton, Mary Kupiec. "The Making of an American Prophet: Emerson, His Audiences, and the Rise of the Culture Industry in Nineteenth-Century America." *American Historical Review* 92 (June 1987): 597–620.

"A Century of Thrills and Chills." *Wilson Library Bulletin*, Apr. 1942, pp. 638–44, 661.

Channing, William Ellery. *Self-Culture*. Boston: James Munroe, 1845.

Charvat, William. *The Profession of Authorship in America, 1800–70*. Columbus: Ohio State University Press, 1968.

Chase, Stuart. "Our Lock-Step Culture." *Forum*, Apr. 1929, pp. 238–42.

Cheney, O. H. *Economic Survey of the Book Industry, 1930–31*. New York: National Association of Book Publishers, 1931.

Christopher Morley: A Biographical Sketch. Garden City, N.Y.: Doubleday, Page, 1922.

Cmiel, Kenneth. *Democratic Eloquence: The Fight over Popular Speech in Nineteenth-Century America*. New York: William Morrow, 1990.

Colum, Mary. "Literature or Propaganda." *New York Herald Tribune Books*, July 24, 1932, pp. 1–2.

"Coming Events." *Radio Guide*, Mar. 9, 1940, p. 3.

Cortissoz, Royal. *The New York Tribune: Incidents and Personalities in Its History*. New York: New York Tribune, 1923.

Coser, Lewis A., Charles Kadushin, and Walter W. Powell. *Books: The Culture and Commerce of Publishing*. New York: Basic Books, 1982.

Coss, John J. Introduction to *Five College Plans*. New York: Columbia University Press, 1931.

Cothran, Andrew H. "The Little Blue Book Man and the Big American Parade." Ph.D. dissertation, University of Maryland, 1966.

"Council's 'Words at War' Program Gets Commercial Sponsor." *Publishers' Weekly*, July 1, 1944, p. 32.

Cousins, Norman. "Birthday Party." *Saturday Review*, Jan. 7, 1978, p. 4.

———. "S.R.L. Award to 'Information Please.'" *Saturday Review of Literature*, Apr. 6, 1940, p. 12.

Covert, Catherine L. "'We May Hear Too Much': American Sensibility and the Response to Radio, 1919–24." In *Mass Media between the Wars: Perceptions of Cultural Tension, 1918–1941*, edited by Catherine L. Covert and John D. Stevens, pp. 199–220. Syracuse: Syracuse University Press, 1984.

Cowley, Malcolm. *After the Genteel Tradition: American Writers, 1910–1930*. Carbondale: Southern Illinois University Press, 1964.

————. *And I Worked at the Writer's Trade: Chapters of Literary History, 1918–1978*. New York: Viking, 1978.

————. "Dr. Canby and His Team." *Saturday Review of Literature*. Aug. 29, 1964, pp. 54–55, 177.

Cowley, Malcolm, and Henry Seidel Canby. "Creating an Audience." In *Literary History of the United States*, 3d ed., edited by Robert E. Spiller, Willard Thorp, Thomas H. Johnson, Henry Seidel Canby, and Richard Ludwig, pp. 1119–34. New York: Macmillan, 1963.

Curti, Merle. *The Growth of American Thought*. 2d ed. New York: Harper and Brothers, 1951.

Czitrom, Daniel J. *Media and the American Mind: From Morse to McLuhan*. Chapel Hill: University of North Carolina Press, 1982.

"Danger: Brains at Work." *Radio Guide*, Sept. 24, 1938, pp. 1, 14, 19.

"Daniel among the Lions." *Commonweal*, Apr. 3, 1929, p. 615.

Darrow, Ben H. *Radio: The Assistant Teacher*. Columbus: R. G. Adams, 1932.

Davis, Elmer. *History of the New York Times, 1851–1921*. New York: New York Times, 1921.

Deitch, Joseph. "About 'Invitation to Learning.'" *New York Times*, July 29, 1951, II, p. 9.

Delaney, C. F. *Mind and Nature: A Study of the Naturalistic Philosophy of Cohen, Woodbridge, and Sellers*. Notre Dame, Ind.: University of Notre Dame Press, 1969.

"Democracy's Poet." *Time*, Oct. 31, 1938, p. 57.

"Department Store Methods for Radio Promotion of Books." *Publishers' Weekly*, May 15, 1947, p. 2484.

"Designed for Listening." *Radio Guide*, Feb. 12, 1938, p. 9.

"Detours of Billy Phelps: Rambling Autobiography Paints the Portrait of an Era." *Newsweek*, Apr. 17, 1939, p. 44.

Dewey, John. *Reconstruction in Philosophy*. New York: Henry Holt, 1920.

DiMaggio, Paul. "Cultural Entrepreneurship in Nineteenth-Century Boston: The Creation of an Organizational Base for High Culture in America." *Media, Culture and Society* 4 (1982): 33–50.

————. "Cultural Entrepreneurship in Nineteenth-Century Boston, Part II: The Classification and Framing of American Art." *Media, Culture and Society* 4 (1982): 303–22.

Dorothy Canfield Fisher: In Memoriam. New York: Book-of-the-Month Club, 1958.

"Doubleday Book Shops Put on Radio Program." *Publishers' Weekly*, Nov. 1, 1947, p. 2169.

Douglas, Susan J. *Inventing American Broadcasting*. Baltimore: Johns Hopkins University Press, 1987.

Duffus, R. L. *Books: Their Place in a Democracy*. Boston: Houghton Mifflin, 1930.

Durant, Will. *Adventures in Genius*. New York: Simon and Schuster, 1931.

———. "The Breakdown of Marriage." *Pictorial Review*, Nov. 1927, pp. 4, 94, 97–98, 112.

———. "The Failure of Philosophy." *Harper's*, Dec. 1926, pp. 80–90.

———. "In Defense of Outlines." *Forum*, Jan. 1930, pp. 8–14.

———. "Is America's Age of Art Dawning?" *New York Times Magazine*, Aug. 29, 1926, pp. 1, 20.

———. "Is Our Civilization Dying?" *Saturday Evening Post*, May 5, 1934, pp. 8–9, 77–78, 81–82.

———. "I Want to Be Happy." *Cosmopolitan*, July 1929, pp. 80, 214–16.

———. "Letter to the Editor." *Saturday Review of Literature*, Aug. 3, 1935, pp. 9, 18.

———. *The Mansions of Philosophy: A Survey of Human Life and Destiny*. New York: Simon and Schuster, 1929.

———. "The Modern Woman." *Century*, Feb. 1927, pp. 418–29.

———. "One Hundred Best Books." *American Magazine*, Dec. 1929, pp. 26–28, 109, 112, 115–16, 118.

———. *Philosophy and the Social Problem*. New York: Macmillan, 1917.

———. *Socialism and Anarchism*. New York: Albert and Charles Boni, 1914.

———. *The Story of Civilization: Caesar and Christ*. New York: Simon and Schuster, 1944.

———. *The Story of Civilization: The Life of Greece*. New York: Simon and Schuster, 1939.

———. *The Story of Civilization: Our Oriental Heritage*. New York: Simon and Schuster, 1935.

———. *The Story of Philosophy*. New York: Simon and Schuster, 1926.

———. "The Ten Greatest Thinkers." *American Magazine*, Mar. 1927, pp. 7–9, 103–4, 106, 108, 110.

———. *Transition: A Mental Autobiography*. New York: Simon and Schuster, 1927.

Durant, Will, and Ariel Durant. *A Dual Autobiography*. New York: Simon and Schuster, 1977.

———. "The Durant History: Letters to the Editor." *New York Times Book Review*, Oct. 6, 1963, pp. 36–37.

"E. P. Dutton Starts Radio Program on WQXR." *Publishers' Weekly*, Apr. 22, 1944, pp. 1597–98.

"Ed Fitzgerald's Broadcasts Sell Books." *Publishers' Weekly*, Apr. 27, 1940, pp. 1658–69.

Eliot, Charles W. "The New Definition of the Cultivated Man." *World's Work*, Aug. 1903, pp. 3806–11.

Eliot, Charles W., ed. *The Harvard Classics*. 50 vols. New York: P. F. Collier, 1909–10.

Eliot, T. S. "Tradition and the Individual Talent." In *Selected Essays, 1917–32*, pp. 13–22. London: Faber and Faber, 1932.

Emerson, Ralph Waldo. *The Early Lectures of Ralph Waldo Emerson, 1836–38*, edited by Stephen E. Whicher, Robert E. Spiller, and Wallace E. Williams. Cambridge: Harvard University Press, 1964.

———. *The Works of Ralph Waldo Emerson.* 14 vols. Boston: Houghton Mifflin, 1883–93.

Erskine, John. "Adult Education in Music." *School and Society* 32 (Nov. 15, 1930): 647–53.

———. *American Character and Other Essays.* Chautauqua, N.Y.: Chautauqua Press, 1927.

———. "Can Hollywood Stars Afford to Be Good Actors?" *Liberty*, Dec. 2, 1939, pp. 14–16.

———. "Clark Gable's Secret Wish." *Liberty*, Jan. 27, 1940, pp. 14–16.

———. *The Complete Life.* New York: Julian Messner, 1943.

———. *The Delight of Great Books.* Indianapolis: Bobbs-Merrill, 1927.

———. *Democracy and Ideals: A Definition.* New York: George H. Doran, 1920.

———. "English in the College Course." *Educational Review* 40 (Nov. 1910): 340–47.

———. "The Future of Broadcasting." In *Radio and Education*, edited by Levering Tyson, pp. 146–55. Chicago: University of Chicago Press, 1934.

———. "General Honors at Columbia." *New Republic*, Oct. 25, 1922, supplement, p. 13.

———. *The Influence of Women—and Its Cure.* Indianapolis: Bobbs-Merrill, 1936.

———. "Literature." In *A Century of Progress*, edited by Charles A. Beard, pp. 400–423. New York: Harper and Brothers, 1932.

———. "MacDowell, Edward." In *Dictionary of American Biography*, 12:24–27. New York: Charles Scribner's Sons, 1933.

———. *The Memory of Certain Persons.* Philadelphia: J. B. Lippincott, 1947.

———. "Mickey Mouse—Supported by Stokowski." *Liberty*, Oct. 28, 1939, pp. 10–12.

———. *The Moral Obligation to Be Intelligent and Other Essays.* New York: Duffield, 1915.

———. *My Life as a Teacher.* Philadelphia: J. B. Lippincott, 1948.

———. *My Life in Music.* New York: William Morrow, 1950.

———. "Outlines." *Bookman*, Mar. 1925, pp. 29–32.

———. *The Private Life of Helen of Troy.* Indianapolis: Bobbs-Merrill, 1925.

———. *Prohibition and Christianity and Other Paradoxes of the American Spirit.* Indianapolis: Bobbs-Merrill, 1927.

———. "Spotlight or Fame?" *Bookman*, July 1922, pp. 449–51.

———. "The Teaching of Literature in College." *Nation*, Sept. 3, 1908, pp. 202–5.

———. "There's Fun in Famous Books." *Delineator*, Dec. 1926, pp. 14–15.

———. "The Twilight of the Specialist: A Program for Mastering Our Own Lives." *Journal of Adult Education* 4 (June 1932): 229–33.

———. *Unfinished Business*. Indianapolis: Bobbs-Merrill, 1931.

———. "Why Films Have So Many Authors." *Liberty*, Nov. 18, 1939, pp. 13–15.

"Evolution." In *Catholic Encyclopedia*, edited by Charles G. Herbermann, Edward A. Pace, Condé B. Pallen, Thomas J. Shahan, and John J. Wynne, 5:654–69. New York: Encyclopedia Press, 1907–12.

Fadiman, Clifton. *Any Number Can Play*. New York: Avon, 1957.

———. *Party of One*. Cleveland: World Publishing, 1955.

———. *Reading I've Liked*. New York: Simon and Schuster, 1941.

———. "Two Lives and Some Collected Hemingway." *New Yorker*, Oct. 22, 1938, pp. 81–83.

"Fadiman Quits." *Time*, Sept. 27, 1943, p. 46.

Feldman, Ruth Dushkin. *Whatever Happened to the Quiz Kids?: The Perils and Profits of Growing Up Gifted*. Chicago: Chicago Review Press, 1982.

Filler, Louis. "Van Loon, Hendrik Willem." In *Dictionary of American Biography, Supplement Three, 1941–45*, pp. 789–91. New York: Charles Scribner's Sons, 1973.

"The Fireside Hour." *Publishers' Weekly*, Nov. 24, 1934, p. 1917.

Fisher, Dorothy Canfield. "Book Clubs." In *Dorothy Canfield Fisher: In Memoriam*. New York: Book-of-the-Month Club, 1958.

———. *The Brimming Cup*. New York: Harcourt, Brace, 1921.

———. *Memories of Arlington, Vermont*. New York: Duell, Sloan and Pearce, 1957.

———. *Our Young Folks*. New York: Harcourt, Brace, 1943.

———. *Seasoned Timber*. New York: Harcourt, Brace, 1939.

———. *Self-Reliance: A Practical and Informal Discussion of Methods of Teaching Self-Reliance, Initiative, and Responsibility to Modern Children*. Indianapolis: Bobbs-Merrill, 1916.

———. "Teen Age Children and Grown Up Books." *Book-of-the-Month Club News*, Sept. 1946.

———. *Vermont Tradition: The Biography of an Outlook on Life*. Boston: Little, Brown, 1953.

———. "What Makes It Worth While." *Delineator*, Sept. 1920, p. 8.

———. "What My Mother Taught Me." In *A Harvest of Stories*, pp. xi–xxix. New York: Harcourt, Brace, 1956.

———. *Why Stop Learning?* New York: Harcourt, Brace, 1927.

Fitzgerald, F. Scott. *The Great Gatsby*. New York: Charles Scribner's Sons, 1925.

Foerster, Norman. *Towards Standards: A Study of the Present Critical Movement in American Literature*. New York: Farrar and Rinehart, 1930.

Ford, James L. "The Fad of Imitation Culture." *Munsey's*, Oct. 1900, pp. 153–57.

Forman, Henry James. "Will Durant Takes All Civilization as His Province." *New York Times Book Review*, Aug. 4, 1935, p. 3.

"Four Best-Selling Personalities." *Literary Digest*, Jan. 11, 1936, p. 28.

Fox, Richard Wightman. "Character and Personality in the Protestant Republic." 1988. Unpublished paper in author's possession.

"Frederick, John T(owner)." *Current Biography*, 1941, pp. 309–11.

Freeman, Joseph. Introduction to *Proletarian Literature in the United States: An Anthology*, edited by Granville Hicks, Joseph North, Michael Gold, Paul Peters, Isidor Schneider, and Alan Calmer. New York: International Publishers, 1935.

Frith, Simon. "The Pleasures of the Hearth: The Making of BBC Light Entertainment." In *Formations of Pleasure*, pp. 101–23. London: Routledge and Kegan Paul, 1983.

Gaines, James. *Wit's End*. New York: Harcourt Brace Jovanovich, 1977.

Gannett, Lewis. "A Quarter Century of a Weekly Book Review . . . and of the World." *New York Herald Tribune Books*, Sept. 25, 1949, pp. 4–5.

Garrison, Dee. *Apostles of Culture: The Public Librarian and American Society, 1876–1920*. New York: Free Press, 1979.

Gerould, Katharine Fullerton. "The Plight of the Genteel." *Harper's*, Feb. 1926, pp. 310–19.

"Get in the Quiz Game." *Radio Guide*, Oct. 27, 1939, p. 8.

Gilkeson, John S., Jr. *Middle-Class Providence, 1820–1940*. Princeton: Princeton University Press, 1986.

Gilmer, Walker. *Horace Liveright: Publisher of the Twenties*. New York: David Lewis, 1970.

"Gloria Chandler Recordings, Inc., to Record Book Dramatizations." *Publishers' Weekly*, Apr. 26, 1947, p. 2219.

Godkin, Edwin Lawrence. "Chromo-Civilization." In *Reflections and Comments, 1865–1895*, pp. 192–205. New York: Charles Scribner's Sons, 1895.

———. "The Organization of Culture." *Nation*, June 18, 1868, pp. 486–88.

Goffman, Erving. *The Presentation of Self in Everyday Life*. Garden City, N.Y.: Doubleday, 1959.

Goldman, Eric F. *The Crucial Decade—and After: America, 1945–60*. New York: Vintage, 1960.

Goldsmith, Alfred N., and Austin C. Lescarboura. *This Thing Called Broadcasting*. New York: Henry Holt, 1938.

Golenpaul, Dan, ed. *Information, Please!* New York: Simon and Schuster, 1939.

Gordon, George N. *Educational Television*. New York: Center for Applied Research in Education, 1965.

Graff, Gerald. *Professing Literature*. Chicago: University of Chicago Press, 1987.

Gray, William S., and Ruth Monroe. *The Reading Interests and Habits of Adults: A Preliminary Report*. New York: Macmillan, 1929.

Green, Martin. *The Problem of Boston: Some Readings in Cultural History*. New York: Norton, 1966.

Greenberg, Clement. "The State of American Writing." *Partisan Review* 15 (Aug. 1948): 876–83.

Greenslet, Ferris. *Under the Bridge: An Autobiography*. Boston: Houghton Mifflin, 1943.

Gregory, Horace. "Criticism from the Left." *New York Herald Tribune Books*, Oct. 13, 1935, p. 16.

Griffith, Sally Foreman. *Home Town News: William Allen White and the Emporia Gazette*. New York: Oxford University Press, 1989.

Gross, John. *The Rise and Fall of the Man of Letters: Aspects of English Literary Life since 1800*. London: Weidenfeld and Nicolson, 1969.

Gross, Robert A. "Much Instruction from Little Reading: Books and Libraries in Thoreau's Concord." *Proceedings of the American Antiquarian Society* 97 (Part 1, 1987): 129–88.

Haldeman-Julius, E. *The First Hundred Million*. New York: Simon and Schuster, 1928. Reprint. New York: Arno Press, 1974.

———. *My Second Twenty-Five Years: Instead of a Footnote*. Girard, Kans.: Haldeman-Julius Publications, 1949.

Hall, Benn. "Radio Outlets for Author Publicity." *Publishers' Weekly*, Sept. 12, 1942, pp. 926–31.

Hall, David D. "The 'Higher Journalism' and the Politics of Culture in Mid-Nineteenth Century America." 1988. Unpublished paper in author's possession.

———. "The Uses of Literacy in New England." In *Printing and Society in Early America*, edited by William L. Joyce, David D. Hall, Richard D. Brown, and John B. Hench, pp. 1–47. Worcester, Mass.: American Antiquarian Society, 1983.

———. "The Victorian Connection." *American Quarterly* 27 (Dec. 1975): 561–74.

———. *Worlds of Wonder, Days of Judgment: Popular Religious Belief in Early New England*. New York: Knopf, 1989.

Hall, Peter Dobkin. *The Organization of American Culture, 1700–1900: Private Institutions, Elites, and the Origins of American Nationality*. New York: New York University Press, 1982.

Halttunen, Karen. *Confidence Men and Painted Women: A Study of Middle-Class Culture in America, 1830–1870*. New Haven: Yale University Press, 1982.

———. "From Parlor to Living Room: Domestic Space, Interior Decoration, and the Culture of Personality." In *Consuming Visions: Accumulation and Display of Goods in America, 1880–1920*, edited by Simon J. Bronner, pp. 157–89. New York: Norton, 1989.

Hammerton, J. A., ed. *The Universal History of the World*. 8 vols. London: Amalgamated Press, 1927–28.

Hansen, Harry. "Book Reviews Resist Commercialism." *Editor and Publisher*, July 21, 1934, pp. 105, 128.

Hardwick, Elizabeth. "The Decline of Book Reviewing." *Harper's*, Oct. 1959, pp. 138–43.

"Hardy Perennial." *Time*, June 6, 1938, p. 43.

Harris, Neil. "The Drama of Consumer Desire." In *Yankee Enterprise: The Rise of the American System of Manufactures*, edited by Otto Mayr and Robert C. Post, pp. 192–212. Washington: Smithsonian Institution, 1981.

———. "Lay Mastery in America." Unpublished paper in author's possession. Presented at the Conference on Popular Culture in Europe and America, Cornell University, Apr. 1982.

Hart, James D. *The Popular Book*. New York: Oxford University Press, 1950.

Hart, Joseph K. "Radiating Culture." *Survey*, Mar. 18, 1922, pp. 948–49.

"Has America a Literary Dictatorship?" *Bookman*, Apr. 1927, pp. 191–99.

Hawkins, Hugh. *Between Harvard and America: The Educational Leadership of Charles W. Eliot*. New York: Oxford University Press, 1972.

Hawkins, Stuart. "Broadcasting and Literature." *Publishers' Weekly*, Jan. 12, 1935, pp. 127–28.

Hawley, Ellis. *The Great War and the Search for a Modern Order*. New York: St. Martin's, 1979.

Hayes, Carlton J. H. "The Other-Worldly Mr. Wells." *Freeman*, Mar. 16, 1921, pp. 18–21.

Heald, Morrell. "Business Thought in the Twenties: Social Responsibility." *American Quarterly* 13 (Summer 1961): 126–29.

"Helen and Galahad under Fire." *Literary Digest*, Jan. 8, 1927, pp. 26–27.

Hellman, Geoffrey T. "How to Win Profits and Influence Literature (Part I)." *New Yorker*, Sept. 30, 1939, pp. 22–28.

———. "How to Win Profits and Influence Literature (Part II)." *New Yorker*, Oct. 7, 1939, pp. 24–30.

Hendricks, Luther V. *James Harvey Robinson: Teacher of History*. New York: King's Crown Press, 1946.

Herder, Dale M. "Haldeman-Julius, the Little Blue Books, and the Theory of Popular Culture." *Journal of Popular Culture* 4 (Spring 1971): 881–91.

Higginson, Thomas Wentworth. "Literature as an Art." *Atlantic Monthly*, Dec. 1867, pp. 745–54.

———. "A Plea for Culture." *Atlantic Monthly*, Jan. 1867, pp. 29–37.

Higham, John. "The Matrix of Specialization." In *The Organization of Knowledge in Modern America, 1860–1920*, edited by Alexandra Oleson and John Voss, pp. 3–18. Baltimore: Johns Hopkins University Press, 1979.

"High-Brow, Low-Brow, Middle-Brow." *Life*, Apr. 11, 1949, pp. 99–102.

Hill, Frank Ernest. *Listen and Learn: Fifteen Years of Adult Education on the Air*. New York: American Association for Adult Education, 1937.

Hill, John D. "A Business Man Views the Classics." *American Mercury*, Aug. 1945, pp. 167–74.

Hinshaw, A. W. "Philosophy Is Still the Aristocrat of Literature." *New York Times Book Review*, July 26, 1926, pp. 6, 18.

A History of Columbia College on Morningside. New York: Columbia University Press, 1954.

Hoeveler, J. David. *The New Humanism: A Critique of Modern America, 1900–40*. Charlottesville: University Press of Virginia, 1977.

Hofstadter, Richard. *Anti-Intellectualism in American Life*. New York: Vintage, 1963.

Hollander, John. "Some Animadversions on Current Reviewing." *Daedalus* 92 (Winter 1963): 145–54.

Hollinger, David A. "The Canon and Its Keepers: Modernism and Mid-Twentieth-Century American Intellectuals." In *In the American Province*, pp. 74–91. Bloomington: Indiana University Press, 1985.

———. *Morris R. Cohen and the Scientific Ideal*. Cambridge: MIT Press, 1975.

"Hoover Reveals Presidents Fish So They Can Get Away from It All." *New York Times*, May 19, 1947, p. 1.

Horowitz, Daniel. *The Morality of Spending: Attitudes toward the Consumer Society in America, 1875–1940*. Baltimore: Johns Hopkins University Press, 1985.

Houghton, Walter E. *The Victorian Frame of Mind*. New Haven: Yale University Press, 1957.

Howe, Daniel Walker. *The Unitarian Conscience: Harvard Moral Philosophy, 1805–1861*. Cambridge: Harvard University Press, 1970.

"How to Avoid the Mental Draft." *Radio Guide*, Jan. 29, 1938, p. 10.

"How to Make People Read." *Time*, Oct. 21, 1940, p. 58.

Hoyt, Edwin P. *Alexander Woollcott: The Man Who Came to Dinner*. London: Abelard-Schuman, 1968.

Hutchens, John K. "Who Thought Up the Quiz Show?" *New York Times Magazine*, Aug. 23, 1924, pp. 12–13, 31.

Hutchins, Robert M. *The Higher Learning in America*. New Haven: Yale University Press, 1936.

———. *No Friendly Voice*. Chicago: University of Chicago Press, 1936.

Hyman, Stanley Edgar. *The Armed Vision: A Study in the Methods of Modern Literary Criticism*. New York: Knopf, 1948.

"Ignorance Loves Company." *Newsweek*, May 13, 1946, p. 64.

"Information, Please, Yes." *Saturday Review of Literature*, Mar. 11, 1939, p. 8.

"In the Book Market." *Publishers' Weekly*, June 26, 1926, pp. 2036–37.

"Irita Van Doren, Editor of Books, Herald Tribune Review, Is Dead." *New York Times*, Dec. 19, 1966, p. 37.

Jackson, Joseph Henry. "Radio and Reading." *Publishers' Weekly*, Apr. 27, 1929, pp. 2000–2004.

———. "The Technique of Radio Book Reviews." *Publishers' Weekly*, Nov. 26, 1938, pp. 1890–93.

"Jackson, Joseph Henry." In *Twentieth Century Authors: A Biographical Dictionary of Modern Literature*, edited by Stanley J. Kunitz and Howard Haycraft, pp. 710–11. New York: H. W. Wilson, 1942.

James, William. *Letters of William James*. Vol. 2. Edited by his son Henry James. Boston: Atlantic Monthly Press, 1920.

"Jan Valtin Explains." *Wilson Library Bulletin*, Nov. 1941, pp. 213–14, 219, 223.

"Jim M'Williams, Ran Quiz Show on Radio." *New York Times*, Oct. 15, 1955, p. 15.

Johnson, Edgar. "Brother Cheeryble." *New Republic*, May 17, 1939, pp. 53–54.

Johnson, Walter. *William Allen White's America*. New York: Henry Holt, 1947.

"Join Ted Malone's 'Pilgrimage of Poetry.'" *Radio Guide*, Dec. 9, 1939, pp. 24–26.

Jones, Howard Mumford. "The Cult of Short-Cut Culture." *Forum*, Jan. 1930, pp. 5–8.

Jones, William Frank. *Nature and Natural Science: The Philosophy of Frederick J. E. Woodbridge*. Buffalo: Prometheus Books, 1983.

"Junior Guild Broadcasts." *Broadcast Advertising*, Dec. 1930, p. 30.

Kaplan, Milton. *Radio and Poetry*. New York: Columbia University Press, 1949.

Karsner, David. *Sixteen Authors to One: Intimate Sketches of Leading American Story Tellers*. New York: Lewis Copeland, 1928.

Kasson, John F. *Amusing the Million: Coney Island at the Turn of the Century*. New York: Hill and Wang, 1978.

———. *Rudeness and Civility: Manners in Nineteenth-Century Urban America*. New York: Hill and Wang, 1990.

Katz, James C. "An Afternoon with Clifton Fadiman." *Columbia College Today*, Fall 1982, pp. 30–32, 57.

Kaufman, Samuel. "Backstage in Broadcasting." *Radio News*, Feb. 1934, p. 485.

Killikelly, Sarah Hutchins. *Curious Questions in History, Literature, Art, and Social Life, Designed as a Manual of General Information*. 3 vols. Pittsburgh: Privately printed, 1886–1900 (vols. 1, 2); Philadelphia: McKay, 1900 (vol. 3).

Kluger, Richard. *The Paper: The Life and Death of the New York Herald Tribune*. New York: Knopf, 1986.

Kramer, Dale. *Heywood Broun*. New York: Current Books, 1949.

Kronenberger, Louis. "Down with Woollcott." *Nation*, Dec. 18, 1935, pp. 720–21.

Kuklick, Bruce. *The Rise of American Philosophy: Cambridge, Massachusetts, 1860–1930*. New Haven: Yale University Press, 1977.

Lasch, Christopher. *The Culture of Narcissism: American Life in an Age of Diminishing Expectations*. New York: W. W. Norton, 1978.

———. *The New Radicalism in America, 1889–1963: The Intellectual as a Social Type*. New York: Vintage, 1965.

Lazarsfeld, Paul F. *Radio and the Printed Page*. New York: Duell, Sloan and Pearce, 1940.

Lazarsfeld, Paul F., and Harry Field. *The People Look at Radio*. Chapel Hill: University of North Carolina Press, 1946.

Lears, T. J. Jackson. "From Salvation to Self-Realization." In *The Culture of Consumption: Critical Essays in American History, 1880–1980*, edited by Richard Wightman Fox and T. J. Jackson Lears, pp. 1–38. New York: Pantheon, 1983.

———. *No Place of Grace: Antimodernism and the Transformation of American Culture, 1880–1920*. New York: Pantheon, 1981.

Lee, Charles. *The Hidden Public: The Story of the Book-of-the-Month Club*. Garden City, N.Y.: Doubleday, 1958.

Lehmann-Haupt, Hellmut, Lawrence C. Wroth, and Rollo G. Silver. *The Book in America: A History of the Making and Selling of Books in the United States*. New York: R. R. Bowker, 1951.

Leland, Charles Godfrey. *The Art of Conversation, with Directions for Self Education*. New York: Carleton, 1866.

LeMahieu, D. L. *A Culture for Democracy: Mass Communication and the Cultivated Mind in Britain between the Wars*. Oxford: Clarendon Press, 1988.

"Leon Levine Will Produce 'Of Men and Books' Program." *Publishers' Weekly*, Jan. 25, 1947, p. 434.

Levine, David O. *The American College and the Culture of Aspiration, 1915–1940*. Ithaca: Cornell University Press, 1986.

Levine, Lawrence W. *Highbrow/Lowbrow: The Emergence of Cultural Hierarchy in America*. Cambridge: Harvard University Press, 1988.

Levinthal, Sonia. "Daytime Radio Programs as a Medium for Book Publicity." *Publishers' Weekly*, June 18, 1949, pp. 2448–52.

Lewis, Sinclair. *Babbitt*. New York: Signet, 1961.

———. "William Lyon Phelps." *Saturday Review of Literature*, Apr. 1, 1939, pp. 3–4.

"Listening to Learn." *Radio Guide*, June 27, 1939, p. 40; Oct. 27, 1939, p. 14; Nov. 17, 1939, p. 15; Dec. 1, 1939, p. 17; Feb. 16, 1940, p. 17.

"Literary Guild Drops Books on Trial Program." *Publishers' Weekly*, July 20, 1946, p. 290.

The Literary Marketplace. New York: R. R. Bowker, 1940–60.

Lohman, Sidney. "Radio Row: One Thing and Another." *New York Times*, Sept. 29, 1946, II, p. 9; Feb. 2, 1947, II, p. 11.

Lowell, James Russell. "Criticism and Culture." *Century*, Feb. 1894, pp. 515–16.

———. "The Five Indispensable Authors." *Century*, Dec. 1893, pp. 223–24.

Lowenthal, Leo. "The Triumph of Mass Idols." In *Literature and Mass Culture: Communication in Society*, vol. 1, pp. 203–35. New Brunswick, N.J.: Transaction Books, 1984.

Lynes, Russell. "Highbrow, Lowbrow, Middlebrow." *Harper's*, Feb. 1949, pp. 19–28. Reprinted in *The Tastemakers*, pp. 310–22, 331–33. New York: Harper and Brothers, 1954.

Mabie, Hamilton Wright. "Mr. Mabie's Answers to Questions." *Ladies' Home Journal*, Apr. 1906, p. 26.

McBride, Mary Margaret. *Out of the Air*. Garden City, N.Y.: Doubleday, 1960.

McConnell, Stuart. "E. Haldeman-Julius and the Little Blue Bookworms: The Bridging of Cultural Styles, 1919–1951." *Prospects* 11 (1987): 59–79.

Macdonald, Dwight. "The Book-of-the-Millennium Club." *New Yorker*, Nov. 29, 1952, p. 171.

———. "Masscult and Midcult: I." *Partisan Review* 27 (Spring 1960): 203–33.

———. "Masscult and Midcult: II." *Partisan Review* 27 (Fall 1960): 589–631.

———. "The Romantic Lecturers of Yale." *Yale Record*, May 4, 1927, pp. 1–2.

McDonald, Florin L. "Book Reviewing in the American Newspaper." Ph.D. dissertation, University of Missouri, 1936.

MacDonald, J. Fred. *Don't Touch That Dial*. Chicago: Nelson-Hall, 1979.

Mackenzie, Norman, and Jeanne Mackenzie. *H. G. Wells: A Biography*. New York: Simon and Schuster, 1973.

Madison, Charles A. *Book Publishing in America*. New York: McGraw-Hill, 1966.

"The Man in the Street Protests." *New York Herald Tribune Books*, Feb. 22, 1925, p. 12.

Marchand, Roland. *Advertising the American Dream: Making Way for Modernity, 1920–40*. Berkeley: University of California Press, 1985.

Martin, Everett Dean. *The Meaning of a Liberal Education*. New York: Norton, 1926.

Matthiessen, F. O. *The Responsibilities of the Critic*. New York: Oxford University Press, 1952.

Mattingly, Garrett. "Storytelling Historian." *Saturday Review*, Nov. 9, 1957, p. 20.

"Max Lincoln Schuster, Editor and Publisher, Dies." *New York Times*, Dec. 21, 1970, p. 38.

May, Henry F. *The End of American Innocence: A Study of the First Years of Our Own Time, 1912–1917.* Chicago: Quadrangle Books, 1964.

Mayer, Milton. "Great Books." *Life*, Oct. 28, 1946, pp. 2–8.

"Medal of Merit." *Radio Guide*, Jan. 5, 1940, p. 2.

Mencken, H. L. "The Motive of the Critic." *New Republic*, Oct. 26, 1921, pp. 249–51.

Miller, Merle. "Your Regular Moderator." *Theatre Arts*, Sept. 1950, pp. 40–45.

Mix, Jennie Irene. "Is Radio Standardizing the American Mind?" *Radio Broadcast*, Nov. 1924, pp. 48–50.

"Mobilizing Readers." *Saturday Review of Literature*, Sept. 29, 1931, p. 81.

"The Modern Woman." *Century*, Feb. 1927, pp. 418–29.

Monahan, James, and Tom Davis. *Guess Again.* New York: Duffield, 1927.

Moorhead, Hugh S. "The Great Books Movement." Ph.D. dissertation, University of Chicago (Department of Education), 1964.

Mordell, Albert, comp. *The World of Haldeman-Julius.* New York: Twayne, 1960.

Morgan, Charles. *The House of Macmillan (1843–1943).* New York: Macmillan, 1944.

Morgan, Joy Elmer. "A National Culture—By-Product or Objective of National Planning?" In *Radio as a Cultural Agency*, edited by Tracy F. Tyler, pp. 23–32. Washington: National Committee on Education by Radio, 1934.

———. "Radio and Education." In *Radio and Its Future*, edited by Martin Codel, pp. 68–82. New York: Harper and Brothers, 1930.

Morley, Christopher. *Ex Libris Carissimus.* Philadelphia: University of Pennsylvania Press, 1932.

———. *Forty-Four Essays.* New York: Harcourt, Brace, 1925.

———. *The Haunted Bookshop.* Philadelphia: J. B. Lippincott, 1951.

"Morley, Christopher." In *Twentieth-Century Authors: A Biographical Dictionary of Modern Literature*, edited by Stanley Kunitz and Howard Haycraft, pp. 986–87. New York: H. W. Wilson, 1942.

Morris, Lloyd. *Not So Long Ago.* New York: Random House, 1949.

———. *A Threshold in the Sun.* New York: Harper and Brothers, 1943.

Morrison, Theodore. *Chautauqua: A Center for Education, Religion, and the Arts in America.* Chicago: University of Chicago Press, 1974.

Mott, Frank Luther. *Golden Multitudes: The Story of Best Sellers in the United States.* New York: Macmillan, 1947.

———. *A History of American Magazines.* 5 vols. Cambridge: Harvard University Press, 1939–68.

"Mr. Wells Discovers the Past." *Nation*, Feb. 9, 1921, pp. 224–31.

Mumford, Lewis. *The Golden Day: A Study in American Literature and Culture*. New York: Dover, 1968.

Murphy, Cullen. "The Venerable Will." *Atlantic*, Nov. 1985, pp. 22, 24.

Murry, J. Middleton. "A Critical Credo." *New Republic*, Oct. 26, 1921, pp. 251–52.

Nadal, E. S. "Newspaper Literary Criticism." *Atlantic Monthly*, Mar. 1877, pp. 312–17.

Neavill, Gordon B. "The Modern Library Series and American Cultural Life." *Journal of Library History* 16 (Spring 1981): 247–48.

Nevin, Thomas. *Irving Babbitt: An Intellectual Study*. Chapel Hill: University of North Carolina Press, 1984.

Nevins, Allan. *The Evening Post: A Century of Journalism*. New York: Boni and Liveright, 1922.

"A New Battle of the Books." *Literary Digest*, June 1, 1929, pp. 27–28.

Newman, Frances. "One of the Wistful Young Men." *New York Herald Tribune Books*, Apr. 25, 1926, p. 4.

Nobile, Philip. *Intellectual Skywriting: Literary Politics and the New York Review of Books*. New York: Charterhouse, 1974.

Norton, Charles Eliot. *Letters of Charles Eliot Norton*. 2 vols. Edited by Sara Norton and Mark A. DeWolfe Howe. Boston: Houghton Mifflin, 1913.

———. "Notices of Gillett's Huss." *North American Review*, July 1864, pp. 269–74.

———. "The Paradise of Mediocrities." *Nation*, July 13, 1865, pp. 43–44.

———. Review of *Le Prime Quattro Edizione della Divina Commedia*, by G. G. Lord Vernon. *Atlantic Monthly*, May 1860, pp. 622–29.

"Notes." *Nation*, Nov. 1, 1917, p. 490.

O'Brien, Sharon. "Becoming Noncanonical: The Case against Willa Cather." In *Reading in America: Literature and Social History*, edited by Cathy N. Davidson, pp. 240–58. Baltimore: Johns Hopkins University Press, 1989.

O'Connor, Richard. *Heywood Broun: A Biography*. New York: Putnam, 1975.

"Of Men and Books," Dec. 27, 1941. In *Northwestern University on the Air*, 1:2–8. Evanston, Ill.: Northwestern University, 1941.

Oleson, Alexandra, and John Voss, eds. *The Organization of Knowledge in Modern America, 1860–1920*. Baltimore: Johns Hopkins University Press, 1979.

"Opera: 'Rigoletto' Is Put to Work Booming Coffee Sales." *Newsweek*, Dec. 8, 1934, p. 33.

Ordway, Warren. "Books in the Air." *Radio News*, Jan. 1925, pp. 1153, 1284–87.

Orrick, James. "Reviewers, Reviewing, and Book Promotion." *Publishers' Weekly*, Dec. 19, 1931, pp. 2631–34.

"Orson Welles Begins Radio Book Series." *Publishers' Weekly*, Mar. 4, 1939, p. 956.

Paterson, Isabel M. "Turns with a Bookworm." *New York Herald Tribune Books*, Oct. 19, 1924, p. 12; Jan. 3, 1926, p. 17; Sept. 5, 1926, p. 15.

———. "Up to the Minute." *New York Herald Tribune Books*, Apr. 19, 1925, p. 6.

Paul, Sherman. *Emerson's Angle of Vision: Man and Nature in American Experience*. Cambridge: Harvard University Press, 1952.

Paulsen, Friedrich. *Introduction to Philosophy*. 2d ed. New York: Henry Holt, 1906; reprint, 1924.

Peiss, Kathy. "Comment: Consumer Culture in Historical Perspective." 1989. Unpublished paper in author's possession.

Perry, Bliss. "The American Reviewer." *Yale Review* 4 (Oct. 1914): 3–24.

———. "Literary Criticism in American Periodicals." *Yale Review* 3 (July 1914): 635–55.

Perry, Lewis. *Intellectual Life in America: A History*. New York: Franklin Watts, 1984.

Persons, Stow. *The Decline of American Gentility*. New York: Columbia University Press, 1973.

"Person to Person." *Radio Guide*, May 29, 1939, p. 19.

Peyre, Henri. "What Is Wrong with American Book-Reviewing?" *Daedalus* 92 (Winter 1963): 128–44.

Phelps, William Lyon. *Appreciation*. New York: E. P. Dutton, 1932.

———. *As I Like It*. New York: Charles Scribner's Sons, 1923.

———. *Autobiography with Letters*. New York: Oxford University Press, 1939.

———. *Yearbook*. New York: Macmillan, 1935.

"Philco Television Playhouse to Feature Book Adaptations." *Publishers' Weekly*, Aug. 31, 1949, pp. 661–62.

Plumb, J. H. "Some Personalities on the Paths of History." *New York Times Book Review*, Sept. 15, 1963, pp. 3, 44.

Porter, Noah. *Books and Reading, or What Books Shall I Read and How Shall I Read Them*. New York: Charles Scribner, 1871.

"Preliminary Report of Committee on Instruction." *Columbia College Gazette*, Dec. 1916, pp. 1–7.

Purdy, Kenneth W. "Bright Young Man." *Radio Guide*, Sept. 29, 1939, p. 4.

Purdy, Theodore, Jr. "Snows of Yesteryear." *Saturday Review of Literature*, Aug. 28, 1937, p. 11.

"Q. & A." *Literary Digest*, Dec. 26, 1936, p. 32.

"Radio Broadcasts Sell Books for Gill." *Publishers' Weekly*, June 19, 1937, pp. 2473–74.

"Radio Notes." *Publishers' Weekly*, Apr. 17, 1948, p. 1690; Sept. 13, 1947, p. 1158; Oct. 4, 1947, p. 1782; Nov. 1, 1947, pp. 2160–61; Dec. 6, 1947, p. 2533; Jan. 17, 1948, p. 217.

"Radio Reviewer's Christmas List in Demand." *Publishers' Weekly*, Dec. 16, 1939, p. 2186.

"Radio Reviews Sell Books." *Publishers' Weekly*, Sept. 19, 1931, pp. 1252–54.

"Radio Stories from Children's Books." *Publishers' Weekly*, Feb. 25, 1939, p. 871.

Radway, Janice. "The Book-of-the-Month Club and the General Reader." In *Reading in America: Literature and Social History*, edited by Cathy N. Davidson, pp. 259–84. Baltimore: Johns Hopkins University Press, 1989.

———. "The Scandal of the Middlebrow: The Book-of-the-Month Club, Class Fracture, and Cultural Authority." *South Atlantic Quarterly* 89 (Fall 1990): 703–36.

Raleigh, John Henry. *Matthew Arnold and American Culture*. Berkeley: University of California Press, 1957.

Randall, John H., Jr. "The Department of Philosophy." In *A History of the Faculty of Philosophy*, edited by John H. Randall, Jr., pp. 108–29. New York: Columbia University Press, 1957.

Rascoe, Burton. *Before I Forget*. Garden City, N.Y.: Doubleday, Doran, 1937.

———. *We Were Interrupted*. Garden City, N.Y.: Doubleday, 1947.

"Reading and Reviewing." *Harper's*, Jan. 1960, pp. 8, 10.

"Recent Experiments in Radio Advertising." *Publishers' Weekly*, July 6, 1946, pp. 47–48.

"Recommended Programs." *Radio Guide*, Jan. 29, 1938, p. 11.

Redman, Ben Ray. "No: Not without Socrates." *Saturday Review of Literature*, Dec. 9, 1950, pp. 6–7, 32–35.

———. "Old Wine in New Bottles." *New York Herald Tribune Books*, Dec. 29, 1935, p. 10.

Reilly, Joseph J. "'Billy' Phelps of Yale." *Commonweal*, Jan. 28, 1938, pp. 376–78.

Riesman, David, with Nathan Glazer and Reuel Denney. *The Lonely Crowd: A Study of the Changing American Character*. 1950. New Haven: Yale University Press, 1971.

Roberts, R. Ellis. "The Personal Preferences of John Erskine." *Saturday Review of Literature*, Apr. 24, 1943, p. 8.

Robinson, David. *Apostle of Culture: Emerson as Preacher and Lecturer*. Philadelphia: University of Pennsylvania Press, 1982.

Robinson, Henry Morton. "John Erskine as I Knew Him." *Columbia Alumni News*, Mar. 1957, pp. 8–10.

Robinson, James Harvey. *The Humanizing of Knowledge*. New York: George H. Doran, 1923.

———. *An Introduction to the History of Western Europe*. 2 vols. Boston: Ginn, 1902–3; rev. ed. 1924–26, 1934.

———. *The Mind in the Making*. New York: Harper and Brothers, 1921.

Robinson, James Harvey, and Charles Beard. *Outlines of European History*. Boston: Ginn, 1907–19.

"Romberg: Composer for Stage and Screen Wins Air Laurels." *Newsweek*, Dec. 1, 1934, p. 28.

Rorty, James. "Free Air: A Strictly Imaginary Educational Broadcast." *Nation*, Mar. 9, 1932, pp. 280–82.

Rosenfield, Leonora Cohen. *Portrait of a Philosopher: Morris R. Cohen in Life and Letters*. New York: Harcourt, Brace and World, 1962.

Ross, Ishbel. *Ladies of the Press: The Story of Women in Journalism by an Insider*. New York: Harper and Brothers, 1936.

Ross, Mary. "Dos Passos Writes a Symphony of Wartime." *New York Herald Tribune Books*, Mar. 13, 1932, p. 5.

Rourke, Constance. *American Humor*. New York: Harcourt, Brace, 1931.

Rugg, Harold. "The Artist and the Great Transition." In *America and Alfred Stieglitz: A Collective Portrait*, edited by Waldo Frank, Lewis Mumford, Dorothy Norman, Paul Rosenfeld, and Harold Rugg, pp. 179–98. New York: Literary Guild, 1934.

Ruland, Richard. *The Rediscovery of American Literature: Premises of Critical Taste, 1900–40*. Cambridge: Harvard University Press, 1967.

Russell, Charles Edward. "Take Them or Leave Them: Standardization of Hats and Houses and Minds." *Century*, June 1926, pp. 168–77.

Sackheim, Maxwell. *My First Sixty Years in Advertising*. Englewood Cliffs, N.J.: Prentice-Hall, 1970.

———. "Why the Book Clubs Are Successful." *Advertising and Selling*, Aug. 1947, pp. 38, 68.

Salpeter, Harry. "Fatal to Review: How Does One Review Books over the Air?" *Publishers' Weekly*, May 16, 1931, pp. 2417–19.

Santayana, George. *The Genteel Tradition: Nine Essays by George Santayana*. Edited by Douglas L. Wilson. Cambridge: Harvard University Press, 1967.

Sargeant, Winthrop. "In Defense of the High-Brow." *Life*, Apr. 11, 1949, pp. 99–102.

"Saturday Review and WNEW Launch New Weekly Book Program." *Publishers' Weekly*, Apr. 19, 1947, p. 2113.

Schapiro, J. Salwyn. "History Wise and Witty." *Nation*, Dec. 28, 1921, pp. 759–60.

———. "Mr. Wells Discovers the Past." *Nation*, Feb. 9, 1921, pp. 224–31.

Scherman, Harry. "What the Record Means." *Book-of-the-Month Club News*, Apr. 1949.

Schroth, Raymond A., S.J., "The Excommunication of Will Durant." 1986. Unpublished paper in author's possession.

Schudson, Michael. *Advertising, The Uneasy Persuasion: Its Dubious Impact on American Society*. New York: Basic Books, 1984.

Schwed, Peter. *Turning the Pages: An Insider's Story of Simon & Schuster, 1924–84*. New York: Macmillan, 1984.

Scott, Donald M. "The Popular Lecture and the Creation of a Public in Mid-

Nineteenth Century America." *Journal of American History* 66 (Mar.
1980): 791–809.

"Search-Light" [Waldo Frank]. "Poor Little Rich Boy." *New Yorker*, June
19, 1926, pp. 19–20.

"Seaver Starts Book-of-the-Month Radio Service." *Publishers' Weekly*, Mar.
22, 1941, p. 1301.

Seldes, Gilbert. *The Great Audience*. New York: Viking, 1950.

Sennett, Richard. *The Fall of Public Man*. New York: Knopf, 1977.

Sherman, Stuart P. *Americans*. New York: Charles Scribner's Sons, 1922.

————. "Anatole France." *New York Herald Tribune Books*, Oct. 26, 1924,
pp. 1–3.

————. "The 'Big' Novels of Charles Norris." *New York Herald Tribune
Books*, Mar. 14, 1926, pp. 1–3.

————. *Critical Woodcuts*. New York: Charles Scribner's Sons, 1926.

————. "Don Marquis—What Is He?" *New York Herald Tribune Books*,
Feb. 8, 1925, pp. 1–3.

————. "Education by the People." *Nation*, May 9, 1913, pp. 461–64.

————. *The Emotional Discovery of America*. New York: Farrar and
Rinehart, 1932.

————. "Farewell, New England Gentleman." *New York Herald Tribune
Books*, Dec. 7, 1924, pp. 1–3.

————. "Finding the Intelligent Public and Enlarging It." *Publishers'
Weekly*, May 29, 1926, pp. 1781–84.

————. "Five Years with the American Intelligentsia." *New York Herald
Tribune Books*, June 6, 1926, pp. 1–3.

————. *The Genius of America*. New York: Charles Scribner's Sons, 1923.

————. "George Moore." *Nation*, Apr. 8, 1912, pp. 385–88. Reprinted with
additions as "The Aesthetic Naturalism of George Moore," in *On
Contemporary Literature*, pp. 120–68. New York: Henry Holt, 1917.

————. "Here Is a Novelist Who Will Please You." *New York Herald
Tribune Books*, Oct. 11, 1925, pp. 1–3.

————. "Indifferent? No!" *New York Herald Tribune Books*, Sept. 21, 1924,
pp. 1–2.

————. "An Irish Epicure Caviare for the Million." *New York Herald
Tribune Books*, Nov. 9, 1924, pp. 1–3.

————. "Lawrence Cultivates His Beard." *New York Herald Tribune Books*,
June 14, 1925, pp. 1–3.

————. *Letters to a Lady in the Country*. New York: Charles Scribner's
Sons, 1925.

————. "A Man against the Sky." *New York Herald Tribune Books*, Jan. 11,
1925, pp. 1–3.

————. "Mark Twain's Last Phase." *New York Herald Tribune Books*, Nov.
2, 1924, pp. 1–2.

————. *Matthew Arnold: How to Know Him.* Indianapolis: Bobbs-Merrill, 1917.

————. "Middle Class Strategy or a Call to the Converted." *New York Herald Tribune Books*, Feb. 22, 1925, pp. 1–3.

————. "Miss Sinclair Presents Magnanimous Love." *New York Herald Tribune Books*, Oct. 5, 1924, pp. 1–2.

————. "The 'Modern' Soul in Poetry." *New York Herald Tribune Books*, Dec. 6, 1925, pp. 1–3.

————. *My Dear Cornelia.* Boston: Atlantic Monthly Press, 1924.

————. "O Brave Sea Captain." *New York Herald Tribune Books*, Dec. 28, 1924, pp. 1–3.

————. *On Contemporary Literature.* New York: Henry Holt, 1917.

————. "Philosophy and the Average Man's Adult Education." *New York Herald Tribune Books*, June 20, 1926, pp. 1–3.

————. *Points of View.* New York: Charles Scribner's Sons, 1924.

————. "Recognizing One of Our Contemporaries." *New York Herald Tribune Books*, Oct. 12, 1924, pp. 1–2.

————. "R.L.S. Encounters the 'Modern' Writers on Their Own Ground." *New York Herald Tribune Books*, Oct. 25, 1926, pp. 1–4.

————. *Shaping Men and Women: Essays on Literature and Life.* Edited by Jacob Zeitlin. New York: Doubleday, Doran, 1928.

————. "A Sick Man's Vision or the Naked Truth?" *New York Herald Tribune Books*, Oct. 18, 1925, pp. 1–3.

————. "Style or the Quest of Perfection." *New York Herald Tribune Books*, Oct. 19, 1924, pp. 1–2.

————. "Supermen." *New York Herald Tribune Books*, Dec. 14, 1924, pp. 1–3.

————. "An Uncommon Essayist to the Common Reader." *New York Herald Tribune Books*, July 5, 1925, pp. 1–2.

————. "Vanity Fair in 1924." *New York Herald Tribune Books*, Nov. 16, 1924, pp. 1–2.

————. "What People Want." *New York Herald Tribune Books*, Sept. 28, 1924, pp. 1–2.

————. "What Transforms Life." *New York Herald Tribune Books*, May 10, 1925, pp. 1–2.

Shove, Raymond Howard. *Cheap Book Production in the United States, 1870–91.* Urbana: University of Illinois Library, 1937.

Showalter, Elaine, ed. *The New Feminist Criticism.* New York: Pantheon, 1985.

Sidorsky, David, ed. *John Dewey: The Essential Writings.* New York: Harper Torchbooks, 1977.

Silverman, Al, ed. *The Book of the Month: Sixty Years of Books in American Life.* Boston: Little, Brown, 1986.

Simon, Richard L. "About Those Essandess Cards." *Publishers' Weekly*, Oct. 24, 1936, pp. 1676–77.

Skinner, Constance Lindsay. "What the Well-Dressed Women Are Reading." *North American Review*, Apr. 1929, pp. 430–34.

Smith, David C. *H. G. Wells: Desperately Mortal*. New Haven: Yale University Press, 1986.

Smith, Helen Huntington. "Professor's Progress." *New Yorker*, Dec. 10, 1927, pp. 27–29.

Smith, James Steel. "The Day of the Popularizers: The 1920's." *South Atlantic Quarterly* 62 (Spring 1963): 297–309.

Snow, Wilbert. "A Literalist of the Imagination." *New York Herald Tribune Books*, May 17, 1925, p. 3.

"So You Want to Dream?" *Radio Guide*, Nov. 27, 1937, p. 20.

"'Speaking of Books' Radio Program Gets Audience." *Publishers' Weekly*, June 7, 1941, pp. 2298–99.

Spiller, Robert E. "The Battle of the Books." In *Literary History of the United States*, 3d ed., edited by Robert E. Spiller, Willard Thorp, Thomas H. Johnson, Henry Seidel Canby, and Richard M. Ludwig, pp. 1135–56. New York: Macmillan, 1963.

Spiller, Robert E., Willard Thorp, Thomas H. Johnson, Henry Seidel Canby, and Richard M. Ludwig, eds. *Literary History of the United States*. 3d ed. New York: Macmillan, 1963.

Spingarn, Joel. "Woodberry, George Edward." *Dictionary of American Biography*, 20:478–81. New York: Charles Scribner's Sons, 1936.

Sprague, Jesse Rumford. "The Chain-Store Mind." *Harper's*, Feb. 1929, pp. 356–66.

Sproul, Kathleen. "Dialing Civilization." *Saturday Review of Literature*, Aug. 19, 1950, pp. 19–21.

Squires, Radcliffe. *Allen Tate: A Literary Biography*. New York: Pegasus, 1971.

"SRL Series Ties In with NBC Classics Broadcasts." *Publishers' Weekly*, Sept. 23, 1950, pp. 1389–90.

Stearns, Harold. *Civilization in the United States*. New York: Harcourt, Brace, 1922.

Stevens, Austin. "Scholars Discourse on the Classics." *New York Times Book Review*, Sept. 27, 1942, p. 14.

Stevenson, Louise L. *Scholarly Means to Evangelical Ends: The New Haven Scholars and the Transformation of the Higher Learning in America, 1830–1890*. Baltimore: Johns Hopkins University Press, 1986.

"Stone, Producer of 'Author Meets the Critics,' Refused Injunction." *Publishers' Weekly*, June 8, 1946, p. 3019.

Story, Ronald. "Class and Culture in Boston: The Athenaeum, 1807–1860." *American Quarterly* 27 (May 1975): 185.

Strasser, Susan. *Satisfaction Guaranteed: The Making of the American Mass Market*. New York: Pantheon, 1989.

"Stress the Bookshop in Radio Reviews." *Publishers' Weekly*, May 17, 1930, pp. 2521–22.

Sugrue, Thomas. "A Civilized Man's Guide to Culture." *New York Times Book Review*, Apr. 25, 1943, p. 9.

Sullivan, Mark. "Will Radio Make the People the Government?" *Radio Broadcast*, Nov. 1924, pp. 19–25.

Summers, Harrison B. *A Thirty-Year History of Programs Carried on National Radio Networks in the United States, 1926–1956*. Columbus: Ohio State University, 1958.

Susman, Warren I. *Culture as History*. New York: Pantheon, 1984.

Sussman, Aaron. "See the Pretty Birdie." *Publishers' Weekly*, July 21, 1934, pp. 187–95.

Swan, Carroll J. "How the Book-of-the-Month Club Has Thrived on Direct-Selling Copy." *Printers' Ink*, Feb. 19, 1943, pp. 58, 60–62.

Tebbel, John. *A History of Book Publishing in the United States*. 4 vols. New York: R. R. Bowker, 1972–81.

Tedlow, Richard. "Intellect on Television: The Quiz Show Scandals of the 1950s." *American Quarterly* 28 (Fall 1976): 483–95.

"There Is No Formula to Life." *Wilson Library Bulletin*, Apr. 1943, pp. 609–15.

"They Stopped Hitler." *Wilson Library Bulletin*, Dec. 1942, pp. 285–91.

Thomas, Lorraine. "Meet Mr. Weeks." *Radio Guide*, Dec. 29, 1939, p. 26.

Tompkins, Jane. *Sensational Designs: The Cultural Work of American Fiction, 1790–1860*. New York: Oxford University Press, 1985.

Tomsich, John. *A Genteel Endeavor: American Culture and Politics in the Gilded Age*. Stanford: Stanford University Press, 1971.

"Town Crier." *Newsweek*, Feb. 1, 1943, pp. 62–64.

Trachtenberg, Alan. *The Incorporation of America: Culture and Society in the Gilded Age*. New York: Hill and Wang, 1982.

Trilling, Lionel. "The Van Amringe and Keppel Eras." In *A History of Columbia College on Morningside*, pp. 14–47. New York: Columbia University Press, 1954.

"Tune in on 'The Early Bookworm.'" *Publishers' Weekly*, Sept. 13, 1930, pp. 1038–39.

"Twenty-Seven Great Books of the World." *New York Times Book Review*, July 6, 1941, p. 6.

"20,000 Per Cent Increase." *Fortune*, Jan. 1934, pp. 51, 100.

"Two Views of the Reviews." *Harper's*, Nov. 1959, pp. 6, 8.

"Up-to-Date Book Reviewing." *Independent*, Dec. 27, 1900, pp. 3096–99.

Vanderbilt, Kermit. *Charles Eliot Norton: Apostle of Culture in a Democracy*. Cambridge: Harvard University Press, 1959.

Van Doren, Carl. "Day In and Day Out." *Century*, Dec. 1923, pp. 308–15.

———. "The Literary Spotlight." *Bookman*, June 1922, pp. 354–58.

———. *Many Minds*. New York: Knopf, 1926.

———. "Stuart Sherman: 1881–1926." *New York Herald Tribune Books*, Aug. 29, 1926, pp. 1–2.

"Van Doren, Irita Bradford." *Current Biography*, 1941, pp. 881–82.

Van Doren, Mark. *The Autobiography of Mark Van Doren*. New York: Harcourt, Brace, 1958.

———. "High in the Air, But They Don't Talk Down." *New York Times*, Nov. 16, 1941, IX, p. 12.

———. "Jewish Students I Have Known." *Menorah Journal*, June 1927, pp. 264–68.

———. "A Listener's Guide to Invitation to Learning." Summer 1942, pp. 3–4. Pamphlet in author's possession.

———. *The New Invitation to Learning*. New York: Random House, 1942.

———. *The Selected Letters of Mark Van Doren*. Edited by George Hendrick. Baton Rouge: Louisiana State University Press, 1987.

Van Loon, Gerard Willem. *The Story of Hendrik Willem Van Loon*. Philadelphia: J. B. Lippincott, 1972.

Van Loon, Hendrik Willem. *Air-storming*. New York: Harcourt, Brace, 1935.

———. *How I Came to Publish with S & S*. New York: Simon and Schuster, 1937.

———. *The Story of Mankind*. New York: Boni and Liveright, 1921.

———. *What Is Civilization?* 1926. Reprint. Freeport, N.Y.: Books for Libraries Press, 1968.

"Varieties of Book Reviewing." *Nation*, July 2, 1914, p. 8.

Veysey, Laurence R. *The Emergence of the American University*. Chicago: University of Chicago Press, 1965.

———. "The Plural Organized Worlds of the Humanities." In *The Organization of Knowledge in America, 1860–1920*, edited by Alexandra Oleson and John Voss, pp. 51–106. Baltimore: Johns Hopkins University Press, 1979.

"Views of Roosevelt and Thomas Debated." *New York Times*, Oct. 24, 1932, p. 10.

"Voice of the Listener." *Radio Guide*, May 27, 1939, p. 19.

Wagar, W. Warren. *H. G. Wells and the World State*. New Haven: Yale University Press, 1961.

Wagner, Geoffrey. "The Decline of Book Reviewing." *American Scholar* 26 (Winter 1956–57): 23–36.

Wallach, Mark, and Jon Bracker. *Christopher Morley*. New York: Twayne, 1976.

Waller, Judith C. *Radio: The Fifth Estate*. Boston: Houghton Mifflin, 1946.

Waples, Douglas, and Ralph W. Tyler. *What People Want to Read About: A Study of Group Interests and a Survey of Problems in Adult Reading*.

Chicago: University of Chicago Press and the American Library Association, 1931.

Warren, Dale. "'Weeks'—of the *Atlantic.*" *Publishers' Weekly*, Aug. 12, 1939, pp. 448–51.

"Wartime Washington: 1861–65." *Wilson Library Bulletin*, Mar. 1942, pp. 521–28.

Washington, Ida. *Dorothy Canfield Fisher: A Biography*. Shelburne, Vt.: New England Press, 1982.

Weber, William. "Wagner, Wagnerism, and Musical Idealism." In *Wagnerism in European Culture and Politics*, edited by David Large and William Weber, pp. 28–71. Ithaca: Cornell University Press, 1984.

Weeks, Edward. *In Friendly Candor*. Boston: Little, Brown, 1959.

———. *My Green Age*. Boston: Little, Brown, 1973.

———. *Writers and Friends*. Boston: Little, Brown, 1981.

Weiss, Paul. "Human, All Too Human." *New Republic*, July 28, 1926, p. 286.

Wells, H. G. *Experiment in Autobiography: Discoveries and Conclusions of a Very Ordinary Brain (since 1866)*. New York: Macmillan, 1934.

———. *The Outline of History*. Garden City, N.Y.: Garden City Publishing, 1920.

Wertheim, Arthur Frank. *Radio Comedy*. New York: Oxford University Press, 1979.

Westbrook, Robert B. *John Dewey and American Democracy*. Ithaca: Cornell University Press, 1991.

Whicher, Stephen E., ed. *Selections from Ralph Waldo Emerson*. Boston: Houghton Mifflin, 1957.

Whipple, Leon. "Books on the Belt." *Nation*, Feb. 13, 1929, pp. 182–83.

White, Morton. *Science and Sentiment in America: Philosophical Thought from Jonathan Edwards to John Dewey*. New York: Oxford University Press, 1972.

———. *Social Thought in America: The Revolt against Formalism*. Boston: Beacon Press, 1957.

Whitman, Walt. "Democratic Vistas." In *Complete Poetry and Collected Prose*, pp. 929–94. New York: Library of America, 1982.

Widdemer, Margaret. "Message and Middlebrow." *Saturday Review of Literature*, Feb. 18, 1933, pp. 433–34.

Wiebe, Robert H. *The Search for Order, 1877–1920*. New York: Hill and Wang, 1967.

———. *The Segmented Society: An Inquiry into the Meaning of America*. New York: Oxford University Press, 1975.

Wiggam, Albert Edward. *The Marks of an Educated Man*. New York: Blue Ribbon Books, 1925.

Williams, Raymond. *Culture and Society, 1780–1950*. New York: Harper Torchbooks, 1958.

Wilson, Christopher P. *The Labor of Words: Literary Professionalism in the Progressive Era*. Athens: University of Georgia Press, 1985.

———. "The Rhetoric of Consumption." In *The Culture of Consumption: Critical Essays in American History, 1880–1980*, edited by Richard Wightman Fox and T. J. Jackson Lears, pp. 39–64. New York: Pantheon, 1983.

Wilson, Daniel J. "Science and the Crisis of Confidence in American Philosophy, 1870–1930." 1986. Unpublished paper in author's possession.

Wilson, Edmund. "The All-Star Literary Vaudeville." *New Republic*, June 30, 1926, pp. 158–63.

———. "Critics of the Middle Class." *New York Herald Tribune Books*, Feb. 14, 1932, pp. 1, 6, 18.

Windelband, Wilhelm. *A History of Philosophy with Especial Reference to the Formation and Development of Its Problems and Conceptions*. New York: Macmillan, 1896.

Winterich, John T. "This Is Woollcott. . . ." *Saturday Review of Literature*, Feb. 23, 1935, p. 505.

Wolf, Robert. "In Our Time." *New York Herald Tribune Books*, Feb. 14, 1926, p. 3.

Woodberry, George Edward. *The Appreciation of Literature*. New York: Baker and Taylor, 1907.

———. *Heart of Man*. New York: Macmillan, 1899.

Woodford, Jack. "Radio—A Blessing or a Curse?" *Forum*, Mar. 1929, pp. 169–71.

Woolf, Virginia. "Middlebrow." In *The Death of the Moth*, pp. 180–84. New York: Harcourt, Brace, 1942.

Woollcott, Alexander. "Books." *McCall's*, Dec. 1932, pp. 20, 56.

———. "Reading and Writing." *McCall's*, Sept. 1931, pp. 2, 41; Oct. 1931, pp. 22, 138; Dec. 1931, pp. 17, 53.

"WOR Starts Radio Book Program." *Publishers' Weekly*, May 5, 1939, p. 1921.

Wright, Milton. *The Art of Conversation and How to Apply Its Technique*. New York: Whittlesey House, 1936.

Zeitlin, Jacob, and Homer Woodbridge. *Life and Letters of Stuart P. Sherman*. 2 vols. New York: Farrar and Rinehart, 1929.

Zinsser, William K. *Revolution in American Reading*. New York: Book-of-the-Month Club, 1966.

INDEX

Aaron, Daniel, 13
Adams, Franklin P. (F.P.A.), 136,
137, 139, 142, 218, 252, 291, 320,
323–24
Adams, James Truslow, 30, 32, 90,
146–47
Adler, Felix, 225, 226
Adler, Mortimer, xiv, 178, 183, 186–
96, 238, 239, 267, 309, 327, 329, 350
(n. 49), 353 (n. 100)
Aesthetic training, xix, 12, 13, 27, 28,
32, 37, 39, 53, 54, 88, 105, 118, 130–
31, 133, 155, 286, 288, 325
Allport, Gordon W., 287
Angell, James Rowland, 273
Arnold, Matthew, 14–15, 17, 18, 30,
45–48, 52–54, 56, 66–67, 91, 94,
110, 115, 120, 121, 138, 144, 149,
154, 155, 173, 174, 176, 185, 190,
195, 223, 236–37, 244, 249, 279,
295. See also Genteel tradition
Atlantic Monthly, 37, 38, 40, 59, 60,
301–2

Babbitt, Irving, 44–47, 48, 49, 51, 54,
56, 65, 74, 112, 339 (n. 49)
Bagehot, Walter, 37
Bakeless, John, 283
Barr, Stringfellow, 189, 193, 194, 308,
312
Barton, Bruce, 74, 158
Barzun, Jacques, 326, 353 (n. 100)
Bascom, John, 20, 43–44
Bates, Ernest Sutherland, 242, 250

Beard, Charles, 160, 257, 258
Becker, Carl, 213, 218
Becker, May Lamberton, 86–87, 108
Beebe, Lucius, 281
Bell, Daniel, 171
Bell, Lisle, 88, 91
Benedict, Ruth, 296
Benét, Stephen Vincent, xiv, 91, 313
Benét, William Rose, 114, 122, 266
Bennett, Charles A., 254
Bennett, James Gordon, 38
Benton, William, 193, 195–96
Bloom, Allan, 176
Bodenheim, Maxwell, 86
Bok, Edward, 282
Boni, Albert, 94, 95, 216. See also
Boni and Liveright
Boni, Charles, 64, 94, 95
Boni and Liveright, 218, 355–56 (n.
22). See also Boni, Albert; Live-
right, Horace
Book-of-the-Month Club, xi, xiv, xv,
xvi, xix, 71, 93, 231, 251, 274, 299,
304, 327, 328, 329, 331 (n. 10), 360–
61 (n. 102); origins of, 94–95; struc-
ture of, 95–96, 100–101; responses
to, 96–98; advertising for, 98–101,
104–10, 133, 137, 182, 195, 237,
254, 305; Selecting Committee
(Board of Judges), 102–4, 107, 110–
43, 174, 325; selection procedures,
144–47. See also Genteel tradition
Book-of-the-Month Club News, 96,
101–3, 104, 109, 288, 294

Book reviewing, 34; as criticism, 35, 37, 39, 43, 102–4; as "news," 35–37, 40–43, 69–71, 77, 88, 90–92, 93, 122, 136–38; in nineteenth and early twentieth centuries, 35–42. *See also* Radio: book broadcasts on commercial stations

Books, xi, xvi, 42, 48, 61–92, 101, 103, 105, 114, 249, 328. See also *New York Herald Tribune*

Bourne, Randolph, 23, 55, 57, 148–49, 156, 159–60, 163, 171–73

Breasted, James H., 257, 262

Brett, George P., 212, 215, 245, 246

Brockway, Wallace, 193, 195, 249

Brooks, Van Wyck, xii, xvii, xx, 23, 26, 55, 56, 57, 91, 152, 171–73, 174, 217, 218, 331 (n. 10)

Broun, Heywood, 61, 96, 110, 133, 137, 138–41, 144, 184, 218, 242, 245, 249, 252, 267, 291, 293, 295, 315, 320

Brown, John Mason, 295, 307

Brownell, W. C., 39, 56, 68

Bryant, William Cullen, 36, 38

Bryson, Lyman, 308, 313–14

Buchanan, Scott, 186–87, 189, 193, 194, 308, 313, 350 (n. 40)

Buckminster, Joseph Stevens, 5, 6, 7

Burrill, Edgar White, 276–77, 281, 316, 325

Busey, Garreta, 78

Bush, Wendell, 226

Bushman, Richard, 16

Bushnell, Horace, 4

Butler, Nicholas Murray, 157, 158, 160, 178, 181, 184, 186, 189, 231

Cairns, Huntington, 308–10, 312, 314

Cairns, Timothy, 222, 224

Calkins, Earnest Elmo, 104, 136

Canby, Henry Seidel, xii, xv, xvi, xviii, 42, 60, 64, 68, 69, 90, 96, 98, 109, 126, 134–50 passim, 170, 176, 182, 212, 217, 227, 247, 295; career of, 110–15; as critic, 115–23, 141, 144, 146, 147, 293, 299, 323, 346 (nn. 56, 62), 360 (n. 97); on radio, 266, 267, 304, 305, 315

Cane, Melville, 158

Canfield, Cass, 35

Canfield, James, 124, 141

Canon formation, xviii, 49, 55–56, 115, 121, 167, 171, 194, 284

Cantril, Hadley, 287

Carlin, Phillips, 323

Carmer, Carl, 299, 315

Carnegie, Dale, 170, 191, 192

Cerf, Bennett, 265, 293, 304, 305

Chaffee, Rev. Edmund B., 224

Chamberlain, John, 293, 296

Chambers, Whittaker, 187

Channing, William Ellery, 5, 6, 7, 17, 20, 24

Character, xviii, 3–4, 11, 13, 22, 23–25, 32, 43, 47, 58–59, 60, 63, 105, 106, 109, 126, 129, 131, 142, 169, 176, 228, 254, 268, 286, 325, 327, 335 (n. 51), 350 (n. 38). *See also* Culture; Genteel tradition; Selfhood

Cheney, O. H., 32

Cheney, Sheldon, 81

Chiappe, Andrew, 308–9

Civilization, 32, 47, 56, 125, 129, 164, 171–74, 196, 209, 210, 212–13, 218–19, 235, 241–42, 251, 259–60, 264, 265, 266, 272, 284, 289–90, 307, 331 (n. 10), 351 (n. 75)

Cmiel, Kenneth, 331 (n. 10)

Cohen, Morris, 254

Colum, Mary, 86

Columbia University, 48, 124, 148, 149, 153–58, 160, 162, 164, 176, 178, 181, 184, 247, 308, 327; and "great books" curriculum, 164–68; and Will Durant, 225–27, 230

Conversation, 170, 175, 190–91, 278–81, 284, 295, 300–301, 302–3, 306,

308, 310–11, 313, 322, 324, 326, 327
Cortissoz, Royal, 40, 62–63, 65, 89
Coué, Emile, 260
Cousins, Norman, 261, 326
Cowan, Louis, 318, 326
Cowley, Malcolm, xvii, 80, 84, 91, 97, 135, 147, 293, 301
Craig, Samuel, 95
Crane, Frank, 215
Crosby, Bing, 267
Cross, Milton, 321
Cross, Wilbur, 113
Culture: definition in colonial period, 1–2; and consumption, 2–5, 7, 11, 24–25, 30–33; and inner virtue, 2–5, 8, 21–22, 28, 105, 170, 192; definition in nineteenth century, 2–15; and women, 4; and Unitarianism, 5–7; and democracy, 6–7, 14, 17, 86; and "sacralization," 16–17; as liberal education, 20, 28–29, 31, 39, 43, 70, 209, 235, 250, 265, 268; as news or information, 77, 79, 211, 229, 244, 248, 251, 252, 261, 286–87, 288–89, 294, 302, 307, 312, 318–20, 323, 325, 326, 328. See also Middlebrow culture; Character; Personality; Selfhood
Cuppy, Will, 88, 91
Curtis, George William, 11, 38
Czitrom, Daniel, 271

Damrosch, Walter, 273
Debs, Eugene, 315
Dell, Floyd, 40
Dewey, John, 24, 147, 160, 161, 166–67, 189, 225, 226–28, 229, 236, 238, 239, 254, 257, 258, 272, 315, 317, 357 (n. 36)
Dewey, Melvil, 124
Discipline. See Aesthetic training
Duffus, R. L., 104
Durant, Ariel, 223, 232, 239, 257, 262

Durant, Will, xii, xvi, 64, 211, 217, 267, 284, 295, 302, 307; The Story of Philosophy, xi, 74, 98, 210, 224, 231–45, 249–51, 252, 253, 254, 255, 256, 258; and emphasis on unity, 51, 234–35, 239–41, 244, 261, 265; The Story of Civilization, 210, 255–64, 329; childhood and education, 219–21; vocational crisis, 221–25, 255; and pragmatism, 225–31; and Simon and Schuster, 246–54, 263–64, 286; and genteel tradition, 253, 255, 261; in late 1920s, 254–56

Edman, Irwin, 61, 80, 224, 247, 353 (n. 100)
Eggleston, George Cary, 36, 37, 38
Elbert Hubbard Scrapbook, 100
Eliot, Charles W., 19, 20, 27–29, 77, 94, 95, 105, 286, 345 (n. 33). See also "Five-Foot Shelf of Books"
Eliot, T. S., 171
Emerson, Ralph Waldo, 4, 8–11, 12, 19, 20, 21, 24, 56, 111, 126, 146, 156, 172, 181, 185, 194, 227, 237, 255, 327; and role of the literary critic, 10, 25
Erskine, Eliza Jane Hollingsworth, 149, 151, 152–53, 162–63, 183
Erskine, James Morrison, 149, 150, 151, 154, 157, 186
Erskine, John, xv, xvi, xviii, 49, 52, 64, 80, 83, 148, 187, 191, 196, 211, 212, 217, 221, 227, 228, 243, 247, 259, 261, 282, 284, 289, 310, 320, 326; and "great books," xi, 48, 149, 162, 164–78, 188, 189, 190, 193, 194–95, 240, 279, 308, 311, 327, 350 (n. 40), 353 (n. 100); The Private Life of Helen of Troy, xi, 179–81; and search for experience, 51, 159–61, 163–64, 178, 182–83, 185–86, 197; childhood of, 149–53; and gen-

teel tradition, 149–53, 156–61, 163, 169–71, 175–76, 190; education of, 153–57; as teacher, 157–60, 184; "The Moral Obligation to be Intelligent," 161, 169; and World War I, 161–64, 186; as novelist and public figure, 178–85; and radio, 184–85, 267, 269, 363 (n. 12); *The Complete Life*, 185–86

Experience, 9, 32

Expertise, 32, 70, 87, 100, 102–4, 106, 107, 144, 167, 174, 190, 214–15, 217, 219, 230, 235–37, 242–43, 247, 250, 251, 261, 268, 271, 286, 290, 311, 314, 318–22, 324–25. *See also* Literary critics: role of

Fadiman, Clifton, xiv, xvi, 103, 144, 186, 187, 249, 267, 298, 316, 320–27, 353 (n. 100)

Fashion, 4, 25

Field, Harry, 275

Fields, James T., 36, 37

Fisher, Dorothy Canfield, xi, xii, xv, xvi, 78, 96, 110, 123–33, 134, 135, 136, 138, 140–41, 144, 145, 147, 149, 173, 267, 271, 298, 328, 346–47 (n. 68), 347 (n. 75)

Fisher, John, 124, 125, 301

Fitzgerald, Ed and Pegeen, 299

Fitzgerald, F. Scott, 23, 81

"Five-Foot Shelf of Books," 27–29, 70, 94, 98, 100, 105, 194, 286, 345 (n. 33). *See also* Eliot, Charles W.

Foerster, Norman, 70, 86, 93, 122

Ford, Gerald, 264

Ford, James L., 26

Forman, Henry James, 209, 211

Frank, Waldo, 217–18

Frederick, John Towner, 300, 305–8, 325

Freeman, Joseph, 86

Frith, Simon, 268, 269

Fuller, Margaret, 36

Gaines, James, 296

Gannett, Lewis, 80, 91, 304

Garrison, Wendell Phillips, 38, 39

Genteel tradition, xvi–xviii, xx, 11–15, 21, 28, 31, 58, 60, 77, 78, 190, 227, 331 (n. 10); early nineteenth-century antecedents, 3, 8, 17; and politics, 6–7, 14, 31; and "higher journalism," 15, 46–47; and publishing, 17–19, 248, 264; and public lecturing, 21–22; challenges to, 22–26; as humanistic reform, 26–27, 30, 37, 43; and Stuart Pratt Sherman, 53–55, 58–59, 65–67, 77; and Book-of-the-Month Club, 105, 106–7, 110, 112, 120–21, 133, 143–44; and John Erskine, 149–53, 156–61, 163, 169–71, 175–76, 190; and Will Durant, 253, 255, 261; and radio, 269, 279, 281, 282, 90, 296, 301, 308, 310, 319, 322, 326, 328. *See also* Character

Gerould, Katharine Fullerton, 331 (n. 10)

Gilder, Richard Watson, 11, 156

Gilkeson, John S., 109

Gilman, Daniel Coit, 20

Godkin, E. L., 11, 13, 15, 18, 19, 26, 38, 47

Godwin, Parke, 38

Golenpaul, Dan, 320, 323

Graff, Gerald, xv, xviii, 114, 165, 350 (n. 49)

"Great books" movement, 231, 248, 251, 308–9, 312, 314, 327, 351–52 (n. 76). *See also* Erskine, John; Adler, Mortimer; Radio: programs—"Invitation to Learning"

Great Books of the Western World, xiv, 175, 193–97, 249, 329

Greeley, Horace, 36

Greenberg, Clement, xiii, xiv, xv

Gross, John, 333 (n. 25)

Gunther, John, 324

Haas, Robert K., 95, 120
Hackett, Francis, 40, 41, 55, 57
Haldeman-Julius, Emanuel, 232–34, 235, 246, 247, 358 (n. 55)
Hale, Ruth, 140
Hall, David D., xvi, 11, 15, 27
Halsey, Francis Whiting, 40
Halttunen, Karen, 278–79
Hamilton, Edith, 259
Hammerton, J. A., 256–57
Hansen, Harry, 41, 250, 263, 304
Hardwick, Elizabeth, 34–35, 40, 70
Harris, Neil, 264
Hart, James, 250
Harvard Classics. See "Five-Foot Shelf of Books"
Hayes, Carlton J. H., 213–14
Hays, Will, 184
Heald, Morrell, 108
Hellman, Geoffrey, 246, 248
Hettinger, Herman, 296
Hicks, Granville, 85–86
Higginson, Thomas Wentworth, 12, 13
Higher education, 19–20
"Higher" journalism, 15, 34–92, 115–23. See also Sherman, Stuart Pratt; Genteel tradition
Hoeveler, J. David, 45
Hollinger, David, 194, 227
Hollingsworth, William, 150, 151, 154, 159, 186
Hoover, Herbert, 314
Howe, Daniel Walker, 6, 7
Howe, Will D., 54
Howells, William Dean, 23, 36, 170
Hurst, Fannie, 267, 305
Hutchens, John K., 91, 323
Hutchins, Robert M., 184, 187–89, 193–95
Hutchinson, Ellen Mackay, 40
Hyman, Stanley Edgar, 35

Ives, Pauline, 160–61

Jackson, Joseph Henry, 278, 281, 325
Jaffee, Bernard, 320
James, William, 48, 156, 159, 166, 168, 194, 227, 228, 235
Johnson, Walter, 142–43
Jones, Howard Mumford, 254

Kasson, John, 18
Kazin, Alfred, 62, 84
Kielty, Bernadine, 103, 123
Kieran, John, 320
Kittredge, George Lyman, 44
Kluger, Richard, 84, 92
Kronenberger, Louis, 293
Krutch, Joseph Wood, 312
Kudner, Arthur, 302
Kuklick, Bruce, 226

LaFollette, Robert M., 20, 43
Lamont, Hammond, 48
Lamont, Thomas W., 114
Lazarsfeld, Paul F., 274–75, 296, 299, 302, 319–20, 363 (n. 17)
Lears, Jackson, 23, 51, 99, 159
Lecturing, public, xii, 20–22
Lee, Charles, 97, 101, 110
Lee, Margaret, 315
Levant, Oscar, 320, 323
Levine, Lawrence W., xvi, 16, 22, 26
Levine, Leon, 308, 312, 313
Lewis, R. J., Jr., 303
Lewis, Sinclair, 30, 56, 74, 79
Lewisohn, Ludwig, 57, 59, 90
Literary critics: role of, 6–7, 9, 10, 13, 18, 19, 31–32, 45, 46, 48, 53–54, 59, 65–74, 86, 115–23, 130–33, 138, 139–41, 168, 174, 182, 269, 279, 297–98, 306, 324–25; women as, 83, 87, 131–33
Literary Guild, 95, 96, 100, 105, 109, 280, 284, 305, 311, 322, 343 (n. 5)
Literary modernism, 32, 71–72, 81, 88, 119–20, 144, 147, 171, 190, 193–94, 282

Liveright, Horace, 216, 245, 246, 253, 264. *See also* Boni and Liveright
Loveman, Amy, 87, 114, 123, 132, 144, 266, 299
Lowell, James Russell, 11, 12, 13, 14, 18, 21, 38, 48, 154, 302–3
Lowenthal, Leo, 236
Luce, Clare Boothe, 196
Lynes, Russell, xiii, xiv, xix

Mabie, Hamilton Wright, 1, 15, 87
McBride, Mary Margaret, 267, 314
McCaffery, John K. M., 304–5
Macdonald, Dwight, xiv, xv, xix, 97, 175, 196, 364–65 (n. 32)
McDonald, Florin L., 41
MacDowell, Edward, 154, 158
Macfadden, Bernarr, 222
Macrae, John, 62, 90, 96–97
MacWilliams, Edward (Jim), 318
Malone, Ted, 316–17
Maloney, Russell, 308
Marchand, Roland, 101, 107, 252, 280, 284, 296
Marquis, Don, 63, 72, 136, 137, 139
Martin, Everett Dean, 29, 105
Marx, Groucho, 184
Matheson, Hilda, 273
Matthews, Brander, 39, 157
Matthiessen, F. O., xix-xx
Mattingly, Garrett, 261, 262, 264
May, Henry F., xvii, 223
Mencken, H. L., 55, 57, 301
Middlebrow culture, xi; commentators on, xii–xiv; and consumer culture, xiii–xv, xix, 66, 70, 73, 75, 89, 90, 100, 102–6, 108, 109–10, 125, 131, 135–36, 138, 142–44, 172–76, 191–93, 195–96, 237, 241–42, 244–45, 250, 253, 262, 264, 268, 280, 284, 286, 296–97, 325–26, 329, 335–36 (n. 53); scholars' neglect of, xv; "middleness" of, xviii, xx, 33, 43,

61, 72, 98, 143–44, 147, 149, 159–61, 171, 181, 221, 253, 268, 279, 296–97, 325; and democratic values, xix, xx, 33, 55–56, 116–18, 122, 126, 129, 140, 164, 176–78, 188–90, 191–93, 230–31, 243–44, 268–69, 287–89, 296–97, 303. *See also* Culture; Genteel tradition
Modern Library, 95, 216, 244, 265
Montague, William P., 224, 225
Montessori, Maria, 124–25
Montgomery, Richard G., 279–80
More, Paul Elmer, 39, 40, 41, 44–47, 49, 51, 54, 56, 59, 60, 69, 74, 85
Morgan, Joy Elmer, 272
Morley, Christopher, 96, 110, 114, 122, 133–38, 139, 142, 144, 147, 252, 266, 267, 293
Morris, Lloyd, 160, 161
Morrow, William, 124
Mumford, Lewis, 84, 91, 210, 224
Murphy, Cullen, 259, 260, 261, 262, 264, 360–61 (n. 102)

Nadal, E. S., 37
Nation, 37, 38, 39, 40, 41, 42, 46, 48, 49, 51–52, 53, 54, 59, 61, 64, 66, 69, 77, 82, 115
Nearing, Vivienne, 327
Nevin, Thomas R., 44
Nevins, Allan, 36, 37, 57, 70
New Haven Scholars, 7–8, 19
New Humanism, xv, 39, 43, 44–47, 56, 65, 68, 70, 72, 118
New York Evening Post, 36, 38–40, 41, 42, 48, 62, 70, 86, 114, 134
New York Herald, 291
New York Herald Tribune, xi, 34, 35, 42, 62–65, 92, 93; and advertising, 62, 89–91, 115, 306. See also *Books*; *New York Herald*; *New York Tribune*
New York Times, 34, 35, 40, 42, 62, 92, 115, 249, 251, 291, 310

New York Tribune, 36, 40, 61, 62, 138, 139
Norton, Andrews, 5, 6
Norton, Charles Eliot, 4, 11–15, 18, 20, 22, 26, 27, 38, 47, 56, 115, 126, 154, 302

O'Brien, Howard Vincent, 279, 284
Ochs, Adolph, 40
Olmsted, Frederick Law, 11, 13, 15, 26, 38
Orrick, James, 90
Oursler, Fulton, 184
"Outline" volumes, xii, 37, 54, 182, 209–65, 288, 315, 360 (n. 97)

Parsons, Geoffrey, 62, 91–92
Paterson, Isabel M., 77, 79–80, 91, 104, 122, 136, 252, 341 (n. 96)
Paulsen, Friedrich, 234–35, 237, 239, 256
Peattie, Elia W., 40
Peiss, Kathy, 335 (n. 53)
Perry, Bliss, 40, 41, 89, 146
Personality, xviii, xx, 23–25, 29, 32, 58, 60, 61, 70, 77, 78, 84, 91, 104, 106, 109, 122–23, 136–37, 140, 144, 155, 169, 176, 181, 184, 186, 188, 211, 218, 237, 251, 327, 335 (n. 51); and radio programs, 268, 273, 286–87, 290, 291, 292, 295–96, 297, 302, 310, 319, 323–26. *See also* Culture; Selfhood
Persons, Stow, 152
Phelps, William Lyon, xi, xvi, 54, 112, 281–90, 293–94, 296, 297, 298, 299, 300, 301, 303, 304, 310, 311, 317, 320, 325, 350 (n. 49), 363 (n. 12)
Philosophical idealism, 226–27, 229–30, 239, 241
Pitkin, Walter, 247
Plumb, J. H., 258, 262, 264
Porter, Noah, 7, 18, 19
Pound, Ezra, 90

Pragmatism, 227–30, 238, 239
Publishing, 17, 18, 22, 31, 41
Pynchon, Adelene, 180, 182

Radio: book broadcasts on commercial stations, xi, 31, 266–329; educational, 270–76;
—Programs: "An American Fireside," 266; "American Scriptures," 267; "Kraft Music Hall," 267; "Let's Talk It Over," 267; "Sunday Evening at Fannie Hurst's," 267; "World Security Workshop," 267; "The Author Meets the Critics," 267, 300, 304–5, 318, 327; "Invitation to Learning," 267, 300, 308–14, 326; "Information, Please!," 267, 302, 320–24, 327; "Adventure in Reading," 267, 315; "Invitation to Reading," 271; "Little Red Schoolhouse of Radio," 271; "The Ohio School of the Air," 271; "Major Bowes," 275; "Literary Vespers," 276–77; "Footlight and Lamplight," 277–78; "Reader's Guide" ("Bookman's Notebook"), 278; "The Swift Hour," 281, 283–90, 293; "The Town Crier," 291, 292–99, 303; "The Early Bookworm," 292; "The Best Books of the Month," 299; "Books and Authors," 299; "The Reader's Almanac," 299; "The Ten Best Non-Fiction Books of 1937," 299; "Of Men and Books," 300, 305–8; "The Human Side of Literature" ("Meet Mr. Weeks," "Meet Edward Weeks"), 300–303, 305; "Speaking of Books," 304; "Books on Trial," 305; "Author's Round Table," 314; "Conversation at 8," 314; "Treasures Next Door," 315; "WEVD University of the Air," 315; "Between the Bookends," 316; "A

Book a Week," 316; "NBC University of the Air" ("NBC University Theatre"), 316; "Pilgrimage of Poetry," 316; "Professor Quiz's Night School of the Air," 317–18; "Ask-It Basket," 318; "Dr. I. Q.," 318; "It Pays to be Ignorant," 318; "Kay Kyser's Kollege of Musical Knowledge," 318; "Pot O' Gold," 318; "Quiz Kids," 318; "Uncle Jim's Question Bee," 318; "Conversation," 326; "Let's Balance the Books," 371 (n. 112)

Radway, Janice, xv, xviii, 102, 331 (n. 7)

Randall, John H., Jr., 227

Rascoe, Burton, 55, 62, 68, 341 (n. 93)

Rauschenbush, Walter, 23

"Reader's Guide," 86–87, 108

Redman, Ben Ray, 85

Refinement. See Culture

Reid, Helen Rogers, 62, 65, 77, 83, 86, 89, 90

Reilly, Joseph J., 282, 283

Reith, Sir John, 273, 363 (n. 15)

Riesman, David, 4, 23, 335 (n. 51)

Ripley, George, 36

Robinson, Henry Morton, 158, 178, 182

Robinson, James Harvey, 160, 213, 237, 257–58

Romberg, Sigmund, 281, 283, 284, 289

Rorty, James, 275

Roscoe, William, 3

Rosenbaum, Belle, 83

Ross, Ishbel, 88

Rourke, Constance, 80, 173

Royal, John F., 273, 369 (n. 98)

Royce, Josiah, 226, 227, 241

Rubicam, Raymond, 196

Rugg, Harold, 241

Ruland, Richard, 42, 46, 49, 68, 72

Sackheim, Maxwell, 94, 95, 98, 99, 100, 105, 246, 251

St. John's College (Annapolis), 189, 308, 327

Salpeter, Harry, 279

Santayana, George, xvii, xx, 26, 46–47, 166, 227, 242, 250

Saturday Review of Literature, xii, xiv, 42, 68, 86, 87, 114, 116, 118–20, 134, 135, 249, 250, 251, 266, 323, 346 (n. 56), 371 (n. 112)

Sayler, Oliver M., 277–78, 281

Schapiro, J. Salwyn, 218

Scherman, Harry, 82, 94–110 passim, 120, 121, 129–30, 140, 145, 146, 195, 216, 246, 251, 343–44 (n. 10)

Schudson, Michael, 106

Schuster, Max Lincoln, 234, 235, 236, 245–49, 250, 251, 253, 263–64, 314. See also Simon and Schuster

Schwartz, Delmore, 97

Seaver, Edwin, 299

Sedgwick, Catharine M., 4

Sedgwick, Ellery, 59, 60

Seldes, Gilbert, xiv, 79, 274, 288, 300, 322, 324, 326

Selfhood, xx, 9, 22–25, 27, 44, 46, 47, 51, 70, 99–100, 104, 107–8, 119–20, 133, 152–53, 154, 156, 158–60, 168–71, 182–83, 185–86, 191, 221, 223, 240, 262, 265. See also Character; Culture; Personality

Sennett, Richard, 335 (n. 51)

Sherman, Stuart Pratt, xi, xvi, xviii, 42, 94, 97–98, 103, 112, 114, 115, 117, 120, 121, 123, 152, 159, 182, 221, 227, 250, 251, 254, 294, 327; My Dear Cornelia, xi, 60–61; and New Humanism, 43, 47–49, 51, 52, 55, 57; childhood and youth, 43–44; education, 43–44, 47; and democracy, 47, 49, 54, 55, 56, 70–71, 74, 85, 176, 231; and literary canon, 49, 55–56; and search for experience,

50–51, 53, 57–60, 63–64, 67, 68–69, 75–76, 78, 149; *Matthew Arnold: How to Know Him*, 52–55, 68; and genteel tradition, 53–55, 58–59, 65–67, 77; *On Contemporary Literature*, 54–57; and *Books*, 61–77, 79, 81, 82, 86, 87, 89, 91, 92; *Critical Woodcuts*, 69; prose style, 73–74, 75; death, 75–76, 81; "Letters to a Lady in the Country," 77–79. *See also* Literary critics: role of
Simon, Richard L., 245–47, 248, 249, 251, 253, 301. *See also* Simon and Schuster
Simon and Schuster, 189, 193, 233, 236, 249, 251–54, 263–64, 265, 286, 292, 320. *See also* Schuster, Max Lincoln; Simon, Richard L.
Skinner, Constance Lindsay, 80, 132, 269, 287
Slade, John A., 70
Smith, James Steel, 358 (n. 66)
Specialization, 12, 19–20, 25–26, 28–29, 112–14, 115, 118, 138, 143, 155, 157, 166–67, 178, 181, 185, 188, 210, 212, 219, 265, 306, 311
Spingarn, Joel, 45, 67
Standardization, 29, 31, 98, 116, 117, 120, 121–22, 129, 264, 272
Stearns, Harold, 32, 173
Stempel, Herbert, 327
Stone, Martin, 303
Sugrue, Thomas, 314
Susman, Warren, 24, 99

Taste, 4, 5, 8, 11, 12, 25, 172, 252
Tate, Allen, 309–13
Taylor, Bayard, 154
Taylor, Deems, 290, 365 (n. 44)
Taylor, Frederick Winslow, 70
Thompson, John R., 36
Ticknor, George, 3
Trilling, Lionel, 153, 176, 184, 194, 316, 353 (n. 100)

"Turns with a Bookworm," 77–79, 288. *See also* Paterson, Isabel M.

Unitarianism, 5–7, 9, 11, 13, 17, 23, 37
University of Chicago, 168, 187–89, 306
Untermeyer, Louis, 371 (n. 112)

Van Doren, Carl, 47–48, 49, 55, 57, 59, 64, 65, 72, 75, 78, 80, 83, 135, 224, 267, 282, 297, 298, 299, 313, 316
Van Doren, Charles, 327–28
Van Doren, Irita, xvi, 64–65, 67, 75–76, 78, 80, 82–86, 87–92, 94, 267, 304, 339 (n. 61)
Van Doren, Mark, xvi, 48, 64, 80, 82, 83, 84, 186, 188, 193, 194, 224, 267, 307, 309–14, 316, 320, 325, 327–28, 353 (n. 100)
Van Loon, Hendrik Willem, 80, 209, 211, 216–19, 245, 246, 250, 253–54, 263, 264, 291; on radio, 267, 314–15, 320, 323–24, 355–56 (n. 22), 369 (n. 98)
Veysey, Laurence, 114
Villard, Henry, 38
Villard, Oswald Garrison, 282

Waller, Judith C., 300
Walpole, Helen, 315
Warner, Charles Dudley, 18
Weeks, Edward, 300–303, 306, 316, 325
Weiss, Paul, 242, 243, 244
Wells, H. G., 113, 209–10, 211–16, 217, 218–19, 246, 250, 251, 257, 329
Wendell, Barrett, 20
White, Morton, 257
White, William Allen, 96, 110, 133, 141–43, 144, 145, 146
Whitman, Walt, 24, 56, 65, 194
Widdemer, Margaret, xii

Wiggam, Albert Edward, 29, 185
Wilbur, Ray Lyman, 272
Williams, Raymond, 2
Willkie, Wendell, 83
Wilson, Christopher P., 341 (n. 96)
Wilson, Edmund, 72, 86, 91, 147
Windelband, Wilhelm, 234–35, 237, 256
Woodberry, George Edward, 39, 54, 154–58, 159, 160, 165, 168, 171, 174, 177, 186, 188, 226, 350 (n. 49)
Woodbridge, F. J. E., 225, 226, 227
Woodbridge, Homer, 49, 50, 58

Woolf, Virginia, xiii, xiv
Woollcott, Alexander, xi, xvi, 136, 142, 290–99, 300, 302, 304, 307, 310, 311, 316, 320, 325
Woolsey, Theodore Dwight, 6
Worden, Helen, 162, 163, 182–83, 184, 186
Wylie, Elinor, 79, 146

Yale Review, 113

Zeitlin, Jacob, 49, 58, 82
Zinsser, William, 146

PERMISSIONS

9 6/06